W9-BAP-876

Contemporary Cases
in U.S. Foreign Policy

Contemporary Cases in U.S. Foreign Policy

From Terrorism to Trade

Fifth Edition

Ralph G. Carter
Texas Christian University

Los Angeles | London | New Delhi
Singapore | Washington DC

Los Angeles | London | New Delhi
Singapore | Washington DC

FOR INFORMATION:

CQ Press

An Imprint of SAGE Publications, Inc.

2455 Teller Road

Thousand Oaks, California 91320

E-mail: order@sagepub.com

SAGE Publications Ltd.

1 Oliver's Yard

55 City Road

London EC1Y 1SP

United Kingdom

SAGE Publications India Pvt. Ltd.

B 1/I 1 Mohan Cooperative Industrial Area

Mathura Road, New Delhi 110 044

India

SAGE Publications Asia-Pacific Pte. Ltd.

3 Church Street

#10-04 Samsung Hub

Singapore 049483

Acquisitions Editor: Charisse Kiino

Editorial Assistant: Lauren Johnson

Production Editor: Stephanie Palermini

Copy Editor: Diana Breti

Typesetter: C&M Digitals (P) Ltd.

Proofreader: Rae-Ann Goodwin

Indexer: Jennifer Pairan

Cover Designer: Edgar Abarca

Marketing Manager: Erica DeLuca

Permissions Editor: Jennifer Barron

Copyright © 2014 by CQ Press, an Imprint of SAGE Publications, Inc. CQ Press is a registered trademark of Congressional Quarterly Inc.

All rights reserved. No part of this book may be reproduced or utilized in any form or by any means, electronic or mechanical, including photocopying, recording, or by any information storage and retrieval system, without permission in writing from the publisher.

Printed in the United States of America

Library of Congress Cataloging-in-Publication Data

Contemporary cases in U.S. foreign policy : from terrorism to trade / [edited by] Ralph G. Carter, Texas Christian University. — Fifth edition.

pages cm.
Includes bibliographical references and index.

ISBN 978-1-4522-4154-8 (pbk. : alk. paper)
ISBN 978-1-4833-0082-5 (web pdf)

1. United States—Foreign relations—1989—Case studies.
I. Carter, Ralph G.

E840.C66 2014
327.73—dc23   2013009507

This book is printed on acid-free paper.

Certified Chain of Custody
SUSTAINABLE FORESTRY INITIATIVE
Promoting Sustainable Forestry
www.sfiprogram.org
SFI-01268

SFI label applies to text stock

13 14 15 16 17 10 9 8 7 6 5 4 3 2 1

Contents

PART I   INTERVENTION POLICY

The "war on terrorism" began in the early 1990s, escalated with the 1998 bombings of the U.S. embassies in Kenya and Tanzania, and came into full fruition with the terrorist attacks on New York City and the Pentagon on September 11, 2001. As a result, two U.S. administrations made war on Osama bin Laden's al Qaeda network and the Taliban regime in Afghanistan that provided it sanctuary. Following years of warfare in Afghanistan, the Obama administration employed a surge strategy against the Taliban in order to pacify the country sufficiently to enable U.S. troops to come home.

Targeted killings have become a staple in the U.S. war on terrorism. However, U.S. foreign policymakers took a bold step by authorizing the assassination of Osama bin Laden. Although the intelligence clues were tantalizing, officials could not be sure the potential target in the house in Abbottabad was actually bin Laden, so a decision had to be made under conditions of high uncertainty. Policy failure was a real possibility if the target proved not to be bin Laden, and the mission risked long-term damage to U.S. relations with the government and military of Pakistan, as well as raising again the ethical questions about targeted killings as a policy tool.

Obama administration officials were initially torn between support for Mubarak and the message that sent to other allies in the region and support for the Egyptian masses, but they finally sided with the people.

Supporting human rights in China has long been a U.S. concern, but in 2012 that concern took on a very human face. Chen Guangcheng, a blind Chinese dissident under long-term house arrest for challenging the regime's actions, unexpectedly sought asylum in the U.S. Embassy in Beijing. Suddenly, his situation confronted U.S. diplomats with a crisis-like challenge: how to do the right thing by him and his family without embarrassing the Chinese government, hurting US-China trade, damaging overall US-China relations, or sabotaging an upcoming visit by Secretary of State Hillary Clinton. Ultimately, a solution was found that seemed to satisfy all concerned.

PART IV   ECONOMIC AND TRADE POLICY

In 2007, a housing bubble began to burst in the United States. As a result, more and more banks and financial institutions became the holders of "toxic" assets, the true values of which were unknown. Not knowing their exposure, banks and financial institutions cut back on lending to protect themselves, creating a credit crisis that quickly spread around the world. The outgoing Bush administration had to find a way to bail out the banks and get credit moving again, and the new Obama administration had to find a way to coordinate international responses to promote global economic recovery. This case demonstrates both the interconnectedness of the global economy and the rise of state capitalism.

Thirty years after the United States and China established economic relations, the two continue to exchange complaints about each other's trade practices. China moved from the status of a "strategic partner" under the Clinton administration to a "strategic competitor" under the Bush administration. Now the Obama administration is dealing with China as an emerging economic power, seeking the appropriate balance between protecting U.S. interests and taking advantage of all China offers.

12   **The Politics of Climate Change: Will the US Act to Prevent Calamity?**   347

RODGER A. PAYNE AND SEAN PAYNE

The George Bush, Clinton, George W. Bush, and Obama administrations have struggled with the issue of how to respond to global climate change. The U.S. government's reluctance to reduce fossil fuel emissions to the levels dictated by the 1997 Kyoto Protocol led some states and cities to set their own emissions reduction targets. The Obama administration participated in follow-up meetings, but due to the entrenched and widely divergent positions taken by both developed and developing states, it was only able to attain informal, voluntary pledges of future emissions reductions.

PART V   NATIONAL AND INTERNATIONAL LEGAL POLICY

13   **National Security Surveillance: Unchecked or Limited Presidential Power?**   378

LOUIS FISHER

In late 2005, news reports revealed that after the September 11 attacks, the Bush administration's National Security Agency was authorized to eavesdrop on international telephone calls by U.S. citizens and residents. Although in 1978 a special federal court had been created for just such circumstances, Bush administration officials had chosen not to seek court warrants to authorize the eavesdropping. Facing a near revolt in Congress, the Bush administration pledged to seek court warrants before intercepting the calls of U.S. citizens in the future, but it was not clear to what extent such warrantless wiretapping was curtailed by the Bush administration. The Obama administration and the federal courts continue to try to find the right balance between civil liberties and unilateral executive power in the name of national security.

14   **The Rights of Detainees: Determining the Limits of Law**   409

LINDA CORNETT AND MARK GIBNEY

What legal rights do detainees in the "war on terrorism" have? Are they prisoners of war, criminals, or something else entirely? The Bush administration's policies that such detainees largely lacked legal rights have been generally overturned by the courts, so the Bush administration sought to try them before military tribunals. Although the Obama administration initially sought to try these cases in the U.S. criminal court system, that effort largely failed, and the legal rights of detainees remain unclear.

Despite the U.S. characterization of itself as "a nation of laws," it has long wanted to protect U.S. officials and citizens from frivolous prosecution by the UN's International Criminal Court. President Clinton was enthusiastic about the Court so long as indictments had to be approved by the UN Security Council—where the United States could protect itself with a veto. George W. Bush rejected the idea of the court, and President Obama has shown he is not keen on signing treaties the Senate will not support. All the while, the court continues to take on new cases, the majority of them involving African states. How far do international legal norms extend?

Preface

The terrorist attacks of September 11, 2001 and events thereafter demonstrate that post–Cold War expectations of a more peaceful world built on a foundation of liberal democracies are, at the very best, premature. Military conflicts and national security issues continue to occupy the spotlight, while less traditional foreign policy concerns have also emerged. Human rights, trade matters, and the U.S. role in the international community have moved to the forefront, as foreign policy making has become a much more complex and crowded affair than it was during the Cold War.

Just as the types of foreign policy issues that seem important have changed, the relative roles played by different policymakers have been in flux as well. Although presidents still act unilaterally when possible—as in decisions to use military force—presidential preeminence in overall foreign policy making has generally diminished. Domestic and international groups, nongovernmental organizations, and members of Congress now actively challenge the executive branch's ability to direct foreign policy. In the post–Cold War period, public opinion also seems to play a greater role in policymakers' decisions.

This historic shift in the policy process raises a number of questions: Can international institutions contain terrorism or ethnic and religious violence? How can the United States protect its citizens and interests from global terrorist threats? Are unilateral U.S. responses to global threats appropriate, or do they just compound the problem? Will disgruntled domestic actors define new enemies or foreign policy challenges? After the Great Recession, will the international economy be marked by trade wars between regions and free trade within them? What is more important to U.S. foreign policy: human rights or corporate profits and market share? These questions and similar concerns prompted the conception of this book.

Each of the fifteen case studies included here speaks to a foreign policy process that has become more open, pluralistic, and partisan. With the dramatic increase in the number of congressional subcommittees in the 1970s, followed by the explosive growth of the electronic media in the 1980s and 1990s and the social media of the twenty-first century, individuals and groups now have more points of access through which to participate in policy making. These new actors have their own needs, interests, and agendas. They are generally more partisan in their behavior as well, with Democrats and Republicans vying to put their own foreign policy agendas or policy alternatives forward. In short, U.S. foreign policy making now resembles U.S. domestic policy making: It is overtly political.

Most of the cases in this volume reflect the reality of jurisdictional competition between the president and Congress (and, at times, the courts) over the control and direction of foreign policy in the contemporary era. Not only do members of the president's opposition party often challenge his foreign policy initiatives, but even members of his own party resist executive leadership when they think that the White House tramples on legitimate congressional responsibilities or that the public overwhelmingly opposes administrative policies. Such circumstances have often led to "bad blood" between the branches, a situation that cannot help but strain the policymaking process. White House controversies—or fundamental changes in governmental direction, such as the 2008–2009 bailouts of banks and financial institutions—can further open presidents up to challenge by other policy-making actors. These themes combine to reveal the chinks in the armor of the presidential preeminence model of foreign policy making.

Using Case Studies in the Classroom

Although many excellent U.S. foreign policy texts exist, most fall short in their coverage of recent events and debates. This book aims to cover contemporary events, so that instructors can raise issues confronting today's policymakers. Each case study is written expressly for this volume and is organized in a format that emphasizes the substance of events. A textbook's general description of foreign policy making simply cannot capture all of the intricacies, nuances, and subtleties involved in the events chronicled here. The cases starkly reveal the human dimension of policy making and also help instructors show how administrations often take pains to attempt to do things differently than their predecessors. In addition to showing students the human, political, and organizational faces of policy making, these case studies also introduce them to the wide variety of issues and actors found in the post–Cold War, post–September 11, and now post–Great Recession periods. Students are presented with a "good story," full of compelling characters and daunting challenges, and information on the relevance of issues and why particular policy choices were made.

The pedagogical benefits of the case study approach have spurred its use within the international studies community, joining military, business, public policy, and public administration schools that have long used this approach. For college graduates to compete and perform effectively in the real world, they must first see the world as it is. Simplified models of reality may be necessary at times, but they are rarely sufficient in and of themselves. Theoretical models alone do not capture the messy nature of foreign policy making. If instructors are to facilitate an understanding of the political arena, in which everything seemingly affects everything else, they must confront students with the policy-making dynamics that real-world cases illustrate. Were policymakers trying to make rational choices? Were they trying to balance power concerns on a regional or global basis? Were they more responsive to external threats or opportunities, or to internal political pressures at home? Were they reacting to widely shared perceptions of reality? Did analogies mold their decisions, or were they merely used to convey or defend decisions to the public? These and other theoretical concerns are addressed through the case study method.

Case studies also promote critical thinking and encourage active intellectual engagement. None of their recognized advantages can be realized unless students ask themselves *why* things occurred as they did. Reasoning, considering alternatives, deciding on one alternative rather than another, and communicating the reasoning behind a choice are skills that are integral to lifelong learning and success in any professional career.

Because different educational environments—for example, seminars versus large lecture courses, upper-level courses versus introductory classes—require different teaching approaches, this collection includes a number of aids to help students and instructors get the most out of each case study. "Before You Begin"—a series of critical questions at the beginning of each case—serves as a touchstone, giving students ideas to consider and later review. Each case includes a brief chronology noting the important events covered and a list of key figures in the case. Our shared goal here is to walk a fine line: to encourage students to think without telling them what to think. To provide instructors with guidance in using the studies, the online, password-protected instructor's manual (http://ccusfp.cqpress.com) includes a section on the nuts and bolts of case-based teaching as well as separate entries for analyzing and discussing each case study.

The Cases

The case studies in this book were selected to illustrate two important realities of the post–Cold War, post–September 11, and now post–Great Recession era: (1) the range and diversity of the old and new issues facing U.S. foreign policymakers and (2) the variety of the participants in the current policy-making process. The first set of cases concerns the ongoing questions of when and how the United States should intervene militarily and how terrorist threats should be confronted. Military interventions have always been considered "high politics"—decisions typically made in the White House. As the "war on terrorism," assassinating bin Laden, and Iraq intervention cases show, presidents still largely dominate these issues. However, as always, domestic criticism arises swiftly if presidential policies are not seen as successful or raise other troubling issues—like the use of unmanned drones and targeted killings.

Changing nuclear security situations prompt another set of cases. How to deal with nuclear weapons proliferation in North Korea, and potentially Iran, has bedeviled policymakers at both ends of Pennsylvania Avenue during the Clinton, Bush, and Obama administrations. Then there's the Bush administration's nuclear agreement with India, which did not generate that much controversy despite reversing three decades of U.S. nonproliferation policy.

Diplomacy continues to be integral to the implementation, and at times the formation, of U.S. foreign policy. Three cases reach into this arena. After a series of contentious issues marked US-Russian relations during the Clinton and Bush administrations, President Barack Obama sought a highly publicized "reset" of those relations, beginning with a New START Treaty. Multiple challenges frustrated that effort. Also during his presidency, Obama and other policymakers were largely blindsided by the Arab Spring, and its spread to Egypt suddenly pitted U.S. promotion of democracy and support for a long-time ally against each other. Finally, sometimes stuff just happens. In 2012, routine diplomatic relations with China were upset as a blind Chinese dissident sought refuge in the U.S. Embassy in Beijing just before a long-planned visit to China by Secretary of State Hillary Clinton.

Another set of cases deals with issues involving economic and trade matters. The financial crisis that caused the Great Recession challenged global policymakers, particularly those in the US, where many of the problems began. Trade with China can be routinely contentious, as it involves complex U.S. relations with the world's second-largest economy and often runs the risk of being sidetracked by diverging political agendas on each side. Finally, the increasingly high-profile issue of global climate change cannot be divorced from its economic aspects, as U.S. federal, state, and local policymakers seek to address global climate change without sacrificing U.S. jobs or productivity in the process.

The last set of cases focuses on difficult legal issues that have emerged in recent years. The war on terrorism renewed an old debate: What's more important? Personal security or personal liberties? The case in point involved electronic surveillance of potential terrorism suspects and the need for court warrants to engage in eavesdropping. The global effort against terrorism after September 11 also created another challenge: What legal rights to due process of law did detainees have—whether in the United States, on foreign soil, or on U.S. bases abroad? This case thrust the nation's highest courts into a political battle involving both the administration and Congress. Finally, is the United States a "nation of laws" as U.S. political culture suggests? If so, why did the United States choose not to join the newly created International Criminal Court in the late 1990s and why does it continue to oppose U.S. membership? Why would three U.S. presidents—two of them lawyers—resist cooperating with the world's foremost court for trying individuals accused of war crimes, crimes against humanity, genocide, or aggression?

Acknowledgments

As is usually the case in publishing, this book benefits from the efforts of many individuals. First, my thanks go to the authors of the case studies. Not only were they willing to write the studies requested, but they also graciously agreed to make the changes that the CQ Press editors and I suggested. Much appreciated is the timeliness with which they produced their chapters, particularly as the situations covered in some cases continued to evolve as they wrote. Second, a number of colleagues and friends provided valuable assistance at various stages of this process. This collection also benefits from the helpful feedback over the years from many members of the Active Learning in International Affairs Section of the International Studies Association. Having good help when you need it is a treasure, and this volume is better as a result of their respective contributions.

Luckily for me, the professionals at CQ Press have also been great partners. We began this edition with Elise Frasier's guidance, but she has since moved on to other professional opportunities. Luckily, Charisse Kiino picked up the baton without a hitch, not surprising since Charisse guided the first edition of this volume. Careful copyediting by Diana Breti further improved the writing. Stephanie Palermini took great care in shepherding the book through the production process and into print.

Finally, I must thank those closest to me. First, Nita has been wonderful throughout the long life of this project. Her advice, understanding, and encouragement, particularly on the many nights and weekends when I had to work, helped me keep my focus on the job at hand. Her consistent support has been instrumental to the successful completion of this project. Second, I also need to thank my extended family and friends. They, too, have been supportive and understanding when my work pulled me away at times. I am truly fortunate to be surrounded by such caring individuals.

Contributors

RALPH G. CARTER is professor and former chair of the Political Science Department at Texas Christian University. His research interests center on the domestic sources of U.S. foreign policy. He is the coauthor of *IR* (2013), *Choosing to Lead: Understanding Congressional Foreign Policy Entrepreneurs* (2009), and *Making American Foreign Policy* (1994, 1996), and he served as an associate section editor for the foreign policy entries of *The International Studies Encyclopedia* (2010). Carter is a past president of both the International Studies Association's Foreign Policy Analysis Section and ISA's Midwest Region. He served as one of the inaugural editors of *Foreign Policy Analysis* and was the 2006 recipient of the ISA's Quincy Wright Distinguished Scholar Award. In 2012, he was named one of *The Best 300 Professors* in the United States by Princeton Review. He holds a PhD from Ohio State University.

LINDA CORNETT is associate professor and chair of political science at the University of North Carolina Asheville, where her classes include international organization, international political economy, and the political economy of development. She earned her BA from Transylvania University, Lexington, Kentucky, and a MA and PhD in political science from the University of Washington, Seattle.

PRIYA DIXIT is an assistant professor in the Department of Political Science at Virginia Tech. Her research interests focus on the study of war, especially terrorism and counterterrorism. She is the coauthor of the book *Critical Terrorism Studies: An Introduction to Research* (2013) and of various journal articles in *International Studies Perspectives, International Relations,* and *Studies in Conflict and Terrorism*. She is currently working on theorizing a critical approach to terrorism, as well as studying the role of "local troops" from small states in global conflicts. She has a PhD from the School of International Service, American University.

LOUIS FISHER is Scholar in Residence at the Constitution Project. Previously he worked for four decades at the Library of Congress as senior specialist in separation of powers at Congressional Research Service and specialist in constitutional law at the Library of Congress. He retired in August 2010 after testifying more than fifty times before congressional committees on a range of constitutional issues. He received his doctorate at the New School for Social Research in 1967 and has taught at a number of universities and law schools. Currently he is adjunct professor at the William and Mary Law School. He is the author of more than twenty books, including *Presidential War Power*, 2nd ed. (2004), *Constitutional Conflicts between Congress and the President*, 5th ed. (2007), coauthor with Katy Harriger of *American Constitutional Law*, 10th ed. (2013), and author of a forthcoming treatise on *The Law of the Executive Branch: Presidential Power*, to be published by Oxford University Press in 2013.

FRÉDÉRICK GAGNON is a professor in the Department of Political Science and director of the Centre for United States Studies of the Raoul Dandurand Chair at the University of Quebec at Montreal. He was visiting scholar at the Woodrow Wilson International Center for Scholars (Washington, DC) and at the Center for American Politics and Citizenship (University of Maryland) and visiting professor at the Center for Canadian-American Studies at Western Washington University. His research and teaching interests focus on the U.S. Congress, American foreign policy, legislative-executive relations, congressional and presidential elections, U.S. culture wars, U.S. popular culture, and Quebec-US relations. He is the author of a French-language textbook on the U.S. Congress (*Le Congrès des* États-Unis, 2006), and coauthor of another textbook on U.S. Government (*Les États-Unis d'Amérique: Les Institutions Politiques*, 2011). He is currently preparing a book on the influence of the chairs of the Senate Foreign Relations Committee since 1945.

MARK GIBNEY is the Belk Distinguished Professor at UNC Asheville. His most recent book projects include *The Handbook of Human Rights* (co-edited with Anja Mihr; forthcoming); *Watching Human Rights: The 101 Best Films* (forthcoming); *Litigating Transnational Human Rights Obligations: Alternative Judgments* (co-edited with Wouter Vandenhole; forthcoming); *The Politics of Human Rights: The Quest for Dignity* (with Sabine Carey and Steven Poe; 2010); *Universal Human Rights and Extraterritorial Obligations* (co-edited with Sigrun Skogly; 2010); and *The Global Refugee Crisis* (2010). Since 1984, Gibney has directed the Political Terror Scale (PTS), which measures levels of physical integrity violations in more than 185 countries (www.politicalter rorscale.org).

RYAN C. HENDRICKSON is professor of political science at Eastern Illinois University. His research and teaching interests focus on American military action abroad and leadership at NATO. He is the author of *The Clinton Wars: The Constitution, Congress, and War Powers* (2002) and *Diplomacy and War at NATO: The Secretary General and Military Action after the Cold War* (2006). He received his PhD from the University of Nebraska, Lincoln.

STEVEN W. HOOK is professor and former chair of the Political Science Department at Kent State University. He is co-author of *American Foreign Policy Since World War II*, 19th ed. (2013) and author of *U.S. Foreign Policy: The Paradox of Power*, 4th ed. (2013) and *National Interest and Foreign Aid* (1995). His edited books include *U.S. Foreign Policy Today: American Renewal?* (2012), *Routledge*

Handbook of American Foreign Policy (2012), and Democratic Peace in Theory and Practice (2010), and he has published in the leading journals of the field. He received a BA degree in journalism and political science at the University of Michigan and an MA and PhD in international studies at the University of South Carolina. At Kent State, he received the university's Distinguished Teaching Award in 2007. He is a past president of the Foreign Policy Analysis sections of the American Political Science Association and the International Studies Association.

DONALD W. JACKSON recently retired as the Herman Brown Professor of Political Science at Texas Christian University but returned as the Green Distinguished Emeritus Tutor teaching classes on American constitutional law and international human rights law. His recent research has focused on transnational dimensions of the rule of law, especially on the protection of human rights. He was an observer at the UN conference leading to the adoption of the Rome Statute and the creation of the International Criminal Court. He is the author of several books, including *Even the Children of Strangers: Equality under the U.S. Constitution* (1992) and *The United Kingdom Confronts the European Convention on Human Rights* (1997). He was the lead editor of *Globalizing Justice: Critical Perspectives on Transnational Law and the Cross-Border Migration of Legal Norms* (2010). His PhD is from the University of Wisconsin, Madison, and his JD is from SMU School of Law.

PATRICK JAMES is Dornsife Dean's Professor of International Relations and Director of the Center for International Studies at the University of Southern California. He is the author of 22 books and more than 120 articles and book chapters. Among his honors and awards are the Louise Dyer Peace Fellowship from the Hoover Institution at Stanford University, the Lady Davis Professorship of the Hebrew University of Jerusalem, the Quincy Wright Scholar Award from the International Studies Association, and the Eccles Professorship of the British Library. He has been Distinguished Scholar in Ethnicity, Nationalism, and Migration and in Foreign Policy Analysis for the International Studies Association. He has been president (2007–2009) of the Association for Canadian Studies in the United States, president of the International Council for Canadian Studies (2011–2013), and vice president (2008–2009) of the ISA. He served a five-year term as editor of *International Studies Quarterly*.

JOYCE P. KAUFMAN is professor of political science and director of the Center for Engagement with Communities at Whittier College. She is the author of *Introduction to International Relations* (2013); *A Concise History of U.S. Foreign Policy*, 2nd ed. (2010); and *NATO and the Former Yugoslavia: Crisis, Conflict and the Atlantic Alliance* (2002); and co-editor (with Andrew M. Dorman) of *The Future of Transatlantic Relations: Perceptions, Policy and Practice* (2011). She is also the author of numerous articles and papers on U.S. foreign and security policy. With Kristen Williams, she is co-author of *Challenging Gender Norms: Women and Political Activism in Times of Crisis* (2013); *Women and War: Gender Identity and Activism in Times of Conflict* (2010); and *Women, the State, and War: A Comparative Perspective on Citizenship and Nationalism* (2007). She holds a BA and MA in political science from New York University and a PhD from the University of Maryland.

THOMAS D. LAIRSON is Gelbman Professor of International Business and professor of political science at Rollins College in Winter Park, Florida. His courses focus on the political economy and business systems of East Asia, and he has published books and articles on international political economy, Chinese business, Asian economic growth, and technology and economy. He served as the first Ford Foundation Professor of International Relations in Hanoi, Vietnam, in 1994; was awarded a Fulbright Fellowship in 2011 for Singapore; and has taught and lectured at Fudan University, Jiaotong University, and Wuhan University in China and at Jindal Global University in India. Lairson earned his PhD from the University of Kentucky.

JEFFREY S. LANTIS is professor of political science and international relations at The College of Wooster, Wooster, Ohio. His teaching and research interests include foreign policy analysis, nuclear nonproliferation, and international cooperation and conflict. A past president of the Active Learning in International Affairs Section of the International Studies Association, he is the author or co-editor of seven books, including most recently *U.S. Foreign Policy in Action: An Innovative Teaching Text* (2013) and *Foreign Policy in Comparative Perspective* (2012), as well as numerous journal articles and book chapters. He has served as a Fulbright Senior Scholar at The Australian National University and the University of New South Wales and a visiting scholar at other universities. He earned his PhD from The Ohio State University.

FRANKLIN BARR LEBO recently earned a PhD in transnational and comparative politics and policy from Kent State University. His dissertation is titled "Between Bureaucracy and Democracy: Regulating Administrative Discretion in Japan." His research and teaching interests center on East Asia and environmental policy. Lebo received a BA in political science and East Asian studies at Brandeis University and a JD with an International Law concentration from the University of California, Hastings College of the Law. He is also an adjunct instructor in the Political Science Department at Baldwin Wallace University, teaching environmental policy and sustainability courses. Lebo is the author of "The Lake Erie Energy Development Corporation (LEEDCo)" in the *Northeast Ohio Sustainability Case Studies Project* (2013) and is the co-author (with Steven W. Hook) of "Development/Poverty Issues and Foreign Policy Analysis" in *The International Studies Encyclopedia* (2010).

ERIC MOSKOWITZ is associate professor of political science and urban studies at The College of Wooster, Wooster, Ohio. His research interests center on presidential decision making, the public policy-making process, and racial politics. He has also published on housing and neighborhood policy and contemporary U.S. decision making on foreign policy. He received his PhD from Indiana University.

ÖZGÜR ÖZDAMAR is deputy chairperson and director of graduate studies at Bilkent University's Department of International Relations. He has taught at the University of Missouri-Columbia, Stephens College, Turkey's Ministry of Foreign Affairs, TOBB-ETÜ, the Turkish Military Academy, and the National Security College. Dr. Özdamar's research focuses on foreign policy analysis, international relations theories, and security studies. Specifically, he has written articles on Turkish, American, Syrian, and Iranian foreign policies; Black Sea regional security; EU energy security; and ethno-religious conflicts and religion in world politics. Dr. Özdamar's articles have been published in academic journals such as *Foreign Policy Analysis, Social Science Quarterly, Terrorism and Political Violence, Middle East Policy, Uluslararası İlişkiler,* and *International Studies Review.* He currently serves as executive officer at the International Studies Association-ENMISA, on the editorial board of *Foreign Policy Analysis,* and as editor of *All Azimuth: Journal of Foreign Policy and Peace.*

RODGER A. PAYNE is professor and chair of the Department of Political Science at the University of Louisville. He is the coauthor of *Democratizing Global Politics* (2004) and *The Power of Ideas* (2008) and author of forty journal articles or book chapters, focusing primarily on security politics. From 1994–2011, Payne directed the Grawemeyer Award for Ideas Improving World Order. He previously taught at Northwestern University and was a visiting research fellow at Harvard's Belfer Center for Science and International Affairs; Stanford's Center for International Security and Cooperation; and the Program on International Politics, Economics, and Security at the University of Chicago. Payne's awards include an International Peace and Security Studies Fellowship cosponsored by the Social Science Research Council and MacArthur Foundation. He was a member of the two-person 1983 National Debate Tournament championship team from the University of Kansas. He holds a PhD from the University of Maryland, College Park.

SEAN PAYNE is a doctoral candidate in the School of Urban and Public Affairs at the University of Louisville. His research interests include environmental politics, international development, and urban policy.

THOMAS PRESTON is the C. O. Johnson Distinguished Professor of Political Science and Director of The School of Politics, Philosophy, and Public Affairs at Washington State University. A specialist in security policy, foreign affairs, and political psychology, he is the author of *The President and His Inner Circle: Leadership Style and the Advisory Process in Foreign Affairs* (2001), *From Lambs to Lions: Future Security Relationships in a World of Biological and Nuclear Weapons* (2007, 2009), *Pandora's Trap: Presidential Decision Making and Blame Avoidance in Vietnam and Iraq* (2011), and co-author of *Introduction to Political Psychology* (2004, 2010). He frequently serves as an independent consultant for various U.S. government departments and agencies.

JAMES M. SCOTT is the Herman Brown Chair and professor of political science at Texas Christian University. He is the author, coauthor, or editor of seven books and more than fifty articles, chapters, and other publications. A former president of both the International Studies Association's Midwest Region (2000) and its Foreign Policy Analysis Section (2001), he is currently a coeditor of *Foreign Policy Analysis*. He is the recipient of the 2012 Quincy Wright Distinguished Scholar Award from the International Studies Association and he has directed the annual NSF-funded Democracy, Interdependence, and World Politics Summer Research Experience for Undergraduates Program since 2004.

GERALD FELIX WARBURG is professor of public policy and assistant dean for external affairs at the University of Virginia's Batten School of Leadership and Public Policy. His research interests center on the U.S. national security policy-making process and best practices for NGO leaders. As legislative assistant to members of the U.S. House and Senate leadership, he played a lead staff role in drafting such public laws as the Nuclear Non-Proliferation Act, the Comprehensive Anti-Apartheid Sanctions Act, and the Bingham Amendment, leading to the abolition of the Joint Committee on Atomic Energy. He is author of *Conflict and Consensus: The Struggle Between Congress and the President Over Foreign Policymaking* (1990), *The Mandarin Club* (2006), chapters on Congress and lobbying in *The National Security Enterprise: Navigating the Labyrinth* (2011), and *Dispatches from the Eastern Front: A Political Education from the Nixon Years to the Age of Obama* (2014). He holds degrees from Hampshire College and Stanford University.

STEPHEN ZUNES is professor of politics and coordinator of Middle Eastern Studies at the University of San Francisco. His research interests focus on U.S. Middle East policy, human rights, and nonviolent civil insurrections. He is the principal editor of *Nonviolent Social Movements* (1999), the author of *Tinderbox: U.S. Middle East Policy and the Roots of Terrorism* (2003), and co-author (with Jacob Mundy) of *Western Sahara: War, Nationalism and Conflict Irresolution* (2010). He serves as a senior policy analyst for the Foreign Policy in Focus project of the Institute for Policy Studies, an associate editor of *Peace Review*, a contributing editor of *Tikkun,* and chair of the academic advisory committee for the International Center on Nonviolent Conflict. He received his PhD from Cornell University.

Introduction

Ralph G. Carter

The Greek philosopher Heraclitus may have been the first person to put in writing the notion that "the only constant is change."[1] Since the days of the Greek city-states, foreign policy has involved reacting to both threats and opportunities that arise in a changing international environment. However, the pace of those changes in the international system has varied considerably over time. From 1947–1989, there were only incremental changes in the issues typically perceived as most important by U.S. foreign policy makers. The Cold War rivalry dominated their discussions, and, regardless of the subjects involved, most foreign policy-related issues sooner or later came down to this question: How does this affect our relations with the Soviet Union and its allies?[2]

When the Cold War rivalry ended with the fall of the Berlin Wall and the fragmentation of the Soviet Union, some expected a new international system marked by more harmonious relationships among states. Instead, a period of rapid and at times violent change ensued. New policies had to be forged for dealing with Russia and the former Soviet states. More unexpectedly, without the glue of anticommunism as a bond, the United States and its traditional allies and trading partners faced the task of redefining their relationships. New, post–Cold War policies had to be found for the African, Asian, and Latin American states.

Long overshadowed by the Cold War, global issues moved to the forefront of U.S. foreign policy. How should the United States react to regional conflicts, the challenges involved in nation building, attempted genocide, poverty, and threats to the environment? To what extent should the United States depend on international organizations in the pursuit of its goals? What place should international actors like the United Nations, NATO, the European Union, and regional organizations in Asia, Africa, and Latin America have in U.S. foreign policy? Should the United States lead these international organizations, or should it act as a "first among equals" in a team-like environment?

The September 11, 2001, terrorist attacks on New York City and the Pentagon brought home the message that many of those beyond U.S. borders were fundamentally opposed to the main currents of U.S. foreign policy, if not to the basic themes in U.S. culture itself. While many Americans were shocked to learn that others resented, if not hated, U.S. policies, dealing with the challenges of terrorist threats quickly dominated the attention of top policy makers.

If thereafter any Americans needed reminders that all are affected by events in other countries, the consequences of the global recession of 2007–2009 reiterated that message. Suddenly, the basics of the global economy were at risk. Fundamental questions about debt, credit, and trade took on new importance and perhaps changed the thinking of an entire generation of young adults.

As the international environment has changed, so have U.S. foreign policy processes. These changes in the internal policy-making process are as evident as the changes in the external environment. Understanding the dynamics of this process is the goal of this volume.

The "Old" Foreign Policy System

With the exception of a few periods of "thaw," the Cold War dominated U.S. foreign policy from 1947 until the fall of the Soviet Union in late 1991. The threat of nuclear war between the US- and Soviet-led blocs put a premium on national security policy, and the U.S. foreign policy process evolved to meet that threat. As commander in chief, the president was at the heart of this process. Moreover, the National Security Act of 1947 gave the chief executive considerable assistance by creating a unified Defense Department as well as the Central Intelligence Agency, National Security Council, and the post of national security adviser.

Not surprisingly during this period, the focus of the policy-making process became the presidency and the executive branch. This process was well represented by the presidential preeminence model of foreign policy making, which views foreign policy as the result of decisions and actions by the president and his closest advisers and relevant other officials in the executive branch.[3] Other theoretical approaches were developed within the presidential preeminence model to reflect the processes by which presidential administrations made foreign policy. These included seeing administration actions and decisions as

- optimal choices of a rational calculation of costs and benefits;
- choices between various bureaucratic routines appropriate to the situation; or

- the result of political processes played out within the administration by actors with differing degrees of power and interests in a particular issue.[4]

Members of Congress, interest groups, the media, and the public were seen as playing little or no role in the making of foreign policy.[5]

The "New" Foreign Policy System

The post–Cold War era triggered changes in the ways in which U.S. foreign policy is made. With the exception of the war power, the ability of the president to play a predominant role in shaping policy diminished, and the roles played by a host of other actors increased.[6] Two factors were crucial to these changes. First, the global economy became more interdependent, and decisions made elsewhere had greater influence on the United States. In short, intermestic issues—those that occur in the international environment but are reacted to as if they are domestic policy issues—are more common than was previously the case. Take, for example, the possible ways of formulating policy toward China: Should U.S. policy be defined primarily as national security policy, thus mobilizing the State and Defense Departments to rein in China's ability to threaten U.S. security interests? Should it increasingly be defined as trade policy, mobilizing officials in the Commerce Department, national and state chambers of commerce, trade groups, and US-based multinational corporations that want to sell more to the enormous Chinese market? Should China policy be defined as monetary policy, thus empowering the Treasury Department and possibly the Federal Reserve to be major players? Should China policy be seen as "jobs policy," thus mobilizing members of the Labor Department and labor unions, whose members and leaders fear the loss of U.S. jobs to lower-paid Chinese workers? Should it be defined as human rights policy, thus mobilizing the State Department's under secretary for civilian security, democracy, and human rights and interest groups like Amnesty International, Human Rights Watch, and Freedom House? In short, *how an issue is defined determines who will play active roles in the resolution of the matter.*

Second, during the Cold War foreign and national security policy was deemed too important and too risky to let non-experts play a significant role. Primary policy-making actors included the president, his close White House advisers, and key officials from the foreign and defense bureaucracies—the members of the National Security Council and their staff, the State Department, the Defense Department, and the Central Intelligence Agency and other parts of the intelligence community. Congressional and public roles were generally relegated to supporting the actions of the White House, except in those instances of a major policy mistake or when no policy emerged from the White House.[7]

With the exception of protecting the United States from al Qaeda affiliates and their supporters, there is now no clear domestic political consensus regarding the central aims of U.S. foreign policy. Without widely shared norms to exclude their participation, more and more domestic actors can be expected to try to shape foreign policy. Hence one can expect more foreign policy activity by members of Congress through legislation and other actions that administrations often resent (such as holding critical committee hearings, using oversight roles to monitor the administration's foreign policy performance, requiring extensive briefings and reports by administration actors, and making speeches critical of administration policy). Members of the opposition party can particularly be expected to challenge the president's foreign policy in terms of ends pursued and means employed. Interest groups and other nongovernmental organizations will become more involved as well, lobbying government officials on behalf of their policy preferences, using the written and electronic media to get their policy positions before the public and government officials, engaging in letter-writing campaigns to influence officials, using campaign contributions to help friendly officials get elected, and so on. Members of the media and other pundits will use their access to editorial pages, television, and the expanding constellation of news and information outlets to influence foreign policy in their preferred direction. Grassroots activists, online bloggers, public opinion pollsters, and others who claim to represent the public will also become involved. Even the ability of the president to control his own administration may weaken, as bureaucratic actors become more active in policy making or find themselves the targets of other actors.[8]

Thus the unifying theme of this volume is that the U.S. foreign policy process is becoming more open, more pluralistic, and more intensely partisan. It resembles more the decade leading up to World War II than the four decades that followed the war. One leading scholar summarizes the current period as follows:

> [T]here now seems to be a *post–cold war dissensus* predicated on societal disagreement on the nature and extent of U.S. leadership, policy disagreement on the proper role, strategy, goals, and instruments of U.S. foreign policy, and procedural decentralization away from presidential leadership to more widely diffused involvement of actors from a wider circle of bureaucratic agencies, members of Congress, and nongovernmental actors.[9]

In short, the foreign policy process is becoming more like the domestic policy process, and thus it is becoming more political. As President Bill Clinton said in 1995, "The more time I spend on foreign policy . . . the more I become convinced that there is no longer a clear distinction between what is foreign and domestic."[10] More actors are involved, and they have their own foreign policy needs, interests, and agendas. Although presidents still have impressive formal and informal foreign policy roles and powers, they are now less able to dominate foreign policy processes and outcomes than was the case during the Cold War.[11] Presidential foreign policy "wins" may be less frequent than previously was the case, and they will almost always represent hard-fought victories.

A number of other themes unify this volume as well. Jurisdictional competition between the president and Congress over the control and direction of foreign policy is commonplace. Even members of the president's own party will resist his policies if they think the White House is trampling on the legitimate jurisdictional responsibilities of Congress to legislate policy or appropriate funds. The opposition party can be expected to challenge the president's wishes, and does so often. For example, during the 1990s congressional Republicans developed a visceral dislike for President Clinton. It seemed that Republican Party leaders Trent Lott, Dick Armey, and Tom DeLay, along with powerful committee chair Jesse Helms, opposed nearly anything Clinton supported. White House scandals, including the Monica Lewinsky affair and allegations of illegal campaign contributions, gave critics another reason to oppose Clinton's policy goals. The high-water mark of their opposition was Clinton's impeachment. More recently, the Democratically controlled Congress of 2006–2008 seemed just as skeptical of the George W. Bush administration, particularly when the White House refused to share requested information and documents with Congress or invoked executive privilege in the face of congressional subpoenas to get top administrative officials to testify under oath on Capitol Hill. Now, in the Obama era, former vice president Dick Cheney has been quick to criticize many of the new president's foreign and national security policy decisions, and a number of congressional Republicans have done so as well. Partisan attacks between the two branches cannot help but strain the policy-making process. The themes discussed here reveal some of the chinks in the presidential preeminence model of policy making.

The Case Study Approach

One often hears statements like "Today Washington announced . . ." or "The United States responded by. . . ". Such pronouncements obscure the fact that individuals "announce" and decide how to "respond." Saying "The United States decided to do X" is shorthand for the more accurate statement that a number of people acting in the name of the state decided to do X, usually for a variety of different reasons. Case studies are perhaps the best way to illustrate how such individuals cooperate, compete, and often compromise in order to produce foreign policy.

The fifteen studies that comprise this volume are teaching cases. The definition of a teaching case is that it tells the story of what happened, "who was involved, what they contended with, and, sometimes, how it came out."[12] Rather than provide instant analysis of why things happened as they did, teaching cases rely on the reader to determine why individuals took the stances or engaged in the actions discussed. They vividly illustrate how policy making brings together individuals who see matters from different perspectives and who are motivated by an assortment of goals and objectives. Such cases also help show that these policy makers live in a political environment in which everything affects everything else; foreign policy decisions are not made in a vacuum. They affect and are affected by other foreign and domestic policy issues at the time the policy is devised and into the foreseeable future. Like the rest of the political process, foreign policy making can be a messy affair, and case studies help to realistically illustrate the process.

One advantage of the cases in this volume is their contemporary nature. Textbooks usually cover the broad themes and theoretical issues involving foreign policy making, but often do not have many contemporary illustrations of what happens or how things play out in the policy-making process. These cases focus on issues and events that confronted U.S. policy makers from the last decade of the twentieth century through the first decade of the twenty-first century. A second advantage of these studies is their range. They were chosen to represent the array of external challenges and opportunities, substantive issues, internal political situations, and policy-making dynamics that seem likely to repeatedly confront U.S. foreign policy makers in the post–Cold War, post–September 11th, and now post–Great Recession world.

Each case study offers a unique perspective on the events, issues, and policy makers involved, but beyond their uniqueness are patterns in the influences at work. Where do the causal factors for U.S. foreign policy arise? According to realists and neorealists, the answer typically lies beyond U.S. borders. These observers see foreign policy as a state's reaction to events taking place in an international system based on anarchy and lacking a strong legal structure. In essence, states can be expected to pursue their self-defined interests in ways that are, at least on some level, rational.[13] On the other hand, advocates of liberalism argue that what happens within a state's borders also matters, often as much as (or maybe more than) the external situations foreign policy makers face. Thus for liberals and neoliberals, a central belief is "*state structures matter:* the structure of their domestic governments and the values and views of their citizens affect their behavior in international affairs."[14] According to this point of view, one cannot ignore who is in the government, what they think, and what motivates them. In short, different administrations and Congresses will react differently to similar external events. The cases in this volume illustrate the importance of such external and internal factors and help in understanding what U.S. officials have been dealing with in the post–Cold War, post–September 11th, and post–Great Recession eras. In this respect, they provide a realistic understanding of how policy is actually made. They serve as reminders that people often have to make quick decisions based on less-than-complete information, and they help hone critical thinking skills in preparation for real-world situations.[15]

Each case opens with a section titled "Before You Begin," which poses questions about that particular case. These questions help in organizing thoughts and directing attention to important issues. All the cases follow a similar internal organization. Each introduces the case, provides background information, relates relevant events, and offers a conclusion that should help in identifying some of the broader issues or themes involved. Each study is accompanied by a chronology of events and a list of key actors.

Optimally, case-based teaching requires class participation. Instructors ask questions, and students are expected to discuss what happened and, more important, *why* it happened as it did. Such active learning requires that students come to class prepared to contribute to an informed discussion of the case assignment, including putting themselves in the place of the major actors in order to assess issues and events. Why did policy makers do what they did? What internal or external factors affected their decisions? Was the option selected their only option? If not, why was that option chosen over others? What could be gained, and what could be lost? Students will get the most from this approach if they come to class having carefully thought about such things in addition to having reviewed the questions in "Before You Begin." Such preparation will make for a better understanding of the real world of foreign policy making.

As the Cold War was ending, some observers of international politics began speculating about the nature of the post–Cold War world. Many offered the optimistic assessment that international conflict would decline, and widely shared liberal values would become the new glue of international politics.[16] Unfortunately, violent conflict did not disappear, and versions of capitalism were embraced more widely than commitments to liberal values like democracy and human rights.[17] U.S. foreign policy still consequently must deal with difficult issues involving the use of military force and how to protect national interests in an uncertain environment. The first three cases in this volume focus on matters involving U.S. decisions about whether and how to participate in military interventions. In chapter 1, Frédérick Gagnon and Ryan Hendrickson examine the efforts by the Clinton, Bush, and Obama administrations to respond to the terrorist threat represented by Osama bin Laden and the Afghanistan Taliban. In chapter 2, Priya Dixit examines the difficult issues inherent in the use of targeted killings of terrorist leaders. In chapter 3, Jeffrey Lantis and Eric Moskowitz review the Bush administration's efforts to employ coercive diplomacy against, and then topple, the Iraqi regime of Saddam Hussein, as well as the Obama administration's efforts to disengage from that conflict.

The next three case studies examine the challenges posed by the spread of nuclear weapons and nuclear technology. In chapter 4, Thomas Preston chronicles the U.S. efforts to promote a negotiated settlement over Iran's nuclear weapons program, a case posing the fundamental question of whether or not a "rogue" regime should be readily engaged or made to prove its good faith first. In chapter 5, Patrick James and Özgür Özdamar examine the dynamics involved in the Clinton, Bush, and Obama administrations' efforts to confront the threat posed by North Korean nuclear weapons. In chapter 6, Gerald Warburg illustrates how an effort to reshape US-Indian relations resulted in the reversal of thirty years of nuclear nonproliferation policy.

The next section focuses more directly on the use of diplomacy as a tool of statecraft. In chapter 7, Ralph Carter and James Scott detail the poor relationship that developed between the United States and Russia after the end of the Cold War and the Obama administration's goal to "reset" the relationship in a more positive direction. In chapter 8, Stephen Zunes illustrates the difficulties of responding to the Egyptian Revolution and how the Obama administration had to choose between supporting a long-time ally and supporting the people opposing that repressive regime. In chapter 9, Joyce Kaufman shows what can happen when a "situation" shows up on your doorstep–in this case a blind Chinese dissident unexpectedly seeking asylum in the U.S. Embassy in Beijing.

Economic and trade policy has become increasingly important in the post–Cold War and post–Great Recession era. This next section has three cases illustrating some of these challenges. In chapter 10, Thomas Lairson details how the Bush and Obama administrations reacted to the recent global economic crisis and the resulting rise of state capitalism. A range of trade-related issues come to the fore in chapter 11, where Steven Hook and Franklin Lebo look at the impact of a wide array of interest groups across the last three administrations' decisions regarding trade with China. In chapter 12, Rodger Payne and Sean Payne show how economic policy becomes intertwined with environmental issues in the climate change debate.

In our last section, the legal challenges arising from a more globalized world are starkly displayed. In chapter 13, Louis Fisher examines how the Bush administration relied on warrantless wiretapping of overseas phone calls made by U.S. citizens or residents in order to gain intelligence information in the war on terrorism and how the Obama administration tried to reconcile national security needs and the protection of civil liberties. In chapter 14, Linda Cornett and Mark Gibney trace the evolution of Bush administration decisions concerning the detention of "enemy combatants" captured in the war on terrorism and how the Obama administration has sought to modify those controversial decisions. Finally in chapter 15, Donald Jackson and Ralph Carter illustrate the Clinton, Bush, and Obama administrations' political dilemma when faced with the issue of how to react to the creation of the new International Criminal Court and the possibility that U.S. citizens might be tried before it for war crimes, crimes against humanity, or genocide.

These cases represent the wide range of actors, interests, and issues comprising contemporary U.S. foreign policy. The conclusion returns to the book's primary unifying theme—that in the post–Cold War period, U.S. foreign policy making is becoming increasingly open, pluralistic, and partisan. New issues have made their way onto the policy agenda, and many newcomers—agencies, interests, and constituencies—have become involved in addressing them. In short, U.S. foreign policy making looks increasingly like U.S. domestic policy making, and in a world marked by increasing interdependencies among states, perhaps that is to be expected.

Notes

1. See "The Only Thing Constant Is Change," *The Daily Philosopher*, www.thedaily philosopher.org/daily/000011.php.

2. Richard Melanson, *American Foreign Policy since the Vietnam War: The Search for Consensus from Richard Nixon to George W. Bush,* 4th ed. (Armonk, N.Y.: M. E. Sharpe, 2005).

3. James M. Scott and A. Lane Crothers, "Out of the Cold: The Post–Cold War Context of U.S. Foreign Policy," in *After the End: Making U.S. Foreign Policy in the Post–Cold War World,* ed. James M. Scott (Durham: Duke University Press, 1998), 1–25.

4. Graham Allison and Philip Zelikow, *Essence of Decision: Explaining the Cuban Missile Crisis,* 2nd ed. (New York: Longman, 1999).

5. See, for example, Samuel P. Huntington, *The Common Defense: Strategic Programs in National Politics* (New York: Columbia University Press, 1961); Roger Hilsman, *To Move a Nation* (New York: Doubleday, 1967); Morton Halperin, *Bureaucratic Politics and Foreign Policy* (Washington, DC: Brookings Institution, 1974); John Steinbruner, *The Cybernetic Theory of Decision: New Dimensions of Political Analysis* (Princeton: Princeton University Press, 1974); Roger Hilsman, *The Politics of Policy Making in Defense and Foreign Affairs,* 2nd ed. (Englewood Cliffs, N.J.: Prentice Hall, 1990); and Allison and Zelikow, *Essence of Decision.*

6. See Ralph G. Carter and James M. Scott, *Choosing to Lead: Understanding Congressional Foreign Policy Entrepreneurs* (Durham: Duke University Press, 2009); James M. Lindsay and Randall B. Ripley, "How Congress Influences Foreign and Defense Policy," in *Congress Resurgent: Foreign and Defense Policy on Capitol Hill,* ed. Randall B. Ripley and James M. Lindsay (Ann Arbor: University of Michigan Press, 1993), 17–35; James M. Lindsay, *Congress and the Politics of U.S. Foreign Policy* (Baltimore: Johns Hopkins University Press, 1994); and virtually all of the selections in Scott, *After the End.*

7. For more on policy vacuums and policy corrections, see Carter and Scott, *Choosing to Lead.*

8. Scott and Crothers, "Out of the Cold"; James M. Scott, "Interbranch Policy Making after the End," in Scott, *After the End,* 389–407.

9. Scott, "Interbranch Policy Making after the End," 405.

10. Quoted in Ralph G. Carter, "Congress and Post–Cold War U.S. Foreign Policy," in Scott, *After the End,* 129–130.

11. See Carter, "Congress and Post–Cold War U.S. Foreign Policy"; Jerel Rosati and Stephen Twing, "The Presidency and U.S. Foreign Policy after the Cold War," in Scott, *After the End,* 29–56.

12. John Boehrer, quoted in Vicki L. Golich, "The ABCs of Case Teaching," *International Studies Perspectives* 1 (2000): 12.

13. There are lots of sources for realism and neorealism. For reasonably concise discussions of these topics, see David A. Lake, "Realism," in *The Oxford Companion to Politics of the World,* ed. Joel Krieger (Oxford: Oxford University Press, 1993), 771–773; or Allison and Zelikow, *Essence of Decision,* 30–33.

14. Allison and Zelikow, *Essence of Decision,* 39 (emphasis in original).

15. Laurence E. Lynn Jr., *Teaching and Learning with Cases: A Guidebook* (New York: Chatham House Publishers/Seven Bridges Press, 1999), 2.

16. See Francis Fukuyama, "The End of History?" *National Interest* 16 (Summer 1989): 3–16.

17. See Samuel P. Huntington, *The Clash of Civilizations and the Remaking of World Order* (New York: Simon and Schuster, 1996).

1 The United States versus Terrorism: From the Embassy Bombings in Tanzania and Kenya to the Surge and Drawdown of Forces in Afghanistan

Frédérick Gagnon and Ryan C. Hendrickson

Before You Begin

1. What is the traditionally accepted view of Congress's exercise of war powers during the Cold War and after September 11, 2001? How does that view compare to Congress's role leading up to President Bill Clinton's, President George W. Bush's, and President Barack Obama's military actions against terrorism?

2. In the days prior to military action in 1998, 2001, and 2009, how did the diplomatic challenges differ for Clinton, Bush, and Obama?

3. Is Congress's decision to endorse military action against those involved in the September 11 attacks a victory for Congress's war powers? If so, why?

4. Which advisers seem to have the most significant influence on Clinton's, Bush's, and Obama's decisions regarding terrorism, Afghanistan, and al Qaeda? Why?

5. Did President Clinton's military action in 1998 have a "diversionary" intent? What evidence supports such a view? What evidence challenges it?

Introduction: Striking Back at Terrorism

The public, the media, and most members of Congress sometimes are not privy to the process in which U.S. use of force decisions are made. Although Presidents Bill Clinton, George W. Bush, and Barack Obama appear to have vastly different interests in policy matters, and certainly have divergent views of the appropriate role for the United States in international affairs, many similarities exist in the ways they made decisions as commander in chief. On August 20, 1998, when Clinton launched missile strikes against alleged facilities of Osama bin Laden in Sudan and Afghanistan, and on October 7, 2001, when Bush set in motion Operation Enduring Freedom

Timeline

The Clinton, Bush, and Obama Administrations' Strikes against Osama bin Laden

August 23, 1996	Osama bin Laden issues his first *fatwa* against the United States.
February 23, 1998	Bin Laden issues his second *fatwa* against the United States.
August 7, 1998	Bombs explode at the U.S. embassies in Nairobi, Kenya, and Dar es Salaam, Tanzania.
August 14, 1998	Director of Central Intelligence George Tenet presents his agency's assessment that bin Laden and his al Qaeda network were behind the attacks on the embassies.
August 17, 1998	President Bill Clinton admits to the nation that he misled the public about having an extramarital relationship with White House intern Monica Lewinsky.
August 20, 1998	In a 2:00 a.m. telephone conversation with National Security Adviser Sandy Berger, Clinton authorizes strikes against bin Laden. Missiles are launched on alleged al Qaeda sites in Afghanistan and Sudan.
Mid-September 1999	The Clinton administration initiates "the plan," consisting of broader covert operations intended to gather intelligence on bin Laden and disrupt al Qaeda.
October 12, 2000	Al Qaeda launches a suicide boat attack against the USS *Cole* while it is docked in Aden, Yemen. Seventeen Americans are killed.
September 11, 2001	Al Qaeda operatives hijack four commercial aircraft, flying two into the World Trade Center towers and crashing another into the Pentagon. The fourth aircraft crashes in a field in Pennsylvania. The death toll is 2,995.
September 14, 2001	The Senate passes S. J. Res. 23, authorizing George W. Bush to use all necessary and appropriate force against those associated with the September 11 strikes on the United States. The House of Representatives responds the following day by passing the resolution.

September 15–16, 2001	President Bush holds meetings with foreign policy principals at Camp David to discuss military operations in retaliation for the September 11 attacks.
October 6, 2001	Bush gives final approval for military action against Afghanistan.
October 7, 2001	The United States launches Operation Enduring Freedom against the Taliban and al Qaeda in Afghanistan.
December 7, 2001	The Taliban lose Kandahar, the last major city under its control.
August 2003	NATO takes control of security in Kabul, its first-ever operational commitment outside Europe.
October 2006	NATO assumes responsibility for security across the whole of Afghanistan, taking command in the east from a US-led coalition force.
April 2008	NATO leaders meeting in Bucharest say peacekeeping mission in Afghanistan is their top priority. They pledge a "firm and shared long-term commitment" there.
September 2008	President Bush sends an extra 4,500 U.S. troops to Afghanistan, in a move he described as a "quiet surge."
February 2009	President Barack Obama announces the dispatch of 17,000 extra U.S. troops in Afghanistan.
March 2009	President Obama unveils a new U.S. strategy for Afghanistan and Pakistan to combat what he calls an increasingly perilous situation.
December 2009	President Obama announces the dispatch of 30,000 extra U.S. troops in Afghanistan. He also declares that the United States will begin withdrawing its forces by 2011.
January—December 2010	As the surge plan is being implemented, President Obama escalates the use of Unmanned Aerial Vehicle (UAVs)/drone missile strikes against remaining elements of the Taliban and al Qaeda in Pakistan.
June 2010	Gen. Stanley McChrystal is relieved of command of American and NATO forces in Afghanistan. Gen. David Petraeus replaces him.

(continued)

Timeline *(continued)*

The Clinton, Bush, and Obama Administrations' Strikes against Osama bin Laden

November 2010	The United States and its allies announce that all ISAF forces are intended to be withdrawn from Afghanistan by the end of 2014.
May 2, 2011	Osama bin Laden is found and killed in Pakistan by United States Navy SEALs.
June 2011	The American military presence reaches its apex in Afghanistan, with nearly 100,000 troops deployed.
May 2012	The Obama administration announces a Strategic Partnership Agreement with Afghanistan, which will keep approximately 15,000 to 20,000 U.S. military forces in Afghanistan after the 2014 conclusion of the ISAF mission.
July 2012	Afghanistan is named a "Major Non-NATO Ally."
November 2012	Obama wins a second presidential term. Afghanistan has largely moved out of the public and political discussion as the 2012 elections moved forward.[a]

[a]For a complete timeline, read BBC, "Timeline: Afghanistan," http://news.bbc.co.uk/ 2/hi/1162108.stm.

against the Taliban and al Qaeda in Afghanistan, nearly all the critical military decisions were made by the executive branch. In 2009 Obama's "strategic review" of Bush's Afghanistan policy and decision to expand the war on terrorism in Afghanistan and Pakistan were also made primarily by the executive branch, with limited input from other actors. Congress also played a limited role in Obama's decision to reduce the number of troops in Afghanistan. Unlike many other foreign policy issues in the post–Cold War and post-9/11 environments, the center of action concerning terrorism is the White House.

Background: Terrorism and Presidential Powers

The U.S. Constitution grants Congress the power to declare war, as well as other enumerated powers associated with the military. The president is given the explicit authority to act as commander in chief. Most constitutional scholars agree, however, that the president is empowered to use force without congressional approval to "repel sudden attacks" against the United States.[1] In other instances, the president must obtain Congress's approval prior to using force.

For much of U.S. history, Congress's war powers have been respected by the commander in chief.[2] With the Cold War's onset and the widely accepted belief that the Soviet Union and communism represented a threat to the United States, the president's perception of his power as commander in chief became increasingly one of omnipotence. Since 1945 presidents have asserted broad military powers with few recognized limitations. Because members of Congress agreed that communism should be checked, and because it was politically safer to let a president assume full responsibility for U.S. military endeavors, Congress often deferred to executive branch unilateralism in actions by the president as commander in chief.[3] This practice remained the norm until the 1973 passage of the War Powers Resolution, which was designed to reassert the authority that many felt Presidents Lyndon Johnson and Richard Nixon had usurped from Congress during the Vietnam War.[4] The resolution requires that the president "consult with Congress in every possible circumstance" prior to and after the introduction of U.S. forces into hostilities (P.L. 93–148). Despite its intent, the War Powers Resolution has been a failure. All presidents since 1973 have maintained that it is unconstitutional—arguing that it illegally limits their power as commander in chief—and Congress has often failed to enforce it.[5] The Clinton presidency is a good example of this dynamic. Clinton viewed his powers as commander in chief broadly, maintaining that congressional approval was not required for him to take military action.[6] Clinton's outlook is evidenced by U.S. military actions against Iraq, NATO air strikes in Bosnia and Kosovo, military deployments to Haiti and Somalia, and the use of force against bin Laden, all of which occurred without specific congressional approval.

U.S. Embassy Bombings in Tanzania and Kenya: Clinton Strikes Osama bin Laden

On August 7, 1998, 263 people, including 12 Americans, were killed in simultaneous truck bomb explosions at the U.S. embassies in Nairobi, Kenya, and Dar es Salaam, Tanzania. Immediately after the bombings, experts from the Federal Bureau of Investigation (FBI) and the Central Intelligence Agency

(CIA) rushed to East Africa to determine responsibility for the attacks. The evidence quickly pointed to Osama bin Laden, a name most Americans had never heard of but who was no stranger to the U.S. intelligence community. Bin Laden was born in 1957 into a wealthy, conservative family in Saudi Arabia with connections to the Al Saud, the Saudi royal family. In the 1980s, he left Saudi Arabia to go to Afghanistan and support the *mujahidin,* the fighters who were resisting the Soviet takeover and occupation of Afghanistan with critical military assistance from the United States. Toward the end of the Afghan war, bin Laden established an organization of radical Muslims that would become the foundation for al Qaeda, a network of supporters willing to advance their fundamentalist version of Islam using any means necessary. He then moved to Saudi Arabia and Sudan and was suspected of being involved in the bombing of the World Trade Center in New York City in February 1993. The State Department added al Qaeda to its list of terrorist organizations in 1997. One of the first statements by bin Laden to generate international attention occurred on August 23, 1996, when he publicly issued a *fatwa,* or decree (usually by a recognized religious leader), calling for a *jihad* (struggle or holy war) against the United States to oppose its military presence in Saudi Arabia that began with the 1991 Persian Gulf War. In 1998 bin Laden once again caught the eye of the world when on February 23 he issued a second *fatwa* in a fax to a London-based Arabic newsletter. In the communication, he made three central points: the United States should leave the Muslim holy land; the United States should end the "great devastation inflicted" upon the Iraqi people through its continuation of economic sanctions; and the United States was engaged in a religious and economic war against Muslims, while simultaneously serving Israel's interests vis-à-vis the Muslim world. The truck bombings at the U.S. embassies in Kenya and Tanzania occurred less than six months later.

A week after the attacks, on August 14, Director of Central Intelligence (DCI) George Tenet presented his agency's analysis—a "judgment about responsibility"—to President Clinton. According to the CIA, additional evidence suggested that bin Laden was planning another attack on Americans and that an important gathering of bin Laden associates would take place in Afghanistan on August 20, 1998. At the meeting with Tenet, Clinton gave tentative approval to a military response and authorized his senior military advisers to move forward with operational plans.[7]

The bombings and their aftermath occurred at a difficult time for Clinton. On August 17, he testified to the Office of the Independent Counsel and a grand jury, by videoconferencing, that he had had an extramarital relationship with former White House intern Monica Lewinsky. Later that evening, in a national address, Clinton admitted that he had "misled" the American people about his relationship with Lewinsky.[8] After his address, Clinton and his family left for a vacation, but planning continued for military strikes against bin Laden. On Wednesday, August 19, while on Martha's Vineyard, Clinton discussed the strikes with Vice President Al Gore. Senior leaders in Congress were also notified of possible military action. Throughout the day, Clinton spoke on four occasions by phone with his national security adviser, Samuel "Sandy" Berger, who was in Washington. In a call around 2:00 a.m. Thursday, Clinton gave final approval for the strikes.

Beginning on August 20 around 1:30 p.m. EST, seventy-nine cruise missiles were launched at targets in Sudan and Afghanistan from ships stationed in the Arabian and Red Seas. The Sudanese targets included the al-Shifa pharmaceutical plant, which the United States alleged was a chemical weapons factory. Six other sites were struck simultaneously in Afghanistan. Secretary of Defense William Cohen declared that al-Shifa was chosen because bin Laden was heavily involved in Sudan's military-industrial complex and had an interest in acquiring chemical weapons.[9] In discussing the sites hit in Afghanistan, Gen. Henry Shelton, chairman of the Joint Chiefs of Staff, said that one "base camp" that served as the headquarters for bin Laden's organization was struck.

Approximately twenty-five minutes after the strikes, Clinton addressed the nation, providing four justifications for his actions. First, he announced that "convincing evidence" pointed to bin Laden's responsibility for the attacks on the embassies. Second, the president pointed to bin Laden's history of terrorist activities. Third, Clinton argued that "compelling information" suggested that bin Laden was planning another attack against the United States. Fourth, he said that bin Laden sought to acquire chemical weapons.[10] In a second address to the nation later that evening, Clinton expanded on bin Laden's previous declarations and activities and said that his senior military advisers had given him a "unanimous recommendation" to go forward with the strikes.[11] In mentioning the unanimous recommendation Clinton may have been anticipating the reaction from the public, 40 percent of whom believed that the Monica Lewinsky scandal may have influenced the decision to strike. Administration officials responded vehemently with denials that any link existed between the president's domestic troubles and the strikes at bin Laden.[12] Though many Americans thought the "Lewinsky factor" may have entered into the decision to use force, 75 percent still supported the strikes.[13]

Consulting Congress

The night before the attacks, Berger phoned Speaker of the House Newt Gingrich (R-GA) and Senate Majority Leader Trent Lott (R-MS) and presented them with the evidence implicating bin Laden. Senate Minority Leader Tom Daschle (D-SD) also received a phone call before the strikes.[14] Berger attempted to call House Minority Leader Richard Gephardt (D-MO), who was traveling in France. Clinton also phoned these leaders, with the exception of Gephardt, as he flew back to Washington to deliver his second address to the nation.[15] DCI Tenet notified, at minimum, Sen. Bob Kerrey (D-NE), a member of the Senate Intelligence Committee, in advance of the strikes, which Kerrey strongly supported.[16] Other reports contend that Gingrich had been consulted and was privy to intelligence on bin Laden before Berger's first phone calls were made.[17]

In retrospect, it is clear that the most senior leaders in Congress of both parties knew of the impending strikes. White House spokesperson Michael McCurry purposely noted that all requirements of the War Powers Resolution were met, including its consultation mandate.[18] In the aftermath of Clinton's strikes against bin Laden there were no complaints about violations of the War Powers Resolution or Congress's war-making powers. Congress gave broad support to the president on constitutional grounds.

Although these strikes were the last overt military effort to kill bin Laden before the terrorist attacks of September 11, 2001, the Clinton administration did not give up the hunt for bin Laden. Before Clinton left office, he authorized five different intelligence operations aimed at disrupting al Qaeda's planning and preempting terrorist activities.[19]

The most comprehensive intelligence operation was known simply as "the plan" and went into effect around mid-September 1999. The plan sought to focus more attention on human intelligence gathering and expand the CIA's efforts to recruit well-qualified operatives who could be placed on the ground in Afghanistan to gather intelligence on bin Laden. Another critical element of the plan was to develop and use the Predator, an unmanned aerial vehicle with intelligence-gathering and military strike capabilities. On at least two occasions before September 11, and perhaps a third, the Predator sighted bin Laden.[20] Former counterterrorism coordinator Richard A. Clarke maintains that on Clinton's orders, the United States had submarines in place with cruise missiles ready for use against bin Laden, but apparently not at times when "actionable intelligence" and military capability existed at the same time.[21]

From a policy-making perspective, the National Commission on Terrorist Attacks Upon the United States, or the 9/11 Commission, made one especially important finding regarding the Clinton administration's counterterrorism policies: Senior officials of the National Security Council (NSC) and the CIA "differ[ed] starkly" in their assessment of the administration's objectives in regard to bin Laden and therefore what types of actions they should be pursuing. NSC staffers, including Berger, maintained that the administration's policies were clear; authorization had been given to kill bin Laden. In contrast, CIA officials asserted that the administration had sought the capture of bin Laden and that only under certain conditions could he be killed.[22] Although misunderstandings or differences existed among key agencies regarding the effort to get bin Laden, it is clear that the center of action for counterterrorism decisions and use of force was at the White House, with critical assistance provided by the CIA, and that military action was the preferred means of addressing these newfound terrorist challenges.

September 11: Authorization of Force and the War on Terrorism

President George W. Bush was made aware of the events that unfolded on September 11 while visiting with children at Emma E. Booker Elementary School in Sarasota, Florida. Upon hearing that an aircraft had crashed into the Pentagon, Bush later said, he thought to himself, "We're at war. . . . Somebody is going to pay."[23] After the session with the children ended, Bush's Secret Service detail quickly escorted him to Air Force One. As it was not considered safe to fly the president back to Washington immediately, Bush was flown to Offut Air Force Base in Omaha, Nebraska. From there, he spoke by phone with members of his National Security Council, including DCI Tenet, who reported that Osama bin Laden was behind the attacks.[24] By early evening, Bush was back at the White House, where deliberations began on how to address the crisis.

The constitutional dynamics and the authority of the president to respond to the September 11 attacks with military action were considerably different from Clinton's strikes against Afghanistan in 1998. Because the United States was directly attacked on its soil, most constitutional experts would concur that the Constitution allowed Bush, as commander in chief, to respond with force in defense of the nation. In addition, Article 51 of the United Nations Charter permits all member states to act in self-defense if attacked.[25] The Bush administration, however, quickly turned to Congress for formal authorization for the use of force. The public was strongly in favor of a military response, and by approaching Congress the administration could avoid raising constitutional questions about the legitimacy of its forthcoming military actions. At the same time, legitimate constitutional questions existed in terms of whom the United States would be at war with. Part of the difficulty of this issue is that the enemy is not easily defined, identified, or targeted.

When Bush administration officials first met with congressional leaders and their senior staff members on September 12, congressional staffers were initially struck by the sweeping nature of the administration's force authorization proposal. Its request included the authority to "deter and pre-empt any future acts of terrorism or aggression against the United States" and essentially unrestricted financial resources for military responses, which would infringe on Congress's constitutional authority to appropriate money.[26] Key legislators, such as Senate Majority Leader Daschle and Sen. Robert C. Byrd (D-WV), thought it was Congress's duty to avoid giving the president "a blank check to go anywhere, anytime, against anyone."[27] During deliberations over the language of the resolution, administration officials agreed to eliminate *pre-empt* and replace it with *prevent.*[28] The request for unlimited spending powers was deleted.[29] As of late evening on September 13, final agreement on the resolution language had not been reached.[30]

On the morning of September 14, Daschle and Senate Minority Leader Lott met with their respective caucuses. Later that morning, the Senate approved, 98–0, S. J. Res. 23 (P.L. 107–40), granting the president sweeping powers to initiate military action. The key provision of the resolution concerning force authorization stated

> [t]hat the President is authorized to use all necessary and appropriate force against those nations, organizations, or persons he determines planned, authorized, committed, or aided the terrorist attacks that occurred on September 11, 2001, or harbored such organizations or persons, in order to prevent any future acts of international terrorism against the United States by such organizations or persons.

The process by which this resolution was crafted and eventually voted on is uncharacteristic in that it was not passed from a formal committee of the House or Senate, and there was no public debate on the constitutional merits of the resolution. The White House consulted with Congress and revised its original proposal based on congressional input, but all in private sessions. A day after the Senate approved the resolution the House did so as well, in a

420–1 vote. Rep. Barbara Lee (D-CA) was the only member of Congress who voted against the measure, maintaining that it provided a "blank check" to the president and granted him "overly broad powers."[31]

In most cases, senators and representatives commented on the resolution after the vote. A number of senior Democratic senators heralded the resolution as a victory for the principle of checks and balances. There is no doubt that Congress forced some important changes in the resolution's language, exercised and demanded its constitutional prerogatives on appropriations, and even inserted a reference to the War Powers Resolution. Congress also limited the administration's military response to only those "nations, organizations, or persons" associated with the September 11 attacks. These "congressional demands" were noted by Senators Carl Levin (D-MI) and Joseph Biden (D-DE), among others.[32] Regardless, the resolution language remained quite broad and granted considerable discretion to the president to determine who is responsible for the attacks and how an organization or individuals may be related to the events of September 11. It was easy to interpret the resolution in a number of equally legitimate ways. The process was constitutional, with the White House seeking congressional authority to act and the House and Senate voting to grant such authority. At the same time, however, some observers maintain that Congress abdicated much of its war power through the resolution's broad and ambiguous language and by granting the president excessive discretion as commander in chief.[33]

These interactions appear to be the last instance prior to the decision to use force against Afghanistan and al Qaeda when Congress played a substantive role. It is difficult to find any meaningful congressional input between the House vote on September 15 and the initiation of Operation Enduring Freedom on October 7, where a member of Congress had a role in determining whom to go to war against or when to respond militarily.

Whom to Strike

When administration officials first met with the president to discuss the September 11 attacks and devise a response, there was a great deal of confusion and difference of opinion over what should be done.[34] The first weekend following the attacks, Bush convened the principals at Camp David to begin planning for a broad war on terrorism. On the first day of the meetings, Saturday, September 15, Secretary of Defense Donald Rumsfeld and Deputy Secretary of Defense Paul Wolfowitz pressed for making Iraq a target of the planned military response. Secretary of State Colin Powell made the case that bin Laden should be the sole focus of the response, in part because he believed that international support existed for attacking bin Laden but not Iraq. General Shelton was surprised that Iraq was even in consideration and also favored a military response only against bin Laden. Tenet and Vice President Dick Cheney focused their attention on bin Laden. Andrew Card, White House chief of staff, also voiced the opinion that al Qaeda should be the target of the response.[35] During these discussions, National Security Adviser Condoleezza Rice acted as the president's central coordinator at planning sessions. She absorbed information and views and then consulted privately with Bush on the options.[36]

Bush made the decision on September 15 to focus the administration's response on al Qaeda only. After Bush returned to the White House on Monday, September 17, he told his senior principals that Iraq would not be a target for a military response at that time. Former administration officials confirm that it was Bush's view that it was not the appropriate time to strike Iraq, although Bush felt that Iraq was somehow complicit in the September 11 attacks.[37] With Iraq no longer a target, and apparently with heavy input from George Tenet, the Taliban and al Qaeda were increasingly viewed as one entity, ending any lingering debate over whom to strike. The Taliban had come to power in 1996 and governed Afghanistan under an extreme interpretation of the *sharia,* or Islamic law.[38] It provided sanctuary for bin Laden in 1996, when he was expelled from Sudan, and protected him after the 1998 strikes on the U.S. embassies in East Africa. The Taliban also gave him communications equipment and security guards. In exchange, bin Laden helped the Taliban train its military and expand its political control over Afghanistan, and he also provided financial assistance to Mullah Omar, leader of the Taliban.[39]

On September 17, Bush instructed Colin Powell to issue an ultimatum to the Taliban: either turn over bin Laden or face severe consequences from the United States. On Sunday, September 23, the CIA assessed that Mullah Omar would side with bin Laden and refuse to give up the al Qaeda leader. That, indeed, was what happened.[40]

When to Attack

After they decided whom to attack, the question plaguing the Bush administration, and especially President Bush, was when to initiate the strikes. In the first days after September 11, Secretary Rumsfeld offered that it would take at least sixty days to get the military in place and ready for a major offensive. Gen. Tommy Franks, head of Central Command, concurred but more conservatively estimated that it could take several months.[41] President Bush wanted to be aggressive in time and strategy and avoid any comparison with President Clinton's military strikes. He felt that Clinton's strikes amounted to little more than "pounding sand" with cruise missiles.

Bush was attracted to one of the strategies presented by General Shelton. The plan Bush preferred entailed the launch of cruise missiles, air raids on Taliban and al Qaeda defenses, and the use of Special Operations Forces, and thus the insertion of "boots on the ground," all working in concert to combat al Qaeda and the Taliban. In addition, the CIA was to enlist the support of anti-Taliban groups in the northern and southern regions of Afghanistan to attack the Taliban with the assistance of Special Operations Forces and CIA operatives.

As the military plans moved forward, the need for diplomatic allies in the Middle East quickly became clear. To insert Special Operations Forces and to attack from the south, the United States needed access to military bases in the Persian Gulf. Oman, one of the best U.S. allies in the region, had assisted the Clinton administration with the use of its bases in the 1998 air strikes on Iraq. Although Oman did not immediately rush to assist the Bush administration, it ultimately agreed to lend its support, as did Bahrain and the United Arab Emirates. To Secretary Powell's surprise, Pakistani president Gen. Pervez Musharraf, who had had friendly relations with the Taliban, agreed almost immediately to Bush's multiple diplomatic, intelligence, and military requests.[42]

The biggest operational and diplomatic obstacle was securing staging areas for combat and search and rescue operations north of Afghanistan. To obtain permission to operate from military bases in some of the former Soviet republics, the administration requested the assistance of Russian President Vladimir Putin in making diplomatic overtures in the region. Putin, who exercised considerable diplomatic influence with nearly all of the former republics, agreed on the condition that U.S. actions were only temporary and did not represent a long-term military presence in the region.[43]

This Central Asian element was the final piece of the puzzle needed before a military response could be initiated. Uzbekistan—whose president, Islam Karimov, did not have good relations with President Putin—was a preferred site. In responding to the U.S. request, Karimov initially demanded NATO membership, a $50 million loan, and what amounted to a full-fledged security guarantee from the United States. Although the United States did not grant Karimov's every wish, the Uzbeks signed on to assist the United States on October 3. The military launched its first strikes on the Taliban on October 7.

The Taliban regime was brought down 102 days after the terrorist attacks of September 11, and American support for conduct of the war remained near 90 percent for the duration of the fighting in 2001.[44]

After the Initial Strikes

During the initial military strikes on the Taliban and al Qaeda in Operation Enduring Freedom in 2001, war planning directed by the White House, Secretary of Defense Donald Rumsfeld, and the commanding officer for the United States Central Command, Gen. Tommy Franks, had already begun for a possible invasion of Iraq.[45] These actions have led to the argument that U.S. war efforts in Afghanistan suffered from a lack of attention from the rest of the Bush administration, as its central foreign policy ambition and challenge focused first on removing Saddam Hussein from Iraq and then on containing the civil war that ensued in Iraq.[46] Whether this critique is accurate or not, for the remainder of Bush's presidency the U.S. military presence in Afghanistan grew steadily, reaching approximately 32,000 troops by December 2008.[47] During these years, much of the Bush administration's strategic approach to Afghanistan focused on utilizing the North Atlantic Treaty Organization (NATO) to build support for the new Afghan government and on lobbying the NATO allies to conduct more aggressive combat operations against the Taliban and al Qaeda.

In the aftermath of the Taliban's immediate defeat in 2001, the United States turned to the United Nations Security Council to negotiate the presence of an international peacekeeping force in Kabul. UN Security Council Resolution 1386 permitted the presence of UN peacekeepers in Kabul, and created an International Security Assistance Force (ISAF) that sought to provide security for the interim national government. Simultaneously, while this and other diplomatic initiatives unfolded, U.S. military efforts persisted as well. One of the largest military strikes against the Taliban occurred in March 2002 in Operation Anaconda, where U.S. forces struck the Taliban in the Shahi-Kot Valley. At the time, the strikes inflicted considerable damage on Taliban forces, but by some accounts forced the Taliban into the mountainous regions of western Pakistan for refuge.[48] This migration was significant in that it gave the Taliban a new sanctuary to regroup outside of Afghanistan in a region of Pakistan outside of governmental control. This location caused tactical and diplomatic challenges for the military operation.

NATO's formal role in Afghanistan came at the urging of primarily Canada, Germany, and the United States, who sought a continuity of command for

ISAF through NATO rather than the national leadership transitions that came under UN auspices.[49] On August 11, 2003, NATO agreed to take over ISAF. Over the next three years, the peacekeeping mission expanded to include thirteen Provincial Reconstruction Teams (PRTs), which were small groups of civilians and military personnel who spread out across northern and western sections of Afghanistan. The PRTs were deployed to help in the reconstruction of schools and roads, and more generally sought to provide support for economic growth and the national government, which eventually included approximately 10,000 troops from the NATO allies.[50]

Over the course of 2001 to 2006, the U.S. military presence grew gradually as well, as military efforts continued to focus on finding and killing members of the Taliban and al Qaeda. These efforts, though, were dwarfed by the war in Iraq that began on March 20, 2003, which generally consumed the Bush administration for the rest of its tenure. During these same years, Congress was similarly focused on Iraq and otherwise not closely tracking military events in Afghanistan, which is best characterized by the few congressional hearings devoted to Afghanistan and the limited oversight devoted to NATO operations by members of Congress.[51] Nonetheless, the Bush administration continued to work through NATO to wage this war. On July 31, 2006, after intense U.S. lobbying, NATO agreed to oversee the entirety of the Afghan military operation, which now included NATO participation in combat operations along with the PRTs. In agreeing to this revised and more extensive presence in Afghanistan, four NATO members—Canada, the Netherlands, the United Kingdom, and the United States—agreed to wage combat operations in the south. While this new policy indicated that NATO was capable of adapting to new security threats, the change also highlighted the profound differences in how each ally viewed its role in Afghanistan. Some of the allies, notably Germany and Italy, contributed hundreds of peacekeepers to more peaceful regions of Afghanistan in the north and west. These allies, along with other NATO partners, also placed "national caveats" for the kind of military engagement that their countries would permit. Such restrictions included strict prohibitions on the use of force, restriction on aircraft flights during the night, limited patrols that could only be conducted in armed personnel vehicles, and distance limitations on how far patrols could travel from their military bases.[52]

These caveats, and the ensuing casualties that occurred with British, Canadian, and Dutch military forces, produced new and serious diplomatic tensions within NATO. Those states who were experiencing casualties often challenged those allies deployed in safer regions to take on combat operations.[53]

Frustration was also evident in the Bush administration, which was well displayed when Secretary of Defense Robert Gates suggested that some of the current allies did not have the necessary military skills and professionalism to engage in counterinsurgency operations, which later resulted in diplomatic protests from the Netherlands and a subsequent apology from the United States.[54] Although NATO Secretary General Jaap de Hoop Scheffer consistently noted that Afghanistan was NATO's number one priority, the NATO allies continued to adopt very different military approaches for the remainder of the Bush administration, which led to ongoing diplomatic fissures within the alliance.

Despite the ongoing U.S. military operations and NATO's increased military and peacekeeping presence, by the end of the Bush administration most analysts, including U.S. intelligence agencies and the Department of Defense, concluded that the Taliban had successfully regrouped and was capable of waging increasingly advanced military attacks on US and NATO forces.[55] In 2008 the United States suffered 155 casualties in the conflict, the highest number of deaths in one year since the war began. Sen. Barack Obama's (D-IL) presidential campaign often noted that Bush's efforts in Iraq had moved the United States away from what Senator Obama viewed as the real source of global terrorism, which was centered in Afghanistan.

Obama's AfPak Strategy and Troop Surges and Drawdown

When Barack Obama won the 2008 U.S. presidential election, the United States had been fighting terrorism in Afghanistan for more than seven years. The new president did not wait long before starting to implement the changes he had promised during the presidential campaign. As Obama argued during the campaign: "Now is the time for a responsible redeployment of our combat troops that . . . refocuses on Afghanistan."[56] According to Obama, the war in Iraq had distracted the United States from the more important fight against al Qaeda and the Taliban. Obama believed the United States had to change its strategy in Afghanistan in order to win the war against those he labeled "violent extremists."

Obama softened George W. Bush's tone and has been less inclined to use terms such as *evil, brutal,* or *murderers* to define al Qaeda and the Taliban. However, the policies he adopted in the first months of his presidency illustrate his determination to use military force as he deems necessary. In February Obama declared that he would send an additional 17,000 American troops to Afghanistan in the spring and summer of 2009.[57] The president also announced a new "comprehensive" strategy on March 27, 2009, addressing what his administration believed are the major factors that have caused security in Afghanistan to deteriorate since 2006.[58] The strategy—dubbed the "AfPak" strategy—started with what the White House called a "clear, concise, attainable goal": "disrupt, dismantle, and defeat al Qaeda and its safe havens."[59] Moreover, it treated Afghanistan and Pakistan as two countries but one challenge. According to Obama, it was imperative to focus more intensely on Pakistan than in the past, and to increase "U.S. and international support, both economic and military, linked to Pakistani performance against terror."[60] For example, in terms of military cooperation, the Obama presidency has coincided with greater U.S. assistance to the Pakistani army in its push against militants in South Waziristan by providing surveillance video and intelligence gleaned from CIA-operated unmanned aircraft.[61] While it was the first time Islamabad had ever accepted such help from the United States, some have criticized Obama's decision to put Pakistan on the same level as Afghanistan in the war against al Qaeda and the Taliban. For instance, former Pakistani president Pervez Musharraf argued that Pakistan is different from its neighbor, which has no government and is completely destabilized.[62] But United States Special Envoy for Afghanistan and Pakistan Richard Holbrooke—who is believed to be the one who coined the term *AfPak*—provided a different interpretation in March 2009, arguing that the terrorists who attacked New York were in Pakistan, not in Afghanistan.[63]

Obama's AfPak strategy was detailed in a White Paper published by the White House in March 2009. The paper was the product of an overarching sixty-day inter-agency review of the situation in Afghanistan, chaired by South Asian expert Bruce Riedel and co-chaired by Richard Holbrooke and Under Secretary of Defense for Policy Michèle Flournoy.[64] The paper stated that Obama's objectives in Afghanistan and Pakistan were the following: (1) disrupt terrorist networks in Afghanistan and especially Pakistan to degrade any ability they have to plan and launch international terrorist attacks; (2) promote a more capable, accountable, and effective government in Afghanistan that serves the Afghan people and can eventually function, especially regarding internal security, with limited international support; (3) develop increasingly self-reliant Afghan security forces that can lead the counterinsurgency and counterterrorism fight with reduced U.S. assistance; (4) assist efforts to enhance civilian control and stable constitutional government in Pakistan and a vibrant economy that provides opportunity for the people of Pakistan; and (5) involve the international community to actively assist in addressing these objectives for Afghanistan and Pakistan, with an important leadership role for the UN.[65]

When one looks at how the decisions to reshape U.S. strategy in Afghanistan have been made by the Obama administration, one can see two striking similarities between the Democratic president and his two predecessors. On one hand, just like Clinton and Bush, Obama made the White House the center of action concerning the fight against terrorism. Indeed, during the first year of the Obama presidency, the key players of the debate on Afghanistan were the president himself, Defense Secretary Robert Gates, United States Special Envoy for Afghanistan and Pakistan Richard Holbrooke, commanders of U.S. and allied forces in Afghanistan David McKiernan (until June 2009) and Stanley A. McChrystal (from June 2009 to June 2010), Vice President Joseph Biden, Secretary of State Hillary Rodham Clinton, Chairman of the Joint Chiefs of Staff Mike Mullen, Commander of the U.S. Central Command David Petraeus, White House Chief of Staff Rahm Emanuel, and White House National Security Adviser James Jones.[66] On the other hand, just like the members of the Clinton and Bush administrations, Obama's advisers have not always agreed on U.S. strategy to fight terrorism in Afghanistan. In White House sessions, military leaders and civilian officials have clashed over questions of strategy and troop levels, especially in October and November 2009, after the U.S. troops experienced one of their deadliest months in Afghanistan. The rift between Obama and some of his advisers became obvious when General McChrystal, after a four-hour September meeting with Mullen and Petraeus, asked for 40,000 more troops to better protect the Afghan people and train security forces, and pressured the president in public to reject Vice President Biden's proposals to switch to a strategy more reliant on drone missile strikes and special forces operations against al Qaeda.[67] Biden, who has been Obama's "in-house pessimist" or "bull in the china shop" on Afghanistan from the moment the president took office, said he did not favor abandoning Afghanistan; he recommended leaving the U.S. force roughly at what it was in February 2009 (a total of 68,000 troops).[68] According to Biden, al Qaeda had, at the time, reconstituted in Pakistan, and the United States had to concentrate its efforts and resources there. In marketing his strategy, the vice president pointed out that Washington was, during that period, spending approximately $30 in Afghanistan for every $1 it spent in Pakistan.[69]

While some members of the Obama administration, such as Rahm Emanuel and James Jones, were believed to share Biden's pessimism about Afghanistan, others expressed doubts about the vice president's plan and aligned themselves with General McChrystal. Indeed, while Jones said a troop buildup would not be welcome, and while Emanuel told Obama early in 2009 that the war in

Afghanistan could threaten his presidency, Hillary Clinton and her close ally Richard Holbrooke stated that they would back McChrystal's request.[70] Robert Gates appeared more skeptical of further troop increases at first, especially because he thought it could fuel resentment the way the Soviet occupation did in the 1980s. However, he finally backed McChrystal's plan after the general convinced him that the goal of U.S. forces was to protect civilians in major Afghan cities from Taliban attacks, not to dominate Afghanistan like the Soviet Union tried to do during the invasion.[71]

In December 2009, after nine formal war meetings and three months of intense debate within his administration, the president finally announced that he would deploy 30,000 additional troops to Afghanistan within six months to break the Taliban's momentum. The main mission of these new troops was to kill insurgents, protect population centers in the south and east of Afghanistan, and speed up training of Afghan security forces in order to hand over control of the mission to Afghan authorities.[72] In a move that illustrated Obama's willingness to address the critics of those who dubbed the war "Obama's Vietnam," the president also stated that the troop surge did not mean an open-ended commitment. Indeed, Obama declared that his goal was to end the war successfully and quickly, and that after eighteen months, U.S. troops would begin to come home.[73]

Two days after Obama announced his policy, Sens. John Kerry (D-MA) and Richard Lugar (R-IN), who held the positions of chairman and ranking minority member in the Senate Foreign Relations Committee, proved that members of Congress did not want to remain silent or passive in the debate on Afghanistan and Pakistan. Kerry and Lugar held public hearings during which Hillary Clinton, Robert Gates, and Michael Mullen were invited to give more details about Obama's AfPak strategy.[74] These hearings were not the first ones Kerry and Lugar had held since Obama took office. For instance, in May 2009 Kerry set up a debate on Afghanistan within the committee and expressed concerns about the deteriorating security situation in most of the country.[75] Kerry, who was believed to share Biden's pessimism on surging the troops in Afghanistan, also played a fundamental role in the passage of the Enhanced Partnership with Pakistan Act of 2009 in October 2009. The key provisions of this law, dubbed the "Kerry-Lugar bill," were to provide Pakistan $1.5 billion in annual economic assistance for five years, renewable for another five.[76] One key goal of the bill was to counter widespread anti-American sentiment in Pakistan by helping Pakistan's civilian government deliver essential services to its population.[77]

In addition to Kerry and Lugar, Sens. Carl Levin (D-MI) and John McCain (R-AZ), who held the positions of chairman and ranking minority member in the Senate Armed Forces Committee, also organized multiple hearings on Obama's policies in Afghanistan and Pakistan. For instance, on February 26, 2009, the committee held a hearing on "Strategic Options for the Way Ahead in Afghanistan and Pakistan," during which Senator McCain shared Obama's position that the United States needed a troop surge in Afghanistan and a regional strategy to fight al Qaeda and the Taliban.[78] On December 2, 2009, Levin and McCain also invited Hillary Clinton, Robert Gates, and Michael Mullen to discuss Obama's strategy with the full committee. During this meeting, McCain criticized Obama for his decision to set an arbitrary date to begin withdrawing U.S. forces from Afghanistan.[79]

In the House, chairmen of the Permanent Select Committee on Intelligence (Rep. Sylvestre Reyes, D-TX) and of the Committees on International Affairs (Rep. Howard L. Berman, D-CA) and on Armed Services (Rep. Ike Skelton, D-MO) were some of the most dynamic congressional actors in the debate on AfPak. For instance, the three took part in an October 2009 White House meeting to discuss General McChrystal's troop surge proposal. Although Berman said he would consider other options before backing McChrystal, Reyes and Skelton advised Obama to follow his recommendation. Skelton even sent a six-page letter to Obama in which he implored the president to "give the general what he needs."[80] Other House Democrats, such as Rep. John Murtha (D-PA) and Speaker Nancy Pelosi (D-CA), also expressed concerns about Obama's decision to escalate the war.[81] However, the debate between the White House and Congress on the war in Afghanistan revealed that members of Congress had little control over Obama's decision beyond approving the money to pay for it.

By November 2010, Obama had made another important decision at NATO's Lisbon Summit meeting, where the United States and its allies announced that all ISAF forces would be withdrawn by the end of 2014, as NATO forces would work to expeditiously train Afghanistan National Security Forces so that they could lead the way in providing security for the country. This announcement tamped down some of the concerns over the 2011 timeline that Obama had proposed previously. By June 2011, the American military presence reached its apex, with nearly 100,000 troops deployed.[82]

As the surge plan was being implemented, President Obama escalated the use of Unmanned Aerial Vehicle (UAV)/drone missile strikes against remaining elements of the Taliban and al Qaeda in Pakistan, which illustrated a significant policy change compared to that of President Bush. During the entire Bush presidency, a total of 45 drone strikes occurred. Analysts from the New America Foundation, however, calculated that the Obama administration carried out 54 drone missile strikes in 2009, 122 strikes in 2010, and 72 additional strikes in 2011.[83] The use of drones continued, albeit at a slower pace in 2012, though a major increase in missile strikes occurred against al Qaeda targets in Yemen in the same year.[84] Thus, though Barack Obama campaigned aggressively in 2008 against George W. Bush's leadership as commander in chief, Obama himself demonstrated repeatedly his willingness to use force—through a number of means—to address remaining elements of the Taliban and al Qaeda.

From the announcement of the second surge plan in 2009, it was difficult to find many in Washington or the public who could find much good to say about the progress of the military mission. Apart from commanding General David Petraeus, who replaced General Stanley McChrystal after McChrystal's unprofessional interview and conduct was published in *Rolling Stone* magazine in the summer of 2010, few others spoke favorably about the mission. By October 2010, 60 percent of Americans viewed the war as a "lost cause."[85] By 2012, only 27 percent of Americans favored the war in Afghanistan, with 66 percent against.[86]

Liberal congressional Democrats, often led by Dennis Kucinich (D-OH), offered resolutions in 2010 and 2011 aimed at ending America's military presence in Afghanistan. Kucinich's efforts generated a vocal but small following.[87] A number of congressional Republicans also remained opposed to the imposition of a time table for an eventual troop withdrawal. What seemed to unify both Democrats and Republicans was the ongoing concern about corruption within the Afghan government, as well as an interest in limiting financial expenditures for the war.[88] The killing of Osama bin Laden served as a catalyst for such calls. Congressman Steve Cohen (D-TN) noted the "killing of Osama Bin Laden was the biggest deficit reduction action this country has known, if we take advantage of that action," though members of Congress were still hesitant to impose serious financial limitations on Obama's funding requests for the war.[89]

In May 2012, the Obama administration announced a Strategic Partnership Agreement with Afghanistan, which will keep approximately 15,000 to 20,000 U.S. military forces in Afghanistan after the 2014 conclusion of the ISAF mission.[90] In addition, Afghanistan was named a "Major Non-NATO Ally" in July 2012. Though this status has nothing to do with NATO or collective security, the agreement does permit an expedited trade relationship for sharing of sensitive defense technology, training, and weapons development between the two countries.[91] Yet even with these new agreements, conditions on the ground remained grim. Most notably, the number of killings of ISAF military trainers by Afghanistan National Security Forces (the so-called "green on blue" attacks) increased significantly in 2012.[92]

Despite such high levels of dissatisfaction with the war expressed in Washington, across the nation, and even within the military, by many accounts the Afghanistan war largely moved out of the public and political discussion as the 2012 elections progressed. Candidates rarely raised the Afghanistan issue during the congressional elections or even during the presidential contest. Republican presidential candidate Mitt Romney's address at the Republican national convention did not even devote one sentence to Afghanistan.[93] Military historian Andrew Bacevich maintains that Americans have increasingly become accustomed to the use of U.S. military force abroad, and in this respect, have lost some sense of policy discernment of America's military presence abroad today.[94] Though perhaps Americans are comfortable with and support the new Strategic Partnership Agreement, it seems more likely that Bacevich's ideas have some merit, and that American politicians see few political incentives in aggressively challenging the ongoing and foreseeably unending military presence in Afghanistan.

Conclusion: Presidential Leadership in the War on Terrorism

In the Clinton, Bush, and Obama administrations' military actions against al Qaeda, the White House has been the heart of the policy-making process, with limited formal input from others. This finding contrasts sharply with most other cases in this book—and in general with U.S. foreign policy making in the post–Cold War era—in which multiple bureaucratic officials, individual members of Congress, and individuals outside of government often play critical roles. Although Congress has considerable formal leverage through the War Powers Resolution and the Constitution to demand a substantive role for itself in matters concerning the decision to go to war, it is largely the president who controls the policy-making process regarding such a decision. Bush and Clinton, to different degrees, consulted with Congress, but in their formal communications with Capitol Hill, they asserted essentially unlimited powers as commander in chief, as had all presidents during the Cold War. Obama was less inclined to assert unlimited powers as commander in chief, and he consulted with key members of Congress during his policy review on Afghanistan. However, it seems fair to argue that Congress had little direct leverage over Obama. Formally, members of Congress could rely on the power of the purse and refuse to finance Obama's surge plan; instead, most members of Congress supported President Obama, with only a handful of liberal Democrats openly challenging either of Obama's troop surges.

The national security advisers of Clinton and Bush played key roles prior to the use of force. Sandy Berger and Condoleezza Rice, respectively, acted as primary confidants, consulting privately with the commander in chief. It appears that the national security adviser was the most trusted principal among all senior-level foreign policy decision makers in both administrations. Obama's national security adviser also played an important role during the debate on Afghanistan. However, it seems fair to say that other political actors at least matched James Jones's influence, especially Secretary of Defense Robert Gates, who toward the end of the White House debate about the troop surge was instrumental in shaping a plan that would bridge the differences between Hillary Clinton, Joseph Biden, and others.

The public widely supported the military actions of Bill Clinton and George W. Bush. Although many people suspected that Clinton's strikes on al Qaeda may have been a "diversionary military action" related to the Lewinsky scandal, his approval ratings remained high in the days following the strikes.[95] President Bush's political approval ratings soared soon after the September 11 tragedy and remained exceptionally high during the war in Afghanistan. As for Obama, the unveiling of his new military strategy revealed that Americans were not overly confident about the war. The killing of Osama bin Laden (which is examined in more detail in chapter 2) was popular among the American people, but a September 2012 poll showed that only a quarter of them still supported the military effort in Afghanistan.[96]

As of January 2013, the White House nonetheless continued to allege that the war was necessary. For instance, Washington stressed that the remaining leadership of the Afghan Taliban was still based around the city of Quetta, in the Balochistan province of Pakistan.[97] Among these leaders, Mullah Omar has been effective in reorganizing remnants of the Taliban.[98] In November 2009, Omar issued a message in which he rejected peace negotiations while Western forces remain in Afghanistan.[99] The U.S., Afghan, and Pakistani governments have pursued various peace initiatives with the Taliban since, including the December 2012 release of members of the movement from Pakistani prisons.[100] However, Omar's refusal to negotiate a settlement with Kabul reminded Washington that the war in Afghanistan could last longer than Obama would want it to. It could also continue after ISAF forces are withdrawn from the country in 2014.

Key Actors

Samuel "Sandy" Berger National security adviser; principal adviser to President Clinton leading up to strikes in 1998 against Osama bin Laden and his network in Sudan and Afghanistan.

Joseph Biden Vice president; President Obama's "in-house pessimist" and most outspoken critic about an expansive troop-surge policy in Afghanistan.

Osama bin Laden Leader of al Qaeda; which was responsible for the bombings of U.S. embassies in Nairobi, Kenya, and Dar es Salaam, Tanzania, and the September 11 attacks.

George W. Bush President; principal decision maker for initiating Operation Enduring Freedom against the Taliban and al Qaeda in 2001 in Afghanistan.

Richard A. Clarke Counterterrorism coordinator for Presidents Clinton and Bush.

Bill Clinton President; principal decision maker for strikes against bin Laden in 1998.

Hillary Rodham Clinton Secretary of state; advocate for a troop surge in Afghanistan during the first months of the Obama presidency.

Rahm Emanuel White House chief of staff; expressed opposition to an expansive troop surge in Afghanistan during the first months of the Obama presidency.

Robert Gates Secretary of defense; helped President Obama shape a troop-surge plan that would bridge the differences between Hillary Clinton, Joseph Biden, and others.

Richard Holbrooke United States Special Envoy for Afghanistan and Pakistan; coined the term *AfPak* during the first months of the Obama presidency.

James Jones White House national security adviser; expressed opposition to an expansive troop surge in Afghanistan during the first months of the Obama presidency.

Stanley A. McChrystal Commander of U.S. and allied forces in Afghanistan; most aggressive advocate for a troop surge in Afghanistan during the first months of the Obama presidency; relieved of his command due to unprofessional military conduct.

Barack Obama President; principal decision maker for increasing the war effort against the Taliban and al Qaeda after January 2009; in November 2010, announced that all International Security Assistance Force (ISAF) troops would be withdrawn from Afghanistan by the end of 2014.

David Petraeus   Commander of U.S. and allied forces in Afghanistan; replaced Stanley A. McChrystal in the summer of 2010; spoke favorably about the mission in Afghanistan even when it was getting less popular in U.S. public opinion and in Washington.

Condoleezza Rice   National security adviser; principal adviser to Bush in the lead-up to attacking the Taliban and al Qaeda in Afghanistan in 2001.

Hugh "Henry" Shelton   Chairman of the Joint Chiefs of Staff under Clinton and Bush; provided Bush with options for striking the Taliban and al Qaeda after the September 11 attacks.

George Tenet   Director of the Central Intelligence Agency under Clinton and Bush; exercised great influence in determining whom to strike after the September 11 attacks on the United States.

Paul Wolfowitz   Deputy secretary of defense; most aggressive advocate for military strikes on Iraq immediately after September 11.

Notes

1. Charles A. Lofgren, "War-Making under the Constitution: The Original Understanding," *Yale Law Journal* 81 (1972): 672–702.

2. Francis D. Wormuth and Edwin B. Firmage, *To Chain the Dog of War* (Urbana: University of Illinois Press, 1989).

3. Ryan C. Hendrickson, *The Clinton Wars: The Constitution, Congress, and War Powers* (Nashville, TN: Vanderbilt University Press, 2002).

4. Robert David Johnson, *Congress and the Cold War* (Cambridge: Cambridge University Press, 2006), 190–193.

5. Michael J. Glennon, "Too Far Apart: The War Powers Resolution," *University of Miami Law Review* 50 (1995): 17–31; Edward Keynes, "The War Powers Resolution: A Bad Idea Whose Time Has Come and Gone," *University of Toledo Law Review* 23 (1992): 343–362.

6. Hendrickson, *The Clinton Wars,* 104.

7. "Press Briefing with National Security Advisor Berger on U.S. Strikes in Sudan and Afghanistan," August 20, 1998, secretary.state.gov/www/statements/1998/980820.html.

8. Bill Clinton, "Address to the Nation on Testimony before the Independent Counsel's Grand Jury," Weekly Compilation of Presidential Documents, August 28, 1998, 1638, www.gpoaccess.gov/wcomp/index.html; James Bennet, "Testing of a President: The Overview," *New York Times,* August 18, 1998, A1.

9. Defense LINK News, "DoD News Briefing," August 20, 1998, www.defense .gov/transcripts/transcript.aspx?transcriptid=1727.

10. Bill Clinton, "Remarks on Departure for Washington, DC, from Martha's Vineyard, Massachusetts," Weekly Compilation of Presidential Documents, August 28, 1998, 1642.

11. Bill Clinton, "Address to the Nation on Military Action against Terrorist Sites in Afghanistan and Sudan," Weekly Compilation of Presidential Documents, August 28, 1998, 1643.

12. For example, see Secretary of State Madeleine Albright's statements, "Interview on NBC-TV *Today Show* with Katie Couric," August 21, 1998, http://usembassy-israel .org.il/publish/press/state/archive/1998/august/sd4824.htm.

13. For polling data, see Marck Z. Barabak, "The Times Poll," *Los Angeles Times,* August 23, 1998, A1; Bruce Westbrook, "War or a 'Wag'?" *Houston Chronicle,* August 25, 1998, 1; Marcella Bombardieri, "Wagging Dog? Fine, Some Say," *Boston Globe,* August 22, 1998, A8.

14. Office of the Press Secretary, "Press Briefing by Mike McCurry," August 20, 1998, www.presidency.ucsb.edu/ws/index.php?pid=48262; see also Chuck McCutcheon, "Lawmakers Back Missile Strikes Despite a Bit of GOP Skepticism," *CQ Weekly,* August 22, 1998, 2289.

15. McCutcheon, "Lawmakers Back Missile Strikes."

16. "National Commission on Terrorist Attacks Upon the United States, Eighth Hearing," March 24, 2004, govinfo.library.unt.edu/911/archive/hearing8/9–11Commis sion_Hearing_2004–03–24.htm.

17. Office of the Press Secretary, "Press Briefing by McCurry in Gaggle"; see also McCutcheon, "Lawmakers Back Missile Strikes," 2289.

18. See Office of the Press Secretary, "Press Briefing by McCurry in Gaggle."

19. Bob Woodward, *Bush at War* (New York: Simon and Schuster, 2002).

20. Tenet maintains that it is likely that two sightings occurred, but Richard A. Clark, former counterterrorism coordinator, maintains that there were three occasions. "Testimony of Richard A. Clarke before the National Commission on Terrorist Attacks Upon the United States," March 24, 2004, govinfo.library.unt.edu/911/archive/ hearing8/9–11Commission_Hearing_2004–03–24.htm#clarke.

21. Ibid.

22. National Commission on Terrorist Attacks Upon the United States, "Intelligence Policy," staff statement no. 7, March 24, 2004, govinfo.library.unt.edu/911/archive/ hearing8/9–11Commission_Hearing_2004–03–24.htm#statement7.

23. Quoted in Woodward, *Bush at War,* 17. For more information about Bush's reaction to the September 11 attacks, read the chapter "Day of Fire" of his memoir: George W. Bush, *Decision Points* (New York: Crown Publishers, 2010), 126–151.

24. Woodward, *Bush at War,* 26–27.

25. One forceful advocate of this view is Robert F. Turner, "The War on Terrorism and the Modern Relevance of the Congressional Power to 'Declare' War," *Harvard Journal of Law and Public Policy* 25, no. 2 (2002): 519–537.

26. Quoted in David Abramowitz, "The President, the Congress, and Use of Force: Legal and Political Considerations in Authorizing Use of Force against International Terrorism," *Harvard International Law Journal* 43, no. 1 (2002): 73.

27. Tom Daschle (with Michael D'Orso), *Like No Other Time: The Two Years That Changed America* (New York: Three Rivers Press, 2003), 124.

28. Abramowitz, "The President, the Congress, and Use of Force," 73.

29. *Congressional Record,* September 14, 2001, S9424.

30. Dave Boyer, "Some Lawmakers Call for War on Terror," *Washington Times,* September 14, 2001, A13.

31. Barbara Lee, "Why I Opposed the Resolution to Authorize Force," *San Francisco Chronicle,* September 23, 2001.

32. *Congressional Record,* September 14, 2001, S9416, S9417, S9423.

33. Nancy Kassop, "The War Power and Its Limits," *Presidential Studies Quarterly* 33, no. 3 (2003): 513–514.

34. An excellent account about the White House deliberation is provided in Woodward, *Bush at War*. See also Ron Suskind, *The Price of Loyalty: George W. Bush, the White House, and the Education of Paul O'Neill* (New York: Simon and Shuster, 2004); and Richard A. Clarke, *Against All Enemies: Inside America's War on Terror* (New York: Free Press, 2004).

35. Woodward, *Bush at War*, 83–91.

36. Ibid., 158; David Halberstam, *War in a Time of Peace: Bush, Clinton, and the Generals* (New York: Scribner's, 2001), 404–409.

37. Woodward, *Bush at War*, 99. Woodward's account squares with the recollection of former Treasury secretary Paul O'Neill. See Suskind, *The Price of Loyalty*, 184–187.

38. Shawn Howard, "The Afghan Connection: Islamic Extremism in Central Asia," *National Security Studies Quarterly* 6, no. 3 (2000): 28–29.

39. James S. Robbins, "Bin Laden's War," in *Terrorism and Counterterrorism: Under the New Security Environment*, ed. Russell D. Howard and Reid L. Sawyer (Guilford, CT: McGraw-Hill/Duskin, 2004), 396; George Tenet, "Written Statement for the Record of the Director of Central Intelligence Before the National Commission on Terrorist Attacks Upon the United States," March 24, 2004, 6–7, www.9-11commission.gov/hearings/hearing8/tenet_statement.pdf.

40. Woodward, *Bush at War*, 99, 121.

41. Ibid., 32, 43. For more details about Tommy Franks's role in the planning of the war, see Gen. Tommy Franks, *American Soldier* (New York: HarperCollins, 2004), 255–262.

42. Woodward, *Bush at War*, 115–117, 59.

43. Ibid., 117–118.

44. RAND Corporation, "Operation Enduring Freedom: An Assessment," Research Brief, 2005, 1, www.rand.org/pubs/research_briefs/2005/RAND_RB9148.pdf. See also Richard Morin and Claudia Deane, "Most Americans Back U.S. Tactics; Poll Finds Little Worry over Rights," *Washington Post*, November 29, 2001, A1.

45. Michael R. Gordon and Bernard E. Trainor, *COBRA II: The Inside Story of the Invasion and Occupation of Iraq* (New York: Pantheon Books, 2006), 19–23; Thomas E. Ricks, *Fiasco: The American Military Adventure in Iraq* (New York: Penguin Books, 2007), 32–34.

46. Sean Kay, "From COIN to Containment," *ForeignPolicy.com*, September 1, 2009, afpak.foreignpolicy.com/posts/2009/09/01/from_coin_to_containment.

47. Kirk Semple, "U.S. Plans a Shift to Focus Troops on Kabul Region," *New York Times*, December 7, 2008, A1.

48. Eric Schmitt and Thom Shanker, "A Nation Challenged: Strategy: Afghans' Retreat Forced Americans to Lead a Battle," *New York Times*, March 10, 2002, 1.

49. Wallace J. Thies, *Why NATO Endures* (Cambridge: Cambridge University Press, 2009), 304; Sean M. Maloney, "The International Security Assistance Force: The Origins of a Stabilization Force," *Canadian Military Journal* 4 (Summer 2003): 4–7.

50. Michael J. McNerney, "Stabilization and Reconstruction in Afghanistan: Are PRTs a Model or a Muddle?" *Parameters* 35 (Winter 2005–2006): 32–46; Sean M. Maloney, "Afghanistan Four Years On: An Assessment," *Parameters* 35 (Autumn 2005): 21–32.

51. Ryan C. Hendrickson, "L'OTAN et George W. Bush: Perspectives du Congrès Américain sur la Transformation de l'Alliance," Études *Internationales* 38, no. 4 (2007): 475–499.

52. Vincent Morelli and Paul Belkin, "NATO in Afghanistan: A Test of the Transatlantic Alliance," *Congressional Research Service,* August 25, 2009, 10–11.

53. Mike Blanchfield, "U.K. Minister Blasts Dion's Stance on Afghanistan: NATO Needs to 'Get Real,'" *National Post,* December 12, 2006, A6; Bruce Campion-Smith, "Lack of NATO Help Slammed," *Toronto Star,* November 16, 2006, A06.

54. Judy Dempsey, "Defense Secretary, Facing Criticism, Hails NATO's Forces in Afghanistan," *New York Times,* January 18, 2008, A10.

55. Mark Massetti and Eric Schmitt, "U.S. Study Is Said to Warn of Crisis in Afghanistan," *New York Times on the Web,* October 9, 2008; Mark Mazzetti, "Military Death Toll Rises in Afghanistan as Taliban Regain Strength," *New York Times,* July 2, 2008, A6.

56. Barack Obama, "Obama's Remarks on Iraq and Afghanistan," *New York Times,* July 25, 2008, www.nytimes.com/2008/07/15/us/politics/15text-obama.html?page wanted=print.

57. Helene Cooper, "Putting Stamp on Afghan War, Obama Will Send 17,000 Troops," *New York Times,* February 17, 2009, www.nytimes.com/2009/02/18/washington/18web-troops.html?_r=0.

58. Kenneth Katzman, "Afghanistan: Post-Taliban Governance, Security, and U.S. Policy," *Congressional Research Service,* October 6, 2009, 26.

59. The White House, "What's New in the Strategy for Afghanistan and Pakistan," March 27, 2009, www.whitehouse.gov/the_press_office/Whats-New-in-the-Strategy-for-Afghanistan-and-Pakistan.

60. Ibid.

61. "U.S. Drones Aiding Pakistani Military Offensive," Fox News, October 23, 2009, www.foxnews.com/politics/2009/10/23/drones-aiding-pakistani-military-offensive.

62. Spiegel interview with Pervez Musharraf, "Obama 'Is Aiming at the Right Things,'" *Spiegel Online,* June 7, 2009, www.spiegel.de/international/world/spiegel-interview-with-pervez-musharraf-obama-is-aiming-at-the-right-things-a-628960.html.

63. Pascale Mallet, "Les États-Unis Énoncent Leurs Priorités en Afghanistan," *La Presse,* March 21, 2009, www.cyberpresse.ca/international/moyen-orient/200903/21/01–838918-les-etats-unis-enoncent-leurs-priorites-en-afghanistan.php.

64. Katzman, "Afghanistan: Post-Taliban Governance, Security, and U.S. Policy," 26.

65. The White House, "White Paper of the Interagency Policy Group's Report on U.S. Policy Toward Afghanistan and Pakistan," March 27, 2009, 1, www.whitehouse.gov/assets/documents/Afghanistan-Pakistan_White_Paper.pdf.

66. "Key Players in the U.S. Debate on Afghanistan Policy," *Los Angeles Times,* October 17, 2009, www.latimes.com/news/nationworld/world/la-fg-afghan-players17–20090ct17,0,3331018.story.

67. Alex Spillius, "White House Angry at General Stanley McCrystal Speech in Afghanistan," *The Daily Telegraph,* October 5, 2009, www.telegraph.co.uk/news/world news/northamerica/usa/barackobama/6259582/White-House-angry-at-General-Stanley-McChrystal-speech-on-Afghanistan.html.

68. Peter Baker, "Biden No Longer a Lone Voice on Afghanistan," *New York Times,* October 13, 2009, www.nytimes.com/2009/10/14/world/14biden.html; Peter Baker,

"How Obama Came to Plan for 'Surge' in Afghanistan," *New York Times,* December 6, 2009, www.nytimes.com/2009/12/06/world/asia/06reconstruct.html?_r=2&scp=5 &sq=afghan%20surge&st=cse.

69. B. Stoddard, "Biden's Moment," *The Hill,* October 28, 2009, www.thehill.com/ opinion/columnists/ab-stoddard/65273-bidens-moment.

70. *Los Angeles Times,* "Key Players in the U.S. Debate on Afghanistan Policy."

71. "Q. and A. on Obama's Afghan Plan," *New York Times,* December 7, 2009, thecaucus.blogs.nytimes.com/2009/12/07/q-and-a-on-obamas-afghan-plan.

72. "Obama's War," *The Economist,* December 2, 2009, www.economist.com/world/ unitedstates/displayStory.cfm?story_id=15004081&source=features_box1; Sheryl Gay Stolberg, Helene Cooper, and Brian Knowlton, "Obama Team Defends Policy on Afghanistan," *New York Times,* December 2, 2009, www.nytimes.com/2009/12/03/ world/asia/03policy.html?_r=1&hp.

73. Barack Obama, "Remarks by the President in Address to the Nation on the Way Forward in Afghanistan and Pakistan," *The White House,* December 1, 2009, www .whitehouse.gov/the-press-office/remarks-president-address-nation-way-forward -afghanistan-and-pakistan.

74. See U.S. Senate Foreign Relations Committee, "Afghanistan: Assessing the Road Ahead," December 3, 2009, www.gpo.gov/fdsys/pkg/CHRG-111shrg56845/pdf/CHRG -111shrg56845.pdf.

75. John Kerry, "Chairman Kerry Opening Statement at Hearing On Afghanis-tan-Pakistan Strategy, " U.S. Senate Committee on Foreign Relations, May 21, 2009, www.foreign.senate.gov/imo/media/doc/KerryStatement090521a.pdf.

76. U.S. Public Law 111–73, "Enhanced Partnership with Pakistan Act of 2009," October 15, 2009, www.gpo.gov/fdsys/pkg/PLAW-111publ73/pdf/PLAW -111publ73.pdf .

77. Omar Waraich, "How a U.S. Aid Package to Pakistan Could Threaten Zardari," *Time Magazine,* October 8, 2009, www.time.com/time/world/article/0,8599,1929306,00 .html.

78. See U.S. Senate Committee on Armed Services, "Hearing to Receive Testimony on Strategic Options for the Way Ahead in Afghanistan and Pakistan," February 26, 2009, www.gpo.gov/fdsys/pkg/CHRG-111shrg53725/html/CHRG-111shrg53725.htm.

79. John McCain, "Statement of Senator McCain," *Hearing to Receive Testimony on Afghanistan,* U.S. Senate Armed Forces Committee, December 2, 2009.

80. S. A. Miller, "Key Democrats Align with Military on Afghan Buildup," *Washington Times,* October 9, 2009, www.washingtontimes.com/news/2009/oct/09/key-dem ocrats-align-with-military-on-buildup/?feat=article_top10_shared.

81. Karen DeYoung, "Lawmakers Scrutinize New Afghan Strategy," *Washington Post,* December 3, 2009, www.washingtonpost.com/wp-dyn/content/article/2009/12/02/ AR2009120201013.html.

82. Kenneth Katzman, "Afghanistan: Post-Taliban Governance, Security, and U.S. Policy," Congressional Research Service, September 21, 2012.

83. New America Foundation, "The Year of the Drone," accessed December 19, 2012, counterterrorism.newamerica.net/drones.

84. The Long War Journal, "Charting the Data for U.S. Airstrikes in Yemen, 2002–2012," accessed December 19, 2012, www.longwarjournal.org/multimedia/ Yemen/code/Yemen-strike.php.

85. Frank Oliveri and Emily Cadei, "Mission Uncertain," *Congressional Quarterly Weekly* (October 18, 2010): 2382–3.

86. Emily Cadei, "Campaigns Quiet on Afghanistan," *Congressional Quarterly Weekly* (May 21, 2012): 1022.

87. Eugene Mulero, "Kucinich Troop Withdrawal Effort Goes Down to Defeat in House," *Congressional Quarterly Weekly* (March 21, 2011): 635; Eugene Mulero, "House Resolution Calling for Afghanistan Withdrawal Draws Heated Debate but Fails by Large Margin," *Congressional Quarterly Weekly* (March 15, 2010): 636.

88. Emily Cadei and Frank Oliveri, "Capitol Hill's Own Afghanistan War," *Congressional Quarterly Weekly* (January 10, 2011): 100.

89. Quoted in Alexander C. Hart, "House Rejects War Funding Limitations," *Congressional Quarterly Weekly* (July 11, 2011): 1496.

90. White House: Office of the Press Secretary, "Fact Sheet: The U.S.-Afghanistan Strategic Partnership Agreement," May 1, 2012, www.whitehouse.gov/the-press-office/2012/05/01/fact-sheet-us-afghanistan-strategic-partnership-agreement.

91. U.S. State Department, "Major Non-NATO Ally Status for Afghanistan: Fact Sheet," July 7, 2012, www.state.gov/r/pa/prs/ps/2012/07/194662.htm.

92. Alissa J. Rubin, "Audacious Raid on NATO Base Shows Taliban's Reach," *New York Times,* September 16, 2012, www.nytimes.com/2012/09/17/world/asia/green-on-blue-attacks-in-afghanistan-continue.html?pagewanted=all.

93. David E. Sanger and Thom Shanker, "Two Campaigns Skirt Talk of Tough Choices in Afghanistan," *New York Times,* October 21, 2012, www.nytimes.com/2012/10/22/us/politics/candidates-skirt-talk-of-hard-afghanistan-choices.html?pagewanted=all.

94. Andrew J. Bacevich, *The Limits to Power: The End of American Exceptionalism* (New York: Henry Holt and Company, 2009).

95. For an argument expressing doubt about the diversionary theory for these strikes, see Ryan C. Hendrickson, "Clinton's Military Strikes in 1998: Diversionary Uses of Force?" *Armed Forces and Society* 28 (2002): 309–332.

96. Peter Bergen, "Abandon Afghanistan? A Dumb Idea," CNN, January 10, 2013, www.cnn.com/2013/01/10/opinion/bergen-afghanistan-troop-levels/index.html.

97. Augustine Anthony & Haris Anwar, "Bombs Kill 118 People in Pakistan as Sectarian Attacks Surge," *Bloomberg,* January 11, 2013, www.bloomberg.com/news/2013-01-11/bombings-kill-114-people-in-pakistan-as-sectarian-attacks-spiral.html.

98. Hassan M. Fattah, "Bin Laden Re-emerges, Warning U.S. while Offering 'Truce,'" *New York Times,* January 19, 2006. See also Amir Shah, Associated Press, "Taliban Leader Said to Be Reorganizing Group," *Fort Worth Star-Telegram,* September 22, 2003, 6A.

99. "Mullah Omar Gets on Message with Speech Aimed at West," *The Nation,* November 26, 2009, www.nation.com.pk/pakistan-news-newspaper-daily-english-online/international/26-Nov-2009/Mullah-Omar-gets-on-message-with-speech-aimed-at-West.

100. Haris Anwar, "Pakistan Frees Former Taliban Officials to Promote Afghan Peace," *Bloomberg,* December 31, 2012, www.bloomberg.com/news/2013-01-01/pakistan-frees-former-taliban-officials-to-promote-afghan-peace.html.

2 Assassinating bin Laden: Right or Wrong

Priya Dixit

Before You Begin

1. What are some benefits of targeted killings as a tool of foreign policy? What are some drawbacks?

2. Are targeted killings permitted under the U.S. Constitution?

3. What are some key events during the rise of al Qaeda?

4. How did U.S. foreign policy deal with bin Laden and terrorism pre- and post-9/11?

5. How was the raid to kill bin Laden carried out?

6. What are some key foreign policy concerns arising from the killing of bin Laden?

Introduction

The Obama administration has followed the previous policy of George W. Bush in utilizing unmanned aerial vehicles (UAV), commonly called "drones," for achieving its counterinsurgency goals. These include surveillance and targeting and killing suspected terrorists and militants in various parts of the world. The drone program and, especially, the targeted killing program have been both praised and criticized. By December 2012, the administration was discussing plans to draw up a "code book" for the use of drones. With more than 300 strikes that have killed more than 2,500 people (by conservative estimates) since the start of Obama's first term, drone usage to kill suspected militants will continue to be a key issue of U.S. foreign policy.[1] Despite calls for transparency, operation of the drone program remains officially classified. The most well-known targeted killing—that of Osama bin Laden—occurred without the direct use of drones, though they were used in surveillance and mapping prior to the event. Drones were responsible for other high-profile targeted killings, such as that of Anwar al-Awlaki. There is, therefore, more than one method of targeted killing in U.S. foreign policy.

41

Timeline

Key Developments in the Killing of Osama bin Laden

1988	Al Qaeda is established in Afghanistan. Its goal is to act against the US, Israel, and their allies.
1996	Bin Laden returns to Afghanistan from Sudan.
1998	Bombings at the U.S. embassies in Kenya and Tanzania kill more than 200 people.
September 2001	Suicide bombers kill close to 3,000 people in a series of attacks on the World Trade Center in New York and the Pentagon in Washington, DC.
December 2001	The battle of Tora Bora leads to the capture of an al Qaeda base there, but bin Laden remains at large.
October 2004	Bin Laden sends a video to Al Jazeera in which he claims responsibility, for the first time, for organizing 9/11.
2007	U.S. intelligence sources acquire the name of bin Laden's favorite courier. However, his whereabouts remain unknown.
August 2010	Reports of the courier living in a compound in Abbottabad are received. Intelligence analysts suspect a higher-value target is living in the enormous compound. They suspect it is Osama bin Laden himself.
March 2011	President Obama has a series of national security council meetings to decide upon courses of action regarding this compound. The first one is on March 14.
March 29, 2011	The second meeting regarding the Abbottabad operation is held.
April 12, 2011	The third meeting is held.
April 19, 2011	The fourth meeting occurs.
April 28, 2011	The fifth meeting is held.
April 29, 2011	Before going to inspect tornado damage in Alabama, President Obama gives the go ahead for the operation.

| May 1, 2011 | The raid occurs. Obama and his team watch parts of it live at the White House. The raid takes a total of 40 minutes, during which time bin Laden is shot twice and killed. At 7 pm, Obama receives tentative confirmation that bin Laden was killed. |
| May 1, 2011, 11:35 pm | President Obama gives a televised address, saying bin Laden is dead. |

Background: Osama bin Laden and the Rise of al Qaeda

The life of Osama bin Laden has been fairly well publicized. Born in 1951 in Saudi Arabia into a wealthy family, bin Laden became involved in politics during the Soviet-Afghanistan wars in the early 1980s. He supported anti-Soviet forces and eventually ended up establishing al Qaeda. Until his death, he was the head of the organization. Before this, his intellectual views were formed by his contacts with pilgrims who stayed at his family's residence on their way to Mecca, his own visits to Mecca and Medina during his youth, lectures and discussions during his time at university, and his own intellectual interest in the changing role of Islam in the world. Bin Laden also wrote extensively, writing sermons and poems on the role of Islam, and was capable of linking historic verses and prose with current events, making him a persuasive orator.[2] Overall, bin Laden would become influenced by the works of Sayyid Qutb and would form alliances with another radical Islamist scholar, Abdullah Azzam, who was influential in leading bin Laden to initially volunteer in Afghanistan.

In the 1980s, bin Laden was extensively engaged in funding and participating in groups that fought against the Soviets in Afghanistan. In the early days of bin Laden's involvement with the Afghani mujahideen, he encouraged others in Saudi Arabia and elsewhere to go fight in Afghanistan to serve the cause of Islam. Thus, bin Laden was not just personally involved in Afghanistan but he provided financial assistance, helped recruit volunteers, and established the foundations for a network of people and money to be transported from the Middle East to Afghanistan. During this period, it has been well documented that the United States was providing financial and military assistance to help train the Afghani mujahideen.[3] U.S. foreign policy of the time was focused on deterring and combating Soviet influence around the world. Within this framework, the mujahideen were fighting the Soviets, and therefore supporting them in their activities was a U.S. foreign policy goal.[4] Similarly, Saudi Arabia supported the mujahideen in their efforts, and there were widespread fundraising campaigns in Saudi Arabia, as well as official and unofficial assistance to support Afghani efforts against the Soviets.[5] Thus, in the 1980s, bin Laden's goals and that of Saudi Arabia and the US were similar—remove the Soviets from Afghanistan. Overall, bin Laden's knowledge of and interest in unconventional warfare tactics, and his viewpoints regarding how smaller groups could engage and even weaken larger forces, further developed during this period.

On the whole, bin Laden's actions were said to have been motivated by two main goals: First, he viewed the US and its foreign policy as negatively impacting Arabs and Muslim people in the Middle East and elsewhere. He wanted to right the perceived injustices against Muslims. Second, bin Laden was interested in expanding the role and presence of Islam. He is believed to have spent a lot of time learning and interpreting the Koran. He wanted to establish a religious caliphate, where Sharia law would take precedence. In doing so, he believed corrupt influences of Westernization and modernization could be countered.

Al Qaeda: The Early Days

The actual date of al Qaeda's formation remains unclear, but experts claim it was established as a coherent group by 1988. During this initial period, al Qaeda was involved in minor actions in Afghanistan, but its operations were mostly covert. During his time in Afghanistan, bin Laden funded a network of recruits who would come to Afghanistan to fight against the Soviet invaders. After the withdrawal of the Soviets in 1989, bin Laden and al Qaeda continued their operations and moved beyond the borders of Afghanistan. Bin Laden was interested in a global movement, not just involvement in internal battles as in Afghanistan.

Saudi Arabia banned bin Laden after bin Laden criticized Saudi leaders during the First Gulf War for allowing foreign troops—the US and its allies—on Saudi soil. Bin Laden saw Saudi Arabia as sacred to Islam because of the location of Mecca and Medina and claimed the presence of foreign troops was antithetical to Islam. After being banished from Saudi Arabia, bin Laden moved his operations to Sudan. In the early to mid-1990s, bin Laden directed operations from Sudan and allied himself and his organization with local and regional extremist networks. He remained in

Sudan from 1992 to 1996, and various smaller-scale operations were planned and carried out.[6] In 1996, bin Laden issued a fatwa against "the occupation of the land of the two Holy Places . . . by the armies of the American crusaders and their allies."[7]

In May 1996, bin Laden moved back to Afghanistan, where the Taliban had taken control.[8] The Taliban's extremist interpretation of Islam and the establishment of an oppressive state in Afghanistan facilitated the development of al Qaeda. Indeed, the organization grew stronger as alliances with other networks were established and strengthened. One of these alliances was with Egypt's Islamic Jihad, the leader of which was Ayman al-Zawahiri.

The two main al Qaeda–related events that occurred in the 1990s, which are of relevance to U.S. foreign policy, were the 1993 bombing of the World Trade Center in New York and the 1998 embassy bombings in Kenya and Tanzania. In the 1993 World Trade Center bombings, six people died and more than 1,000 were injured when a 500 kg bomb exploded in an underground car park. In 1998, U.S. embassies in Kenya and Tanzania were targeted by suicide bombers. More than 200 people died in Nairobi and around a dozen in Dar es Salaam. More than 4,000 people were wounded in both cities. This incident resulted in bin Laden being placed on the FBI's most wanted fugitives list. In addition, in October 2000, seventeen U.S. sailors were killed when the USS *Cole* was attacked in Aden, Yemen.

In response to the embassy bombings, the US attacked training camps in Sudan and Afghanistan in one of the earliest direct strikes against al Qaeda. In a speech on August 20, 1998, President Bill Clinton said the strikes on "terrorist-related facilities" in Sudan and Afghanistan were "because of the imminent threat they presented to our national security."[9] President Clinton went on to add,

> The groups associated with him come from diverse places, but share a hatred for democracy, a fanatical glorification of violence, and a horrible distortion of their religion to justify the murder of innocents. They have made the United States their adversary precisely because of what we stand for and what we stand against.

Despite this strong statement, U.S. responses to al Qaeda in the 1990s remained low key. It was acknowledged that bin Laden was a threat, but that he could organize and carry off an attack on the scale of the 2001 bombings was not something that U.S. policy makers had imagined.

U.S. Foreign Policy toward bin Laden and al Qaeda: Pre-September 11, 2001

U.S. foreign policy in the late 1970s and the 1980s remained within a Cold War framework in which the major threat to U.S. security was seen as emanating from the ideologies of communism. By the late 1970s, the US was wary of overt wars after the long-drawn, expensive, and ultimately unsuccessful efforts in Vietnam. Therefore, in terms of strategy, U.S. foreign policy focused more on providing indirect assistance to local groups and on training, rather than full-scale "boots on the ground" operations. This meant U.S. involvement in Afghanistan in the 1980s was in the form of "behind the scenes" assistance to those seeking to oust the Soviets from the country.

One could argue that, for the Soviets, Afghanistan's move toward a more extremist Islamist state was a threat to Soviet national security. Thus, occupying Afghanistan to ensure it would not be taken over by Islamist radicals and eventually influence Soviet Muslims made sense for Soviet foreign policy. However, for the United States and its allies, this was yet another indication of aggressive Soviet encroachment into neutral territory. Hook and Spanier argue that the US saw the Soviet invasion of Afghanistan as "the greatest threat to world peace since World War II."[10] Indeed, Carter said, "[The Soviet action] made a more dramatic change in my opinion of what the Soviets' ultimate goals are than anything they've done in the previous time I've been in office."[11] On the whole, the Soviet invasion of Afghanistan was a shock to the U.S. foreign policy of the late 1970s, which had been moving toward more amicable relations between the two superpowers. However, apart from providing military and financial assistance to those fighting the Soviets, the US did not engage in more direct fashion in Afghanistan at the time.

After the end of the Cold War, U.S. foreign policy did not have a direct threat to confront. The breakup of the Soviet Union meant that there was no global enemy. Thus, there was a move toward a more humanitarian and socioeconomic-focused foreign policy for the United States. This was especially the case during the presidency of Clinton, with economic goals taking priority and military interventions (e.g., in the former Yugoslavia) framed in humanitarian terms. Scholars have argued the world moved toward unipolarity during this time, with the US as the sole superpower, a situation that continues today.

Economically, the US grew strong in the 1990s and new alliances, including the North American Free Trade Agreement (NAFTA), were established.

However, this focus on humanitarianism did not translate to financial support for a socioeconomically focused foreign policy. "Congress cut foreign aid. Despite President Bill Clinton's adoption of an ambitious foreign policy agenda based on global 'engagement' and democratic 'enlargement,' the State Department's budget in 1997 fell to its lowest level in twenty years."[12] The goal of "global engagement" did not materialize when the United States and the world was confronted with the massive tragedy of the Rwandan genocide. Bill Clinton would later claim the failure to act to stop this genocide was one of his biggest regrets. At the time, however, the United States and other world powers were reluctant to act.

The First Gulf War would be a pivotal point in terms of impressing upon the Middle East region and global allies the military superiority and efficiency of the U.S. military. In a swift, effective, and short war, the US easily overpowered Saddam Hussein's forces and drove them back into Iraq from Kuwait. This had some key implications for U.S. foreign policy: First, the US realized, in its first major land battle since Vietnam, that it was capable of winning wars quickly. Second, unipolarity became further solidified because the US could have easily defeated the Iraqi army on its own, without any assistance from allies. Third, this was one of the first technological and "instant" wars, when bombings could be viewed in "real time" via the television screens of American (and global) households. Fourth, Saddam Hussein suffered a humiliating defeat as his much-vaunted troops were swiftly defeated and the US and its allies dictated terms of his surrender. Finally, the Middle East region was divided, with discontent among some of the population because foreign invaders had become involved in a situation that was not of their concern.

Al Qaeda was still in its infancy during the First Gulf War, but bin Laden remained active. He already had his supporters, most of whom he had funded and who had fought in the war in Afghanistan. He was allied with Egyptian radicals and others in the Middle East. He could use the situation during and after the First Gulf War, in which the US and its allies were present in the Middle East, to rally support for his cause by claiming foreigners were illegally in the Holy Lands of Muslims.

After the First Gulf War, al Qaeda became stronger as more recruits joined, perceiving foreign intervention into the affairs of Muslims and Arabs in the Middle East. Bin Laden extended his reach, and there have been reports that al Qaeda was involved in the killings of U.S. soldiers in Somalia during the "Black Hawk Down" incident. Other reports claimed bin Laden supporters infiltrated local forces during the civil wars in the former Yugoslavia in the 1990s. A *New York Times* article claimed the "outsiders"—fighters who went to the former Yugoslavia from Saudi Arabia and other parts of the Middle East—were extremists and religiously more hardcore than local Muslims.[13] Here, the spread of ideas can be noted as can the development of a regional and even global network of supporters for bin Laden's cause. By claiming Muslims and Arabs were being oppressed and negatively influenced by foreign forces, bin Laden and his allies could gain support outside their home base.

Bin Laden was popular in many parts of the world, and his actions were seen as countering the injustices faced by Muslims and Arabs due to U.S. foreign policy. Atwan claims there was a "historical inevitability" to the rise of bin Laden, and he can be understood as the emergence of a "resurgent Muslim identity."[14] He adds,

> After centuries of decline, [many Muslims] view bin Laden as having brought hope and dignity back to a people under the shadow of humiliation and exploitation, and having squared up to the bullies of the West, in particular the U.S.[15]

All this, of course, came to a head on September 11, 2001, as al Qaeda members flew hijacked airplanes into the Twin Towers of the World Trade Center in New York and onto the Pentagon in Washington, DC. A fourth plane was foiled in its suicide mission and crashed into fields in Pennsylvania. Almost 3,000 people died in the attacks. Subsequently, the US pursued bin Laden for his role in planning the attacks. Almost immediately after the September 2001 attacks, the US invaded Afghanistan, where al Qaeda had its base. However, despite a swift overthrow of the extremist Taliban government, al Qaeda's leader remained elusive for almost a decade after September 2001, and the closest the US came to capturing him was during the Battle of Tora Bora in December 2001.[16] At that time, bin Laden escaped and, until August 2010, clear leads of his whereabouts were unavailable.

The Killing of Osama bin Laden

During his presidential campaign, Barack Obama pledged that

> if we have Osama bin Laden in our sights and the Pakistani government is unable or unwilling to take him out, then we have to act and we will take him out. We will kill bin Laden; we will crush al-Qaeda. That has to be our biggest national-security priority.[17]

This statement would prove to be the foundation of his government's efforts to find bin Laden after he took office in January 2009. Obama campaigned saying he would not hesitate to make a unilateral decision to order the death of bin Laden. Months after he took office, he prioritized the search for bin Laden and urged then–CIA chief Leon Panetta to provide resources to accomplish this end.[18]

On May 26, 2009, Obama gathered together Director of Central Intelligence Leon Panetta, National Security Adviser Tom Donilon, Chief of Staff Rahm Emanuel, and Director of the National Counterterrorism Center Mike Leiter. Obama said,

> Here's the deal. I want this hunt for Osama bin Laden and al-Zawahiri to come to the front of the line. I worry that the trail has gone cold. This has to be our top priority and it needs leadership in the tops of your organizations. . . . And I want regular reports on this to me, and I want them starting in thirty days.[19]

And that is what occurred. But there was little information until August 2010, when reports emerged of bin Laden's favorite courier living in a compound in Abbottabad, Pakistan. The information resulted from more than a decade of intelligence work and various forms of intelligence gathering. The name of the courier was reportedly received from some of the prisoners at Guantánamo Bay, Cuba. He operated under various aliases, and U.S. officials claimed they found out his commonly used name, Abu Ahmed al-Kuwaiti, in 2007, but it took them another few years to locate him.[20] Although previous information had made it seem as though bin Laden was hiding in the mountainous areas between Pakistan and Afghanistan, this latest information suggested he was inside this compound. Abbottabad is a medium-sized city in northern Pakistan of around 500,000 people, at an elevation of 4,000 feet. Pakistan's main army college is in the city. Peter Bergen described the city: "The overall feeling is a little more country club than that of the rest of Pakistan's heaving, teeming, smog-filled cities."[21]

There were reports of sightings of someone who looked like bin Laden who lived in the building along with his family and some other people. But the information was very limited and a lot of it remained uncertain. We now know that bin Laden had been living in the compound since 2005. He spent most of his time on the upper floors, with very brief walks in the back garden. The building he lived in was new and built specifically for him and those of his family—reportedly three wives and a dozen children and grandchildren—who lived there with him. The compound was almost entirely self-sufficient, with meat, vegetables, eggs, and milk all available without leaving the grounds. The compound was valued at U.S. $1 million.

Between then and March 2011, the compound was kept under surveillance, and efforts were made to confirm whether the person living on the third floor of the main building was bin Laden. It was difficult to tell and not much new information emerged. During this time, Joint Special Operations Commander Admiral William McRaven joined the planning team, providing input from Afghanistan and Pakistan about possible options for dealing with the suspected bin Laden. Decisions had to be made on whether to attack the compound or not.

In the United States, between March 14, 2011 and the end of April, there were a series of meetings at which four different options were discussed. One was to bomb the compound; the second was a targeted strike by a drone; third, to use ground forces in a raid; and fourth, to do nothing and wait for more information. Other less-debated options included a joint raid with Pakistani forces. The bombing option was likely to lead to high numbers of civilian casualties. The force of the bomb could mean bin Laden's remains could not be identified for certain, leading to uncertainty and continued rumors of his existence. Experts argued that even a "surgical" drone strike would still require weaponry and bombs and would not be surgical, and there would still be concerns about identifying bin Laden's remains. Doing nothing was not an option either because any bit of knowledge of what the US was planning could lead to bin Laden disappearing, leading to another decade of searching for him and continued anxiety about his actions.[22]

Still, at this time, no one was sure whether the person inside the compound was actually bin Laden or merely a decoy or someone who looked like him. Later "Red Team" exercises based on the intelligence available at the time reached the conclusion that there was a 40–60 percent chance the person was bin Laden. The CIA's estimate was higher, at 60–80 percent. No matter how one looked at it, the chances that the person who was being kept under surveillance was not bin Laden were still high. There was a distinct possibility that bin Laden was elsewhere. Later, both Gates and Vice President Joe Biden would claim they would not have authorized the raid. Both men, with extensive experience in the government, were hesitant and urged the president to wait until more information could be procured.

But, at the time, a decision had to be made. Corn writes, "Whatever the percentages, Obama and everyone else realized this was the best shot the U.S. government had at finding bin Laden since he escaped at the battle of Tora

Bora in late 2001."[23] The US could wait for more information but in the meantime bin Laden might get knowledge that his hideout had been exposed and he might disappear. Considering how long it took to find information about the compound in Abbottabad, if bin Laden were to leave it, it might be difficult if not impossible for the US to find him again anytime soon.

Regarding possible courses of action, a joint operation with Pakistan was not considered seriously because the president and his team believed Pakistan was not to be trusted and that its secret service was leaking information to extremists. But what if U.S. troops ran into Pakistani soldiers on their way out of the compound after completing their mission? The president was concerned about this and was reassured by McRaven that the U.S. team would be able to hold off Pakistani forces for some hours, at least.

A helicopter raid seemed the best option. But, Gates was hesitant about a helicopter raid because he had previously been at the CIA during the unsuccessful raid to rescue hostages in Iran as well as during the Black Hawk Down incident in Somalia.[24] Both Biden and Gates advised waiting for more intelligence because the latest calculations put the chances of the man in the compound being bin Laden at around 50–50. Despite hesitation by some of his top advisers, Obama gave the go ahead for a helicopter raid on April 29, 2011. McRaven, however, had to wait until conditions were appropriate.

On May 1, 2011, conditions were deemed optimal. Peter Bergen describes the start of the raid as follows:

> At about 11 p.m. local time, the two Black Hawks took off from the Jalalabad airfield and headed east toward the border with Pakistan, which they would cross in about 15 minutes. The choppers were MH-60s, modified so as to remain undetected by Pakistani radar stations, which were in peacetime mode, unlike the radar facilities on the border Pakistan shared with its longtime enemy India, which were always on heightened alert. Painted with exotic emulsions to help them evade detection, the modified MH-60s gave off a low heat signature in flight. Their tail rotors had been designed to make them less noisy and less susceptible to radar identification. On top of that, the helicopters flew "nap of the earth," which means perilously low and very, very fast—only a few feet above the ground, driving around trees and hugging the riverbeds and valleys that lace the foothills of the Hindu Kush mountain range. This also made them harder to detect by radar. After crossing the border, the choppers swung north of Peshawar and its millions of residents and eyeballs. The total flight time to the target was about an hour and a half, the distance about 150 miles.[25]

Potential negative impacts of the raid were high—the U.S. troops might face stiff resistance from those in the compound; the compound may have been booby trapped; Pakistani soldiers might engage the U.S. troops; U.S. relations with Pakistan might be damaged severely. In many of these scenarios, U.S. troops could die. Overall, Obama's presidency was at stake, a claim Vice President Biden made when he expressed his caution about the raid. If things went well, then the raid would be hailed as a success. If things did not go well—if the person was not bin Laden, if there were large-scale casualties, if the relationship with Pakistan was damaged, and especially if there were many U.S. deaths—Obama would take the blame. His chances of gaining a second term would become practically impossible. He would be considered weak and ineffective on issues of national security and foreign policy. The question became whether it was worth taking the risk to order the assault then or to wait until intelligence reports confirmed or denied that the individual living in that compound in Abbottabad was bin Laden.

Further, keeping Pakistan out of the loop meant planning for the raid had to incorporate how U.S. troops would leave the compound as quickly as possible, in addition to planning for entry and securing the area. Admiral McRaven was a key proponent of the helicopter raid option and assured Obama that "if his team could be delivered to the compound, they could clear it and kill or capture bin Laden with minimal loss of life."[26]

The U.S. SEAL team flew from Afghanistan under the cover of darkness and utilizing evasive techniques in order not to be picked up by Pakistani surveillance. Once in Abbottabad, 120 miles within the Pakistani border, the first helicopter crashed in hazy weather conditions. The second landed without any mishap and U.S. Special forces entered bin Laden's compound. There were twenty-three Navy SEALs on board this helicopter from SEAL Team Six, a group whose existence was not publicized before the bin Laden killing.

Along with the SEALs, there was also a translator and a tracking dog called Cairo.[27] The SEALs swiftly moved through the various buildings, reaching bin Laden's building and climbing up to the third floor where the suspected bin Laden lived. There, reports vary about what they found—either bin Laden surprised and without any defense or bin Laden reaching for a weapon.[28] In any case, shots to his head and chest killed bin Laden. There are different accounts about whether he died immediately or whether he was alive when SEALs entered his room and shot him again. Along with him, four other people were shot and killed, including one of his sons. Bin Laden's body was the only one that the U.S. forces took with them, along with his computers and other data found in his rooms. Bin Laden's body was buried at sea, with his corpse "prepared in conformance with Islamic precepts and practice," according to a White House statement. No photograph of the dead bin Laden was released to the public.

Other people in the compound were left for Pakistani security officials to find, and these included bin Laden's wives who were there with him. Pakistani officials later said a 12-year-old daughter of bin Laden had witnessed the killing. On their way out, the U.S. forces destroyed the downed helicopter so its components could not be used by others. The entire operation took around 40 minutes from start to finish. President Obama's reaction to the news of bin Laden's death is reported to have been, "We got him."

Thousands of miles away in Washington, DC, live video of the raid was being broadcast within the White House. Official reports have claimed that the 20–30 minutes of the actual entry and killing of bin Laden were blank and unavailable on the feed, but the approach to the compound, initial strikes, and getaway were all on video and were available to policy makers in the United States. Bowden writes that when then–National Security Adviser Tom Donilon learned that there was a plan to watch a live feed of the raid in the Situation Room of the White House, he wanted it moved to a smaller room.[29] There was concern that Obama might get involved in the raid, and Donilon did not want that to happen. Eventually, when the president himself came to the smaller room to watch the feed, Secretary of State Hillary Clinton was worried about whether the president should watch it. Deputy National Security Adviser Ben Rhodes answered, "He's not going to be directing anything . . . it's just a feed."[30]

After bin Laden's death was confirmed, Obama gave a press conference at 11:35 pm EST on May 1, 2011 in which he said,

> Good evening. Tonight, I can report to the American people and to the world that the United States has conducted an operation that killed Osama bin Laden, the leader of Al Qaeda, and a terrorist who is responsible for the murder of thousands of innocent men, women and children.

Celebrations occurred on the streets of U.S. cities.

The killing of bin Laden, of course, raised other questions as well. An interesting aspect of the raid was its description over Twitter by some local residents of Abbottabad. One man, Sohaib Akhtar, became famous as he live-tweeted the incident, starting with details of the U.S. helicopter flying over Abbottabad and continuing with reports of its crash. This indicates the role of social media in publicizing information in today's networked world. A top secret mission, unknown to even the Pakistani government, was being live-tweeted by residents of Abbottabad. Granted, they had little idea of what was going on— Akhtar speculates about what the helicopters flying around may have been doing and who they belonged to—but the secrecy of the mission could have been compromised if bin Laden's supporters or even the Pakistani government had been monitoring tweets more thoroughly.

The U.S. relationship with Pakistan was also important in discussions about the raid. McRaven suggested that the SEALs should remain quiet and let Washington and Islamabad work things out, in case things did not work out and they were trapped or had to be evacuated. Obama did not want this situation to occur; he insisted throughout the discussions that the SEALs should not only have enough resources to enter the compound and complete their tasks but also to be able to leave, all without Pakistani assistance. Indeed, Obama wanted the U.S. Special Forces team to be able to fight their way out of the situation and out of Pakistan if necessary. Having its SEALs in Pakistani control was not something the US wanted to see.

The killing of bin Laden raises a number of additional issues for the future of U.S. foreign policy. These can be divided into legal, ethical, and operational/military issues. Some experts have argued that the killing of bin Laden, and especially the killing of Anwar al-Awlaki and his son (both U.S. citizens), were extrajudicial and unconstitutional. One could make the point, as many have done, that bin Laden did not deserve to be put on trial, but setting the legal precedent of killing one's enemy even if he or she might have surrendered is something to consider further. Although early news reports claimed bin Laden was armed and was reaching for his weapon, later reports contradicted this and said he remained unarmed.

Again, while it might be somewhat easier to justify the killing of bin Laden without due process and claim "justice was done," this is a more difficult claim with regard to al-Awlaki and his son. After all, mass murderers and serial killers—those who have actively murdered civilians—are placed on trial in the United States. They receive due process for their actions because they are U.S. citizens and their rights are guaranteed under the U.S. Constitution. So, why is it that a person who had, apparently, incited violence through his words but not directly killed anyone (al-Awlaki) and another person who was not on the "kill list" (Samir Khan), and al-Awlaki's son, a minor who was allegedly looking for his father, not receive the same opportunity?

If one is to say that "terrorists" should not receive the same rights as everyone, then is there even a reason to uphold the Constitution? Should it not apply to any and all U.S. citizens by virtue of their citizenship? These are questions that could be further discussed.

With respect to concerns about publicity and lack of resources in domestic courts, it is important to keep in mind that the US is currently prosecuting Khalid Sheikh Mohammed and has tried various other extremists. Although Mohammed is charged in a military court and this remains controversial, the point remains that there is precedent for putting extremists on trial. The U.S. legal system has coped with mass murderers. The case of the most notorious terrorist attack prior to September 11, 2001—the Oklahoma bombings—could be another example: Timothy McVeigh was charged and tried in the U.S. District Court in Denver, Colorado.

Another legal issue, which also falls under the ethical umbrella, is a concern over secrecy. So far, the targeted killing operations as well as drone strikes have operated under a veil of secrecy. There has been no official word on how many civilians have been killed by drones. Although the news that there was a "kill or capture" list of suspected militants was made public, there is little public knowledge of how decisions are made. What is known is that a small group of top-level officials debates who should be on the list. Ultimately, the president makes the decision. One could argue that decisions to kill, especially to kill a U.S. citizen as in the case of al-Awlaki, Khan, and al-Awlaki's son, should be discussed publicly. Toward the end of 2012, the Obama administration said it could codify rules on targeted killings, but what form this will take remains to be seen.

Finally, there are questions of international law and norms in the case of the death of bin Laden. Norms of warfare argue that an unarmed enemy combatant has the right to surrender; there remains doubt over whether bin Laden was given such an opportunity. The issue of Guantánamo Bay and whether it is legal to detain prisoners there remains of ongoing concern in U.S. foreign policy (see chapter 14). Obama pledged to close the detention center when he first took office, but it remained open at the start of his second term. Whether non–state actors are eligible for protection under the rules of war is also a question that has been debated since the inception of the "war on terror." No matter what one's opinion on this issue may be, it is essential for long-term U.S. foreign policy goals to clarify what can and cannot apply in terms of international warfare and legal norms in the context of engaging decentralized groups of militants.

The killing of bin Laden was an operation that was carried out within another sovereign nation state, without the knowledge of that state and without its permission. In the buildup to the operation, President Obama made it clear he wanted U.S. forces not just to enter bin Laden's compound but also to leave it without any assistance from Pakistan. The issue of sovereignty—key in international norms—is important because one could ask whether this action sets a precedent that the US and its allies could operate in a similar fashion in other states. At the same time, states less friendly to the US could also begin operations within the US. There are United Nations–recognized conditions (especially the Responsibility to Protect norm) under which intervention into sovereign states is permissible; however, the killing of bin Laden did not fall under such norms. Some experts have claimed that because bin Laden was the leader of a group the US is at war with, the US was permitted to seek him even within other sovereign states.

Along with legal issues, there are ethical issues to be discussed and debated. The key one—who decides whom to kill, where, and when—has been alluded to above. It is a question that will not go away merely by being ignored; instead, a full discussion in Congress about the existence of the "kill and capture list" and its implications for the US could become part of President Obama's second term.

Furthermore, what if others reciprocate by conducting attacks within the US and its allies upon those they deem "terrorists" or "militants"? Clear guidelines on who is targeted and why could reduce claims by others that the US is acting unethically. Other ethical issues in the bin Laden killing include questions of responsibility to civilians. For example, the Pakistani doctor who was used by the CIA to provide DNA samples of the people living in bin Laden's compound has been arrested by Pakistan and jailed for being a U.S. spy. Future U.S. foreign policy should take into account the possibility that those seen as helping the United States could be in danger, and it should include plans to protect them.

Long-term military goals of the U.S. counterinsurgency policy are obviously key when thinking about future implications of targeted killings as a strategy for U.S. foreign policy. As outlined earlier, there remains debate about whether targeted killings actually reduce terrorism in the long run. Concerns about blowback are also present. For example, information about the whereabouts of bin Laden and his family was collected via a fake vaccination campaign that was led by Pakistani doctor Shakeel Afridi. Not only was Afridi sentenced to 33 years in prison for treason, but there have been attacks against vaccination campaigns in Pakistan since Afridi's actions were made public knowledge. In December 2012, eight vaccination workers seeking to administer the polio vaccine in various parts of Pakistan were killed by suspected militants. One of the unintended consequences of using Afridi to gather information about bin Laden is, therefore, the long-term impact on much-needed vaccination programs in Pakistan. As of December 20, 2012, United Nations agencies have suspended the polio vaccination drive in the country. Pakistan is one of only three countries in the world where polio remains uneradicated.

Operationally, the bin Laden case also indicated the value of different types of intelligence-gathering measures. CIA "black sites" and enhanced interrogation techniques are alleged to have provided early leads about the name and whereabouts of bin Laden's courier. Bowden writes,

> It should . . . be noted this effort did involve torture, or at the very least coercive interrogation methods. The first two mentions of Ahmed the Kuwaiti were made by Mohamedou Ould Slahi and Mohammed al-Qahtani in coercive interrogation sessions. The third, the misleading characterization of the Kuwaiti as retired by Khalid Sheik Mohammed, came during one of his many water-boarding sessions. Hassan Ghul verified the Kuwaiti's central role during secret interrogation sessions at an undisclosed CIA detention center.[31]

Enhanced interrogation techniques were banned and "black sites" shut down when President Obama took office in 2009.

Targeted Killings in U.S. Foreign Policy: Implications for the Future

Overall, targeted killings are not a new tactic in foreign policy. There are different definitions of what "targeted killings" entail, but in general, they are strikes against specific individuals or small groups that have been undertaken with government approval. These strikes usually occur from bombs or, more recently, drone strikes and attempt to minimize collateral damage, including damage to civilians who may be near the target as well as large-scale damage to buildings. Assassinations are related to targeted killings in that the two terms are often used interchangeably, especially with regard to recent U.S. foreign policy. However, one could argue that there are differences in perception between the two. Calling a killing an "assassination" brings up images of it being outside of legal norms and norms of warfare. It also calls to mind historical assassinations and often illegal assassination attempts by the US and its allies on individuals who were deemed unfriendly to the United States. "Targeted killing" would appear to be a more neutral phrase without the negative connotations of "assassinations." Israel, for example, uses "targeted thwarting" or "interceptions" to explain its policies.[32]

Although the use of targeted killings as a tool for U.S. foreign policy is relatively new, other countries, especially Israel, have been using targeted killings as a policy option for decades. Some of Israel's biggest "successes" with respect to alleged Palestinian militants have been targeted killings. Daniel Byman argues, for Israel, targeted killings are often a policy of last resort. He adds that many of the militants the Israeli government wants to arrest remain under protection of neighboring countries. Israel often cannot request extradition or place them on trial, and targeted killings are deemed appropriate within Israel's foreign policy framework. Israel's policy on killing suspected militants is also publicized in the media, and the Israeli public knows about it; it is more transparent than the U.S. policy. Israel has adopted this strategy since the 1970s, and although those killed are generally high-ranking militants, there have been plenty of occasions when civilians have been killed as well. Even for a more experienced country like Israel, targeted killings are not a simple and "clean" tactic and have been condemned by its allies. Byman points out that Israel's practice of targeted killings escalated since the start of the second intifada in 2000:

> Before then, the killings had been carried out relatively infrequently and against a limited number of targets, usually outside Israel's borders. But according to B'Tselem, an Israeli human rights organization, between 2000 and the end of 2005, Israeli security forces successfully targeted 203 Palestinian terrorists, killing an additional 114 people in the process.[33]

For the US, too, targeted killings have intensified in the past few years of the war on terrorism. An often-quoted statistic claims that during the first four years of President Obama's administration, he ordered "more targeted killings than any modern president."[34] Called "the Obama doctrine" by some experts, this shift in counterinsurgency policy from the large-scale attacks and "boots on the ground" approach of previous years to swift and (hopefully) more precise small-scale drone strikes on suspected militants has been noticeable since 2009. These strikes against alleged militants have occurred in areas ranging from Pakistan and Afghanistan to Somalia and Yemen. In Yemen, however, the initial strike in December 2009 controversially killed civilians, including small children. It also left behind numerous smaller bombs that eventually exploded and killed more people. Yemeni officials claimed this incident actually led to increased support for militants in the country and to anti-American sentiments.[35] The increase in targeted killings as a foreign policy option may be partly explained by the sophistication of new technologies and more precise targeting mechanisms, but the expansion of the policy of using targeted killings as a tool for countering extremism and terrorism has not been fully scrutinized.[36]

The existence and development of what some experts have called a "kill list" has also proven controversial. A *New York Times* article on May 29, 2012, reported that the president decides what happens to various suspected militants, some of whom may be children. Although the options are to kill or capture the suspects, recent policy has been to kill rather than capture.[37] The list of suspects is based on intelligence reports and is top secret, except to a small group of government officials. The rest of the government and the general public do not know who is on the list or even how they are placed on the list. Considering definitions of terrorism are not consistent across U.S. departments and agencies (and even less so cross country), notions of who or what is considered "terrorist" could be open to question here.

Different kinds of strikes are authorized during the process of targeted killings. So-called "personality strikes" are directed at militant leaders and their close allies; "signature strikes," used mostly in Pakistan and Afghanistan, target training camps and areas where larger groups of people congregate. In North Africa and Yemen, signature strikes have not often been used. Instead, there is a new type of strike. The *New York Times* article claims,

> The Defense Department can target suspects in Yemen whose names they do not know. Officials say the criteria are tighter than those for signature strikes, requiring evidence of a threat to the United States, and they have even given them a new name—TADS, for Terrorist Attack Disruption Strikes. But the details are a closely guarded secret—part of a pattern for a president who came into office promising transparency.[38]

The highest-value targeted killing from the perspective of the United States, apart from Osama bin Laden, has been that of Anwar al-Awlaki. A U.S. citizen, al-Awlaki was killed in a U.S. drone strike in Yemen in September 2011. Samir Khan, a U.S. citizen who was not on the president's kill list, was also killed by the strike. A couple of weeks later, more strikes killed other alleged militants and also al-Awlaki's 16-year-old son, Abdulrahman. The teenager was also a U.S. citizen. Although the argument can be made that, as al-Awlaki was an extremist who urged violence against the US, legal norms could be subverted, this was not the case with his son.[39] The teenager was killed without due process, without being brought to trial, and he was underage.[40] It can be argued this is not what a government should be doing to its citizens. Indeed, there is little to no evidence to show the boy was a threat to U.S. interests.

And, yet, the positives are seen as outweighing the negatives in using targeted killings as a tool of U.S. foreign policy. Supporters of the policy argue targeted killings save resources, both human (they reduce the need to send troops to war) and financial (the overall cost will be less in the long term than large-scale efforts such as in Iraq and Afghanistan). Furthermore, they are more effective in terms of accuracy and speed than sending in even small teams to assassinate potential targets. Because those killed are usually higher-level officials in extremist groups, targeted killings do a better job of disrupting militant activities and operations. On a related note, targeted killings provide instant results by killing suspected militants, as compared to longer-term options like diplomacy and soft power. Targeted killings also fit in with U.S. public opinion, which is tired of seeing its soldiers dying overseas and of long overseas military operations. The U.S. public remains anxious about terrorism, and by killing militants overseas before they can potentially harm the US, targeted killings satisfy public demand that something is done regarding terrorism.

By taking out leaders of militant groups, targeted killings have a swift and immediate impact on reducing potential extremist threats to the United States. "The purpose of these actions is to mitigate threats to U.S. persons' lives," John Brennan said in an interview.

> It is the option of last recourse. So the president, and I think all of us here, don't like the fact that people have to die. And so he wants to make sure that we go through a rigorous checklist: The infeasibility of capture, the certainty of the intelligence base, the imminence of the threat, all of these things.[41]

As such, targeted killings reduce the number of U.S. deaths and advance U.S. counterterrorism interests. These are all reasons that have been put forward in support of the still-secretive program.

Despite these claims by supporters of the program, there remain concerns about the effectiveness of the policy, and especially about its secretive and extrajudicial nature. Experts have claimed that targeted killings are not effective, especially in decentralized networks of militants in places such as Yemen and Somalia because another person would merely take over the tasks (and post) of the person killed. They are also ineffective in terms of decreasing terrorism and can actually lead to an increase in terrorism and increased popular support for militants. Considering a major part of the U.S. counterinsurgency strategy has been to "win hearts and minds" of local populations, keeping them in a constant state of anxiety with repeated drone strikes might not be the best policy option for the long term. In addition to increasing the legitimacy of and support for militants (especially if and when drone strikes kill civilians), militants could respond to the U.S. drone strikes by killing supporters of the US. This, too, is likely to reduce local support for U.S. actions. Those killed are portrayed as martyrs by militants. It has been alleged that one of the motivations of Faisal Shahzad, who planned to bomb Times Square in May 2010, was revenge for the constant drone strikes in Pakistan.[42]

There have also been criticisms that the U.S. drone strikes are illegal and unconstitutional. They remain shrouded in secrecy, and many aspects of the program, including how many civilians may have died and justifications for targeting specific individuals, remain mostly unpublicized. And although the short-term costs might be lower than the cost of a large-scale military operation, the long-term costs, such as the cost to the U.S. reputation and its image in the world, could be high. In addition, drones are expensive. Good intelligence is necessary to ensure the target is really who it should be and is being targeted. And, in cases such as the killing of Osama bin Laden, well-trained quick response teams are necessary. At the moment, the US is the main user of drones in targeted killings around the world. But what will happen if and when other states and even non–state actors, not all of whom may be friendly to the US, acquire drones? What if they begin their own targeted killing policy? How could and would the US respond? These are questions that need more discussion in the government and public.

Toward the end of 2012, there were plans to codify targeted killings and other options for the US. During the first Obama administration, all military-age males in a strike zone were counted as militants unless there was clear evidence proving they were civilians. However, because they tend to be already dead by the time any evidence is found, proof that they are civilians does not change the decision whether to strike or not.

To the question of whether targeted killings reduce terrorism there is no definitive answer. But a deeper discussion may be necessary just because of this lack of consensus. Some experts have warned that having to live with the sound of drones and hear of drone strikes killing friends and family in places like

Pakistan, Somalia, and Yemen could convince locals to increase their support for militants, thus providing them with legitimacy. This would, of course, weaken the US's and its allies' goals of winning the hearts and minds of the local population. In places like Afghanistan, there has been a rise in the number of "green on blue" attacks; in 2012, numerous deaths of ISAF forces occurred in this way. Green on blue attacks are attacks by members of the Afghani security forces upon international forces. The rise in these attacks is particularly worrisome for the US and its allies because significant sums of money, time, and expertise has been and is being spent training Afghans to ensure their own security and the security of their citizens.

The question of the best way to proceed to achieve foreign policy goals is also relevant in future discussions about targeted killings. Would soft power—the ability to attract others to your side without using military force—be preferable? If so, should there be a strong emphasis on public diplomacy and spreading information about U.S. ideals and values among the population of North Africa, Middle East, and South Asia? After all, it is unlikely that the Taliban are beloved in much of Afghanistan, considering their past actions and current intimidation tactics. Is it more likely a case of "better the devil you know" or even the view that foreign forces will soon leave, thus leaving locals who may have supported them vulnerable and without protection. This is connected to transparency and the need to have a transparent discussion of counterinsurgency and counterterrorism options in the U.S. Congress before strategies such as targeted killings become mainstreamed.

At the international level, too, the US should be concerned about possible human rights and other violations if and when drone use becomes more widespread in the global arena. Finally, as Byman points out, the US needs to maintain good relations with its allies because its drone strikes and targeted killings are occurring outside its territorial borders. Unlike Israel, which employs targeted killings in countries it is not allied with, the US needs the support and permission of countries such as Yemen, Pakistan, Afghanistan, and Somalia to conduct its operations. Therefore, a long-term policy of targeted killing needs to take relations with allies into account. As indicated above, the Yemeni government claimed more people supported militants after the first few U.S. strikes killed civilians. It is only with a close alliance with host governments that targeted killing could be part of an effective counterinsurgency strategy for the United States.

The temptation to think of drones as an "easy solution" was laid out by President Obama. In an interview with Mark Bowden, Obama said,

Creating a legal structure, processes, with oversight checks on how we use unmanned weapons, is going to be a challenge for me and my successors for some time to come . . . There's a remoteness to it that makes it tempting to think that somehow we can, without any mess on our hands, solve vexing security problems.[43]

It is this type of thinking that might lead U.S. foreign policy makers to only focus on the short-term seeming benefits of drones and targeted killings, to the detriment of long-term solutions and caution about long-term impacts on U.S. values and identity.

Key Actors

Joe Biden   U.S. vice president; he remained cautious about the raid on the Abbottabad compound and urged waiting for more information before taking action.

John Brennan   Assistant to the president for homeland security and counter-terrorism; he debated each possible outcome with the president. He was also one of those involved in drawing out and debating the "kill or capture" list. He called the president's decision to authorize a raid a "gutsy call."

Bill Clinton, George W. Bush   Former presidents of the United States; initiated the large-scale intelligence-gathering operation that ultimately led to information about bin Laden's hideout.

Hillary Clinton   Secretary of state; not directly involved in planning the operation, but was present to watch the live feed of the raid.

Tom Donilon   National security adviser who provided regular briefings to the president on various intelligence issues.

Robert Gates   Secretary of defense; similar to the vice president, he supported waiting for more information before attacking the compound.

Barack Obama   President of the United States; despite the odds of the person in the compound being bin Laden ranging around 50–50, he authorized the raid, thinking this was the best chance of catching bin Laden in almost a decade. After the raid was successful in killing bin Laden, Obama claimed "justice is done."

Admiral William McRaven   Commander of the joint special operations command; was confident in his team's ability to carry out the raid; he pushed for it over other options. He planned and implemented the raid very efficiently. Even when one helicopter crash landed, his team adjusted and carried out the operation successfully.

Leon Panetta   Director of central intelligence who was involved in information gathering and planning from the inception. He supported a helicopter-led raid.

Notes

1. Scott Shane, "Election Spurred a Move to Codify U.S. Drone Policy," November 24, 2012, *New York Times*, www.nytimes.com/2012/11/25/world/white-house-presses -for-drone-rulebook.html?pagewanted=all&_r=0.

2. BBC News, "Analysing bin Laden's Jihadi Poetry," September 24, 2008, news .bbc.co.uk/2/hi/middle_east/7630934.stm.

3. National Security Archives, "Interview with Dr. Zbigniew Brzezinski," June 13, 1997, www.gwu.edu/~nsarchiv/coldwar/interviews/episode-17/brzezinski2.html.

4. Donald L. Barlett and James B. Steele "The Oily Americans," May 13, 2003, *Time*, www.time.com/time/magazine/article/0,9171,450997–92,00.html.

5. Greg Bruno, "Saudi Arabia and the Future of Afghanistan," *Council of Foreign Relations*, www.cfr.org/afghanistan/saudi-arabia-future-afghanistan/p17964.

6. For a list of al-Qaeda operations and related incidents, see "The Five Ages of Al Qaeda," September11, 2009, *The Guardian*, www.guardian.co.uk/world/interactive/ 2009/sep/10/alqaida-five-ages-terror-attacks.

7. PBS News Hour, "Bin Laden's Fatwa," August 23, 1996, www.pbs.org/newshour/ updates/military/july-dec96/fatwa_1996.html.

8. U.S. Government, *The 9/11 Commission Report*, July 22, 2004, http://avalon.law .yale.edu/sept11/911Report.pdf, 109.

9. PBS News Hour, "The Presidential Address," August 20, 1998, www.pbs.org/news hour/bb/military/july-dec98/clinton2_8–20.html.

10. Steven W. Hook and John Spanier, *American Foreign Policy Since World War II*, 18th ed. Washington, DC: CQ Press, 2010), 129.

11. Ibid.

12. Ibid., 262.

13. Chris Hedges, "Outsiders Bring Islamic Fervor to the Balkans," *New York Times*, September 23, 1996, www.nytimes.com/1996/09/23/world/outsiders-bring-islamic -fervor-to-the-balkans.html.

14. Abdel Bari Atwan, *The Secret History of Al Qaeda* (Berkeley and Los Angeles: University of California Press, 2008), 39.

15. Ibid., 40.

16. Philip Smucker, "How Bin Laden Got Away," *Christian Science Monitor*, March 4, 2002, www.csmonitor.com/2002/0304/p01s03-wosc.html.

17. Graham Allison, "How It Went Down," *Time*, May 7, 2012, www.time.com/ time/magazine/article/0,9171,2113156,00.html#ixzz2F4YCyKlr.

18. David Corn, "How Obama Got Bin Laden: A Detailed Account from 'Showdown' by David Corn," *Daily Beast*, April 29, 2012, www.thedailybeast.com/articles/2012/04/29/ how-obama-got-bin-laden-a-detailed-account-from-showdown-by-david-corn.html.

19. Quoted in Mark Bowden, "The Hunt for 'Geronimo,'" November 2012, *Vanity Fair*, www.vanityfair.com/politics/2012/11/inside-osama-bin-laden-assassination-plot.

20. Mark Mazzetti and Helene Cooper, "Detective Work on Courier Led to Break-through on Bin Laden," *New York Times*, May 2, 2011, www.nytimes.com/2011/05/02/ world/asia/02reconstruct-capture-osama-bin-laden.html?_r=0.

21. Peter Bergen, "The Last Days of Osama Bin Laden," *Time*, May 7, 2012, www .time.com/time/printout/0,8816,2113155,00.html.

22. Corn, "How Obama Got Bin Laden."

23. Ibid.

24. Ibid.

25. Bergen, "The Last Days of Osama Bin Laden."

26. John A. Gans, Jr. "'This is 50–50': Behind Obama's Decision to Kill Bin Laden," *The Atlantic,* October 10, 2012, www.theatlantic.com/international/archive/2012/10/this-is-50-50-behind-obamas-decision-to-kill-bin-laden/263449.

27. BBC News, "Osama Bin Laden's Death: How It Happened," September 10, 2012, www.bbc.co.uk/news/world-south-asia-13257330.

28. Early U.S. reports said bin Laden was reaching for a weapon and hiding behind one of his wives when he was shot. Later reports admitted he was unarmed and had not taken shelter behind his wife.

29. Mark Bowden, *The Finish: The Killing of Osama Bin Laden* (New York: Atlantic Monthly Press, 2012), 217.

30. Ibid., 225.

31. Ibid., 248.

32. Stephen R. David, "Fatal Choices: Israel's Policy of Targeted Killing," The Begin-Sadat Center for Strategic Studies, September 2002, biu.ac.il/Besa/david.pdf.

33. Daniel Byman, "Do Targeted Killings Work?," *Foreign Affairs,* March/April 2006, 98.

34. Uri Friedman, "Targeted Killings: A Short History," *Foreign Policy,* September/October 2012, www.foreignpolicy.com/articles/2012/08/13/targeted_killings?page=full.

35. Jo Becker and Scott Shane, "Secret 'Kill List' Proves a Test of Obama's Principles and Will," *New York Times,* May 29, 2012, www.nytimes.com/2012/05/29/world/obamas-leadership-in-war-on-al-qaeda.html?pagewanted=all&_r=0.

36. The process behind targeted killing in U.S. foreign policy is outlined here: "The Process Behind Targeted Killing," *The Washington Post,* October 23, 2012, www.washingtonpost.com/world/national-security/the-process-behind-targeted-killing/2012/10/23/4420644c-1d26–11e2-ba31–3083ca97c314_graphic.html.

37. Becker and Shane, "Secret 'Kill List.'"

38. Ibid.

39. Not everyone agrees with this. See David R. Dow, "In Assassinating Anwar Al-Awlaki, Obama Left the Constitution Behind," *Daily Beast,* May 16, 2012, www.thedailybeast.com/articles/2012/03/13/in-assassinating-anwar-al-awlaki-obama-left-the-constitution-behind.html.

40. Conor Friedersdorf, "How Team Obama Justifies the Killing of a 16-year Old American," *The Atlantic,* October 24, 2012, www.theatlantic.com/politics/archive/2012/10/how-team-obama-justifies-the-killing-of-a-16-year-old-american/264028/#; Tom Junod, "Obama's Administration Killed a 16-Year-Old American and Didn't Say Anything About It. This is Justice?" *Esquire,* July 9, 2012, www.esquire.com/blogs/politics/abdulrahman-alawlaki-death-104.

41. Becker and Shane, "Secret 'Kill List.'"

42. Noah Shachtman, "Times Square Terror: Drone Payback?" *Wired,* May 5, 2010, www.wired.com/dangerroom/2010/05/times-square-terror-drone-payback/.

43. Scott Shane, "Election Spurred a Move to Codify U.S. Drone Policy," *New York Times,* November 24, 2012, www.nytimes.com/2012/11/25/world/white-house-presses-for-drone-rule-book.html?pagewanted=all&_r=0.

3 Executive Decisions and Preventive War: Strategies of Intervention and Withdrawal in Iraq (2003–2011)

Jeffrey S. Lantis and Eric Moskowitz

Before You Begin

1. What is the "imperial presidency" model, and what are its implications for U.S. foreign policy making?

2. Why did the Bush administration decide to invade Iraq and topple Saddam Hussein in 2003? What were the justifications for a preemptive war against Iraq, and how well has this stood the test of time?

3. What leaders were particularly influential in shaping the decision to invade Iraq, and what domestic opposition did they face?

4. Why was it so difficult for Congress to have a significant impact on presidential plans for war?

5. What links can you draw between the decision-making process and outcomes in the Iraq war?

6. Does the withdrawal of all U.S. forces from Iraq in December 2011 indicate success for U.S. foreign policy or something else?

7. What are the long-term implications of a doctrine of preemption for U.S. foreign policy?

"It's going to take a long time to win this war."

—President George W. Bush, Speech
at the Pentagon, September 17, 2001

Introduction

The terrorist attacks of September 11, 2001, represented a watershed moment for U.S. foreign policy. September 11 enabled the executive branch to assume an unusual amount of influence over security policy making.

President George W. Bush and his advisers used that influence in a variety of ways, including to implement a new strategy of preemptive strikes against potential enemies. The United States would rely most often on the unilateral exercise of power, rather than on international law and organizations, to achieve its security objectives. Some observers suggest that the Bush doctrine, the larger war on terrorism, and the Iraq war (2003–2010) represented the resurgence of the "imperial presidency." However, these developments raised critical questions about the success of executive dominance at home and the benefits and costs of the global war on terror.

Background: The Rise of the Imperial Presidency

Historian Arthur M. Schlesinger Jr. coined the term *imperial presidency* to describe the dominance of the executive branch in U.S. policy making during the Cold War. Schlesinger identified a pattern of steady accumulation of power in the executive branch, especially "under the demand or pretext of an emergency." He argued that by the early 1970s, "the American president had become on issues of war and peace the most absolute monarch (with the possible exception of Mao Tse Tung of China) among the great powers of the world."[1] Schlesinger viewed this as an *un*constitutional usurpation of authority through "the appropriation by the Presidency, and particularly by the contemporary Presidency, of powers reserved by the Constitution and by long historical practice to Congress."[2] Another scholar, Michael Beschloss, concurred:

> The founders never intended to have an imperial president. Always worried about tyranny, they drafted a Constitution that gives the president limited authority and forces him to use his political skills to fight for influence as he squeezes laws out of Congress and prods the American people to think in new ways.[3]

The imperial presidency may have blossomed in the first decades of the Cold War, but political winds shifted in the 1970s as Americans grew weary of the war in Vietnam and executive excess. The Watergate scandal and resignation of President Richard Nixon in 1974 seemed to mark the demise of the Cold War imperial presidency. A resentful Congress and a mobilized nation began to check the power of the executive branch. Succeeding presidents faced resistance from mobilized institutions that constrained their latitude in foreign policy making. The international security environment

Timeline

U.S. Intervention in Iraq

August 2, 1990	Iraq invades Kuwait.
August 8, 1990	President George H. W. Bush announces the United States is sending troops to Saudi Arabia in response to the Iraqi invasion of Kuwait; UN Security Council later passes a resolution authorizing the use of force if Iraq does not withdraw from Kuwait by January 15, 1991.
January–February 1991	Iraqi president Saddam Hussein's forces remain in Iraq past deadline; UN-sanctioned multinational forces launch a war against Iraq, and Iraqi troops quickly retreat from Kuwait; Bush decides to end the war after one hundred hours.
March 1991	Hussein brutally puts down a Shia revolt in southern Iraq and a Kurdish revolt in the north; the Bush administration sets up "no-fly" zones over Iraq to restrain further assaults on these groups.
April 3, 1991	The UN Security Council passes Resolution 687, which requires the Iraqi government to allow international inspections of all its weapons facilities and to destroy all weapons of mass destruction (WMD).
December 1998	Iraq ends all cooperation with UN weapons inspections. Without Security Council approval, President Bill Clinton orders Operation Desert Fox, a four-day bombing campaign of Iraqi military installations.
September 15, 2001	In a meeting of the George W. Bush war cabinet, Deputy Secretary of Defense Paul Wolfowitz proposes including Iraq as a target of the U.S. military response to the September 11 terror attacks; Secretary of State Colin Powell objects, arguing for a focus on the Taliban and al Qaeda in Afghanistan; President Bush orders Afghanistan as the immediate target, though he indicates that Iraq will be reconsidered later.
January 29, 2002	In the State of the Union address, Bush denounces Iraq, Iran, and North Korea as an "axis of evil." He declares that the United States will act preemptively against nations with WMD that threaten it.
Summer 2002	Debate about regime change in Iraq heats up in the Bush administration. The momentum for war appears to be growing; Powell, the secretary of state, warns Bush about political and economic consequences of a war.

October 11, 2002	Congress passes a joint resolution authorizing Bush to use any means necessary to enforce Security Council resolutions against Iraq and defend U.S. national security.
November 8, 2002	UN Security Council unanimously passes Resolution 1441, warning Iraq of serious consequences unless it submits immediately to unrestricted weapons inspections.
March 19–20, 2003	After an ultimatum for Saddam Hussein to step down goes unheeded, US and coalition forces launch air attacks on Iraq and invade the country.
May 1, 2003	Bush announces that all major combat operations in Iraq have been successfully concluded.
June 28, 2004	Paul Bremer, head of the Coalition Provisional Authority, hands over sovereign authority to an interim Iraqi government.
December 15, 2005	Iraqis elect a permanent government, with the Shia-led United Iraqi Alliance winning a plurality of the seats; Nouri al-Maliki, of the Shiite Dawa Party, is selected prime minister.
December 6, 2006	The Iraq Study Group issues its report calling for an aggressive diplomatic effort and a phased withdrawal of U.S. troops.
January 10, 2007	President Bush announces plans for a "New Way Forward," which includes a surge of 21,500 additional troops to Iraq.
November 2008	The United States accepts a status of forces agreement (SOFA) with Iraq that commits the United States to withdraw all of its troops from Iraq by December 31, 2011.
December 2011	Following the collapse of negotiations for an extension of the SOFA, the Iraqi government orders the withdrawal of all U.S. forces by the end of the month.

was also uncertain, and Washington officials appeared to share a basic consensus that the United States should tread carefully in global affairs in the post–Cold War era. When George W. Bush entered office in 2001, Beschloss characterized him as the United States' first truly "post-imperial president," given public attitudes favoring restraint in foreign affairs and relative peace in the world.

U.S. Foreign Policy after September 11

The attacks of September 11 became a catalyst for fundamental transformations in U.S. foreign policy, however, as key tenets of U.S. strategy in the Cold War—and stewardship in the post–Cold War order—no longer appeared adequate. The United States suddenly seemed vulnerable. Shaping U.S. responses to the terrorist threat would call into question traditional concepts and practices in foreign affairs, including hegemony and multilateral cooperation.

The Bush administration decided to interpret September 11 as a transformative moment for the country. President Bush and his top advisers believed that the attacks represented a "moment of destiny" for the nation. Moreover, they recognized that the attacks had reduced the public's resistance to risk taking and its casualty aversion. National security adviser Condoleezza Rice characterized this new era as similar to the period from 1945 to 1947, when events "started shifting the tectonic plates in international politics." She argued it was "important to try to seize on that and position American interests and institutions and all of that before they harden again."[4]

The administration began to define new avenues for foreign and security policy. The president received congressional support for a broadly worded resolution that authorized him "to use all necessary and appropriate force against those nations, organizations, or persons he determines planned, authorized, committed, or aided the terrorist attacks that occurred on September 11, 2001, or harbored such organizations or persons, in order to prevent any future acts of international terrorism against the United States by such nations, organizations, or persons." The resolution did not prompt much congressional debate at the time, yet this was the beginning of what Ivo Daalder and James Lindsay termed "a revolution in American foreign policy." Bush's advocacy of "the unilateral exercise of American power" and his emphasis on "a proactive doctrine of preemption and [de-emphasis of] the reactive strategies of deterrence and containment" set the path for a dramatic new phase in U.S. foreign policy.[5]

Decision Making and the Iraq War

The idea to invade Iraq as part of a global war against terrorism was first raised just days after the September 11 attacks.[6] On September 15, 2001, President Bush held a meeting of his principal national security advisers, including Rice, Vice President Richard Cheney, Secretary of State Colin Powell,

Secretary of Defense Donald Rumsfeld, Deputy Secretary of Defense Paul Wolfowitz, Director of Central Intelligence (DCI) George Tenet, and Chairman Richard Myers of the Joint Chiefs of Staff. Rumsfeld and Wolfowitz reportedly brought along briefing papers that identified "three potential sets of targets: Taliban, al Qaeda, and Iraq."[7] When given the opportunity, Wolfowitz argued that Iraqi president Saddam Hussein was a tyrant who represented a direct threat to U.S. national security; that his regime supported international terrorism; that Iraq sought to develop weapons of mass destruction (WMD) that could be used against U.S. allies, including Israel; and that he might have been involved in the September 11 plot.

In fact, Iraq had been a primary U.S. security concern since the Persian Gulf War in 1991. After the war, officials in the George H. W. Bush administration authored a Defense Policy Guidance that called for a firm stand against the Iraqi leader and other adversaries and stated that "American power ought to be vigorously asserted to bring order to a potentially disintegrating post–Cold War world."[8] As part of Iraq's 1991 surrender, the United Nations (UN) conducted regular inspections of suspected WMD sites for eight years. After the war, Saddam Hussein cracked down on insurgent groups and political opponents. In response, the United States and its allies established "no-fly" zones over parts of northern and southern Iraq to help protect those groups. U.S. and British planes patrolled the zones from 1991 to 2003, engaging in periodic exchanges of fire with Iraqi antiaircraft missile batteries. In May 1991, President Bush also signed secret orders for the CIA to spend more than $100 million on covert operations to "create the conditions for removal of Saddam Hussein from power."[9]

At the Camp David meeting in mid-September 2001, however, there was little support among the president's other advisers for the Iraq option. When Wolfowitz continued to make his argument, Bush had his chief of staff, Andrew Card, take Wolfowitz aside to tell him to allow the discussion to move on to other, more pressing policy alternatives.[10] Nevertheless, Bush reportedly told his national security adviser the next day that though the first target of the war on terrorism was Afghanistan, "eventually we'll have to return to [the Iraq] question."[11] In late November 2001, the president secretly instructed Rumsfeld to update war plans for Iraq. Senior administration officials later argued that Bush "understood instantly after September 11 that Iraq would be the next major step in the global war against terrorism, and that he made up his mind" on Iraq "within days, if not hours, of that fateful day."[12]

Nevertheless, the administration moved forward with plans to first strike the Taliban and al Qaeda in Afghanistan. Bush launched the war with strong congressional and public support. U.S. and British troops, aided by forces from other countries, conducted a rapid series of campaigns against the Taliban. Special operations troops worked in concert with groups in the Northern Alliance and quickly took control of key regions of the country. By December 2001, the war in Afghanistan seemed near its end, though Osama bin Laden and other leaders of al Qaeda remained at large.

2002: A Year of Decision

Even before the war in Afghanistan wound down, battle lines had been drawn within the Bush administration over Iraq. Officials were divided into two camps: those who favored an invasion of Iraq and those who favored intensified efforts to contain Iraq.[13] In 2002 the camp supporting the invasion of Iraq included Rumsfeld, Cheney, and Wolfowitz. Also sharing their perspective were I. Lewis "Scooter" Libby, Cheney's chief of staff; Zalmay Khalilzad, deputy national security adviser on Iraq; Stephen Hadley, deputy national security adviser; and Wayne Downing, White House counterterrorism adviser. Some members of this faction had been pressuring the government to topple the Iraqi leader since the early 1990s. The call for an attack on Iraq was an important part of the agenda of a group of so-called neo-conservatives, or "neo-cons," inside (and outside) the Bush administration.

Secretary Rumsfeld was a key player in planning the Iraq invasion. He has been described as a "masterful bureaucratic infighter" during this period, "who ruthlessly gained control over the major decisions [of the Iraq war] and marginalized colleagues." The secretary "operated in a secretive fashion [allowing] him to increase control over information that acted to distort and complicate the policy-making process."[14] Rumsfeld was advised by the Pentagon's Defense Policy Board, a private group of consultants led by neo-conservatives including former Pentagon official Richard Perle, former CIA director James Woolsey, and *Weekly Standard* editor William Kristol, the chair of a neo-conservative think-tank called the Project for the New American Century (PNAC). In February 1998, eighteen prominent neo-conservatives from PNAC had sent President Bill Clinton an open letter warning that Saddam Hussein posed an immediate threat to the United States and calling for U.S. support for a popular insurrection in Iraq.[15] Neo-conservatives persuaded Congress to pass the Iraq Liberation Act of 1998, calling for regime change in Iraq as an official policy of the United States.[16] Many of those neo-conservatives were later drafted by Cheney to serve in top positions in the Bush administration. They sought U.S. international hegemony and the democratization of the Middle East. In their calculation, the overthrow of the Iraqi leader could be the start of something larger. After achieving regime change in Iraq, Perle suggested, the United States could more easily intimidate other dangerous states such as Iran and Syria to fall in line by simply delivering "a short message. . . . 'You're next.'"[17]

Secretary Rumsfeld created a new office in the Pentagon, the Counter-terrorism Evaluation Group—later known as the Office of Special Plans—that was to provide the secretary with advanced analysis of intelligence on Iraq and links between Middle Eastern states and terrorist networks. Critics charged that this office was created to find evidence of what Wolfowitz and Rumsfeld already "believed to be true" in the post–September 11 era: "that Saddam Hussein had close ties to al Qaeda, and that Iraq had an enormous arsenal of chemical, biological, and possibly even nuclear weapons that threatened the region and potentially, the United States."[18]

Dick Cheney was, "by common consent, the most powerful vice president in history."[19] And he seemed especially preoccupied with the September 11 attacks and possible links between Saddam Hussein and al Qaeda. Wolfowitz commented that Cheney was "someone whose view of the need to get rid of Saddam Hussein was transformed by September 11, by the recognition of the danger posed by the connection between terrorists and WMDs, and by the growing evidence of links between Iraq and al Qaeda."[20] Soon after September 11, "Cheney immersed himself in a study of Islam and the Middle East," meeting with scholars to discuss whether "toppling Saddam would send a message of strength and enhance America's credibility throughout the Muslim world."[21] His staff was also heavily focused on Iraq, working closely with Rumsfeld and the Pentagon in investigating links between Iraq and al Qaeda and building the case for war. Secretary Powell later said that he had "detected a kind of fever in Cheney. [Cheney] was not the steady, unemotional rock that he had witnessed a dozen years earlier during the run-up to the Gulf War. The vice president was beyond hell-bent for action against Saddam. It was as if nothing else existed."[22]

The group within the administration opposed to an outright invasion of Iraq included State Department officials, who became strong advocates of containment as an alternative, along with some military leaders. Powell was the leading voice for moderation in the cabinet during the winter months of 2001 and 2002. He was supported by Richard Armitage, deputy secretary of state,

Richard Haas, director of policy planning, and retired army general Anthony Zinni, the department's adviser on the Middle East. DCI Tenet also worried about the implications of an invasion for U.S. international security. State Department officials argued that the United States should support a renewed international program of WMD inspections in Iraq and ideally should build a multilateral coalition of countries willing to authorize more stringent UN Security Council resolutions and possibly even threaten the use of force against Saddam Hussein's regime. Thus, while there was a growing consensus that the Iraqi leader should be removed from office, there remained significant disagreement on the means to that end.

Secret Plans

The two camps secretly debated Iraqi policy throughout the fall of 2001. Rumsfeld and Cheney reportedly kept Iraq alive in "freewheeling meetings of the principals," where they discussed possible ties between so-called rogue states, such as Iraq, and terrorist groups. One senior official said of those meetings, "The issue got away from the president. He wasn't controlling the tone or the direction. . . . [Some members of the administration] painted him into a corner because Iraq was an albatross around their necks."[23] On November 21, 2001, while the war in Afghanistan continued, the president ordered Secretary Rumsfeld and Gen. Tommy Franks, head of Central Command (CENTCOM), to begin secretly updating war plans for Iraq. Bush would later say that this order was "absolutely" the first step in taking the nation to war.[24] Between December 2001 and September 2002, Franks would meet with President Bush eight times to present ever more detailed Iraq war plans.

Bush's State of the Union address in January 2002 gave him a platform to articulate the evolution of his foreign policy. In the address, the president's articulation of an "axis of evil"—Iran, Iraq, and North Korea—suggested that there were obvious enemies in the war on terrorism. A few weeks later, the president secretly directed the CIA to begin developing plans for supporting military efforts to overthrow the Iraqi regime. The CIA received almost $200 million for covert activities against Baghdad. President Bush reportedly set a deadline of April 15, 2002, for his advisers to develop a "coagulated plan" for dealing with Iraq. He told top officials he was ready to "take out Saddam."[25]

This new push to develop an operational plan led to serious debates in 2002 over the nature and scope of the operation. Administration officials discussed a number of options for toppling the Iraqi leader, including "providing logistical and intelligence help to [his] enemies in hopes of inciting a mutiny within his military circle; providing air and limited ground support for an assault by opposition groups; or an outright American invasion."[26] CIA officials informed the president that covert action alone could not achieve regime change in Iraq. Civilian leaders at the Pentagon and officials on the National Security Council (NSC) favored an option in the spirit of the "Afghanistan model"—using several thousand Special Forces soldiers and concentrated airpower to support opposition groups' efforts to defeat the Iraqi army. Wolfowitz and Downing were among the most outspoken advocates for the invasion plan, believing that light and technologically advanced forces could swiftly overrun Iraqi opposition.[27] At one point, Rumsfeld argued that perhaps as few as 125,000 troops could win the war.

Meanwhile, the Joint Chiefs of Staff and General Franks of CENTCOM argued strongly against the Pentagon's civilian leadership during this period. The military brass believed that any operation in Iraq would require overwhelming force to confront Iraq's established army. Military leaders were very concerned about Iraq's potential use of chemical or biological weapons and the possibility of prolonged urban warfare. They also questioned the reliability of the Iraqi National Congress as a leader of insurgent forces and the adequacy of plans for a postwar occupation regime. At one point General Franks articulated a plan calling for 380,000 troops for the invasion and occupation. "Nobody knew how long U.S. forces would need to be in Iraq, so CENTCOM war planners wrote that the occupation would last as long as ten years."[28] State Department officials joined the military brass in trying to resist a rush to invade.

To make matters worse, Condoleezza Rice's NSC did not adequately manage the decision process. Kim Holmes, an assistant secretary of state in the Bush administration, said she observed disagreements about foreign policy decisions like Iraq "everywhere, constantly" during this period.[29] Critics charged that Rice was not sufficiently engaged in her management role, opting instead to serve as confidante to the president. According to one report, Rice's management of the NSC, "the principal coordinator and enforcer of presidential decision making," was severely lacking. Another State Department official said, "If you want a one-word description of the NSC since January 21, 2001, [it is] dysfunctional."[30] Because Rumsfeld and Cheney had a close personal relationship, they often teamed up to "roll over national security advisor Rice and Secretary of State Powell" on Iraq policy making.[31]

Finally, though the subject of postwar planning for Iraq might be just as important as war planning, it received far less attention in the buildup to the invasion. The State Department had started a postwar planning initiative in 2002, but its efforts were quickly swept aside by the Pentagon leadership. Rumsfeld successfully argued that his department should be in charge of postwar planning and the occupation. The president signed National Security Presidential Directive NSPD-24 on January 20, 2003, establishing an Iraq Postwar Planning Office in the *Defense* Department.[32] Pentagon leaders blocked input from other agencies. Retired general Jay Garner was appointed to head postwar planning initiatives, but months of preparation only revealed more potential problems. One analysis from a planning simulation in Washington in late February 2003—just one month before the invasion—warned,

> Current force packages are inadequate for the first step of securing all major urban areas, let alone for providing interim police. . . . We risk letting much of the country descend into civil unrest [and] chaos whose magnitude may defeat our national strategy of a stable new Iraq.[33]

Even though Rumsfeld had primary authority, through NSPD-24, the secretary seemed aloof and uninterested in postwar planning, while at the same time micromanaging the war plans.

The Hot Summer

The summer of 2002 was a critical period for Bush administration decision making on Iraq. Officials publicly maintained that there were no war plans on the president's desk, but evidence began to mount that an invasion was in the works. At the graduation ceremony of the U.S. Military Academy at West Point on June 1, the president gave a speech that hinted he had already made up his mind on Iraq. Faced with threats of attack from terrorist groups and rogue states, Bush argued,

> The gravest danger to freedom lies at the perilous crossroads of radicalism and technology. When the spread of chemical and biological and nuclear weapons, along with ballistic missile technology—when that occurs, even weak states and small groups could attain a catastrophic power to strike great nations. . . . They want the capability to blackmail us, or to harm us, or to harm our friends—and we will oppose them with all our power.[34]

Secretary of Defense Rumsfeld also continued to manipulate the policy-making process. According to interviews with former administration members, Rumsfeld tried to advise Bush directly as opposed to engaging in debate with other principal players. He even tried to assert that the chain of command, "which he characterized as running from combatant commanders, to him, to the president, superseded the NSC process."[35] When other members of the administration complained that they were being shut out of the decision process, deputy national security adviser Stephen Hadley reportedly told them "the real work was being done upstairs [in the White House] with the president, Cheney, and Rumsfeld."[36]

The issue came to a head at an August 5 meeting of the NSC. General Franks briefed the president and his advisers on war plans for Iraq, including a new plan for faster mobilization and strikes. At the end of the briefing, Secretary Powell requested time alone with the president and Rice to address his reservations. Powell frankly expressed his concerns about the potential negative consequences of an invasion. He told the president, "You are going to be the proud owner of 25 million people. You will own all their hopes, aspirations, and problems. You'll own it all."[37] Powell and Armitage privately called this "the Pottery Barn rule: You break it, you own it." The secretary went on to warn that an attack on Iraq would "suck the oxygen out of everything. This will become the first term."[38] The best approach, Powell argued, was for the United States to push for UN and allied support.

President Bush, over the next few days, appears to have decided on a two-track strategy. Track one would authorize military deployments and call-ups of reserves to amass troops in the Persian Gulf region for an attack against Iraq. Track two would focus on diplomacy at the United Nations. Should the UN efforts fail, the diplomacy would nevertheless help build international, congressional, and public support for track one. This second track remained controversial inside the administration. Some officials, possibly including the president, simply "didn't believe diplomacy would or could take care of the threat Saddam posed. Going to the UN was a means, not an end."[39] Neo-conservatives in the administration did not want another UN resolution creating new arms inspections in Iraq, fearing that the Iraqi leader would manipulate the inspection process and sidetrack U.S. efforts at regime change. Meanwhile, others in the Bush administration believed there was a chance that a refurbished United Nations inspection regime could work.

Given this policy disarray, it was no surprise that debates over the tracks broke out into the open. State Department officials leaked their concerns to the press, questioning whether the administration had already decided upon an invasion. Leading Republicans also began to challenge the merits of a rush to invade. Brent Scowcroft, the national security adviser under the elder Bush, published an op-ed article warning "an attack on Iraq at this time would seriously jeopardize, if not destroy, the global counter-terrorist campaign we have undertaken."[40] Republican leaders in Congress had concerns about whether the administration had adequately prepared the military or the public for the scope of the undertaking.

In late August, invasion supporters pushed back. Rice gave an interview to the BBC in which she emphasized the growing moral imperative for the United States and its allies to topple Saddam Hussein:

> This is an evil man who, left to his own devices, will wreak havoc again on his own population, his neighbors and, if he gets weapons of mass destruction and the means to deliver them, on all of us. There is a very powerful moral case for regime change.[41]

Vice President Cheney contributed to the war momentum, declaring in an August 26 speech to the convention of the Veterans of Foreign Wars,

> We must take the battle to the enemy. . . . There is no doubt that Saddam Hussein now has weapons of mass destruction; there is no doubt that Saddam is amassing them to use against our friends, against our allies, and against us. . . . Many of us are convinced that Saddam will acquire nuclear weapons fairly soon.[42]

Secretary Powell was blindsided by Cheney's bold assertions. Powell, who was on vacation, had not been briefed on the vice president's speech. He was particularly angered because weeks earlier the president's top advisers had unanimously agreed to take the Iraq issue to the United Nations. Cheney's public assertion that inspections would not prevent Iraq from acquiring WMD was contrary to Bush's yearlong insistence that inspectors should be allowed to resume their work. Powell characterized Cheney's action as "a preemptive attack" on the policy process.[43]

Powell returned to Washington and requested another meeting with Bush to try to convince him of the need for the United States to work with the international community on the Iraq issue. He argued that the United States could gain international support by formulating a UN Security Council resolution to clamp down on Iraq and force compliance with UN demands. The president reassured Powell that he would pursue a new round of diplomacy. The night before Bush's September address to the UN General Assembly, Powell convinced Rice that the president should include the following statement in his speech: "We will work with the UN Security Council for the necessary resolutions, but the purposes of the United States should not be doubted. The Security Council resolutions will be enforced."[44]

Bringing the War to the Home Front

By mid-August 2002, it appeared that war with Iraq might be on the horizon, but the president faced deep-seated skepticism in Congress and the public. Prominent congressional Republicans, including House Majority Leader Richard Armey (R-TX) and Senators Chuck Hagel (R-NE) and Richard Lugar (R-IN), questioned the wisdom of a unilateral, preemptive attack on Iraq. Other congressional representatives, back in their districts for the summer recess, were finding their constituents uncertain about a potential invasion. A *Washington Post/*ABC News poll showed a slip in public support for a war, and only 45 percent of the public thought Bush had a clear policy on Iraq.

On August 26, the White House stirred the pot by asserting that the president needed no authorization from Congress to pursue a preemptive attack against Iraq. Such a strike was validated, a spokesman argued, by the president's constitutional role as commander in chief, as well as the 1991 congressional authorization of the Persian Gulf War and the 2001 congressional authorization to use force after September 11. One administration official said simply, "We don't want to be in the legal position of asking Congress to authorize the use of force when the president already has that full authority." The administration also feared restrictions that Congress might impose on the president's flexibility to move against Iraq.

As one of many rejoinders, Sen. Arlen Specter (R-PA) insisted that the war was "a matter for Congress to decide. The president as commander in chief can act in an emergency without authority from Congress, but we have enough time to debate, deliberate and decide."[45] Sen. Robert Byrd (D-WV) argued that the Persian Gulf War resolutions "ceased to be effective once Iraq capitulated to U.S. and allied forces in April 1991." Sen. Max Cleland (D-GA) maintained that the September 11 use-of-force resolution was "not some blank check to go after any terrorists in the world."[46] Others in Congress conceded the president's legal position but believed it would undermine the war's political support. Said Sen. John McCain (R-AZ), "I believe technically the president is not required to come to Congress; politically, I believe it would be foolish not to."[47]

Significant congressional opposition (even among Republicans) coupled with volatile public attitudes ultimately led the White House to seek congressional approval to act against Iraq. The administration began to make its case to the nation and to Congress through frequent appearances by administration officials on television talk shows, in testimony at congressional hearings, and closed-door briefings for congressional leaders. On September 4, Bush met with a congressional delegation to make the case for the use of force against Iraq and to ask for an authorizing resolution. The president told them he wanted congressional approval soon—before the end of the October recess and before midterm elections—and without conditions.

The Search for Support

Bush's speech to the UN General Assembly on September 12 was designed to address both tracks of policy developed by the White House. While the president offered an olive branch—negotiations with the UN Security Council to reach a multilateral resolution of the Iraq situation—he also issued strong words of warning to Iraq and other nations. Marking the one-year anniversary of the September 11 attacks, he said,

> Our principles and our security are challenged today by outlaw groups and regimes that accept no law of morality and have no limit to their violent ambitions. . . . In one place—in one regime—we find all these dangers, in their most lethal and aggressive forms, exactly the kind of aggressive threat the United Nations was born to confront. . . . Are Security Council resolutions to be honored and enforced, or cast aside without consequence? Will the United Nations serve the purpose of its founding, or will it be irrelevant?[48]

Eight weeks later, on November 8, the UN Security Council unanimously approved Resolution 1441, authorizing a new round of weapons inspections in Iraq. In late fall 2002, dozens of UN inspectors returned to Iraq for the first time in four years.

The UN address was a turning point for Bush in his efforts to build popular support at home for war. Major media outlets noted the favorable congressional response to the speech and suggested that it had generated momentum for quick approval of a resolution authorizing force.[49] The White House sent its formal draft of a resolution to Congress one week after the UN address. It would authorize the president "to use all means that he determines to be appropriate, including force, in order to enforce the United Nations Security Council Resolutions . . . [to] defend the national security interests of the United States against the threat posed by Iraq, and restore international peace and security in the region [the Middle East]."[50] This was designed to give the president maximum flexibility. Reaction in Congress was generally positive, though some were troubled by the breadth of authority requested and withheld their support.

By late September, the executive and legislative branches were engaged in a tug of war over the resolution. Some Democrats pulled back, fearing that the president's insistence on quick passage was being used for partisan advantage in the upcoming election. Though they opposed the president's confrontational strategy toward Iraq, they would "nonetheless support it because they fear[ed] a backlash from voters."[51] Others held firm. For example, Senator Byrd spoke out against "this war hysteria [that] has blown in like a hurricane."[52] And the White House shifted rhetorical focus to national security and the war on terrorism. Rumsfeld publicly asserted that the US had "bulletproof " evidence linking Saddam Hussein to al Qaeda.[53] According to one analysis, themes of war and security made up more than two-thirds of the content of Bush campaign speeches in the fall of 2002.[54] Bush's strategy appeared to work, as polls showed voters more concerned about Iraq than the economy, despite a significant decline in both the stock market and consumer confidence.

Facing charges that the White House was politicizing the Iraq War issue, the president circulated a new compromise resolution in Congress, with the regional security clause eliminated, language invoking the War Powers Act inserted, and a new clause requiring the president to inform Congress promptly of his determination that diplomatic efforts were insufficient. This new version was generally well received, though Senators Joseph Biden (D-DE), Lugar, and other moderates sought to narrow the resolution's justifications for war from the laundry list of UN resolutions to a single justification: Iraq's failure to destroy its WMD. Biden admitted that he probably would vote for even an "imperfect" resolution so as not to undermine the president in the international arena. He added, "I just can't fathom the president going it alone. If I'm wrong, I've made a tragic mistake."[55] The White House saw making WMD the sole justification for war as too restrictive. Bush wanted the flexibility to remove the Iraqi leader from power regardless of whether he was disarmed. The president declared, "I don't want to get a resolution which ties my hands."[56]

House Minority Leader Richard Gephardt (D-MO) also suggested revisions to the White House, which found them far less restrictive than those of Biden and Lugar. On October 2, the White House announced that it had come to an agreement with Gephardt and the Republican Party leadership in the House on a new draft resolution. The agreement isolated Daschle, the only major congressional leader who had not come to terms with the White House, and diminished Biden and Lugar's bargaining position. Bush built on the momentum from the Gephardt agreement with a speech televised on October 7, in which he called for Congress to pass the authorizing resolution. He made the case that Iraq was an urgent threat "because it gathers the most serious dangers of our age in one place." In supporting the principle of a preemptive strike, he argued "we cannot wait for the final proof—the smoking gun—that could come in the form of a mushroom cloud." Bush went on to say that congressional passage did not mean that war was imminent. Rather, a resolution would show "the United Nations and all nations that America speaks with one voice."[57]

The momentum of the Gephardt-Bush agreement and the October 7 speech seemed to sweep away much of the centrist opposition to the revised resolution. Sen. Evan Bayh (D-IN), a strong supporter of regime change in Iraq and a cosponsor of the administration resolution, explained the Democratic shift:

> The majority of the American people tend to trust the Republican Party more on issues involving national security and defense than they do the Democratic Party. We need to work to improve our image on that score by taking a more aggressive posture with regard to Iraq, empowering the president.[58]

And on October 10, the House approved the resolution 296–133, with 127 Democrats and 6 Republicans opposed. The vote was less consensual than expected. Observers saw it as a sign of Democratic dissatisfaction with Gephardt's position and a reaction to the late release of a CIA letter concluding that Iraq was only likely to use WMD against the United States in response to an attack. Early the next day, the Senate voted overwhelmingly, 77–23, in support of the resolution. The most impassioned opposition came from Senator Byrd, who deplored Congress's failure to be faithful to its constitutional duties, asserting, "We can put a sign on top of this Capitol: Gone home, gone fishing, out of business."[59] Senator Daschle summed up the case for supporting the president's resolution: "I believe it is important for America to speak with one voice at this critical moment."[60]

Final Preparations

The Bush administration publicly praised the congressional authorization and supported efforts by international weapons inspectors in Iraq (track two). Behind the scenes, however, the administration was engaged in war preparations. As fall turned to winter, the United States prepositioned more than one hundred thousand troops in the Persian Gulf and called up National Guard and reserve units. President Bush appears to have made his final decision to authorize the war in fall 2002, even as weapons inspectors continued their work in Iraq. In October the Joint Chiefs of Staff sent a strategic guidance memo to combat planning officers in the field, telling them in essence that "a war with Iraq [should] be considered part of the war on terror."[61] CIA director Tenet was also convinced that war was inevitable based on a private conversation with the president in which Bush told him, "We're not going to wait." In a discussion with CIA officials on November 4, Tenet was "asked if it really looked like war with Iraq: 'You bet your ass,' Tenet said bluntly. 'It's not a matter of if. It's a matter of when. The president is going to war. Make the plans. We're going.'"[62]

That winter, the president was briefed on the contents of Iraq's 12,000-page declaration to the United Nations rebutting WMD charges. The administration dismissed Iraq's evidence as implausible. In early January 2003, the president told Rice privately that he felt the inspections were failing and that it was time for more decisive action. Rice interpreted this as the president's final decision: "He had reached the point of no return."[63]

The International Community and the Impending War

The world seemed to come together following the attacks of September 11. U.S. allies in NATO invoked Article V of the Washington Treaty, defining the events as an attack on the entire alliance. During the Afghan war, European countries provided logistical support for operations, emergency food aid, refugee assistance, and stabilization forces.

International cooperation on Iraq was another matter, however. By fall 2002, U.S. and allied perceptions of threats to security had clearly diverged. Many in the Bush administration, especially the neo-conservatives, argued that terrorism, tyranny, and the spread of WMD were the fundamental threats to U.S security. While sympathetic, other world leaders saw their own "homeland security" as economic stability and the management of ethnic and religious tensions. To some, the most pressing issue in the Middle East continued to be the Israeli-Palestinian conflict, not regime change in Iraq.

On January 20, 2003, after intense debate, many European leaders made it clear they would not go beyond Resolution 1441 to endorse an invasion of Iraq based merely on a lack of cooperation with weapons inspectors. Insiders have suggested that this was a turning point for Powell, who felt ambushed by the timing and intensity of international criticism. On February 5, Powell outlined to the UN Security Council suspected WMD sites in Iraq and purported links between Saddam Hussein and al Qaeda. The world listened with interest, but European diplomats concluded Powell had presented no "new" evidence of Iraqi violations.

The Iraq War

On March 17, hours after dropping plans to gain a Security Council resolution authorizing war against Iraq, President Bush issued a public ultimatum to Saddam Hussein: Go into exile within forty-eight hours or risk attack from the United States and its allies. The president made it clear that he expected war and believed that he had a strong base of congressional and public support. In a poll taken hours after the president's speech, 66 percent of Americans said they approved of the ultimatum and the choice of going to war against Iraq if Saddam Hussein did not leave office; 68 percent of respondents said that they believed the United States had done "everything in its power" to reach a diplomatic resolution.[64]

U.S. and coalition forces launched "Operation Iraqi Freedom" on March 19, 2003, and ground troops advanced rapidly into Iraq. The main contingent of ground troops invaded from the south, coupled with a massive aerial bombardment. Invading forces faced challenges such as bad weather, long and insecure supply lines, and hit-and-run attacks, but they made steady progress northward through the country. In early April, U.S. and coalition forces rushed into Baghdad and forced a general surrender of Iraqi forces. On May 1, aboard the USS *Abraham Lincoln,* President Bush stood before a banner proclaiming "Mission Accomplished" and declared the "end of major combat operations" in Iraq. His administration's policy of preemptive attack had proven successful. Iraq had been liberated from a dictator, and the threat of a rogue regime with WMD had been eliminated. The president's made-for-television spectacle was a powerful symbol of the modern imperial presidency.

However, the war and its consequences proved much more difficult to control than its imagery. No evidence of an active WMD program was ever found.

Intelligence reports used by the Bush administration in making its case for urgent action proved false. Critics charged that the administration had "cooked the books" in favor of war. In particular, they asserted that the Pentagon's Office of Special Plans manipulated intelligence to influence public opinion and legitimate the administration's Iraq policies. Most experts now believe that Iraq's WMD capacity did not survive the 1991 Persian Gulf War and subsequent international inspections.[65]

Furthermore, the limitations of postwar occupation planning soon became apparent. Many Bush administration officials simplistically believed that coalition forces would be greeted as liberators of Iraq, but that did not occur. Moreover, U.S. and allied forces were not deployed in sufficient numbers to provide security throughout the country. In the three weeks that followed the fall of the Iraqi government, unchecked looting gutted almost every major public institution in Baghdad. When questioned about the chaos, an exasperated Rumsfeld said, "Stuff happens! Freedom is untidy."[66] Things quickly went from bad to worse, as an insurgency against coalition forces gained momentum.

Some of the consequences of the Iraq war might have been recognized with a more coherent policy-making process. There is no doubt that the tough interagency struggle leading up to the war fostered bitter disagreements between departments in the aftermath of the invasion. Secretary Rumsfeld had fought hard for Pentagon control of the postwar situation, and excluded many regional experts from the process. In May 2003, in an effort to stabilize Iraq, Bush and Rumsfeld installed Paul Bremer, an experienced diplomat, as head of the Coalition Provisional Authority (CPA). While Bremer brought new resources to rebuild Iraq's infrastructure, he was also responsible for two of the most controversial occupation initiatives: the de-Ba'athification of the Iraqi government and the disbanding of the Iraqi army. These actions alienated hundreds of thousands of Iraqis and destroyed an indigenous Iraqi security force. Bremer's actions were part of Rumsfeld's plan to control postwar Iraq, but they had never been cleared at the interagency level. Critics have charged that these actions helped foment the popular insurgency that further destabilized Iraq, and Garner later called them "tragic decisions."[67]

Although "major combat operations" were supposedly over, attacks against coalition troops actually increased in the next two years of the war. More than a thousand U.S. soldiers were killed and several thousand were injured between spring 2003 and fall 2004. Facing the reality of the postwar occupation of Iraq, U.S. public opinion eroded. An April 2004 poll indicated that 46 percent of Americans believed that the United States "should have stayed out of Iraq." One year after the president's announcement of the end of major combat operations, his overall approval rating stood at 46 percent, down from a high of 89 percent just after the September 11 attacks.[68] Despite public doubts about the war, Iraq never became a central issue in the 2004 presidential election, in part because Democratic leaders had voted to authorize the president's use of force in Iraq.

President Bush and top officials nevertheless maintained a resolute attitude in the face of mounting criticism. Indeed, the president was determined to proceed toward restoration of order in Iraq and the consolidation of democracy. Chairman of the Joint Chiefs of Staff Richard Myers observed,

> When any doubt started to creep into the small, windowless Situation Room, the president almost stomped it out. Whether it was alarming casualties, bad news, the current decision on the timing of Iraqi elections, some other problem, or just a whiff of one of the uncertainties that accompany war, the president would try to set them all straight. "Hold it," Bush said once. "We know we're doing the right thing. We're on the right track here. We're doing the right thing for ourselves, for our own interest and for the world. And don't forget it. Come on, guys."[69]

The situation continued to worsen, even as the Bush administration struggled to prop up a new unity government in Iraq. In late April 2004, the press reported on stories and photographs of prisoner abuse by U.S. soldiers at the Abu Ghraib prison outside Baghdad. Attacks on U.S. troops continued to rise. According to a 2006 secret report by the intelligence division of the Joint Chiefs, the insurgency had gained momentum from 2004 to 2006. Attacks on coalition forces were at their highest level, with more than 3,000 in May 2006 alone, and the Joint Chiefs report correctly predicted rising violence in the next year.[70]

Searching for an Endgame: "Tell Me How This Ends"[71]

By 2006, the Bush administration's policies in "postwar" Iraq had become untenable, given the growing and complex pattern of violence emanating from Ba'athist insurgents, Sunni jihadists, and Shiite militias. U.S. casualties and economic costs continued to rise in Iraq. It was also an election year in the United States, and that spring the White House reluctantly agreed to the creation of a bipartisan commission, the Iraq Study Group (ISG), to reevaluate U.S. options in Iraq. Meanwhile, Republican Party prospects seemed to dim. A *New York Times*/CBS News poll taken just before the election showed that the war in Iraq was by far the most important issue for voters. Moreover, only 29 percent of the respondents supported Bush's handling of the war in Iraq, and almost 70 percent believed that he had no plan to end the war.[72]

The election brought a stunning victory for the Democrats, who gained control of the Senate by a margin of 51–49 and the House by 233–202. Not a single Democratic incumbent was defeated in the House. On December 6, 2006, the ISG issued its report. The opening sentence set the tone: "The situation in Iraq is grave and deteriorating." Despite its scathing critique of the situation, the report rejected drastic policy change in the form either of a significant increase in, or an immediate withdrawal of, U.S. troops. But it refused to accept staying the course, either. Instead, the report called for an aggressive diplomatic offensive involving all of Iraq's neighbors, internal political reform in Iraq, and a shift in the role of the U.S. military from direct combat to training Iraqi forces—with the goal, subject to conditions in Iraq, of removing U.S. combat forces by spring 2008.[73]

In public comments, President Bush acknowledged that the ISG report was "worthy of serious study," but he was clearly not comfortable with two of its most significant recommendations: negotiations that included Iran and Syria and setting a timetable for the removal of combat troops.[74] He indicated that he would wait for studies ongoing in his administration before making any decisions about future policy directions. The goal was to complete the review by mid-December so as to have policy alternatives to compete with the ISG report. But the administration found it difficult to build a consensus on a new policy and soon announced that no new policy would be forthcoming before early 2007.[75]

The Surge

Many military leaders, including the Joint Chiefs of Staff; Gen. John Abizaid, head of Central Command; and Gen. George Casey, commander of the coalition forces in Iraq, were highly resistant to any significant increases in troop levels.[76] They believed that an increase would only encourage the Iraqi government to postpone making necessary political, economic, and military reforms. On the other hand, national security adviser Stephen Hadley consistently supported a troop surge to regain control of the security situation in Baghdad, arguing that viable political reforms could not be achieved without that security.[77]

Bush had never seriously considered beginning to withdraw troops from Iraq. By early December, the president was leaning toward some type of surge.[78] Bush's final views were shaped by a White House meeting with retired general Jack Keane, who not only strongly supported an increase in troop levels but confidently outlined a new strategy for the troops based on counterinsurgency doctrine. A White House aide later told Keane,

> The meeting in the Oval Office turned out to be decisive, in terms of your presentation . . . You did two things in there that I haven't seen. You gave them a vision, a way ahead, and you gave them courage.[79]

Meanwhile, the president was disappointed with the Joint Chiefs' opposition to a significant troop surge. He reportedly came away from a meeting with them on December 13, 2006, thinking that the chiefs "were trying to manage defeat rather than find a way to victory."[80] By the end of December, the Joint Chiefs, as well as Casey and Abizaid, accepted a troop surge. But Bush also agreed to a permanent increase of 92,000 soldiers to relieve the stress on the military created by deployments in Iraq and Afghanistan.[81]

As the nation waited for Bush's Iraq policy address, word leaked out that the president was replacing the U.S. diplomatic and military leadership in Iraq—the U.S. ambassador to Iraq, the commander of coalition forces in Iraq, and the head of Central Command. Perhaps most important, Gen. David Petraeus, who had been responsible for revising the army's counterinsurgency policy and who enthusiastically supported a troop surge, was to be the new commander of forces in Iraq.[82]

That "new way forward" was announced on January 10, 2007. The president admitted that his old course had failed, but his new plan did not resemble the recommendations of the ISG report: there was no time frame for withdrawal or even reduction of troops, and there was no ambitious diplomatic initiative to draw Iraq's neighbors into a peace process. Instead, arguing that the mission in Iraq was too important to be abandoned, the president announced that a "surge" of five more brigades (about 21,500 combat troops) would be sent to Iraq. Controlling sectarian violence and providing physical security would become the primary goal of U.S. forces. There would also be an extensive economic development effort to enhance the lives of Iraqis, and the government of Iraqi prime minister Nouri al-Maliki would be given a series of political reform benchmarks to achieve, although, unlike the ISG recommendations, no sanctions were threatened for failure to achieve them.

Most Democrats and some Republicans in Congress denounced the troop increase as a rejection of both the bipartisan ISG recommendations and the public will as expressed in the fall election. An overnight *Washington Post*/ABC News poll found that 61 percent of the public opposed the president's plan.[83] Congress struggled to respond to Bush's initiative, but congressional Democrats were divided. A number of recourses were considered, including a nonbinding resolution opposing the troop increase; a repeal of the original legislation authorizing the use of force in Iraq and its replacement with another, more narrowly drafted, conditional authorization; an appropriation of funds for the war that put conditions on the use of troops in Iraq, such as stipulating a deadline or goal for the removal of combat soldiers; and a refusal to appropriate any future funds for the war.

Each of those options raised political, military, and constitutional problems, however. Some members of Congress rejected a nonbinding resolution as a meaningless symbol that would do nothing to end the war. Others thought that placing restrictions, including time limits, in legislation not only would infringe on the president's constitutional role as commander in chief, but would put the military at risk by limiting the president's ability to make rapid adjustments to changes on the ground. Strong opponents of the war thought conditional appropriations would still let the war continue for too long. Conditional legislation also had the liability of being subject to presidential veto. All sides agreed that Congress had the constitutional authority to refuse to appropriate any future funds for the war, but that such a move might leave members open to charges of failing to support the troops.

President Bush's need in spring 2007 for a $97 billion supplemental appropriation for the wars in Iraq and Afghanistan provided opponents with a vehicle to limit the combat role of U.S. troops in Iraq. But Democratic leaders' attempts to require a timetable for a planned troop withdrawal could not muster the two-thirds vote necessary to override a presidential veto in the House, nor could they gather a consistent sixty-vote majority in the Senate. At the end of May, the Democratic leadership in both houses conceded defeat and agreed to drop any troop withdrawal language from the appropriation bill funding the Iraq war through September 30, 2007. The only concession that Congress was able to win from the Bush administration was the inclusion in the legislation of benchmarks of military, economic, and political progress in Iraq. The bill required that President Bush provide a report to Congress evaluating the progress on those benchmarks on July 15 and September 15—a plan designed to assuage concerns about presidential accountability by both opponents and moderate Republicans.

General Petraeus saw a need to produce quick results in Iraq to address both the politics of the issue in Washington and practical constraints in military manpower that made it unlikely that the surge could continue indefinitely. On the political side, he worried,

> The Washington clock is moving more rapidly than the Baghdad clock. . . . So we're obviously trying to speed up the Baghdad clock a bit and to produce some progress on the ground that can perhaps . . . put a little more time on the Washington clock.[84]

On the troop question, he recognized that all of the surge troops, ultimately numbering about thirty-one thousand, would not arrive until June 2007, and yet they would probably have to rotate out of Iraq by the summer of 2008. Furthermore, the new counterinsurgency strategy entailed not only a surge in the number of troops but a change in military and political policy in Iraq. Much of the new military strategy could not be put into play until all the troops arrived.[85] The new approach would combine a continued, but more focused, attack on the most violent insurgent and sectarian militias with a new emphasis on a far more sustained effort to make secure population centers.

The last and most crucial component of the new strategy was to encourage the political reconciliation of the three major warring factions within Iraq—Sunni, Shiite, and Kurd. In particular, it would require that the Maliki government, which was perceived by many Iraqis as pro-Shia, balance more fairly the needs of the three groups. But such reconciliation was not likely to occur until all sides felt more physically secure.

The first half of 2007 did not go well in Iraq. Violence against both Iraqi civilians and U.S. troops sharply escalated. Petraeus recalled the spring of 2007 as a "horrific nightmare."[86] More American troops (904) died in Iraq in 2007 than in any other year of the war. In addition, almost 24,000 Iraqi civilians were killed. But by the late summer, as the strategy became more fully operational, violence began to diminish significantly. Both troop and civilian casualties were cut in half over the last six months of 2007. Most analysts attributed this significant decline to a number of factors, including the increase in the number of troops; the change to a more population-centric strategy; and, perhaps most important, the successful outreach to insurgent Sunni militias that resulted in almost one hundred thousand of them being placed on the American payroll. Petraeus later testified in congressional hearings that there had been significant military progress in Iraq, with incidents of violence down over 45 percent from its high point in December 2006. Nonetheless, he said the situation was fragile, and a precipitous drop in U.S. troop levels could have "devastating consequences."[87] He then recommended the gradual surge withdrawal approved by Bush.

While most Democrats and some Republicans were still troubled by the lack of a clear strategy to militarily disengage successfully from Iraq in the near term, Petraeus seemed to have bought the new counterinsurgency policy more time on the Washington clock. In 2008 there would be no serious attempt in Congress to set a timetable for disengagement, the security situation in Iraq would continue to improve, and the annual civilian and military violence levels in Iraq would continue to decline.[88]

Ironically, the most effective impetus for a troop withdrawal timetable came from within the *Iraqi* political process. The Maliki government announced that it would not accept an extension of the UN mandate for the multinational forces in Iraq beyond 2008. Iraqis saw the end of the UN mandate as an important recognition of their renewed national sovereignty. Without a UN mandate, there would be no legal basis for the presence of U.S. troops on Iraqi soil. Consequently, the United States and Iraq would need to negotiate a bilateral status of forces agreement (SOFA) for the governance of U.S. troops in Iraq. As the various Iraqi political factions jockeyed for political position for the provincial and national elections scheduled for 2009, the Maliki government sought to use the SOFA to legitimize itself as a government independent of U.S. influence. Maliki sought more Iraqi control over the use and regulation of U.S. troops in Iraq. In addition, under "intense domestic pressure" he insisted on a timetable for withdrawal that would allow him to frame the agreement as one that would set the conditions for "Americans leaving Iraq."[89] In July 2008, Maliki seemed to support Democratic presidential candidate Barack Obama's plan to withdraw troops sixteen months after Obama's inauguration. Faced with the expiring UN mandate and recognizing Maliki's precarious domestic political position, the Bush administration eventually acquiesced and signed an agreement in November 2009 that required the United States to withdraw all of its troops from Iraq by December 31, 2011.

Obama's War in Iraq

The war in Iraq moved into its second presidential administration on January 20, 2009. Barack Obama took office with fourteen combat brigades still in Iraq. He had campaigned on withdrawing all combat troops there by the spring of 2010. Obama had also indicated that he would increase

U.S. military forces in Afghanistan. Given the sharp constraints on U.S. military personnel, these two goals were intertwined. On his first full day in office, Obama met with the military leadership and his national security advisers to discuss plans for the prompt withdrawal of combat troops from Iraq. But Obama faced a tension between his electoral base and the military field commanders (General Petraeus, the new commander of CENTCOM and responsible for both Iraq and Afghanistan, and Gen. Raymond Odierno, who replaced Petraeus as commanding general in Iraq). Voters expected Obama to keep his promise of a steady sixteen-month withdrawal from Iraq, while military leaders favored a much slower and phased pullout. The generals recommended a gradual reduction of troop strength that would remove only two brigades over the next six months and then a reevaluation of conditions on the ground. Odierno was particularly concerned that there be a sufficient U.S. force present during the Iraqi national elections, which were scheduled to be held at the beginning of 2010.

In February 2009, the new president announced he had approved a plan to bring out all the combat troops by August 2010, three months later than his original campaign pledge. Most of the withdrawals would take place after the Iraqi national elections. This nineteen-month time frame was a compromise between those who favored a fairly rapid, sixteen-month withdrawal and others who believed it should take place much more gradually.

The United States began drawing down combat troops in 2009 and 2010. However, while the Obama administration touted the withdrawal as proof that he had fulfilled his promise to end the war, continuing sectarian violence and attacks on U.S. forces showed the fragility of the situation. One of the administration's goals—to leave behind a stable and representative government—was also undermined by sectarian splits among leaders of the Shiite and Sunni factions in Iraq and growing hostility between the Kurds and the Shiite-led government. Many difficult issues remained, including plans to share oil revenues, problems with basic infrastructure, and the drifting foreign policy agenda of the new Iraqi regime. The magnitude of these challenges was symbolized by the nine months it took for negotiations following the contested March 2010 Iraqi parliamentary elections to produce a viable majority coalition. Even with the announcement of a new governing coalition, once more led by Maliki, the Iraqi political system appeared fragile and stalemated.

In January 2011, with a new governing coalition situated in Iraq and the 2010 congressional elections over in the United States, the attention of the

Obama administration turned to the potentially controversial issue of residual troops to be left in Iraq after the SOFA deadline. As noted above, the 2008 agreement negotiated by the Bush administration required all U.S. troops to leave Iraq by December 31, 2011. For any troops to stay beyond that date, a number of issues would need to be worked out by the Obama administration, including the number of troops to remain, their mission, and requirements of their Iraqi hosts.[90]

General Lloyd Austin, the new American commander in Iraq, argued to the Pentagon that these residual U.S. forces would be needed to train Iraqi forces, monitor volatile Kurdish-Iraqi checkpoints in the North, assist Iraqi special forces troops with counterterrorism efforts, protect Iraqi airspace, and protect remaining U.S. military and diplomatic forces in Iraq. He estimated a minimum force level of 20,000–24,000 troops. Civilians in the Pentagon recognized that this recommendation was larger than the White House would accept and worked with Austin to eventually bring the estimate down to about 16,000. The Joint Chiefs of Staff strongly supported this estimate as well.

Nonetheless, the White House, facing the continuing severe economic slowdown and budget crisis as well as its campaign commitment to bring the war in Iraq to a conclusion, was shocked by the military's request. At an April 2011 meeting, national security advisor Donilon convinced the secretary of defense to acquiesce to a figure of 10,000 residual troops. A month later, President Obama set 10,000 troops as the absolute upper limit on American participation. However, negotiations with the Iraqis had been slow to start and time was now growing short. Obama had a videoconference with Maliki on June 2 in which he indicated that Iraq would have to ask for American troops to remain and that the new SOFA would then need to be approved by the Iraqi Parliament in order for it to be constitutionally binding.

The ensuing negotiations dragged on as the administration waited for the Iraqis to take the initiative in asking for a residual American military presence. For domestic political purposes, the Obama administration did not want to appear too eager to continue a significant military presence in Iraq. The biggest stumbling blocks on the Iraqi side were the American requirements that SOFA include legal immunity for U.S. troops and that the agreement be approved by parliament. In the strife-ridden, nationalistic politics of Iraq, these two requirements were seen as politically dangerous. Meanwhile, the U.S. deficit crisis deepened, and the Obama administration's willingness to commit to a significant presence in Iraq diminished. In early August, Obama informed Leon

Panetta, the new secretary of defense; Mullen; and Clinton that he would only approve a limited mission of some training of Iraqi troops, counterterrorism support, and minimal protection of Iraqi airspace requiring only a continuous deployment of 3,500 troops (with an additional 1,500 who would periodically rotate into Iraq).[91]

Yet even this reduced commitment never materialized. In October, the Iraqi leadership approved a request for military trainers but rejected legal immunity for those troops. With time running out for an orderly withdrawal of the remaining 43,000 U.S. troops in Iraq, Obama spoke with Maliki on October 21 and they agreed that the SOFA negotiations were over. Hours later, Obama announced to the nation that, "as promised, the rest of our troops in Iraq will come home by the end of the year. After nearly nine years, America's war in Iraq will be over." He added, "After a decade of war, the nation we need to build—and the nation we will build—is our own."[92] On December 18, 2011 the last remaining U.S. military forces left Iraq.[93]

Conclusion

The Iraq war has provided some important lessons for U.S. foreign policy in the post–September 11 era. In many ways, it seems an ongoing war on terrorism lends itself to an imperial presidency. The Bush doctrine and the wars in Afghanistan and Iraq all suggest the ability of a very strong executive to dominate U.S. foreign policy decision making. The Iraq war and its aftermath also demonstrate some of the problems that result from executive branch dominance in foreign policy making. A highly personalized and aggressive executive decision process, especially with an acquiescent Congress, appears prone to taking action without an adequate range of information. The result can be flawed decisions, including, in the case of U.S. military action against Iraq, underestimating the danger of intervening without adequate international support, failing to make adequate preparations for the occupation of Iraq, and only belatedly recognizing that the occupation strategy, in effect, was failing.

At the same time, constraints on an imperial president may be quite limited. Despite losing the 2006 congressional elections, Bush was still able to go against public opinion and impose a troop surge in 2007. The limits on Congress's ability to influence the situation were also seen in that decision. Party loyalty among congressional members of the president's party and the president's veto power normally limit Congress's ability to check the president. But the most potent constitutional tool available to Congress, a funding cutoff, was under most circumstances considered too blunt a political tool to wield effectively. It may be that imperial presidents can only be checked by their own electoral fate, the presidential two-term limit, or the abandonment of the cause by their own party. These are all slow and uncertain processes.

Observers now have the benefit of hindsight to critically reflect on the lessons and outcomes of the Iraq War. The costs were clearly high: In 2011, government officials estimated that the war had cost the United States over one trillion dollars, plus continuing costs, including refurbishing depleted military equipment and the long-term care of wounded veterans, estimated at two trillion dollars.[94] The human cost included 4,486 American troops killed and more than 32,000 wounded, plus an Iraqi society with over 100,000 civilians killed and 4 million people displaced from their homes.[95] Some also see a strategic cost for the war with Iraq: the historic geopolitical balance with Iran greatly weakened and Iran consequently left much more powerful in the region. Nevertheless, other experts and policy makers quietly tout the benefits of the war. To them, the removal of Saddam Hussein from power, prevention of further terror attacks on U.S. soil, and the war's demonstration of the credibility of U.S. power in the 21st century marked a victory.

Current conditions in Iraq also may serve as markers by which to evaluate the success or failure of the war. In 2012, Iraq operated under a coalition government led by Prime Minister Nouri al-Maliki, which— while taking minimal steps toward sectarian inclusiveness of Sunni, Shiite, and Kurdish parties—has continued to centralize authority within the prime minister's office and has prosecuted political opponents, such as Vice President Tariq al Hashemi, a Sunni opposition leader. Political stability remains fragile.

Finally, within the United States, Iraq has become part of a broader political debate about the focus of Obama's foreign policy. A group of Senators, including John McCain (R-AZ), Lindsey Graham (R-SC), and Joseph Lieberman (I-CT), visited government and opposition groups in Iraq in September 2012 and found serious cause for concern. McCain reported,

> It was all predictable when Obama announced that he was proud we were leaving. Because of his failure, we didn't leave a residual force there and of course the whole thing is unraveling, as many of us predicted. And the tragedy is we wasted so many American lives.[96]

In contrast, Antony Blinken, national security advisor to the vice president, has cited improved statistics on declining violence and increased oil production to argue that criticisms of Iraq policy have been overblown. He supported the Obama administration's move from a military to a diplomatic strategy by noting,

> For more than three decades, Iraq has known nothing but dictatorship, war, sanctions, and sectarian violence. In just three years, its progress toward a more normal political existence has been remarkable. Iraq still has a long way to go, but today it is less violent, more democratic, and more prosperous than at any time in recent history, and the United States remains deeply engaged there.[97]

These different characterizations are well captured by Gordon and Trainor's depiction of Obama's military policy in Iraq. They said Obama "saw America's involvement there not as an opportunity, or even as containing opportunities, but rather as a leftover minefield, a path out of which had to be charted as quickly as possible."[98] Only time will tell which vision was correct.

Key Actors

George W. Bush   President; saw the need after the September 11 attacks for the United States to adopt a policy of preventive strikes against nations that presented a potential security threat; believed that Iraq was such a threat.

Richard Cheney   Vice president; strongly believed that Iraq, because it allegedly possessed weapons of mass destruction and had links to al Qaeda, posed an immediate threat to the security of the United States and that diplomacy would not produce an adequate response.

Thomas Donilon   National security adviser in the Obama administration during negotiations for a new Status of Forces Agreement.

Nouri al-Maliki   Prime minister of the newly formed Iraqi government in 2006; centralized authority in the prime minister's office and negotiated hard line with multinational forces (reelected in 2010).

Barack Obama   President; campaigned for the presidency in 2008 on a platform of removing all combat troops from Iraq in sixteen months and refocusing U.S. efforts to restabilize Afghanistan.

David Petraeus   Commanding general of the Multi-National Forces in Iraq; led the counterinsurgency strategy with the surge troops in 2007–2008;

later served as head of Central Command (CENTCOM) and succeeded Gen. Stanley McChrystal as commander of surge operations in Afghanistan in 2010.

Colin Powell   Secretary of state; argued within the administration that the threat from Iraq could be contained with beefed-up UN weapons inspections and cautioned against the United States intervening militarily in Iraq without international support.

Condoleezza Rice   National security adviser and central foreign policy adviser to President George W. Bush; had difficulty coordinating the policy process within the administration because of strong and conflicting personalities and policy positions; became secretary of state in the second term.

Donald Rumsfeld   Secretary of defense; argued that a transformed U.S. military with precision-guided munitions and a smaller, lighter strike force was the appropriate option to remove the allegedly imminent Iraqi threat.

George Tenet   Director of central intelligence; was skeptical about the need for an invasion of Iraq but later provided intelligence reports that helped the president make the case for war.

Paul Wolfowitz   Deputy secretary of defense; a long-time proponent of a preventive military strategy in general and the use of military force to achieve regime change in Iraq in particular.

Notes

1. Arthur M. Schlesinger Jr., *The Imperial Presidency* (Boston: Houghton Mifflin, 1973), ix.
2. Ibid., viii.
3. Michael Beschloss, "The End of the Imperial Presidency," *New York Times,* December 18, 2000, A27.
4. Nicholas Lemann, "The Next World Order: The Bush Administration May Have a Brand New Doctrine of Power," *New Yorker,* April 1, 2002, accessed January 12, 2004, www.newyorker.com/fact/content/?020401fa_FACT1.
5. Ivo H. Daalder and James M. Lindsay, *America Unbound* (Washington, DC: Brookings Institution Press, 2003), 2.
6. Bob Woodward, *Plan of Attack* (New York: Simon and Schuster, 2004).
7. Michael R. Gordon and Bernard E. Trainor, *Cobra II: The Inside Story of the Invasion and Occupation of Iraq* (New York: Pantheon, 2006), 16.
8. Michael J. Mazarr, "The Iraq War and Agenda Setting," *Foreign Policy Analysis* 3 (2007): 2.
9. Quoted in Jane Mayer, "The Manipulator," *New Yorker,* June 7, 2004, 61.
10. Bill Keller, "The Sunshine Warrior," *New York Times Magazine,* September 22, 2002, 48; Bob Woodward, *Bush at War* (New York: Simon and Schuster, 2002), 85.
11. Woodward, *Plan of Attack,* 26.

12. Quoted in Glenn Kessler, "U.S. Decision on Iraq Has Puzzling Past," *Washington Post,* January 12, 2003, A1.

13. Lawrence F. Kaplan, "Why the Bush Administration Will Go after Iraq," *New Republic,* December 10, 2001, 21.

14. Stephen Benedict Dyson, " 'Stuff Happens': Donald Rumsfeld and the Iraq War," *Foreign Policy Analysis* 5 (2009): 327, 333–334.

15. Seymour M. Hersh, "The Iraq Hawks," *New Yorker,* December 24, 2001, 58.

16. David Rieff, "Blueprint for a Mess," *New York Times,* November 2, 2003, A1.

17. Richard Perle, "Should Iraq Be Next?" *San Diego Union-Tribune,* December 16, 2001, accessed January 22, 2010, www.aei.org/article/13478.

18. Seymour M. Hersh, "Selective Intelligence?" *New Yorker,* May 12, 2003, accessed January 11, 2004, www.newyorker.com/printable/?fact/030512fa_fact.

19. Gordon and Trainor, *Cobra II,* 38.

20. Quoted in Michael Elliot and James Carney, "First Stop, Iraq," *Time,* March 31, 2003, 177; Daalder and Lindsay, *America Unbound,* 130.

21. Daalder and Lindsay, *America Unbound,* 130.

22. Woodward, *Plan of Attack,* 175.

23. Kessler, "U.S. Decision on Iraq Has Puzzling Past."

24. Woodward, *Plan of Attack,* 1–3.

25. Elliot and Carney, "First Stop, Iraq," 173.

26. Christopher Marquis, "Bush Officials Differ on Way to Force Out Iraqi Leader," *New York Times,* June 19, 2002, A1.

27. Woodward, *Plan of Attack,* 72–73.

28. Gordon and Trainor, *Cobra II,* 26.

29. Quoted in Dyson, "Stuff Happens," 332.

30. Glenn R. Kessler and Peter Sleven, "Rice Fails to Repair Rifts, Officials Say," *Washington Post,* October 12, 2003, A1.

31. Mark Hosenball, Michael Isikoff, and Evan Thomas, "Cheney's Long Path to War," *Newsweek,* November 17, 2003, 29.

32. Gordon and Trainor, *Cobra II,* 112.

33. Quoted in Bob Woodward, *State of Denial* (New York: Simon and Schuster, 2006), 125.

34. "President Bush Delivers Graduation Speech at West Point: Remarks by the President at the 2002 Graduation Exercise of the United States Military Academy," West Point, New York, June 1, 2002, accessed January 22, 2004, www.whitehouse.gov/news/releases/2002/06/print/ 20020601–3.html.

35. Dyson, "Stuff Happens," 334.

36. Woodward, *Plan of Attack,* 230.

37. Ibid., 150.

38. Ibid.

39. John Diamond et al., "Bush Set Sights on Saddam after 9/11, Never Looked Back," *USA Today,* March 21, 2003, 8A.

40. Brent Scowcroft, "Don't Attack Saddam," *Wall Street Journal,* August 15, 2002, A14.

41. Glenn Kessler, "Rice Lays Out a Case for War in Iraq," *Washington Post,* August 26, 2002, A1.

42. Elizabeth Pond, *Friendly Fire: The Near-Death of the Transatlantic Alliance* (Washington, DC: Brookings Institution Press, 2004); see also "Vice President Speaks at

VFW 103rd National Convention," accessed January 12, 2004, www.whitehouse.gov/news/releases/2002/08/ 20020826.html.

43. Woodward, *Bush at War,* 44, 161.

44. *Frontline,* "The War Behind Closed Doors," www.pbs.org/wgbh/pages/frontline/shows/iraq.

45. Ibid.

46. Miles Pomper, "Bush Hopes to Avoid Battle with Congress over Iraq," *CQ Weekly,* August 31, 2002, 2255.

47. Allison Mitchell and David Sanger, "Bush to Put Case for Action in Iraq to Key Lawmakers," *New York Times,* September 4, 2002, A1.

48. "President's Remarks at the United Nations General Assembly," accessed July 31, 2003, www.whitehouse.gov/news/releases/2002/09/print/20020912–1.html.

49. Dan Balz and Jim VandeHei, "Bush Speech Aids Prospect for Support by Congress," *Washington Post,* September 13, 2002, A32.

50. "Text of the Proposed Resolution," *Washington Post,* September 20, 2002, A21.

51. Jim VandeHei, "Daschle Angered by Bush Statement," *Washington Post,* September 26, 2002, A1.

52. U.S. Congress, *Congressional Record,* September 20, 2002, 148:S8966.

53. Eric Schmitt, "Rumsfeld Says U.S. Has 'Bulletproof' Evidence of Iraq's Links to Al Qaeda," *Washington Post,* September 28, 2002, A9.

54. Dana Milbank, "In President's Speeches, Iraq Dominates, Economy Fades," *Washington Post,* September 25, 2002, A1.

55. David Nather et al., " 'One Voice' Lost in Debate over Iraq War Resolution," *CQ Weekly,* September 28, 2002, 2500.

56. "Bush Rejects Hill Limits on Resolution Allowing War," *Washington Post,* October 2, 2002, A1.

57. Karen DeYoung, "Bush Cites Urgent Iraqi Threat," *Washington Post,* October 8, 2002, A1.

58. John Cushman, "Daschle Predicts Broad Support for Military Action against Iraq," *New York Times,* October 7, 2002, A11.

59. Dana Milbank, "For Many, a Resigned Endorsement: Attack Authorized with Little Drama," *Washington Post,* October 11, 2002, A6.

60. James VandeHei and Juliet Eilperin, "House Passes Iraq War Resolution," *Washington Post,* October 11, 2002, A1.

61. Thomas Ricks, *Fiasco* (New York: Penguin, 2006), 66.

62. Woodward, *State of Denial,* 89.

63. Woodward, *Plan of Attack,* 254.

64. CNN, "Poll: Two-Thirds of Americans Support Bush Ultimatum," accessed May 6, 2003, www.cnn.com.

65. Hersh, "Selective Intelligence?"; Burrough et al., "The Path to War," 294.

66. Harvey Rice and Julie Mason, "America at War: Anarchy Reigns in Baghdad," *Houston Chronicle,* April 12, 2003, 1.

67. Woodward, *State of Denial,* 219; see also Ricks, *Fiasco,* 158–165.

68. Richard W. Stevenson and Janet Elder, "Support for War Is Down Sharply, Poll Concludes," *New York Times,* April 29, 2004, A1.

69. Woodward, *State of Denial,* 371.

70. Quoted in ibid., 472.

71. Gen. David Petraeus to journalist Rick Atkinson in 2003, as reported in Atkinson's *In the Company of Soldiers* (New York: Henry Holt and Co., 2004), 6.

72. Adam Nagourney and Megan Thee, "With Election Driven by Iraq, Voters Want New Approach," *New York Times,* November 2, 2006, A1.

73. Iraq Study Group, *Iraq Study Group Report* (New York: Vintage, 2006), xiii.

74. Peter Baker and Robin Wright, "Bush Appears Cool to Key Points of Report on Iraq," *Washington Post,* December 8, 2006, A1.

75. Michael Fletcher, "Bush Delays Speech on Iraq Strategy," *Washington Post,* December 13, 2006, A12.

76. Linda Robinson, *Tell Me How This Ends* (New York: Public Affairs, 2008); Thomas Ricks, *The Gamble: General David Petraeus and the American Military Adventure in Iraq, 2006–2008* (New York: Penguin Press, 2009).

77. Glenn Kessler, "Bush's New Plan for Iraq Echoes Key Parts of Earlier Memo," *Washington Post,* January 11, 2007, A13.

78. Michael Abramowitz and Peter Baker, "Embattled Bush Held to Plan to Salvage Iraq," *Washington Post,* January 21, 2007, A1.

79. Linda Robinson, *Tell Me How This Ends,* 35.

80. Ibid.

81. Ann Scott Tyson and Josh White, "Gates Urges Increase in Army, Marines," *Washington Post,* January 12, 2007, A14.

82. Robin Wright and Michael Abramowitz, "Bush Making Changes in His Iraq Team," *Washington Post,* January 5, 2007, A1.

83. Michael Abramowitz and Robin Wright, "Bush to Add 21,500 Troops in an Effort to Stabilize Iraq," *Washington Post,* January 11, 2007, A1.

84. Ricks, *The Gamble,* 148.

85. Robinson, Tell Me How This Ends.

86. Ricks, "Understanding the Surge in Iraq and What's Ahead," *Foreign Policy Research Institute E-Notes,* accessed May 4, 2009, www.fpri.org/enotes/200905.ricks .understandingsurgeiraq.html.

87. Peter Baker and Jonathan Weisman, "Petraeus Backs Initial Pullout," *Washington Post,* September 11, 2007, A1.

88. Brookings Institution, *Iraq Index,* December 11, 2009, www.brookings.edu/ about/centers/saban/iraq=index.

89. Karen DeYoung, "U.S., Iraq Scale Down Negotiations Over Forces," *Washington Post,* July 13, 2008, A1.

90. This account of the Obama administration's handling of the attempted renegotiation of SOFA in 2011 relies heavily on Michael Gordon and Bernard Trainor, *The Endgame* (New York: Pantheon Books, 2012), 651–671.

91. Ibid., 670–671.

92. White House, "Remarks by the President on Ending the War in Iraq," October 21, 2011.

93. It should be noted that the U.S. presence in Iraq will still be substantial, with some 16,000 civilians working under the U.S. ambassador in Iraq. About 80% of the personnel will be private contractors, with approximately 5,000 of those being private security contractors who will protect diplomats; aid workers; and the embassy, consulates, and other important facilities. The State Department will also operate its own air service and hospital system. Estimated annual costs for State operations in Iraq alone

will be about $6 billion; see Mary Beth Sheridan and Dan Zak, "State Department Readies Iraq Operation, Its Biggest Since Marshall Plan," *Washington Post,* October 7, 2012.

94. James Glanz, "The Economic Cost of War," *New York Times,* February 28, 2009, A1; *Iraq Study Group Report,* 32.

95. Some critics charge estimates of the number of wounded in Iraq are downplayed by the Pentagon and ignore the hundreds of thousands of soldiers returning from Iraq with traumatic brain injuries, post-traumatic stress disorder, hearing loss, and other long-term health problems; see Terry Tanielian and Lisa H. Jaycox, eds., *Invisible Wounds of War: Psychological and Cognitive Injuries, Their Consequences and Services to Assist Recovery* (Washington, DC: RAND Corporation, 2010).

96. Quoted in Julian Pecquet, "Iraq 'unraveling' amid renewed sectarian violence, says Sens. McCain, Graham," September 11, 2012, accessed October 9, 2012, http://thehill.com/blogs/global-affairs/middle-east-north-africa/248797-returning-senate-hawks-describe-iraq-on-the-brink-blame-obama.

97. Antony Blinken, "Morning in Mesopotamia," *Foreign Affairs,* 91, no. 4 (July/August 2012): 152–154.

98. Gordon and Trainor, *Endgame,* 689.

4 The Nuclear Standoff between the United States and Iran: Muscular Diplomacy and the Ticking Clock

Thomas Preston

Before You Begin

1. What have been the trends and patterns in U.S.-Iranian relations over the past six decades? Why do history and context matter in foreign policy decision making for U.S.-Iranian relations?

2. How do the United States and Iran view each other, and are those perceptions accurate? Could the perceptions be changed?

3. How has the Obama administration differed from the previous Bush administration in its approach to negotiations with Iran?

4. What are the domestic political constraints, especially in Iran, that may prevent the two countries from improving their relations or compromising on the nuclear issue? With Mahmoud Ahmadinejad's tenure as Iranian president ending, does compromise become more or less possible?

5. What are the policy approaches of the United States, United Nations, European Union, Israel, and Iran regarding the nuclear issue?

6. How can the Obama administration successfully convince China and Russia to apply pressure on Iran? How does the growing threat of Israeli preemptive attack on the Iranian program and increasingly critical IAEA reports on the program influence Iranian behavior?

7. What were the roots of the Iranian nuclear program, the "zone of immunity," and does it really matter, in terms of regional stability, whether Iran obtains nuclear weapons?

Introduction: The Clenched-Fist Metaphor and the Problem of Diplomatic Constraints

In his January 2009 inaugural address, President Barack Obama announced that the United States was prepared to extend a hand in friendship to those adversarial states who "are willing to unclench" their fists.[1] This statement represented a significant departure from the hard-line negotiating approach favored by the previous Bush administration. Obama was intent on reinvigorating America's image abroad and, in particular, establishing a new direction in the United States' relationship with the Islamic world. The statement was also an explicit recognition that the Bush administration policy of nondirect negotiations over Iran's nuclear enrichment program (and its implied threats of military force) had failed to produce any substantive results with Tehran. Instead, the Iranian program had steadily expanded its nuclear facilities and developed new technologies (like IR-2 centrifuges) that improved its ability to produce enriched uranium for nuclear fuel or bombs. Obama's new strategy shift departed substantially from George W. Bush's 2002 "axis of evil" policy direction and viewed direct negotiations with Iran as holding greater potential for yielding a resolution to the nuclear standoff.

Unfortunately, this new strategy was quickly undercut by contested Iranian presidential elections in June 2009, in which Supreme Leader Ali Khamenei declared then-President Mahmoud Ahmadinejad the winner even before the official recount—which hundreds of thousands of Iranian protesters (and most Western observers) saw as the culmination of a fraudulent, rigged election process. Opponents of direct negotiations immediately claimed such talks would amount to U.S. acquiescence to an illegitimate regime. Moreover, Israel continued to demand military action to preempt Iran's program, despite the hard reality that Iran's opaque (and well-dispersed) nuclear program was impossible to preempt or destroy with air strikes alone. Military options were also constrained by war weariness among the American public due to the Afghan and Iraqi conflicts. Moreover, any strike on Iran would have certainly provoked retaliation against U.S. interests in Iraq, Afghanistan, and the Straits of Hormuz; provoked attacks on Israel (either directly or through surrogates in Lebanon and Gaza); negatively impacted oil prices and the world economy; and resulted in a host of other blowback. Further, it would have certainly undercut the Iranian democratic reform movement and provided justification for a conservative crackdown as well as scuttled allied support for harsher UN sanctions.[2] And such support was already difficult to acquire, given Russian and Chinese reluctance to provide any "regime change"-type justifications for the US in UN resolutions. At the same time, accepting a "nuclear" Iran was also seen as politically unacceptable for Obama domestically.

From Iran's standpoint, there were long-standing concerns regarding its regional security—especially given the U.S. military presence in neighboring Iraq

Timeline

US-Iran Relations and the Nuclear Issue

August 1953	A U.S.-supported coup overthrows democratically elected Iranian prime minister Mohammed Mossadeq, and the pro-American Shah is restored to power.
1970s	The Shah of Iran institutes a nuclear program with both civilian and military components.
Mid-1978 through 1979	Iranian revolution overthrows the Shah, who is replaced by Ayatollah Khomeini.
October–November 1979	The Shah is admitted into the United States; Iranian students seize U.S. embassy in Tehran.
April 1980	The United States breaks off diplomatic relations with Iran; U.S. hostage rescue mission fails.
September 1980	Iraq invades Iran, beginning the Iran-Iraq War (1980–1988); the United States supports Iraq.
Mid-1985	Iran begins a secret centrifuge enrichment program.
1987	Iran acquires drawings of centrifuges and component parts from A. Q. Khan smuggling network.
May 1995	President Bill Clinton signs an executive order prohibiting trade with Iran.
August 1997	Moderate cleric and reformer Mohammad Khatami becomes president of Iran.
1999	After assembling and testing centrifuges, Iran enriches uranium for the first time.
June 2001	U.S. Senate extends economic sanctions on Iran an additional five years.
January 29, 2002	President George W. Bush gives his "axis of evil" speech.
August 14, 2002	Opposition group of exiles reveals that Iran has clandestine uranium enrichment facility and heavy water plant.
September 12, 2003	The IAEA calls on Iran to suspend all enrichment-related activity.

October 21–23, 2003	Iran agrees to halt all enrichment and reprocessing activities after negotiations with France, Britain, and Germany.
March 13, 2004	IAEA criticizes Iran for failing to report centrifuge research or suspend all activities.
April 29, 2004	Iran announces it is starting to convert uranium, the step preceding actual enrichment.
September 18, 2004	IAEA tells Iran to cease uranium conversion and implicitly threatens referral to UN Security Council.
November 15, 2004	After further negotiations with the European Union (EU), Iran agrees to cease uranium enrichment.
August 2005	Ahmadinejad becomes Iran's president, campaigning on a pro-nuclear platform.
September 2, 2005	IAEA announces that Iran has not fully cooperated with the agency, despite repeated requests and visits from inspectors.
January 12, 2006	Europeans call off nuclear talks with Iran.
February 4, 2006	IAEA board votes to report Iran to the UN Security Council.
April 11, 2006	Iran announces that it has succeeded in enriching uranium.
May 2006	Ahmadinejad sends his letter to President Bush.
June 2006	UN sanctions are delayed to give Iran time to consider a new package of U.S. and European incentives to end its nuclear program; Iran rejects the proposal and is given an August 31 deadline to implement "full and sustained suspension" of its nuclear activities.
October 2006	North Korean nuclear test; Iran refuses to condemn it and sets up second centrifuge cascade.
December 2006	Security Council unanimously passes resolution banning import or export of materials and technology used in uranium enrichment, reprocessing, or ballistic missiles.
March 2007	Security Council unanimously passes resolution banning all arms exports to Iran and freezing assets of Iranians linked to its military or nuclear program.

(continued)

Timeline *(continued)*

US-Iran Relations and the Nuclear Issue

April 2007	Ahmadinejad boasts Iran is capable of enriching uranium on an industrial scale.
April 2008	Ahmadinejad tours the Natanz site to publicize the testing of a new generation of centrifuge, the IR-2, which may have the capability to enrich uranium at a much faster rate.
January 2009	Bush authorized "Olympic Games," a clandestine cyber-attack campaign against Iran. Barack Obama is inaugurated president of the United States, promising to "extend a hand [to hostile states] if . . . [they] are willing to unclench [their] . . . fist[s]."
June 2009	President Ahmadinejad is reelected in a contested election that is followed by months of street protests challenging the authority of the Islamic Republic's ruling elite.
July 2009	Iranian government's brutal crackdown against political protesters and reformers. Hundreds are jailed and tortured in Evin prison.
September 2009	Iran discloses the existence of the Qum nuclear facility. The site had gone unreported to the IAEA.
October 2009	Iran rejects an IAEA plan to reprocess enriched uranium in Russia and then assemble the uranium fuel into rods in France to be sent back to Iran for use in a medical research facility in Tehran.
November 2009	The Iranian government approves the building of ten additional uranium enrichment facilities in violation of UN demands, which ordered Iran to stop its nuclear program.
2010 (month unknown)	Israeli government under Netanyahu discusses military preemption of Iran's nuclear program, but internal opposition and concerns about military feasibility prevent action.
May 2010	Iran, Turkey, and Brazil issue joint declaration agreeing to send low-enriched uranium to Turkey in return for enriched fuel for its research reactor. U.S. calls for additional sanctions against Iran at the UN.

November 2011	IAEA issues report chronicling Iran's clandestine military-related nuclear research, including work on warhead designs, neutron initiators, and mounting warheads on ballistic missiles.
August 2012	Iran nears completion of underground enrichment facility at Qum, leading Israeli Defense Minister Barak to warn of approaching "zone of immunity" when preemption of the Iranian program will no longer be possible.
September 2012	Israeli Prime Minister Netanyahu gives UN speech warning that time is running out if Iran is to be prevented from becoming a nuclear weapon state.
October 2012	Sanctions devalue Iranian currency by 40%, cut oil exports by half, and drive inflation to 196%. Ahmadinejad states openness to negotiations but insists on Iran's right to its civilian nuclear program.

and Afghanistan—alongside strong, nationalistic desires (even among the Iranian public) to pursue a nuclear program and not be dictated to by the international community. For Ahmadinejad, appealing to Iranian nationalism served to distract attention from criticisms of his domestic policies and maintain the support of Ayatollah Khamenei, which was critical to his political survival. Thus, in some respects, Ahmadinejad needed the impasse over Iran's nuclear program to continue, but only at a low simmer—which backfired as International Atomic Energy Agency (IAEA) reporting and the speed of Iran's enrichment program expansion raised concerns and stiffened sanctions. Considering the constraints facing both sides, it's easy to see why the current standoff over Iran's nuclear program became so enormously complex and difficult to resolve diplomatically.

Background: Patterns of Intervention and Mutual Antagonism

A defining tendency in U.S.-Iranian relations has been a long-standing pattern of American intervention in Iran's domestic affairs. In 1953 the United States backed the overthrow of Iranian prime minister Mohammad Mossadeq's democratically elected government, an action sparked by Mossadeq's efforts to nationalize Iran's oil industry, taking ownership away from British companies. The US subsequently reinstalled the autocratic Shah of Iran, who preserved foreign rights to Iran's oil fields. Although Americans saw Mossadeq's overthrow through the cold war lens of East-West competition and the need to prevent the spread of communism, to Iranians it epitomized U.S. interference in their internal affairs and imperial ambitions in their country. Hostility toward the US for reinstalling the Shah continued long after his overthrow in the 1979 Iranian revolution. Indeed, it is revealing that a key Iranian demand during the subsequent hostage crisis, when militant students seized the American embassy and its staff, was an apology for the 1953 overthrow and a U.S. pledge never again to interfere in Iran's domestic affairs. Since that time, American policy makers have not restored diplomatic relations, have encouraged dissident groups, have spoken favorably of regime change, and have depicted Iran as a rogue state intent on shirking international law to advance its Islamic revolutionary agenda and destabilize the region. The Iranians have responded with unremitting hostility of their own, condemning the "Great Satan," pursuing improved military capabilities, and working to undercut American influence in the Middle East.

The origins of the conflict can be traced to the rise of the Shah of Iran, Mohammad Reza Pahlavi, who replaced his father on the Iranian throne during World War II. After he was deposed by the Iranian people during the early 1950s and Mossadeq was elected, the Shah returned to power in 1953 in a U.S.-backed coup.[3] In return for substantial American military and economic aid, the Shah provided both a steady stream of oil and an important pro-Western ally in the Persian Gulf to help block Soviet expansionism. Iran's strategic position and resources continued to make it a high-priority ally for American presidents throughout the Shah's reign. However, the Shah's rule was also marked by corruption, brutality, and political repression. The Shah's secret police and intelligence service, known as the SAVAK, was particularly hated by the population. It ruthlessly helped maintain the Shah's one-party rule through the torture and execution of thousands of political prisoners, suppression of political dissent, and alienation of the religious masses.[4] U.S. training and support of the SAVAK served to further cultivate anti-Americanism in the decades prior to the Iranian revolution. Moreover, the Shah's efforts to modernize Iran and follow a Western model of development angered the country's conservative religious leaders, who saw Western influences as an affront to their fundamentalist Islamic faith.

Inspired by the fundamentalist cleric Ayatollah Ruhollah Khomeini, whose pro-Islamist and anti-Western message struck a special chord with the Iranian masses, violent demonstrations erupted throughout the country in mid-1978. By January 1979, the Shah (now terminally ill with cancer) abdicated his Peacock Throne and went into exile, and Khomeini returned from exile. The Shah moved first to Egypt, then to Morocco, and by February 1979 was ready to accept an earlier American offer of asylum. On February 14, however, Iranian students "temporarily" overran the American embassy and held U.S. personnel for "several hours," prompting U.S. government concern for all the Americans there. When President Jimmy Carter's Special Coordinating Committee met to discuss the situation, it concluded that if the Shah was permitted to enter the country there might be an Iranian backlash that could threaten U.S. personnel in the country. As a result, Carter decided to rebuff the Shah's request for admission into the United States, but administration officials remained split over the matter. Secretary of State Cyrus Vance argued against receiving the Shah, but national security adviser Zbigniew Brzezinski and a cadre of friends (including former secretary of state Henry Kissinger) pushed for the Shah's admission. Time and the Shah's health interceded in his favor, and Carter eventually acquiesced to the Shah's entry after being told his life could only be saved by medical facilities in New York.[5] The Shah arrived in October 1979, received medical treatment, and was encouraged to leave. He eventually traveled to Egypt, where he died in July 1980. But the damage to U.S.-Iranian relations had been done. On November 4, 1979, thousands of Iranian students overran the U.S. embassy and seized 66 American hostages (53 of whom would be held for 444 days). The ensuing hostage crisis would humiliate and destroy the Carter presidency and cause a rupture in U.S.-Iranian relations that has lasted to the present day. The two countries still do not have diplomatic relations, and the three-decade freeze, in which the relationship has remained set in a mode of mutual hostility and antipathy, is the backdrop against which the current nuclear dispute is playing out. After failed efforts to negotiate, Carter authorized a rescue mission, the ill-fated Desert One operation, which ended in disaster in the Iranian desert. And despite all the sanctions the US imposed, including freezing all Iranian assets, halting military sales, breaking diplomatic relations, and so forth, Iran refused to budge on its demands the United States return its assets, apologize for past misdeeds, and return the Shah (and, after his death, his wealth) to Tehran. Only the full-scale invasion of Iran by Saddam Hussein's Iraq in September 1980 (the start of a bloody eight-year war of attrition) and the election in November 1980 of Ronald Reagan, who had campaigned on a promise to unleash massive military retaliation on Iran if the hostages were not released, convinced the Iranians finally to resolve the crisis on Carter's last day in office in January 1981 and release the hostages.

The U.S.-Iranian relationship continued to deteriorate during the Reagan administration, which threw its support behind Iraq in its war with Tehran (even though Iraq was the aggressor). Concerns about the spread of Iran's radical Islamist politics to moderate Sunni states in the Gulf, which the US depended upon for oil (such as Saudi Arabia and Kuwait), led to framing Iraq as the lesser of two evils. Reagan provided Iraq with economic and military support and encouraged wealthy Gulf states to bankroll the Iraqi war effort with hundreds of billions of dollars throughout the 1980s.[6] The Reagan team established a long-term policy of Iranian containment, which subsequent administrations continued. Obviously, given the enormous number of casualties the eight-year war inflicted on Iran, which some estimates place as high as 1 million, and its economic costs of upwards of $350 billion,[7] it is unsurprising that U.S. support for Saddam's Iraq created further hostility toward America among the Iranian people.

Losing the conflict and its economy in shambles, Iran went to the UN to negotiate a cease-fire with Iraq. The Iranian leadership's feelings toward America at that point were clear, with Khomeini declaring, "God willing . . . we will empty our hearts' anguish at the appropriate time by taking revenge on the Al Saud [monarchy] and America."[8] Relations remained frosty between Iran and the George H. W. Bush and Clinton administrations, both of which claimed Iran was sponsoring terrorism (through its financial and military support of groups such as Lebanon's Hezbollah and the Palestinian group Hamas) and was likely pursuing nuclear weapons.

All U.S. and Iranian leaders must deal with the reality that domestic political constraints encourage mutually hostile policies and that appearing tough is usually rewarded. It has also become a pattern of U.S.-Iranian relations that any move toward moderating the corrosive nature of the current relationship meets significant roadblocks. For example, in seeking to deter Iran from sponsoring terrorism abroad or pursuing nuclear weapons, President Clinton found himself caught between a desire to implement an Iranian trade embargo during the mid-1990s and growing political pressure to pursue a more extreme, regime-change policy. Following the pattern of Reagan's containment policy, Clinton hoped to separate the Middle East into friendly, moderate states versus the more radical, fundamentalist ones—thereby isolating Iran and putting pressure on it to alter its behavior. However, in the months leading up to the trade embargo vote, pressure increased on Clinton to adopt an even tougher policy. Aside from growing intelligence concerns about Iran's nuclear progress (that were leaked to the press), Speaker of the House Newt Gingrich, R-Ga., stated, "The eventual forced replacement of Iran's Islamic regime is the only long-term strategy that makes sense."[9] The US adopted both the trade embargo and a policy implicitly supporting regime change.

Iran's Nuclear Program

Iran's nuclear program began during the mid-1970s under the Shah, who embarked on an ambitious effort to obtain the know-how and materials required for weapons, as well as plans to construct twenty-three nuclear power reactors.[10] The Shah openly said Iran would have nuclear weapons "without a doubt and sooner than one would think."[11] Documents found after the Iranian revolution revealed the Shah's government and Israel discussed plans to adapt an Israeli surface-to-surface missile to carry nuclear warheads.[12] Iran began a clandestine uranium enrichment program in 1985 and sought to develop a scientific cadre capable of pursuing a weapons program; 15,000 to 17,000 Iranian students were sent abroad to study nuclear-related subjects.[13] Iran also actively recruited nuclear technicians from the former Soviet Union and other countries, offering salaries of up to $20,000 a month to skilled (but impoverished) nuclear scientists.[14] In addition to building a gas centrifuge uranium enrichment program at Natanz, which former IAEA director general Mohamed El Baradei described as "sophisticated," Iran acknowledged intending to build both a forty-megawatt thermal heavy-water reactor at Arak and a fuel fabrication plant for the reactor at Esfahan.[15] The pilot plant at Natanz was designed to hold about 1,000 centrifuges and produce ten to twelve kilograms of weapons-grade uranium per year. The main enrichment facility at Natanz was envisaged to hold up to 50,000 centrifuges and produce about 500 kilograms of weapons-grade uranium annually (enough for twenty-five to thirty nuclear weapons per year). This facility, if operated at full capacity, could "produce enough weapons-grade uranium for a nuclear weapon in a few days."[16] In addition, Pakistan (through the illegal A. Q. Khan smuggling network) provided Iran not only with advanced centrifuge technology and advice, but also with essential data on bomb design.[17] In total, this infrastructure has the capability (if completed) to transform Iran rapidly into a nuclear weapon state with a substantial arsenal.

As the program's development demonstrates, Iran's interest in nuclear weapons has continued regardless of the nature of the current regime.[18] Estimates within the U.S. intelligence community about Iran's nuclear program have varied widely (in some ways mirroring the worst-case assumptions found in prewar Iraqi WMD estimates). For example, in January 2000 the CIA reported that Iran might be able to make a nuclear weapon, but other intelligence agencies hotly disputed the claim.[19] Estimates of Iranian nuclear capabilities routinely overestimated the speed of Tehran's progress, with U.S. and Israeli intelligence in 1992–1993 predicting an Iranian nuclear bomb by 2002 and in 1995 predicting a bomb within "7–15 years."[20] Although a presidential commission reported in March 2005 that U.S. "intelligence on Iran is inadequate to allow firm judgments about Iran's weapons programs," an August 2005 National Intelligence Estimate (NIE) concluded Iran was "determined to build nuclear weapons" but unlikely to possess them until 2010–2015.[21] But while the speed and scope of the program was subject to conjecture and debate, Western intelligence services all agreed on the fundamental point: that Tehran likely had "a long-term program to manufacture nuclear weapons."[22] In the views of many experts, Iran already possessed the basic nuclear technology, infrastructure, and expertise to build weapons and lacked only adequate stockpiles of fissile material to become a nuclear state.[23]

However, Tehran signed the Nuclear Non-Proliferation Treaty, placing its existing (declared) civilian nuclear power industry under IAEA inspection. By treaty, Iran is obligated to report all nuclear activities to the IAEA, and when rumors surfaced regarding a hidden program, Tehran (after intense outside pressure) was eventually forced to allow inspectors into the country in October 2003. Inspections revealed a long-running Iranian nuclear program that had effectively concealed itself from outside scrutiny for decades and which, unmolested, had the potential to provide the country with substantial weapons capabilities. Although the U.S. position on Iran remained hostile, befitting Iran's status within the "axis of evil," Britain, France, and Germany embarked on a five-year diplomatic effort to peacefully resolve the dispute over Iran's nuclear program.

The Bush Approach: Lost Opportunities after September 11

It should be noted that in the months following the September 11 attacks, the Bush administration had an opportunity to expand cooperation with Iranian president Mohammad Khatami's government. Khatami, a reformer, believed that a window of opportunity had opened. Mohammad Hossein Adeli, a deputy at the Iranian Foreign Ministry, began intense contacts with higher officials in the Iranian government. Adeli explains, "We wanted to truly condemn the [September 11] attacks but we also wished to offer an olive branch to the United States, showing we were interested in peace."[24] Adeli was even able to convince Ayatollah Khamenei that the proposals would be productive. A Khamenei assistant noted, "The Supreme Leader was deeply suspicious of the American government. . . . But [he] was repulsed by these [September 11] terrorist acts and was truly sad about the loss of the civilian lives in America."[25]

In the weeks following 9/11, American and Iranian representatives met several times. The Iranian delegation pushed for action because it opposed the Taliban and supported the opposition Northern Alliance (also a U.S. ally against the Taliban and al Qaeda). Iran was instrumental in convincing the Northern Alliance to accept Hamid Karzai, a Pashtun from the south, as the new president of Afghanistan and to form a coalition government. Iran also committed $500 million to rebuild Afghanistan. But, while the US and Iran had common interests and a willingness to open up dialogue, a series of gaffes derailed this opportunity. One week after Iran's pledge to provide aid to Afghanistan, Tehran was included in the "axis of evil" speech at the urging of National Security Council (NSC) Adviser Condoleezza Rice. Mohammad Adeli, a deputy at the Iranian Foreign Ministry, noted that the speech immediately marginalized Iranian officials who were seeking better relations with the US: "The speech exonerated those [hard-liners] who had always doubted America's intentions."[26]

There had also been a history of American legislative antagonism toward Iran. In July 2001, the Senate approved legislation extending sanctions against Iran for another five years—a move undercutting efforts by moderate Iranian president Khatami to improve relations and emboldening hard-liners. In October 2006, Congress passed and Bush signed into law the Iran Freedom Support Act, which placed sanctions on countries assisting Iran's nuclear program, even if the technical support was legal under the Nuclear Non-Proliferation Treaty (NPT).[27] Critics noted the similarity of this legislation to the 1998 Iraq Liberation Act, which helped provide the Bush administration with authority to take action in the buildup to the 2003 war.

Yet, before leaving office, it became obvious to Bush that military action against Iran's nuclear facilities would only complicate his efforts to achieve stability in Iraq and Afghanistan. In January 2009, senior American officials disclosed that Bush had denied Israeli requests for special bunker-buster bombs and to fly over Iraq to strike the Iranian Natanz nuclear complex.[28] Late in his presidency, Bush became convinced a strike against Iran would "prove ineffective, lead to the expulsion of international inspectors, and drive Iran's nuclear effort further out of view."[29] In its place, Bush directed a covert program to sabotage the Iranian nuclear program.

In sum, the Bush presidency could be characterized as a period of missed opportunities with recurring episodes of conflict and misunderstanding. Domestic constraints on both sides have added to the diplomatic malaise. Since 1979, any U.S. president seeking to soften policy toward Iran, normalize relations, or engage in direct talks has risked attack by domestic opponents of such moves. Similarly, in Iran, limited efforts by two Iranian presidents—Ali Akbar Hashemi Rafsanjani during the 1990s and Mohammad Khatami prior to 2005—to improve U.S.-Iranian relations brought both men under attack at home from conservative clerics, who forced them to maintain the existing hostile pattern. Both sides are trapped with a hostile image of the other, locked into place like a bug in amber by the historical relationship they share and by strategic and political factors that make it almost impossible to escape.

US-Iran Nuclear Standoff (2005–2009): The European Union and United Nations as Negotiating Agents

During the Bush years, the Europeans viewed diplomacy as the best way to resolve the dispute, maintain international support for whatever sanctions might be necessary, and avoid provoking a conflict that might cause Iran to leave the Nuclear Non-Proliferation Treaty and cease cooperation with the IAEA. Although the US left the direct diplomatic efforts to the Europeans and refused to discuss incentives for Iran, it did not discourage Britain, Germany, and France from pursuing their efforts, judging that any efforts to gain international support for harsher measures against Tehran would require an effort at diplomacy first (especially after the controversial lead-up to the Iraq war).[30]

In June 2005, hard-line conservative Mahmoud Ahmadinejad was elected president of Iran, replacing the moderate reformist Khatami. Ahmadinejad insisted Iran's nuclear program was purely peaceful but warned,

> Nuclear energy is a result of the Iranian people's scientific development and no one can block the way of a nation's scientific development. . . . This right of the Iranian people will soon be recognized by those who have so far denied it.[31]

Over the following months, Iran adopted a much tougher stance in its negotiations with the Europeans and IAEA. Although Ahmadinejad became the visible, public face of this more confrontational approach, he was not entirely responsible for the shift because the policy was actually decided by the Supreme Leader Ayatollah Khamenei.[32] Tehran not only refused the IAEA's demand to halt its uranium conversion program, but stated that "making nuclear fuel for civilian purposes was its right under the Nuclear Nonproliferation Treaty (NPT)."[33] By beginning work on its uranium conversion facilities in Isfahan, where raw uranium is converted into a gas that is fed into centrifuges for enrichment, Iran explicitly rejected giving up its right to develop nuclear fuel indigenously.[34] Iranian officials warned the West that Iran would not negotiate over its uranium conversion plants, but was willing to discuss the uranium enrichment facilities at Natanz in future talks.[35] The IAEA responded by setting a deadline of September 3, 2005, for Iran to "reestablish full suspension of all enrichment-related activities."[36] When Iran failed to comply, the Western allies found their options limited. Although not immediately referring Iran to the UN Security Council, they sought a tough new IAEA resolution accusing Iran of "noncompliance" with treaties governing its nuclear program. But Russia and China still objected because the IAEA draft proposal signaled that Iran's case would eventually be sent to the Security Council.

For its part, Iran continued to say it was willing to negotiate with the Europeans, but did not back away from its earlier declaration that referral to the UN might lead to its withdrawal from the NPT.[37] Between June 2003 and September 2005, the IAEA passed seven resolutions criticizing Iran's activities and urging it to grant unfettered access to inspectors.[38] Yet, although Iran's nuclear activities were suspicious, the IAEA lacked conclusive proof Iran was pursuing a weapons program—despite its lack of cooperation with inspectors, its failure to provide a full accounting of its efforts to acquire centrifuges for uranium enrichment, or an explanation for the discovery of recently produced plutonium (which were inconsistent with claims its plutonium separation experiments only ran between 1988 and 1993).[39] In the absence of conclusive proof, Russia, India, Brazil, South Africa, and many developing countries opposed U.S. and European calls for a referral of Iran to the Security Council, where sanctions (either military or economic) could be imposed.[40]

With international pressure on Tehran growing, and the US and Europeans adopting a more united front over the issue, Ahmadinejad upped the ante in January 2006 by announcing the uranium enrichment complex at Natanz would reopen after a fourteen-month halt in operations. That facility had sparked the original crisis over the Iranian nuclear program, when inspectors discovered plans in February 2003 for more than 50,000 centrifuges at the site—enough to produce up to twenty nuclear weapons per year. Not only did the Western allies send messages warning against such a move, but Russia and

China did as well—a stark indication to Iran that their resistance to a referral to the Security Council might be waning.[41] Nevertheless, within days Iran broke open the internationally monitored seals on three of its nuclear facilities, clearing the way for uranium enrichment and derailing any new negotiations with the Europeans. Combined with Iran's harsh rhetoric, its actions met general condemnation by the international community. One European diplomat commented,

> The Iranians have behaved so remarkably badly, it's hard to believe that the international community will do anything other than put them in front of the ultimate court of international public opinion [the UN Security Council]. . . . That is where the Iranians are heading.[42]

For their part, the Iranians defended their actions as peaceful and involving research activities permitted under the NPT.[43] Later, during a press conference, the German foreign minister, Frank-Walter Steinmeier, noted, "Our talks with Iran have reached a dead end. . . . From our point of view, the time has come for the UN Security Council to become involved."[44] Pressing its advantage, the US announced its full support for the European action, with Secretary of State Rice declaring Iran's actions "have shattered the basis for negotiation."[45]

In response to the renewed movement toward referring it to the Security Council, Iran turned up the heat still further in April 2006 by announcing its nuclear engineers had advanced to "a new phase in the enrichment of uranium," allowing it to speed production of nuclear fuel on an industrial scale. In a nationally televised broadcast, Ahmadinejad declared that "Iran has joined the nuclear countries of the world," leading the White House to announce that the US would work with the Security Council "to deal with the significant threat posed by the regime's efforts to acquire nuclear weapons." Given that earlier in the week Bush had repeated his "stated goal" not to allow "the Iranians to have a nuclear weapon, the capacity to make a nuclear weapon, or the knowledge as to how to make a nuclear weapon," Ahmadinejad's announcement represented a serious setback for U.S. foreign policy.[46]

Although nuclear analysts quickly dismissed Iran's claims as exaggerated "political posturing" meant to invoke Iranian nationalism to firm up domestic political support for Ahmadinejad, this did nothing to reduce growing international concern.[47] Iran refused to answer IAEA questions about the previously unknown secret uranium enrichment program (based on P-2 centrifuges obtained on the black market through the A.Q. Khan network) unwisely disclosed by Ahmadinejad. He rejected a UN deadline to suspend the nuclear program, as well as a proposal by Moscow to enrich Iranian uranium on Russian soil, declaring that sanctions would hurt Western nations more than Iran.[48] In response, the US announced it would ask the Security Council to require Iran to stop enrichment, based on Chapter VII of the UN Charter, the section making resolutions mandatory and opening the way for either sanctions or military action—a move opposed by both Russia and China.[49]

Over the following months, with no movement on either the diplomatic or sanctions front, the Europeans began pressing Bush to make a "dramatic gesture" to reenergize talks, rally world opinion against Iran, and avoid having America blamed for not doing its utmost to defuse the crisis.[50] An eighteen-page letter from Ahmadinejad to Bush in May 2006, although filled with religious language and declarations that Western democracy had failed, was seen by many foreign policy experts as an attempt by the Iranian leader to open a new dialogue.[51] After an internal White House debate, in which Secretary Rice overcame the skepticism of Vice President Cheney to convince Bush of the need for "a third option" apart from "either a nuclear Iran or an American military action," the president agreed to engage in substantive talks with Iran—the first major negotiations in the twenty-seven years since the hostage crisis. Although Cheney and other hard-line officials were "dead set against it," preferring a strategy to isolate Iran enough to force "regime change," they were finally persuaded that if military action was eventually necessary, it would be easier to gain international approval if negotiation efforts preceded it.[52] As a result, in June 2006 punitive action by the Security Council was shelved until Iran could respond to a new package of incentives (still minus U.S. security guarantees) presented by the US, Europe, Russia, and China.[53] Although the Iranians immediately stated they would "not negotiate over our nation's natural nuclear rights," they struck a slightly conciliatory tone by noting they were "ready to hold fair and unbiased dialogue and negotiations over mutual concerns within the context of a defined framework," and Ayatollah Khamenei (long an opponent of direct talks with Washington) gave his blessing to talks "if there was respect for mutual interests."[54] Even so, the UN Security Council issued a call for Iran to implement a "full and sustained suspension" of its nuclear activities by August 31 or face sanctions.[55]

Iran ignored those calls, and after North Korea's nuclear test in October 2006, the European Union (EU) supported limited UN sanctions.[56] The IAEA reported Iran had successfully set up a second centrifuge cascade and expanded its enrichment capabilities, though IAEA director El Baradei maintained, "The jury is still out on whether they are developing a nuclear weapon."[57]

Although it suggested "France organize and monitor the production of enriched uranium inside Iran" (a proposal rejected as falling short of Security Council demands for a freeze on all nuclear activities), Tehran maintained it would not comply with UN demands and refused to condemn North Korea for its nuclear test.[58] Raising tensions further, Ahmadinejad declared in November 2006 that Iran's program was nearing the milestone of mastering the nuclear fuel cycle and that "we can have our celebration of Iran's full nuclearization this year."[59] This announcement increased Western concerns because mastering the fuel cycle implies the ability not only to enrich uranium but also to reprocess plutonium from spent fuel, potentially providing Iran with two sources of material for nuclear weapons.

Finally, in December 2006 the Security Council unanimously passed a resolution against Iran, banning the import or export of materials and technology used in uranium enrichment, reprocessing, or ballistic missiles. Although the measure was softened to gain Russian and Chinese support (and excluded any sanctions against the Bashehr nuclear power plant being built by Russia in southern Iran), it still froze the assets of twelve Iranians and eleven companies involved in Tehran's nuclear and ballistic missile programs.[60] That led to friction with U.S. allies in Europe, who resisted subsequent Bush administration demands to increase financial pressure on Iran by curtailing exports, loan guarantees, and many business transactions because of their far greater commercial and economic ties with Tehran.[61] The Europeans believed they were being asked to sacrifice far more than the Americans for the sanctions (given limited U.S. business interests), and their resistance provided Tehran with a continued economic lifeline in the face of the UN penalties. In February 2007 Russia announced it would consider OPEC-like cooperation with Tehran on sales of natural gas, and President Putin noted "the people of Iran should have access to modern technologies, including nuclear ones" while complying with their NPT commitments to avoid weaponization.[62] One of the greatest hurdles for the US in marshaling international support for harsh economic sanctions remained the reality that other states had tremendous economic interests in Iran and much to lose from such measures—ranging from the Russians and Chinese, who feared losing access to Iranian oil and gas, to the Europeans, who had long-standing business interests with Tehran.

Even so, in the face of Iran's continued defiance, on March 24, 2007, the Security Council unanimously passed Resolution 1747 barring all arms exports to Iran and freezing the financial assets of twenty-eight Iranians linked to its military and nuclear programs. This provoked Khamenei to warn that not only was the nuclear program "more important than the nationalization of oil in 1958," but "if they want to treat us with threats and use of force or violence, the Iranian nation will undoubtedly use all its capabilities to strike the invading enemies."[63] Ahmadinejad warned if pressure on Iran was not ended, he would consider halting all cooperation with the IAEA, observing that "the Iranian nation will defend its right and that this path is irreversible."[64] The US intended to try gradually increasing the severity of sanctions, while refusing to take military options off the table, but Iran showed no willingness to give in and sped up installation of centrifuges. In 2007 it was estimated 8,000 centrifuges were added at Natanz, enough to enrich sufficient material for at least two nuclear weapons a year.[65] Throughout 2008 and 2009, Iran expanded its nuclear enrichment facilities. Ahmadinejad's visit to Natanz in April 2008 showcased new-generation IR-2 centrifuges that enhanced Iran's capability to separate out U-235 for fuel or bombs.[66]

Later, in fall 2009, Iran disclosed to the IAEA that it had not reported an enrichment site near the city of Qum, within the confines of a Revolutionary Guard base. The underground plant was estimated to eventually hold "3,000 centrifuges" of the P-1 type.[67] The new disclosure, coupled with the fact Iran's nuclear program had been dispersed and literally gone underground, caused great concern in the West. U.S. Defense Secretary Robert Gates noted a military strike "would only slow Iran's nuclear ambitions by one to three years."[68] The Qum site, about one-half complete, was "buried inside a mountain."[69] Finally, in October 2009, the IAEA reported Iran had acquired "sufficient information to be able to design and produce a workable atom bomb."[70] The report suggested Iran's work was geared toward a nuclear payload to be delivered using the Shahab 3 (medium-range) missile system.[71] Despite UN sanctions and an engaged West seeking accommodation over the enrichment issue, Iran stayed the course on its nuclear path. When the Qum site was disclosed, both the British and French quickly condemned Iran's deception.[72] At the same time, in January 2009, Bush authorized "Olympic Games," a clandestine cyber-attack effort against Iran's nuclear program targeting critical electrical and computer systems. The program continued under Obama and may have resulted in the Stuxnet computer worm attack on the Natanz centrifuges later that year.[73]

The Obama Approach and the Rise of Muscular Diplomacy

Barack Obama was elected president in November 2008 and campaigned on a pledge to open direct negotiations with the Iranians over the nuclear standoff.

In his inaugural address, and later in the Cairo Address, Obama hinted at the possibility of the UN reaching accommodation with Iran by allowing it to retain some limited nuclear enrichment capability for peaceful purposes. Obama explained, "Any nation—including Iran—should have the right to access peaceful nuclear power if it complies with its responsibilities under the Nuclear Non-Proliferation Treaty."[74] This was a clear departure from the Bush policy of nonengagement and denial of Iran's ability to enrich uranium. Obama sent a letter to Ayatollah Khamenei, the real power broker in Iranian politics, outlining a framework for talks to resolve the standoff. However, this strategy was frustrated by the failure of Iran to accept a proposed IAEA reprocessing deal, its persistent human rights abuses after the contested presidential election, and the lack of will on the part of the UN Security Council to place added pressure on Iran.

In the IAEA proposal Iran rejected in October 2009, Tehran was to send 2,600 pounds of its enriched uranium to Russia for reprocessing and then on to France for assembly into fuel rods—a move significantly reducing the amount of material that could be diverted for weapons purposes. The fuel rods would then be sent back to Iran for use in a medical research facility in Tehran. In July 2009, Obama traveled to Moscow to meet with Russian president Medvedev to persuade the Kremlin to cooperate in placing pressure on Iran to accept limits on its enrichment program. However, by October 2009, Russian foreign minister Lavrov stated, "Threats, sanctions and threats of pressure in the current situation, we are convinced, would be counterproductive."[75] As one of Iran's closest trading partners, Russia insisted Iran had made good faith efforts to deescalate the conflict. Nevertheless, Moscow was dismayed by the disclosure in September of the Iranian Qum nuclear site—yet another new, undisclosed enrichment facility and a discovery that increased its willingness to consider some additional sanctions.

For its part, China also resisted tough new sanctions against Iran. China has "invested heavily in Iranian oil and gas reserves" and worries sanctions may adversely affect its commercial relationship.[76] Chinese-Iranian trade has escalated in recent years with "Iran awash in Chinese products . . . and [Iran supplying] . . . 15 percent of China's oil."[77] These facts, taken in concert with Iranian counteroffers of an incremental reprocessing agreement in December 2009, effectively kept China from moving toward the position of the Western powers. In this proposal, Iran would "hand over 400 kilograms, or 882 pounds, of uranium initially—about a third of the amount proposed in the draft agreement reached under UN auspices in October [2009]—in exchange for an equivalent amount of enriched material to fuel a medical research reactor."[78] Critics argued this was simply a technique to divide the UN Security Council.

Obama also faced the difficulty of negotiating with Iran in the aftermath of the June 2009 contested presidential election and the brutal crackdown that followed. On June 12, 2009, Iranians went to the polls to elect a new president, which pitted the incumbent Ahmadinejad against several reformer candidates, including former prime minister Mir Hussein Moussavi (whose position on nuclear enrichment did not diverge substantially from Ahmadinejad's). Moussavi had a wide following and was clearly expected to challenge Ahmadinejad in the polls. However, by early nightfall on election day, Ahmadinejad was announced as the overwhelming victor. Given Moussavi's popularity and clear evidence of irregularities, many supporters saw the election result as a sham, provoking tens of thousands of dissenting Iranians into the streets. Khamenei quickly backed Ahmadinejad, though many reformers and clerics alike believed the election had been stolen. Almost immediately, Iranian police and Basij militiamen began to violently suppress the street demonstrations. Over the course of several weeks, hundreds were jailed, with reports of torture, rape, and murder in prisons.

Throughout all of 2010, the Iranians refused to cooperate with the IAEA, provide details of their nuclear program, or address the troubling evidence of offensive military dimensions to Tehran's efforts highlighted in numerous IAEA reports.[79] At the same time, it engaged in a strategy of delay to ward off further sanctions being proposed in Washington. In May 2010, Iran issued a joint declaration with Brazil and Turkey, agreeing to send low-enriched uranium to Turkey in exchange for enriched fuel for its research reactor (in a rehash of the earlier Russian proposal)—a step Tehran hoped would show compromise and prevent additional sanctions, while masking its continued refusal to cease enrichment of additional uranium to high levels or slow its program.[80] However, the US quickly responded by announcing a new push for additional sanctions against Iran in the UN Security Council, a move criticized by both Turkey and Brazil, and continued its strategy of muscular sanctions to try force Tehran into serious negotiations.[81]

But even as Iran continued its pattern of delay and limited engagement in any negotiations over its growing nuclear program, Israeli fears of Tehran possessing nuclear weapons began to crystallize in Tel Aviv's continuing calls for military preemption if progress were not made quickly. In 2008, the Bush administration refused to consider Israeli requests that the US attack Iran's nuclear facilities (given the probable negative blowback) and discouraged Tel Aviv from attacking on its own.[82] Yet, despite sanctions and efforts at negotiation, Iran's construction of enrichment facilities and growing stocks of uranium enriched to 20 percent (a level that could easily be further enriched to weapons-grade levels) continued and accelerated. In response, in 2010 Israeli Prime Minister Benjamin Netanyahu and Defense Minister Ehud Barak ordered the Israeli military to prepare plans to attack Iran's facilities—a move provoking opposition from other top ministers, including Gabi Ashkenazi, the head of the Israeli Defense Forces, and Meir Dagan, head of Israel's Mossad intelligence service, who questioned both the legality of these orders and the ability of the Israeli military to carry them out.[83] With continued opposition from the Obama administration to such a strike, and a lack within the Israeli military of the kind of "bunker-buster" weapons needed to strike at the hardened Iranian facilities, Israel refrained from launching an attack while continuing to threaten unilateral action and called upon the international community to act immediately. But as Admiral Michael Mullen, the chairman of the Joint Chiefs of Staff, observed (in a view reflecting the general consensus within the Obama administration),

> Iran getting a nuclear weapon would be incredibly destabilizing. Attacking them would also create the same kind of outcome. . . . In an area that's so unstable right now, we just don't need more of that.[84]

In November 2011, the IAEA released a startling report accusing Tehran of violating its NPT commitments by engaging in clear nuclear weapons-related research that included testing detonators used in creating nuclear implosions and developing (with the aid of foreign nuclear scientists) spherical warhead designs geared to fit Iranian Shahab-3 missiles, about which IAEA analysts concluded "any payload option other than nuclear . . . can be ruled out."[85] Iran immediately denounced the IAEA as an American stooge making use of fabricated evidence provided by Washington in its report, while vowing to not be "bullied into abandoning its nuclear program."[86] Though the French, British, and Germans immediately announced they would join with the US to seek increased UN sanctions against Iran, Russia continued to block any new measures despite the reports' conclusions.[87] Throughout 2011–2012, the IAEA continued to report on Iran's accelerating program, its vast expansion of uranium enrichment facilities, and increasing evidence of military dimensions to its program. But these reports always resulted in further Iranian denials and continued unwillingness by Moscow or Beijing to back stiffer sanctions.

Nevertheless, though not bringing the Iranians to the negotiating table, the Obama administration's strategy of muscular economic sanctions against Tehran was beginning to have an enormous negative impact upon the Iranian economy—though only time will tell whether sanctions are sufficient to force it to change course on its nuclear program. By October 2012, sanctions had caused the Iranian rial to fall 40 percent against the U.S. dollar and other foreign currencies (panicking the markets), increased the costs of imported goods (forcing a ban on all luxury imports), and led to an inflation rate as high as 196 percent![88] The sanctions banned Iran's purchase of weapons, constricted Tehran's ability to conduct international financial transactions, and drastically reduced its main source of foreign revenue, oil exports, by nearly half.[89] As Dennis Ross, the Obama administration's chief adviser on Iran, observed, 2013 will be "a decisive year, one way or another" as Iranian leaders decide between negotiations and economic catastrophe.[90] As Iran continues expanding its centrifuge work at its uranium enrichment facilities, refusing IAEA access to the Parchin military site (suspected of hosting tests of neutron initiators used in nuclear weapon chain reactions), and condemning IAEA reports of its weapons-related activities, it remains uncertain whether Ahmadinejad's rhetorical willingness to engage in bilateral negotiations with the US will be enough to sway hardliners in the Iranian establishment, especially Ayatollah Khamenei, to compromise on the nuclear program.[91] In particular, accelerated work at its uranium enrichment facility at Fordow near Qum, buried deep inside a mountain, leads many analysts (including Israeli Defense Minister Ehud Barak) to worry about what Barak called a "zone of immunity"—a point at which the Iranian program can no longer be effectively preempted militarily and Tehran's march toward the bomb will be impossible to stop.[92] Of course, it is important to distinguish between possession of infrastructure enabling development of weapons (enrichment facilities, 20 percent enriched material, etc.) and actual weapons capability (nuclear weapon(s), delivery systems, etc.)—all of which would take some time to develop *if* Iranian leaders made the decision to go ahead. So while Iran has already produced enough nuclear fuel to potentially manufacture about four weapons if further enriched, the last two U.S. National Intelligence Estimates (NIEs) of 2007 and 2010 both concluded that the Iranian leadership had made no political decision yet to build a bomb.[93]

Still, though Ahmadinejad has expressed a willingness to negotiate (while steadfastly maintaining Iran's right to continue its peaceful program), it seems unlikely that this longstanding Iranian delaying tactic will continue to be effective over the coming year, given Tehran's continuing nuclear-related work.

As Robert Wood, chargé d'affaires at the U.S. mission to the IAEA warned, "If by March (2013) Iran has not begun substantive cooperation with the IAEA . . . the United States will work with other board members to pursue appropriate board action."[94] Similarly, Israeli Prime Minister Netanyahu strongly warned in his September 27, 2012, speech at the United Nations that time was running out to prevent Iran from possessing nuclear weapons and that action was required before the spring of 2013 if that outcome were to be prevented—unilaterally by Israel if necessary.[95] Yet as sanctions continued to bite heavily into the Iranian economy, and with war fatigue high in the US and Europe after long wars in Iraq and Afghanistan, there exists no desire in Western countries to support military action, except as a last resort. Seeming to back away from the threat to take immediate, unilateral action, in October 2012 Israeli Defense Minister Barak noted IAEA reports showing Iran had converted a large amount of its stockpile of 20 percent enriched uranium into fuel rods for civilian use, thereby "delaying the moment of truth by 8 to 10 months."[96] Nevertheless, all signs point to 2013 as being a critical year in shaping the path to be taken by the Iranian nuclear program and determining whether muscular sanctions or military action can prevent the arrival of a new nuclear weapon state on the world stage.

Conclusions and Policy Options

What are the viable policy options to pursue regarding the Iranian nuclear program? Though world leaders (from Bush and Obama to European leaders to Israeli policy makers) routinely remark that Iran obtaining nuclear weapons is totally unacceptable, the reality is that this outcome may be unavoidable. Though policy "hawks" will loudly proclaim the need to take military action to preempt the Iranian nuclear program, this tough rhetoric often refuses to face the harsh reality of the serious constraints and potential blowback from such actions that severely limit it as an option, including (1) the inability of even combined U.S./Israeli military attacks to successfully find and destroy all of the hidden, dispersed, and deeply buried parts of the Iranian program (resulting in only a delay, not an end to Tehran's nuclear ambitions); (2) the likelihood of Iran retaliating directly (against the oil traffic moving through the Strait of Hormuz, Israel, or U.S. military assets in region) or indirectly through Hezbollah and Hamas against Israel, sparking a regional military conflict; (3) the immediate cessation of Iranian cooperation with the IAEA, the removal of its inspectors, and a continuing nuclear program completely hidden from sight; (4) the creation of immense hostility in the Arab world to the US/Israel, leading to further attacks on Western interests and difficulties dealing with ongoing regional problems like Syria; (5) the probability of Iranian destabilization of neighboring Afghanistan, Iraq, and other Gulf States, harming regional stability and inflating the price of oil; (6) the fact that only complete military occupation of Iran could uncover and prevent a determined nuclear program from eventual success; and (7) the constraints imposed by war-weary publics in the US and Europe, after a decade of conflict in Iraq and Afghanistan, who would be unwilling to support the kind of massive military operation required to successfully interdict the Iranian nuclear program or the economic costs it would entail.

For all of these reasons, the strategy of muscular sanctions (and negotiations) pursued by the Obama administration represents a more realistic policy approach—though, if successful, one that will still require compromise with Iran and likely not entail the complete elimination of Iran's nuclear program. Ideally, the bite of economic sanctions and international pressure will eventually lead Tehran to (1) open up all of its nuclear facilities to rigorous IAEA inspections; (2) agree to cease enrichment of uranium to high levels and place a moratorium on the construction of further enrichment or other nuclear facilities; and (3) cease any research efforts having a military dimension and implement a policy not to pursue nuclear weapons. Any negotiations between the West and Iran would also have to include "face-saving" provisions for the Iranian leadership, such as the acknowledgement of Iran's right under the NPT to possess a peaceful nuclear program, develop civilian nuclear energy, and possess enrichment capabilities sufficient to provide fuel to that civilian program, in return for robust IAEA oversight. Such an outcome, while not totally satisfying to policy hawks, represents the "best" possible outcome from a selection of less than optimal choices—something real-world policy makers often must deal with in addressing the messy realities of actual foreign policy making. It would contain the Iranian nuclear program, defuse the current crisis, and effectively halt Tehran's rapid march toward obtaining nuclear weapons. Moreover, it would enable diplomacy and the transformation of Iranian politics by the reform-minded Green Movement to hopefully create a less antagonistic Iranian government. And while these may be optimistic outcomes, with the alternatives to a strategy of sanctions/negotiations being either military preemption (with all the serious negative blowback this entails) or the acceptance of a nuclear-armed Iran (which is politically unacceptable, though potentially unavoidable in reality), clearly the current approach holds the possibility of avoiding the worst of both worlds. But if the choice becomes one of launching a major war or making "lemonade from lemons" by adopting a deal that merely slows or halts Iran's current nuclear progress, it is likely the latter will be the preferred option. In all likelihood, the chosen path will be embarked upon during the coming year.

Key Actors

Mahmoud Ahmadinejad   Iran's current president (2005–present), a conservative opposed to the social reforms pushed by Khatami. He has strongly pursued a more aggressive negotiating position in support of Iran's continued nuclear enrichment program, which he claims is for peaceful purposes. Ahmadinejad was victorious in the contested presidential election of June 2009. His internal position was weakened due to street protests challenging his legitimacy in the aftermath of the election.

George W. Bush   Former U.S. president who took a hard line on negotiations with Iran over its nuclear program, demanding that Iran stop nuclear enrichment before negotiations could go forward.

Jimmy Carter   U.S. president during the Iranian revolution and the hostage crisis.

Bill Clinton   Former U.S. president who signed an executive order in 1995 prohibiting trade with Iran to force it to stop supporting terrorism and developing a nuclear weapons program.

Supreme Leader Ali Khamenei   Iran's current supreme leader, who wields tremendous power to step into the political process and make important decisions for the country. He has strongly supported Iran's nuclear program and has been largely opposed to normalizing relations with the United States.

Mohammad Khatami   Iranian president (1997–2005) who tried unsuccessfully to reform the political system and establish better relations with the West.

Ayatollah Ruhollah Khomeini   Iranian revolutionary leader who became Iran's first supreme leader. His anti-Western policy became the inspiration behind the Iranian revolution and the storming of the American embassy in Tehran.

Mir Hussein Moussavi   Former Iranian prime minister and presidential challenger to Ahmadinejad. Moussavi lost the June 2009 contested presidential election but quickly became the symbol of resistance to the Iranian regime. His followers have continued to engage in political dissent throughout the country.

Barack Obama   Current U.S. president; campaigned on a platform of opening up dialogue directly with the Iranian government. His clenched-fist metaphor was intended to send a message to the Iranian government that the United States desired a less confrontational and more cooperative relationship with the Islamic republic. After the contested election, his position became much more difficult due to resistance to negotiations within the U.S. government.

Benjamin Netanyahu   Israeli Prime Minister who is calling for military action against Iran's program.

Ali Akbar Hashemi Rafsanjani   Former Iranian president and powerful cleric who has challenged the legitimacy of the current Iranian regime; viewed the June 2009 presidential election as fraudulent.

Ronald Reagan   Former U.S. president who adopted a containment strategy versus Iran and supported Iraq in its war against Iran (1980–1988).

Notes

1. Barack Obama, "Inaugural Address," January 21, 2009, www.whitehouse.gov/blog/inaugural-address.

2. See Thomas Preston, *From Lambs to Lions: Future Security Relationships in a World of Biological and Nuclear Weapons* (Boulder: Rowman and Littlefield, 2009).

3. See William J. Daugherty, "Jimmy Carter and the 1979 Decision to Admit the Shah into the United States," AmericanDiplomacy.org, January 2003, www.unc.edu/depts/diplomat/archives_roll/2003_01–03/daugherty_shaw.

4. GlobalSecurity.org, "Ministry of Security SAVAK," www.globalsecurity.org/intell/world/iran/savak.htm.

5. Daugherty, "Jimmy Carter."

6. John King, "Arming Iraq and the Path to War," March 31, 2003, www.parstimes.com/news/archive/2003/arming_iraq.html.

7. Farhang Rajaee, *The Iran-Iraq War: The Politics of Aggression* (Gainesville: University Press of Florida, 1993), 1.

8. Ibid.

9. Ibid.

10. Seymour M. Hersh, "The Iran Game," *New Yorker,* December 3, 2001, 42–50; Elaine Sciolino, "Nuclear Ambitions Aren't New for Iran," *New York Times,* June 22, 2003, WK 4.

11. Sciolino, "Nuclear Ambitions," 4.

12. Ibid.

13. Terrence Henry, "Nuclear Iran," *Atlantic Monthly,* December 2003, 45.

14. Ibid.; Jack Boureston and Charles D. Ferguson, "Schooling Iran's Atom Squad," *Bulletin of the Atomic Scientists* 60, no. 3 (May/June 2004): 31–35.

15. David Albright and Corey Hinderstein, "Iran, Player or Rogue?" *Bulletin of the Atomic Scientists* 59, no. 5 (September/October 2003): 54–56.

16. Ibid.

17. Hersh, "The Iran Game," 50; William J. Broad, David E. Sanger, and Raymond Bonner, "A Tale of Nuclear Proliferation: How Pakistani Built His Network," *New York Times*, February 12, 2004, A1.

18. For a detailed discussion of Iran's postrevolution pursuit of nuclear, biological, and chemical weapons, see Gregory F. Giles, "The Islamic Republic of Iran and Nuclear, Biological, and Chemical Weapons," in *Planning the Unthinkable: How New Powers Will Use Nuclear, Biological, and Chemical Weapons*, ed. James J. Wirtz, Peter R. Lavoy, and Scott D. Sagan (Ithaca, NY: Cornell University Press, 2000), 79–103.

19. James Risen and Judith Miller, "No Illicit Arms Found in Iraq, U.S. Inspector Tells Congress," *New York Times*, October 3, 2003, A1.

20. Joseph Cirincione, *Deadly Arsenals: Tracking Weapons of Mass Destruction* (Washington, DC: Carnegie Endowment for International Peace, 2002), 257. Indeed, a January 2005 briefing to the Israeli Knesset by Meir Dagan, head of the Mossad intelligence agency, warned that Iran could build a bomb in less than three years and, if it successfully enriched uranium in 2005, could have a weapon two years later. See BBC News, http://news.bbc.co.uk/go/pr/fr/-/2/hi/middle_east/4203411.stm, January 24, 2005. By August 2005, Israeli intelligence had adjusted its estimate to Iran's having the bomb as early as 2008, "if all goes well for it," but probably by 2012. Orly Halpern, "New Estimates on Iranian Nukes," *Jerusalem Post*, August 1, 2005, jpost.com/servlet/Satellite?page name=Jpost/JPArticle/ShowFull&cid=1122776414371&p=1101615860782.

21. Douglas Jehl and Eric Schmitt, "Data Is Lacking on Iran's Arms, U.S. Panel Says," *New York Times*, March 9, 2005, A1; Steven R. Weisman and Douglas Jehl, "Estimate Revised on When Iran Could Make Nuclear Bomb," *New York Times*, August 3, 2005, A8. Agreeing with this assessment, London's International Institute for Strategic Studies concluded that Iran would not be expected to build nuclear weapons before the next decade.

22. Alan Cowell, "Nuclear Weapon Is Years Off for Iran, Research Panel Says," *New York Times*, September 7, 2005, A11. See Cirincione, *Deadly Arsenals*, 255. The IAEA, after two years of inspections, has stated it has not found evidence of any weapons program. See Jehl and Schmitt, "Data Is Lacking on Iran's Arms."

23. Cirincione, *Deadly Arsenals*, 255.

24. Michael Hirsh, Maziar Bahari, et al., "Rumors of War," *Newsweek*, February 19, 2007, 30.

25. Ibid., 31.

26. Ibid.

27. Azar Nafisi, "The Veiled Threat," *The New Republic*, February 22, 1999, 27.

28. David E. Sanger, "U.S. Rejected Aid for Israeli Raid on Iranian Nuclear Site," January 11, 2009, www.nytimes.com/2009/01/11/washington/11iran.html.

29. Ibid.

30. Steven R. Weisman, "U.S. in Talks with Europeans on a Nuclear Deal with Iran," *New York Times*, October 12, 2004, A16.

31. David E. Sanger, "Iranian Upset, U.S. Challenge," *New York Times*, June 26, 2005, A1.

32. Nazila Fathi, "Iran Tells Europe It's Devoted to Nuclear Efforts and Talks," *New York Times*, August 4, 2005, A6.

33. Nazila Fathi, "Iran Warns the West Not to Use the U.N. to Penalize It," *New York Times*, September 12, 2005, A7.

34. Nazila Fathi, "Iran Rejects European Offer to End Its Nuclear Impasse," *New York Times,* August 7, 2005, A11.

35. Nazila Fathi, "Iran's New Leader Turns to Conservatives for His Cabinet," *New York Times,* August 15, 2005, A3.

36. Thomas Fuller and Nazila Fathi, "U.N. Agency Urges Iran to Halt Its Nuclear Activity," *New York Times,* August 12, 2005, A8.

37. Steven R. Weisman, "West Presses for Nuclear Agency to Rebuke Iran, Despite Russian Dissent," *New York Times,* September 23, 2005, A6.

38. Mark Landler, "Nuclear Agency Expected to Back Weaker Rebuke to Iran," *New York Times,* September 24, 2005, A3.

39. Mark Landler, "U.N. Says It Hasn't Found Much New about Nuclear Iran," *New York Times,* September 3, 2005, A3.

40. Steven R. Weisman, "Wider U.S. Net Seeks Allies against Iran's Nuclear Plan," *New York Times,* September 10, 2005, A3.

41. Elaine Sciolino, "Iran, Defiant, Insists It Plans to Restart Nuclear Program," *New York Times,* January 10, 2006, A11.

42. Steven R. Weisman and Nazila Fathi, "Iranians Reopen Nuclear Centers," *New York Times,* January 11, 2006, A1.

43. Ibid.

44. Richard Bernstein and Steven R. Weisman, "Europe Joins U.S. in Urging Action by U.N. on Iran," *New York Times,* January 13, 2006, A1.

45. Ibid.

46. Nazila Fathi, David E. Sanger, and William J. Broad, "Iran Reports Big Advance in Enrichment of Uranium: U.S. Warns of 'Significant' Arms Threat as Tehran Says It Will Defy the UN," *New York Times,* April 12, 2006, A1.

47. William J. Broad, Nazila Fathi, and Joel Brinkley, "Analysts Say a Nuclear Iran Is Years Away," *New York Times,* April 13, 2006, A1.

48. David E. Sanger and Nazila Fathi, "Iran Is Described as Defiant on 2nd Nuclear Program," *New York Times,* April 25, 2006, A6.

49. Elaine Sciolino, "U.N. Agency Says Iran Falls Short on Nuclear Data," *New York Times,* April 29, 2006, A1.

50. Steven R. Weisman, "U.S. Is Now Ready to Meet Iranians on Nuclear Plan," *New York Times,* June 1, 2006, A1.

51. Michael Slackman, "Iranian Letter: Using Religion to Lecture Bush," *New York Times,* May 10, 2006, A1; David E. Sanger, "U.S. Debating Direct Talks with Iran on Nuclear Issue," *New York Times,* May 27, 2006, A1.

52. David E. Sanger, "Bush's Realization on Iran: No Good Choice Left Except Talks," *New York Times,* June 1, 2006, A8.

53. Thom Shanker and Elaine Sciolino, "Package of Terms (No Sanctions Included) for Iran," *New York Times,* June 2, 2006, A12.

54. Ibid.

55. Elissa Gootman, "Security Council Approves Sanctions against Iran," *New York Times,* December 24, 2006, A8.

56. "Europeans Back Gradual Steps against Iran's Nuclear Program," *New York Times,* October 18, 2006, A11.

57. David E. Sanger, "U.N. Official Says Iran Is Testing New Enrichment Device," *New York Times,* October 24, 2006, A8.

58. Elaine Sciolino, "Iran's Proposal to End Nuclear Standoff Is Rejected by the West," *New York Times,* October 4, 2006, A6; Navila Fathi, "Iran Defies Call to Drop Nuclear Plans," *New York Times,* October 13, 2006, A11.

59. William J. Broad and Nazila Fathi, "Iran's Leader Cites Progress on Nuclear Plans," *New York Times,* November 15, 2006, A8.

60. Gootman, "Security Council Approves Sanctions."

61. Steven R. Weisman, "Europe Resists U.S. on Curbing Ties with Iran," *New York Times,* January 30, 2007, A1.

62. Steven Lee Myers, "Pact with Iran on Gas Sales Is Possible, Putin Says," *New York Times,* February 2, 2007, A8.

63. Nazila Fathi, "Iran Says It Can Enrich Uranium on an Industrial Scale," *New York Times,* April 10, 2007, A3.

64. David E. Sanger, "Atomic Agency Confirms Advances by Iran's Nuclear Program," *New York Times,* April 19, 2007, A10.

65. David E. Sanger, "Inspectors Say Iran Is Advancing on Nuclear Front," *International Herald Tribune,* May 15, 2007, A1.

66. Broad, "A Tantalizing Look at Iran's Nuclear Program."

67. David E. Sanger and William J. Broad, "U.S. and Allies Warn Iran over Nuclear 'Deception,'" September 26, 2009, www.nytimes.com/2009/09/26/world/middleeast/26nuke.html.

68. William J. Broad, "Iran Shielding Its Nuclear Efforts in Maze of Tunnels," January 6, 2010, www.nytimes.com/2010/01/06/world/middleeast/06sanctions.html.

69. Ibid.

70. William J. Broad and David E. Sanger, "Report Says Iran Has Data to Make a Nuclear Bomb," October 4, 2009, www.nytimes.com/2009/10/04/world/middleeast/04nuke.html.

71. Ibid.

72. Sanger and Broad, "U.S. and Allies Warn Iran Over Nuclear 'Deception.'"

73. David E. Sanger and Rick Gladstone, "Iranian Says Nuclear Sites Were Targets of Explosions," *New York Times,* September 18, 2012, A4.

74. Barack Hussein Obama, "A New Beginning: Cairo University, Cairo, Egypt," June 4, 2009, www.whitehouse.gov/the-press-office/remarks-president-cairo-university-6-04-09.

75. Mark Landler and Clifford J. Levy, "Russia Resists U.S. Position on Sanctions for Iran," October 14, 2009, www.nytimes.com/2009/10/14/world/europe/14diplo.html.

76. Ibid.

77. Roger Cohen, "The Making of an Iran Policy," August 2, 2009, www.nytimes.com/2009/08/02/magazine/02Iran-t.html.

78. Robert F. Worth, "Iran Avows Willingness to Swap Some Uranium," December 13, 2009, www.nytimes.com/2009/12/13/world/middleeast/13iran.html.

79. International Atomic Energy Agency, "Implementation of the NPT Safeguards Agreement and Relevant Provisions of Security Council Resolutions 1737 (2006), 1747 (2007), 1803 (2008), and 1835 (2008) in the Islamic Republic of Iran" May 31, 2010, www.iaea.org/Publications/Documents/Board/2010/gov2010-28.pdf.

80. "Nuclear Fuel Declaration By Iran, Turkey, and Brazil," BBC, May 17, 2010, news.bbc.co.uk/2/hi/middle_east/8686728.stm.

81. "Clinton Attacks Turkey-Brazil Deal With Iran," *The Financial Times*, May 18, 2010, www.ft.com/cms/s/0/58caa4b4-62a4-11df-b1d1-00144feab49a.html.

82. Jeffrey Goldberg, "The Point of No Return," *The Atlantic,* September 2010, 60.

83. Jodi Rudoren, "Israeli Report Cites a Thwarted 2010 Move on Iran," *New York Times,* November 5, 2012, A3.

84. Goldberg, "The Point of No Return," 65–66.

85. Oren Dorell, "UN Agency Issues Red Alert Over Iran's Secret Nuke Program," *USA Today,* November 9, 2011, 8A.

86. Robert F. Worth and Rick Gladstone, "Iran Frames UN Nuclear Report as U.S. Bullying," *New York Times,* November 10, 2011, A6.

87. Ibid.; Ellen Barry, "Russia Dismisses Calls for New UN Sanctions on Iran," *New York Times,* November 10, 2011, A6.

88. Thomas Erdbrink, "Iran Places New Curbs on Trading of Currency," *New York Times,* October 9, 2012, A9.

89. Ibid; Joby Warrick, "Iran Locked in Internal Debate Over Whether to Talk to U.S.," *The Washington Post,* November 13, 2012, A1.

90. Warrick, "Iran Locked."

91. Ibid; "Satellite Images Indicate Iranian Nuke Cleanup," *USA Today,* March 8, 2012, 7A.

92. David E. Sanger, "Signs That Iran Is Speeding Up Nuclear Work," *New York Times,* August 24, 2012, A1, A10.

93. David E. Sanger, "Iran Trumpets Nuclear Ability at a Second Location." *New York Times,* January 9, 2012, A1, A3.

94. Jason Rezaian, "Ahmadinejad Proves Resilient in Iran," *The Washington Post,* November 30, 2012, A1.

95. Jodi Rudoren, "Netanyahu Says He'd Go It Alone on Striking Iran," *New York Times,* November 6, 2012, A5.

96. Rick Gladstone, "Israeli Defense Chief Says Iran Postponed Nuclear Ambitions," *New York Times,* October 31, 2012, A8.

5 The United States and North Korea: Avoiding a Worst-Case Scenario

Patrick James and Özgür Özdamar

Before You Begin

1. Why has North Korea been trying for about three decades to achieve nuclear weapons capability?

2. If incentive-based diplomacy had been pursued initially, would it have had a chance of resolving the issue before North Korea acquired nuclear weapons?

3. Is the Agreed Framework a good arrangement? Is the agreement an example of appeasement or of diplomatic and peaceful management of an international problem?

4. How did President George W. Bush's labeling North Korea a member of the "axis of evil" change U.S.–North Korean relations? How did five years of confrontation policy by the Bush administration contribute to security in East Asia and the world?

5. Was the deal reached in February 2007 another form of "appeasement" or a new hope for resolution of the issue? Did this deal send the wrong message to other states hoping to produce nuclear weapons?

6. Which foreign policy options are available to the Obama administration in dealing with North Korea?

7. What does U.S. policy on North Korea teach us about nuclear proliferation in general?

Introduction: Surprising Intelligence

In March 1984 satellite images of North Korea revealed a nuclear reactor under construction at Yongbyon, one hundred kilometers north of the capital, Pyongyang. The photographs shocked the Reagan administration, as this small but militarily powerful communist country in East Asia might be preparing to produce some of the world's deadliest weapons. The images also showed a reactor-type chimney rising from the site. In June 1984, additional intelligence identified a cooling tower, limited power lines, and electrical grid connections for the local transfer of energy. Analysts suggested that the reactor probably used uranium and graphite, both of which were available locally. This evidence could not establish conclusively that North Korea had the capacity to produce nuclear weapons; further intelligence in 1986, however, showed the construction of buildings similar to reprocessing plants used for separating plutonium, a step needed to produce atomic weapons. That same year, new photographs revealed circular craters of darkened ground, assumed to be the residue of high-explosive tests. The pattern suggested a technique used to detonate a nuclear device. A check of earlier photographs revealed the aftereffects of similar tests since 1983.[1]

When intelligence sources discovered construction in 1988 of a fifty-megawatt-capacity reactor—one much larger than the reactor photographed in 1984—the United States became even more alarmed. Estimates held that the older, smaller reactor could produce enough plutonium for up to six weapons a year, whereas the larger plant would make enough for up to fifteen weapons. Finally confident of the existence of a nuclear program, the administration of George H. W. Bush approached Soviet and Chinese officials in February 1989 and Japanese and South Korean authorities in May 1989 about putting pressure on North Korea to meet its obligations as a member of the International Atomic Energy Agency (IAEA). The administration specifically wanted North Korea to sign a safeguards agreement allowing inspections of its nuclear facilities.[2] Thus began more than two decades of roller coaster U.S.–North Korean relations concerning nuclear nonproliferation.

Background: North Korea's Nuclear Quest

The Korean Peninsula was ruled as a single entity from the time the Shilla Kingdom unified it in the seventh century until the end of World War II.[3] Japan colonized Korea in 1910, but when Japan surrendered in 1945, the Soviet Union and United States temporarily divided Korea at the 38th parallel. Thus a communist system evolved in the north, and a capitalist system in the south. Soon thereafter, the peninsula experienced the Korean War. Fought between communist North Korea (the Democratic People's Republic of North Korea [DPRK]) and anticommunist South Korea (the Republic of Korea [ROK]) for domination of the peninsula, the war lasted from June 1950 to July 1953 and stands out as a major proxy war between the United States and Soviet Union.[4] The principal combatants were Australia, Canada, South Korea, Turkey, the

Timeline

Key Developments in
U.S.–North Korean Relations

1977	The Soviet Union supplies North Korea with a small, experimental nuclear reactor.
March 1984	Satellite images of North Korea reveal a nuclear reactor under construction at Yongbyon, 100 kilometers north of the capital, Pyongyang.
1985	North Korea accedes to the Nuclear Non-Proliferation Treaty (NPT).
1988	U.S. intelligence identifies the construction of a large-capacity reactor in North Korea.
1989	The United States leads in calling on North Korea to meet its obligation to sign a safeguards agreement with the International Atomic Energy Agency (IAEA).
September 1991	The United States announces its withdrawal of tactical nuclear arms from the Korean Peninsula.
December 1991	North Korea and South Korea sign the Basic Agreement, concerning the end of hostilities between them, and the Joint Declaration on the Denuclearization of the Korean Peninsula, agreeing to forgo nuclear weapons–related activities.
January 1992	North Korea concludes a safeguards agreement with the IAEA.
1993	The crisis over North Korea's nuclear program escalates.
March 1993	Political and military issues erode North Korea's relations with South Korea and the United States. As a result, North Korea declares its intent to withdraw from the NPT in ninety days.
June 1993	The United States eases tensions with North Korea by offering to hold high-level talks on nuclear issues. The North suspends its withdrawal from the NPT.
January 1994	The CIA asserts that North Korea may have built one or two nuclear weapons.
June 13, 1994	North Korea announces its withdrawal from the IAEA.
June 15, 1994	Former president Jimmy Carter negotiates a deal in which Pyongyang confirms its willingness to freeze its nuclear program and resume high-level talks with the United States.

June 20, 1994	The Clinton administration sends a letter to the North Korean government stating its willingness to resume high-level talks if the North Koreans proceed in freezing their nuclear program.
July 8, 1994	North Korean leader Kim Il Sung dies. He is succeeded by his son Kim Jong Il.
October 21, 1994	The United States and North Korea sign the Agreed Framework in Geneva. The agreement involves dismantling Pyongyang's nuclear program in return for heavy oil supplies and light water reactors.
March 1995	Japan, South Korea, and the United States form the Korean Peninsula Energy Development Organization (KEDO) as part of the Agreed Framework.
1996–2000	North Korea and the United States hold several rounds of talks concerning the North's missile program. Washington suggests that Pyongyang adhere to the Missile Technology Control Regime (MTCR). The talks prove unproductive.
August 1998	North Korea generates unfavorable international attention by testing the Taepodong 1 rocket, which flies over Japan. The missile has a range of 1,500 to 2,000 kilometers.
June 15, 2000	At a historic summit, North Korea and South Korea agree to resolve the issue of reunification for the Korean Peninsula.
June 19, 2000	Encouraged by the Korean summit, the United States eases sanctions on North Korea.
January 29, 2002	President George W. Bush labels North Korea a member of a so-called axis of evil. The North Korean government reacts negatively.
October 3–5, 2002	James Kelly, assistant secretary of state for East Asian and Pacific affairs, visits North Korea and informs officials that the United States is aware of its clandestine nuclear program.
October 16, 2002	North Korea admits to having had a clandestine program to enrich uranium (and plutonium) for nuclear weapons development.
November 2002	KEDO stops shipping oil to North Korea. The IAEA asks North Korea for clarification on its nuclear program.

(continued)

Timeline *(continued)*
Key Developments in
U.S.–North Korean Relations

December 2002	North Korea responds to KEDO's oil stoppage by restarting its frozen nuclear reactor and orders IAEA inspectors out of the country.
January 10, 2003	North Korea withdraws from the NPT.
April 2003	At a meeting held in Beijing with China, South Korea, and the United States, North Korea announces that it has nuclear weapons.
2003–2004	Negotiations involving China, Japan, North Korea, Russia, South Korea, and the United States fail to produce any effective results.
July 4–5, 2006	North Korea conducts seven missile tests, including a long-range Taepodong 2.
July 15, 2006	The UN Security Council unanimously votes to impose sanctions that ban selling missile-related material to North Korea by all member states.
October 3, 2006	North Korea conducts its first nuclear detonation test ever. The world condemns this provocative act.
October 14, 2006	The UN Security Council unanimously votes to impose both military and economic sanctions on North Korea to protest the nuclear test.
February 13, 2007	Announcement comes from the six-party talks, continuing in Beijing, that North Korea has agreed to freeze its nuclear reactor in Yongbyon in return for economic and diplomatic concessions from the other parties.
June 2008	As an important step in the denuclearization process, North Korea announces its nuclear assets.
October 2008	United States removes North Korea from its sponsors of terrorism list; in return, North Korea agrees to allow inspectors in its key nuclear sites.
April 2009	North Korea fires a rocket carrying a satellite. Suspected for testing a long-range missile by regional countries and criticized by the UN Security Council, North Korea declares it will no longer participate in six-party talks.
May 2009	North Korea tests a nuclear device for the second time in its history; protests from all around the world.

January 2010	North Korea claims to work for ending hostilities with US and a nuclear-free Korean peninsula.
May 2010	South Korea declares that one of its warships was sunk by North Korean torpedo fire.
November 2010	North Korea fires dozens of artillery rounds at a South Korean island, Yeonpyeong. Two South Korean soldiers die. South fires eighty shots in response.
December 17, 2011	North Korean leader Kim Jong Il dies. His youngest son, Kim Jong Un, is declared the "Great Successor."
February 2012	Obama administration agrees to provide food aid to North Korea in return for the North's suspension of its nuclear program. The agreement was broken following an unsuccessful satellite launch by the North.
October 2012	North Korea declares that its missiles can now reach the U.S. mainland.
December 2012	North Korea tests a long-range missile and puts a satellite into orbit. The development was condemned by South Korea and other regional countries, including China.

United Kingdom, the United States, and other allies under a UN mandate, and on the other side North Korea and the People's Republic of China. The Soviet Union sided with North Korea, but it did not provide direct military support in the form of troops.[5] After three years of fighting, a cease-fire established a demilitarized zone (DMZ) at the 38th parallel, a demarcation still defended by substantial North Korean forces on one side and South Korean and U.S. forces on the other. More than fifty years after the fighting ended, the adversaries have yet to sign a peace treaty.

North Korea is ruled by one of the last remaining communist regimes and has had only three leaders in more than a half century: Kim Il Sung, from 1948 till his death in 1994; his son Kim Jong Il until his death in December 2011; and currently Kim Jong Un, who appeared as the "Great Successor." The Korean Worker's Party of North Korea is the last example of a classic Stalinist, communist party. The regime in North Korea is extremely autocratic, and the country has perhaps the most closed political system in the world.[6] After decades of mismanagement, the North relies heavily on international food aid to feed its population and avert mass starvation.[7] It is estimated that nearly 2 million people may have died of starvation between 1995 and 1998.[8]

Despite severe economic crises over the last two decades and widespread famine, North Korea continues to feed one of the largest armies in the world, with more than a million personnel.[9] In addition, North Korea's interest in nuclear power apparently began in the 1960s, when Kim Il Sung asked China to transfer nuclear technology to North Korea after China's first nuclear tests. Chinese leader Mao Zedong rejected such requests in 1964 and in 1974. The Soviet Union also refused to transfer nuclear technology to North Korea, but in 1977 the Soviets gave it a small, experimental reactor and insisted that it be placed under IAEA safeguards.[10] In all likelihood, the North persisted in efforts to go nuclear for two primary reasons: the Korean War experience and South Korean efforts to obtain nuclear weapons. During the war, North Korea experienced the threat of U.S. nuclear power, a menace that remained in Pyongyang's consciousness after the war concluded. According to one observer, "No country has been the target of more American nuclear threats than North Korea—at least seven since 1945." South Korea had attempted to gain nuclear weapons in the 1970s, but the United States prevented it from doing so. That venture by the South strongly influenced North Korean policy makers' security perceptions and pushed them to seek the nuclear option. In 1995, Walter Slocombe, U.S. under secretary of defense for policy in the Clinton administration, itemized the threats that North Korea's going nuclear posed, saying that it

- could be coupled with the oversized conventional force to extort or blackmail South Korea and greatly increase the costs of a war on the Korean Peninsula;
- could ignite a nuclear arms race in Asia;
- could undermine the Nuclear Non-Proliferation Treaty (NPT) and the IAEA safeguards system of inspections; and
- could lead to the export of nuclear technologies and components to pariah states and terrorists worldwide, and could project the nuclear threat across most of Northeast Asia if the government was successful in upgrading missile delivery systems.[11]

For these reasons, nuclear proliferation by North Korea became one of the foremost foreign policy challenges for the United States in the late twentieth century, and it still is today.

The Policy of George H. W. Bush

In the 1980s and early 1990s, most senior officials in the first Bush administration—including national security adviser Brent Scowcroft, his deputy and later CIA director Robert Gates, Secretary of State James Baker, Secretary of Defense Dick Cheney, and Under Secretary of Defense Paul Wolfowitz—believed that diplomatic means would not work with North Korea. Domestic political reasons, such as pressure to focus on the economy, along with Congress's and the foreign policy establishment's obvious distaste for dealing with North Korea, reinforced their reluctance to employ cooperative measures. Because Washington did not want to engage in diplomatic give and take, it adopted a crime and punishment approach that arguably led to crisis and subsequent deadlock.[12] In other words, from 1989 through 1992, the United States primarily, though not exclusively, used the stick rather than the carrot to deal with North Korea.

The Bush administration relied on the IAEA to monitor North Korea's nuclear program and the UN Security Council to enforce compliance with the NPT, to which North Korea had acceded in 1985 on the advice of the Soviet Union.[13] Although Pyongyang was supposed to sign the IAEA safeguards treaty within eighteen months of signing the NPT, it delayed for six years and signed the agreement only in January 1992. In other words, through various actions (or inaction), the North Korean government gave the impression that it had an ongoing interest in producing nuclear weapons.

Efforts by the Bush administration significantly influenced North Korea's ultimate signing of the IAEA safeguards agreement. By 1990, South Korea and the United States both worried that North Korea might already have developed one or two nuclear weapons. Unknown to U.S. officials, Soviet intelligence also had been receiving signals about the North Korean project. A KGB document from February 1990 (revealed in 1992) suggested that the North actually had completed a bomb:

> Scientific and experimental design work to create a nuclear weapon is continuing in the DPRK. . . . According to information received, development of the first atomic explosive device has been completed at the DPRK Center for Nuclear Research, located in the city of Yongbyon in Pyongan-pukto Province. At present there are no plans to test it, in the interests of concealing from world opinion and from the controlling international organizations the actual fact of the production of nuclear weapons in the DPRK. The KGB is taking additional measures to verify the above report.[14]

Beginning in 1991, South Korea and the United States implemented different elements of an integrated political, economic, and military campaign designed to persuade North Korea to allow inspections of its nuclear facilities.

U.S. actions appear, however, to have been somewhat ad hoc, developing according to circumstances,[15] most notably in reaction to getting nowhere by using the stick alone.

During 1991, U.S. strategy concerning North Korean nuclearization consisted of four primary elements. The first was an unequivocal statement of a reduced U.S. military position on the Korean Peninsula.[16] In 1990, the United States had initiated limited troop withdrawals from South Korea as part of its East Asian Strategic Initiative (and had taken steps to ease the trade embargo on the North). Then, in part because the Cold War was coming to an end, the United States announced in September 1991 the withdrawal of nuclear warheads, shells, and bombs from South Korea.[17] Second, Washington reaffirmed its security relationship with South Korea, to convince the North Koreans that delaying inspections would gain them nothing; this was conceived as an assertive element to balance the more pacific announcement about its forces and nuclear arsenal. Third, the annual U.S.–South Korean Team Spirit Military Exercise, which had been condemned by North Korea as provocative, was suspended for a year. Fourth, U.S. officials agreed to begin direct talks with North Korea, albeit only for a single session, with more to follow if North Korea cooperated and allowed nuclear inspections.[18]

This diplomatic approach produced some relatively positive consequences. In December 1991, North Korea and South Korea began talks at the level of prime minister that resulted in two agreements, which were welcomed by the United States. The Basic Agreement, signed on December 10, appeared to provide a strong basis for ending hostility between the two Koreas. Its main terms are as follows:

- mutual recognition of each other's systems and an end to mutual interference, vilification, and subversion
- mutual efforts "to transform the present state of armistice into a solid peace," with continued observance of the armistice until this is accomplished
- a mutual commitment not to use force against each other and the implementation of confidence-building measures and large-scale arms reductions
- economic, cultural, and scientific exchanges, free correspondence between divided families, and the reopening of roads and railroads severed at the border[19]

After signing the Basic Agreement, the North and South reached a nuclear accord in only six days. The Joint Declaration on the Denuclearization of the Korean Peninsula states that both countries agree not to "test, manufacture, produce, receive, process, store, deploy or use nuclear weapons" or "process nuclear reprocessing and enrichment facilities."[20]

In January 1992, North Korea concluded a safeguards agreement for inspection of its nuclear facilities by the IAEA, another result of a diplomatic initiative. At the end of April, almost everything stood ready for inspections to begin at Yongbyon.

Some observers argue that the fundamental lesson from the negotiations was that diplomacy works when dealing with North Korea about its nuclear program, so such an approach should continue. According to this line of argument, the gradual, nuanced strategy of pressure and incentives had persuaded the North to allow inspections.[21] Other observers argue, however, that the Bush administration had not provided any substantial incentive to the North to truly convince policy makers there to comply fully with the agreement. In fact, they say that the administration's handling of North Korea caused the deadlock that led to the more serious upheavals years later.[22] This line of argument also suggests that North Korea actually wanted to open direct talks with the United States, to obtain assistance to ameliorate its economic problems and to build light water reactors to solve its energy problem.[23] Quite possibly because of a reluctance to show the carrot, the Bush administration preferred to ignore North Korea's true goals.

Analysis of the situation in greater depth suggests that it is very likely that North Korea attempted to use its nuclear program as a bargaining chip to lure the United States into direct talks and into supplying it with light water reactors. The United States and South Korea, however, perceived the nuclear threat to be real. The differences between Washington's and Pyongyang's perceptions of the North's nuclear program stood during this phase as the main obstacles to a genuine resolution of North Korean nuclearization. Administration hawks—among them the national security adviser, Brent Scowcroft, and Under Secretary of State for Political Affairs Arnold Kanter—lobbied hard for military action against North Korea. In a more general sense, the administration had assembled a foreign policy team whose members believed that diplomacy would be wasted on North Korea because its leadership understood only the use of force. This view may have been indicative of a Munich syndrome, a disposition against appeasement of presumably dangerous states. Approaching elections also encouraged the Bush administration to play hardball with North Korea.

From Bush to Clinton

The agreements reached between the two Koreas, along with the North's announcement that it would allow IAEA inspections, represented two quite positive developments in terms of nonproliferation and peace on the Korean Peninsula. As early as February 1992, however, CIA director Gates alleged—and, it turned out, with good reason—that the North had not been honest about its nuclear program. After Pyongyang accepted inspections, the head of the IAEA, Hans Blix, traveled to North Korea in May 1992 for a guided tour of its nuclear facilities in advance of the formal IAEA inspection teams. Although North Korea aimed to show Blix the most nonthreatening aspects of its program, large buildings suspected of being used for processing plutonium turned out to be exactly that. Blix's visit served to confirm suspicions that the North's nuclear weapons program might still be active. Later in 1992 the IAEA revealed that North Korea had not been truthful about its activities. Pyongyang had declared that it had processed ninety grams of plutonium for research purposes only. Analysis by the IAEA, however, revealed that it had processed plutonium at least three times—in 1989, 1990, and 1991. A sample of nuclear waste, supposedly from the separation process, did not match any of the separated plutonium, which led the IAEA to believe that more plutonium than was revealed had to have been produced. Neither the IAEA nor the CIA, however, could determine how much plutonium the North possessed at the time.[24]

In 1993, the dialogue between North Korea and the actors trying to denuclearize it gradually began to collapse. In January, the IAEA began informing the international community that it might ask to inspect two other suspected North Korean sites, an unusual measure for the organization. The CIA provided the IAEA with photographs of certain sites that had not been inspected and that it thought might contain the hidden plutonium. North Korea, as anticipated, rejected further inspections on the grounds that the suspected structures were only conventional military buildings and that permitting further IAEA inspections would be a breach of sovereignty and a threat to North Korean security. The IAEA's desire for additional investigations isolated North Korea and set back the newly developing relations between Pyongyang and the world.

Despite the cooperation agreements between the North and South, by February 1993 growing evidence of the North's undocumented nuclear activities, combined with other events, reduced hopes for an amicable solution to the problem of North Korean nuclearization. In fall 1992, South Korea had revealed evidence of a North Korean spy ring in the ROK. The South Korean Agency for National Security Planning (ANSP) asserted that a conspiracy against the South—involving labor organizations and even lawmakers in the

National Assembly—intended to disrupt its politics to facilitate unification with the North in 1995, an action that was viewed unfavorably in the South. The ANSP alleged that more than 400 people were involved in the spy operation. North Korea rejected the allegations.

Although South Korea had a legitimate right to investigate espionage against it, the timing of the announcement could not have been worse in the context of long-term relations with the North. Bilateral talks and cooperation were canceled and their future prospects significantly damaged. As might have been expected, the suspended Team Spirit military exercises resumed. In spite of the spy ring incident, it is difficult to understand why South Korea and the United States would renew the military exercise. North Korea had long protested Team Spirit and had even used it as an excuse for delaying imminent IAEA inspections. Put simply, the gains hard won by diplomacy were lost as a result of the Team Spirit exercises. In fact, just a day before the exercises began, the "Dear Leader," Kim Jong Il, heightened tensions all around when he ordered that "the whole country, all the people and the entire army shall, on March 9, 1993, switch to a state of readiness for war."[25]

Thus the diplomatic "spring" of 1992 gradually eroded in 1993. After six months of IAEA inspections, the North had obtained no tangible benefits from the process: no economic aid, no direct talks with the United States, no broader dialogue with the South, and no ability to verify that U.S. nuclear weapons had, in fact, been withdrawn from the South. The increasing demands from the IAEA and South Korea to allow short-notice inspections of virtually any military site in North Korea, combined with the spy ring incident and Team Spirit, led some observers to speculate that the South's moves were designed to force the North to back away from negotiations.[26] Despite all of these developments, it is not possible to place full blame for the disintegration of relations in 1993 on South Korea or the United States. The North had apparently violated international agreements and did not want to make additional concessions on denuclearization. The absence of any sign by the United States that it might be interested in rapprochement might also have contributed to the shift toward disintegrating relations. North Korea's actions ultimately influenced U.S. and South Korean policy makers to revert to a hard-line approach.

Withdrawal from the NPT and Reactor Refueling

The Clinton administration inherited a developing crisis in its first days in office. By January 1993, North Korea already had begun maneuvering around IAEA inspections. The administration did not, however, make any significant policy shifts, choosing instead to retain Bush administration policies, which stressed adherence to the NPT. This legalistic approach merely held that North Korea had certain obligations under the NPT and must therefore fulfill them. Direct talks with the North or benefits related to nonproliferation might come if the North complied with inspection requirements.

Secretary of Defense Les Aspin and officials from his office suggested initiating direct contact with Pyongyang in the form of a high-level delegation in early 1993 and offering the North Koreans concrete benefits as incentives to cooperate. They argued that if North Korea still refused to cooperate after getting the carrot, then the United States would use the stick of sanctions and possibly even military action. For the Clinton administration, this represented not appeasement but a rather balanced approach. One U.S. official described the policy as a "sugar-coated ultimatum."[27] President Bill Clinton did not pursue this option at first because it seemed like rewarding the North for not doing something it should have already done. The conservative media and some members of Congress had been attacking the administration for its seemingly left-of-center disposition toward gays in the military, and conservatives argued that perceived weakness in dealing with North Korea was unacceptable among much of the public.

The first crisis for the Clinton administration began in March 1993 when, during the Team Spirit exercises, Pyongyang asserted that such operations endangered nonproliferation efforts and threatened its security. It announced its opposition to additional nuclear inspections on its territory, claiming that the IAEA worked for U.S. interests. That same month, North Korea stated its intention to withdraw from the Nuclear Non-Proliferation Treaty in ninety days. Both the Clinton administration and the South Korean government of Kim Yong Sam were relatively new in March 1993 and not well prepared for such a development, but with the support of South Korea, the United States eased tensions by offering to hold talks with Pyongyang on nuclear issues. In return, North Korea suspended its withdrawal from the NPT in June. Thus the Clinton administration effectively adopted the Defense Department's previously articulated approach of direct, high-level talks, and North Korea attained one of its goals: to sit at the negotiating table with the United States. With this success, the North proposed to relinquish its entire nuclear program in return for light water reactors. The United States acknowledged the North's interest but then stated that it should first comply with IAEA inspections and renew its dialogue with South Korea. The dialogue with the United States continued in 1993 but did not resolve any existing problems. The IAEA continued to have difficulties with North Korea. The IAEA referred the issue to the UN Security Council and even claimed that it would be better for North Korea to be excluded from the NPT than to compromise the treaty's integrity.[28]

The North ignited another crisis as the international community discussed what to do about matters already under review. While ideas about how to punish North Korea for its nuclear program preoccupied leading members of the world community, Pyongyang declared in May 1994 that the reactor would be refueled. This meant removing the existing rods, from which weapons-grade plutonium could then be produced.[29]

The Carrot

In response to North Korea's decision to refuel, in early summer 1994 President Clinton threatened to halt the U.S. dialogue and impose economic sanctions, which would have significantly damaged the North's already terrible economy. He also considered air strikes. The North announced that sanctions would mean war.[30] Before implementing punitive action, the administration decided to take a diplomatic tack. Former president Jimmy Carter had previously communicated to the White House his interest in visiting North Korea to seek a peaceful solution to the looming nuclear crisis. The Reagan and Bush administrations had earlier rejected his requests to travel to North Korea.[31] This time, however, Carter found support in the Oval Office. A White House official referred to Carter's visit as an opportunity for "a face-saving resolution" to the tensions.[32] Clinton did not designate Carter as an official U.S. representative, so he would travel to North Korea with the status of a private citizen. The State Department, however, briefed him and dispatched a career Foreign Service officer to accompany him. State Department spokesperson Michael McCurry pointed out that Carter would not be "carrying any formal message from the United States."[33]

The Carter mission had two primary goals: to defuse the immediate tensions related to the North Korean nuclear program and to jumpstart the talks between the United States and North Korea. Carter left for Pyongyang on June 12, North Korea announced its withdrawal from the IAEA on June 13, and on June 16 the Clinton administration laid out its vision of economic sanctions. Madeleine Albright, the U.S. ambassador to the United Nations, called for restricting arms exports from North Korea, cutting UN assistance, and encouraging further diplomatic isolation. These measures would be followed by economic sanctions if the North did not comply with the IAEA inspection regime. Carter's diplomatic efforts, however, yielded positive results, with North Korea expressing a willingness to freeze its nuclear program and resume high-level talks with the United States. On June 20 the United States sent a letter to Pyongyang officially proposing such talks.[34]

The Carter visit elicited both praise and criticism. Conservatives perceived it as appeasement, and even some Democrats in the administration became outraged when Carter renounced the possible use of sanctions. One point cannot, however, be ignored: Carter's visit prevented the use of force and perhaps a war with enormous costs. According to one State Department official, "If Jimmy Carter had not gone to Korea, we would have been damned close to war."[35] If the prevention of war is the criterion of success, then at least for the short term Carter's mission must be regarded as a success, indeed. Carter's efforts led both sides to conclude that negotiations constituted the best option available to them, but Kim Il Sung's death on July 8 delayed the start of talks that month. They instead began on August 5.

The Agreed Framework and KEDO

On October 21, 1994, the United States and North Korea signed the Agreed Framework to resolve the issues surrounding Pyongyang's nuclear program. The agreement included a bilateral structure for negotiations—which represented a major change in the nature of U.S.–North Korean relations—and was to be implemented in phases, allowing the two sides to assess each other's compliance at each step before moving on to the next. The Agreed Framework required North Korea to undertake the following:

- eliminate its existing capability to produce weapons-grade plutonium
- resume full membership in the NPT, including complying completely with its safeguards agreement with the IAEA, which mandates the inspectors to investigate suspected nuclear waste sites and to place any nuclear material not previously identified under IAEA safeguards
- take steps to consistently execute the Joint Declaration on the Denuclearization of the Korean Peninsula
- engage in a dialogue with the South

The Korean Peninsula Energy Development Organization (KEDO)—a consortium of Japan, South Korea, and the United States officially established in March 1995 to coordinate the agreement—was by 2003 to provide two 1,000 megawatt, light water reactor power plants (priced around $4 billion) and supply North Korea with 500,000 tons of heavy oil annually to compensate for the capacity forfeited by freezing its graphite-modulated reactors. The United States and North Korea agreed to open liaison offices in each other's capitals and reduce barriers to trade and investment. The United States also agreed to provide formal assurances that it would not threaten North Korea with nuclear weapons.[36] North Korean negotiator Kang Sok Ju remarked to his American counterpart, Robert Gallucci, that the North's bargaining chip was continuing production of plutonium and preventing IAEA inspections if the United States did not comply with the agreement. In turn, U.S. leverage rested on the prospect of establishing political and economic ties valuable to North Korea.[37]

The Agreed Framework was a loose agreement in the sense that its implementation was left to the states' own volition. Implementation initially ran rather smoothly. In August 1998, however, North Korea launched over Japan a Taepodong 1 rocket with a range of 1,500 to 2,000 kilometers. Pyongyang announced that the rocket had successfully placed a small satellite into orbit, but that claim was contested by the U.S. Space Command. Japan responded to this invasion of its air space by suspending the signing of a cost-sharing agreement for the Agreed Framework's light water reactor project until November 1998. The development came as a shock to the U.S. intelligence community, which admitted being surprised by North Korea's advances in missile-staging technology. On October 1, 1998, U.S.–North Korean missile talks held in New York made little progress. The United States requested that Pyongyang terminate its missile programs in exchange for the lifting of some remaining economic sanctions. North Korea rejected the proposal, asserting that the lifting of sanctions was implicit in the Agreed Framework.

On November 12, 1998, President Clinton appointed former secretary of defense William Perry as his policy coordinator on North Korea. A policy review that Perry undertook noted that the situation in East Asia was not the same as it had been in 1994, when the Agreed Framework was signed. He observed that the North's missile tests had substantially increased Japanese security concerns and that the passing of North Korea's leadership to Kim Jong Il had created further uncertainty. On a more positive note, the new South Korean president, Kim Dae Jung, had embarked on a policy of engagement with North Korea. Based on his policy review, Perry ultimately devised a two-path strategy. The first path involved a new, comprehensive, and integrated approach to negotiations. In return for the North's full compliance with the NPT, Missile Technology Control Regime, and export of nuclear and missile technologies, Japan, South Korea, and the United States would reduce pressures that the North perceived as threatening. Perry argued that reduction of those threats would give the regime confidence about coexisting with other states in the region. If the North did as it should, according to Perry, the United States should normalize relations and relax sanctions.

Perry's second path focused on what to do if North Korea did not want to cooperate. If there was no chance of continuing relations with the North, the United States would sever relations, contain the threat, and enforce the provisions outlined in the first path.[38] Perry's report also observed that the North had complied with the NPT and had not produced plutonium in the preceding five years, which provided grounds for encouragement about the feasibility of the first path.

Overall, the first five years of the Agreed Framework revealed a mixed record. The North did not advance in producing nuclear weapons, but it did significantly improve its missile technology. The United States supplied crude oil as agreed, but the light water reactors remained far from being finished as scheduled. Maintaining the Agreed Framework was not to be an easy job.

The Critics

Clinton's policy of "engagement" met severe criticism in Congress and from conservative columnists. Critics argued that it was unacceptable to compromise with a so-called rogue state that threatened U.S. allies. From that point of view, unless the North capitulated, coercion in general, sanctions in particular, and even military action would be preferred to negotiation. Moreover, considering North Korea's economic problems, any deal effectively supported an already sinking regime. Putting together a deal such as the Agreed Framework, according to critics, was immoral and set a terrible precedent for other rogue states.[39] In an October 1994 letter to Clinton, four Republicans on the Senate Committee on Foreign Relations summed up the more critical view of policy at the time: "We are left wondering how to distinguish such a deal from U.S. submission to North Korean nuclear blackmail."[40] Other concerns focused on the timing of reciprocal concessions and actions under the framework.

Clinton administration officials and supporters of the Agreed Framework responded that although the United States made some concessions, the outcome, if successful, would meet U.S. strategic objectives. Key achievements for the United States as a result of the agreement were enumerated as follows: (1) being able to estimate the amount of plutonium produced by the North in the past and dismantling any nuclear weapons already produced; (2) convincing North Korea to halt its nuclear program; (3) keeping North Korea within the NPT and its safeguards agreement; (4) enticing the North out of international isolation; and (5) supporting stability and security in the region.[41]

Largely through Ambassador Gallucci, the administration also countered the critics with six arguments. First, the framework did not amount to appeasement or, even worse, submission to blackmail because North Korea had made even more concessions than the United States. Second, the conditions the North agreed to fulfill met U.S. objectives, such as its remaining within the NPT and respecting obligations under the safeguards agreement. Third, the agreement pertained to the North's past nuclear program and aimed to find plutonium already produced. Fourth, whether Pyongyang met the requirements of the safeguards agreement could be verified by IAEA and U.S. assets, and no benefits would be provided before proof of full compliance. Fifth, the agreement needed to be viewed as a compromise, meaning that significant but not unreasonable costs were entailed to obtain such benefits as reduction of the threat of nuclear proliferation and instability in Northeast Asia. Sixth, the agreement set a precedent only to the degree that other situations involve similar elements, an unlikely event.[42]

The United States, like other great powers before it, has tended toward a basic action-reaction pattern: "Our first reaction to somebody's doing something we don't like is to think of doing something unpleasant to them."[43] In partial contrast to that generalization, the Clinton administration's Agreed Framework with North Korea on nuclear proliferation serves as an example of incentive-based diplomacy. Despite some legitimate criticisms, by signing the framework the United States accomplished its immediate goals at a bearable cost. The agreement, despite the political and financial problems of domestic criticism and the cost of supplying crude oil to North Korea, functioned until (for better or worse) President George W. Bush designated North Korea, Iraq, and Iran an "axis of evil" in 2002.

The Policy of George W. Bush

Dialogue with North Korea slowed as the new George W. Bush administration took some time to review policy toward it in early 2001. Although Republicans, including some Bush aides, engaged in harsh rhetoric about the North, after three months of review, the president announced in June 2001 that his administration would stick with the basic outlines of the existing policy in the form of the Agreed Framework. Lobbying by Japan and South Korea, combined with Secretary of State Colin Powell's successful fending off of the more conservative Bush advisers, were influential in bringing about this decision.[44]

Although the administration reaffirmed its intent to supply the two light water reactors that the framework specified in return for North Korea's restraint of its nuclear development, it found domestic opposition to fulfilling that requirement difficult to bear. From the beginning of the administration, some members of Congress and commentators in academia and the media argued repeatedly that one of the two reactors should be replaced with a thermal power station. The reasoning was that nuclear weapons–grade plutonium could be extracted from them. Another, hidden reason might have been the increasing cost of the heavy oil the United States had provided to North Korea since 1995, and which it was slated to continue to provide until the new reactors were completed.

Republican partisans did not want to fund a regime that they believed was hostile to the United States. The South Korean government, which bore 70 percent of the construction costs for the two reactors, maintained its opposition to their replacement with thermal power stations because: (1) that would violate the most critical agreement between the United States and the North; (2) it would further delay the project and result in additional costs; and (3) it would be impossible for North Korea to extract plutonium of nuclear weapons grade from the light water reactors because, although extraction remains theoretically possible, it would not be able to obtain the extremely sophisticated reprocessing technology needed. North Korea also opposed such a change in the Agreed Framework. Although the Bush administration initially gave no indication of a significant change in U.S. policy, the simple act of reviewing the agreement was enough to upset the North. On March 17, 2001, the North Korean Central Broadcasting Station issued the following warning: "If the Bush administration feels it burdensome and troublesome to perform the Geneva Agreed Framework, we don't need to be indefinitely bound by an agreement that is not honored. We will go on our way in case the agreement is not honored."[45] *Rodong Sinmun,* the state-controlled newspaper, observed, "North Korea would take 'countermeasures' if the United States does not perform its obligations under the agreement. We will also demand compensation for the delay in construction of the LWRs [light water reactors]."[46] At the end of 2001, there appeared to be reason to believe that bilateral talks would continue, although the North was suspicious of a renewed dialogue.

Another year of tense relations between the United States and North Korea unfolded in 2002. The attacks of September 11, 2001, on the United States transformed the Bush administration's foreign policy into one that would deal with unfriendly regimes more decisively, and if necessary, unilaterally and forcefully. The watershed event of 2002 for U.S.–North Korean relations occurred on January 29, when President Bush, in his State of the Union address, accused North Korea of being one of three members of a so-called axis of evil that threatened U.S. and even world security. In this highly controversial speech, Bush described North Korea as "a regime arming with missiles and weapons of mass destruction, while starving its citizens. . . . The United States of America will not permit the world's most dangerous regimes to threaten us with the world's most dangerous weapons."[47] Bush's speech sent shock waves around the world, as leaders waited to see what it might mean in practice.

Shortly after the speech, the State Department and the U.S. ambassador to South Korea, Thomas C. Hubbard, insisted that the president's statement did not represent a policy shift. The United States, according to them, remained fully open to resuming bilateral talks with North Korea without any preconditions.

North Korea, however, responded harshly and directly to the speech with rhetoric aimed to match Bush's:

> Mr. Bush's remarks clearly show what the real aim [sic] the U.S. sought when it proposed to resume talks with the DPRK recently. . . . We are sharply watching the United States [sic] moves that have pushed the situation to the brink of war after throwing away even the mask of "dialogue" and "negotiation." . . . The option to strike impudently advocated by the United States is not its monopoly.[48]

Thus, with Bush's speech and Pyongyang's reaction to it, what guarded hopes there were for a renewed diplomatic exchange between the United States and North Korea disappeared, at least for the foreseeable future.

In South Korea and Japan, various political groups accused the United States of destroying the North-South dialogue and threatening the peace in East Asia. Although the State Department, and Secretary Powell himself, asserted on several occasions that the United States was ready to resume a dialogue with North Korea at "any time, any place, or anywhere without preconditions," that did not convince the North Koreans.[49] A memorandum from President Bush stated that he would not certify North Korea's compliance with the Agreed Framework; because of national security considerations, however, Bush waived the provision that would have prohibited Washington from funding KEDO.[50] Continuation of that support under such hostile conditions, however, did not bring North Korea back to the negotiation table.

The United States warned North Korea in August 2002 to comply as soon as possible with IAEA safeguard procedures. The North replied that it would not do so for at least three more years. Developments that fall raised the tension between the United States and North Korea and led to the confrontation that continues today. In October, James Kelly, assistant secretary of state for East Asian and Pacific affairs, visited North Korea and presented U.S. concerns about its nuclear program as well as its ballistic missile program (which at the time the North Koreans themselves had delayed), export of missile components, conventional force posture, human rights violations, and overall humanitarian situation. Kelly informed Pyongyang that a comprehensive settlement addressing these issues might be the way to improve bilateral relations. North Korea called this approach "high-handed and arrogant" and maintained its noncooperative stance.[51]

More important, the United States announced on October 16 that North Korea had admitted to the existence of a clandestine program to enrich uranium (in addition to plutonium) for nuclear weapons, after Kelly had informed the North Koreans that the United States had knowledge of it. Such a serious violation of the Agreed Framework raised immediate and intense reactions around the world. In November, KEDO announced the suspension of oil deliveries, and the IAEA asked North Korea for clarification on its nuclear program. North Korea rejected these demands and announced that because of the halt to KEDO's supply of oil, it would reopen the frozen nuclear reactors to produce electricity. In December, North Korea cut all seals on IAEA surveillance equipment on its nuclear facilities and materials and ordered inspectors out of the country.

North Korea continued to abrogate its international agreements with the announcement of its withdrawal from the NPT on January 10, 2003. The following month, the United States confirmed that North Korea had in December restarted a nuclear reactor previously frozen by the Agreed Framework. The North also conducted two missile tests in February and March 2003.[52] Perhaps most ominous was an incident in which North Korea sent a fighter jet into South Korean airspace and shadowed a U.S. reconnaissance plane.[53]

Trilateral talks among China, North Korea, and the United States in April 2003 and six-party talks (with Japan, Russia, and South Korea) in September 2003 and February 2004 did not bring a resolution to the crisis.[54] Little was produced diplomatically in 2004 and 2005. Leaders of the two nations occasionally railed against each other, while diplomats achieved next to nothing. In August 2004, in response to President Bush's portraying Kim Jong Il as a "tyrant," North Korea described the president as an "imbecile" and a "tyrant that puts Hitler in a shade." Then on September 28, North Korea announced that it had produced another nuclear weapon from eight thousand spent fuel rods for self-defense against U.S. nuclear threats. On September 13, 2005, six-party talks resumed. On September 19, another "historic" statement was issued that North Korea agreed to give up its nuclear activity and rejoin the NPT. This time the good atmosphere did not even survive a day: on September 20, North Korea declared it would not give up its nuclear program if light water reactors were not supplied. This eventually ended the fifth round of six-party talks, without progress, a month later.[55]

The international community experienced a more turbulent year concerning the North Korean nuclear program in 2006. Two major acts by the DPRK shocked observers: on July 4 and 5, the DPRK test-fired seven missiles including a Taepodong 2, whose suspected range covers the western coast of the United States. The UN Security Council responded quickly, on July 15, 2006, with unanimous Resolution 1695, which demanded that North Korea return to the six-party talks without precondition, comply with the September 2005 joint statement "in particular to abandon all nuclear weapons and existing nuclear programmes," and return to the NPT and IAEA safeguards soon. In addition, the Security Council required all member states "to exercise vigilance and prevent missile and missile-related items, materials, goods and technology being transferred to DPRK's missile or WMD programmes."[56]

North Korea's response to the sanctions was even more provocative. On October 9, 2006, North Korea conducted its first nuclear weapon test ever. Sending shock waves around the world, the DPRK administration argued that the test was against "U.S. military hostility." The UN Security Council adopted Resolution 1718, condemning the action and demanding similar compromises from the DPRK. The UN also imposed military and economic sanctions.[57]

There were contending commentaries and intelligence about this test. On October 13, U.S. intelligence asserted that the air sample obtained from the test site contained radioactive material; yet the size of the explosion was less than one kiloton, which is quite small compared to nuclear detonations by other states, which usually ranged from ten to sixty kilotons.[58] On the other hand, a recent comment by CIA director Michael Hayden suggests that the October 2006 test was a failure, and the United States does not recognize North Korea as a nuclear weapon–maintaining state.[59] Obviously, the DPRK conducted some kind of a nuclear detonation, but the success of the test is open to debate.

While the international community was upset by the latest developments in the DPRK's nuclear program and the failure of diplomacy at the six-party talks, the world was stunned, once again, with a new development: on February 13, 2007, "The Third Session of the Fifth Round of the

Six-Party Talks" issued a statement that North Korea had agreed to a new arrangement. According to this, "yet another" historic agreement,

1. The DPRK will shut down and seal the Yongbyon nuclear facility in sixty days, including the reprocessing facility, and invite back IAEA personnel for monitoring and verifications.
2. The DPRK will discuss with other parties a list of all its nuclear programs.
3. The DPRK and the United States will start bilateral talks aimed at solving issues between them and advance toward full diplomatic relations. In this context, the United States will begin the process of removing the DPRK from its state sponsor of terrorism list and terminate its application of the Trading with the Enemy Act to the DPRK.
4. The DPRK and Japan will start bilateral talks aimed at taking steps to normalize their relations.
5. The parties agree to send economic, energy, and humanitarian assistance to the DPRK. Initially, fifty thousand tons of heavy fuel oil will be given to DPRK within the next sixty days.[60]

During 2007 and 2008, there were major developments in the denuclearization of North Korea. In July 2007, North Korea shut down its Yongbyon reactor in return for fuel aid by the South. In June 2008 the country announced it dismantled the cooling tower of the same facility. In return, the United States removed North Korea from its state sponsors of terrorism list. However, with North Korea launching a rocket on April 5, 2009, U.S.–North Korean relations worsened again. Protesting the UN Security Council's condemnation of the rocket launch, North Korea declared it would not participate in six-party talks and would not be bound by any agreement signed before. On May 25, 2009, North Korea made a second nuclear test, generating protests from all around the world.

Critics of George W. Bush's Policies

The international community welcomed the new 2007 agreement, but it was publicly criticized by U.S. policy makers across the political spectrum. The most frequently expressed objection was that, despite the fact that Republicans had voiced their contempt for the Agreed Framework of 1994 for a decade, the new deal that the Bush administration agreed to looked almost identical to it; that is, North Korea would suspend its nuclear program in return for economic and diplomatic incentives by the other parties. Perhaps the only difference was that now North Korea seemed to have achieved greater nuclear capabilities than before. Therefore many analysts asked what had been the use of the confrontation policy that the Bush administration had followed for five years, which simply gave North Korea additional time to build more weapons. A South Korean regional expert's comment was informative: "We have lost four or five years and now we have to start again with North Korea—except the situation is worse because they have now tested a nuclear device."[61]

Critics of the Bush administration were not the only ones dissatisfied with the agreement. John Bolton, a Republican and former U.S. ambassador to the UN, criticized the deal harshly:

> It sends exactly the wrong signal to would-be proliferators around the world: If you hold out long enough and wear down the State Department negotiators, eventually you get rewarded. . . . It makes the [Bush] administration look very weak at a time in Iraq and dealing with Iran it needs to look strong.[62]

Many Republicans in Congress also criticized the deal on similar grounds.

The Bush administration rejected the assertion that the agreement was an example of appeasement because it was based only on staggered incentives. That is, if North Korea did not fulfill the requirements, it would not receive any economic or diplomatic concessions. However, one should also remember that the heavily criticized Agreed Framework was based on similar terms. In sum, it could be argued that the confrontation policy of the Bush administration ended up favoring the North Korean regime. Between 2007 and North Korea's missile and nuclear device tests in 2009, the agreement seemed to work quite well. However, with apparent escalations from the North Korean side, the talks and dismantling of nuclear reactors have been curbed. A solution to the problem seems more difficult than before.

The Obama Administration and North Korea

In the first year of the Obama administration, North Korea did not appear to be at the top of the foreign policy agenda. Obama's election rhetoric (i.e., engagement with hostile nations) suffered a setback with North Korea's second nuclear test. After the inauguration in January 2009, the Obama administration appointed Stephen Bosworth, the former ambassador to South Korea, as the U.S. Special Representative for North Korea Policy, a post he kept until October 2011. Although Secretary of State Hillary Clinton used harsh rhetoric and warned the country, President Obama and his administration seemed only to hope that North Korea would rejoin the six-party talks by itself. Of course, the Obama administration inherited a multiparty diplomatic process from the previous administration that has been suspended due to the North's behavior in early 2009. Yet the administration seemed to focus heavily on other issues, such as Afghanistan and Iraq, and did not seem to pay much attention to the Korean peninsula. Besides, Obama's attitude toward the issue can be seen as softening; he announced the US would not place North Korea on the State Department's list of state sponsors of terrorism because it does not meet the statutory criteria.[63] However, after a crisis over a sunken warship began in 2010 between the North and South, the Obama administration became involved more actively in inter-Korean affairs. Allegedly, North Korea sank a South Korean navy ship and forty-six South Korean sailors died.[64] Although the North rejected accusations against it, South Korea's report on the incident showed that the torpedo parts perfectly matched the North Korean manufacturers'. As a first response, the Obama administration condemned the attack and described it as an act of aggression that challenged international peace and security. Later, the Obama administration intensified its efforts to promote cooperation among the neighboring countries. White House Spokesman Robert Gibbs said that the US believes it is necessary "to intensify their [regional countries] cooperation to safeguard peace and stability in the region against all provocations."[65] In the following months, the Obama administration refused to remove the sanctions on North Korea due to its perceived acts of aggression.

On November 23, 2010, bombardment of a South Korean island, Yeonpyeong, triggered some of the most serious tensions between the South and North since the Korean War ended in 1953. In response, the South fired back and sent a fighter jet to the area.[66] According to some sources, the attack aimed to press regional powers to return to negotiations on the North Korean nuclear program. Following the attack, the White House immediately condemned the North and called on it to "halt its belligerent action."[67] The action by Pyongyang, which suggested that the North was intensifying its efforts to expand its nuclear capacity, constituted a serious challenge for the Obama administration. The attack—and especially its timing—directly challenged Obama's disarmament discourse. The concern that the attack was a signal of the North's acceleration of its nuclear program created a challenge for Obama's policy on gradual global disarmament. According to some analyses, the attack was aimed at getting the attention of Washington, which "turned to a deaf ear to Pyongyang."[68]

On December 17, 2011, the death of Kim Jong Il started a new phase on the Peninsula. Kim Jong Il's youngest son, Kim Jong Un, came into power as the "Great Successor." The first response of the Obama administration was to call on North Korea to let a democratic transition take place.[69] Behind the scenes, the major concern of South Korea and the US was the new leader's possible intention to prove himself through assertive actions.

In February 2012, the Obama administration agreed to continue to provide food aid to North Korea in return for suspension of its nuclear program. However, the positive atmosphere did not last long. Following an unsuccessful rocket launch by North Korea in March, the Obama administration declared that it would not move forward with the food aid program. Ben Rhodes, the spokesman for the National Security Council, asserted that "their efforts to launch a missile clearly demonstrates that they could not be trusted to keep their commitments."[70]

In October 2012, an agreement between the US and South Korea was reached to extend the range of the South's ballistic missiles. Two days after the agreement was reported, the North declared that its missiles now could reach the U.S. mainland. [71]

Recently, in December 2012, North Korea announced that it had successfully launched a satellite into orbit.[72] Also coinciding with the first anniversary of Kim Jong Il's death, this development was perceived as Kim Jong Un's first serious show of strength.

In general, Obama's policy regarding the North Korean nuclear program has been seen by some as indifferent and ineffective. It is very likely that Obama will face further criticisms about his failure to prevent further nuclearization of North Korea.

Conclusion: Options

North Korea's nuclear status has been an issue of varying salience in U.S. foreign policy for the last three decades. Presidents have used a range of tactics, from the stick to the carrot and varying combinations thereof, to cope with North Korea's quest for status as a nuclear power. It is not clear that any particular approach can be labeled an unqualified success. However, the dealings of various administrations with North Korea have one characteristic in common: their inclination to repeat the same mistakes over and over again. "U.S. administrations have a tendency to start from scratch in their dealings with North Korea—and then relearn, step by step, the tortuous lessons."[73]

The George W. Bush administration significantly changed U.S. policy on North Korean nuclear proliferation, replacing engagement with confrontation, which led to the breakdown of bilateral relations and undermined the gains of the Agreed Framework of 1994. North Korea's uncompromising attitude and provocative behavior did not help the situation. Opponents of the Clinton administration's way of dealing with North Korea questioned the likelihood that Pyongyang could be trusted to implement the framework and relinquish its quest for nuclear weapons. The Bush administration's undermining of the Agreed Framework without providing a better alternative, however, hurt the United States and its allies. As North Korean vice foreign minister Kim Gye Gwan noted, North Korea can develop a nuclear arsenal without the limitations of any international agreement or monitoring: "As time passes, our nuclear deterrent continues to grow in quality and quantity."[74] Free from the limitations of the Agreed Framework, North Korea may have quadrupled its arsenal of nuclear weapons.[75] As of 2012, North Korea is estimated to have six to twelve nuclear bombs.

None of the options for the future is without difficulties. One option is to do nothing: accept the North as a nuclear power (as is done with India, Israel, and Pakistan) and hope not to aggravate the situation. That entails the danger of North Korea's further developing long-range missiles that can hit U.S. soil or selling nuclear material to terrorists. North Korea announced in 2012 that it had already developed such capabilities. Moreover, allowing the North to have nuclear weapons would set an unacceptable precedent for future cases of nuclear proliferation. Japan and South Korea, for example, might want to produce such weapons in response to the North Korean threat. The presence of multiple nuclear powers in Asia could lead to an enormously costly war in the region and place China in a difficult position in terms of choosing a side. Countries like Iran may also use North Korea as an example of legitimate nuclear programs.

Second, the North Korean nuclear facilities could be destroyed, if that is still feasible strategically. Such an action might cause collateral damage and radioactive fallout over China, Japan, and South Korea. Third, sanctions and international pressure, led by China, Japan, Russia, and the United States, could eventually pressure North Korea into giving up its nuclear program. The North, however, already is being pressed hard, and escalation of such tactics could lead to another war on the Korean Peninsula.

The fourth option is to try to make the February 2007 deal work in a way that would provide assurances to the North Korean regime about its security and deliver the economic and diplomatic aid that the country desperately needs.

This could fit into President Obama's engagement policy promises during his first election campaign. However, judging from three decades of U.S.–North Korean relations on the nuclear issue, no "carrot policy" seemed to work perfectly. North Korea, as a military dictatorship, prefers the benefits of nuclear deterrence over economic and political gains. The leadership change in North Korea may not lead to the positive developments some expected. Only a North Korean leader who really wants to cooperate can change the outcome. From U.S. foreign policy makers' perspective, North Korea seems to be an unsuccessful example.

Key Actors

George H. W. Bush　First U.S. president to deal with North Korea as a nuclear problem; employed a confrontation policy and avoided direct talks.

George W. Bush　President; publicly referred to the Korean leadership as part of a so-called axis of evil (along with Iran and Iraq), hastening the breakdown of relations and of implementation of the Agreed Framework.

Jimmy Carter　President; actions as a self-appointed ambassador to help ease tensions between the United States and North Korea in summer 1994 led to a resumption of talks that produced the Agreed Framework.

Bill Clinton　President; advocated engagement and direct negotiation with North Korea.

Robert L. Gallucci　Ambassador-at-large and chief U.S. negotiator during the 1994 crisis with North Korea.

International Atomic Energy Agency　UN agency that promotes safe, secure, and peaceful nuclear technologies for member states; active in keeping the North Korean nuclear program in check.

Kim Il Sung　The "Great Leader" of North Korea from 1948 to 1994; chairman of the Korean Workers' Party, which has ruled the country for more than five decades.

Kim Jong Il　The "Dear Leader" of North Korea from 1994 to 2011; successor of Kim Il Sung, his father, and general secretary of the Korean Workers' Party and chairman of the National Defense Committee.

Kim Jong Un　The "Great Successor"; Kim Jong Il's son; leader of North Korea since 2011.

Korean Peninsula Energy Development Organization　Grouping of Japan, South Korea, and the United States, established in 1995 to advance implementation of the Agreed Framework; was to provide North Korea with heavy fuel oil and light water reactors in return for dismantling its nuclear program.

Barack Obama President; criticized for not focusing enough on nuclearization of North Korea.

William J. Perry US–North Korea policy coordinator and special adviser to President Bill Clinton; reviewed North Korean policy in 1999.

Notes

1. David Reese, *The Prospects for North Korea's Survival,* International Institute for Strategic Studies Adelphi Papers, 323 (Oxford: Oxford University Press, 1998).
2. Ibid.
3. "Korea's History/Background," *AsianInfo.org,* www.asianinfo.org/asianinfo/korea/pro-history.htm.
4. "Korean War," *Encyclopedia4u.com,* www.encyclopedia4u.com/k/korean-war.html.
5. "Korean War," *Wikipedia,* en.wikipedia.org/wiki/Korean_War.
6. "Communist Party of Korea," *TheFreeDictionary.com,* encyclopedia.thefree dictionary.com/Korean%20Communist%20Party.
7. Central Intelligence Agency, "North Korea," *World Factbook,* www.cia.gov/cia/publications/factbook/geos/kn.html.
8. May Lee, Associated Press, "Famine May Have Killed Two Million in North Korea," August 19, 1998, www.cnn.com/WORLD/asiapcf/9808/19/nkorea.famine.
9. Facts on International Relations and Security Trends, first.sipri.org/index.php.
10. Reese, *The Prospects for North Korea's Survival,* 42.
11. Walter B. Slocombe, "The Agreed Framework with the Democratic People's Republic of Korea," *Strategic Forum,* 23 (Washington, DC: National Defense University, Institute for National Strategic Studies, 1995), www.ndu.edu/inss/strforum/SF_23/forum23.html.
12. Leon V. Sigal, *Disarming Strangers: Nuclear Diplomacy with North Korea* (Princeton: Princeton University Press, 1998).
13. Ibid.
14. Michael J. Mazarr, *North Korea and the Bomb: A Case Study in Nonproliferation* (New York: St. Martin's Press, 1995), 56–57.
15. Ibid.
16. Ibid.
17. Curtis H. Martin, "The U.S.–North Korean Agreed Framework: Incentives-Based Diplomacy after the Cold War," in *Sanctions as Economic Statecraft: Theory and Practice,* ed. Steve Chan and A. Cooper Drury (New York: St. Martin's Press, 2000).
18. Mazarr, *North Korea and the Bomb.*
19. Reese, *The Prospects for North Korea's Survival,* 45.
20. Ibid., 46.
21. Mazarr, *North Korea and the Bomb.*
22. Sigal, *Disarming Strangers.*
23. In terms of nonproliferation, light water reactors are preferred to the North Korean graphite-modulated reactors because producing the necessary waste for the development of nuclear weapons is much more difficult.
24. Mazarr, *North Korea and the Bomb.*

25. Ibid., 98.

26. Ibid.

27. Ibid., 102.

28. Reese, *The Prospects for North Korea's Survival.*

29. Ibid.

30. Sigal, *Disarming Strangers.*

31. Rod Troester, *Jimmy Carter as Peacemaker: A Post-Presidential Biography* (Westport, CT: Praeger, 1999), 76.

32. D. Jehl, "U.S. Is Pressing Sanctions for North Korea," *New York Times,* June 11, 1994, A7, cited in Troester, *Jimmy Carter,* 76.

33. Stone, "Citizen Carter, the Statesman," *USA Today,* June 15, 1994, A4, as cited in Troester, *Jimmy Carter,* 76.

34. Troester, *Jimmy Carter.*

35. Sigal, *Disarming Strangers,* 132.

36. Thomas L. Wilborn, "Strategic Implications of the U.S.-DPRK Framework Agreement," U.S. Army War College, Washington, DC, April 3, 1995, www.milnet .com/korea/usdprkp1.htm#B22.

37. Reese, *The Prospects for North Korea's Survival.*

38. William J. Perry, "Review of United States Policy toward North Korea: Findings and Recommendations," unclassified report, Washington, DC, October 12, 1999, bcsia .ksg.harvard.edu/publication.cfm?program=CORE&ctype=book&item_id=6.

39. Wilborn, "Strategic Implications."

40. Alfonse D'Amato, Jesse Helms, Mitch McConnell, and Frank Murkowski, October 19, 1994, in Wilborn, "Strategic Implications," 6.

41. Wilborn, "Strategic Implications."

42. Ibid.

43. R. Fisher, *International Conflict for Beginners* (New York: Harper and Row, 1970), as quoted in Martin, "The U.S.–North Korean Agreed Framework."

44. John Diamond, "On Foreign Policy Bush Moving to Clinton Views," *Chicago Tribune,* June 8, 2001.

45. Yonhap News Agency, *North Korea Handbook* (Armonk, NY: M. E. Sharpe, 2003), 553.

46. Ibid.

47. Donald G. Gross, "Riding the Roller-Coaster," *Comparative Connections: An E-Journal on East Asian Bilateral Relations,* April 2002, www.csis.org/pacfor/cc/ 0201Qus_skorea.html.

48. Ibid., 1.

49. Arms Control Agency, "Chronology of U.S.–North Korean Nuclear and Missile Diplomacy," fact sheet, June 2003, www.armscontrol.org/factsheets/dprkchron.asp.

50. Ibid.

51. Ibid.

52. Ibid.

53. Donald G. Gross, "Tensions Escalate in Korea as the U.S. Targets Iraq," *Comparative Connections: An E-Journal on East Asian Bilateral Relations,* April 2003, www .csis.org/pacfor/cc/0301Qus_skorea.html.

54. Donald G. Gross, "In the Eye of the Beholder: Impasse or Progress in the Six-Party Talks?" *Comparative Connections: An E-Journal on East Asian Bilateral Relations,* April 2004, www.csis.org/pacfor/cc/0401Qus_skorea.html.

55. "Timeline: North Korea Nuclear Stand-Off," BBC News, accessed April 9, 2007, news.bbc.co.uk/2/hi/asia-pacific/2604437.stm.

56. "Security Council Condemns Democratic People's Republic of Korea's Missile Launches," *United Nations,* July 15, 2006, www.un.org/News/Press/docs/2006/sc8778 .doc.htm.

57. "Resolution 1718 (2006)," IAEA News Center, October 14, 2006, www.iaea.org/ NewsCenter/Focus/IaeaDprk/unscres_14102006.pdf.

58. Associated Press, "U.S. Confirms North Korea's Nuclear Test," October 16, 2006, www.iht.com/articles/ap/2006/10/16/america/NA_GEN_US_NKorea.php.

59. Lee Jin-woo, "U.S. Judges N. Korean Nuclear Test Failure," *Korea Times,* March 28, 2007, times.hankooki.com/lpage/nation/200703/kt2007032821284011990.htm.

60. Ministry of Foreign Affairs of PRC, "Initial Actions for the Implementation of the Joint Statement," February 13, 2007, www.fmprc.gov.cn/eng/zxxx/t297463.htm.

61. Jun Bong-geun, of the Institute of Foreign Affairs and National Security in Seoul, as quoted in Charles Scanlon, "The End of a Long Confrontation?" BBC News, February 13, 2007, news.bbc.co.uk/2/hi/asia-pacific/6357853.stm.

62. "Rice Calls North Korean Deal 'Important First Step,'" CNN News, February 13, 2007, www.cnn.com/2007/WORLD/asiapcf/02/13/nkorea.talks/index.html.

63. "U.S. Keeps North Korea Off Terror List," *New York Times,* February 23, 2010, www.nytimes.com/2010/02/04/world/asia/04terror.html.

64. "'North Korean Torpedo' Sank South's Navy Ship," BBC News, May 20, 2010, www.bbc.co.uk/news/10129703.

65. Ibid.

66. "North Korea Shells South in Fiercest Attack in Decades," *Reuters,* November 23, 2010, www.reuters.com/article/2010/11/23/us-korea-north-artillery-idUSTRE6AM0Y S20101123.

67. "'Crisis Status' in South Korea After North Shells Island," *New York Times,* November 23, 2010, www.nytimes.com/2010/11/24/world/asia/24korea.html?page wanted=all.

68. Ibid.

69. "Kim Jong Il Dead: White House Reaction," ABC News, December 19, 2011, abcnews.go.com/GMA/video/north-korea-kim-jong-il-dead-white-house-reaction -15186935.

70. "Obama Team: No Food Aid to North Korea," *USA Today,* April 13, 2012, content.usatoday.com/communities/theoval/post/2012/04/obama-aide-no-food-aid-to -north-korea/1#.UNIc3W8z0b0.

71. "North Korea Says Its Missiles Can Reach U.S. Mainland," *New York Times,* October 9, 2012, www.nytimes.com/2012/10/10/world/asia/north-korea-says-its-missiles -can-reach-us-mainland.html.

72. "North Korea Launches Successful Rocket in Face of Criticism," *Guardian,* December 12, 2012, www.guardian.co.uk/world/2012/dec/12/north-korea-launches -rocket.

73. Scanlon, "The End of a Long Confrontation?"

74. Charles L. Pritchard, "What I Saw in North Korea," *New York Times,* January 21, 2004.

75. Ibid.

6 Nonproliferation Policy Crossroads: The US-India Nuclear Cooperation Agreement

Gerald Felix Warburg

Before You Begin

1. How have nuclear nonproliferation issues affected the important US-India relationship over the last forty years?

2. Why did the George W. Bush administration seek to change the status quo on US-India relations?

3. Which national political leaders supported or opposed the US-India nuclear agreement, and why?

4. What were the roles and responsibilities of the Bush administration and Congress in negotiating and ultimately approving the controversial US-India nuclear deal?

5. What special interest groups were involved in lobbying for this deal, and what strategies did they use to convince members of Congress?

6. What have been the results of the US-India nuclear deal, both for the countries involved and in terms of their impact upon global nuclear nonproliferation efforts?

Introduction: A Policy Reversal

Irony abounds in the story of how the George W. Bush administration realized its improbable 2008 victory in securing final congressional approval of the US-India Civil Nuclear Cooperation Initiative. The accord represented a diplomatic coup for Indian Prime Minister Manmohan Singh, granting de facto recognition to India's status as a nuclear weapon power and ending New Delhi's three decades as a pariah on nuclear proliferation issues. For Washington, the concessions on nuclear nonproliferation, made expressly to pursue a new strategic relationship with India, constituted, as a leading journalist noted, "one of the boldest initiatives ever launched by a secretary of state . . . nothing less than a repudiation of three decades of U.S. policy."[1] At the elaborate White House signing ceremony, President Bush shared credit with an emergent Indian-American lobby. Also applauding at the October 8, 2008, event were representatives from General Electric and Westinghouse, eager to secure U.S. nuclear sales to India, touted as having a potential value as high as $150 billion.[2]

Critics concluded that the revolutionary pact "fundamentally reverses half a century of U.S. nonproliferation efforts, undermines attempts to prevent states like Iran and North Korea from acquiring nuclear weapons, and potentially contributes to an arms race in Asia."[3] Opponents maintained that the deal violated essential congressional requirements, failed to restrain India's nuclear weapons program, and appeared as "an unprincipled naked grab for lucrative trade and geopolitical advantage."[4]

The precedents set by the US-India deal were soon tested. Pakistan sought similar nonproliferation exceptions from Washington and then contracted to import nuclear reactors from the Chinese.[5] In resisting UN sanctions on their nuclear program, Iranian negotiators cited India's special treatment, while some nonaligned powers have also charged the agreement constitutes a clear double standard employed by the United States.[6] Japan and Australia debated whether to maintain their own, now eroded, policies prohibiting cooperation with India, justified because New Delhi continued to reject full-scope International Atomic Energy Agency (IAEA) safeguards.

The May 18, 1974, Indian nuclear explosion was the single event, more than any other, that gave rise to a series of congressional initiatives to tighten international export controls, controls weakened by the US-India nuclear agreement completed in 2008. The two events serve as bookends for a generation of nonproliferation laws. It is thus crucial to assess lessons learned from recent US-India nuclear cooperation.

Background: US-India Nuclear Relations

Many U.S. nonproliferation efforts have been designed specifically to thwart the nuclear ambitions of emerging powers such as India. The conflict over nuclear policy accelerated after India's use of civil nuclear assistance from the United States and Canada in the 1950s to clandestinely develop nuclear explosives. It persists with India's present position as a nuclear-armed nation that rejects the Treaty on the Non-Proliferation of Nuclear Weapons (NPT). India's recent emergence as a valued U.S. ally in South Asia—and an important trading partner with growing military connections to the United States—has

Timeline

Key Developments in
US-India Nuclear Relations

1974	India detonates a nuclear explosive device, fabricated in a clandestine program that benefited from U.S.-source material provided years earlier under the Atoms for Peace program.
1978	Congress crafts and President Jimmy Carter signs the Nuclear Non-Proliferation Act, which prohibits nuclear trade with nations such as India, which divert materials to domestic programs not subject to UN inspection.
2001	Al Qaeda-sponsored terrorist attacks against the US lead to a series of U.S. military responses in the Middle East and Southwest Asia. Support from India, the world's most populous democracy, becomes an important Washington objective.
2005	At a Washington summit between U.S. and Indian leaders, the Bush administration outlines a proposed agreement that would advance US-India ties and open the way for nuclear energy technology exports.
April 2006	Secretary of State Condoleezza Rice testifies before the Senate Foreign Relations Committee in support of a new US-India nuclear accord.
Summer 2006	House Foreign Affairs Committee Democrats and Republicans object to the administration proposal that Congress approve an accord yet to be negotiated.
Fall 2006	Congress passes the Hyde Act, establishing goals for the forthcoming accord, but requiring its subsequent submission to Congress for formal approval.
2007	Bush administration negotiations with India on pact terms stall, while U.S.-based interest groups supporting an accord expand targeted U.S. lobbying efforts.
Mid 2008	A change in India's governing coalition frees Prime Minister Singh to conclude an agreement.
September 2008	Bush administration lobbies the multinational Nuclear Supplier Group to accommodate new precedents set by emerging US-India accord.
October 1, 2008	The U.S. Congress approves entry into force of a sweeping new agreement on US-India nuclear cooperation.
October 8, 2008	Bush signs the legislation approving the agreement.

put substantial pressure on decades-old U.S. nonproliferation policies. These were embodied in statutes many believe are now dated.

Policy history is crucial here: In an effort to woo leaders of newly independent India, the United States sent twenty-one tons of heavy water in 1956, while Canada provided reactor technology.[7] India's subsequent detonation of a nuclear device violated, spectacularly, the basic principle of Atoms For Peace, the policy first defined by President Dwight D. Eisenhower in 1953 that committed the United States to sharing nuclear technology, materials, and know-how for peaceful purposes. India's action remains the most egregious abuse of peaceful nuclear assistance. President Richard M. Nixon's emissaries had explicitly warned India against diversion of U.S. nuclear energy assistance for a weapons program.[8] US-India relations had been poor for some time, as a consequence of the tepid U.S. response to Chinese border clashes with India, India's role in the dismemberment of Pakistan, as well as the close relations nonaligned leaders in New Delhi were developing with Moscow. India's May 18, 1974, nuclear weapons test froze in place a breach with Washington that lasted thirty years and spurred sweeping nuclear export reforms in Washington.

These initiatives included efforts led by Representative Jonathan Bingham (D-NY) to abolish the powerful Joint Committee on Atomic Energy that championed nuclear exports; in 1976, Congress scattered its jurisdiction to several panels led by skeptics of unfettered nuclear commerce.[9] Legislators such as Senator John Glenn (D-OH) and Bingham cited Indian abuse of U.S. nuclear assistance as a central rationale for enactment of the 1978 Nuclear Non-Proliferation Act (NNPA) that tightened Atomic Energy Act (AEA) standards for U.S. trade. The NNPA required states seeking U.S. nuclear technology to first accept IAEA inspection of *all* nuclear materials.[10] The measure exhorted nuclear suppliers to exercise restraint, even as they competed for export markets. Nations were discouraged from incentivizing sales by waiving full-scope safeguards requirements or sweetening reactor offers by including the export of weapons-usable technologies.[11]

The 1974 Indian nuclear test proved to be the first of a series of blows to nuclear export markets. Until then, American companies had cornered nearly 90 percent of the market for reactor exports. Foreign competition to adopt least-common-denominator standards was accelerating. To win reactor sales, the French and the West Germans had proposed to include sensitive enrichment and reprocessing facilities capable of producing weapons-grade nuclear material. Surging oil prices and doubts about the reliability of uranium supplies also created pressures to develop fuels based on weapons-usable plutonium.[12]

By the 1980s, new orders for U.S.-built power reactors fell due to a number of reasons, including soaring interest rates and construction costs for such capital-intensive plants, plunging growth rates for energy demand after the 1973 Middle East oil price shocks, the 1979 Three Mile Island nuclear accident, the failure to resolve reactor waste disposal issues, and the growth of anti-nuclear nongovernmental organizations (NGOs).[13]

Through subsequent decades, India's nuclear program colored *all* aspects of its relations with the United States. Although some U.S. allies, including Israel, enjoyed strong Washington relations despite their nuclear ambitions, the Indian psyche was deeply scarred by NNPA and by Nuclear Suppliers Group (NSG) restrictions requiring technologically advanced nations to deny India assistance. For India, post-colonial sensitivities remained a prominent dimension of the national identity; they had no sympathy for the nonproliferation zeal of Washington.[14] The Indian nuclear test also, predictably, produced a nuclear arms race on the subcontinent, accelerating Pakistan's nuclear weapons program, and ultimately climaxing in a series of Indian and Pakistani nuclear tests in 1998.[15] Subsequently, efforts by the Clinton administration to restore dialogue with New Delhi served only to underscore India's insistence that it receive nondiscriminatory treatment as a nuclear weapon state.

President George W. Bush was determined to engage India on new terms. As his key international strategist, Secretary of State Condoleezza Rice argued that the US-India nuclear dispute had produced for a generation "a bedeviled relationship, a structural ambivalence between the world's leading democracy and the world's largest democracy."[16] Bush acted not just because he was encouraged by Rice and other senior advisors to view India as a democratic counterweight to growing Chinese power, but also because the "global war on terror," launched in the fall of 2001, gave new urgency to the U.S. search for allies in South Asia.[17] The genesis of the Bush initiative can be traced back to 2001, when State Department officials—including Counselor Philip D. Zelikow, U.S. Ambassador to India Robert D. Blackwill, and Senior Adviser to the Under Secretary of State for Political Affairs Ashley J. Tellis—outlined in considerable detail the potential benefits of a robust nuclear-armed democratic ally for the United States in South Asia.[18] Also important was the need for U.S. diplomats to have something to offer an anxious New Delhi government after Rice told Pakistan the United States would provide Islamabad advanced fighter planes, as one consequence of US-Pakistan cooperation after the September 11, 2001, attacks. (Rice later wryly observed that India and Pakistan had become "linked as the poster children for crimes against the non-proliferation regime.")[19] Noteworthy in this history is the fact that few U.S. strategists argued rapprochement with India would bring substantial nonproliferation benefits. More than a generation after India's 1974 test, the needs of *realpolitik* spurred President Bush's determination to build a stronger U.S. alliance with India, despite the consequent costs to nonproliferation efforts.

The emerging proposal advanced by the White House in 2005 was quite simple in its central elements. The United States would agree to division of the Indian nuclear complex and engage in routine commerce with the segregated civilian program, which would be placed under IAEA inspection, while accepting the continuation of the uninspected Indian military program. In return, India would endorse NSG export controls and offer private pledges to refrain from further testing of nuclear explosives. India would become a de facto nuclear power, even though it had tested—after the NPT came into force—nuclear explosives developed from "peaceful" international assistance.

Beginning in 2005, critics maintained that a weak US-India nuclear accord could harm nonproliferation efforts by exalting selective nonenforcement. They also worried that U.S. concessions might reward India merely for endorsing export standards all responsible NSG members adopted—and which India has long adhered to as a matter of national self-interest.[20] Renewed international nuclear trade with India also threatened to allot a greater share of limited Indian uranium supplies for its military program, as Indian proponents publicly noted.[21]

The New Bush-Rice Approach

The case of the turbulent US-India nuclear relationship offers a stark illustration of how general multilateral causes, such as nuclear nonproliferation, are often sacrificed to the specific requirements of bilateral diplomacy. By 2005, President Bush felt an acute need to create a "strategic partnership" with India as his administration struggled to maintain international support for prolonged, controversial military engagements in Iraq and Afghanistan.[22] Competing policy-making factions in the executive and legislative branches created tense dichotomies between the sober calculation of the State Department and the ideological passions of veteran arms control advocates—the latter of which Rice would deride as the "high priests of nonproliferation."[23]

Rice aggressively advocated the transformation of US-India relations. Yet by 2005, it also became a presidential initiative. President Bush pushed his negotiating team hard, both before and after the July 2005 summit with Indian leaders.

"How are we coming on India?" President Bush would ask Rice with some frequency during his second term, even at meetings unrelated to South Asia.[24] The fact that political elites in Washington were skeptical may, in fact, have made the risky endeavor more attractive to the notably contrarian president. Bush welcomed the chance to try a different diplomatic approach, a "game-changer," from time to time. Bush led a team staffed by numerous skeptics of the multilateral arms control efforts his predecessors had embraced. Furthermore, in the vigorous Indian democracy, Bush could see both a poster child for his "democracy initiative" as well as a potential counterweight to China.[25]

Rice personalized the negotiations; after they stalled in July 2005, she declared she "wasn't ready to surrender."[26] She pressed Prime Minster Singh directly in a July 18 breakfast meeting at the Willard Hotel in Washington, DC, successfully reopening talks, which yielded further U.S. concessions. In defending the agreement before Congress, Rice would later declare conclusively, "President Bush has made his choice, and it is the correct one."[27]

The White House team gave Indian negotiators what Singh wanted during key bilateral discussions on July 18, 2005. Under acute time pressures—with summit discussions proceeding in the Oval Office even as staff negotiators were deadlocked in the nearby Roosevelt Room—Indian negotiators pressed their U.S. counterparts. According to former senior Bush administration officials, the Indians reportedly insisted, "We need more if we are to sell this deal back home."[28] The more the Indians pushed, the more the U.S. team backpedaled. "The Indians were incredibly greedy that day. They were getting ninety-nine percent of what they asked for," one senior U.S. negotiator conceded to the *Washington Post,* "and still they pushed for one hundred."[29] The Indians rejected an explicit no explosion pledge, reserved numerous facilities as military—off-limits to IAEA inspectors—and balked at making commitments on securing timely action on liability protection, essential before the U.S. nuclear industry could gain access to the Indian nuclear market. Appraising how badly the U.S. team was out-negotiated, one senior Bush appointee subsequently quipped, "It almost makes me glad the Bush team would not sit down with the Iranians or North Korea"—fearing what similar concessions might have ensued.[30]

Why did the U.S. team agree? They relented because President Bush had already made the basic decision to engage India on India's terms. Bush saw this as a matter of U.S. national interest and an opportunity to build an alliance at a time when the U.S. positions in Iraq, Afghanistan, and Pakistan were suffering increased international isolation and domestic opposition. With the costs of a summit negotiation failure apparent, the president apparently concluded that the compromise of abstract nonproliferation principles would gain specific commercial and security benefits from alliance with India. Rice sold an agreement to negotiate on favorable terms to the Indian Prime Minister as "a deal of a lifetime," while Under Secretary of State for Political Affairs Nicholas Burns told India's foreign minister that "the United States wants to take this thirty-year millstone from around your neck."[31] The Indians had walked away from the negotiations, but then the United States made an offer so generous that the Indians could not refuse.

Critics maintained that the Bush administration's push for the deal was driven by President Bush's quest for a legacy. This was an opinion shared by some skeptical Indian officials. The proposed pact was not popular with opposition politicians in India, yet the Indian negotiators often heard from their U.S. counterparts that "the deal had to be completed while Bush was still in office" and that Bush's successor might renege on the deal, or be unable to secure final congressional approval.[32]

The Indians had made clear in 2005 that nondiscriminatory acceptance of their status as a nuclear weapon state was required to improve relations with Washington. The post-9/11 dilemmas the United States faced gave the Washington–New Delhi talks new urgency. Prime Minister Singh embraced the U.S. initiative at some risk to his governing coalition. Nationalist critics in Parliament, as well as India's vocal Communist Party, vigorously opposed India's renewed ties with Washington, claiming, among other things, that it would lead to violations of Indian sovereignty and nonaligned status.

Just as the 1974 Indian test proved damaging to U.S. nuclear exporters, the Bush administration's proposal to reopen the India nuclear market represented the best hope in decades for U.S. nuclear sales. Nuclear power advocates also took heart from the Obama administration's subsequent proposal of billions of dollars in loan guarantees to jumpstart domestic nuclear power sales. One express rationale for such initiatives was to reduce carbon emissions and create more "green" jobs in the United States. As a consequence, the effectiveness of nuclear export controls and the durability of nonproliferation standards will now grow markedly in importance.

The accord outlined in July 2005 provided only the framework for an agreement. Before the agreement could take effect, Congress would have to approve waiving numerous conditions in nonproliferation law in a multistep process. The first step in this process yielded the Henry J. Hyde United States-India Peaceful Atomic Energy Cooperation Act of 2006, commonly known as the

Hyde Act. This measure approved negotiation of a US-India pact that would waive the full-scope IAEA safeguards requirements required by Section 123 of the Atomic Energy Act—while first requiring the president to determine that a number of conditions had been met.

Nearly two years of bilateral negotiations with India followed, along with the alteration of multilateral NSG standards and a second vote by Congress, before the US-India Civil Nuclear Agreement (the "123 Agreement") could enter into force. Critical to U.S. hopes of new reactor sales, India would also have to adopt legislation limiting U.S. manufacturers' liability before nuclear sales could proceed. Each of these developments would ensue at a time of waning popularity for President Bush, demonstrated by the loss of Republican control of both houses of Congress in the fall of 2006, renewed congressional challenges to presidential authority, and heightened U.S. concern about nuclear proliferation in Iran, Pakistan, and North Korea.

Keys to the Lobbying Campaign

How did the Bush team assemble support for the proposed deal waiving nonproliferation requirements for the India accord? Bush administration officials decided early in 2006 that they might as well risk everything, given that the lobbying on Capitol Hill would be difficult under any circumstances considering the sweeping nonproliferation concessions they proposed. Insiders called this element of strategy for dealing with Congress the "big bang" theory.[33] The administration kept congressional leaders in the dark about the details of bilateral negotiations as long as possible. "The agreement had already been made a central part of U.S. foreign policy before we even heard about it," one congressional nonproliferation expert lamented.[34]

Administration strategists made one false start, attempting to sell Congress a proposal to get final legislative approval for an agreement amending Section 123 of the AEA—even though the terms of the agreement had yet to be negotiated. Critics in Congress assailed the proposal; one Democratic House leader (who ultimately voted for the accord) circulated to his colleagues the *Washington Post* account of the July 2005 summit negotiations as an illustration of how badly the U.S. team had been outmaneuvered.[35] Leaks from internal dissenters in the executive branch fueled congressional opposition. Indeed, it was often the nonproliferation benchmarks for US-India negotiations State Department staff had spelled out—but failed to secure—that became congressional critics' talking points. In a House International Relations Committee hearing on May 11, 2006, the proposal for blank check approval was criticized by leading Democrats.[36]

Why then did Congress later that year approve the Hyde Act—authorizing conclusion of an agreement—and then, in the fall of 2008, vote overwhelmingly to pass the final 123 Agreement? Many in Congress were restrained; legislators feared that the diplomatic downsides of rejecting an accord with India outweighed the costs of conditionally permitting it to proceed. Most members wanted better relations with India. A move to kill the deal outright would set back US-India relations for another generation. The fact that Indian Prime Minister Singh faced leftist opprobrium in Parliament just for engaging with the United States also became a selling point on Capitol Hill.

The logic cited by the Bush lobbying team in 2006 went beyond the desire to court India as a regional ally. Administration spokespersons addressed congressional critics head on. Asked about pressures to offer the same deal to such unstable nations as Pakistan, officials said the deal set no enduring precedents, arguing that India has never shared nuclear weapons–usable technology and know-how. Pakistan, on the other hand, has the shameful legacy of A.Q. Khan, who notoriously assisted Iran and North Korea's clandestine nuclear efforts.[37] And what about North Korea and Iran, asked the critics? They are not transparent democracies like India, responded the administration. When Congress asked how weakening critical standards would "enhance" nonproliferation, the Bush team replied that convincing India, a long-standing nuclear power, to embrace NSG export requirements, would do just that.[38]

Given the tortured history of US-India nuclear relations, the challenges facing the Bush administration in securing legislative approval were formidable. As in many international presidential negotiations, bypassing the foreign policy bureaucracy and keeping Congress ill-informed had short-term benefits and long-term costs. When Democrats won majorities in both the House and the Senate in the November 2006 elections, the gauntlet for approving the accord grew longer, requiring elaborate choreography from New Delhi to Washington.

The campaign to get Capitol Hill support for the India nuclear deal minimized interagency consultation. Internal executive branch skeptics were effectively marginalized. Nonproliferation experts within the bureaucracy were excluded from key meetings or vastly outranked and outnumbered.[39] Few of the U.S. negotiators were well-versed in the history of U.S. nuclear nonproliferation laws. Many of the benchmarks proposed by the State Department staff were not accomplished. As noted above, these same unmet standards were used by members of Congress as arguments against approval of the accord.

The key discussions with Congress were led by Rice, who leaned on Under Secretary Burns and Assistant Secretary of State for Legislative Affairs Jeffrey Bergner. Bergner had served for years under Indiana's Senator Richard Lugar, who was the senior Republican on the Senate Committee on Foreign Relations. This panel was initially viewed as the source of the most significant potential opposition, but Bergner, who had previously been the committee's respected staff director, helped to overcome this.

The lobbying ground game evolved, after the initial setback, into a classic campaign. The State Department team sought first to secure support from congressional leadership, then to isolate critics, and finally to minimize legislated conditions. By the summer of 2006, a consensus began to emerge among key legislators supporting a two-step conditional approval process.

Congress works often via a tacit division of labor. A handful of committee chairs and issue experts can shape options and sway scores of votes, especially on technical security matters.[40] For an issue as complex as the US-India nonproliferation policy—one burdened with a long and tortured diplomatic history, but which riled few local constituencies in the US—this phenomenon proved especially true. Accordingly, Bush administration strategists targeted three principal groups of legislators: the House and Senate leadership, committee chairs, and senators weighing presidential bids. These tactics proved sound: Absent a visible deal opponent, a majority in Congress would likely acquiesce.

The State Department team coordinated advocates from three camps. The first consisted of business leaders. Legislators from states with many potential job benefits were visited by General Electric, Westinghouse, and other nuclear suppliers. Lobbyists cited estimates the pact would produce 27,000 U.S. jobs and $150 billion in sales.[41] Their case was reinforced by defense and telecommunications lobbyists, eager for new sales to India. Indian industries hosted a series of visits by U.S. congressional delegations. Washington's largest law/lobbying firm, Patton Boggs, was hired by the US-India Business Council. Robert Blackwill, who left government service in November 2004, soon secured a seven-figure annual lobbying retainer for his consulting firm to lobby Congress to approve the accord. Yet State Department strategists deliberately kept Indian lobbyists from Capitol Hill, fearing their enthusiasm would fuel perceptions that U.S. negotiators had been outmaneuvered.[42]

A second group included veteran India hands and respected global strategists. They argued it was time to "get over" the 1974 test because bringing India into the nuclear fold could advance other U.S. security objectives; to do otherwise was "to cling to a futile principle—isolating India as a nonproliferation punishment—unattached to the reality that the United States needed Indian support on a host of global concerns."[43] Better to have India "inside the tent" directing its fire outward, than the reverse.[44] Bush administration officials orchestrated a sustained series of lobbying visits, letters, and phone calls from U.S. foreign policy establishment leaders designed to encourage congressional approval of the US-India accord. Proponents also made significant use of clean energy arguments for nuclear sales to India, noting that India relies on dirty coal for 70 percent of its electricity needs. With Indian demand projected to double by 2030, carbon emissions could grow sevenfold. The latter argument proved successful in converting holdouts, especially Democrats.[45]

The third set of supporters included Indian-American community leaders. A relatively small cohort representing just 2.2 million U.S. citizens, it nevertheless emerged as a reasonably sophisticated, highly educated, wealthy community just beginning to have an impact. "They were full of good intentions," one senior Bush administration official noted, "but had never done this kind of work before. They were exhilarated; they needed guidance, and they were very helpful."[46] These leaders were steered toward key legislators, stressing U.S. interests in creating a new India relationship. Indian-Americans also hosted substantial fundraisers, including for Senators Richard Lugar, Joseph Biden (D-DE), Hillary Clinton (D-NY), and John Kerry (D-MA).[47]

Also active was the congressional US-India Caucus. Although such caucuses rarely have a significant impact, this one proved effective in mobilizing its 187 members. The Indian-Americans modeled themselves after the aggressive and influential American-Israel Public Affairs Committee. "This is huge," the president of the US-India Business Council declared. "It's the Berlin Wall coming down. It's Nixon in China . . . the bounty is enormous."[48] As a *Washington Post* profile noted,

[lobbying for] the nuclear pact brought together an Indian government that is savvier than ever about playing the Washington game, an Indian-American community that is just coming into its own and powerful business interests that see India as perhaps the single biggest money-making opportunity of the 21st century.[49]

Long-time nonproliferation advocates, such as Representative Edward Markey (D-MA) and Senator Barbara Boxer (D-CA) were unyielding. Opponents maintained that the proposed deal would reward a nation for scorning the NPT while undermining the longstanding international norm requiring full-scope safeguards on nuclear exports to nonnuclear weapon states. Critics pointed out that commercial interests were being used to justify erosion of nuclear export standards—*precisely* the practice that the NNPA had been designed to inhibit. Skeptics noted that the proposed agreement placed no limits on India building new nuclear explosives. It failed to secure IAEA inspection of many Indian nuclear facilities. It did not cap production of fissile material. Indian facilities left unsafeguarded had the capacity to produce fissile material sufficient for an estimated fifty new nuclear bombs each year.

Nevertheless, other nonproliferation champions, from Senators Biden and Kerry, to Representatives Tom Lantos (D-CA) and Howard Berman (D-CA), proved receptive. The administration argued that the NNPA had worked for a generation, buying time and reducing the danger that scores of nations—including Brazil, Argentina, Libya, Syria, Iraq, South Africa, and South Korea—might breach the nuclear threshold. Nevertheless, in the post-9/11 world, they maintained, India could be a strategic ally if brought "inside the club."

Congress's institutional memory rests with its staff. Thus the State Department faced its toughest questions from experts reporting to successive House Foreign Affairs Committee chairmen, Representatives Henry Hyde (R-IL), Lantos, and Berman. "Freelancing staffers steeped in esoteric minutiae sought to create insuperable obstacles," one lobbyist lamented. "They were competing to ask the cleverest questions—all of which missed the central point: the United States *needed* India, and we were better off with India inside the nonproliferation tent than outside."[50] For the State Department, the most worrisome criticism came from Republicans. Rather than trying directly to block the agreement—and thereby take responsibility for the diplomatic consequences—the House sought, before the 2006 election, to approve the negotiation of an agreement with detailed conditions.[51] This reliance on legislative conditionality is typical of many foreign policy struggles. Congressional leaders are reluctant to stand in front of a fast-moving foreign policy train. On most contentious national security issues, Congress opts for conditionality and delay, not outright rejection.[52] This reality supported State Department officials' decision to go for the "big bang" rather than a piecemeal approach to rapprochement with India.

Legislators used procedural options to ensure Congress would have a second look at the detailed agreement after it was negotiated. The Hyde Act set benchmarks, including a ban on plutonium extraction from U.S.-supplied material and an explicit termination of nuclear trade if India tested another nuclear weapon, a provision already in the NNPA, but which members insisted be made explicit in the forthcoming agreement text. The Bush team was irked by the Hyde requirement of yet *another* congressional vote—which would come in 2008, after details of the nuclear trade pact were hammered out. Nevertheless, with this key proviso, the Hyde Act received final congressional approval in November 2006 by a vote of 85–12 in the Senate, following a 330–59 vote in favor in the House earlier that July.

With this conditional victory in hand, the U.S. negotiating team worked with India over two long years to write the detailed text of the 123 Agreement. The executive branch used some of the congressional conditions to limit further U.S. concessions to Indian negotiators. However, U.S. diplomats failed to get explicit Indian agreement on several of the conditions set forth in the Hyde Act. Rather, the negotiators finessed central issues, such as approval for India to reprocess U.S.-source fuel and an automatic nuclear trade cut-off in the event of another Indian nuclear explosion, despite the fact that several veteran State Department aides were concerned from the outset by such U.S. concessions.[53] Rice advised Congress of the intent to terminate U.S. supply if India violated its unilateral testing moratorium, but insisted a binding requirement would constitute a "poison pill" certain to kill the agreement. Indeed, it was likely the Indian Parliament, where Prime Minister Singh governed by a fragile coalition, would reject any such requirement, which would be viewed as an infringement on India's sovereignty.

The breakthrough in US-India negotiations to complete the 123 Agreement was achieved in mid-2008; it came only after changes occurred within India's governing coalition. Leftist opponents of the deal in New Delhi, who felt it conceded too much of India's sovereign program to international inspection, abandoned Singh's government. The move freed Singh's hand just when Bush administration aides saw their last chance to conclude the deal on their watch. Racing against both the clock and review requirements set in law, the pact was completed and hurriedly submitted to Congress for final U.S. approval late in the summer of 2008.[54]

Congressional skeptics, including those who had overcome concerns in 2006 to support the Hyde Act, were infuriated by the emerging Bush administration strategy, which proposed getting the forty-five members of the NSG to waive prohibitions against trade with India before Congress approved the US-India agreement.[55] In September 2008, critics focused once again on the agreement's failure to cap India's unsafeguarded production of plutonium, to place the Indian breeder reactor program under IAEA inspection to insure against diversion of weapons-grade fuel to the military program, or to explicitly state U.S. supply would terminate if India tested another nuclear explosive. The 123 Agreement left to New Delhi sole discretion to decide what future facilities would be inspected. It could free India to use its limited domestic uranium reserves for weapons, but it obliged the United States to help secure alternative uranium supplies for India if there was ever a U.S. supply cut-off.[56]

Ironically, even members of Congress concerned about the unfavorable terms conceded the bill now needed to be acted upon quickly. As Chairman Berman noted, after the NSG's members waived in early September multilateral sanctions against nuclear trade with India, Russian and French firms would have an overwhelming competitive advantage. The NSG vote was preceded by a last-ditch effort by critics to slow final approval; Capitol Hill opponents implored such NSG member states as Austria and Ireland to hold out.[57] Once again, an effective and unusually forceful personal effort by Rice prevailed. In her memoir, she recounts her all-night lobbying-by-phone campaign to secure the unanimous NSG vote required.[58] As John Isaacs, a leading Washington nonproliferation advocate, noted, "The Bush administration exerted unprecedented political pressure at the NSG to clinch the deal, including phone calls from U.S. cabinet members to their counterparts during negotiating sessions."[59]

Once the NSG waived restrictions on commercial trade with India's nuclear program, many felt it was incumbent upon Congress to approve the final agreement. Washington-based opponents sought to build a coalition to block passage. However, signatories on a September 19, 2008, letter to Congress assailing the agreement came from a loosely organized group of arms control NGOs. It called for delay and renegotiation of terms, noting that the conditions set by Congress in 2006 hadn't been met. Representative Edward Markey's denunciation was far more pointed, declaring on the eve of the September 26 roll call vote in the full House,

> With this vote, we are shattering the nonproliferation rules, and the next three countries to march through the broken glass will be Iran, and North Korea, and Pakistan . . . [This] is an absolutely crazy situation for us to be engaging in . . . this deal is ripping [the NPT] foundation up by its roots.[60]

The weaknesses of the agreement that had been negotiated were apparent even to supporters, but it had the power of momentum—joined with the desire of many exhausted members to get out of Washington and onto the campaign trail. A leading opponent later conceded,

> I believe that critics would have accepted the deal if all Indian facilities were opened to international inspections, if there were assurances that India could not use the deal to produce more nuclear weapons [and] if U.S. nuclear cooperation were automatically cut off if India conducts a nuclear test explosion.[61]

A politically weakened Bush team managed once again to gain overwhelming support in Congress for the India deal. Why? Many legislators felt the Congress had *already* spoken on the issue with the 2006 Hyde Act. Members hate to appear to "flip-flop," and a majority accepted the administration argument that U.S. negotiators had pushed the Indians as far as they could go to meet many of the act's benchmarks. Having already gained the benefits—and weathered modest criticism for a "yes" vote in 2006—few legislators saw a reason to vote "no" in 2008. Proponents warned that failure to approve would cause grievous harm to the budding US-India friendship. They argued that a sufficient number of Hyde conditions had been met and that India was on notice that another nuclear test would produce renewed isolation in the international marketplace. In its rush to adjourn, as one authoritative analysis concluded, "Congress failed to adequately review the US-India nuclear cooperation agreement."[62]

Democrats had many foreign policy issues to contrast themselves with Republicans. Arms control and nonproliferation concerns were muted in a campaign centered on the economy and Iraq. By the fall of 2008, most Democratic leaders had already declared support for the deal; privately some conceded a preference for approval that year, before a new administration arrived to face what would have been a thorny unresolved problem.[63] Thus, the White House was successful in achieving an agreement to secure final congressional approval following the election in November, even as most other White House legislative priorities died. Despite their lame duck status, President Bush and Secretary Rice prevailed upon Democratic leaders to expedite approval. They presented legislators with a *fait accompli* and dared Congress to block it.[64] Ironically, the pressure the Bush negotiating team placed most heavily—and effectively—was not on their Indian interlocutors, but on Congress.

Outcome: Ironies Abound in the US-India Nuclear Deal

Many benefits of a new strategic partnership between the United States and India will take decades to develop. Nevertheless, eight years offer sufficient perspective for evaluating the U.S. decision to re-engage India's nuclear program.

Bush officials downplayed the purported nonproliferation benefits of renewing nuclear trade with India; yet they understandably felt they could not speak only of the theoretical geostrategic benefits of closer India ties for fear of appearing to have abandoned nonproliferation concerns. In her 2006 Hill testimony, Secretary Rice delineated potential arms control gains only on page eleven—last among her stated reasons for moving ahead.[65] Similarly, a disconnect occurs in the authorizing legislation: The preamble of the Hyde Act declares that "sustaining the NPT . . . is the keystone of United States nonproliferation policy." The measure proceeds, however, to provide means to reward India for rejecting the NPT.[66]

How then to evaluate the wisdom of the initiative? The US-India deal was advanced primarily to build ties between two democracies—while trying to *contain* the associated damage to worldwide nonproliferation standards. Rice testified that the Bush administration sought to "deepen the U.S.-India strategic partnership; enhance energy security; benefit the environment; create opportunities for U.S. business; and enhance the international nuclear nonproliferation regime."[67] This was a broad U.S. diplomatic initiative that made major nonproliferation concessions in an attempt to realize potential bilateral benefits, including expanded defense and technology trade, cooperation on energy and security issues, and collaboration on antiterrorism initiatives—each of which has, to some degree, occurred.

Against this list of benefits, the challenges created by the US-India deal are numerous. It rewarded India despite its refusal to sign the NPT. This discriminatory double standard codifies a U.S. nonproliferation policy that actually offers two sets of rules—one for friends, one for adversaries. It reversed decades-long U.S. and NSG policies requiring full-scope IAEA inspections as a condition of supply. It secured Indian access to international markets for uranium; India now might choose to dedicate scarce domestic uranium supplies to the stockpiling of weapons-grade material.[68]

Irony is ever-present in the US-India nuclear deal case study. Proponents lamented that India had been "isolated" for decades by the NNPA. Yet that was precisely the objective of U.S. policy for three decades. Insisting on full-scope IAEA inspections remains the centerpiece of crucial U.S. diplomatic campaigns to impose multilateral sanctions on such nations as Iran and North Korea, efforts that were weakened by U.S. inconsistency.

Another irony is the fact that although the United States led the controversial effort to remove barriers to nuclear trade with India, other states have been the principal beneficiaries. French and Russian firms have signed lucrative nuclear contracts in India. Because these exports come from state-owned monopolies, no liability limitations are required from India. U.S. nuclear commerce with India has yet to commence because legislation curbing reactor manufacturers' liability has taken years to work its way through the Indian Parliament, where post-Bhopal fears have made this a major national sovereignty issue.[69] The Indian Parliament has passed a watered-down bill that demonstrably does not meet U.S. manufacturers' concerns.[70] Rice's decision to press for NSG changes helped to get Congress to approve the Bush deal in the short run, but it hurt U.S. firms in the long run.

Many arguments made by proponents of the US-India deal proved weak, especially the alleged nonproliferation benefits. Proponents noted that the deal places 65 percent of Indian nuclear reactors under IAEA inspection. Safeguards, however, require 100 percent application to provide any measure of security against military diversion. The most serious failure of U.S. negotiators remains their unwillingness to balk, in July 2005 or the summer of 2008, at concluding an unsatisfactory deal by insisting on more effective nonproliferation conditions that would proscribe India's nuclear weapons program.

The most compelling argument for pursuing US-India rapprochement is the disutility of continuing to punish India thirty-five years later for *how* India entered the "club" of nuclear weapon–capable nations. After the United States developed nuclear weapons in World War II, several other nations, perceiving existential threats to their survival, followed course. These nations employed a variety of means, and even "responsible" members of the emergent nuclear club—UN Security Council members with whom the United States worked to contain proliferation—engaged in clandestine proliferation, including France with Israel and China with Pakistan.[71] With the development of the NPT regime, U.S. policy makers believed national interests required vigilance in blocking *any* new members of the club. Dual standards were inevitable; hypocrisy was an inescapable byproduct. The United States ignored Israel's nuclear weapons and engaged in nuclear commerce with communist China's energy sector, while shunning democratic India—all because of when and how India acquired a weapons capability. In the proponents' view, the U.S. initiative was required to alter this "unhelpful" status quo.

The post-1974 global nonproliferation sanctions regime—designed to deter any others who might follow New Delhi's course—has served many U.S. interests. It succeeded in limiting how many nations possess nuclear weapons. It bought time, subjecting would-be proliferators to global opprobrium.

The Indian decision made four decades ago to violate its peaceful use commitments remains a reprehensible fact. However, international policies must evolve to recognize new realities. U.S. interests *are* best served by building upon the many common interests that will drive U.S. and Indian policies in the century ahead. These range from reducing greenhouse gas emissions to collaborating on antiterrorist initiatives, from cooperation on Afghanistan and Pakistan issues to containing the power of a one-party China. Looking at the recent US-India nuclear accord in such a broad diplomatic context clarifies the long-term potential of closer US-India ties.

Consider the rapprochement—as Bush loyalists prefer—as parallel, though not comparable, to more momentous policy reversals of the Cold War era.[72] These include President John F. Kennedy's post-Cuban Missile Crisis opening to the Soviet Union and President Nixon's opening to communist China. Intellectual inconsistencies abound in each case. Some similarities, however, are striking. These patterns are discernible and highly relevant to evaluation of the US-India nuclear deal. In each, the White House kept much of its own foreign affairs bureaucracy—and Congress—in the dark, then presented a *fait accompli* to U.S. legislators. Congressional leaders were confronted by enormous pressure not to reverse a new national course set by the president. The Cuban Missile Crisis underscored the urgency of dialogue with adversaries in Moscow. The United States could not forever maintain the fiction that Beijing did not govern China. So, too, one concludes, U.S. policy makers could not cling forever to the notion that the nations that joined the nuclear club *before* 1970—when the NPT entered into force—would enjoy, in perpetuity, privileges denied to such latecomers as India.

Conclusion

Was the pursuit of US-India nuclear rapprochement a good idea? Yes. It was time to move the US-India relationship into the twenty-first century. Painful U.S. nonproliferation concessions were undeniably the cost. Long-term US-India interests in regional and global security issues; in environmental protection; in democracy and antiterrorism; and, indeed, in nuclear nonproliferation—though not necessarily an anti-China condominium—will continue to converge.[73]

Were U.S. interests well-served by the Bush administration negotiators? No. Too often Bush and Rice compromised key points without extracting meaningful Indian concessions. Holding out for a more balanced deal would have been a wiser option, though there should be no illusion that all items on the U.S. wish list were achievable.

Was the Bush administration's strategy well-executed in Washington? Yes. After a false start—with the brazen proposal that Congress give final approval to a pact not yet negotiated—the Bush administration team got the job done. Secretary Rice coordinated a complex, multiplayer lobbying campaign that offers a case study in tough, unrelenting, and effective policy advocacy.

Were the promised commercial benefits realized in a timely fashion? No. More than eight years later, U.S. companies had not completed a single reactor sale to India. True, U.S. military exports to India had grown to nearly $10 billion and commercial deals have been concluded for telecommunications and aviation exports.

Was the agreement a net plus for nonproliferation? No. It eroded standards without securing sufficient parallel benefits. Bush administration officials did not press Congress to approve the agreement on primarily nonproliferation grounds, and they were reluctant to justify the accord on any basis other than improving prospects for long-term diplomatic and security cooperation.

It is easy for scholars and policy makers who have championed nonproliferation standards to find the terms of the US-India agreement wanting. Yet the diplomatic opening the pact facilitated shouldn't be dismissed for what it does *not* do. Critics lament U.S. negotiators' failure to extract Indian support for the NPT, the Comprehensive Nuclear-Test-Ban Treaty (CTBT), or for full-scope IAEA safeguards on the Indian nuclear program. Yet some of these goals were not going to be accepted by Indian negotiators, who had to answer to their own domestic opponents.

Effective diplomacy requires the wisdom to know when to change course. Intellectual consistency can indeed become, as Emerson warned, the "hobgoblin of little minds." U.S. leaders reached out to the Soviet Union at the height of the Cold War. The United States moved grudgingly, more than fifteen years after departing from Vietnam, to restore bilateral trade ties. An eye toward future opportunities required similar realism in considering ways to strengthen US-India ties. That is why one can conclude that US-India rapprochement remains a good idea, but one burdened by flawed negotiations poorly pursued and explained by a U.S. team working under self-imposed deadlines.

A final irony arises from this sober conclusion, one that should serve as a caution to future policy makers. The US-India nuclear deal was pressed by an administration staffed by members of a neoconservative school who embrace unilateralism. "Neo-cons" spent the better part of the past decade scorning multilateral diplomatic initiatives—from the CTBT, to the Anti-Ballistic Missile Treaty, to efforts to combat climate change. Yet it is often international norms the US cites when seeking multilateral support of U.S. national interests. From the Gulf War to the Iraq War, the response to 9/11 to military strikes in Afghanistan and Pakistan, the efforts to block North Korea's nuclear program, and sanctions against Iran, U.S. leaders repeatedly justified international actions with agreed principles of acceptable international behavior.

Those who diminish the NPT complain that some signatories have cheated. This argument misses the point. It was *in response* to such cheating that multilateral sanctions have been applied. Isolation of miscreants has helped in several cases. Libya abandoned its weapons of mass destruction (WMD) program under international pressure. Isolation of Iraq over its alleged nuclear weapons program was central to the Bush administration case in building international support for sanctions. Pressing respect of nonproliferation norms has proved, in many cases, a viable alternative to preventive war or diplomatic capitulation.

Global nuclear nonproliferation efforts are at a crossroads. Dangers posed by increasing carbon emissions now create intense pressure to expand nuclear trade. Even in the wake of the March 2011 Fukushima disaster in Japan, dozens of nations continue to pursue nuclear technology. New burdens were placed on the global nonproliferation regime just as a central pillar was weakened.

Advancing relations between the world's most populous democracy and the world's most powerful democracy made U.S. compromise with India desirable. A tactical nonproliferation retreat by U.S. diplomats was necessary to secure long-term objectives to strengthen bilateral ties. But in the rush to negotiate the accord and secure final congressional approval of the agreement before the end of President George W. Bush's second term, U.S. diplomats and lawmakers failed to secure solid terms and reliable conditions. The flawed US-India nuclear accord became, regrettably, the embodiment of worthy hopes for closer US-India ties. A vote in Congress to reject the agreement became equivalent to rejecting the promise for strengthened bilateral cooperation. As a consequence, the accord has weakened essential nonproliferation standards without yet establishing diplomatic gains sufficient to justify the risks incurred. The initiative was a worthy idea, poorly executed.

Key Actors

President George W. Bush   The driver of U.S. efforts to transform US-India relations. He saw India as a potential strategic partner for the US in South Asia, and was willing to compromise the cause of nuclear nonproliferation to bolster bilateral relations.

Prime Minister Manmohan Singh   Outlined India's positions, securing major concessions from the United States. He later faced opposition from leftists within India's Parliament for supporting the deal and rapprochement with the US.

Secretary of State Condoleezza Rice   Acted as the lead negotiator for the Bush administration in talks with India, engaging directly with Prime Minister Singh. Rice also played a crucial role in advising President Bush and defending the product of the negotiations before Congress.

Representative Henry Hyde   Chairman of the House Foreign Affairs Committee; authored the bill (known therefore as the "Hyde Act") that authorized the conclusion of a US-India nuclear agreement.

Representative Howard Berman   Senior Democrat on the House Committee in 2006; was highly critical of the initial Bush Administration proposal but ultimately supported the final pact.

Senator Joe Biden   Chairman of the Senate Foreign Relations Committee in 2006; was one of several Democratic candidates for president, including **Senator Hillary Clinton** and **Senator Barack Obama**, who supported strong nonproliferation measures yet ultimately decided to endorse the US-India agreement.

**An earlier version of this chapter appeared in the *Nonproliferation Review*. The author wishes to acknowledge most helpful editorial assistance from Max West, Caitlin Carr, and Stephen Schwartz.

Notes

1. Glenn Kessler, "India Nuclear Deal May Face Hard Sell," *Washington Post,* April 3, 2006, 1; Glenn Kessler, *The Confidante: Condoleezza Rice and the Creation of the Bush Legacy* (New York: St Martin's, 2007), 49.

2. President Bush declared, "I appreciate the work of Indian-Americans across the nation." georgewbush-whitehouse.archives.gov/news/releases/2008/10/20081008–4 .html.

3. Jayshree Bajoria and Esther Pan, "The U.S.-India Nuclear Deal," Council on Foreign Relations, November 5, 2010, www.cfr.org/india/us-india-nuclear-deal/p9663.

4. Leonard Weiss, "U.S.-India Nuclear Cooperation: Better Later than Sooner," *Nonproliferation Review* 14 (November 2007), 453.

5. Howard LaFranchi, "U.S. Objects to China-Pakistan Nuclear Deal. Hypocritical?" *The Christian Science Monitor,* June 16, 2010, www.csmonitor.com/USA/Foreign -Policy/2010/0616/US-objects-to-China-Pakistan-nuclear-deal.-Hypocritical.

6. As a senior Iranian official declared, "What the Americans are doing is a double standard. On the one hand, they are depriving an NPT member [Iran] from having peaceful technology, but at the same time they are cooperating with India, which is not a member of the NPT, to their own advantage." See Simon Tisdall, "Tehran Accuses US of Nuclear Double Standard," *Guardian*, July 27, 2005, www.guardian.co.uk/world/2005/jul/28/iran.usa.

7. The Indians used some twenty-one tons of U.S.-supplied heavy water and a Canadian-U.S. (CIRUS) reactor imported in the mid-1950s in their illicit nuclear weapons program.

8. See prepared statement of Senator Alan Cranston for the Senate Committee on Foreign Relations hearing on "Tarapur Nuclear Fuel Export Issue," 96th Cong., 2nd sess. June 18–19, 1980, 8.

9. Bingham's ploy required only majority support in the House Democratic Caucus to bar referral of any legislation to the Committee. See Edward Cowan, "Joint Atomic Panel Stripped of Power," *New York Times*, January 5, 1977, 16.

10. The NNPA followed the discriminatory NPT notion of "grandfathering" existing nuclear weapons states and permitting unsafeguarded military programs in those nations. The independent efforts by Senator Glenn and Representative Bingham built upon several legislative proposals, including, in the House, an amendment by Clement Zablocki (D-WI) and Paul Findley (R-IL) and various proposals by Senators Charles Percy (R-IL), Abraham Ribicoff (D-CT) and Stuart Symington (D-MI).

11. This feature of the NNPA codified the work of the Nuclear Suppliers Group.

12. Sharon Squassoni, "Looking Back: Nuclear Nonproliferation Act of 1978," *Arms Control Today*, December 2008, www.armscontrol.org/print/3470.

13. See Lawrence Wittner, *Confronting the Bomb: A Short History of the World Nuclear Disarmament Movement* (Stanford, CA: Stanford University Press, 2009), 113–77.

14. Weiss argues convincingly that U.S. nonproliferation statutes helped check India's "bomb lobby," especially in the mid-1990s. Weiss, "U.S.-India Nuclear Cooperation," 430.

15. The latter was followed by weak U.S. sanctions, then an unsuccessful Clinton administration regional initiative to engage India, as well as Pakistan. See Saroj Bishoyi, "India-U.S. High Technology Cooperation: Moving Forward," Institute for Defence Studies and Analyses, February 16, 2011, idsa.in/idsacomments/IndiaUSHighTechnology CooperationMovingForward_sbishoyi_160211.

16. Prepared statement of Secretary of State Condoleezza Rice for the Senate Committee on Foreign Relations hearing, "United States-India Peaceful Atomic Energy Cooperation: The Indian Separation Plan and the Administration's Legislative Proposal," 109th Cong., 2nd sess., April 5, 2006, reprinted in Senate Committee on Foreign Relations, "United States-India Peaceful Atomic Energy Cooperation and U.S. Additional Protocol Implementation Act," Report 109–288, July 20, 2006, 110, www.gpo.gov/fdsys/pkg/CRPT-109srpt288/pdf/CRPT-109srpt288.pdf.

17. Rice insists in her voluminous memoir that seeking a counterweight to China was not the principal motivating factor. See Condoleezza Rice, *No Higher Honor: A Memoir of My Years in Washington* (New York: Crown Publishing Group, 2011), 436.

18. Tellis is widely credited with focusing most intently at the State Department on the benefits of improving ties with India. See Ashley J. Tellis, "India as a New Global Power: An Action Agenda for the United States," Carnegie Endowment for International Peace, July 2005, carnegieendowment.org/files/CEIP_India_strategy_2006.FINAL.pdf.

19. Rice, *No Higher Honor,* 437.

20. George Perkovich, "Global Implications of the U.S.-India Deal," *Daedalus* 139 (Winter 2010), 20–31.

21. See, for example, K. Subrahmanyam, "India and the Nuclear Deal," *Times of India,* December 12, 2005, articles.timesofindia.indiatimes.com/2005–12–12/edit-page/27856485_1_nuclear-energy-nuclear-power-nuclear-deal.

22. Scholars note that Congress tends to champion the former, while the executive branch—especially the State Department—supports the latter. See Stanley J. Heginbotham, "Dateline Washington: The Rules of the Games," *Foreign Policy* 53 (Winter 1983–84), 157.

23. Rice, *No Higher Honor,* 437.

24. Former State Department official, personal interview with author, Washington, DC, July 10, 2010.

25. The attraction of "game-changer" moves are discussed throughout George W. Bush, *Decision Points* (New York: Crown Publishing Group, 2010).

26. Rice, *No Higher Honor,* 439.

27. Prepared statement of Secretary of State Condoleezza Rice for the Senate Committee on Foreign Relations hearing, "United States-India Peaceful Atomic Energy Cooperation: The Indian Separation Plan and the Administration's Legislative Proposal."

28. As described by former senior State Department and intelligence community officials, personal interviews with author, Washington, DC, July 8, 2010.

29. Kessler, "India Nuclear Deal May Face Hard Sell."

30. Former senior State Department and intelligence community officials, personal interviews with author, Washington, DC, August 10, 2010.

31. Rice, *No Higher Honor,* 439.

32. John Newhouse, "Diplomacy, Inc.: The Influence of Lobbies on U.S. Foreign Policy," *Foreign Affairs* 88 (May-June/2009), 73–92.

33. Kessler, *The Confidante,* 55.

34. House of Representatives Committee on International Relations, majority and minority staffers, personal interviews with author, Washington, DC, July 21, 2010.

35. Representative Howard Berman, "The U.S.-India Nuclear Deal: Striking the Right Balance," May 8, 2006, www.house.gov/list/speech/ca28_berman/India_nuke.shtml.

36. See, for example, United News of India, "Democrats Spearhead Opposition to U.S.-India Nuclear Deal," May 12, 2006, news.oneindia.in/2006/05/12/democrats-spearhead-opposition-to-us-india-nuclear-deal-1147421922.html.

37. According to House staffers, then-Chairman Tom Lantos (D-CA) insisted that India set "a precedent of one," noting that there is no other democracy with nearly one billion citizens seeking a nuclear deterrent.

38. One maneuver backfired: the State Department failed to respond to pointed congressional inquiries about alleged Indian cooperation with Iranian missile programs until hours before a key vote. Representative Henry Hyde (R-IL) was so incensed that he initially sought a criminal investigation of the failure to meet its legal obligation to keep Congress "fully and currently informed."

39. House of Representatives Committee on International Relations, majority and minority staffers, personal interviews with author, Washington, DC, July 21, 2010.

40. See Gerald Warburg, "Congress: Checking Presidential Power," in *The National Security Enterprise: Navigating the Labyrinth,* ed. Roger Z. George and Harvey Rishikof (Washington, DC: Georgetown University Press, 2011), 233.

41. J. Sri Raman, "The U.S.-India Nuclear Deal—One Year Later," *Bulletin of the Atomic Scientists,* October 1, 2009, www.thebulletin.org/web-edition/features/the-us -india-nuclear-deal-one-year-later.

42. Former State Department official, personal interview with author, Washington, DC, July 10, 2010.

43. Remarks by Dr. Jeffrey Bergner at University of Virginia Frank Batten School of Leadership and Public Policy Forum, November 10, 2011.

44. Effectively pressing this point was former U.S. Ambassador to India Robert Blackwill, on retainer at the BGR lobbying firm. A veteran nonproliferation policymaker noted that Blackwill and colleagues "argued that the rule preventing India from getting United States nuclear technology was an artifact of an earlier epoch, which no longer was relevant." See Leonard S. Spector, interview by Bernard Gwertzman, "Symbolism Tops Substance in US-India Nuclear Agreement," Council on Foreign Relations, July 15, 2008, www.cfr.org/india/symbolism-tops-substance-us-india-nuclear-agreement/p168033.

45. Data cited from the U.S. Energy Information Agency, as quoted in Richard Dobb, "Key Cities," *Foreign Policy* 91 (September/October 2010), 134.

46. Former senior State Department and intelligence community officials, personal interviews with author, July 8, 2010.

47. See Newhouse, "Diplomacy, Inc."

48. Mira Kamdar, "Forget the Israel Lobby. The Hill's Next Big Player is Made in India," *Washington Post,* September 30, 2007, www.washingtonpost.com/wp-dyn/ content/article/2007/09/28/AR2007092801350.html.

49. Ibid.

50. Senior Bush administration State Department official, personal interview with author, Washington, DC, July 6, 2010.

51. Former State Department official, personal interview with author, Washington, DC, July 10, 2010.

52. Consider, for example, congressional consideration of the Taiwan Relations Act and the Panama Canal treaty of 1977, and the 2002 vote authorizing the use of force against Iraq.

53. See Fred McGoldrick, Harold Bengelsdorf, and Lawrence Scheinman, "The U.S.-India Nuclear Deal: Taking Stock," *Arms Control Today,* October 2005, 6–12.

54. Under the NNPA, proposed agreements must be provided to Congress sixty days before voting, a requirement that was waived in the September 2008 legislation approving the U.S.-India nuclear cooperation agreement.

55. Rep. Berman blasted the strategy as "incomprehensible" in an August 5, 2008, letter to Rice; see www.carnegieendowment.org/files/Berman_NSG_letter_to_Rice 20080805.pdf. Remarkably, in recounting these events before a U.S.-Indian industry gathering in Mumbai on September 30, 2011, Principal Deputy Assistant Secretary of State for South and Central Asian Affairs Geoffrey Pyatt reversed the sequence of events, stating that Congress passed the final 123 Agreement *before* the NSG action. See Geoffrey Pyatt, "Taking Stock of the U.S.-India Nuclear Deal," U.S. Department of State, September 30, 2011, www.state.gov/p/sca/rls/rmks/2011/174883.htm.

56. See Leonard Weiss, "India and the NPT," *Strategic Analysis* 34 (March 2010), 255–71.

57. House of Representatives Committee on International Relations, majority and minority staffers, personal interviews with author, Washington, DC, July 21, 2010, and Paul Kerr, "U.S. Nuclear Cooperation with India: Issues for Congress," Congressional Research Service, November 5, 2009.

58. Rice, *No Higher Honor*, 698.

59. John Isaacs, Executive Director, Council for a Livable World, e-mail correspondence with the author, August 28, 2010. See Barry Blechman, et al., "The U.S.-Indian Nuclear Cooperation Agreement: A Bad Deal," letter to members of Congress, September 19, 2010, from the files of the Council for a Livable World.

60. Statement by Representative Edward Markey to the House of Representatives, September 26, 2008, markey.house.gov/press-release/sep-26-2008-markey-breaking -nuclear-rules-india.htm.

61. E-mail correspondence with John Isaacs.

62. Squassoni, "Looking Back: Nuclear Nonproliferation Act of 1978."

63. Senate Foreign Relations committee staffers, personal interviews with author, Washington, DC, July 21, 2010.

64. Ironically, members of Congress supporting a strong NNPA in 1978 employed similar brinksmanship against the executive branch. After a tough draft of the NNPA passed the House of Representatives in 1977, industry lobbyists, working with State Department lawyers, convinced senators to open a number of issues for compromise in an anticipated House-Senate conference. Those pushing for less stringent export controls hoped to wrest control from Senator Glenn over the Senate conference delegation. But Representative Bingham outmaneuvered them; he convinced House leaders to adopt the Senate version of the bill, which was developed independently by Senators Percy and Glenn, by voice vote, thus bypassing conference. The Carter administration was presented a *fait accompli* on a take-it-or-leave-it basis. President Jimmy Carter signed the bill, while taking written exception to several of the stronger provisions.

65. Prepared statement of Secretary of State Condoleezza Rice for the Senate Committee on Foreign Relations hearing, "United States-India Peaceful Atomic Energy Cooperation: The Indian Separation Plan and the Administration's Legislative Proposal," 109th Cong., 2nd sess., April 5, 2006, reprinted in Senate Committee on Foreign Relations, "United States-India Peaceful Atomic Energy Cooperation and U.S. Additional Protocol Implementation Act," Report 109–288, July 20, 2006, 110, www.gpo.gov/ fdsys/pkg/CRPT-109srpt288/pdf/CRPT-109srpt288.pdf.

66. United States-India Nuclear Cooperation Approval and Non-proliferation Enhancement Act, H.R. 5682, 1.

67. Prepared statement of Secretary of State Condoleezza Rice for the Senate Committee on Foreign Relations hearing, "United States-India Peaceful Atomic Energy Cooperation: The Indian Separation Plan and the Administration's Legislative Proposal."

68. Henry Sokolski, executive director of the Nonproliferation Policy Education Center, makes this point in Bajoria and Pan, "The U.S.-India Nuclear Deal."

69. On December 2–3, 1984, a major leak of methyl isocynate gas and other chemicals from a pesticide plant in Bhopal, India, owned by the Indian subsidiary of Union Carbide, killed more than 2,200 people immediately (and perhaps more than 5,000 others soon thereafter) and injured more than 558,000 people overall. Although Union Carbide and the government of India reached an out of court settlement in 1989 totaling $470 million in damages, civil and criminal cases seeking additional compensation and punishment for the employees responsible are still pending in U.S. and Indian courts.

70. See B. Muralidhar Reddy, "PM Proposes Joint Group to Iron out Difficulties for U.S. Nuclear Suppliers," *The Hindu,* November 18, 2011, www.thehindu.com/news/national/article2638487.ece. See also Sharon Squassoni, "The U.S.-Indian Deal and Its Impact," *Arms Control Today,* July/August 2010, www.armscontrol.org/act/2010_07–08/squassoni; Lisa Curtis, "India's Flawed Nuclear Legislation Leaves U.S.-India Partnership Short," Heritage Foundation, August 31, 2010, www.heritage.org/research/reports/2010/08/indias-flawed-nuclear-legislation-leaves-us-india-partnership-short.

71. On French and Chinese proliferation records, see, for example, Seema Gahlaut, "U.S.-India Nuclear Deal Will Strengthen Nonproliferation," *PacNet,* No. 37, Pacific Forum CSIS, August 31, 2005, csis.org/files/media/csis/pubs/pac0537.pdf.

72. Relations with Moscow and Beijing were certainly more crucial than those with India, and it is true New Delhi had few other superpower suitors. Yet the challenges confronting U.S. security interests in the twenty-first century—nuclear arms control in South Asia, greenhouse gases, and terrorism—also involve existential threats.

73. On the limits of a U.S.-India anti-China condominium, see, for example, Harry Harding, "The Evolution of the Strategic Triangle: China, India, and the United States," in *The India-China Relationship: What the United States Needs to Know,* ed. Harry Harding and Francine R. Frankel (New York: Columbia University Press, 2009), 321–50.

7 Hitting the Russian Reset Button: Why Is Cooperation So Hard?

Ralph G. Carter and James M. Scott

Before You Begin

1. Why did the U.S.-Russian relationship deteriorate after the Cold War ended? Why didn't these former adversaries see eye-to-eye?

2. What changed to cause these regimes to reach out to each other? Did policies change, or did leaders?

3. Who initiated this outreach, and why? What was to be the basis of a new and better relationship?

4. What was accomplished in this outreach? Which issues got addressed and which didn't? Why?

5. Why has cooperation proved to be so difficult? What does this case suggest about other contentious relationships?

Introduction

The George W. Bush administration often refused to engage "rogue" or problematic regimes unless preconditions were met, arguing that to engage them without preconditions gave them added legitimacy. In the 2008 presidential campaign, Barack Obama promised a new emphasis on engagement with other international actors. Obama believed the United States should be willing to talk with anyone, and thus his administration would reach out to both friends and enemies. Despite the end of the Cold War, the new friendship between the two former rivals grew increasingly tense after 1991. Shortly after arriving in office, the Obama administration announced its desire to "hit the reset button" on the U.S.-Russian relationship. "Resetting" relations between major powers—and longtime rivals—proved far more difficult than senior administration officials ever imagined.

Background: A Bumpy Post–Cold War Ride

When the Soviet Union dissolved and the Cold War ended in 1991, a brief euphoria was followed by a period marked by missed opportunities and

Timeline

Key Developments in Post–Cold War U.S.-Russian Relations

December 1991	The Soviet Union dissolves, leaving the Russian Federation as the most important component of the old USSR.
1992	The George H. W. Bush administration's foreign assistance package for Russia is seen as "too little, too late" by most Russian elites, some of whom interpret the U.S. offer as an American hope for Russia's economic failure.
1992–1995	NATO alarms the Russians by intervening in the Bosnian civil war against Russia's traditional ally, Serbia. Russia demands to participate in the peacekeeping force in Bosnia following the war's end, and NATO agrees to allow Russian troops as part of the peacekeeping component.
April 1993	New U.S. President Bill Clinton and Russian President Boris Yeltsin create a U.S.-Russian Joint Commission on Economic and Technological Cooperation (the Gore-Chernomyrdin Commission) to coordinate U.S.-Russian cooperative relations.
1997	NATO invites Hungary, Poland, and the Czech Republic to join the alliance. NATO seeks to pacify Russian objections by providing Russia more economic aid and inviting Russia to join the Group of Seven (G-7) major industrial nations.
1999	NATO conducts a bombing campaign against Serbia in response to its ethnic cleansing operations in the Serbian province of Kosovo. With the war's end, Russian peacekeeping troops in Bosnia race into Kosovo and take control of the major international airport there, establishing a presence as peacekeepers without authorization from NATO.
2002	NATO invites former communist Eastern European states Bulgaria, Romania, Slovakia, and Slovenia as well as former Soviet states Latvia, Lithuania, and Estonia to join NATO.
2002–2003	Russia opposes the George W. Bush administration's efforts to get UN authorization for the use of force against Iraq and may have provided Iraq with information on U.S. military plans prior to the 2003 invasion of Iraq.

(continued)

Timeline *(continued)*

Key Developments in Post–Cold War U.S.-Russian Relations

2005	Local Russian security forces in Perm force a three-hour standoff when they demand the right to inspect the military aircraft carrying a delegation of U.S. senators, one of whom is freshman Senator Barack Obama.
2006	Russia hires a U.S. public relations firm to improve its image.
2007–2008	The Bush administration announces an anti–ballistic missile system to be based in Poland and the Czech Republic to protect allies in Europe from a missile attack by a rogue Middle Eastern state. The Russians reply with provocative military maneuvers.
February 2008	The United States recognizes Kosovo's independence from Serbia.
April 2008	NATO invites Albania and Croatia to join the alliance and notes former Soviet republics Georgia and Ukraine will join the alliance at some later date.
August 2008	Russian troops defeat Georgian forces in a five-day war over the status of Georgia's breakaway provinces Abkhazia and South Ossetia.
January 2009	Russian President Dmitry Medvedev calls and writes newly inaugurated U.S. President Barack Obama, seeking to improve U.S.-Russian relations.
February 2009	Russian and U.S. officials sketch out a "reset" agenda, including a New START Treaty, a bilateral commission to coordinate relations, and support for Russia's entry into the World Trade Organization; President Obama and Defense Secretary Robert Gates publicly link Russian assistance on Iran's nuclear weapons program to the planned missile defense system in Poland and the Czech Republic.
April 2009	Obama and Medvedev meet in London for the Group of Twenty (G-20) major economies meeting and profess their desire for a New START Treaty. In Prague, Obama calls for a nuclear-free world.
Summer 2009	Prime Minister Vladimir Putin, Vice President Joe Biden, and State Department officials make a series of statements that alarm the other side.

September 2009	Obama announces the discontinuation of plans for missile defense systems in Poland and the Czech Republic; Medvedev announces that Russia will consider new sanctions against Iran.
December 2009	Obama and Medvedev generally agree on the numbers of warheads and launchers to be allowed under the New START Treaty.
January 2010	The Russians link missile defense issues to the New START Treaty; Romania's announcement that it will host short-range interceptor missiles in the new Obama missile defense system alarms Russian elites.
March 2010	Medvedev and Obama agree to add separate statements to the New START Treaty clarifying their positions regarding missile defense.
April 8, 2010	Obama and Medvedev sign the New START Treaty in Prague.
December 2010—January 2011	Congress approves an agreement allowing U.S.-Russian cooperation in commercial trade in nuclear fuel, technology, and research. The U.S. Senate approves the New START Treaty by a 71–26 vote, while the Russian State Duma approves the treaty by a 350–56 vote.
March 2011	In Moscow, Biden calls for free and fair elections, an end to corruption, and greater protection of civil and political rights in Russia.
October 2011	Russia and China veto a UN Security Council resolution condemning the Syrian regime for violence against the Syrian people and calling for an end to human rights abuses.
February 2012	Russia and China veto another UN Security Council resolution condemning the Syrian regime for violence against the Syrian people. Ten days later the Obama administration announces that it is considering three different options to cut the number of deployed nuclear warheads below the totals in the New START Treaty.
March 2012	Despite protests and allegations of massive fraud, Putin is re-elected as president, and Medvedev takes the post of prime minister.
June 2012	Russia sells combat arms to the Syrian regime. The U.S. House of Representatives passes legislation to sanction Russian officials accused of human rights abuses.

(continued)

Timeline *(continued)*

Key Developments in Post–Cold War U.S.-Russian Relations

July 2012	Russia sends eleven warships carrying hundreds of marines to its naval base in Tartus, Syria. Russia and China veto another UN Security Council resolution authorizing sanctions on Syria. Russia announces it is in negotiations to establish naval bases in Cuba, the Seychelles, and Vietnam.
August 2012	Russia announces the addition of 600 new combat aircraft and 1,000 combat helicopters to its military arsenal and signs an agreement to sell Iraq $4.2 billion in new arms, making Russia Iraq's number two arms supplier after the United States. Three members of the punk band Pussy Riot are convicted of hooliganism for their anti-Putin demonstration in a Moscow church and sentenced to two years in prison. Russia joins the WTO with U.S. support.
September 2012	Russia forgives North Korean debts. Putin orders major Russian corporations doing business abroad not to provide information to foreign regulators without Moscow's permission. As Russian officials accuse U.S. officials of meddling in Russian domestic politics, USAID is ordered to cease funding civil society groups in Russia, including the largest Russian election monitoring organization. Putin endorses Obama for re-election over Governor Mitt Romney.
October 2012	Russia orders UNICEF to cease its operations in Russia by the end of the year. An immigrant from Kazakhstan is indicted in New York for illegally exporting electronic microchips to the Russian military. Russia announces it will not renew the Nunn-Lugar Cooperative Threat Reduction Program when it expires in 2013. The State Duma holds hearings on U.S. human rights abuses.
December 2012	Putin calls for an end to the Syrian civil war but continues to oppose outside military intervention. The US repeals the 1974 Jackson-Vanik amendment and normalizes trade with Russia and Moldova; the act includes sanctions on Russian officials responsible for the death in prison of Sergei Magnitsky, who exposed a $230 million tax fraud. Russian lawmakers respond with legislation to prohibit the adoption of Russian orphans by Americans, effective January 1, 2013.

misperceptions.[1] Facing economic collapse, Russians expected significant foreign assistance as a "reward" from the capitalist West for abandoning communist ideology. While some aid was forthcoming, particularly from Germany, the amount of U.S. aid provided was widely perceived as too little, too late by Russian elites. President George H.W. Bush and other senior U.S. officials felt it would not be prudent to engage Russia with a large infusion of foreign aid until the true colors of the new regime had been revealed. Although President Boris Yeltsin proclaimed his friendship with the United States, other Russian elites called for a reestablishment of the former Russian empire, and some Russian military officials said the U.S. aim was to cripple the new Russian regime so it could never be a rival again. Thus, in a very short time, the seeds of mistrust had been planted.

At a summit conference in Vancouver in April 1993, new president Bill Clinton and Yeltsin agreed to the creation of a U.S.-Russian Joint Commission on Economic and Technological Cooperation, to be led by U.S. Vice President Al Gore and Russian Prime Minister Viktor Chernomyrdin.[2] With that structure in place, Clinton delegated Russian issues to Gore and the commission, and except for moments of attention to a few major issues, Clinton's personal approach to Russian concerns became almost one of benign neglect.

Post–Cold War alliance politics quickly became a point of friction. When the Soviet Union dissolved, its military alliance—the Warsaw Pact—did as well, and the Russians could not understand why NATO continued as before. In the 1992–1995 Bosnian civil war, NATO began out-of-area operations for the first time. As a historical ally of the Serbs, the Russians were upset when NATO launched air strikes against Serbian forces and then sent peacekeeping forces to Bosnia after the war.[3] Russian troops were subsequently allowed to participate in the NATO peacekeeping mission in Bosnia.[4]

In 1997, NATO invited three former Warsaw Pact members—Poland, the Czech Republic, and Hungary—to join the alliance.[5] NATO's goal was to preserve and institutionalize democratic reforms in those states, but Russians perceived an anti-Russian alliance creeping closer to their borders. American and NATO leaders sought to assuage Russian concerns by increasing economic assistance to Russia and inviting Russia to participate as a nonvoting member in the Group of Seven (G-7) advanced industrial countries. With Russia's inclusion, the G-7 became known as the G-8, and the three former Warsaw Pact members formally joined NATO in 1999.

In 1999, NATO engaged in a bombing campaign against the Serbian-dominated Yugoslavian government in the war over the Serbian province of Kosovo, which the Russian government bitterly opposed. Following a cease-fire, Russian peacekeeping troops in Bosnia entered Kosovo and took up an unauthorized presence at its main international airport.[6] Russian foreign policy makers saw a link between the Kosovo operation and a possible future NATO intervention in Chechnya, a breakaway Islamic province where the Russian army was accused of serious human rights violations. New Russian president Vladimir Putin's harsh military response to crush the Chechen militants was not challenged by the United States following September 11, 2001, as new U.S. President George W. Bush accepted Putin's definition of Chechen militants as Islamic terrorists and thus part of Bush's call for a global war on terrorism.

In spite of some common interests in the global war on terrorism, U.S.-Russian relations deteriorated further during the Bush years. NATO expansion arose again. Despite strong objections from Russia, in 2002 the former communist states of Bulgaria, Romania, Slovakia, and Slovenia were invited to join NATO, as were Estonia, Latvia, and Lithuania—three former republics of the Soviet Union. Those seven states became new NATO members in 2004, and NATO planned for further expansion by inviting in Albania and Croatia in 2007 (they joined in 2009). President Bush pushed for former Soviet republics Ukraine and Georgia to be included as well, but Russian opposition led to an indefinite postponement of their membership.[7]

Other national security differences arose over Iraq and Iran. Fears of an emerging unipolar world dominated by the US led Russia to oppose the Bush Doctrine of preemptive military strikes and join with France and China to block a UN Security Council resolution authorizing the use of force against Iraq in 2002.[8] During the 2003 intervention in Iraq, reports indicated that Russian diplomats even forwarded information on U.S. military strategy and troop movements to Saddam Hussein's regime.[9] Moreover, as George W. Bush pushed for tighter economic sanctions against Iran to limit its nuclear program, Putin resisted such sanctions, perhaps in part due to the many Russian commercial contracts with Iran—including Russia's construction of a nuclear reactor there.[10] When Bush proposed an antiballistic missile (ABM) defense system to protect Europe from long-range, intercontinental ballistic missiles (ICBMs) launched by Iran, Putin viewed it as a threat to Russian national security and proposed that the ABM system be relocated to Azerbaijan, a former Soviet republic closer to Iran.[11]

These and other tensions continued in 2008, with Putin threatening to target missiles at the Ukrainian capital if it joined NATO and Russia engaging in a series of provocative flights near NATO airspace and over U.S. naval vessels.

As Russia refused to support new sanctions against Iran, the US refused to finalize a treaty sharing the lucrative business of storing spent civilian nuclear fuel. On the campaign trail, 2008 presidential hopefuls John McCain, Hillary Clinton, and Barack Obama all criticized President Bush for being too soft on Putin for his actions abroad and repression of human rights at home.[12] After the Russians invaded Georgia in August 2008 to protect the separatist enclaves of Abkhazia and South Ossetia from a Georgian military advance, both candidates Obama and McCain called for a ceasefire and UN Security Council action, and Obama called for Russia to respect Georgian territory.[13]

In sum, as President-elect Obama prepared to enter office, U.S.-Russian relations were deteriorating. Although Konstantin Kosachev, a Russian parliamentarian, optimistically said "Barack Obama. . . . [is] not infected with any Cold War phobias,"[14] even Obama had personally experienced new U.S.-Russian tensions as a freshman senator in 2005. On his first trip to Russia with members of the Senate Foreign Relations Committee, Russian security forces in the city of Perm demanded the right to board and inspect their U.S. military aircraft. The senators refused, and a three-hour standoff ensued before Washington and Moscow officials defused the situation, for which the Russian Foreign Ministry later apologized.[15] By 2006, the Russian government realized its image in the United States was so poor it hired a public relations firm to try to create a more positive image.[16] Yet while the Russians sought to present a better image, their actions often alarmed the West. President Medvedev later said that by late 2008 "I felt that we had reached a dead end and had almost slid to the level of a Cold War."[17] For Obama, the question was how to reverse the trend.

Phase I: Courtship, January 2009–Mid-March 2009

President Obama was inaugurated on January 20, 2009. Less than a week later, Dmitry Medvedev called him and suggested that two "young, new presidents" should be able to work together. Medvedev followed up the call with an eight-page letter to Obama and another phone call to discuss substantive issues affecting U.S.-Russian relations. Obama's initial response was to list Iran's nuclear program, nuclear proliferation, and Middle East matters as issues where their interests coincided.[18] On February 7, at an international security conference in Munich, Vice President Joe Biden said the Obama administration wanted to "press the reset button" on relations with Russia.

"The last few years have seen a dangerous drift in relations between Russia and members of our alliance," he added. "The U.S. and Russia can disagree but still work together where its interests coincide."[19] Later, at the Munich conference, Biden met with Russian Deputy Foreign Minister Sergei Ivanov, who asked if the "reset" initiative was real. Biden assured him it was, and the two then had a substantive discussion of the issues involved in Afghanistan, Iran, and arms control.[20] In February, Under Secretary of State (and former ambassador to Russia) William Burns met with Russian leaders and agreed on major elements of a "reset" agenda: a new treaty to replace the expiring Strategic Arms Reduction Treaty (START), re-creating bilateral committees to promote cooperation similar to those of the Gore-Chernomyrdin Commission, and U.S. support for Russia's entry into the World Trade Organization (WTO). Burns added that if the Russians could help reduce the threat from Iran's nuclear weapons program, the need for an ABM system in Europe could be reconsidered.

Yet beyond these positives, there were obstacles to overcome. The United States would have to overlook the fact that Russia had offered Kyrgyzstan $2.1 billion to put the Manas airbase off-limits for the resupply of NATO forces in Afghanistan. (Putin offered NATO an overland route to Afghanistan through Russia, which could put resupply at risk of Russian interference or blockage. Only a subsequent U.S. offer to increase aid to Kyrgyzstan renewed the U.S. right to use the airbase.) Also, Russia's repression of human rights (such as the suppression of dissidents, murder of opposition journalists, etc.) would have to be overlooked or decoupled from the "reset" initiative. Reports also indicated that Russia was making military preparations to "finish the job" of regime change in Georgia by toppling the government of Mikheil Saakashvili by force the following summer. Finally, the plummeting Russian economy could mobilize public opposition to the Medvedev/Putin regime and deprive Russia of the funds to undertake new initiatives.[21]

Despite these potential obstacles, the momentum was still positive. In mid-February, Obama sent Medvedev a letter offering to reconsider the Polish/Czech ABM system if Russia could help with the issue of Iran's nuclear program, a proposal reinforced by Secretary of Defense Robert Gates during a NATO defense ministers' meeting in Krakow that month.[22] The Russians responded by placing a hold on the delivery of an S-300 antiaircraft missile system Iran had already contracted to purchase from Russia.[23] On March 1, Medvedev optimistically told reporters in Spain that he expected the United States and Russia to deal with the issue of missile defense in Europe "in a more inventive and partnership-like" way now that the new administration was in place.[24] By the end of February, Obama administration officials were putting together a formal package of potential issues that would structure U.S.-Russian relations on a firmer foundation.[25]

These positive statements generated pushback from critics at home, and both Obama and Medvedev held press conferences on March 1 to clarify their positions. Obama said that any decision about missile defense in Europe would be based on estimations of Iran's threat to Europe, not on any deal with Russia. He said the United States remained steadfast in its position of defending Poland and the Czech Republic from missile attacks with shorter-range Patriot missile batteries, even if the Bush administration's more ambitious long-range missile defense program was scrapped. For his part, Medvedev told reporters that Russia would continue building a nuclear reactor in Iran and continue opposing harsher sanctions against the Iranian regime; he also denied that there was a deal in which the Russians would change their position in return for a favorable decision on missile defense in Europe.[26]

On March 5, 2009, NATO foreign ministers met in Geneva and decided to resume relations between NATO and Russia, which had been broken off following the August 2008 war with Georgia. The next day in Geneva, Secretary of State Clinton met Russian Foreign Minister Sergei Lavrov for the first time. Clinton talked of the need for a "fresh start" in U.S.-Russian relations, and identified a potential "reset" agenda including Iran's nuclear program, the ABM system in Poland and the Czech Republic, Afghanistan, START, and NATO expansion.[27] Their two hours of talks began awkwardly as Clinton presented Lavrov a symbolic reset button as a gift, but State Department translators had gotten the Russian word for "reset" wrong. Instead, it was identified as the "overloaded" or "overcharged" button rather than the "reset" button. Both laughed off the somewhat prophetic incident.[28] Clinton said that both sides needed to "translate words into deeds." While Lavrov agreed, he also took the opportunity to criticize U.S. recognition of Kosovo and defend Russia's sale of missile components to Iran.[29] In contrast, in mid-March Medvedev told visiting American scholars that the recent successful Iranian launch of a satellite was alarming for both the US and Russian governments. At about that same time, reports surfaced that the Obama administration was considering delaying NATO membership for Ukraine and Georgia and pushing for repeal of the Jackson-Vanik Amendment, which imposed U.S. trade sanctions on Russia and other countries accused of human rights violations.[30] Thus the momentum of the "reset" initiative still seemed positive.

Phase II: Reality Sets In, Mid-March–July 2009

Beginning in mid- to late March, pessimistic signals seemed as likely as more optimistic ones. On March 17, Medvedev announced that Russia would begin a large-scale military rearmament program and would upgrade Russia's nuclear forces beginning as soon as the START agreement expired in December 2009.[31] Three days later, while Medvedev stated that he was hoping the Obama administration would live up to its pledge to "reset" relations, the Russian deputy foreign minister told reporters that the European ABM issue had to be linked to START negotiations.[32] Just a few days later in Brussels, Foreign Minister Lavrov told a group of current and past European policy makers that the West had lied to Russia and that NATO was still a threat to Russia and should be replaced by the Organization for Security and Cooperation in Europe (OSCE). He cautioned against too many demands on Russia, noting that there were plenty of customers in Asia for the Russian natural gas now purchased by Europeans. He finished his remarks by questioning the assumption that Iran's nuclear program was meant for military purposes.[33]

Amid these more ominous tones, Obama and Medvedev met during the G-20 economic summit in London, where they renewed their pledge to complete an arms treaty to replace START when it expired in December.[34] On April 5, Obama used an opportunity in Prague to issue the call for a nuclear-free world.[35] However, just two weeks after the G-20 meeting, Russia sent thousands of troops, with air and armor support, to Abkhazia and Ossetia; added an additional deployment in early June; and conducted large-scale military exercises close to the Georgian border in late June.[36] At the same time, Russia used its power as one of the permanent members of the UN Security Council to veto a resolution extending the stay of UN peacekeepers in Georgia.[37] NATO responded with joint military exercises with Georgian forces, which Russian leaders immediately denounced.[38] One Russian diplomat ticked off a list of Russian grievances to Western visitors, including the failure to provide significant aid during the 1990s, support for Chechen "terrorists" after September 11, NATO's expansion to Russia's borders, and provocative missile defense system plans for Poland and the Czech Republic.[39] Thus, on the eve of a planned summit conference between Obama and Medvedev in Moscow, tensions were growing.

The Moscow summit began on July 6, 2009, just one day after the Russian military exercises on the Georgian border ended. Obama sought to reestablish momentum toward the "reset," as well as play on potential dissension or competition between President Medvedev and Prime Minister Putin, in part by casting Medvedev as the reasonable partner and Putin as the obstructionist.[40] However, as a veteran journalist reported, although Obama and his advisers sought to treat Medvedev as a Russian version of Obama, other indicators pointed to the Medvedev-Putin strategy as a high-level "good cop—bad cop" pair.[41] At the same time, Obama delivered a grim message about the road to a meaningful reset. While urging progress on nuclear arms and other matters, Obama also pressed Medvedev to respect Georgia's territorial integrity and said the United States did not accept the idea of a privileged position or sphere of influence for Russia among the former Soviet republics.[42] In response, Medvedev praised Obama's new approach to diplomacy without making any concessions, while Putin challenged Obama with a list of slights and grievances.[43] Just a week after the summit, both the United States and Russia conducted military exercises near Georgia (with the United States coordinating with the Georgian military), even as UN peacekeepers left Georgia, where they had been stationed for sixteen years to help reinforce the cease-fire between Russia and Georgia.[44] Hence, by mid-summer, optimism over a speedy "reset" in relations had given way to the realities of cold, hard interests and diverging perspectives.

Phase III: Fault Lines Reappear, July–August 2009

In the aftermath of the Moscow summit, efforts toward resetting U.S.-Russian relations entered a third phase, in which both presidents contended with a complex set of conflicting interests and cross-pressures. Both presidents found themselves struggling to balance pressures at home and from abroad, while maintaining positive momentum toward resetting U.S.-Russian relations.

One issue concerned countries around Russia's perimeter. Just two weeks after the Moscow summit, Mikheil Saakashvili, Georgia's president, asked the United States for advanced defensive weapons in the face of Russian troops massed in Abkhazia and South Ossetia. While the Obama administration did not make such a commitment, the news did little to ease the growing tensions.[45] At the same time, Lech Walesa and Václav Havel, the well-known former leaders of Poland and the Czech Republic, sent an open letter to Obama, urging him not to forget Eastern Europe in the process of "resetting" relations with Russia. These highly regarded individuals articulated the growing concern in countries of the region that Russia's needs—and U.S. interests in improved relations and progress on arms control—would be prioritized above the rest of the region.[46]

The United States responded in several ways. In one track, administration officials painted an optimistic and reassuring picture of progress. For example, U.S. diplomats told the House Foreign Affairs Subcommittee on Europe that the Obama administration was open to the idea of possible Russian admission to NATO; stressed that NATO was neither an anti-Russian alliance nor a strategic threat to Russia; and noted that Russia made it clear that it wanted to cooperate with NATO despite differences over Ukraine and Georgia.[47] Alexander Vershbow, assistant secretary of defense for International Security Affairs, told a hearing of the House Armed Services Committee that the Obama-Medvedev summit had gone better than anticipated, stressing agreements to allow shipments of both lethal and nonlethal cargoes across Russian airspace to resupply NATO forces in Afghanistan and pledges of cooperation on nuclear nonproliferation as examples. Vice Adm. James A. Winnefeld Jr., director for strategic plans and policy for the U.S. Joint Chiefs of Staff (JCS), told the committee that these and other summit agreements would improve military-to-military cooperation with the Russians and help reduce tendencies to see the U.S.-Russian military relationship in zero-sum terms. Vershbow also announced that a U.S. military team had traveled to Russia for discussions on the establishment of an early warning system in Russia to evaluate missile threats from places like Iran and North Korea. According to Vershbow, these discussions were partly intended to reduce paranoia and worst-case scenario assumptions among Russian elites about U.S. actions and intentions in Europe.[48]

At the same time, Vice President Joe Biden was dispatched to Georgia and Ukraine, where he delivered a number of key messages. In Kiev, Biden told his hosts, "As we reset the relationship with Russia, we reaffirm our commitment to an independent Ukraine."[49] Biden also renewed U.S. support for Ukraine's entry into NATO. However, he also urged Ukrainian leaders to end their factional infighting and commit to a package of political and economic reforms recommended by the International Monetary Fund and Western governments.[50] In Georgia, Biden sharply criticized Russia's military intervention and expressed U.S. support, but also stressed the U.S. view that Georgia could not pursue a military solution to the problem. He also urged speedier democratic reforms, and offered further U.S. support for Georgia's entry into NATO, saying, "We understand that Georgia wants to join NATO. We fully support that aspiration."[51]

Biden sparked controversy in his post-visit remarks to the press. In typical fashion, the vice president was especially candid, telling the *Wall Street Journal* that while it would be unwise to embarrass them publicly, Russia's poor economy gave its leaders little choice but to go along with the U.S. position on a START extension. As Biden put it,

> [They] have a shrinking population base, they have a withering economy, they have a banking sector and structure that is not likely to be able to withstand the next 15 years, they're in a situation where the world is changing before them and they're clinging to something in the past that is not sustainable.[52]

Not surprisingly, Russian newspapers and Russian leaders strongly objected to Biden's remarks. Secretary Clinton tried to downplay the comments, noting that the Obama administration considered Russia a great power. Clinton also said, "Every country faces challenges. We have our own challenges, Russia has their challenges. There are certain issues that Russia has to deal with on its own."[53] In another signal that revealed the delicate balancing act in which the Obama administration was engaged, the State Department's daily press briefing on July 27, 2009, announced that the Obama administration was pursuing high-level reengagement discussions with the governments of China and India, with structured presidential and secretarial participation—just like the approach to the Russians at the Moscow Summit on July 6–8. Russian leaders interpreted this as a signal that closer U.S.-Chinese and U.S.-Indian relations would lessen the American need for closer ties with Russia, as well as the fact that Russia had not been singled out for a privileged relationship as many in Russia had perceived at the Moscow Summit.[54]

Russian leaders responded to this mixed bag of signals, assurances, carrots, and sticks with their own mixed bag. On the one hand, Medvedev called Obama on the phone on August 4 to wish him a happy birthday and to push the idea that both of them should order their negotiators to increase the pace of their work so New START could be ready in December.[55] Russian Foreign Minister Sergei Lavrov also asserted that U.S.-Russian differences over the Georgian war were resolved and would not impair U.S.-Russian relations, as indicated by the Moscow Summit in July.[56] At the same time, Lavrov also asserted that Georgia was trying to destabilize the entire Caucasus region by inviting U.S. participation in the EU's mission monitoring the Georgia-Abkhazia-South Ossetia borders.[57] Russian deputy foreign minister Grigoriy Karasin criticized the U.S. decision to sell "defensive" arms to Georgia.[58] Putin visited Abkhazia and pledged Russian military support in the case of a future Georgian attack. He also announced over $800 million in military and economic aid to Abkhazia and urged the OSCE and UN to recognize Abkhazia's independence.[59] Additionally, in early August Medvedev posted an open letter on his Kremlin Web site to Ukrainian president Viktor Yushchenko. In it he listed a number of Russian complaints against Ukraine, including its efforts to join NATO over Russian objections.[60] These and other statements prompted the Obama administration to deny that U.S. support for Georgia or Ukraine was aimed at Russia or involved lethal military assistance.[61]

Amidst this impasse, both presidents faced stirrings of domestic political opposition. For example, in Russia Medvedev faced signs of public concern. According to the Russian Public Opinion Research Center, a July 18–19 poll showed 54 percent of Russians expected U.S.-Russian relations to improve following the recently completed summit meeting in Moscow.[62] Similarly, on the anniversary of the war in Georgia, a poll showed that, while most respondents believed Western countries supported Georgia in an effort to push Russian influence out of the Transcaucasus region, for the first time slightly more Russians held Georgia to blame for the conflict (35 percent) than the United States (34 percent). Previous polls had put the number holding the United States to blame at 49 percent.[63] In the United States, rumblings from members of Congress signaled to the Obama administration that patience was ebbing and that more progress in resetting U.S.-Russian relations was desired. For example, Rep. Robert Wexler (D-PA), chairman of the House Foreign Affairs subcommittee on Europe, pressed for progress on arms control negotiations while resisting Russian pressure in the region, and fellow committee member Rep. Dana Rohrabacker (R-CA) stressed that Russia had been taken for granted since the end of the Cold War and relations needed to be mended.[64]

Phase IV: ABM Reset—An Opening and Opportunity, August–October 2009

By the late summer, the Obama administration was forced to come to grips with the complicated realities of U.S.-Russian relations and difficulties in overcoming the differences that had plagued the relationship since the heady optimism at the end of the Cold War. With prospects for a quick "reset" fading, the administration considered options to spur progress and produce tangible gains. After intense deliberation, Obama elected to change U.S. missile defense plans to better address Iran's threat and capabilities. Driven by new intelligence and the Defense Department's assessment and recommendation, the decision also carried the prospect of focusing Russian leaders on two areas of potential cooperation that would help make the reset a reality: New START negotiations and cooperation to address Iranian nuclear programs.

According to press reports, the missile defense shift was "years in the making,"[65] and U.S. officials strenuously denied that they were simply accommodating Russian objections.[66] However, Obama also noted,

> If the byproduct of it is that the Russians feel a little less paranoid and are now willing to work more effectively with us to deal with threats like ballistic missiles from Iran or nuclear development in Iran, you know, then that's a bonus.[67]

With review and discussion stretching back into early 2009, the critical period occurred in August and early September when new and updated intelligence assessments on Iran were provided to top officials in the White House, Defense and State Departments, and elsewhere. This intelligence indicated that Iran had experienced expensive setbacks in its ICBM research and development program and was opting instead to produce larger numbers of short- and medium-range missiles that, when launched in large numbers, could threaten Europe and the Middle East. The new intelligence caused Secretary Gates to reverse his prior endorsement of the Bush administration's Poland/Czech-based ABM system.[68] As Gates put it, he did not want the United States committed to a defense system against Iranian ICBMs when the real threat was Iranian shorter-range missiles.[69]

Obama and his top foreign policy advisers met on September 10 to consider the new intelligence and review missile defense plans. At that meeting, officials discussed an "upper tier" system that combined long-range interceptor missiles in California and Alaska with ten interceptor missiles in Poland, and a "lower tier" system that featured a combination of shorter-range, already deployed, or capable of deployment missiles: the Aegis seaborne SM-3 missiles, the Terminal High Altitude Air Defense System (THAAD) about to be deployed to Israel, and Patriot antimissile batteries already deployed. Defense Department experts recommended the "lower tier" system, as its components were considerably cheaper and capable of being deployed years earlier. In the meeting, Marine Gen. James Cartwright, vice chairman of the JCS, raised objections to the "upper tier" system, based on his prior service in charge of the Pentagon's missile and space weapons programs. He believed the Defense Department was about to embark on a very expensive investment to meet an Iranian ICBM threat that might never materialize. He was a persuasive opponent of the status quo, as was Defense Secretary Gates.[70] After discussion, the president made the decision to abandon the planned "upper tier" system in favor of the "lower tier" option based on more mobile systems located closer to Iran and the Middle East, and both Poland and the Czech Republic were so advised, although they had been consulted on the matter earlier.[71] The president announced the decision on September 17.

Although the official line was that the missile defense decision was not linked to Russian concerns or the desire to facilitate progress in U.S.-Russian relations, privately U.S. administration officials acknowledged the connections. In particular, policy makers expressed their hopes that Russia would cooperate on UN sanctions directed against Iran's nuclear program and, especially, that the decision to cancel the ABM system in Poland/Czech Republic would facilitate progress on a New START Treaty.[72]

If so, the administration was swiftly rewarded. Medvedev immediately praised the decision and said, "We will work together to develop effective measures against the risks of missile proliferation, measures that take into account the interests and concerns of all sides and ensure equal security for all countries in European territory."[73] According to observers, the Obama decision to scrap the ABM system in Europe opened the door for Russian cooperation on the New START agreement and nuclear nonproliferation, which Russian elites saw as linked. Russian commentators expected the Medvedev regime to reciprocate quickly, and they praised the Obama administration for taking Russian views into consideration. Furthermore, Russian Foreign Ministry sources said the Americans expected Russia to support tougher UN sanctions on Iran and to stop delivery of the S-300 antiaircraft missile defense system to Iran.[74] As military expert Viktor Baranets explained on a Russian government-controlled television news program, in addition to pressure for Russian help on Iran,

> We can say that today is an historic day because a real step towards real reset was made. . . . By taking this step, which we welcome, Obama at the same time has put us in a difficult situation. Such steps never come free of charge. Naturally, Russia will have to pay for it in a big way. I can't rule out concessions in the nuclear missile department.[75]

Moreover, Russia's *Interfax* reported that Russian leaders had decided to reverse their decision to place short-range Iskander antiaircraft missiles and strategic bombers in Kaliningrad, near Poland. Polish Defense Minister

Radoslaw Sikorski applauded this decision as a significant improvement in Poland's security situation, and he welcomed the U.S. decision to send Patriot missile batteries to Poland instead.[76]

Just a few days after the announcement of the policy change, both Obama and Medvedev met privately at the Waldorf Astoria Hotel during the opening session of the UN General Assembly. Media reports indicated that Medvedev agreed to greater UN pressure on Iran, which Russian pundits interpreted as a response to Obama's abandonment of the Polish/Czech ABM system.[77] According to Medvedev,

> We believe we need to help Iran to make a right decision. As to . . . sanctions, Russia's belief is very simple, and I stated it recently. Sanctions rarely lead to productive results. But in some cases sanctions are inevitable. Finally, it is a matter of choice.[78]

Furthermore, two days later, in an address at the University of Pittsburgh, Medvedev said Russia was ready to significantly cut its number of nuclear delivery vehicles and that the time may have come for tougher sanctions on Iran.[79] White House officials were extremely pleased with his remarks. According to the National Security Council's Russia expert, Michael McFaul,

> To me, that's a very big change in their position. I can't improve on what President Medvedev said. . . . It was not that long ago where we had very divergent definitions of the threat and definitions of our strategic objectives vis-à-vis Iran.[80]

In a press conference after their meeting, McFaul told reporters that he believed Obama and Medvedev now shared a two-track approach, with diplomacy being the preferred track but with coercive sanctions as a fallback in case Iran did not cooperate.[81]

There were notes of caution, however. For example, while Prime Minister Putin called Obama's decision on the ABM system in Europe brave, he also added that he now expected other brave decisions from Obama, such as ending trade barriers between the countries and championing Russia's joint bid with Kazakhstan and Belarus to join the WTO.[82] Russian military experts agreed that an ABM system based on the U.S. Navy's Aegis system would not threaten Russia, but they also expressed concerns that technological upgrades in the weapons and radars suggested by Obama could potentially threaten Russian interests, particularly if they involved space-based weapons. Similarly, although Russian legislators expressed appreciation for the decision, calling it a victory for common sense, they also warned that no deal had been struck with the United States and that reciprocal Russian policy shifts regarding Iran should not be expected in Washington.[83] Focusing on Russia's increasing reliance on its nuclear forces for security as it downsized its conventional forces, one Russian defense analyst went so far as to call Obama's linkage of Russia to his calls for a nuclear free world "idiotic. . . . They strengthen those in Russia who said you can't believe him—that he is laying traps for us."[84] And in October, Russian officials expressed concern that the possible use of an early-warning radar in Ukraine as part of an anti-Iranian missile defense system could hurt U.S.-Russian relations.[85]

Phase V: The New START Endgame, November 2009–January 2011

In the wake of the missile defense decision, the Obama administration focused on efforts to conclude the New START agreement as the central and most tangible prize of efforts to reset U.S.-Russian relations. However, hopes that it would be completed by December, when the earlier START provisions expired, swiftly disappeared.

Negotiations moved forward in November when Russian and U.S. negotiators met for an eighth time to work on New START. According to Russia's chief of the General Staff, Gen. Nikolai Makarov, one stumbling point was the fact that the U.S. side wanted to continue on-site monitoring of the construction of Russia's Topol and Topol-M missile systems. The Russians saw such inspections as an affront that had been forced on Russia in the last agreement, and so the Russian side resisted on-site monitoring in Russia without similar on-site monitoring in the United States.[86] According to one account, the Russians stalled in the late fall and early winter, convinced that Obama "would be so eager to have a new treaty by the time he traveled to Oslo later that month to accept his Nobel Peace Prize that he would accept concessions."[87] Even direct meetings between Obama and Medvedev during the Asia-Pacific Economic Cooperation (APEC) meetings in Singapore a short time later failed to produce agreement. The two could not break the deadlock, and Obama would not concede in advance of his trip to Oslo.[88]

Obama and Medvedev met again in December during the UN climate change conference in Copenhagen. Accord to press accounts, the two leaders came very close to resolving their key differences. They agreed to the following:

They would cut deployed warheads to 1,550 per side, down from the current limit of 2,200. They would cut deployed heavy bombers and missiles to 700 each. They would conduct 18 inspections a year, up from 10 originally proposed by Moscow. Even on the technical telemetry issue, they found agreement. "Let's just do it on an annual basis," Mr. Obama proposed spontaneously. "I don't see any problem with that," Mr. Medvedev said. Mr. Obama turned to his own advisers and asked, "You guys good with that?"[89]

Optimistic about what appeared to be a critical breakthrough, Gen. James L. Jones, the national security adviser; Adm. Mike Mullen, the chairman of the Joint Chiefs of Staff; Rose Gottemoeller, the lead New START negotiator; Michael McFaul, the president's Russia adviser; and Gary Samore, the nonproliferation adviser followed with a trip to Moscow in January to address the remaining issues. During these talks, the two sides agreed to cap launchers at 800 each, and the U.S. team left believing they had completed the agreement. When they discussed the results with President Obama on their return, they reported, "We're done, sir."[90]

Yet another delay ensued. Returning again to the issue of missile defense, the day after what had appeared to be the final breakthrough, a lead Russian negotiator told Rose Gottemoeller that any agreement had to include a commitment to lock missile defense plans to their current status. According to one account, "The renewed dispute intensified two weeks later when Romania unexpectedly announced that it would host interceptors from the new system, putting the reconfigured missile defense system right in Russia's geopolitical backyard."[91] These delays apparently also resulted in a conversation between Clinton and Lavrov, in which she urged the Russian foreign minister to speed up the pace of negotiations and help break the impasse.[92] However, on February 24, 2010, Medvedev telephoned Obama to raise the issue and insist that a joint statement on missile defense be included in the treaty. Obama reportedly objected angrily, "Dmitri, we agreed. . . . We can't do this. If it means we're going to walk away from this treaty and not get it done, so be it. But we're not going to go down this path."[93] According to Dmitri V. Trenin, director of the Carnegie Moscow Center, Russian leaders again calculated that Obama would agree to their demands in order to secure the agreement in advance of international nuclear summit meetings planned for April. "They believed Obama could be put under pressure and concessions could be extracted from him. . . . He needed the treaty more than the Russians in the short term."[94]

They calculated incorrectly. Instead, Obama dispatched negotiators for further talks, finally reaching agreement in mid-March to issue separate statements on missile defense at the signing ceremony. According to one account,

> Ultimately, Russia backed down. Mr. Medvedev called Mr. Obama on March 13, and Secretary of State Hillary Rodham Clinton then traveled to Moscow. Negotiators finished drafting their separate statements on Tuesday, with Russia warning that it reserved the right to withdraw from the treaty if it deemed American missile defenses a threat, while the United States said it would build the defenses as it saw fit but was not making a target of Russia.[95]

The treaty was signed on April 8, 2010. Although some Senate conservatives opposed the treaty, they could not overcome the endorsements by people like former President George H.W. Bush, Defense Secretary Gates, and members of the Joint Chiefs of Staff.[96] New START was approved by a vote of 71–26 in the Senate on December 22, 2012.[97] It was approved by a vote of 350–56 by the Russian State Duma on January 25, 2011, although Russian legislators added their reservation that the two sides agreed to disagree over missile defense.[98]

Phase VI: New Discord and Policy Challenges, March 2011-October 2012

Unfortunately, the treaty failed to prompt even greater cooperation. Instead, multiple issues continued to plague the U.S.-Russian relationship. On March 10, 2011, Vice President Biden used a speech at Moscow State University to criticize lack of progress in Russia's legal and political systems. He said,

> Russians want to be able to choose their national and local leaders in competitive elections. They want to be able to assemble freely, and they want the media to be independent of the state. And they want to live in a country that fights corruption. . . . Mr. Medvedev said last week—and I quote him— "Freedom cannot be postponed." Joe Biden didn't say that. The president of Russia said that.[99]

When the Arab Spring produced a brutal crackdown on pro-democracy demonstrators by the Assad regime in Syria, Russian-U.S. differences were again highlighted. As the Syrian regime killed thousands of civilians, the Russians (with China) repeatedly blocked UN Security Council resolutions condemning the violence and the Assad regime and calling for an end to human rights abuses there. Despite this disappointment, the Obama administration revealed that it was considering more nuclear warhead cuts. Options considered included cutting the current limit of 1,550 deployed warheads by 300–400, 700–800, or 1,000–1,100 deployed warheads.[100]

As the Syrian situation deteriorated in the early spring of 2012, Russians were preparing for a presidential election. With Medvedev saying he would step down, Putin ran for reelection as president. Thousands of protesters came out before the election, but on March 4, 2012—before 30 percent of the votes were counted—Putin declared victory despite the allegations of massive voter fraud. Hundreds of protesters were arrested or detained by police and security forces.[101] Putin then appointed Medvedev to take the post of prime minister.

Violence in Syria dominated concerns in the summer of 2012. As civil war set in, Secretary of State Clinton accused Russia of selling attack helicopters to the Syrian regime. Foreign Minister Lavrov denied the charge and counter-charged that the United States was arming the Syrian rebels, which the Obama administration denied.[102] A few days later, the Russian government announced it was selling anti-ship and anti-aircraft missiles to Syria.[103] In July, Russia announced a fleet of eleven warships carrying hundreds of marines was moving to its naval base in the Syrian port of Tartus.[104] Then on July 19, Russia and China vetoed yet another UN Security Council resolution that would have sanctioned the Syrian regime.[105] After meeting privately with Putin for ninety minutes at the APEC summit in Vladivostok in September 2012, Secretary of State Clinton said, "We haven't seen eye to eye with Russia on Syria. That may continue." Foreign Minister Lavrov responded by saying,

> Our American partners have a prevailing tendency to threaten and increase pressure, adopt ever more sanctions against Syria and against Iran. Russia is fundamentally against this, since for resolving problems you have to engage the countries you are having issues with and not isolate them.[106]

Other issues arose in the summer that posed obstacles to closer cooperation. In June, the Russian government cracked down further on domestic dissent. For its part, the House of Representatives sent a bill to the Senate which would authorize sanctions for Russian officials accused of human rights abuses.[107] In July, the State Duma passed a law putting limits on access to the Internet.[108] In August, three members of the all-female punk band Pussy Riot were convicted of "hooliganism based on religious hatred" after their demonstration they called a "punk prayer" in a Moscow church, calling for the Virgin Mary to save Russia from Putin. They received two-year prison terms.[109]

Other national security announcements also created potential tensions. In July, Russia acknowledged that it had entered negotiations regarding the establishment of new naval bases in Cuba, the Seychelles, and Vietnam. Moscow observers linked the potential Cuba base to U.S. plans for a European missile defense system.[110] In August, Putin announced that 600 new combat aircraft and 1,000 new helicopters would be added to the Russian military by 2020, paid for by increased oil and gas revenues.[111] In August, Russia and Iraq reached final agreement on a $4.2 billion arms purchase, which included both attack helicopters and surface-to-air missiles. The deal made Russia Iraq's second-leading arms supplier after the United States and was also seen as a way for Russia to keep its military presence in the region if the Assad regime in Syria lost power.[112]

Some positive steps were taken when Russia finally joined the WTO in August after an eighteen-year wait, in part due to successful U.S. pressure on Georgia to resolve its trade differences with Russia.[113] Furthermore, at the Vladivostok summit of APEC in September, Secretary Clinton announced the United States would end its Cold War–era trade sanctions—the Jackson-Vanik amendment—on Russia. However, her pledge came in the face of congressional efforts to sanction Russian officials accused of human rights abuses by denying them visas and freezing their financial accounts.[114] As the fall of 2012 wore on, more contentious events arose. In September, Russia forgave North Korea's debts left over from the Soviet era, which Moscow observers interpreted as an attempt to clear the way for new Russian investments in that isolated country.[115] Putin also ordered important Russian corporations operating abroad— such as Gazprom—not to disclose information to foreign regulators without Moscow's approval.[116]

Yet perhaps the most surprising action was the Russian regime's decision to order the United States Agency for International Development (USAID) to cease its funding of Russian nongovernmental organizations trying to create a more liberal, civil society. Although only amounting to $50 million, this assistance was crucial to these small NGOs' continued operations. Prominent among the groups affected was Golos, the only independent election monitoring group in Russia, which provided thousands of Russian election monitors for the 2012 presidential election. The decision was communicated first to Secretary Clinton on September 8 by Foreign Minister Lavrov at the APEC meeting in Vladivostok and then again to Washington through (now) U.S. Ambassador to Russia Michael McFaul on September 11. The State Department response was mild: If Russia didn't want the money, others could use it. However, Senator McCain responded,

The Russian government's decision to end all U.S.A.I.D. activities in the country is an insult to the United States and a finger in the eye of the Obama administration, which has consistently trumpeted the alleged success of its so-called "reset" policy toward Moscow.[117]

More mixed signals came on other issues. In September, the State Duma passed a law stiffening penalties for those convicted of libel or slander directed at public officials, a move widely interpreted as a clamp-down on dissent.[118] Yet, on the other hand, Putin weighed in on the U.S. presidential election, calling Obama a "very honest man" and deriding Mitt Romney for his statement that Russia was "our No. 1 geo-political foe." Putin went on to say that Russian fears of a US-led missile defense system for Europe would likely come true if Romney was elected, while Obama was more open to compromise on such issues. Putin added that the U.S. Departments of State and Defense were obstacles to a deal on the missile defense system as well.[119]

In October, a positive note was struck that was then overshadowed by more negative news. Russian judges released one of the jailed members of Pussy Riot from prison, suspending her sentence because she had been arrested in the church even before she could open her guitar case![120] More negatively, the Russian Foreign Ministry ordered UNICEF to cease its programs by the end of the year, and Alexander Fishenko, an immigrant from Kazakhstan who owned an electronics firm in Houston, was indicted on charges of illegally exporting microchips to Russia without the required licenses. Essentially, he was seen as a spy for the Russian military.[121] Worse for the relationship, the Russian foreign ministry announced that the Nunn-Lugar Cooperative Threat Reduction Program would not be extended when it expired in 2013. Under this twenty-year-old program, the United States had largely funded the deactivation of over 7,600 nuclear warheads along with huge stocks of chemical weapons, missiles, and launchers left over from the Soviet Union. Despite the Obama administration's desire to continue the program, the Foreign Ministry said Russia could now afford to do the job itself.[122]

In December 2012, the mixed signals continued from both sides. On the one hand, Putin announced that changes were needed in Syria to avert a never-ending civil war, and he said he was not concerned about the fate of the Assad regime itself. However, he said such changes could not be the result of outside military intervention, as such interventions caused as many problems as they solved.[123] In Washington, Congress passed and Obama signed the Russia and Moldova Jackson-Vanik Repeal and Sergei Magnitsky Rule of Law Accountability

Act of 2012. While the Russians were pleased that Jackson-Vanik was repealed and trade with Russia normalized, they were not happy about the Magnitsky part of the legislation. Sergei Magnitsky was a Russian lawyer who uncovered what he said was a $230 million tax fraud case involving Russian officials and was beaten to death in prison in 2009, and the 2012 legislation imposed U.S. travel and banking sanctions on any Russian officials involved in his death. Outraged, Russian legislators passed a law prohibiting Americans from adopting Russian orphans, which Putin signed on December 28. Citing the deaths of 19 Russian children adopted by U.S. citizens since the 1990s without satisfactory prosecutions of the parents, the law banned U.S. adoptions as of January 1, 2013, banned political activity by nongovernmental organizations funded by the United States if deemed harmful to Russia's interests, and authorized travel sanctions against any U.S. citizen suspected of human rights abuses.[124]

Conclusion: What Reset?

The presidencies of Barack Obama and Dmitry Medvedev began with high hopes of achieving cooperation on a number of fronts and involving multiple different issues. Yet despite encouragement and support from the top two officials in each country, cooperation has seemed painfully elusive. The two worked closely on a personal level to override obstacles to achievements like the New START Treaty and Russian admission to the WTO, but differing values and entrenched national interests prevailed on most other issues. Moreover, the fact that Obama had made it clear that he strongly preferred dealing with Medvedev rather than Putin came back to haunt him when Putin regained the Russian presidency. Only time will tell whether these two former Cold War rivals can overcome entrenched obstacles to cooperation in the near future.

Key Actors

Joe Biden   U.S. vice president whose candid comments on the weakness of the Russian state and society jeopardized the warming relationship between the two regimes.

George H. W. Bush, Bill Clinton, George W. Bush   U.S. presidents who presided over a deteriorating U.S.-Russian relationship.

Hillary Rodham Clinton and Sergei Lavrov   The U.S. secretary of state and Russian foreign minister, respectively, who pressed for each country's national interests in the New START negotiations.

Robert Gates   The U.S. defense secretary who said setbacks in Iran's long-range missile program allowed him to change his previous support for a missile defense system in Poland and the Czech Republic to favor a more mobile system located closer to Iran.

Dmitry Medvedev   Russian president who reached out to the United States to change the direction of the relationship.

Barack Obama   U.S. president who pledged to change the U.S.-Russian relationship.

Boris Yeltsin, Vladimir Putin   Russian presidents who presided over a deteriorating U.S.-Russian relationship.

Notes

1. For more on this period, see Robert H. Donaldson and Joseph L. Nogee, *The Foreign Policy of Russia: Changing Systems, Enduring Interests,* 4th ed. (Armonk, NY: M. E. Sharpe, 2009) and Stephen K. Wegren and Dale R. Herspring, eds., *After Putin's Russia: Past Imperfect, Future Uncertain,* 4th ed. (Lanham, MD: Rowman and Littlefield, 2009).

2. James Martin, "Russia: Gore-Primakov (Gore-Chernomyrdin) Commission (GCC)," *Nuclear Threat Initiative,* www.nti.org/db/nisprofs/Russia/forasst/otherusg/gcc .htm.

3. Bureau of Public Affairs, U.S. Department of State, "Fact Sheet—Bosnia: NATO Involvement in the Balkan Crisis," November 1, 1995, dosfan.lib.uic.edu/ERC/bureaus/ eur/releases/951101BosniaNATO.html.

4. "World: Europe: Russian Troops Camp in Pristina," BBC News, June 12, 1999, news.bbc.co.uk/2/hi/europe/367490.stm.

5. "NATO Enlargement," *NATO,* www.nato.int/cps/en/natolive/topics_49212.htm.

6. "World: Europe: Russian Troops Camp in Pristina," BBC News.

7. "NATO Enlargement," *NATO.* For more on this, see Ronald D. Asmus, *A Little War That Shook the World: Georgia, Russia, and the Future of the West* (New York: Palgrave Macmillan, 2010).

8. Chris Baldwin, "Putin Says Russia Threatened by 'Unipolar World,'" *Reuters,* November 4, 2007, www.reuters.com/article/idUSL0449803320071104; "The War in Iraq: Legal Issues," Human and Constitutional Rights Resource, May 15, 2007, www .hrcr.org/hottopics/Iraq.html.

9. Jamie McIntyre and Ryan Chilcote, "Pentagon: Russia Fed U.S. War Plans to Iraq; Russian Official: Report Unfounded," CNN, March 26, 2006, www.cnn.com/2006/ WORLD/meast/03/25/saddam.russia/index.html.

10. "Target Iran: Countdown Timeline," *GlobalSecurity.org,* www.globalsecurity .org/military/ops/iran-timeline.htm.

11. William Douglas and Jonathan S. Landay, "Putin Expands Missile Defense Offer but Division Remains," *McClatchy,* July 2, 2007, www.mcclatchydc.com/ 2007/07/02/17556/putin-expands-missile-defense.html.

12. Peter Baker, "U.S.-Russia Relations Chilly Amid Transition—Stalled Nuclear Pact Is Just One Sign of Unease," *Washington Post,* March 1, 2008, A1.

13. Peter Finn, "Russian Air, Ground Forces Strike Georgia—Military Action Follows Georgian Offensive to Reassert Control over Separatist South Ossetia," *Washington Post*, August 9, 2008, A1.

14. Kevin Sullivan, "Overseas, Excitement over Obama; In Presumptive Nominee, Many See Chance for New Direction and New Attitude," *Washington Post*, June 5, 2008, A10.

15. Peter Finn, "Delegation Led by U.S. Senators Detained Briefly at Russian Airport," *Washington Post*, August 29, 2005, A16; Joby Warrick, "U.S. to Aid Ukraine in Countering Bioweapons—Pact Focuses on Security at Labs—Russia Apologizes for Delay of Senate Delegation," *Washington Post*, August 30, 2005, A11.

16. Peter Finn, "Russia Pumps Tens of Millions into Burnishing Image Abroad," *Washington Post*, March 6, 2008, A1.

17. "Medvedev Calls for Better Relations with U.S., Ex-Soviet Countries," *PRIME-TASS* report, September 25, 2009, on *Johnson's Russia List*, September 25, 2009, www .cdi.org/russia/johnson.

18. Jim Hoagland, "Obama vs. Clenched Fists," *Washington Post*, February 22, 2009, A19.

19. Craig Whitlock, "'Reset' Sought on Relations with Russia, Biden Says," *Washington Post*, February 8, 2009, A18.

20. David S. Broder, "Biden Is Surprised at Criticism of Plan," *Washington Post*, February 11, 2009, A6.

21. Karen DeYoung, "U.S. Envoy Indicated Flexibility with Russia on Missile Defense," *Washington Post*, February 14, 2009, A8; Jackson Diehl, "A 'Reset' That Doesn't Compute," *Washington Post*, February 23, 2009, A13.

22. Michael A. Fletcher, "Obama Makes Overtures to Russia on Missile Defense," *Washington Post*, March 3, 2009, A2.

23. Philip P. Pan, and Karen DeYoung, "Russia Signaling Interest in Deal on Iran—Still, Obama Effort Faces Obstacles," *Washington Post*, March 18, 2009, A10.

24. Michael A. Fletcher, "Obama Makes Overtures to Russia on Missile Defense," *Washington Post*, March 3, 2009, A2.

25. Karen DeYoung, "Obama Team Seeks to Redefine Russia Ties—U.S. Aiming at Strategic Goals with Proposals on Arms Reduction, Missile Defense, Economic Support," *Washington Post*, March 4, 2009, A11.

26. "No Deal—Barack Obama and Dmitry Medvedev Offer Welcome Clarity on Iran and Missile Defense," *Washington Post*, March 4, 2009, A14.

27. Paul Reynolds, "Pressing the U.S.-Russia Reset Button," BBC News, March 5, 2009, www.bbc.co.uk.

28. "Button Gaffe Embarrasses Clinton," BBC News, March 7, 2009, www.bbc.co.uk.

29. Glenn Kessler, "Clinton 'Resets' Russian Ties—and Language," *Washington Post*, March 7, 2009, A6.

30. Pan and DeYoung, "Russia Signaling Interest in Deal on Iran," A10.

31. "RF, U.S. Have Disagreements on START Talks—Gen. Staff Chief," *ITAR-TASS* report, November 12, 2009, on *Johnson's Russia List*, November 13, 2009, www.cdi.org/russia/johnson.

32. Philip P. Pan, "Medvedev 'Counting on a Reset' with U.S.—Russia Again Raises Missile Shield Issue," *Washington Post*, March 21, 2009, A10.

33. Anne Applebaum, "For Russia, More than a 'Reset,'" *Washington Post*, March 24, 2009, A13.

34. "Clinton Urges Russia to 'Push Hard' for Arms Treaty," *Ria Novosti*, February 24, 2010, http://en.rian.ru.

35. Jonathan Weisman and Peter Spiegel, "Cost Concerns Propelled U.S. Missile Pivot: Obama Decision Is Aimed at Saving Pentagon Funds While Helping Nonproliferation Push; Shift Was Years in the Making," *Wall Street Journal*, September 19, 2009, on *Johnson's Russia List*, September 20, 2009, www.cdi.org/russia/johnson.

36. See Jackson Diehl, "A World of Trouble for Obama," *Washington Post*, April 20, 2009, A15; "Another Summer in Georgia—Once Again Russia Masses Troops and Stages Provocations," *Washington Post*, June 4, 2009, A20; Misha Dzhindzhikhashvili, "U.S.-Russian Tensions Rise over Georgia," *Washington Post*, July 14, 2009, www.washington post.com.

37. Tom Esslemont, "UN Monitors to Leave Georgia," BBC News, July 15, 2009, www.bbc.co.uk.

38. Dzhindzhikhashvili, "U.S.-Russian Tensions Rise over Georgia."

39. David Ignatius, "What a 'Reset' Can't Fix," *Washington Post*, July 5, 2009, A19.

40. "Why Obama Visited Russia: Experts Claim That the Main Objective of U.S. President Barack Obama's Visit to Moscow Was to Identify a Key Counterpart to Deal With," *Argumenty Nedeli* 31, August 7, 2009, on *Johnson's Russia List*, August 7, 2009, www.cdi.org/russia/johnson; "President Dmitry Medvedev Told CNN He Felt Comfortable Communicating with Barack Obama," *ITAR-TASS* Report, September 20, 2009, on *Johnson's Russia List*, September 21, 2009, www.cdi.org/russia/johnson; Michael A. Fletcher and Philip P. Pan, "U.S.-Russia Summit Brings Series of Advances," *Washington Post*, July 8, 2009, A6.

41. Jim Hoagland, "The Two Faces of Russia," *Washington Post*, September 20, 2009, on *Johnson's Russia List*, September 20, 2009, www.cdi.org/russia/johnson.

42. Dzhindzhikhashvili, "U.S.-Russian Tensions Rise over Georgia"; David J. Kramer, "Resetting U.S.-Russian Relations: It Takes Two," *The Washington Quarterly* 33 (January 1, 2010), www.twq.com/10january/index.cfm?id=375.

43. Gregory L. White and Marc Champion, "No Quick Thaw in Russia Ties," *Wall Street Journal*, September 18, 2009, on *Johnson's Russia List*, September 19, 2009, www.cdi.org/russia/johnson.

44. Dzhindzhikhashvili, "U.S.-Russian Tensions Rise over Georgia"; Esslemont, "UN Monitors to Leave Georgia."

45. Philip P. Pan, "Georgia's Saakashvili Seeking U.S. Weapons to Deter Russia," *Washington Post*, July 22, 2009, A8.

46. Samuel Charap, "Anxiety and Recommitment in Russia's Neighborhood," *Center for American Progress*, July 21, 2009, www.americanprogress.org.

47. "Obama Administration Says Russia Could Join NATO," *Associated Press*, July 29, 2009, www.ap.org.

48. Dan Robinson, "U.S. Lawmakers Concerned About 'Reset' of U.S.-Russian Relations," *Voice of America*, July 31, 2009, on *Johnson's Russia List*, July 31, 2009, www.cdi.org/russia/johnson; Walter Pincus, "U.S. Takes Steps to Boost Security Cooperation with Russia," *Washington Post*, July 31, 2009, A17.

49. "Mr. Biden's Diplomacy—The Vice President Pays Important Visits to Ukraine and Georgia," *Washington Post*, July 25, 2009, A16.

50. Sabina Zawadzki, "Stop Infighting, Biden Tells Ukraine's Leaders," *Reuters*, July 22, 2009, www.reuters.com.

51. "Mr. Biden's Diplomacy." See also Philip P. Pan, "Biden Offers Georgia Solidarity—Russian Invasion in 2008 Decried," *Washington Post*, July 24, 2009, A12.

52. "Biden Takes Aim at Russia," *Washington Post*, July 26, 2009, A8.

53. Lynn Berry, "Vice President Biden Hits Nerve in Russia," *Associated Press*, July 27, 2009, www.ap.org.

54. Yevgeniy Aleksandrovich Klochikhin, "From Multipolar World to Multipartner One," *Nezavisimaya Gazeta*, August 3, 2009, on *Johnson's Russia List*, August 3, 2009, www.cdi.org/russia/johnson.

55. "Russian News Agency Carries Fuller Account of Medvedev-Obama Phone Conversation," *Interfax* report on *Johnson's Russia List*, August 5, 2009, www.cdi.org/russia/johnson.

56. "Georgia Issue No Longer Impedes RF-West Relations–Lavrov," *ITAR-TASS* report on *Johnson's Russia List*, August 5, 2009, www.cdi.org/russia/johnson.

57. "Russia Accuses Georgia of Trying to Destabilize Caucasus," *Ria Novosti* report on *Johnson's Russia List*, August 5, 2009, www.cdi.org/russia/johnson.

58. "Russia Will Not Shut Eyes to USA Supplying Arms to Georgia–Top Diplomat," *Interfax* report on *Johnson's Russia List*, August 5, 2009, www.cdi.org/russia/johnson.

59. Indira Bartsits, "Putin Promises Military Backing for Abkhazia," *Agence France-Presse*, August 12, 2009, on *Johnson's Russia List*, August 12, 2009, www.cdi.org/russia/johnson; Philip P. Pan, "Putin Visits Breakaway Georgian Region, Unveils Plan for Military Base," *Washington Post*, August 13, 2009, A8.

60. Kramer, "Resetting U.S.-Russian Relations: It Takes Two."

61. For example, "DoD Official on Military Cooperation with Georgia," *Civil Georgia* report on *Johnson's Russia List*, August 5, 2009, www.cdi.org/russia/johnson; "U.S. Renders Military Assistance to Georgia but Does Not Supply Weapons–Vershbow," *Interfax* report on *Johnson's Russia List*, August 12, 2009, www.cdi.org/russia/johnson.

62. *Interfax* report on *Johnson's Russia List*, July 22, 2009, www.cdi.org/russia/johnson.

63. "Russians Blame Georgia, USA for War over South Ossetia–Poll," *Interfax* report on *Johnson's Russia List*, August 4, 2009, www.cdi.org/russia/johnson.

64. Robinson, "U.S. Lawmakers Concerned About 'Reset' of U.S.-Russian Relations"; Robert Wexler, "Opening Statement: The Reset Button Has Been Pushed: Kicking Off a New Era in U.S.-Russian Relations," Hearings before the House Foreign Affairs Subcommittee on Europe, July 28, 2009, on *Johnson's Russia List*, July 29, 2009, www.cdi.org/russia/johnson.

65. Weisman and Spiegel, "Cost Concerns Propelled U.S. Missile Pivot."

66. Robert M. Gates, "A Better Missile Defense for a Safer Europe," *New York Times*, September 20, 2009, on *Johnson's Russia List*, September 20, 2009, www.cdi.org/russia/johnson; "Remarks by the President on Strengthening Missile Defense in Europe," Diplomatic Reception Room, White House, September 17, 2009, on *Johnson's Russia List*, September 19, 2009, www.cdi.org/russia/johnson.

67. Ben Feller, "Obama: Missile Defense Decision Not about Russia," *Associated Press*, September 20, 2009, on *Johnson's Russia List*, September 20, 2009, www.cdi.org/russia/johnson.

68. Weisman and Spiegel, "Cost Concerns Propelled U.S. Missile Pivot."

69. Gates, "A Better Missile Defense for a Safer Europe."

70. Weisman and Spiegel, "Cost Concerns Propelled U.S. Missile Pivot."

71. "Report: U.S. to Scrap E. Europe Missile Shield Bases," *Agence France-Presse*, August 27, 2009, on *Johnson's Russia List*, August 27, 2009, www.cdi.org/russia/johnson; Weisman and Spiegel, "Cost Concerns Propelled U.S. Missile Pivot."

72. Gregory L. White and Marc Champion, "No Quick Thaw in Russia Ties," *Wall Street Journal,* September 18, 2009, on *Johnson's Russia List,* September 19, 2009, www .cdi.org/russia/johnson; Mary Beth Sheridan and Philip P. Pan, "Obama Missile Decision May Smooth U.S.-Russia Arms Talks," *Washington Post,* September 21, 2009, A7.

73. Philip P. Pan, "A Cautious Russia Praises Obama Move," *Washington Post,* September 18, 2009, on *Johnson's Russia List,* September 19, 2009, www.cdi.org/russia/johnson.

74. Vladimir Soloviov, Alexander Gabuyev, and Nargiz Asadova, "Curtailment of the ABM System in Europe Requires a Symmetric Response from Russia," *Kommersant,* September 18, 2009, on *Johnson's Russia List,* September 19, 2009, www.cdi.org/russia/ johnson; "ROAR: New Bargaining Looms as U.S. Scraps Missile Shield Plan," *Russia Today,* September 18, 2009, www.russiatoday.com.

75. BBC Monitoring, "Expert Ponders Price Russia May Pay for U.S. Decision on ABM," Center TV, September 20, 2009, on *Johnson's Russia List,* September 19, 2009, www.cdi.org/russia/johnson.

76. "Russia's Plan to Abandon Missile Project Good for Poland–Defence Minister," PAP (Polish Agency Press), September 18, 2009, on *Johnson's Russia List,* September 20, 2009, www.cdi.org/russia/johnson; Gleb Bryanski, "Russia's Putin Hails U.S. Shield Move, Calls for More," *Reuters,* September 18, 2009, on *Johnson's Russia List,* September 19, 2009, www.cdi.org/russia/johnson.

77. Andrei Terekhov, "Dmitry Medvedev's Response: Russia Appeared to Have Promised Washington Support in Dealing with Iran," *Nezavisimaya Gazeta,* September 25, 2009, on *Johnson's Russia List,* September 25, 2009, www.cdi.org/russia/johnson.

78. "Remarks by President Obama and President Medvedev of Russia after Bilateral Meeting," Office of the Press Secretary, The White House, September 23, 2009, www .whitehouse.gov/the-press-office/remarks-president-obama-and-president-medvedev -russia-after-bilateral-meeting.

79. "Medvedev Calls for Better Relations with U.S., Ex-Soviet Countries," *PRIME-TASS* report, September 25, 2009, on *Johnson's Russia List,* September 25, 2009, www .cdi.org/russia/johnson.

80. Josh Gerstein, "W.H. Hails Russia/Iran Breakthrough," www.politico.com, September 23, 2009, on *Johnson's Russia List,* September 25, 2009, www.cdi.org/russia/ johnson.

81. "Press Briefing by Gary Samore, National Security Council Coordinator for Arms Control and Non-Proliferation; Ambassador Alex Wolff, Deputy Permanent Representative to the United Nations; and Mike McFaul, Senior Director for Russian Affairs on Thursday's UN Security Council Meeting and the President's Meeting Today with President Medvedev of Russia," The White House, Office of the Press Secretary, September 23, 2009, on *Johnson's Russia List,* September 25, 2009, www.cdi.org/russia/johnson.

82. Bryanski, "Russia's Putin Hails U.S. Shield Move, Calls for More."

83. Pan, "A Cautious Russia Praises Obama Move."

84. Jim Hoagland, "Nuclear Pushback," *Washington Post,* September 27, 2009, A2.

85. "Russia," *Washington Post,* October 16, 2009, A10.

86. "RF, U.S. Have Disagreements on START Talks—Gen. Staff Chief," *ITAR-TASS* report, November 12, 2009, on *Johnson's Russia List,* November 13, 2009, www.cdi.org/ russia/johnson; Peter Baker, "Twists and Turns on the Way to Arms Pact with Russia," *New York Times,* March 26, 2010, www.nytimes.com/2010/03/27/world/europe/ 27start.html.

87. Baker, "Twists and Turns on the Way to Arms Pact with Russia."

88. "Medvedev, Obama to Continue Efforts to Settle START Issue—Official," *ITAR-TASS* report on *Johnson's Russia List,* November 13, 2009, www.cdi.org/russia/johnson.

89. Baker, "Twists and Turns on the Way to Arms Pact with Russia."

90. Ibid.

91. Ibid.

92. "Clinton Urges Russia to 'Push Hard' for Arms Treaty," *Ria Novosti,* February 24, 2010, http://en.rian.ru.

93. Baker, "Twists and Turns on the Way to Arms Pact with Russia."

94. Ibid.

95. Ibid.

96. Peter Baker, "A Former President Weighs In," *New York Times,* December 9, 2010, A33; Donna Cassata, "U.S. Military Leaders Say Treaty Won't Hurt Defense," *Fort Worth Star-Telegram,* December 17, 2010, 11A.

97. James Oliphant, "Senate Approves New START Treaty and Help for 9/11 First Responders," *Los Angeles Times,* December 22, 2010, articles.latimes.com/2010/dec/22/nation/la-na-congress-20101223.

98. Andrew E. Kramer, "Arms Treaty Advances in Russia, *New York Times,* January 26, 2011, A9.

99. Ellen Barry, "Plain Speaking From Biden in Moscow Speech," *New York Times,* March 11, 2011, A4.

100. Robert Burns, "US Weighing Steep Nuclear Arms Cuts," *Boston Globe,* February 14, 2012, www.boston.com/news/nation/washington/articles/2012/02/14/ap_newsbreak_us_weighing_steep_nuclear_arms_cuts/.

101. Miriam Elder, "Putin Makes His Presence Felt As Protesters Take to Moscow's Streets," *The Guardian,* March 5, 2012, www.guardian.co.uk/world/2012/mar/05/putin-protesters-moscow.

102. Joby Warrick and Will Englund, "Helicopter Allegations Roil U.S.-Russia Ties," *Washington Post,* June 13, 2012, www.washingtonpost.com/world/national-security/helicopter-allegations-roil-us-russia-ties/2012/06/13/gJQApsCvaV_story.html.

103. Andrew E. Kramer, "Russia Sending Missile Systems to Shield Syria," *New York Times,* June 15, 2012, www.nytimes.com/2012/06/16/world/europe/russia-sending-air-and-sea-defenses-to-syria.html.

104. Andrew E. Kramer and Rick Gladstone, "Russia Sending Warships on Maneuvers Near Syria," *New York Times,* July 10, 2012, www.nytimes.com/2012/07/11/world/middleeast/russia-sends-warships-on-maneuvers-near-syria.html.

105. Culum Lynch, "Russia, China Veto U.N. Sanctions Resolution on Syria," *Washington Post,* July 19, 2012, www.washingtonpost.com/world/national-security/new-shelling-pessimism-in-syria-a-day-after-bomb-kills-top-government-aides/2012/07/19/gJQAJzszvW_story.html.

106. David M. Herszenhorn and Steven Lee Myers, "For Putin, a Flight of Fancy at a Summit Meeting's Close," *New York Times,* September 10, 2012, A9.

107. Steven Lee Myers and David M. Herszenhorn, "Clinton Tells Russia That Sanctions Will Soon End," *New York Times,* September 8, 2012, www.nytimes.com/2012/09/09/world/europe/clinton-tells-russia-trade-sanctions-will-end.html.

108. Kathy Lally, "Russia Passes Law Curbing Internet," *Washington Post*, July 11, 2012, www.washingtonpost.com/world/europe/russia-passes-law-curbing-internet/2012/07/11/gJQAvkzPdW_story.html.

109. Andrew E. Kramer, "2 Band Members in Russia Said to Flee to Avoid Arrest," *New York Times*, August 27, 2012, A4.

110. Henry Meyer and Anatoly Temkin, "Russia Seeks Naval Bases in Cold War Allies Cuba, Vietnam," Bloomberg News, July 27, 2012, www.bloomberg.com/news/2012–07–27/russia-seeks-naval-supply-bases-in-cold-war-allies-cuba-vietnam.html.

111. Vladimir Isachenkov, "Putin Promises to Boost Russian Air Force," *Associated Press*, August 11, 2012, news.yahoo.com/putin-promises-boost-russian-air-force-142925431—finance.html.

112. "Russia to Become Iraq's Second-Biggest Arms Supplier," BBC News, October 9, 2012, www.bbc.co.uk/news/world-europe-19881858.

113. Laura Mills, "Russia Joins WTO After 18 Years of Negotiation," *USAToday*, August 22, 2012, usatoday30.usatoday.com/money/economy/trade/story/2012–08–22/russia-joins-world-trade-organization/57207664/1.

114. Myers and Herszenhorn, "Clinton Tells Russia That Sanctions Will Soon End."

115. David M. Herszenhorn and Ellen Barry, "Russia Halting Groups' Access to U.S. Money," *New York Times*, September 19, 2012, A1.

116. Andrew E. Kramer, "Putin Impedes European Inquiry of State Fuel Supplier," *New York Times*, September 12, 2012, A9.

117. Herszenhorn and Barry, "Russia Halting Groups' Access to U.S. Money."

118. Ibid.

119. David M. Herszenhorn, "Putin Says Missile Deal Is More Likely With Obama," *New York Times*, September 7, 2012, A7.

120. "Pussy Riot Case: One Defendant Freed in Russia," BBC News, October 10, 2012, www.bbc.co.uk/news/world-europe-19893008.

121. Andrew E. Kramer, "F.B.I. Says Russians Smuggled out U.S. Microchips," *New York Times*, October 5, 2012, A10; "UNICEF To End Russian Operations By End Of Year," *Radio Free Europe Radio Liberty*, October 9, 2012, www.rferl.org/content/unicef-end-russia-operations/24733634.html.

122. David M. Herszenhorn, "Russia Won't Renew Pact on Weapons With U.S.," *New York Times*, October 11, 2012, A10.

123. Sergei L. Loiko and Patrick J. McDonnell, "Putin Further Distances Russia From Syria's Assad," *Los Angeles Times*, December 20, 2012, www.latimes.com/news/nationworld/world/middleeast/la-fg-syria-putin-refugees-20121221,0,2772996.story.

124. "Russia's Putin Signs U.S. Anti-Adoption Bill," CNN, December 28, 2012, www.cnn.com/2012/12/28/world/europe/russia-us-adoptions/index.html?hpt=hp_t3.

8 Friendly Tyrants? The Arab Spring and the Egyptian Revolution

Stephen Zunes

Before You Begin

1. How does the U.S. government respond to totally unexpected events in regions of critical strategic importance?

2. How should the United States respond when an allied dictator is challenged by his own people?

3. What tools does the United States have to influence events when the key players are not soldiers on the battlefield or government officials around conference tables, but activists in the streets?

4. Does the United States risk being on the wrong side of history when an allied government proves itself unwilling to respond to popular demands for justice and democracy?

5. What do the largely nonviolent civil insurrections teach us about the real nature of political power?

Introduction

Egypt is by far the largest country in the Arab world and traditionally the center of Arab media, scholarship, and popular culture. Its identity as a nation is perhaps the oldest in the world, going back more than 5,000 years. Despite limited oil or other natural resources, the country has one of the stronger economies in the region due to tolls from the Suez Canal, tourism, and the largest industrial capacity in the Arab world. The center of a left-leaning pan-Arab nationalism under the leadership of Gamal Abdul-Nasser in the 1950s and 1960s, which included an informal alliance with the Soviet Union, the country dramatically swung to a pro-Western orientation under his successor, Anwar Sadat. Under the leadership of President Jimmy Carter, Egypt and Israel signed a peace treaty in 1978, returning the Sinai Peninsula—which had been captured by Israel in the June 1967 war—to

Egypt and establishing full diplomatic relations, the first Arab country to do so. Though most peace treaties result in a reduction in militarization, the Camp David Treaty included an annex whereby the United States would provide billions of dollars' worth of U.S. arms to both countries.

Sadat was assassinated in October 1981 and was succeeded by his vice president, career military officer and former air force chief Hosni Mubarak. Despite the shift in its geopolitical orientation and change in leadership, however, Egypt remained autocratic. And U.S. policy remained relatively constant under both Democratic and Republican administrations. Despite its many problems, the assumption was that Egypt would remain stable and dependent on the more than $1.7 billion in annual U.S. military and economic assistance.

However, U.S. diplomatic history is replete with examples of strategic analysts, State Department officers, and other Washington officials engaging in detailed policy planning dealing with almost any conceivable contingency—except for ordinary people mobilizing to create change. This certainly appears to have been the case regarding the pro-democracy insurrections in the Middle East early this decade, which caught Washington completely off guard.

For example, in Tunisia—the first Arab country to experience the wave of pro-democracy protests—the U.S. ambassador, in preparation for then–Secretary of State Condoleezza Rice's visit in 2008, spoke in glowing terms about the authoritarian regime of Zine El-'Abidine Ben Ali. A memo read, "Tunisia styles itself as a country that works," adding, "While Tunisians grumble privately about corruption by the first lady's family, there is an abiding appreciation for Ben Ali's success in steering his country clear of the instability and violence that have plagued Tunisia's neighbors."[1] According to Bush officials, "the lack of Tunisian political activism, or even awareness, seems to be a more serious impediment. While frustration with the First Family's corruption may eventually lead to increased demands for political liberalization, it does not yet appear to be heralding the end of the Ben Ali era."[2]

The Obama administration seemed similarly oblivious to the desire for change in Arab countries. Even during the early days of the Egyptian revolution, Secretary of State Hillary Clinton insisted that the country was stable.[3] As the popular pro-democracy struggle escalated, a top White House official acknowledged, "We're struggling to figure all this out."[4] Another major White House source noted, "We've had endless strategy sessions for the past two years on Mideast peace, on containing Iran. And how many of them factored in the possibility that Egypt moves from stability to turmoil? None."[5]

Though just as unexpected as the Tunisian and Egyptian revolutions, similar pro-democracy uprisings had been largely welcomed by the United States when they targeted autocratic governments that challenged U.S. interests in their respective regions, such as the successful uprisings in Serbia (2000), Georgia (2002), and Ukraine (2004) and the US clearly had hoped for the success of what proved to be failed uprisings, such as Iran's aborted Green Revolution in 2009. It is more problematic when such uprisings target regimes the United States sees as strategic allies.

The Obama administration quickly recognized that the pro-democracy revolutions were not seeking American leadership and that any efforts to become too deeply involved would be counterproductive. Criticism that the United States had not exercised sufficient leadership in more directly supporting the uprising is seriously misplaced because to do so would have almost certainly created a backlash that would have harmed these movements. Similarly, members of the Obama administration correctly realized they could not stop the uprisings either, despite criticisms from the right that they bear responsibility for the downfall of staunch U.S. allies. Indeed, as with former Soviet leader Mikhail Gorbachev in the face of the pro-democracy uprisings in Eastern Europe in 1989, Obama recognized there were limits to what a declining hegemonic power could control in an increasingly pluralistic and complex region.

There were times when it appeared that President Obama genuinely supported the aspirations of the revolutionaries, even while recognizing that public opinion in the Arab world—which would matter much more in the case of democratization—was generally less favorably aligned to U.S. policy goals than were allied autocratic regimes. However, there were other times when it appeared that his administration was reluctant to end its support of autocratic allies or support the aspirations of the largely youthful pro-democracy protesters in the streets.

This chapter examines the shift in U.S. policy regarding the largest and most important Arab country, Egypt, long America's most important Arab ally, when it was faced with a popular revolution against its US-backed dictator Hosni Mubarak.

U.S. Support for Mubarak

Though U.S. policy makers had a number of concerns regarding Washington's relations with Egypt, human rights and democracy were never high on the list.

Timeline

Key Developments in U.S.-Egyptian Relations

1952	A coup overthrows the pro-Western monarch and establishes a republic led by nationalist military officers.
1953	Egypt rejects U.S. offer of military aid in return for signing a security pact.
July 1956	Concerned by Egypt's growing relations with the Soviet Union and the Eastern Bloc, US withdraws tentative offer to help finance the construction of the Aswan High Dam. President Gamal Abdul-Nasser nationalizes Suez Canal to raise revenue.
November 1956	British, French, and Israeli forces invade Egypt. Fearing an anti-Western backlash and the weakening of the United Nations system, Eisenhower pressures U.S. allies to withdraw from occupied Egyptian territory.
June 1967	Israel invades and occupies the Sinai Peninsula, closing down the Suez Canal. Egypt, charging U.S. complicity in the Israeli conquest, breaks diplomatic relations with the United States.
1972	U.S. Secretary of State Henry Kissinger successfully convinces Israel to ignore peace overtures from Egyptian president Anwar Sadat.
October 1973	US launches largest military airlift in history to support Israeli efforts to defeat Egyptian forces, which had launched a war to reclaim occupied Egyptian territory.
1974	U.S. Secretary of State Henry Kissinger negotiates a series of disengagement agreements leading to partial Israeli withdrawal from the Sinai and the reopening of the Suez Canal.
September 1978	President Jimmy Carter negotiates a peace agreement between Egypt and Israel, leading to an Israeli withdrawal from occupied Egyptian territory and cementing large-scale foreign aid and strategic cooperation between Egypt and the United States.
October 1981	Sadat is assassinated. Former presidents Nixon, Ford, and Carter attend the funeral in an unprecedented display of support for the United States' new Arab ally. U.S. pledges support for the new president, Hosni Mubarak.

(continued)

Timeline *(continued)*

Key Developments in U.S.-Egyptian Relations

1990–91	Egypt supports US-led international effort against the Iraqi invasion and occupation of Kuwait, dispatching troops to Saudi Arabia in Operation Desert Shield.
2003	Egypt joins other Arab states in opposition to the U.S. invasion of Iraq. Left-leaning youth-led protest movements against the war emerge, which eventually would coalesce into Kefaya and other pro-democracy groups.
September 2005	The Bush administration praises Egypt's presidential election, in which Mubarak claims 88% of the vote, despite massive fraud and other irregularities.
June 2009	President Barack Obama visits Egypt, delivering a major speech on U.S. Middle East policy at Cairo University calling for greater democracy in the region but refraining from criticizing the Mubarak regime.
November 2010	Increased repression and another fraudulent election result in little reaction from Washington, leading to increasing pressure from human rights activists for a change in U.S. policy.

Under the Mubarak dictatorship, a simple gathering of five or more people without a permit was considered illegal. Peaceful pro-democracy protesters were routinely beaten and jailed. Martial law was in effect for nearly thirty years. Independent observers were banned from monitoring the country's routinely rigged elections, in which the largest opposition party was banned from participating and other opposition parties were severely restricted in producing publications and other activities. Corruption was rampant. Amnesty International and other reputable human rights groups documented gross and systematic human rights abuses against perceived opponents of the regime, including massive detention without due process, torture on an administrative basis, and extrajudicial killings. Targets of government repression included not just radical Islamists but leftists, liberal democrats, feminists, gay men, independent-minded scholars, Coptic Christians, and human rights activists.

As with other autocratic allies in the region, U.S. military, economic, and diplomatic support for the regime continued through both Republican and

Democratic administrations. In an effort to rationalize the U.S. invasion and occupation of Iraq, the Bush administration claimed that it was recalibrating U.S. policy to support greater freedom in the Middle East. In 2004, the Bush administration began to press Mubarak on a number of human rights issues, and Secretary of State Condoleezza Rice met with leading dissidents on a visit to Cairo. This effort was short-lived and never very substantive, however, and little was done or said regarding democracy and human rights in Egypt for the remainder of the Bush administration's time in office.

There was hope among pro-democracy activists that there might be a change in U.S. policy under the new administration of Barack Obama, who came to office in January 2009, and that the United States might finally apply real pressure on the regime. That hope did not last very long, however. For example, in an interview with Justin Webb of the BBC in June of that year, just prior to his first and only visit to Egypt, President Obama was asked, "Do you regard President Mubarak as an authoritarian ruler?" Obama's reply was "No," insisting that, "I tend not to use labels for folks." Obama also refused to acknowledge Mubarak's authoritarianism, saying, "I haven't met him." In further justifying his refusal to acknowledge the authoritarian nature of the Egyptian government, Obama referred to Mubarak as "a stalwart ally, in many respects, to the United States." He praised Egypt's despotic president for having "sustained peace with Israel, which is a very difficult thing to do in that region." Obama went on to insist, "I think he has been a force for stability. And good in the region." When Webb asked Obama how he planned to address the issue of the "thousands of political prisoners in Egypt," he answered only in terms of the United States being a better role model, such as closing the prison at Guantánamo Bay, and of the importance of the United States not trying to impose its human rights values on other countries. Obama said nothing about the possibility of linking even part of the more than $1.7 billion in annual U.S. aid to the Mubarak regime to providing freedom for prisoners of conscience. The most negative assessment Obama could muster for Mubarak's dictatorial regime in the interview was this: "Obviously, there have been criticisms of the manner in which politics operates in Egypt." Given that there have also been criticisms of the manner in which politics is conducted in every country of the world, including the United States, it was hardly the public display of disapproval pro-democracy forces in Egypt had hoped for. The Washington-based Freedom House ranked Egypt in the bottom quintile of the world's countries in terms of political rights and civil liberties.

Furthermore, Webb's question was not about whether there have been criticisms of the manner in which politics operates in Egypt, but whether Mubarak was an authoritarian leader. Obama, however, not only refused to label the Egyptian president as an authoritarian, he refused to even acknowledge that Mubarak led an authoritarian government.[6]

In the months prior to the uprising, Egyptian journalist Ibrahim Eissa complained that "Obama is not pressuring Mubarak at all" to end the repression, nor was Obama "realizing that society is going to implode on itself and destroy those regimes."[7] Particularly disappointing to pro-democracy activists was the administration's tepid response to the regime's blatantly fraudulent parliamentary elections in late November 2010, which were severely compromised by the refusal by the regime to allow independent monitors and mass arrests and escalated media suppression just prior to the vote. Daniel Calingaert of Freedom House, in testimony before Congress, observed how the stolen elections posed "a clear-cut choice for the Obama administration—whether to side with the Egyptian government or with the Egyptian people."[8] The administration made its choice clear in successfully pushing for a renewal of the multibillion dollar aid package to the Mubarak regime just weeks later.

Despite its decades of support for the Mubarak regime, the United States had also—through the National Endowment for Democracy (NED) and other congressionally funded foundations—provided a limited amount of aid to civil society organizations addressing women's issues, working conditions, human rights, election monitoring, and other pro-democracy efforts. An audit by the United States Agency for International Development (USAID) concluded that economic assistance to these independent civil society organizations was far more effective than the far greater amount of U.S. aid to government-controlled aid recipients. On coming to office, however, Obama slashed such funding by 75 percent while maintaining the $1.3 billion in military assistance. Michele Dunne, a senior associate at the Carnegie Endowment, observed that "[m]embers of the administration have made it clear that they did not want economic assistance to irritate the Egyptian government."[9] Funding was shifted to an endowment that could only allocate to groups approved by the Mubarak regime. According to Safwat Girgis, leader of the Egyptian Centre for Human Rights, Obama's decision was "in the best interest of the Egyptian government, not the people nor civil society organizations."[10] Such "pro-democracy" funding from the U.S. government-backed agencies has been controversial among some opposition groups, who fear that dependency on such assistance could make them susceptible to a U.S. political agenda and could discredit them in the eyes of the many Egyptians suspicious of U.S. motives. Many other activists, however, did feel abandoned by the Obama administration's decision to suspend much of this support.

Some U.S. Embassy staffers had sporadic contacts with pro-democracy activists and, despite the cutbacks and restrictions on such "pro-democracy" funding, there was still limited financial assistance to a number of civil society organizations. Subsequently, some have tried to credit (or blame) such foreign support for the subsequent uprising. This small amount of U.S. "democracy assistance," however, did not include any support for training in strategic non-violent action or the other kinds of grassroots mobilization that proved decisive in the anti-Mubarak struggle, and most of the key groups that organized the protests refused U.S. funding on principle. In any case, the amount of U.S. funding for NED and related programs in Egypt and the periodic contact between embassy personnel and Egyptian activists paled in comparison with the billions of dollars' worth of military and economic assistance to the Mubarak regime and the close and regular interaction among U.S. officials and leading Egyptian political and military leaders.

Indeed, direct U.S. support for Egypt's armed forces, paramilitary units, and secret police—altogether numbering nearly 2 million—remained at more than $1.3 billion annually under Obama. Throughout Mubarak's nearly thirty years as Egypt's president, his regime received more aid than any other country except Israel. Despite the prodding of US-based human rights groups, it was extremely difficult for anyone in Republican or Democratic administrations or on either side of the aisle on Capitol Hill to even raise questions about American support for the Egyptian dictatorship. For example, a proposed non-binding Senate resolution in 2010 calling on the Egyptian regime to liberalize and hold free elections was blocked by Senate Intelligence Committee chairwoman Dianne Feinstein (D-CA).

When Obama visited Egypt in 2009, he did engage in a few symbolic efforts to demonstrate a concern for human rights. He didn't praise Mubarak, his Egyptian host, from the podium in his University of Cairo speech, as is generally customary on such occasions. Nor did he physically embrace the dictator or otherwise offer visual displays of affection, as is typical during such visits to leaders in that region. The Obama administration invited some leading critics of the regime, including both secular liberals and moderate Islamists, to witness his speech and insisted that the regime allow them to attend. However, Kefaya,

Egypt's leading grassroots pro-democracy group, boycotted the speech, demanding that Obama show his commitment to democracy in deeds, not words.

In his speech, Obama proclaimed his

> unyielding belief that all people yearn for certain things: the ability to speak your mind and have a say in how you are governed; confidence in the rule of law and the equal administration of justice; government that is transparent and doesn't steal from the people; the freedom to live as you choose.

Emphasizing that such concepts are not just American ideas but basic universal human rights, he pledged that the United States "will support them everywhere." Though the American president's comments were well-received, few of the human rights activists who would lead the revolution eighteen months later appeared willing to believe the United States actually supported human rights in their country because Obama's rhetoric was not matched by action, specifically an end to the arming and funding of one of the most repressive governments in the Middle East. As journalist Shirin Sadeghi commented, "Obama's inevitable message to the Muslim world" was that "the United States will look the other way at your governments' repressive policies because a working relationship with them is more important than a consideration of the peoples' rights."[11]

In rejecting the problematic neoconservative ideology of his predecessor, Obama had largely fallen back onto the realpolitik of previous administrations by continuing to support Mubarak and other repressive allies in the region through unconditional arms transfers and other security assistance. Although the Obama administration, like much of the international community, was understandably skeptical of externally mandated, top-down approaches to democratization through "regime change"—a key element in the foreign policy of the outgoing Bush administration—as of the end of the first half of Obama's first term, there appeared to be no alternative policy in place.

At the same time, there was a subtle, but important, shift in the U.S. government's discourse on human rights when Obama came into office in January 2009. The Bush administration pushed a rather superficial structuralist view. It focused, for instance, on elections—which can easily be rigged and manipulated in many cases—in order to change certain governments for purposes of expanding U.S. power and influence. Indeed, Bush praised the transparently fraudulent 2005 presidential elections in Egypt as "important steps" toward freedom and democracy.[12] Obama, by contrast, took on more of an agency view of human rights, emphasizing such rights as freedom of expression and the right to protest, recognizing that true democracy can only come from below and not be imposed from above.

Until early 2011, however, this had not translated into much in the way of tangible policy changes. Military aid and arms sales to Mubarak in Egypt and other repressive Arab regimes continued unabated. However, the White House's statement in the early days of the Egyptian uprising calling for the regime to support "universal rights, including the right to peaceful assembly, association, and speech"[13] was indicative that the administration was ready to see the possible fall of the regime because it presumably recognized that the free exercise of such rights could very well mean the end of Mubarak's rule. The Obama administration seemed to recognize that democracy would not come to the Arab world from foreign intervention or sanctimonious statements from Washington, but from Arab peoples themselves.

Still, given that the Mubarak regime was an important U.S. ally and the Egyptian people had largely negative views on U.S. policy in the Middle East, there were still questions in Washington as to whether greater democracy was even desirable.

The Tunisian Precedent

Although the United States was the primary foreign backer of the autocratic regimes in Egypt, Bahrain, and Yemen—all of which would experience pro-democracy uprisings in early 2011—in Tunisia, the United States played a secondary role relative to France, the former colonial power. Still, Washington had traditionally seen the regime of Ben Ali as an ally, and strategic cooperation with the regime had been increasing.

During the first weeks of the Tunisian protests, rather than praise the pro-democracy movement and condemn the country's repressive regime, Secretary of State Hillary Clinton instead expressed her concern over the impact of the "unrest and instability" on the "very positive aspects of our relationship with Tunisia," insisting that the United States was "not taking sides" and that she would "wait and see" before even communicating directly with the Tunisian dictator or his ministers.[14] Furthermore, just days after the popular uprising against the Ben Ali dictatorship began on December 17, 2010, Congress weighed in with support for the regime by passing a budget resolution that included $12 million in security assistance to Tunisia, one of only seven foreign governments (the others being Israel, Egypt, Iraq, Afghanistan, Jordan, and Colombia) provided direct taxpayer-funded military aid.[15]

Along with limited political freedom and government accountability, the poor economic situation in Tunisia was a major focus of the protests, particularly among unemployed educated youth. Secretary Clinton acknowledged this issue on January 11, 2011—nearly four weeks after the outbreak of the uprising—noting that "one of my biggest concerns in this entire region are the many young people without economic opportunities in their home countries." Rather than calling for a more democratic and accountable government in Tunisia, however, her suggestion for resolving the crisis was that the economies of Tunisia and other North African states "need to be more open."[16] Ironically, Tunisia under the Ben Ali regime—more than almost any country in the region—had been following the dictates of Washington and the International Monetary Fund in instituting "structural adjustment programs," privatizing much of its economy and allowing for an unprecedented level of "free trade." The US also backed IMF efforts to push the Tunisian government to eliminate the remaining subsidies on fuel and basic food stuffs and further deregulate its financial sector. Countries that have adopted this neoliberal model often see increased economic output, but it can also exacerbate inequality. This was certainly the case in Tunisia, where some publicly owned enterprises were simply transferred to the family of the president's wife, and the gap in economic opportunity grew between the relatively prosperous coastal areas and the impoverished interior and southern regions, where the protests originated. Indeed, it is probably no accident that the suicide of Mohamed Bouazizi, the unemployed young man from central Tunisia forced to sell fruit on the street, only to be abused by police and have his wares seized, became the spark that led to the revolution.

These policies, which increased rather than decreased unemployment while enriching those close to the country's top ruling families, was privately acknowledged by the U.S. embassy, which labeled the Ben Ali regime as a "kleptocracy." Cables described Tunisia as a "police state, with little freedom of expression or association, and serious human rights problems" and stated that "President Ben Ali is aging, his regime is sclerotic and there is no clear successor."[17] The country's elites were described as almost Mafia-like in their complex networks of control, stealing enormous wealth from almost every sector of the economy, and a series of WikiLeaks documents vividly described the extravagant lifestyle and related egregious behavior of the families of the president and his in-laws.

Neither the Obama administration nor its predecessors apparently shared the embassy's concern over the regime's persistent pattern of gross and systematic human rights violations. Indeed, Tunis became the home of the Middle

East Partnership Initiative, a regional office for the State Department's "democratic reform program." U.S. officials justified their support for Ben Ali's dictatorship in the name of the "war on terror," even though radical Islamist movements had been weaker in Tunisia than in practically any other Arab country. Ben Ali's regime assisted the United States in "extraordinary rendition," in which suspected Islamist radicals captured by U.S. forces or kidnapped by intelligence services were brought to Tunisia for interrogation and torture. Tunisia was also one of the governments more willing to cooperate with the U.S. Africa Command (AFRICOM) in its efforts to extend U.S. military operations in and military relations with African countries.

After official silence followed more than two weeks of protests and increasingly severe repression by the government, the State Department began to issue some mildly worded rebukes over the police attacks against demonstrators. Even though most of the protests had been nonviolent, State Department spokesman P. J. Crowley chose to represent the movement by its most unruly components, stating that the Obama administration was "concerned about government actions, but we're also concerned about actions by the demonstrators, those who do not have peaceful intentions."[18]

U.S. policy began to shift as the pro-democracy movement gained momentum, however. Just two days after the interview in which she appeared to back the Ben Ali regime, Clinton took a more proactive stance at a meeting in Qatar, where she noted that "people have grown tired of corrupt institutions and a stagnant political order" and called for "political reforms that will create the space young people are demanding, to participate in public affairs and have a meaningful role in the decisions that shape their lives."[19] Both out of recognition that France still had more influence on Tunisia than did the United States and that events inside the country would ultimately decide the country's fate, the United States recognized there were limits to the actions that could be taken to impact the outcome.

The following day, January 14, as Ben Ali was fleeing the country for exile in Saudi Arabia, President Obama came forward with the most pointed declaration in support of democracy in the Arab world since he became president:

> I condemn and deplore the use of violence against citizens peacefully voicing their opinion in Tunisia, and I applaud the courage and dignity of the Tunisian people. The United States stands with the entire international community in bearing witness to this brave and determined struggle for the universal rights that we must all uphold, and we will long remember the

images of the Tunisian people seeking to make their voices heard. . . . Each nation gives life to the principle of democracy in its own way, grounded in the traditions of its own people, and those countries that respect the universal rights of their people are stronger and more successful than those that do not. I have no doubt that Tunisia's future will be brighter if it is guided by the voices of the Tunisian people.[20]

The Egyptian Revolution

President Obama also spoke eloquently, if briefly, in support of Tunisia's pro-democracy uprising during his January 25 State of the Union address, yet he was silent regarding the dramatic developments in Egypt that day, as hundreds of thousands of pro-democracy activists massed in Tahrir Square in Cairo and elsewhere around the country in an unprecedented display of opposition to the US-backed dictatorship. Secretary of State Clinton insisted that the Mubarak regime was "looking for ways to respond to the legitimate needs and interests of the Egyptian people,"[21] despite the miserable failure of the regime to do so during its nearly thirty years in power. Asked whether the United States still supported Mubarak, White House spokesman Robert Gibbs said that Egypt remained a "close and important ally." As during the Tunisian protests, the Obama administration tried to equate the scattered violence of some pro-democracy protesters with the far greater violence of the dictatorship's security forces, with Gibbs saying, "We continue to believe first and foremost that all of the parties should refrain from violence."[22] Similarly, Vice President Joe Biden, when asked what role the United States should play in regard to the burgeoning insurrection, responded, "I think the role we have to play is continuing to make it clear . . . that we think violence is inappropriate on the part of either party—either of the parties, the government or the protesters."[23]

On the third day of the uprising, the regime cut off all cell phone and Internet communication. Even when Clinton finally issued a statement urging "Egyptian authorities not to prevent peaceful protests or block communications including on social media sites,"[24] the administration simply called for the regime to reform from within rather than supporting pro-democracy protesters' demand that the dictator step down. As Clinton put it, "We believe strongly that the Egyptian government has an important opportunity at this moment in time to implement political, economic and social reforms to respond to the legitimate needs and interests of the Egyptian people."[25]

As the protests grew over the next couple of days, as well as the prospects that the regime might actually be facing a serious challenge, Vice President Biden rushed to Mubarak's defense, rejecting calls that he step aside, simply saying that he needed to be "more responsive to some of the needs of the people out there" and expressing his belief that Mubarak "is going to respond to some of the legitimate concerns that are being raised." In addition, the vice president insisted, in response to a question by veteran journalist Jim Lehrer, "I would not refer to him as a dictator." And, despite explicit calls by the large and diverse protesters for the regime to step down, Biden claimed that they were simply "middle-class folks who are looking for a little more access and a little more opportunity."[26]

The reluctance to more openly support the pro-democracy movement or demand Mubarak's resignation likely came from a belief that the regime could probably survive the challenge and that it would react negatively to what it perceived as any wavering of U.S. support, as would other autocratic allies in the region. There was undoubtedly also concern that, should the popular movement succeed in bringing down the dictatorship, they would probably not be as supportive of U.S. foreign policy priorities in the region. There was still a belief in Washington that Mubarak could survive, but the need to enact meaningful reforms was urgent to quell the uprising. On January 28, Obama spoke on the phone with Mubarak and pressed him to enact meaningful reforms and to end the repression by security forces.

In the White House, aides were debating about how aggressively the United States should pressure Mubarak to resign or get serious about having free and early elections. There was a growing sense that Mubarak might be forced out, but the US would not want to be seen as trying to engineer a successor, particularly if the regime somehow survived. One senior administration official was quoted as saying,

> It's just a very tough line to straddle. If he guts this out and stays, we're going to continue to need him and work with him, and he might not appreciate that we pushed. Bottom line, Egypt's destiny is Egypt's to decide, and we'll work with whoever emerges or is left standing.

Another problem was the lack of any obvious successor. The official noted, "There isn't a natural successor. And if we were to embrace a particular person, it does more harm than good. It's a classic dilemma for America."[27] As a result, Obama's calls for democratic reforms still rested on the hope that needed changes could take place under President Mubarak, as when he noted how the Egyptian president "has a responsibility to give meaning" to his promises to build "a better democracy and greater economic opportunity" and to "take concrete steps and actions that deliver on that promise."[28]

The U.S. refusal to either defend Mubarak or demand his ouster was met with frustration by both supporters and opponents of the Egyptian dictator. However, as former U.S. Defense Secretary William Cohen put it, Obama eventually "will have to make the decision on standing with Mubarak. Too soon is a mistake. And too late is mistake. No one can say at this particular point in time."[29]

Despite questions as to how to respond to the situation, President Obama did recognize the significance of the ongoing protests, monitoring the situation closely and requesting multiple daily briefings. Unlike his predecessor, Obama solicited advice from Middle Eastern scholars and others who knew the region well. One senior administration official told a story of how the president

> dropped into a previously scheduled Principals Committee meeting on a different topic so that he could discuss Egypt with his top foreign policy advisors. At that meeting, the President decided to call President Mubarak and to make a statement to the American people.[30]

There were those within the administration who apparently believed that, even if Mubarak had to step down, the regime could largely remain intact. Some called for backing security chief Omar Suleiman, whom Mubarak had named as his vice president on January 29, as a logical successor. Suleiman had worked closely with the United States on the extraordinary rendition program, on security issues involving the besieged Hamas-controlled Gaza Strip, and other issues of mutual interest and was well-known in Washington as a skilled negotiator and a friend of the United States. Others expressed concern that his notorious reputation for human rights abuses (which had given him the nickname of "torturer-in-chief") and his close personal ties to Mubarak and the more corrupt elements in the Egyptian military would make him unacceptable to the masses of Egyptians in the streets across the country, now numbering well into the millions. Though skeptical of Suleiman, Obama recognized that the Egyptian military had been a key player in Egyptian politics since the Free Officers coup of 1952, and he believed they needed to be seen as a partner in determining the future of the strategically important country.

On January 30, the fifth day of the Egyptian demonstrations, as the protests continued to gain momentum, the Obama administration started speaking in terms of an eventual transition to democratic rule and telling the regime that large-scale repression of nonviolent protesters—which would presumably be implemented with US-supplied weaponry—would be unacceptable. As George Washington University professor Marc Lynch, who advised the White House during the uprising, observed during that period, there was a growing sense within the administration that

> Mubarak's regime has been wounded at its core, and even if he survives in the short run the regime will have to make major internal changes to regain any semblance of normality. An Egyptian regime which spends the next years in a state of military lockdown will hardly be a useful ally.[31]

It was at this point that Obama directed his aides to maintain close contact with Egyptian opposition activists and other leaders outside the government,[32] and the Obama administration began speaking openly about a transition to democracy.

On the Sunday morning talk shows that day, Secretary Clinton pressed for restraint by security forces and called for an "orderly, peaceful transition" to a "real democracy" in Egypt, but she still refused to call for Mubarak to step down, insisting that "it's not a question of who retains power. That should not be the issue. It's how are we going to respond to the legitimate needs and grievances expressed by the Egyptian people and chart a new path." On the one hand, she recognized that whether Mubarak would remain in power "is going to be up to the Egyptian people." On the other hand, she continued to speak in terms of reforms coming from the regime, stating that U.S. policy was to

> help clear the air so that those who remain in power, starting with President Mubarak, with his new vice president, with the new prime minister, will begin a process of reaching out, of creating a dialogue that will bring in peaceful activists and representatives of civil society to . . . plan a way forward that will meet the legitimate grievances of the Egyptian people.[33]

Given the ambivalent signals from the administration in the first few days of the uprising and continued support for Mubarak by some prominent Republican congressional leaders and influential media pundits, within the White House there was a growing concern whether the Egyptian regime had gotten the message that the United States had lost faith in its longtime ally.

Also, Republicans on Capitol Hill and elsewhere appeared to be building the foundations of an "Obama lost Egypt" attack, to be launched in the next election cycle should a democratic transition lead to an anti-American government or serve as a precedent for further instability in the Middle East. Consequently, there were also concerns that the Egyptian regime might believe that Obama—who had been quick to pull back on some foreign policy issues in the face of attacks from the right—might not be serious. Similarly, human rights advocates and other critics of the Obama administration on the left—worn cynical from the longstanding U.S. support for the Mubarak dictatorship—were underscoring earlier statements by Clinton and Biden that appeared to be defending the regime. As a result, the administration recognized an urgency in going public with its shift in thinking.

The White House then announced that the president's position was that he wanted "an orderly transition to a government that is responsive to the aspirations of the Egyptian people." Recognizing the regional significance of these developments, Obama personally called the leaders of Great Britain, Turkey, Israel, and Saudi Arabia to discuss the situation. On January 31, the *Washington Post* reported, "The Obama administration firmly aligned itself on Sunday with the protest movement that has overtaken Egypt, calling for an 'orderly transition' to a more representative government." Fearing that such unrest could spread to other countries in the region, the article noted that "[i]n telephone calls to Egyptian and regional leaders, President Obama and his top national security advisers tried to reassure them that their countries remain vital U.S. strategic partners, while warning that the political status quo is not sustainable."[34]

Indeed, though never actually calling on Mubarak to step down, President Obama became even more explicit regarding the shift in policy by announcing on February 1 that U.S. policy was for there to be "an orderly transition" of power in Egypt and that it "must be meaningful, it must be peaceful, and it must begin now."[35] To emphasize this sentiment still further, White House spokesperson Robert Gibbs said on February 2—in response to Mubarak's promise to step down when his term expired in September—that "now means yesterday."

The change in the administration's approach likely came from the belated realization that nothing short of a Tiananmen Square–style massacre would probably stop the protests, and that such measures using US-provided weaponry would inflame anti-Americanism throughout Egypt and the entire Arab world and could drive the anti-Mubarak resistance underground into the arms of violent extremists. The Obama administration made it clear to the Egyptian military that any large-scale repression would have seriously negative implications for the U.S.-Egyptian relationship, presumably meaning severing U.S. military aid and cooperation. It also began to press the military to force Mubarak to step down.

To underscore that this dramatic shift in U.S. policy went beyond the administration, Democratic Senator John Kerry and Republican Senator John McCain, both of whom have served as leading spokesmen of their respective parties on foreign policy issues on Capitol Hill, called on Mubarak to hand over power to a caretaker government.

The pressure was met with great resistance, of course, as the regime continued to downplay the significance of the protests and exaggerate the threat from Islamists, but the administration persisted. Although there was disappointment among pro-democracy activists and their American supporters that the Obama administration had not moved earlier, some U.S. analysts, such as Marc Lynch, defended the more gradualist approach, noting how Mubarak had been a U.S. ally for thirty years and "needed to be given the chance to respond appropriately. . . . Obama saying 'Mubarak must go' would not have made Mubarak go, absent the careful preparation of the ground so that the potential power-brokers saw that they really had no choice." However, as Lynch also noted, as the regime's desperation and its violence against the protesters escalated, it became both possible and necessary to increase the pressure.[36]

The administration began quietly working on convincing leading military and civilian figures in the regime to distance themselves from Mubarak, negotiate with the opposition, and to consider drafting constitutional revisions they could quickly push through the parliament.[37]

Quiet pressure from Washington and—more significantly—the massive and largely nonviolent resistance in the streets of Egypt increased over the next week and a half until Mubarak resigned on February 11, handing power over to the Supreme Council of the Armed Forces. President Obama, in response to the news, stated,

There are very few moments in our lives where we have the privilege to witness history taking place. This is one of those moments. This is one of those times. The people of Egypt have spoken, their voices have been heard, and Egypt will never be the same. . . . This is the power of human dignity, and it can never be denied. Egyptians have inspired us, and they've done so by putting the lie to the idea that justice is best gained through violence. For in Egypt, it was the moral force of nonviolence—not terrorism, not mindless killing—but nonviolence, moral force that bent the arc of history toward justice once more. . . . The word *Tahrir* means liberation. It is a word that speaks to that something in our souls that cries out for freedom. And forevermore it will remind us of the Egyptian people—of what they did, of the things that they stood for, and how they changed their country, and in doing so changed the world.[38]

The Shift in Policy

Throughout the eighteen-day uprising, particularly during the first week, there were some major divisions within the administration regarding U.S. policy toward Egypt, with some officials still insisting on backing Mubarak or supporting a handover to Suleiman and the military. Secretary of Defense Robert Gates, a holdover from the Bush administration, initially appeared to support continued U.S. backing of the Egyptian regime, as did Secretary of State Clinton, who—even during the height of the repression—insisted "[t]here is no discussion of cutting off aid."[39] As late as February 6, Clinton was publicly advocating a leadership role for the notorious General Suleiman.[40] Vice President Biden, who has been more influential than most vice presidents on foreign policy matters, initially allied with the more conservative elements of the administration, but eventually he recognized the need for the United States to distance itself from its long-time ally. In an embarrassing moment emblematic of these divisions, President Obama's special envoy, retired veteran diplomat Frank Wisner, who had ostensibly been dispatched to Cairo to pressure Mubarak to step down, instead insisted during a stopover in Europe on his way home on February 6 that "President Mubarak's continued leadership is critical" in the interest of "stability."[41] This forced an embarrassed State Department to disavow earlier claims that he was actually a U.S. envoy, saying he was merely an available conduit, and they firmly distanced themselves from his statement.[42]

Historically, the National Security Council—based in the White House and reporting directly to the president—has taken a somewhat more hawkish position in regard to support for allied dictatorships, while the State Department—made up largely of career diplomats—has sometimes been more willing to challenge autocratic regimes. During the Obama administration's first term, however, the situation seemed to be reversed, as the president appointed to the NSC somewhat younger and more innovative thinkers from academia, such as Michael McFaul and Samantha Power, who had a particularly strong concern for human rights and an appreciation of the power of nonviolent pro-democracy struggles. Meanwhile, he granted Hillary Clinton the power to effectively name key appointees in the State Department, who tended to be somewhat older and more traditional representatives of the foreign policy establishment who had served in her husband's administration in the 1990s. These included Undersecretary of State for Political Affairs Bill Burns, who had served as ambassador to Jordan and in other posts under the Clinton administration and assistant secretary of state for Near Eastern affairs under the Bush administration; he was a major supporter of Mubarak.

These differences came to the fore in discussions during the Egyptian uprising and subsequent revolts. Although Obama's personal sympathies appeared to lean toward more open support for human rights and democracy, he was also willing—as he had demonstrated in such cases as the 2009 coup in Honduras, the ongoing Moroccan occupation of Western Sahara, and elsewhere—to sometimes defer to the realpolitik orientation of officials in the State Department and the Pentagon. However, when a foreign policy issue has been deemed of critical national security interest, the White House has had no problem asserting its primacy. This is what prevailed regarding the U.S. response to the Egyptian revolution.

Indeed, Obama pretty quickly recognized that the future of Egypt would come not from Washington and other Western capitals, but from the streets of Cairo and other Egyptian cities. He also recognized that when an unarmed insurrection advances to the stage it had in Egypt by the second week of the protests, the United States could no more suppress or co-opt pro-democracy forces than the Soviet Union could do in regard to similar movements in Eastern Europe in 1989. He did realize, however, that the United States could have an impact on the Egyptian military, with which U.S. officials had worked closely for more than three decades and in which administration officials had cultivated personal relationships with important officers at various levels. Indeed, during those critical days the Obama administration played its most important role in maintaining near-constant communication with its contacts throughout the ranks of the Egyptian military, pressuring them not to massacre protesters. The administration made clear that the use of large-scale force against nonviolent protesters would sever their close working relationship and jeopardize the flow of new military equipment, the junkets to the United States for meetings and advanced training, and other perks Egyptian officers enjoyed, which undoubtedly had an impact.[43] Although it is quite possible that Egyptian soldiers would have refused such orders anyway, as they did in Tunisia and elsewhere, this was fortunately never tested. More than 800 protesters were killed during the eighteen days of the uprising, but the slaughter could have been far worse.

Despite decades of U.S. support for the Mubarak regime, the Egyptian protests featured virtually no explicit anti-Americanism, a striking contrast with the Iranian revolution of 1978–1979, the last time a popular civil insurrection in a large Middle Eastern country ousted a US-backed dictatorship. Indeed, the Egyptian protests focused almost exclusively on Mubarak's misrule rather than the U.S. role in enabling it. Despite efforts by the Egyptian regime and its U.S. supporters to frighten American policy makers into thinking that the only alternative to Mubarak and other Western-backed Arab dictators would be Islamist extremists, Egyptian protest leader Ahmed Salah noted,

> It is clear those revolutions encompass all elements of society and seek values aspired to by people around the world—the most important of which is freedom. We were systematically punished for decades for a notion that only resides in the minds of western politicians and the lies of tyrants. We lived in a police state, occupied by a two million-strong militarised police force. Given this, isn't there now a moral responsibility that the west bears?[44]

Indeed, Salah, in an interview with Jackson Diehl of the *Washington Post,* was frank about his disappointment (shared by many Egyptian activists) with the U.S. government's failure to support them initially and its slowness to respond when the pro-democracy struggle finally became a mass movement.[45]

Still, Obama appeared to have recognized that the future of Egypt did not necessarily belong in the hands of corrupt authoritarian rulers. In 2002, back when he was an Illinois state senator, he had argued that support for Egypt was counter to U.S. interests, saying,

> Let's fight to make sure our so-called allies in the Middle East . . . the Egyptians, stop oppressing their own people, and suppressing dissent, and tolerating corruption and inequality and mismanaging their economies so that their youth grow up without education, without prospects, without hope, the ready recruits of terrorist cells.[46]

It would be fair to surmise, then, that before he was put in a position of having to battle with the State Department, the Defense Department, intelligence agencies, Congress, the Israel Lobby, arms exporters, and other powerful interests that support propping up Arab dictators, Obama had an innate understanding of the reality of Egypt under Mubarak and its consequences and thus genuinely supported the forces seeking his ouster.

Obama also appears to have recognized that the United States could not afford be on the wrong side of history. Indeed, Obama—perhaps influenced by his experience as a community organizer in his youth—is open to recognizing human agency and that political power comes not just from those in formal positions of authority or those who have the guns, but from civil society as well.

Conclusion

The dramatic change in U.S. policy, from supporting the Ben Ali and Mubarak dictatorships to belatedly supporting a democratic transition in Egypt and Tunisia, illustrated a radical shift in understanding of the power dynamics in the region. Despite the longstanding sense of fatalism among Arabs that Washington would ultimately impact what happened on the "Arab street," the Arab street proved itself capable of impacting what happened in Washington. Indeed, after scrambling to play catch-up during the events unfolding in the two allied North African countries, President Obama finally made eloquent statements praising the pro-democracy demonstrators in Tunisia and Egypt—right after those countries' dictators fled.

Much has been written about how the uprisings of the "Arab Spring" have discredited the radical Islamist narrative that pro-Western dictatorships could only be toppled by subscribing to reactionary interpretations of Islam and supporting violence and even terror. Indeed, Salafi extremists and allied groups have never come close to threatening US-backed autocratic regimes and, if anything, have strengthened them by providing a justification for further militarization and repression. The dramatic decline in support for al Qaeda and related groups in recent years has been largely attributed to the success of these unarmed insurrections.[47]

In addition, though, the pro-democracy struggles in the Arab world have also challenged radical ideologues on the other extreme: the neo-conservatives and other supporters of the Iraq War who insisted that only by Western invasion and occupation could Arab dictators be toppled and democracy take hold. Even putting aside how the repressive and corrupt US-backed regime in Baghdad has fallen well short of virtually any reasonable standard of democracy, it is now clear that there are more effective and far less destructive means of bringing down autocratic regimes.

President George W. Bush called for spreading democracy from "Damascus to Tehran." And, although most observers would certainly agree that Syria and Iran could use more democracy, it is noteworthy that he did not call for spreading democracy from Tunis to Cairo. Or from Riyadh to Manama to Muscat to Rabat, or to the capitals of any allied dictatorship. Despite President Bush's pro-democracy rhetoric, the Bush administration provided more support to more dictatorships in the greater Middle East and North Africa than any previous U.S. administration. Most pro-democracy activists in the region believed that calls for democratic change by the Bush administration were insincere and were employed as an excuse for its imperialist ambitions, arguing that it actually set back indigenous pro-democracy struggles. In many respects, these liberal democrats argued, Bush did for democracy in that region what Stalin did for socialism in Eastern Europe, associating these ideals with foreign conquest, occupation, and domination and giving regimes an excuse to label any pro-democracy agitation as part of a foreign imperialist plot.

It is generally recognized that the Bush administration, and possibly most previous administrations as well, would have been less willing than the Obama administration to accept Mubarak's downfall. At the same time, the Obama administration has continued to support the repressive monarchy in Bahrain, with the occasional stern rebuke, despite its brutal suppression of a nonviolent pro-democracy movement with the help of the Saudi military in the months following the Egyptian revolution. And while playing an active role in forcing the resignation of Yemeni dictator Ali Abdullah Salih in early 2012, the United States appeared to steer the transition process in favor of the autocratic president's elite former allies, rather than the pro-democracy activists. Still, perhaps the most important lesson from the Egyptian revolution and other civil insurrections is that it may force the United States to reevaluate longstanding assumptions about the nature of political power.

The emphasis in the West on cultural or religious explanations for the paucity of democracy and liberty in the greater Middle East tends to minimize other factors that are arguably more important. These include the legacy of colonialism, high levels of militarization, and uneven economic development, much of which can be linked to the policies of Western governments, including the United States. Arms transfers and the diplomatic and economic support from Washington have always played an important role in keeping these regimes in power.

As the world's most militarized region and the region with the most military-backed dictatorships, the Middle East and North Africa have long exemplified the realist paradigm that power rests with whoever has the guns, which has traditionally been correlated with the backing of foreign industrialized powers, primarily the United States. The dramatic civil insurrections in Egypt and other Arab countries, however, have permanently challenged that assumption. Indeed, these largely nonviolent revolutions remind us that even a monopoly of military force and the support of the one remaining superpower may not suffice to retain power in the face of massive popular nonviolent resistance. Even the most brutal regime armed with massive weaponry from the United States or another major power is still ultimately powerless if the people refuse to recognize its authority. Despite the defeat of the pro-democracy struggle in Bahrain and the incomplete pro-democracy struggle in Yemen, the dramatic events in recent years have underscored the fact that through general strikes, filling the streets, mass refusal to obey official orders, and other forms of nonviolent resistance people can overthrow even the most brutal and autocratic regime.

Indeed, one of the most significant aspects of the unarmed pro-democracy insurrections in the Arab world is that they are indicative that—however outside powers may choose to respond—the United States and other foreign governments are less relevant today in determining the future of the region than they have been in more than century. Both critics and supporters of a strong U.S. role in the world often exaggerate American power. Despite the understandable disappointment of some human rights activists that the United States did not do "more" to support the revolutions once they were launched, the Obama administration, after a number of initial missteps, seems to have recognized that the future of the Middle East is ultimately in the hands of the people of the region and, perhaps more important, once an uprising reaches a critical mass, there is little the United States or any foreign government can do about it.

Key Actors

Barak Obama   President of the United States who ultimately supported pro-democracy protesters in Egypt.

Hosni Mubarak   President of Egypt who resisted the pro-democracy movement.

Joe Biden   Vice president of the United States who initially sided with the pro-Mubarak officials in the Obama administration.

Hillary Clinton   U.S. secretary of state who initially sided with the pro-Mubarak officials in the Obama administration.

Kefaya, the **April 6 Movement,**   and other pro-democracy groups in Egypt, which provided impetus for the public movement to demand Mubarak's ouster.

Notes

1. Scott Shane, "Cables from American Diplomats Portray U.S. Ambivalence on Tunisia," *New York Times,* January 15, 2011, A14.

2. WikiLeaks, Cable reference id: #06TUNIS1673.

3. "U.S. Urges Restraint in Egypt, Says Government Stable," *Reuters,* January 25, 2011, www.reuters.com/article/2011/01/25/ozatp-egypt-protest-clinton-idAFJOE 70O0KF20110125.

4. Mike Allen, "Behind the Curtain: Egypt Erupts in the WH," *Politico,* January 31, 2011, www.politico.com/blogs/laurarozen/0111/Behind_the_curtain_Egypt_erupts_in_ the_WH.html.

5. David E. Sanger, "As Mubarak Digs In, U.S. Policy in Egypt Is Complicated," *New York Times,* February 5, 2011, A12.

6. Justin Webb's America, BBC, "An Interview with President Obama," June 1, 2009.

7. David Lepeska, "Gag Time in Cairo: An Interview with Egyptian Journalist Ibrahim Eissa," *Columbia Journalism Review,* November 9, 2010, www.cjr.org/cam paign_desk/gag_time_in_cairo.php.

8. Hearing before the Subcommittees on Africa, Global Health, and Human Rights of the Committee On Foreign Affairs, U.S. House of Representatives, 112th Congress, 1st session, December 8, 2011.

9. Mitt Bradley, "Egypt's Democracy Groups Fear Shift in U.S. Policy Will Harm Their Work," *The National,* January 29, 2010.

10. Ibid.

11. Shirin Sadeghi, "View From Cairo: What about the People, Obama?" *Huffington Post,* June 4, 2009, www.huffingtonpost.com/shirin-sadeghi/view-from-cairo-what -abou_b_211323.html.

12. Stephen Zunes, "Bush at the UN: Annotated," *Foreign Policy In Focus,* September 20, 2006, www.fpif.org/articles/bush_at_the_un_annotated.

13. Office of the Press Secretary, "Remarks by the President on the Situation in Egypt," The White House, January 28, 2011.

14. Hillary Rodham Clinton, Interview with Taher Barake of Al Arabiya—Dubai, UAE, January 11, 2011.

15. Alexis Arieff, "Political Transition in Tunisia," Report for Congress, Congressional Research Service, June 18, 2012, www.crs.gov.

16. Clinton, Interview with Taher Barake.

17. "U.S. Embassy Cables: Tunisia—A U.S. Foreign Policy Conundrum," *Guardian*, December 7, 2010, www.guardian.co.uk/world/us-embassy-cables-documents/217138.

18. Tim Lister, "Tunisian Protests Fueled by Social Media Networks," CNN, January 21, 2011, www.cnn.com/2011/WORLD/africa/01/12/tunisia/index.html.

19. Hillary Clinton, "Forum for the Future: Partnership Dialogue Panel Session," Department of State, January 13, 2011.

20. The White House, Office of the Press Secretary, "Statement by the President on Events in Tunisia," January 14, 2011.

21. "U.S. Urges Restraint in Egypt."

22. "White House Monitoring Egypt Situation Closely," *Reuters*, January 26, 2011, www.reuters.com.

23. Joe Biden, cited in PBS NewsHour, "Biden: Mubarak Is Not a Dictator, But People Have a Right to Protest," January 27, 2011.

24. "As Arabs Protest, U.S. Speaks Up," *The Washington Post*, January 27, 2011, www.washingtonpost.com/wp-dyn/content/article/2011/01/26/AR2011012608075.html.

25. "Egypt Has Chance to Make Political Reforms: U.S.," *Reuters*, January 26, 2011, www.reuters.com.

26. "Biden: Mubarak Is Not a Dictator."

27. Mike Allen, "White House Scrambles to Keep Up with Crisis," *Politico*, January 31, 2011, www.politico.com/news/stories/0111/48492.html.

28. Nicholas Johnston and Kate Andersen Brower, "Obama Tells Mubarak He Must Stick to Pledge of Democratic Reforms in Egypt," *Bloomberg*, January 28, 2011, www.bloomberg.com/news/2011-01-28/obama-says-mubarak-must-take-concrete-steps-to-deliver-pledge-on-reforms.html.

29. Hans Nichols and Mike Dorning, "Obama's Words Put to Test in U.S. Response to Egypt," *Bloomberg*, January 31, 2011, www.bloomberg.com/apps/news?pid=2065100&sid=afLY5iKR5Cto.

30. Allen, "Behind the Curtain."

31. Marc Lynch, "Washington Eyes a Fateful Day in Egypt," *Foreign Policy*, January 28, 2011, lynch.foreignpolicy.com/posts/2011/01/28/a_fateful_day_in_egypt.

32. Nichols and Dorning, "Obama's Words Put to Test."

33. Brian Knowlton, "Clinton Urges Diplomacy with Mubarak, New Government," *New York Times*, January 30, 2011, www.nytimes.com.

34. Karen DeYoung, "Obama Administration Aligns Itself with Protests in Egypt with Call for 'Orderly Transition,'" *Washington Post*, January 31, 2011, www.washingtonpost.com/wp-dyn/content/article/2011/01/30/AR2011013004401.html.

35. Office of the Press Secretary, "Remarks by the President on the Situation in Egypt," The White House, February 1, 2011.

36. Marc Lynch, "Egypt Endgame," *Foreign Policy*, February 3, 2011, lynch.foreignpolicy.com/posts/2011/02/03/the_closing_egyptian_window.

37. Sanger, "As Mubarak Digs in."

38. "Obama's Remarks on the Resignation of Mubarak," *New York Times*, February 11, 2011.

39. Michael Falcone and Amy Walter, "The Note: White House Seeking Clarity on Egypt," ABC News, January 31, 2011, abcnews.go.com/blogs/politics/2011/01/-the-note-white-house-seeking-clarity-on-egypt.

40. Julian Borger and Chris McGreal, "Egypt Protests: Hosni Mubarak's Power Fades as U.S. Backs His Deputy," *Guardian*, February 5, 2011, www.guardian.co.uk/world/2011/feb/06/egypt-protests-hosni-mubarak-sulieman.

41. Julian Borger, "The Egyptian Crisis: Another Day, Another Two U.S. Policies," *Guardian*, February 6, 2011, www.guardian.co.uk/world/julian-borger-global-security-blog/2011/feb/06/egypt-obama-administration.

42. Kareem Fahim, Mark Landler, and Anthony Shadid, "West Backs Gradual Egyptian Transition," *New York Times*, February 5, 2011, www.nytimes.com/2011/02/06/world/middleeast/06egypt.html.

43. Marc Lynch, *The Arab Uprising: The Unfinished Revolutions of the New Middle East* (New York: Public Affairs), 96.

44. Ahmed Salah, "The West's Debt to Egypt," *Guardian*, February 9, 2011, www.guardian.co.uk/commentisfree/2011/feb/10/the-west-has-debts-to-egypt.

45. Jackson Diehl, "An Egyptian Revolutionary Seeks Obama's Support," *Washington Post*, March 1, 2011, voices.washingtonpost.com/postpartisan/2011/03/egypt_protest_ahmed_maher.html.

46. Barack Obama, "Transcript: Obama's Speech Against the Iraq War," NPR, January 20, 2009, www.npr.org/templates/story/story.php?storyId=99591469.

47. Sami Yousafzai and Ron Moreau, "Al Qaeda on the Ropes: One Fighter's Inside Story," *Newsweek*, January 2, 2012, www.thedailybeast.com/newsweek/2012/01/01/al-qaeda-on-the-ropes-one-fighter-s-inside-story.html.

9 Chen Guangcheng: The Case of the Blind Dissident and US-China Relations

Joyce P. Kaufman

Before You Begin

1. Why did one individual, Chen Guangcheng, have such an impact on US-China relations?

2. Why was Chen an important figure in China?

3. How did the negotiations about Chen unfold?

4. What were the possible outcomes of the negotiations?

5. How much of the outcome of this case was based on circumstances and coincidence (e.g., Secretary of State Hillary Clinton happened to be in China at that time)?

6. In what ways might the story of Chen Guangcheng change China's human rights policy?

Introduction

The story of the escape of forty-year-old blind human rights activist Chen Guangcheng from house arrest in a remote village in China, ending with his flight to and resettlement in the United States, has the makings of a great spy novel. It is not an exaggeration to say that as the events unfolded over just a few weeks in April and May 2012, the story riveted the public around the world. And there are details of the escape that still remain unknown. Since settling in the United States, Chen Guangcheng has continued to speak out about human rights violations in China. The question remains whether China's new leadership will alter its human rights policies in any way.

Who Chen Guangcheng is and how he gained the notoriety he did is far more than the story of a single individual, although that in itself is fascinating. The story became greater than any one person as the United States and China, two major international powers, negotiated a resolution that would save face for China, support the U.S. position on human rights, and ensure the safety of

Timeline

Key Developments in the
Chen Guangcheng Case

1996	Chen Guangcheng files a grievance against local officials about the agricultural tax in support of his parents and others in his village
1998	Helps organize protest against paper factory for pollution violations
2005	Documents abuses by local government officials of forced abortions and sterilizations in Shandung Province
September 2005	Placed under house arrest
June 2006	Arrested and brought to trial
August 2006	Sentenced to four years and three months imprisonment
2007	Wins Ramon Magsaysay Award while in prison
September 2010	Released from prison and placed under house arrest
April 22, 2012	Escapes from house arrest and flees to Beijing
April 23, 2012	Arrives in Beijing where he is protected by friends
April 26, 2012	Takes refuge in American Embassy in Beijing
May 2, 2012	Leaves American Embassy after six days to go to hospital
May 3, 2012	Apparent change of heart
May 3-4, 2012	Third annual meeting of the US-China Strategic Dialogue that brings Secretary of State Hillary Clinton and Treasury Secretary Timothy Geithner to Beijing
May 4, 2012	New agreement apparently reached that allows Chen and his family to leave China with protections for his family still in China
May 19, 2012	Arrives in New York
November 15, 2012	Chinese Communist Party ends 18th Party Congress with new leadership in place
November 30, 2012	Chen's nephew, Chen Kegui, arrested in China, tried, and sentenced to more than three years in prison
December 2012	From New York, Chen speaks out against the Chinese government's handling of his nephew's case

Chen and his family. In many ways, the case of Chen Guangcheng reveals a great deal about the impact an individual can have on the direction of foreign policy and, perhaps even more important, about the ways in which unanticipated events and circumstances can change the actions of nations.

Background

China has become a model of economic growth and development, but that has come at a price. China's extensive human rights abuses have been documented consistently by a number of sources, including NGOs such as Amnesty International and Human Rights Watch; even the United States Department of State has extensive documentation of abuses by the Chinese government. In a lengthy and detailed background briefing on China (including Tibet, Hong Kong, and Macau) published by the State Department in March 2007, the point made repeatedly was that although the Chinese constitution and law technically provide for basic freedoms (e.g., association, academic freedom, access to Internet), the reality is that the government restricts these rights, often controlling what can or cannot be said or done.[1]

In a very detailed document, the State Department provided examples of a number of groups and individuals who were detained, tortured, and imprisoned in China for alleged acts of misconduct against the state. The State Department begins with the assertion that

> [a]lthough the [Chinese] constitution asserts that "the state respects and preserves human rights," the government's human rights record remained poor, and in certain areas deteriorated. There were an increased number of high profile cases involving the monitoring, harassment, detention, arrest and imprisonment of journalists, writers, activists and defense lawyers, many of whom were seeking to exercise their rights under law.[2]

And then the State Department uses the document to detail a number of cases that prove these points. For example, despite constitutional provisions for freedom of religious belief and the freedom not to believe, the Chinese government sought to limit or control religious practice. The crackdown on the group Falun Gong, starting in 1999, became an international symbol of China's hostility toward religious groups, but more particularly, toward any group that could potentially gather supporters who could threaten the state. Although the Chinese government position was clear that Falun Gong represented a dissident group that had to be controlled, others saw them as a religious group that was singled out by the government in order to send a signal to other such groups.

Similarly, discontent continues to simmer in China among ethnic Tibetans who are spread throughout China. Sichuan has two "autonomous provinces" with large Tibetan populations, and the neighboring provinces of Gansu, Qinghai, and Yunnan are affected as well. Authorities have been trying to keep journalists and tourists out of these areas, which have seen an increase in protests, including the self-immolation of Tibetan Buddhist monks and nuns. The unrest that started more than three years ago in Tibet and Tibetan-inhabited parts of Sichuan, Qinghai, Gansu, and Yunnan provinces is now concentrated primarily in Sichuan's highlands, where the authorities are struggling to contain the discontent. Authorities are concerned that if news of the immolations spreads, it will further arouse tensions among the more than 1 million Tibetans living there.[3]

In addition, China has become far more aggressive at asserting its military power, especially projecting power in the South and East China Seas. In 2011 and 2012, disputes escalated over the Paracel and Spratly Islands, which Vietnam and the Philippines claim as well as China; the Macclesfield Bank, claimed by the Philippines and China; and the Diaoyu/Senkaku Islands, claimed by both China and Japan, causing fear of an armed conflict in the region. This has prompted the United States to take a more active position in Asia. For example, on a trip to Australia in November 2011, President Obama pledged "that the United States will take an expanded role in shaping the Asian Pacific region, with an increased military presence one step of that policy."[4] According to a CNN news analysis, "the speech on the second day of his two-day trip to Australia, Obama's first as president, signaled a policy objective to compete head-on with China for influence in the region while also providing security assurances for allies."[5] Referencing the United States' presence as a Pacific power, the president noted that under a new agreement with Australia, the US will deploy marines to Australia for military exercises and training, with the number expected to climb to about 2,500 over the next several years.[6] The result will be a clear assertion of U.S. presence in the region, apparently to counter China's increased role. When official Chinese spokesmen questioned the wisdom of this move by the US, the Obama administration made it clear that this area of the Pacific was within the United States' sphere of influence and is a region in which the US has a number of allies. In short, this sent a strong signal to U.S. allies as well as to China about the U.S. role in the Pacific in particular, and globally in general.

Attempts have been made to balance this assertion of military power by both the United States and China with the economic realities of these two critical trading partners. This point was emphasized in July 2012 during a visit to Asia by Secretary of State Hillary Clinton, who made trade between the US and Asia-Pacific countries a centerpiece of her trip. According to press coverage of her trip,

> It has become more common these days for the nation's chief diplomat to play a role as a business booster. But the extra attention devoted to economics is intended to send a message that Washington recognizes that it initially overemphasized the military component of its new focus on Asia, setting up more of a confrontation with China than some countries felt comfortable with.[7]

Despite the accusations made during the 2012 presidential election about China as a currency manipulator as well as stealer of jobs from Americans, the reality is that the two countries, the United States and China, are not only dependent upon one another but are important sources of trade and economic stability in the region.

Also of interest by way of background are the attitudes of the Chinese people toward the United States, as evidenced by a recent poll by the Pew Global Attitudes Project, which shows a shift in Chinese perceptions over time. The 2012 survey shows that only about 39 percent describe the US-China relationship as one of "cooperation," down from 68 percent in the previous 2010 poll, and 26 percent characterize the relationship as one of hostility, up from 8 percent previously. But more than half (52 percent) indicate that they like American ideas, especially about democracy, and about 70 percent in higher income categories "have a positive opinion about American democratic ideals."[8] Perhaps more revealing are Chinese attitudes toward their own country. Although the majority see themselves as better off now than they were five years ago, and 92 percent say their standard of living is better than their parents' at a similar age, there is also acknowledgment that not all have benefited equally, as well as general concern about rising corruption.[9] The concerns raised about their own country are especially revealing as they come at a time of major political change in China.

The 18th Communist Party Congress in November 2012 introduced a new generation of Chinese leaders. In its second major orderly handover of power during more than sixty years of Communist rule, Xi Jinping, age 59, assumed the role of general secretary of the Communist Party. He became state president in March 2013 and also the chairman of the Central Military Commission. In a speech televised live, Xi pledged

> to improve citizen's lives, including offering "better schooling, more stable jobs, more satisfying incomes, more reliable social security, higher levels of health care, more comfortable housing conditions and a more beautiful environment" so they can "look forward to their children growing up in better circumstances, finding better work and living in better conditions."[10]

Although some spoke glowingly of his speech and what Xi might do for China, others were more critical and noted that his speech did not address any issues related to law, human rights, democracy, or freedom. According to news coverage,

> No one can know for sure whether Mr. Xi favors fundamental political changes of that kind—he has given no clear indication that he does. What is clear is that his fellow members of the Standing Committee are longtime party veterans whose track records provide no evidence of a strong impulse to change the way China is governed.[11]

Xi is facing a call from some members of the Chinese elite to support more openness in China's economic and political systems, "which critics say have stagnated in the last decade under the departing party chief Hu Jintao, despite the country's emergence as the world's second largest economy and a growing regional power."[12] Xi is one of the so-called "princelings," who see themselves as the heirs of the revolution of 1949 because of their parentage. As such, they are "endowed with the mandate of authority that that status confers."[13] Despite their relatively young age, it remains unclear whether Xi or other potential leaders of his generation will work for, or be able to implement, major change. "Even those princelings who support liberalizing the economy of the political system still believe in the primacy of the party, and their push for various reforms is seen as an effort to ensure the party's survival."[14] And it will still be a while before the full impact of the changes in leadership will even be felt or new policies implemented.

In many ways, as was the case with the United States and Russia during the Cold War, although there might be tensions between the United States and China, there is recognition that the two countries need and depend upon one another as well as grudging recognition of the critical international role played by both. Although the United States has not hesitated to criticize China's human rights record, pragmatically the US has not allowed that to affect the two countries' economic and even security relationships. In many ways, when the Chen Guangcheng situation unfolded as it did, it placed into stark relief not only China's record on human rights, but also the importance of the relationship between the two countries. Thus, it was in both countries' interest to arrive at a resolution.

This background sets the stage for the case of Chen Guangcheng and the events leading up to the dénouement in May 2012, and it should be seen against the background of China's overall record of human rights abuses, which is considerable.

Introduction to Chen Guangcheng

Chen Guangcheng was a noted lawyer and dissident who worked on human rights issues in parts of rural China. Born in a tiny village in Shandong Province, the youngest of five brothers, he lost his eyesight as an infant because of a fever that destroyed his optic nerves. Denied schooling because of his condition, he absorbed knowledge by listening to the radio and through stories read to him by his family. He entered a school for the blind when he was 17 and then continued his education at a high school for the blind. Always interested in the law, when it affected him personally he began the first of what would be many legal crusades to redress inequities. In 1996, when he was about twenty five, Chen filed a grievance against local officials for refusing to honor a law exempting disabled persons from an agricultural tax, which had imposed an additional burden on his parents. He gained some measure of fame when he won, and others started to seek his advice. He continued to "study" law by having law books read to him by others, and he became more of an activist in the causes he took on.

In 1998 he led a protest in his home county against a paper factory that had been dumping toxic waste into the local river, which was affecting both people and wildlife. He organized the people in his village and others who were affected and won his case. As his fame was growing, local authorities were also following his activities, and he was investigated as well as harassed by the authorities.

In 2004–2005 the government began a repressive crackdown on violators of the state's one-child policy by coercing mothers-to-be to have abortions and forcing thousands of women to undergo sterilization. Local officials were promoted if they met their targets and, conversely, punished for noncompliance. In 2005, Chen's home area of Linyi City, Shandung Province was among the areas most affected.

> International press reports alleged that local officials detained some 13,000 persons and forced them to submit to abortions or sterilization procedures. At least 7,000 persons were forcibly sterilized. . . . Local rights activists documented several cases of forced late-term abortions.[15]

This was all in violation of existing Chinese laws requiring consent.

According to the citation for the Ramon Magsaysay Award for Emergent Leadership,[16] which Chen was awarded when he was in prison, when he learned of the human rights abuses noted above, Chen "meticulously documented the abuses and worked with the victims and lawyers to organize a class-action lawsuit against the responsible officials—the first of its kind in China and also the first concerted domestic challenge to the use of violence in China's population policy."[17] Although the suit failed, it led to an investigation by the State Family Planning Commission, and Chen took the issue to the press and diplomatic corps and eventually to the Internet, which led to international attention and exposure of the abuses.

Although the attention led to public exposure and a tacit admission of the abuses by local officials, it also provided ammunition for the authorities to respond with impunity against Chen, whose fame was growing. His cell phone was jammed, and he and his wife were beaten repeatedly. In September 2005, Chen was placed under house arrest and held without charge or trial for nine months. On June 10, 2006, Chen was formally arrested and brought to trial. Attorneys and law professors who offered to defend him were threatened, and authorities obstructed efforts of lawyers who tried to gather evidence in his defense. The night before his trial was scheduled to begin, his lawyers were detained on spurious charges that were later dropped. "The following day, court-appointed attorneys effectively conceded the case against Chen. On August 24, Chen was sentenced to four years and three months imprisonment on dubious charges of obstructing traffic and inciting others to destroy public property."[18]

Chen appealed the guilty verdict but, according to Amnesty International, "because he's blind, he needed help from his wife or lawyer to prepare; authorities only allowed him one 30-minute visit per month, making that difficult." Amnesty's account continues that "[a]t an appeal hearing several key defense witnesses—who claim that they were tortured into providing testimony against Chen Guangcheng—were detained and prevented from attending by police or men linked to the police. The court upheld the original verdict."[19] Chen's case "was later remanded to retrial, where he was represented by his own lawyers. However, courts affirmed Chen's original conviction and sentence on retrial and then again on appeal."[20] In an indicator of the notoriety that Chen had already acquired, an Internet essayist who had traveled to Shandong Province to cover Chen's trial was detained, and although he was subsequently released, his computer and mobile telephone were confiscated by the authorities.

While in prison, Chen "was severely kicked and beaten by fellow inmates on the orders of the guards after he refused to have his head shaven—the symbol of a criminal in China. He was planning a hunger strike to protest his treatment."[21] In 2007, when his wife Yuan Weijing tried to fly to the Philippines to collect Chen's Ramon Magsaysay Award, she was stopped at Beijing Airport and escorted home.

Chen was finally released from prison in September 2010, but he and his family were immediately placed under house arrest once again, although there were no formal charges pending. They were confined behind the walls of his farmhouse in Shandung province, where sheets of metal covered the windows and they were guarded twenty four hours a day. Chen gained international prominence at the end of April 2012 when he managed to escape, making his way to Beijing, where he ultimately sought refuge at the American embassy. After negotiations between the Chinese government and U.S. State Department officials, an agreement was reached that allowed Chen and his family to leave China and to go to the United States, where he settled in New York. Chen, his wife, and two children have been given a faculty apartment at New York University where he will be allowed to study at the US-Asia Law Institute. The entire situation was embarrassing for both countries, especially because it escalated as they were preparing for their annual Strategic and Economic Dialogue.

Since Chen's escape, China has undergone a leadership transition that many hope will lead to some liberalization of policies and respect for human rights. However, Chen is not optimistic. At the end of November 2012, his nephew Chen Kegui was arrested, allegedly for assaulting officials who had forced their way into his home. His trial took place four hours later, and he was quickly sentenced to three years and three months in prison for "intentional injury."[22] Human rights activists, including Chen's friend and lawyer Jerome Cohen, talked about how this was really an extension of the Chen Guangcheng case and suffered from the "same pathologies." And speaking from New York, Chen stated that "the conviction of his nephew in China was retribution for Chen's escape from house arrest and move to the United States." He said,

> With this sentence, Chen Kegui is being made a scapegoat for my situation. . . . Based on the information I have now, especially in light of Chen Kengui's case, I think the new leadership offers no reason for people to put any faith in them.[23]

It is clear that the case of Chen Guangcheng will not go away quickly, even with the activist safely resettled in New York.

Phase I: The Escape, April 2012

Chen's imprisonment at home following his release from prison in September 2010 was orchestrated by local government officials to ensure that Chen could not continue to engage in his legal work against coercive family planning policies and also to keep the couple cut off from the world outside the walls of the house. According to one report, "When the Chens broke the rules—by trying to sneak out messages or secretly detailing their mistreatment in a homemade video—they were viciously beaten."[24] When Chen's escape finally occurred, it quickly became clear that it had been meticulously planned for months and involved a number of people who put themselves at great risk to help him.

Apparently, as part of the escape plan, Chen feigned illness for weeks in an attempt to convince his guards that he was bedridden. "Then, on a moonless night on April 22 [2012], he began his mad dash from Dongshigu village, heaving himself over the first of several walls while the guards slept." In the course of the initial scramble over the wall, he injured his foot. "In all, he told friends he fell 200 times as he made his way to a predetermined pickup point."[25]

Once he reached that point, he contacted He Peirong, also known as "Pearl," a former English teacher and one of the network of human rights activists who had tried to draw attention to Chen's plight for more than a year. She had tried to contact and visit Chen and his wife several times in the previous months but was stopped by guards. At various times she, too, was beaten and had also been robbed and dumped in a field. By her own account, she got a call from Chen early in the morning of April 23 after he had escaped from Dongshigu. She then drove about twenty hours to meet him and drove him more than 300 miles to Beijing. She declined to offer further details beyond noting that she believed at least six people were involved with the escape, but that Chen himself was the driving force behind the plan.[26] After his escape she was detained and interrogated by police for almost a week before being released.

Once in Beijing, Chen was looked after by a group of close supporters who moved him around daily, making sure that he slept in a different apartment each night while they came up with a plan. He was in great pain from the injury to his foot that he sustained while escaping, so a priority became to get him to someplace safe where his injury could be treated. It was decided that only the American Embassy could provide that protection.

Phase II: The American Embassy/American Involvement

Once it was determined that only the American Embassy could provide the protection needed, one of Chen's friends contacted the embassy to explain the situation, including the fact that Chen had a serious foot injury and needed help. According to official reports,

> [The matter] was quickly brought to the attention of Harold Koh, the State Department legal advisor who was in China on another matter. After consulting with senior State Department officials, Mr. Koh determined that Mr. Chen's injury and blindness qualified him for short-term humanitarian assistance in a good Samaritan way.[27]

They agreed on a rendezvous point where an official embassy car would meet Chen's vehicle and then the transfer would be made.

"But as the two vehicles were about to converge, the Americans noticed Chinese security cars tailing them, one behind the embassy car, the other behind the car with Mr. Chen and his friend." To evade capture, the two vehicles pulled into an alley and Chen was pulled into the embassy car and taken to a United States Marine dormitory.[28] At that point, American officials imposed an information blackout as they negotiated Chen's fate.

It is here that the US and China's versions of the story diverge. According to the United States, when Chen was asked about his preferences, he made it clear that he did not want to request asylum.

> Instead, during talks with Mr. Koh, the State Department legal advisor, and Kurt Campbell, assistant secretary [of State] for East Asian and Pacific Affairs, he spoke fervently of his desire to stay in China, to be reunited with his wife and two children, and to start a new life away from Shandung.[29]

The American ambassador, Gary Locke, returned from vacation to participate in the negotiations, spending hours each day talking to Chen. American officials said that Chen's wishes became the basis for the negotiations with Chinese diplomats. But there was also pressure on the Americans to resolve the situation prior to scheduled high-level talks involving China and the United States. Secretary of State Clinton and Secretary of Treasury Timothy Geithner were both to participate in the bilateral Strategic and Economic Dialogue, scheduled for May 3 and 4, 2012, and were already on their way to Beijing.[30] This added time constraints that also affected what unfolded.

On the Chinese side, Chen's escape was a significant public relations challenge. Despite the government's attempts "to relegate him to obscurity, confining him to his home in the remote village of Dongshigu and surrounding him with plainclothes security guards,"[31] the escape raised his profile dramatically. Initially a spokesman for China's foreign ministry indicated that he had no information about the escape, "but one intelligence officer expressed bewilderment that Mr. Chen had evaded his local government captors and had probably entered the embassy."[32]

China's negotiations were led by Vice Foreign Minister Cui Tiankai, who initially sought to play down the incident. Rather, his focus was on the upcoming Strategic and Economic Dialogue, scheduled for the following week. The United States was also concerned about the impact of the incident on the bilateral U.S-China relationship. The US had been working hard to improve relations between the two countries, which had been bearing fruit as China was being more supportive of U.S. moves to pressure Iran and North Korea over their nuclear programs. State Department spokeswoman Victoria Nuland "said she would make no comment on Mr. Chen's escape or his whereabouts. The White House also declined to comment."[33] This is consistent with the Obama administration's desire to keep itself removed from China's internal politics.

As the negotiations about Chen's status began, the concern on the U.S. side was that "if an accord agreeable to Mr. Chen was not speedily attained, hardliners in the Chinese government would take over from the more amenable Foreign Ministry."[34] The Americans also noted that Chen was informed that his wife had been brought to Beijing "and that Chinese officials had threatened to return her to Shandong if he did not reach a deal that included his exit from the embassy."[35] In one of the early negotiation sessions, apparently the US suggested that Chen be allowed to move to Shanghai, where New York University was planning to open a law school, but this option was rejected by the Chinese. However, this gambit provided an opening in the negotiations that both sides wanted to take advantage of.

The two sides agreed on a list of seven cities in China in which Chen could continue his law studies. Chen agreed on Tianjin, the fourth largest city in China. Because it is relatively close to Beijing—about 75 miles—Chen and the Americans agreed that it would also ensure that the spotlight would be kept on him, with frequent visits from both reporters and diplomats. The Chinese also appeared to agree to this option.

Prior to Chen's departure from the embassy, Ambassador Locke spelled out the specific terms under which he would be leaving the embassy, and Chen did not hesitate to agree. According to one official, when asked if he was ready to leave and to go to the hospital where his wife and children were waiting for him, "Mr. Chen replied, 'zou,' using the Chinese for 'let's go.'"[36] But upon arriving at the hospital and talking with his wife, who said that she had been threatened by officials, Chen seemed to have a change of heart. "Friends say he was also spooked by the presence of plainclothes police officers at the hospital." Chen's fears continued to grow after a conversation with Teng Biao, a former legal advisor as well as prominent human rights advocate, who "expressed alarm at Mr. Chen's decision to reject asylum in the United States and urged him to reconsider for the sake of his family."[37] Teng warned of retaliation against Chen should he decided to remain in China, raising again the specter of house arrest or even jail.

Phase III: Change of Heart, May 3–4, 2012

At the hospital where he was recovering from his injuries, Chen admitted that his decision to leave the protection of the U.S. embassy and to live in China had "not been fully voluntary." Rather, in a phone interview from the hospital, Chen said that "he had left the embassy on his own volition after the Chinese government guaranteed that his rights would be protected. But he also said he had felt some pressure because he was told that Chinese officials had threatened to beat his wife to death if he remained under American protection."[38] He also said that he felt that the United States government "was not proactive enough."[39] And in an interview with journalists, he questioned whether his safety or that of his family would be guaranteed should he stay in China, a position that differed sharply from the U.S. rationale for releasing him from the protection of the embassy.

This turn of events proved embarrassing for the United States, which was just beginning the Strategic Dialogue discussions with China.

> It also exposed the Obama administration to criticism from Republicans and human rights groups that it had rushed to resolve a delicate human rights case so that it would not overshadow other matters on the bilateral agenda that Mrs. Clinton previously called more important, including the Iranian and North Korean nuclear programs and China's currency and trade problems.[40]

In addition, it left the United States open to criticism from human rights activists at home and abroad who claimed that the US had abandoned Chen at a time when the country should have been sensitive to his fears and concerns.

This also contradicts what State Department officials had said earlier, that Chen had repeatedly insisted that he wanted to remain in China and that the Chinese officials had "made concessions to make that possible." Specifically, the Chinese had promised that he could start a new life "free of the harassment and intimidation he had suffered for years at the hands of security officials in the rural village of Shandong province."[41] Secretary Clinton, who by then had arrived in Beijing for the Strategic Dialogue discussion, said that China had provided these "understandings" about the future.

It was apparent that the agreement made was quickly coming apart "as the Chinese government issued a blistering statement to domestic news media saying that the role the United States had played in the matter 'is totally unacceptable to China.' The Foreign Ministry statement insisted that Washington offer an apology and punish officials involved in taking Mr. Chen into American protection."[42] U.S. State Department officials denied saying that they had passed along a message "that Mr. Chen's wife, Yuan Weijing, would be sent back to Shandong if he remained under American care, and that American officials could do nothing to ensure her safety there."[43] State Department spokeswoman Nuland also denied that U.S. officials spoke to Chen about any physical or legal threats to his wife or children but did confirm that the US had made it clear that if Chen chose to stay at the embassy, Chinese officials would return his family to Shandung.

But what was most baffling was that "Mr. Chen's statement that he no longer wanted to stay in China contradicted what American officials said he had told them while in their care, and public statements Mr. Chen had made before he sought American protection."[44] It was unclear whether this apparent change of heart or contradiction was due to the impact of being alone in the hospital in Beijing following a long ordeal, whether it was really second thoughts, or whether the contradictions reflected the U.S. rush to have the issue settled prior to the start of important economic and security talks. Jerome Cohen, the lawyer as well as friend of Chen's from New York, indicated that Chen was panicked after being taken to the hospital where he was denied visitors and apparently had only limited phone calls. But it also was becoming clear that Chen was rethinking his decision, perhaps even reconsidering the option of emigrating to the US.

By May 4, a spokesman for China's Ministry of Foreign Affairs who previously had condemned the United States for its role in this affair, in answer to a question about whether Chen might be allowed to study abroad, responded that he could. According to Cohen,

> That was the signal that a solution had been reached—not by letting Chen rot indefinitely in the U.S. Embassy nor by subjecting him to the considerable risks of staying active in China, as the two governments had initially agreed. No, Chen's family was granted an opportunity that had previously been off the table.[45]

Thus, this opened the possibility that Chen and his family could leave China for the United States.

Phase IV: A New Deal, May 4, 2012

According to a report published in the British magazine *The Economist*, while he was in the hospital Chen "appealed through journalists for the Americans to help him and his family leave the country."[46] By May 4, it appeared that a new deal was struck and he and his family would be permitted to leave China. China agreed to an application from Chen to allow him to study in the US along with his wife and children. The agreement was reached on the last full day of Secretary Clinton's trip to China, although at a news conference she was guarded about the outcome, saying, "We are encouraged by the progress we have seen today. . . . But there is more work to be done." Moments later, the State Department spokeswoman released a statement that "China was expected to issue travel documents to Mr. Chen 'expeditiously' and that the United States would speed visa requests by his wife and two children."[47]

Jerome Cohen added that Chen had been offered a fellowship to study at New York University.

According to press reports,

> The statement [by Victoria Nuland] was the coda to what was, by all appearances, a carefully choreographed series of declarations by Mr. Chen, the Chinese government, and American officials that committed all three parties to a mutually agreeable settlement of Mr. Chen's future.[48]

At that point, it was not clear *when* Chen and his family would be able to leave China, although it was also apparent that the Chinese government was eager to see him leave.

> Indeed, as part of their negotiating tactics with the Chinese government, State Department officials seemed to have used the argument that Mr. Chen's departure would ease a major headache for Beijing both abroad and at home. Unlike the former Soviet Union, China has *encouraged* outspoken dissidents to go into exile, knowing that they would lose their influence inside China once they left.[49]

Similarly, it was clear that the United States was also working behind the scenes to resolve the crisis. Secretary Clinton wanted to have the issue resolved rather than face the perception that she was leaving China with a disturbing and very public human rights case unresolved. According to a news report, "as Mrs. Clinton moved from one session to another at the high-level gathering, she and her top aides messaged each other about how to persuade the Chinese to fulfill Mr. Chen's new wish to go to the United States."[50] Clinton met with then-Chinese President Hu Jintao and Prime Minister Wen Jiabao late in the morning of May 4. Although they did not discuss the Chen case, a few hours later,

> the Chinese Foreign Ministry announced that Mr. Chen, as a Chinese citizen, could apply for a passport in the same manner as the 340,000 students who studied abroad last year. It was the first public sign that a deal was in motion.[51]

Criticized for the way in which the earlier deal had unraveled, this time the State Department detailed the basic terms for Chen's departure. The official release said that

> the Chinese government "would make accommodations for his medical condition," a reference to the fact that Mr. Chen is blind and would not have to travel to his hometown for his passport application. . . . The statement said

that once Mr. Chen had his passport, the United States would expedite visa requests from him and his family. The statement ended, "This matter has been handled in the spirit of a cooperative US-China partnership."[52]

In a statement published on May 6, 2012, as the standoff was coming to its climax, Jerome Cohen said,

> If Chen had been allowed to talk to his Chinese friends before leaving the U.S. Embassy last Wednesday [May 2] as he says he requested, the heroic law professor Teng Biao and other rights activists who have endured abuse from security thugs would have told Chen the same things they said after his American escorts left him at a Beijing hospital: Don't give up the safety of the embassy, even if it means further separation from your family and indefinite isolation.[53]

But Cohen also notes that had any of that happened, Chen would never have been preparing to leave China with this family, "And U.S.-China relations would have grown increasingly hostile in the politically volatile struggle over his fate."[54] Thus, Cohen's assessment is that American exhaustion coupled with China's limiting Chen's access and a dose of luck and timing all contributed to the turn of events that, ultimately, allowed Chen and his family to leave China.

Phase V: The United States, May 19, 2012 to Present

Chen Guangcheng arrived in the United States on May 19 and held a hastily arranged press conference in the heart of Greenwich Village, New York. At the time, he said "he was grateful to the American Embassy and the Chinese government, which allowed him to leave China, and thanked Chinese officials for 'dealing with the situation with restraint and calm.' "[55] Yet just weeks prior, it was unclear whether he would be allowed to leave,

> and the United States' role in his evading the authorities threatened to cause a diplomatic breach just as American officials were seeking China's cooperation on a range of economic and security issues it considers crucial. Mr. Chen's departure from Beijing on Saturday, and the arduous negotiations that led up to it, appeared to reflect careful calculations in both countries that the episode was not worth jeopardizing relations.[56]

In retrospect, it is clear that the Chinese engaged directly with Secretary Clinton and a team of U.S. diplomats to resolve the situation, which was made possible only because both the US and China concluded that a successful outcome would benefit both nations. Conversely, neither side would benefit from failure.

Chen was permitted to leave China to attend law school on a fellowship rather than seeking asylum, which would have been an affront to China. His departure also averted a major embarrassment for the US at a time when Secretary Clinton especially was seeking to reset the relations between the two countries. Although his wife and children left with him, Chen also expressed concern for relatives who remained behind in China.

Shortly after arriving in the United States, Chen published an Op-Ed piece in the *New York Times*. He begins the piece by noting,

> I have come here to study temporarily, not to seek political asylum. And while I pursue my studies, I hope that the Chinese government and the Communist Party will conduct a thorough investigation of the lawless punishment inflicted on me and my family over the past seven years.[57]

And then he continues that after asking for this investigation while hospitalized in Beijing after leaving the U.S. embassy, "High officials from the Chinese government assured me that a thorough and public investigation would take place and that they would inform me of the results."[58] But at the heart of this piece is a condemnation of the Chinese government:

> The fundamental question the Chinese government must face is lawlessness. China does not lack laws, but the rule of law. As a result, those who handled my case were able to openly flout the nation's laws in many ways for many years.[59]

Chen then documents incidents of violations of the law using his nephew, Chen Kegui, as an example. And he concludes,

> This issue of lawlessness may be the greatest challenge facing the new leaders who will be installed this autumn by the 18th National Congress of the Chinese Communist Party. . . . China stands at a critical juncture. I hope its new leaders will use this opportunity wisely.[60]

One month later, in June 2012, during an interview Chen expressed anger at the failure of the Beijing government to investigate the local officials who persecuted him and beat him and his relatives, despite promises that they would do so. Both Chen and his wife also were "desperately worried about the harsh treatment of those they left behind in Shandong Province."[61] Chen and his wife are now studying English, and Chen is learning about American constitutional law and has been working with Jerome Cohen and others at NYU who have tailored a law curriculum for him. As he has learned about America's path, he also ponders how China might learn from this country's experiences. He has not given up on the idea of returning to China at some point, but that "may depend partly on what he says and how far he goes in his activism while in the United States. Barely a month into his stay, the prospect of going back to China looms large in his mind."[62]

In September 2012, about four months after leaving China to come to New York, Chen gave another interview, this one over lunch with Jamil Anderlini of *The Financial Times.* In that interview, Chen notes that he has thought about how his stay in the US will affect his ability to work for human rights and justice at home. His "first demand" is

> that the Chinese government obeys its own laws and its own constitution, which ostensibly guarantees human rights, freedom of speech and many other values that are taken for granted in the west. . . . "When you read China's constitution, you realize that if we could only fulfill those basic requirements then China would be a great country," he says. "China's laws themselves are not the problem; the problem is that they are not properly enforced in real life." This is what makes Chen's case so poignant and what makes him so dangerous for China's rulers—his activism is based on simply asking the authorities to live up to their own pronouncements.[63]

At the end of November 2012, it appeared that Chen's fears about the safety of those left behind in China, especially his nephew, were well founded. On November 30, Chen's nephew Chen Kegui was arrested, tried, and convicted of "intentional infliction of injury" and sentenced to three years and three months in prison. In response to charges that Chen Kegui had injured officials with a kitchen knife, his defense was that they had broken into his house in the middle of the night and attacked his family. Chen Kegui claimed that he was trying to protect himself and his family. This latest incident provoked another outpouring of condemnation of China; "Amnesty International called the conviction of Chen Kegui 'appalling' and retribution for his uncle's escape." And a researcher for Human Rights Watch said that the trial "failed to meet minimum standards for fair trial under domestic of international standards."[64] Chen Guangcheng's friend and lawyer Jerome Cohen said of this latest case, "This is the ultimate example of judicial farce in China, not a happy example of how human rights will be protected by China's new leadership."[65]

Chen Guangcheng, in an interview with CNN in New York, noted that "authorities in China want to perpetuate fear." And in addition to seeing it as an extension of his own case, he also said that "before this, they tried many times to provoke me, but I didn't fall for their trick."[66]

In an interview that Chen Guangcheng gave to *Foreign Policy* magazine at the end of November 2012, prior to his nephew's arrest, he stated clearly that "China is at a stage where it has to change," and predicted that "[w]hether it's civilized or government-driven, and potentially violent, a transformation is inevitable."[67] Whether, when, or how such change will happen remains to be seen.

Conclusion

The case of Chen Guangcheng illustrates how one individual can have a dramatic impact on the relations between two major international powers. It is unusual for any single individual to have the kind of effect that Chen did, with the United States and China negotiating at the highest levels of government not only for his emigration from China, but for his wife's and children's as well. But in this case, there was a confluence of events that contributed to the arc of the story: A compelling hero, blind activist Chen Guangcheng, who was not afraid to take on the authorities in the face of injustice regardless of the cost to him and who was able to build a cadre of supporters who worked with him and helped him escape; and the story of the escape itself, meticulously planned and well executed to ensure that he was able to get to the U.S. embassy.

But it is also the story of circumstance and coincidence. Because Chen had only limited access to the world beyond his home when he was under house arrest, it seems highly unlikely that he had planned his escape to coincide with the start of the US-China Strategic and Economic Dialogue that would bring high-level U.S. government officials, including Secretary of State Hillary Clinton, to China. Nonetheless, it cannot be denied that the Dialogue and the high-level officials who were participating raised the stakes considerably and put additional pressure on the governments of both China and the United States to resolve the situation quickly and satisfactorily. It is impossible to speculate whether the outcome would have been the same without that additional pressure. So whether the escape was carefully planned or a happy coincidence, the result was the same: Chen Guangcheng and his immediate family now live in New York, where the activist will keep fighting for human rights in China. And, as the case of Chen Kegui shows, his family remains within the reach of the Chinese government unless or until the new leadership makes a significant change.

Key Actors

Chen Guangcheng   Blind activist for human rights who is the key player in the story.

Chen Kegui   Nephew of Chen Guangcheng, arrested in China in November 2012, tried and imprisoned on dubious charges, allegedly as a form of retribution by the Chinese government against Chen Guangcheng.

Hillary Clinton   U.S. secretary of state who happened to be in Beijing, China for the Strategic and Economic Dialogue talks with China on security and economic relationships.

Jerome Cohen   Law professor at NYU and expert on Chinese human rights as well as friend and supporter of Chen, who helped negotiate his release from China.

Cui Tiankai   China's vice foreign minister and the leader on the Chinese side of the negotiations.

He Peirong   English teacher and friend of Chen's who picked him up after his escape and drove him to Beijing. She is also known as "Pearl."

Harold Koh   State Department legal advisor who happened to be in Beijing when Chen escaped and worked on the negotiations with China.

Gary Locke   U.S. ambassador to China.

Teng Biao   Chinese lawyer and human rights activist, as well as friend of Chen.

Yuan Weijing   Chen's wife, who left China with him and their two small children.

Notes

1. Extensive background can be found in the U.S. Department of State March 6, 2007, country report on human rights practices, "China (includes Tibet, Hong Kong, and Macau)," accessed November 22, 2012, www.state.gov/j/drl/rls/hrrpt/2006/78771 .htm.

2. Ibid.

3. See "China's Restive Tibetan regions: No Mercy," *The Economist*, November 12, 2011, 47.

4. Dan Lothian and Lesa Jansen, "Obama Pledges U.S. Military Power in the Pacific," CNN, November 16, 2011, www.cnn.com/2011/11/16/world/asia/australia-obama-trip/index.html.

5. Ibid.

6. Ibid.

7. Jane Perlez, "Clinton Makes Effort to Rechannel the Rivalry with China," *New York Times,* July 7, 2012, accessed November 22, 2012, www.nytimes.com/2012/07/08/world/asia/for-clinton-an-effort-to-rechannel-the-rivalry-with-china.html.

8. Pew Global Attitudes Project, "Growing Concerns in China about Inequality, Corruption," October 16, 2012, www.pewglobal.org/.

9. Ibid.

10. Ibid.

11. Ibid.

12. Edward Wong, "Ending Congress, China Presents New Leadership Headed by Xi Jinping," *New York Times,* November 12, 2012, www.nytimes.com/2012/11/15/world/asia/communists-conclude-party-congress-in-china.html.

13. Ibid.

14. Ibid.

15. U.S. Department of State, "China."

16. The Ramon Magsaysay Award is Asia's equivalent of the Nobel Peace Prize. Chen was awarded it in 2007 while in prison for his work on these cases.

17. The 2007 Ramon Magsaysay Award for Emergent Leadership, "Citation for Chen Guangcheng," Ramon Magsaysay Award Presentation Ceremonies, August 31, 2007, accessed November 22, 2012, www.rmaf.org.ph/Awardees/CitationGuangcheng Che.htm.

18. U.S. Department of State, "China."

19. Amnesty International, "Chen Guangcheng—Human Rights Defender and Legal Advisor," May 8, 2008, accessed November 22, 2012, www.wmnesty.org.au/china/comments/11237.

20. U.S. Department of State, "China."

21. Amnesty International, "Chen Guangcheng."

22. Tania Branigan, "Chen Guangcheng's Nephew Jailed after Snap Trial," *The Guardian,* November 30, 2012, www.guardian.co.uk/world/2012/nov/30/chen-guangcheng-nephew-jailed-trial.

23. "Prominent Chinese Activist Blasts Nephew's Conviction," CNN, December 1, 2012, www.cnn.com/2012/11/30/world/asia/china-chen-nephew-convicted/index.html.

24. Jane Perlez and Andrew Jacobs, "A Car Chase, Secret Talks and Second Thoughts," *New York Times,* May 2, 2012, accessed November 22, 2012, www.nytimes.com/2012/05/03/world/asia/a-car-chase-secret-talks-and-second-thoughts.html.

25. Ibid.

26. Clifford Coonan, "He Peirong: The Heroine Behind the Dissident Chen Guangcheng," *The Independent,* May 2, 2012, accessed November 22, 2012, www.independent.co.uk/news/world/asia/he-peirong-the-heroine-behind-the-dissident-chen-guangcheng-7718706.html.

27. Jane Perlez and Andrew Jacobs, "A Car Chase."

28. Ibid.

29. Ibid.

30. According to the U.S. Department of Treasury web site (www.treasury.gov/initiatives/Pages/china.aspx), "The U.S.-China Strategic and Economic Dialogue was established by President Obama and Chinese President Hu in April 2009 and represents the highest level bilateral forum to discuss a broad range of issues between the two nations. The Dialogue is an essential step in advancing a positive, constructive, and comprehensive relationship between the two countries." Treasury Secretary Timothy Geithner and Secretary of State Hillary Clinton serve as special representatives of President Obama to the talks.

31. Andrew Jacobs and Jonathan Ansfield, "Challenge for U.S. after Escape by China Activist," *New York Times,* April 27, 2012, accessed November 22, 2012, www.nytimes.com/2012/04/28/world/asia/chen-guangcheng-blind-lawyer-escapes-house-arrest-china.html.

32. Ibid.

33. Ibid.

34. Jane Perlez and Andrew Jacobs, "A Car Chase."

35. Ibid.

36. Ibid.

37. Ibid.

38. Jane Perlez and Sharon LaFraniere, "Chinese Dissident Is Released from Embassy, Causing Turmoil for U.S.," *New York Times,* May 2, 2012, accessed November 22, 2012, www.nytimes.com/2012/05/03/world/asia/chen-guangcheng-leaves-us-embassy-in-beijing-china.html.

39. Ibid.

40. Ibid.

41. Ibid.

42. Ibid.

43. Ibid.

44. Ibid.

45. Jerome A. Cohen, "Chen's Silent Partner: Luck," *Washington Post,* May 6, 2012, accessed November 22, 2012, www.cfr.org/china/chens-silent-partner-luck/p28175.

46. "Human Rights: Blind Justice," *The Economist,* May 5, 2012, 25–6.

47. Jane Perlez and Michael Wines, "Nascent Deal Would Let Dissident from China Study in U.S.," *New York Times,* May 4, 2012, accessed November 23, 2012, www.nytimes.com/2012/05/05/world/asia/chen-guangcheng-study-abroad-china.html.

48. Ibid.

49. Ibid. Emphasis added.

50. Ibid.

51. Ibid.

52. Ibid.

53. Jerome A. Cohen, "Chen's Silent Partner: Luck."

54. Ibid.

55. Thomas Kaplan, Andrew Jacobs, and Steven Lee Myers, "Dissident from China Arrives in U.S., Ending an Ordeal," *New York Times,* May 19, 2012, accessed November 23, 2012, www.nytimes.com/2012/05/20/world/asia/china-dissident-chen-guangcheng-united-states.html.

56. Ibid.

57. Chen Guangcheng, "How China Flouts Its Laws," *New York Times,* May 29, 2012, www.nytimes.com/2012/05/30/opinion/how-china-flouts-its-laws.html.

58. Ibid.

59. Ibid.

60. Ibid.

61. Erik Eckholm, "Even in New York, China Casts a Shadow," *New York Times,* June 18, 2012, www.nytimes.com/2012/06/19/world/asia/chen-guangcheng-is-safe-in -new-york-but-thinks-of-china.html.

62. William Wan, "Chen Guangcheng Adjusts to Life in America," *Washington Post,* June 18, 2012, www.washingtonpost.com/world/national-security/chen-guangcheng -adjusts-to-life-in-america/2012/06/18/gJQAzPF31V_story.html.

63. Jamil Anderlini, "Lunch with the FT: Chen Guangcheng," *Financial Times,* September 21, 2012, www.ft.com/cms/s/2/686002fe-0188-11e2-83bb-00144feavdc0 .html.

64. "Prominent Chinese Activist Blasts Nephew's Conviction."

65. Branigan, "Chen Guangcheng's Nephew."

66. "Prominent Chinese Activist Blasts Nephew's Conviction."

67. Isaac Stone Fish, "A Change is Gonna Come: Chen Guangcheng on Freedom, Violence, and the Possibility of a Revolution in China," *Foreign Policy,* December 2012, www.foreignpolicy.com/articles/2012/11/26/a_change_is_gonna_come.

10 The Global Financial Crisis: Governments, Banks, and Markets

Thomas D. Lairson

Before You Begin

   1. What are the long-term and short-term causes of the financial crisis?

   2. Whose actions and decisions contributed to the crisis?

   3. Why did governments intervene in the economy and bail out banks?

   4. What are some potential negative consequences of such actions?

   5. What foreign policy choices are involved in efforts to solve problems created by the crisis?

   6. How do the efforts to create a new regulatory regime affect power relations and foreign policies?

   7. Does the concept of state capitalism expand our understanding of financial statecraft?

Introduction

The interactions among powerful states during the time of the global financial crisis, from August 2007 to March 2009, and the continuing aftermath, were marked by great drama. The collapsing values of equities, real estate, and currencies combined with the potential for bankruptcy of the financial and credit systems of many nations to create considerable fear and anxiety. Fears were raised about a possible repeat of the depression of the 1930s and about the viability of capitalism itself. The chance of a global economic system spiraling out of control was not small, and political and ministerial leaders made decisions in an atmosphere of genuine crisis. Missteps could have catastrophic consequences.[1]

In the end, there was much reason for worry. The cost of the crisis in various forms of governmental support was $15 trillion, equal to nearly one-quarter of the global gross domestic product (GDP).[2] In addition, the losses in

Timeline

The Global Financial Crisis

March 1973	Bretton Woods system of fixed exchange rates ends and a system of floating exchange rates for many nations' currencies begins. This opens the way to large foreign exchange markets and futures markets.
August 1982	Mexico declares a default on its foreign debt. After years of rapid growth and rising debt from large budget deficits, the Mexican government is forced to default when oil prices begin to fall. The loans to Mexico come from large U.S. banks, creating a systemic crisis. The Reagan administration, in conjunction with the International Monetary Fund (IMF), provides loans and helps extend the payment schedule for Mexican debt.
October 1982	Garn–St. Germain Depository Institutions Act of 1982. Provides for a substantial deregulation of savings and loan banks, reducing capital requirements and eliminating restrictions on investment options.
October 1987	Global stock market collapse. After several years of rapid increases in prices, the stock market suffers a large and rapid decline (U.S. markets fall 23 percent in one day). The newly appointed chairman of the Federal Reserve, Alan Greenspan, acts quickly to lower interest rates and increase the money supply to restore confidence and prevent a systemic crisis.
August 1989	Establishment of the Resolution Trust Corp. Facing a substantial disintegration of savings and loan banks, President George H. W. Bush and Congress create an agency with $150 billion to purchase the bad assets of the banks and close many of them.
December 1994	Mexican peso crisis. Limited financial crisis involves large budget deficits, repayment of governmental debt, and the collapse of the Mexican peso. The Clinton administration provides loans to Mexico to support the peso.
July 1997–June 1998	Asian financial crisis. Beginning in Thailand and spreading to many Asian nations, the crisis focuses on current account deficits, exchange rates, and levels of private and governmental debt. Supported by the U.S. government, the IMF provides loans to several Asian nations.

June 1998	Russian financial crisis. Linked to the Asian financial crisis, the focus is on debt repayment, government default, and collapse of the Russian currency—the ruble. Supported by the U.S. government, the IMF provides loans to support the ruble.
September 1998	Long-Term Capital Management (LTCM) crisis. Led by Nobel Prize–winning economists, this large hedge fund uses sophisticated investment strategies, based on high levels of leverage. The failure of these strategies, mostly from the Russian financial crisis, brings on fears of a systemic crisis and leads the New York Federal Reserve to arrange loans by major Wall Street firms to prevent a loss of confidence.
November 1999	Gramm-Leach-Bliley Act. Repeals important parts of the Depression-era regulation of U.S. banks, the Glass-Steagall Act, which prevents the combination of commercial and investment banks. With these restrictions removed, new financial institutions combining various parts of finance, such as insurance, banking, and investment, are created.
March 2000	Dot-com stock market crash. Collapse of stock prices, especially of information technology companies, following years of very large price increases.
December 2000– December 2001	Argentine financial crisis relating to international debt repayment and breakdown of fixed exchange rate. Supported by the U.S. government, the IMF provides loans to support the Argentine peso.
September 2001	World Trade Center attacks. With the U.S. economy already weakened by the stock market declines, this event leads the Federal Reserve under Alan Greenspan to lower interest rates to nearly zero and boost the money supply to promote economic growth.
2002–2006	Rapid expansion of subprime mortgage loans and increases in house prices tied to expansion of collateralized debt obligations (CDOs) and credit default swaps (CDSs). This is fueled by low interest rates and large financing of the U.S. budget deficit by China. Debt levels for households, governments, and businesses rise substantially across much of the world.
June 2004	Federal Reserve begins a three-year process of raising interest rates. This affects homeowners with subprime mortgages who begin to default and enter foreclosure in larger and larger numbers. House prices peak and begin to fall in 2006.

(continued)

Timeline *(continued)*
The Global Financial Crisis

August 2007	Federal Reserve begins to lower interest rates based on worries about the effects of declining home prices on the derivatives market.
March 2008	Facing bankruptcy, Bear Sterns is sold to JP Morgan Chase in a deal engineered by the Federal Reserve.
April 2008	Unemployment levels begin to rise from 5 percent to 10 percent by October 2009. This leads to more foreclosures and more declines in housing prices.
July–September 8, 2008	The potential failures of Fannie Mae and Freddie Mac lead first to direct support by the U.S. government, and when that fails to the September 8 takeover of these firms by the U.S. government.
September 14, 2008	Merrill Lynch, the world's largest brokerage firm, is sold to Bank of America in a sale engineered by Secretary of the Treasury Henry Paulson. Facing massive losses from derivatives trading, Merrill Lynch is deemed too big and too interconnected to fail.
September 15, 2008	Lehman declares bankruptcy after the Federal Reserve is unable to find a buyer. Beset by huge losses from derivative investments, Lehman's collapse sends a shock wave through financial markets.
September 16, 2008	Reversing course, the Federal Reserve acts to provide emergency lending to AIG of $85 billion (eventually $182 billion). Deeply involved in the CDOs and CDSs, AIG is too big and too interconnected to be allowed to fail.
September 19–October 15, 2008	Secretary Paulson proposes that Congress create a $700 billion fund for a Troubled Asset Relief Program (TARP). Congress first rejects the proposal, but on October 3 passes the law and President George W. Bush signs it. On October 15 the terms for application of the fund are modified.
September 2008–February 2010	Federal Reserve initiates a multitrillion-dollar program to inject liquidity into financial institutions by purchasing bad assets and sustaining global liquidity through arrangements with other central banks.
October 2008	The banking system in Iceland collapses and is nationalized by the government.

October 2008	The British government enacts a 500 billion pound rescue package for British banks.
November 9, 2008	China announces a $586 billion stimulus package to bolster its economy.
November, 2008 to November 2012	Seven Summit Meetings of the G20
	Forty-one meetings of G20 Finance Ministers and Central Bank Governor and Deputies
December 19, 2008	President Bush announces that TARP funds will be used to help U.S. automakers.
February 17, 2009	President Barack Obama signs a $787 billion stimulus plan for the U.S. economy.
June 2009	President Obama proposes new banking regulation legislation.
July 2010	President Obama signs into law the Dodd-Frank Act, with potentially sweeping effects on bank regulation and consumer protection.
August 2010– December 2012	Implementation regulations for Dodd-Frank are written.
December 2009– December 2012	Eurozone crisis—centered on high debt, large budget deficits in Greece, Portugal, Spain and Italy, with potential bank insolvencies and substantial funds devoted to national bailouts—persists without clear resolution.
June 2010– December 2012	Economic recovery in the United States is very slow, with unemployment near 8 percent; recovery in Europe is even slower, with unemployment for most nations above 10 percent; recovery in Asia is much stronger, with Chinese growth at or above 7.5 percent.

home equity and in investments (potentially recoverable) were as much as $28 trillion.[3] Financial institutions sustained several trillion dollars in losses, as would many firms operating in other areas of the economy. Unemployment rates around the world rose substantially, driven up by the severe economic downturn that followed. Even after several years, significant negative effects of the crisis linger.

The origins of the crisis in the United States, hitherto the nation providing leadership in global affairs and the nation perhaps most damaged by the crisis, complicated a global response to the crisis. The rapid accumulation of economic resources by China, and its relative insularity from the crisis created the potential for a stunning shift of global power away from the United States. Tracing the sources and consequences of the crisis illuminates the capacities of governments, the power of financial interests, and the political and power relationships between the United States and China; it also raises important questions about the sustainability of contemporary forms of capitalism.

Background: Financialization of the Global Economy

The global economic crisis emerged out of a three-decade era of financialization: a rapid global expansion of financial transactions that assumed a vastly greater size and geographic scope.[4] This generated substantial changes in the structure of the financial industry and greatly intensified global competition.[5] The political leadership for this effort came from the government and financial industry of the United States, which pressed hard over thirty years for a liberalization of national policies concerning the movement of goods and money.

Globalization involves a rapid expansion of trade relative to domestic production, but it also leads to a tighter integration of global financial markets, increasing the potential for changes in one market to cascade across the system and affect many nations and markets. The financial crisis of 2007–2009 was by no means the first during this era of globalization; indeed, the expansion of markets and number of market players is usually associated with an increase in the frequency of such crises. Financial crises involving governmental borrowing from global banks occurred in 1982, 1994, 1998, 1999, and 2001; crises involving private sector borrowing occurred in the United States from 1988–1991 and in Asia from 1997–1998; global stock market collapses took place in 1987 and 2000; and the massive collapse of stocks, real estate, and debt instruments came upon us in 2007–2009.[6]

This era of globalization and financialization was also one in which governmental responsibilities for regulatory oversight of financial institutions changed character: both expanding in consistency across nations and contracting in practice within many nations.[7] Though international efforts to coordinate regulatory rules for banking increased, the effect of those rules produced an overall relaxation of regulatory restraints across many nations and a decline in effective regulatory consistency.

Perhaps the most striking element of the financialization of the global economy was innovations in the types of financial instruments and in the processes by which investments were made. Ever since the end of fixed exchange rates for most advanced nations in the 1970s, foreign exchange markets and especially futures markets have grown enormously. By mid-2007, daily turnover in these markets exceeded $3 trillion, more than three-fourths of which involved dollars, euros, yen, and pounds sterling.[8]

Using much the same logic as foreign exchange futures, complex derivatives were developed and expanded as primary trading instruments in global financial markets.[9] A derivative is a security whose value is a time-based result of the value of some other security, asset, or event. Derivatives usually are highly leveraged[10] so that small changes in the value of the underlying asset lead to large changes in the value of the derivative. A derivative could be based on a stock price or on the flow of income coming from bundling together a variety of mortgages on houses (collateralized debt obligations, or CDOs). Even more exotic derivatives are credit default swaps, which are insurance policies that pay off in the event that a particular borrower fails to pay the interest or principal of a bond. These are securitized and traded in shadow markets, based on the market-based risk of defaulting on a bond.[11] In 2008, before the financial crisis had begun in earnest, total global derivatives contracts pending (excluding foreign exchange) were more than $600 trillion, or about nine times the entire global GDP for 2008.[12]

Financialization was also enhanced by the enormous globalization of production, in particular the shift of manufacturing to several Asian nations and the resulting imbalances of trade. Complementarities between the U.S. economy and the economies of several Asian states led to large and persistent imbalances in the global economy.[13] U.S. firms shifted manufacturing capabilities to Asia through foreign direct investment and then exported these products back to eager U.S. consumers, thereby creating large and growing trade deficits for the United States. However, surplus nations in Asia often chose to retain the accumulating dollars as foreign exchange reserves rather than exchange them and push up the value of their currency. Moreover, high growth rates over several decades meant much higher incomes for Asians. When combined with high savings rates, the foreign exchange reserves produced an enormous pool of capital for investment. High budget deficits and large private borrowing in the United States created a large demand for borrowed funds. But low savings rates in the United States (the flip side of high consumption levels) meant U.S. resources could not meet this demand. Much of the Asian capital pool found its way back into purchases of U.S. government debt and an unlikely supply of capital from "poor" nations to "rich" nations.[14] Many of these investment decisions were the result of choices made by Asian governments. Thus the globalization of production and trade combined with financialization to see initial flows of U.S. investment into Asia to finance production of goods for sale in the United States. U.S. money then flowed to Asia to pay for the products and then flowed back to the United States in exchange for debt. The United States financed much of its consumption spree with debt owed to Asian governments.[15]

Globalization and financialization created many important consequences that contributed to the global economic crisis.[16] Perhaps most significant were the vast size of the markets and the giant role in those markets of highly leveraged assets vulnerable to risks not appreciated by most investors.[17] Some scholars and analysts trace the crisis to the rise of "money manager capitalism," a system involving highly leveraged investments aiming at maximizing profits even as investment managers have incentives to underestimate the risk of loss.[18] Also, imbalances of trade and finance were inherent in a system based on dramatic asymmetries of capabilities and interests, as between the United States and China. These imbalances were unsustainable in the long run but continued as a result of the preferences of powerful states and firms. Finally, the vast size of both markets and profits generated interests in governments and private actors intensely committed to preserving and extending the system.[19]

The global economic crisis emerged out of a particular global regime of political economy, involving trade and production, global finance and investment, deregulation, and political relations that began to emerge in the 1970s. The explosion of global finance created high demand for new investment opportunities, which was increasingly met with exotic derivatives that were thought to manage risk even while providing high returns. These securities rested on the ability to expand high-risk home mortgage lending based on expectations of rising home prices. An unprecedented rise in public and private debt in the West was financed in significant part by the resources of relatively poor nations selling manufactured products to rich nations.

Background: The Nature of Financial Markets
Scholars have debated the degree to which financial markets are prone to instability and crisis or whether crises are the result of factors external to markets that affect them negatively. This debate has considerable implications for whether governments accept a limited or proactive role in regulating markets.[20]

Table 10.1   Global Imbalances from US Current Account, 1999–2011

Year	US current account total ($ U.S. millions)	US-Asia current account ($ U.S. millions)	US-China current account ($ U.S. millions)	US-China % total current account	US-Asia % total current account
1999	−301,630	−216,071	−72,743	24.1	71.6
2000	−417,426	−246,690	−88,043	21.1	59.1
2001	−398,270	−225,945	−88,658	22.3	56.7
2002	−459,151	−249,558	−109,899	23.9	54.3
2003	−521,519	−260,713	−131,825	25.3	50.0
2004	−631,130	−325,465	−172,343	27.3	51.6
2005	−748,683	−377,908	−219,196	29.3	50.5
2006	−803,547	−437,434	−259,490	32.3	54.4
2007	−726,573	−452,594	−293,105	40.3	62.3
2008	−706,068	−430,534	−308,474	43.7	61.0
2009	−381,896	−339,372	−263,024	64.9	88.9
2010	−441,951	−383,909	−300,356	67.7	86.7
2011	−465,926	−395,296	−315,033	67.6	84.8

Source: Author's calculations, based on data from the Bureau of Economic Affairs, http://www.bea.gov/iTable/index_ita.cfm

On one side are those with a strong belief in the efficacy of free markets for allocating resources (in this case, capital) rationally and efficiently to those best able to use it. Such a view counsels minimal efforts to regulate or manage markets by government, believing such actions always make things worse in terms of efficiency. This assertion rests on one of two alternative assumptions: that market participants are themselves rational and their choices produce the efficient allocation of resources, or, alternatively, that markets are themselves rational and always reflect the best available information. Consequently, free markets always generate a "correct" price.[21]

Countering this position is a collection of scholars who study markets and market crises and those who examine the actual behavior of market participants. The examination of past market panics reveals a set of common features, including a strong tendency for investors to follow and emulate winners, especially when a new and successful product or technology emerges. When this coincides with substantial expansion of credit and several markets are interdependent, the resulting overinvestment can ultimately lead to panic selling in an effort to escape losses. The consequent cascading of prices across several markets leads to damage to the entire economy.[22] Others have looked at the behavior of market participants, finding considerable evidence for the view that many investors exhibit significant limits to rationality and invest based on emotion as much as clear calculation.[23] One study modeling a stock market composed of players with limited information who form expectations based on the expectations of others found a high frequency of booms and busts in prices.[24]

Background: Regulatory Environments

Financial markets and banking systems have been regulated by governments since the 1930s and even earlier. Central banks (all government-controlled) were designed to manage the money supply in part through the ability to regulate the lending behavior of private banks. Various government institutions have long been involved in guaranteeing banking deposits and in regulating the activities of investment banks and stock markets. But the degree of enforcement of these restrictions has varied according to the government in power and in terms of political and ideological trends. And the ability of central bankers to manage monetary policy to promote economic growth without either inflation or financial crises has been questioned.[25]

During the era of rapid globalization after the 1970s, governments generally retreated from strict regulations and enacted new rules that reduced or eliminated barriers to the international movement of money. This included establishing flexible or floating exchange rates, eliminating controls on capital movements, broadening investment options for banks, and opening financial markets to foreign competition. Financial policies coincided with the privatization of state-owned enterprises, reductions in welfare spending, and the liberalization of trade.[26] At the same time, not all advanced or developing nations were equally committed to such policies. For example, in Europe liberalization of capital was related to constructing an integrated regional market and a single currency requiring more rules to manage and coordinate policies and actions.[27]

Governments and global financial firms interact in more than just a regulatory setting; choices and policy actions are deeply embedded in political and power relationships. Government macroeconomic policies are greatly affected by the actual and anticipated reactions of stock, bond, and foreign exchange markets. Even more important, capital is the lifeblood of a capitalist economy, and those who control its allocation have enormous structural power.[28] The rate of economic growth is contingent on the effectiveness of financial firms in providing capital in sufficient volume to those who can best use it for economic activity. This structural power means two things: first, governments and financial firms must engage in a de facto partnership that both regulates and enhances the competitiveness of the financial sector; second, this requires substantial forms of political governance to prevent abuse and errors from damaging national and global economies, but not so much as to harm growth itself. Regulators are conscious of the possibility that controls on the actions of financial actors can reduce opportunities for profit and innovation.[29] Therefore, the nature and application of regulations are both a necessity and a negotiated outcome between financial and political interests.

The financialization of the world economy in recent decades means that regulation of financial institutions must be coordinated across many nations to be effective in protecting the financial system from cascading processes of crisis-induced breakdown. The core of the international coordination of regulation has been a series of negotiated rules designed to prevent bank failures. Each is named for the agreements reached in Basel, Switzerland, among central bank officials of the richest nations.[30] The first was in 1988 (Basel I), the second in 2004 (Basel II), and the most recent in 2011 (Basel III). National governments are responsible for enacting these rules and enforcing them.[31]

The development of regulatory rules and enforcement practices takes place within political and power environments and reflects the structural power of financial institutions in providing the capital for economic growth. In addition, the rapid globalization of finance increased competition among financial firms. After the 1970s, the regulatory environment had been increasingly defined by a deepening elite consensus in the United States and Great Britain on the value and effectiveness of freer markets for trade and finance. This meant the considerable international power of the United States was behind the move to freer markets. Sometimes referred to as the "Washington consensus," these views called for less regulation and restrictions based on the assertion that free markets were self-regulating. This meant the economic gains from free and unregulated markets were not at significant risk from a financial collapse because market players themselves were the best judges of the riskiness of their decisions and would adjust their actions accordingly.

Regulatory decisions in the decades leading up to the crisis increasingly reflected this thinking. We see considerable evidence of change in government thinking: moving from a regime of intrusive examination and regulation developed in the 1930s to one in which financial institutions themselves defined and measured the risk associated with their actions. An important dynamic in this process was competition between New York and London to attract financial business by creating an environment most favorable to business. This meant a "race to the bottom" in enforcing regulations and in deregulation of finance.[32] This competition came against a background of increasing quantitative sophistication in measuring and managing risk.[33] Moreover, in a series of steps the U.S. government loosened restrictions on the sources of funds and on the investment options for banks. This culminated in the 1999 repeal of the Glass-Steagall Act of 1933 that restricted banks to commercial banking and prevented them from acting as investment banks. Over the years after 1980, banks became multipurpose and complex financial firms operating in virtually all of the rapidly expanding global financial arenas.[34]

The efforts at international regulatory coordination reflect the shifting environment of global finance. The focus of the Basel agreements has been on defining calculations for capital adequacy: How large should bank reserves be as protection against failure? This question has increasingly been defined by the nature of the evolving partnership between governments and banks. That partnership has focused on government guarantees of depositors and even guarantees for the losses of some banks. Over time, this means the "acceptable" level of capital for banks has declined dramatically. In the 1970s and before Basel, the largest banks normally operated with 5 percent of capital as reserves, declining to about 4 percent.[35] The Basel I agreements focused on defining a set of risk categories for bank assets (loans and investments) and required that a certain level of liquid reserves be held as protection against losses.[36] The Basel II agreement in 2004 redefined the risk categories but, most important, placed responsibility for assessing the risk in the hands of the banks themselves. This was premised on assumptions about the validity of new efforts to quantify, with great precision, the risk of loss associated with particular kinds of assets.[37] Reversing previous trends, Basel III increases the requirements for capital adequacy, liquidity, and leverage to be implemented beginning in 2013.[38]

Trajectory of the Global Financial and Economic Crisis

Explanation and Summary

The best explanations for the crisis focus on the factors that contribute to the inherent instability of financial markets, showing how policies and actions of firms and governments contributed to creating and intensifying those circumstances to the point that a systemic crisis erupted:

- Financial markets are inherently unstable. This is especially the case when markets expand rapidly in size and incorporate new players with less investment sophistication. Couple this with an expansion of credit and rising prices, and asset bubbles are a likely result. In markets such as banking systems, with high levels of interdependence from cross investments and cross lending, there is a high potential for downward price cascades when these bubbles pop. The inherent instability of financial markets is enhanced because of the role of confidence in the ability of the various firms to repay their debt. Substantial doubt about repayment leads to panicked efforts to get money from possibly bankrupt firms—much like a "run" on the banks. Loss of confidence can also produce a breakdown in the continuous process of credit allocation that is the heart of financial capitalism, and when credit stops flowing the negative consequences cascade even further.
- More specific to this crisis, the deregulation of financial markets spread over several decades led to many financial innovations that required much higher leverage and thus risk-taking. Financial markets in the decade after 1999 became much more interdependent, took on much more debt, and assumed much greater risk. The leveraging of securities based on subprime (high-risk) mortgages is but one example of this.
- The monetary policy of the Federal Reserve, combined with global financial imbalances, supplied large amounts of cheap credit to the investing community. Seeking higher returns, higher risk investments were made that created an increasing potential for a bubble and collapse.

These features of an explanation for the crisis can be seen in a brief review of the events of the crisis.

The global financial crisis began with a small downturn in the price of homes in the United States, mostly resulting from increasing foreclosures that followed a rise in interest rates. A large number of mortgage borrowers were unable to make the changing payments on their mortgages. These price declines reduced the value of and confidence in the large system of derivative securities, the value of which was based on these mortgages. Once derivatives came under doubt, the viability of the banks and investment institutions (such as hedge funds) with large positions in these securities also came under doubt. This doubt was confirmed as some of the weakest firms began to fail, which created a significant financial panic in which confidence in all lending broke down. Firms that in a normal market were solvent became insolvent in a panicked environment, as all creditors wanted payment at once.

The U.S. government chose to step into the situation with funding to restore confidence and stop the panic that could lead to a breakdown of the entire global financial system. Large sums were used to purchase bad assets, support the liquidity of failing firms, and place the government into the position of lender of last resort. Once the financial collapse began to drag down purchasing power of consumers and thereby led to a rapid decline of the overall economy, the governments of many countries began to act to shore up the economy through stimulus spending. In the aftermath of the immediate crisis, nations continue to consider how to act to prevent a future crisis.

Crisis Sequence

U.S. Origins. The near-confluence of the bursting of the "dot-com" bubble in 2000 and the attacks of September 11, 2001, created a significant economic downturn in the U.S. economy. The Federal Reserve responded with a policy of easy money, lowering interest rates to near zero. Interest rates were similarly low in most other advanced economies. In addition, global liquidity—the supply of investment funds looking for returns—continued a rapid rise. There was considerable political pressure from the U.S. Congress to expand mortgage loans, especially to low-income borrowers. This led to Fannie Mae and Freddie Mac (government-sponsored, but private firms) providing backing to mortgages of questionable value and then to rapid growth of exotic financial instruments tied to these mortgages. This flow of funds to housing led to a rapid increase in house prices.

In the years leading up to the crisis, the amount of debt in the United States reached levels not seen for seventy-five years.[39] But in much of the developed world debt levels were even higher. By 2007 total indebtedness in the United States and across the nations of Europe was three times the size of GDP, a ratio that surpassed the record set in the years of the Great Depression. From 2001 to 2007 alone, U.S. domestic financial debt grew to $14.5 trillion from $8.5 trillion, and home mortgage debt ballooned to almost $10 trillion from $4.9 trillion, an increase of 102 percent. A very large proportion of the mortgage debt increase came from subprime loans, among the riskiest of these loans. In Europe, debt reached similar proportions of GDP, driven as much by business borrowing as by home mortgages. Britain was the largest borrower; even after the crisis, borrowing there rose to 350 percent of GDP.[40] A very large and increasing portion of the government debt was held by Asian governments eager to sustain trade surpluses by holding dollar assets.

Directly connected to this vast increase in debt was the even larger expansion of derivatives, the value of which was often tied to the value of the income streams from the debt. These derivatives were themselves leveraged, usually traded in dark markets where values were not publicly known, and mostly carried by firms operating in unregulated settings and in off-the-books accounts. This "shadow market" was designed to attract global investments seeking higher returns, and was usually rated as very safe based on the theory that the issuers of derivatives had been able to manage and reduce the risks of such securities.[41]

Financialization of the global economy had a major consequence: It created a vast global pool of investment capital constantly searching for higher-yielding but safe investments. One estimate from an IMF official is that this pool totaled about $70 trillion.[42] The major players in these securities were the investment bank wings of the great banks and insurance companies: JP Morgan Chase, Citigroup, Goldman Sachs, AIG, Bear Sterns, Lehman, Merrill Lynch, Bank of America, and Wachovia. Also deeply involved were numerous global investment firms seeking to raise yields.

Much of the decision making regarding lending for homes and creating a variety of securitized instruments built on home mortgages was premised on the long-term trend for steadily rising home prices. The large expansion of funding for homes began by 2003 to drive home price increases well above this long-term trend line. The rising prices of houses and the easily available credit pulled more persons into borrowing to purchase a house, thereby driving up prices even further and pulling more persons into the process. Expansion of the number of mortgages also supported an expansion of the derivative securities built on mortgages. Banks and investment firms seeking better yields purchased enormous amounts of the derivatives relating to mortgages, with confidence provided by the high ratings given by agencies such as Moody's.[43] For two to three years an expanding but unsustainable bubble of lending, buying, and securitization continued.

In the summer of 2004, the Federal Reserve began to reverse its policy of extremely easy credit by raising the discount rate, leading to a process of steadily increasing interest rates that took the discount rate from 2 percent in 2004 to 6.25 percent in 2006.[44] Interest rates throughout the economy rose, including the adjustable rates on many subprime mortgages. Many borrowers had also been borrowing a portion of the interest payments for their mortgage. So when the adjustment of mortgage payments included not only higher interest, but now payment for the old accruing interest, new payments were much higher. Housing prices peaked in many parts of the United States in 2005–2006 and then began to fall as more and more homeowners defaulted on their mortgages, taking them into foreclosure.[45]

The decline in house prices and rise in mortgage foreclosures slowly, and then with a rush, began to unwind the derivatives market, along with placing a new drag on the overall economy. Even small increases in unemployment contributed to the emerging housing crisis as problems in one area began to feed back into other areas. In mid-2007, some U.S. and European high-profile hedge funds and banks with large investments in derivations linked to subprime loans declared bankruptcy, with others making ominous announcements about the value of these investments. The result was a 90 percent decline in new issues of derivatives of CDOs by the end of 2007.

The first large bank failure was the British bank Northern Rock, which was taken over by the government. Several central banks responded with efforts to boost the money supply and lower key interest rates. The U.S. government also attempted to stem the tide with a series of similar but ultimately ineffectual actions. The global credit system began to break down, as many lenders were unable to judge the risks and simply stopped extending credit.

By March 2008, the reinforcing cycles of declining home prices and foreclosures, collapsing derivative values, and bankruptcy for banks and investment firms reached a crisis level when the major Wall Street investment bank Bear Sterns faced bankruptcy. In an arrangement engineered and partly financed by the Federal Reserve, JP Morgan Chase purchased Bear Sterns. This action was taken to prevent losses by Bear Sterns from creating a cascade of losses by other large financial firms.[46] Even so, the process increased fears of a massive crisis. In the late spring of 2008, the financial crisis began to have a significant impact on unemployment, with rates beginning a rapid rise from 5 percent in April 2008 to above 10 percent in late 2009.[47]

Though these are government-sponsored enterprises, Fannie Mae and Freddie Mac are also private and profit-oriented firms resulting from an effort to privatize government enterprises. These enterprises issued bonds and provided guarantees for mortgages and hedge contracts totaling more than $7 trillion in July 2008. The operations of Freddie and Fannie show the deep and profound interconnections in global financial markets, with these obligations held by purchasers such as banks, state and local governments, insurance companies, and foreign governments. Fannie and Freddie began to collapse under huge losses in mid-2008. In July 2008, the U.S. government, led by Treasury

Secretary Henry Paulson, reversed its previous position on providing backing to Freddie and Fannie and provided billions of dollars in support. This came as confidence in the financial system was threatened by the potential failure of the two firms. Soon, however, this proved insufficient, and these two privatized, government-sponsored entities were taken over by the government on September 8, 2008.[48]

The takeover of Freddie and Fannie ushered in the most intense period of the crisis, in which the deep fragility of the global financial system was nakedly exposed and in which government ingenuity in saving this system was severely tested. Policy actions throughout the crisis were premised on the proposition that some financial institutions were so deeply linked to other firms that failure of a major firm would set off a panic and produce a set of domino-like failures that could not be controlled and would lead to a terrible depression. This view was tested by the decision not to rescue Lehman, perhaps the largest underwriter of subprime mortgage–backed securities, which declared bankruptcy on September 15.[49] This decision brought on the feared nightmare scenario with rising panic, collapsing financial firms, and a near-disintegration of the U.S. credit system.[50]

In quick order, government policy makers at the Treasury and Fed reversed their position. After Lehman filed for bankruptcy and panic levels rose, a government-arranged deal allowed Bank of America to purchase the venerable Merrill Lynch, and the insurance giant AIG was rescued with an $85 billion government loan.[51] The panic in financial markets that followed was evident in rapid and large declines in global stock markets.[52] A global run on money market funds indicated not only a rush to liquidity but widespread fears that all financial institutions were on the brink of collapse. A global financial panic was in the offing, as Secretary Paulson stated, "We're at the precipice."[53]

Recognizing the new level of potential disaster, almost immediately the Fed and U.S. Treasury began to press for new resources to stem the crisis. Secretary Paulson proposed that Congress authorize creation of a $700 billion fund to purchase the troubled (some would say toxic) assets of financial firms in order to clear the way for these firms to avoid bankruptcy and resume lending. After initially failing in the U.S. House, which prompted a dramatic drop in U.S. stocks, the bill authorizing funding for the Troubled Asset Relief Program (TARP) passed the Congress.[54] Soon these funds were being used to purchase preferred stock and thereby government ownership positions in these firms. In addition, the program was extended to nonbank financial institutions.

A much larger and unprecedented effort was undertaken by the Federal Reserve, under Bush appointee Ben Bernanke, who moved aggressively into uncharted waters involving use of the monetary power of a central bank. The Fed used its ability to create money to purchase assets directly in markets so as to inject liquidity into the most fragile areas of financial markets. This involved guarantees of money market funds; liquidity for commercial paper markets; $1.25 trillion in purchases of mortgage-backed securities (derivatives, usually CDOs); $300 billion of special purchases of longer-term Treasury bonds; $175 billion purchases of debt of Freddie and Fannie; swap agreements with foreign central banks to provide dollar liquidity in global markets; a Primary Dealer Credit Facility (PDCF), which provided short-term loans to investment banks; and a Term Securities Lending Facility (TSLF), which provided liquidity in credit card, student loan, auto loan, and home equity loan markets.[55] The collective effects of these efforts demonstrate the capacity of the U.S. central bank for rapid and innovative actions in the face of a crisis. Perhaps more important, such capabilities involve a significant extension and deepening of the essential partnership between the central bank and private finance in the governance and operation of contemporary capitalism.

Internationalization of the Crisis. In October 2008, the crisis shifted to Europe and focused on Iceland, the smallest member of the EU and the one most exposed to global finance and the effects of the financial crisis. Faced with a panic run on its banks, Iceland nationalized its banking system and prevented withdrawals. Other European nations were forced to guarantee the banking deposits of their nation's banks, and some bank takeovers occurred. A pan-Euro area meeting in mid-October produced a set of common principles for responding to the crisis. Outside of Europe, the Korean government acted to protect its banks with a $130 billion commitment, and the IMF moved to provide support to several nations.[56]

A backwash effect of the crisis emerged in Europe only later, when in 2010 confidence in the national debt of several nations came into question. It is in the area of macroeconomic policy that the deep problems of the Eurozone have been exposed by the global financial crisis. There are dramatic differences in the macroeconomic positions of the different states in the EU and in the Eurozone, making for great difficulties. The Eurozone makes it possible for individual nations to borrow money at the same interest rate, in spite of the wide differences in their economic position. Compare, for example, the Netherlands and Austria, with debt levels between 60 percent and 79 percent of

GDP, and Greece, with debt levels at 175 percent of GDP. Each nation uses the same currency and has the same central bank. Prior to the crisis, there was no clear path for the Eurozone to deal with a situation in which the uncertainties about the sovereign debt of a member state could threaten the survival of the euro itself. From late 2009 and continuing through to 2012, the euro crisis has remained unresolved because several member states have exceeded the willingness of markets to provide them with loans.

The crisis in the Eurozone focused initially on the fiscal problems in Greece, with national debt in 2009 at 113 percent of GDP and a budget deficit at almost 13 percent of GDP. Doubts about Greece escalated when rating agencies downgraded its debt, thereby undermining its ability to borrow more money, as interest rates on its debt rose drastically. The nations in the EU (especially Germany), along with the IMF, were called on to provide loans to permit Greece to make interest payments, refinance its debt, and avoid default. The crisis expanded when rating agencies downgraded the sovereign debt of Portugal and Spain in late April 2010. Funds to restore confidence in all three nations were projected to reach as high as $500 billion, which generated considerable diplomatic interaction among international organizations and states.[57] The issues were familiar, with opposition to bailouts for countries unable to control their spending countered by fears that doing nothing would metastasize into a crisis for the EU and the euro.[58] Despite the opposition, agreement on Greece was reached in May 2010 on a $146 billion package of loans from the EU and IMF, tied to requirements for drastic reductions in the Greek budget deficit. Later in 2010, a similar arrangement was reached for Ireland, followed by another package for Portugal in 2011.

Though important, these actions failed to quell the crisis because four large uncertainties remained unresolved. One is whether Greece will be able to make the needed cuts in spending and collect tax revenues so as to receive the sequence of loans available to it. Failure of this process would lead to a Greek exit from the euro, damaging confidence in the currency's viability. Second, other much larger nations, such as Italy and Spain, also face a possible cutoff from global credit markets, prompting fears of a potential default on their debt. Third, private banks in Europe own much of the threatened sovereign debt, which extends the effects of the crisis even further. A default by one or more nations would surely force many banks into bankruptcy and threaten another significant global crisis. And finally, the continuing crisis and actions to impose austerity have reduced economic growth in Europe, which also contributes to larger budget deficits and the need for more borrowing.

Eurozone nations have attempted to address some of these persistent issues. In February 2011, an expanded funding system totaling $676 billion was approved to support nations in crisis, and in May 2011, part of the fund was used for a bailout of Portugal. In July 2011, another round of funding for Greece was approved and tied to additional Greek actions to reduce its budget deficit. Nevertheless, the crisis would not go away. The role of global bond markets remains significant, with the loss of confidence in national finances reflected in large increases in the interest rates for the bonds of these nations. Italy, Spain, and even France have come under question, and the European Central Bank has pledged to make large purchases of these nations' bonds to reduce borrowing costs. At the end of 2012, some stability seems possible, with large resources committed to protecting the system and some hope for improving economic conditions. At the same time, the Eurozone crisis reflects a similar pattern of national governments engaged in a close partnership with private banks to manage a deeply unstable system.

Economic Consequences of the Global Crisis. The economic effects of the financial crisis became most apparent in the fall of 2008, when the global economy began a steep slide. Much of this was the result of the near-collapse of the credit system in the United States. Companies facing declines in sales, along with those unable to finance their normal operations, instituted massive layoffs. This led to rapid and steep increases in unemployment and an equally rapid and steep decline in GDP and global trade, the sharpest and deepest since before the 1960s.[59] Unemployment jumped quickly, with hundreds of thousands of jobs lost each month.

The transition from the Bush to the Obama administration in early 2009 came in the midst of ongoing and continuing economic deterioration. Perhaps most disturbing was the rapid acceleration of job losses and the consequent rise in unemployment. In the four months from December 2008 to March 2009, the U.S. economy lost jobs at the rate of more than seven hundred thousand per month, with a total for that time of almost 3 million lost jobs.[60] Analysts commonly asserted the possibility of a depression that would rival that of the 1930s. The Obama administration, operating with traditional macroeconomic thinking, acted quickly to increase government spending in order to boost economic demand and blunt the downturn. Congress passed a $787 billion stimulus package of spending increases and tax cuts in February 2009. By the end of 2009, most analysts concluded the stimulus had made a significant contribution to a return to economic growth and had saved or created many jobs.[61] The rapid loss of jobs in early 2009 had been reversed by early 2010. Though the unemployment rate remained very high, the U.S. economy began creating jobs, and by 2012 the unemployment rate fell below 8 percent.[62]

The crisis did not affect all nations in the same way and to the same extent. The degree to which a nation experienced an economic downturn was influenced by the level of its involvement in the global financial boom and by the ability to adjust to adversity. This was especially true for emerging economies. The nations with a combination of rapid growth in debt, including governmental debt, and an exchange rate of low flexibility suffered the worst. Trade levels were less important for generating economic declines.[63]

Almost all of the most advanced economies adopted a stimulus program to counteract the downturn. Negotiations to coordinate stimulus policies were generally unsuccessful, due to the differential effects of the crisis. Further, the size and the emphases of these programs varied considerably, with the typical size at about 2.5 percent of GDP. Among rich nations, the U.S. stimulus was the largest in absolute and proportional terms, at $787 billion and 5.5 percent of GDP. The emphasis of this program was on income maintenance and tax cuts, with substantial spending for infrastructure.[64] The programs for Norway, Italy, France, and Switzerland were below 1 percent of GDP, while those for Canada, Korea, Australia, and New Zealand were between 4 percent and 5 percent of GDP. The stimulus programs for several emerging economies were dramatically larger as a proportion of GDP. For example, China ($585 billion, 19 percent of GDP), Brazil ($152 billion, 15 percent of GDP), and Russia ($101 billion, 8 percent of GDP) dwarf that of many richer nations.[65] The focus of Chinese spending was on infrastructure (roads, airports, power grid), earthquake recovery (housing for the poor), health care, education, and tax reform to spur business investment.[66] Not surprising, the combination of increased spending and falling tax revenues produced much bigger budget deficits and government debt.[67]

Perhaps the most striking result of the global financial crisis was that the impending and expected global depression did not happen, in spite of the severe damage done to the banking and financial industry and the spillover effects for the rest of the economy. The reason is that government efforts to blunt financial collapse, through injections of money into banks via central bank actions and into demand stimulus through government fiscal policies, were large enough to prevent a more catastrophic decline. Nonetheless, the crisis inflicted severe damage on credit markets, asset markets, and the investment process in many nations. These effects can be seen in the especially long period of economic decline and slow recovery. Five years after the crisis began, many advanced nations remain mired in significant economic difficulty. Though emerging economies experienced cuts in growth rates, most weathered the crisis much better.[68] The Chinese economy experienced a significant decline and contains many serious imbalances, but is in a much better position than is the United States.[69] The speed of the Chinese recovery is partly the result of structural differences in Chinese capitalism, in which large and strategic parts of the economy are state owned and state influenced and can be coordinated quickly with state policies. Furthermore, the Chinese economy has low levels of debt (government and private) and high savings, providing a flush of funding.[70]

There are many lasting and unresolved legacies from the crisis: huge fiscal deficits, uncertainty about how to change institutions to reduce the chances of future financial crises, negative effects on the world's poorest, a reshuffling of power relations, and determining how to redesign the economic system for sustained and more equitable growth.[71]

Foreign Policy Arenas of the Global Economic Crisis

The global financial crisis has important effects on a wide array of global issues, organizations, political struggles, and power relationships; these are distributed across a set of crucial foreign policy arenas. The global financial crisis affects foreign policy choices, the definition of problems and issues, and short-term and long-term power relationships; it also restructures strategic relations. We will examine these arenas as a way of identifying the consequences of the economic crisis for foreign policy and global political economy. The arenas include economic prosperity and global security, global cooperation and coordination, US-China relations, and changes in the nature of capitalism.

Implications for Economic Prosperity, Security, and Power

The ability of the United States to preserve its national security through economic prosperity for itself, its allies, and the many nations linked together through global economic relationships was significantly tested and probably damaged by the economic crisis. Many issues are linked to this broad question:

- role of the dollar as key currency;
- global competitiveness of U.S. firms;
- continuing growth of U.S. GDP and finance-led globalization;
- credibility of free market ideology;
- U.S. global economic and political leadership position; and
- redistribution of global power.

The global financial crisis of 2007–2009 created significant questions for each of these areas. Equally important, the crisis demonstrated the scale and depth of global financial markets and the degree of global interdependence, upon which the economic security of most nations rests. Also of profound importance is the differential impact of the crisis and the speed and size of the economic recovery by different nations, the most important being China.[72]

The crisis reopened and redefined some of the most basic questions of political economy and global politics: Can existing forms of cooperation among governments, in conjunction with global organizations, provide the political governance adequate to manage global markets? Is the goal of expanding economic openness, especially for capital, appropriate for most nations? What new forms of governance and regulation are needed? Does the crisis elevate the importance of state capitalism, in various forms of public-private partnerships, as the dominant system of political economy for all advanced nations?

Role of the Dollar as Reserve Currency

After World War II, the Bretton Woods institutions enshrined the U.S. dollar as the key currency, which meant many nations were willing to hold dollars instead of exchanging them for their own currency. A normal nation would find that operating a long-term current account deficit, as the United States has done for decades, would result in a large depreciation of its currency. But the United States has mostly avoided this fate because of its currency's special status and has consistently used this enormous advantage to pursue its foreign policy and domestic economic goals and shift an important part of the costs to other nations.[73] The large imbalances in trade between the United States and Asia are the latest round in this process.

Many of the nations that have borne the burden of holding dollars have preferred some alternative model in which multiple reserve currencies exist. Expectations of a significantly changed role for the dollar can be found beginning in the 1960s, yet the United States has been able to retain the benefits of a key currency. Several factors stand in the way of change, including the global weight of the U.S. economy and its capital markets and the absence of a viable alternative to the dollar. Nonetheless, in the years leading up to the financial crisis there were many predictions of coming limits to a willingness to hold dollars and a financial crisis resulting from panic-selling of dollars.[74]

To what extent, if any, has the global economic crisis brought about circumstances for a change in the global role of the U.S. dollar? Perhaps the main political element in the role of the dollar is the determined effort of the United States and its political and financial leaders to retain the dollar as the key currency. The gains from this position are simply too great to give them up willingly. Of course, the increasingly bald abuse of the dollar has alienated many nations, especially when this contributes to financial and economic crisis.[75]

The financial crisis could undermine the role of the dollar if it affected negatively the market power or political power relationships that have supported the dollar for decades.[76] The financial industry of the United States continues to hold a dominant position in global markets, one that both facilitates the dollar as key currency and serves as a barrier to any alternative currency.[77] The global scale and liquidity of U.S. financial markets is unmatched. However, the giant imbalances in the U.S. current account (though in decline as a result of the global economic downturn) continue to raise questions about the stability of the dollar. The position of the dollar has also been supported by the political economy of U.S. trade: Mostly Asian nations are able to expand exports to the United States, which then pays for the exports with U.S. dollars.[78] This permits cheap products for U.S. consumers and rapid growth for Asian exporters. The financial crisis demonstrated the risks of such an arrangement but did not lead to a large decline in the dollar. But certainly, a central element underlying many of the negotiations for rebalancing the U.S. and Asian economies (discussed below) will be the dollar's key currency role.[79]

Global Regulatory Policy

The globalization of the world economy and the expanding weight of financial transactions in this process engage contradictory pressures regarding the international coordination for the management of these new economic relationships. The inherent instability of financial markets and the potential for financial crisis is a constant threat lurking in the background that frequently emerges as a dramatic and real challenge. Typically, the pressure for new global regulatory efforts and for economic policy coordination is highest in the immediate aftermath of such events. More often in the forefront of thinking are the gains to be had from the expansion of financial markets. The political and financial leadership of the United States has aggressively sought those gains for decades through policies and negotiations pressing for deregulation and lax interpretation of existing rules. Historically coordination has come from a "follow the leader" process, where the United States sets the standards and others follow along. The current financial crisis has created loud demands for reform and new regulation, usually tempered by fears of undermining the profits and competitiveness of U.S. finance.[80]

The contexts for regulatory policy making and coordination are somewhat fragmented, and the power and position of the actors have been complex and varied. There are two main fronts for new policy relating to the regulation of banks: the Dodd-Frank Act in the United States and the Basel III regulations relating to international regulatory standards. At the same time, three arenas have been the focus of efforts at global policy coordination: interactions among central bankers, the expansion of the economic forum for political leaders from the G-8 (the seven largest industrial economies and Russia) to the G-20 (the twenty largest economies, including some large but developing states like China, India, and Brazil), and discussion of regulatory policies in the Financial Stability Board (FSB). If past patterns hold true, the reelection of President Obama will lead to greater speed and consistency in rule making for the implementation of Dodd-Frank, and those rules and standards will filter into international deliberations and coordination arrangements.

The financial crisis has affected the power relations among the various players in making policy, mainly by enhancing the importance of central banks. Financial crises create intense fears about the possible collapse of an always-fragile financial system leading to dramatic systemic effects. Central banks have long had as a central purpose the management of financial systems in crisis, based in large part on the ability to affect interest rates and create money. In a crisis, central banks can act with some independence of normal political processes and possess the knowledge and resources to affect outcomes. It was central bankers who were able to act most quickly and decisively to address the crisis, and can probably be credited with stopping the momentum toward the abyss generated by the collapse of confidence in global finance. Though the U.S. Federal Reserve certainly made many mistakes and failed to act in anticipation of the crisis, its actions afterward were bold and effective. Once the financial crisis subsided, other actors involved in financial statecraft sought to reestablish their role and power in relation to central banks.[81] Much of the subsequent struggle over the nature of the new regulatory regime was the result of different actors seeking to reassert or extend their authority.

A near-immediate result of the financial crisis was a shift of the locus of efforts to coordinate international political efforts to manage economic issues such as a financial crisis from the G-8 to the G-20. This reflects the opening of the club of global economic discussion to a much bigger group of formerly poor and now emerging nations. The G-8 has traditionally been an informal and "clubby" setting for "fireside chat" discussions among the leaders of the richest nations. It has had some successes in arranging for the public coordination of policy initiatives among these nations. But it is a forum rather than an organization. And the new size of the group, while commendable in recognizing the importance of new, emerging economies, may be too large for effective discussion and decision.[82]

Between 2008 and 2012, the G-20 met seven times.[83] The results of these meetings were limited but important. A set of principles to guide efforts to resolve the crisis was adopted, discussion of economic stimulus plans produced some baseline agreement, substantial new resources were committed to the IMF, and arrangements for coordinating financial regulation were strengthened. But many of the commitments made have not been fulfilled, and major issues, such as providing real authority to the FSB, have lagged.[84] One other important area of failure for the G-20 was in getting nations to carry through on the pledge not to enact additional protectionist measures.[85]

The Dodd-Frank Act was signed into law in 2010, and regulatory agencies have devoted the time since to writing specific rules for its implementation.[86] This is a very complicated law, with a multitude of implications.[87] Its most important parts include the following:

- Enhancing transparency for derivatives trading by requiring trading on public exchanges
- Identifying systemically important firms and permitting a special government role in dealing with them
- Creating a consumer protection bureau to prevent abusive lending practices
- Altering the risk-taking activities of financial institutions

Defining the specific regulations and the process of applying them has turned into a three-sided political bargaining relationship among regulatory officials, Congress, and the financial institutions.[88] The effect of the resulting regulatory regime on the behavior of financial institutions will depend on whether a strong or weak regulatory government is in office. This places regulation even further into a political environment.[89] Perhaps most important, the new regulatory system more deeply institutionalizes the partnership between the largest financial institutions and the national government.

The effort to achieve greater international coordination of financial regulation has achieved some successes, but the Dodd-Frank law increases future uncertainty. The previous U.S. approach to deregulation and limited application of existing regulatory rules has been completely discredited, at least outside the United States. Though the United States may be able to develop a new and more effective regulatory regime, its ability to coordinate adoption across many nations is in doubt unless there is considerable movement toward a model more acceptable elsewhere. Regulatory decisions come against a backdrop of global competition among banks, and competition among nations for being the locations for financial firms and their operations. Affecting these location decisions by banks are a number of considerations, among which are the regulatory standards of the nation. Competition between London and New York was fierce in the years before the crisis, but with a new regulations environment in the offing states cannot help but consider the effect on financial firms who can vote with their feet.[90]

The focal points for international coordination of new arrangements for financial regulation include the Basel Committee on Banking Supervision and the FSB. The former is a committee of national officials responsible for bank supervision and the FSB is composed of senior representatives of national financial authorities (central banks, regulatory and supervisory authorities, and ministries of finance), international financial institutions, standards-setting bodies, and committees of central bank experts. The FSB was initially created as the Financial Stability Forum (FSF) following the 1997 Asian financial crisis. The FSF worked on developing measures to promote global financial stability, though the record of success before 2007 was limited.[91] Nonetheless, the FSF was able to act during the current crisis to formulate a series of proposals that won the support of national leaders and as a result was converted into the FSB in April 2009.[92] The ability to translate a new regulatory system for the US into a system for global coordination through the FSB is, at best, uncertain. Multilateral regulatory coordination awaits the outcome of political struggles over regulation within nations, primarily the United States.

US-China Relations

The decade or so before the economic crisis produced a deepening economic interdependence between China and the United States.[93] However, this relationship yielded trade and financial imbalances sustained by an implicit political bargain: The large Chinese trade surplus with the United States was allowed to grow because it was offset by the willingness of the Chinese to hold U.S. dollar–denominated assets, especially U.S. government debt. The financial crisis has intensified this relationship: U.S. budget deficits have tripled from an already very high level, and the threat of a declining dollar and the actual downgrading of U.S. debt hangs over the relationship.[94] A crucial and unusual feature of this relationship—the financial part of it—is that almost all Chinese purchases of U.S. Treasury bonds are by the Chinese government and not by private Chinese actors. This is not a free market relationship.[95] Moreover, the massive Chinese current account surplus is partly a result of the exchange rate policies of the Chinese government to peg the exchange rate between the Chinese currency—the renminbi (RMB)—and the dollar.[96] At a deeper level, the financial crisis has accentuated examination of the global subsidies pro- vided to sustaining high levels of U.S. consumption for many years. These sub- sidies have come from Europe as well as from Asia.

Estimates of the size of China's holdings of foreign assets vary because of limited transparency from Chinese sources (see Figure 10.1). The $2.3 trillion of Chinese-held foreign assets in the spring of 2009 included approximately $1.5 trillion of dollar assets, or about two-thirds of these foreign assets. These dollar assets are composed of approximately $1.25 trillion in U.S. government debt, with the remainder primarily in U.S. corporate debt and equities.[97] Data from 2011 indicate Chinese holdings of U.S. government debt at $1.5 trillion and total holdings of U.S. assets at $1.7 trillion.[98]

The financial crisis demonstrated these imbalances are unsustainable. However, any realistic strategy for fixing imbalances built up over several decades will require a coordinated effort gradually to shift macroeconomic arrangements in the United States and in Asia.[99] In the United States, consump- tion must fall and savings must rise; in China, the reverse must happen. There is an enormous gap between the savings rates in the two nations, which fuels high consumption in the United States and low consumption in China. The result of rebalancing this arrangement should be a decline in the large trade volume and resulting financial imbalances between them.[100] However, forcing such a set of changes will be painful and will require substantial structural and institutional changes. For U.S. economic growth to continue, increasing saving in the United States must be offset by increased exports, which may require considerable investment in improving U.S. competitiveness. Moreover, the U.S. government, households, and businesses must engage in a difficult process of reducing reliance on debt.[101] In China, consumers must begin to purchase a larger proportion of Chinese products, which may require some restructuring

Figure 10.1 Chinese Foreign Assets, Including Hidden Reserves, 2000–2009

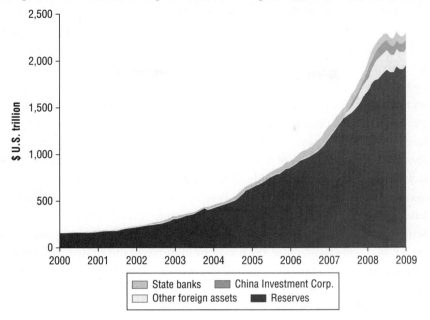

Source: Brad W. Setser and Arpana Pandey, "China's $1.5 Trillion Bet: Understanding China's External Portfolio," Council on Foreign Relations Working Paper, May 2009, 3. Copyright © 2009 by the Council on Foreign Relations, Inc., www.cfr.org. Reproduced by permission.

of Chinese industry. Yet China's current account surplus in 2012 is now one-half as large as in 2008.[102]

An associated strategy is to rely on a financial solution, mainly through a significant shift in exchange rates. China has long maintained a controlled exchange rate, mostly pegged to the U.S. dollar but occasionally allowed to adjust. For example, after 2005 the RMB rose in value from 8.1 to 6.8 to the dollar and after 2009 rose to 6.3. The United States has threatened to define China as a currency manipulator and has attempted to pressure China to let its currency rise to a market-based level. Should this happen, rising prices of Chinese exports and falling prices of U.S. exports could rebalance some of the trade gap.[103] Importantly, such a change will also reduce the Chinese ability and willingness to hold U.S. government debt, which will likely push up interest rates in the United States without a comparable reduction in new borrowing.[104] Even so, some political circles in the United States favor such a strategy, to prevent more painful forms of adjustment.

A related U.S. strategy has been a series of actions by the Federal Reserve to increase the money supply by purchasing financial assets, typically of a longer maturity, directly from banks and other private institutions. Between 2008 and 2012, the Fed purchased several trillion dollars of securities in a policy known as *quantitative easing.* One likely effect of these actions is to depreciate the exchange rate of the dollar and thereby the value of dollar-denominated bonds. As the largest foreign creditor of the US, the Chinese have been especially critical of quantitative easing and have expressed concern over the value of their investments in U.S. government securities. They have raised many questions about the size and trends of the U.S. budget deficit, even as the United States has taken some pains to provide them with reassurance.[105] By contrast, the head of the Chinese central bank, the People's Bank of China, Zhou Xiaochuan, has called for an alternative to the US dollar for international reserves. Such an action would considerably reduce U.S. economic freedom and U.S. economic power. In a more basic sense, the power relationship of the United States and China cannot but be affected, given the enormous holdings of dollar-denominated assets.[106]

Perhaps the most important and lasting consequence of the financial and economic crisis will be the altered relationship between the United States and China. The enormous accumulation of wealth in China, coming as a result of U.S. consumption, is an unprecedented event in global affairs. Though the United States retains enormous strengths, the trends of the relationship with China in the thirty years after 1981 have not been favorable. The United States was able to raise its level of consumption and generate GDP growth, but at a large price, primarily through the accumulation of immense levels of debt.[107] The foreign policy relationship between the United States and China will be deeply colored for years to come by the process of unwinding the effects of that era. Even more significant, the global economic crisis is an important event in the longer-term power shift between the United States and China. This is not a simple "China up and US down" process. Instead, it is better seen as a shift from asymmetrical interdependence favoring the United States, in which U.S. structural power determines outcomes, to a system of more symmetrical interdependence, with growing Chinese structural power partly offsetting that of the United States.[108]

Much of China's newfound structural power comes from its form of state capitalism, in which control over financial resources is concentrated in the state. This position greatly enhances the power of the Chinese state in using domestic policy to promote economic growth and in influencing outcomes in global affairs. Put simply, there are no global financial issues that can now be settled apart from China's interests. Moreover, the almost certain diversification of China's financial assets away from the dollar can undermine the power of U.S. financial markets. China is likely to be able to rebalance the structural advantages of U.S. monetary power as a consequence of reducing global imbalances.[109]

Conclusion: State Capitalism

Because the crisis originated in the United States, there has been considerable criticism around the world of US-style free market capitalism. This cannot be surprising, as U.S. government and business leaders had aggressively pressed their version of capitalism on much of the rest of the world for several decades. In addition to moral condemnations of the system, others have expressed doubts about the viability of such a transactions-based free market system for globalized finance.[110]

Beyond questioning the continuity of Anglo-American-style financial capitalism, we need to examine in more depth the actual workings of such a system. The global financial crisis operates much like lightning on a dark night to illuminate arrangements previously unclear. Specifically, it has served to highlight the relationships of states, financial firms, and global markets in ways that had been largely obscured by the rampant free market rhetoric related to globalization. The pronouncements about the decline of the state and the capabilities of free markets ring as hollow ideology in the face of the clear dependence of the largest financial firms and the entire capitalist system on state support and bailout when times get tough.[111] Much clearer from the crisis is a more accurate picture of the nature of contemporary capitalism, namely the undeniable partnership of states and firms that provides the real governance for globalization.[112] We need to expand our categories of analysis to include the long-standing and expanding role of state capitalism in our understanding of the global economy. For our purposes, the rise of state capitalism increases the role of negotiated outcomes for global economic and financial relationships. These negotiations take place among nations and firms, and are a complex mixture of market-regarding and market-managed arrangements.[113]

State capitalism refers to state-organized and state-directed operations to manage markets, often in cooperation with the largest firms, and thereby promote and manage the governance and functioning of capitalism. These arrangements differ across the world, but the underlying similarity is the deep and profound role played by the central government as a player in capitalism, including the operation of state firms.[114] The concept of state capitalism expands our thinking beyond the simplicities of the liberal state and permits us to reexamine the relationships among firms and nations as different forms of state capitalism.[115]

For example, in all capitalist economies the aggregation and allocation of finance capital is the lifeblood of the economy, and for more than a century governments have assumed a central role in regulating this process and in providing emergency resources when these inherently fragile markets break down. The current financial crisis is simply the latest of many examples of this process, and we should not be surprised that banks and the economic stability of capitalism require this role for government. At the same time, financialization has augmented the role for private finance, as well as the financial operations of states themselves. The financial "power brokers" now include an unlikely set of players, with Goldman Sachs, the Chinese central bank, hedge funds, state petrodollar funds, and other sovereign wealth funds all in a new game of global finance.[116]

Furthermore, the processes of financialization and globalization that contributed to the crisis were a result of the interaction of two different forms of state capitalism: U.S. "market-emphasis capitalism" and Asian "state-emphasis capitalism."[117] In the midst of this process of development, another financial crisis occurred—the Asian financial crisis of 1997–1998.[118] Each crisis was the result of excesses and problems in state capitalism: overconsumption and debt in the current case and overinvestment and debt in the earlier case. And in each instance the government was deeply involved both in creating the problems and in saving the economic system from collapse. The large fiscal stimulus used by almost all capitalist nations to stabilize the impending economic depression is hardly surprising. Governments have long provided between one-quarter and one-half of the spending that drives all capitalist economies.

The really interesting and relevant question is not whether governments should be involved in managing capitalism, but in what ways governments can increase competitiveness and economic growth without generating economic and financial crises and, at the same time, manage the deepening interdependence that defines the global economy. The overheated rhetoric about free markets does little to define and evaluate the real issues and choices for policy. It not only misunderstands the actual nature of markets, but it ignores the role of states in capitalist economies, a role that the financial crisis makes clear will only increase and deepen. We can better understand economic statecraft when we see it as interactions of different forms of state capitalism.

Key Actors

AIG, Morgan Stanley, Lehman Brothers, Bear Stearns, Bank of America, Goldman Sachs, and various hedge funds   Investment firms heavily involved in the subprime mortgage market and its derivative investments, and thus heavily damaged by the collapse of the housing bubble.

Ben Bernanke   Chairman of the Federal Reserve Board; worked creatively to restore liquidity to the U.S. credit and financial markets.

Fannie Mae   The Federal National Mortgage Association; a government-sponsored enterprise that purchases and secures home mortgages. It came under heavy industry and political pressures in the 1990s to expand home loans to more Americans and, as a result of the subprime mortgage crisis, was taken over by the U.S. government.

Financial Stability Board   Originally created as the Financial Stability Forum following the Asian financial crisis of 1997–1998, this entity—comprised of representatives of national financial authorities, international organizations, and financial experts—helps to coordinate international regulation seeking to prevent future financial crises.

Freddie Mac   The Federal Home Loan Mortgage Company; a government-sponsored enterprise that buys home mortgages and bundles them into mortgage-backed securities, which it then sells to investors. As a result of the subprime mortgage crisis, the company was taken over by the U.S. government.

Timothy Geithner   Secretary of the treasury under President Barack Obama and former president of the New York Federal Reserve Bank; defended the Obama stimulus program and sought Chinese assistance in coordinating the two countries' financial and economic policies.

International Monetary Fund (IMF)   The United Nations–based international organization created to help countries experiencing runs on their currency. Following the global financial crisis, it is the international entity most likely to coordinate new regulation or supervision of global financial markets.

Henry Paulson   Secretary of the treasury under President George W. Bush, advocated a governmental bailout of Fannie Mae, Freddie Mac, and the $700 billion Troubled Asset Relief Program.

Mario Draghi President of the European Central Bank (ECB); has taken steps to expand the power of the bank in dealing with the Eurozone crisis.

Zhou Xiaochuan Governor of the People's Bank of China; has acted to expand the role of the RMB in global finance.

Notes

1. For a sense of the crisis atmosphere, see Todd Purdum, "Henry Paulson's Longest Night," *Vanity Fair,* October 2009, www.vanityfair.com/politics/features/2009/10/henry-paulson200910.

2. Matthew Valencia, "The Gods Strike Back: A Special Report on Financial Risk," *The Economist,* February 13, 2010, 1.

3. Charles Roxburgh et al., *Global Capital Markets: Entering a New Era* (McKinsey Global Institute, 2009), 7.

4. Ronald Dore, "Financialization of the Global Economy," *Industrial and Corporate Change* 17, no. 6 (December 2008): 1097–1112. See also Gerald Epstein, ed., *Financialization of the World Economy* (Aldershot, U.K.: Edward Elgar, 2005). From the 1980s to 2005, gross international capital flows increased from 4 to 6 percent of global GDP to more than 16 percent. Richard Deeg and Mary O'Sullivan, "The Political Economy of Global Finance Capital," *World Politics* 61, no. 4 (October 2009): 731.

5. Arnould Boot and Matej Marinc, "The Evolving Landscape of Banking," *Industrial and Corporate Change* 17, no. 6 (December 2008): 1173–1203.

6. For a detailed overview of the savings and loan crisis, see Michael A. Bernstein, "The Contemporary American Banking Crisis in Historical Perspective," *The Journal of American History* 80, no. 4 (March 1994): 1382–1396. Over the period of greatest globalization—1980–2010—financial crises happened about every three years.

7. For a review of deregulation in the United States from 1980–2008, see Fiona Tregenna, "The Fat Years: The Structure and Profitability of the U.S. Banking Sector in the Pre-Crisis Years," *Cambridge Journal of Economics* 33 (2009): 610–611. An overview of the movement toward deregulation in the United States, including finance, is by Joshua Green, "Inside Man," *The Atlantic,* April 2010, www.theatlantic.com/magazine/archive/2010/04/inside-man/7992.

8. Bank for International Settlements, *Survey of Foreign Exchange and Derivatives Markets,* April 2007, 5–7.

9. For a readable and thorough discussion of derivatives, see Randall Dodd, "Derivatives Markets: Sources of Vulnerability in U.S. Financial Markets," in Epstein, *Financialization of the World Economy,* 149–180. A more sophisticated review is by Robert C. Merton, "Observations on the Science of Finance in the Practice of Finance," *MIT World,* http://mitworld.mit.edu/video/659. An analysis of financial innovations is by Saskia Sassen, "Mortgage Capital and Its Peculiarities: A New Frontier for Global Finance," *Journal of International Affairs* 62, no. 1 (Fall 2008): 187–212.

10. This means some significant amount of the investment in a derivative comes from borrowed money, often with various layers of borrowing across the different parts of a derivative.

11. For an excellent short description of the derivatives associated with the financial crisis, see Dave Kansas, *The Wall Street Journal Guide to the End of Wall Street as We Know It* (New York: HarperCollins, 2009), 25–46. A particularly dangerous and even fraudulent security was the synthetic derivative. This was a derivative linked to credit default swaps (CDS), in which the security was based on the value of insurance policies that paid off if CDOs went bad. This permitted two different investments: one a bet that the mortgage-backed CDOs would succeed, the other that they would fail. Joe Nocera, "A Wall Street Invention Let the Crisis Mutate," *New York Times,* April 16, 2010, www .nytimes.com/2010/04/17/business/17nocera.html?ref=global-home.htm.

12. Recent data on the size and composition of derivative markets come from Bank for International Settlements, "Detailed Tables on Semiannual OTC Derivatives Statistics at End-June 2009," www.bis.org/statistics/derdetailed.htm. See specifically Table 19: "Amounts Outstanding of Over-the-Counter (OTC) Derivatives." See also Dore, "Financialization of the Global Economy," 1099. Measuring the flows of derivative investments across borders shows figures of $5 trillion annually. See Ceyla Pazarbasioglu et al., "The Changing Face of Investors," *Finance and Development* 44, no. 1 (March 2007), www .imf.org/external/pubs/ft/fandd/2007/03/pazar.htm.

13. Maurice Obstfeld and Kenneth Rogoff, "Global Imbalances and the Financial Crisis: Products of Common Causes," October 2009, http://scholar.harvard.edu/files/ rogoff/files/global_imbalances_and_financial_crisis.pdf; Simon Cox, "The Long Climb," *The Economist,* October 1, 2009, www.economist.com/specialreports/display-story.cfm?story_id=E1_TQVPDDJP.htm.

14. In 2009, China and Japan combined owned more than $1.5 trillion of U.S. government debt. "A Wary Respect," *The Economist,* October 24, 2009, 5. See also Pazarbasioglu et al., "The Changing Face of Investors." China's dollar assets in 2009 totaled more than $2.3 trillion, which includes investment in other U.S. government and agency debt of $1.5 trillion. Brad Setser and Arpana Pandey, "China's $1.5 Trillion Bet," Council on Foreign Relations Working Paper Update, May 2009.

15. The size of the imbalances is astonishing. The cumulative U.S. current account deficit from 1999 to 2007 was $4.6 trillion and gross U.S. foreign debt reached $13.4 trillion, a four-fold increase from 1998. Bank for International Settlements, *Annual Report,* June 2009, 5. Giselle Datz, "Governments as Market Players: State Innovation in the Global Economy," *Journal of International Affairs* 62, no. 1 (Fall 2008): 35–49; Gregory Chin and Eric Helleiner, "China as a Creditor: A Rising Financial Power?" *Journal of International Affairs* 62, no. 1 (Fall 2008): 87–102; Paul Bowles and Baotai Wang, "The Rocky Road Ahead: China, the U.S., and the Future of the Dollar," *Review of International Political Economy* 15, no. 3 (August 2008): 335–353; Mark Lander, "Dollar Shift: Chinese Pockets Filled as Americans' Emptied," *New York Times,* December 25, 2008; Knowledge@Wharton, "Attached at the Wallet: The Delicate Financial Relationship between the U.S. and China," April 29, 2009, http://knowledge.wharton.upenn.edu/article.cfm?articleid=2230.htm; Eswar Prasad et al., "The Paradox of Capital," *Finance and Development* 44, no. 1 (March 2007), www.imf.org/external/pubs/ft/fandd/2007/03/prasad.htm. Debt levels have risen dramatically in almost all advanced countries in the past twenty years. See Susan Lund et al., "The Looming Deleveraging Challenge," *McKinsey Quarterly,* January 2010, 3.

16. For the contrary view that global imbalances were not related to the financial crisis, see Michael Dooley et al., "Breton Woods II Still Defines the International Monetary System," *Pacific Economic Review* 14, no. 3 (2009): 297–311.

17. For an analysis of the effort to measure and manage risk, see Felix Salmon, "Recipe for Disaster: The Formula That Killed Wall Street," *Wired,* February 23, 2009, www.wired.com/techbiz/it/magazine/17–03/wp_quant?currentPage=all.htm.

18. L. Randall Wray, "The Rise and Fall of Money Manager Capitalism: A Minskian Approach," *Cambridge Journal of Economics* 33 (2009): 807–828.

19. Simon Johnson, "The Quiet Coup," *The Atlantic,* May 2009, 46–56. For a longer-term perspective on the political power of finance, see Gerard Dumenil and Dominique Levy, *Capital Resurgent* (Cambridge: Harvard University Press, 2004). For an examination of enterprise capitalism versus speculative capitalism, see Wray, "The Rise and Fall of Money Manager Capitalism."

20. A readable review of this debate is by John Cassidy, *How Markets Fail* (New York: Farrar, Straus, and Giroux, 2009).

21. Knowledge@Wharton, "Efficient Markets or Herd Mentality: The Future of Economic Forecasting," November 11, 2009, http://knowledge.wharton.upenn.edu/article.cfm?articleid=2383.htm.

22. Charles Kindleberger et al., *Manias, Panics, and Crashes: A History of Financial Crises* (New York: Wiley, 2005).

23. George Akerlof and Robert Shiller, *Animal Spirits* (Princeton: Princeton University Press, 2010).

24. W. Brian Arthur et al., "Asset Pricing under Endogenous Expectations in an Artificial Stock Market," in *The Economy as an Evolving Complex System II,* ed. W. Brian Arthur et al. (Reading: Perseus, 1997), 15–44. See also Mark Buchanan, "Crazy Money," *New Scientist* 199, no. 2665 (July 19, 2008): 32–35.

25. For an indictment of the policies of the Federal Reserve in managing monetary policy in the years before the crisis, see John B. Taylor, *Getting Off Track* (Stanford: Hoover Institution Press, 2009).

26. Steven Vogel, *Freer Markets, More Rules* (Ithaca: Cornell University Press, 1996); Eric Helleiner, *States and the Reemergence of Global Finance* (Ithaca: Cornell University Press, 1994).

27. Rawi Abdelal, *Capital Rules* (Cambridge: Harvard University Press, 2007).

28. Layna Mosley, *Global Capital and National Governments* (Cambridge: Cambridge University Press, 2003); Susan Strange, *Mad Money: When Markets Outgrow Governments* (Ann Arbor: University of Michigan Press, 1998).

29. Not only do regulations need address the riskiness of financial lending and investing practices, but the use of borrowed funds to expand leverage and thus potential profit margins creates the additional risk for failures to cascade across financial systems. This second form of risk is referred to as "systemic risk." The current financial crisis should have settled any questions about whether such risk exists.

30. Daniel K. Tarullo, *Banking on Basel: The Future of International Financial Regulation* (Washington, DC: Peterson Institute, 2008), 15–44.

31. "Base Camp Basel," *The Economist,* January 23, 2010, 66–68.

32. Knowledge@Wharton, "A 'Race to the Bottom': Assigning Responsibility for the Financial Crisis," December 9, 2009, http://knowledge.wharton.upenn.edu/article.cfm?articleid=2397.htm.

33. Valencia, "The Gods Strike Back." The chairman of the Federal Reserve from 1987–2006, Alan Greenspan, was an aggressive proponent of the self-regulatory effectiveness of firms and markets.

34. Tarullo, *Banking on Basel,* 33–35; James R. Barth et al., "The Repeal of Glass-Steagall and the Advent of Broad Banking," *Journal of Economic Perspectives* 14, no. 2 (Spring 2000): 191–204.

35. This compares with a capital ratio of 15 percent in the 1920s. Tarullo, *Banking on Basel,* 31–32.

36. For details on Basel I, see ibid., 45–85.

37. For details on Basel II, see ibid., 87–130. At the onset of the global financial crisis, the Basel II rules were still in the implementation stage in most countries. Salmon, "Recipe for Disaster."

38. http://player.vimeo.com/video/45431290.

39. Debt had become the major driving force of economic growth in advanced nations from the early 1980s. Debt became a substitute for savings: saving is painful, debt is easy. The economic problems in the 1970s were "solved" by increasing debt, at first governmental and later household and corporate. The increasing levels of debt contributed to the rise of finance in the U.S. economy and to financialization of the global economy. Much of the funding for U.S. debt was supplied at first by Japan and later by other Asian nations, especially China. Debt was used to expand consumption in the United States. Between 1982 and 2005, consumption as a percentage of U.S. GDP rose from 61 percent to 71 percent, and personal savings fell from 10 percent of income to nearly zero. See U.S. Department of Commerce, Bureau of Economic Analysis, www .bea.gov and www.bea.gov/national/nipaweb/PrintGraph.asp?Freq=Year.htm.

40. Roxburgh et al., *Global Capital Markets,* 21–22; Anastasia Nesvetailova and Ronen Palan, "A Very North Atlantic Credit Crunch: Geopolitical Implications of the Global Liquidity Crunch," *Journal of International Affairs* 62, no. 1 (Fall 2008): 165–185.

41. Dodd, "Derivatives Markets."

42. Chicago Public Radio, *This American Life,* episode transcript, program no. 355, "The Giant Pool of Money," March 2008, www.pri.org/business/giant-pool-of-money. html. See also Roger Altman, "The Great Crash, 2008: A Geopolitical Setback for the West," *Foreign Affairs* 88, no. 1 (January–February 2009): 2–14.

43. Roger Lowenstein, "Triple A Failure," *New York Times,* April 27, 2008, http:// query.nytimes.com/gst/fullpage.html?res=9900EFDE143DF934A15757C0A96E9 C8B63.htm.

44. Federal Reserve Bank of New York, "Historical Changes of the Target Federal Funds and Discount Rates," www.newyorkfed.org/markets/statistics/dlyrates/fedrate.html.

45. For data on the differential impact of foreclosures through early 2008, see Helen Fairfield, "In the Shadow of Foreclosures," *New York Times,* April 6, 2008, www.nytimes .com/2008/04/06/business/06metricstext.html.

46. Associated Press, "In Bear Bailout, Fed Says It Tried to Avert Contagion," *New York Times,* June 28, 2008, www.nytimes.com/2008/06/28/business/28fed.html?_r=1.htm.

47. For data on unemployment in the United States, see the Bureau of Labor Statistics database, http://data.bls.gov/PDQ/servlet/SurveyOutputServlet?series_ id=LNS14000000.htm.

48. Stephen Labaton, "Scramble Led to Rescue Plan on Mortgage," *New York Times,* July 15, 2008, www.nytimes.com/2008/07/15/washington/15fannie.html.

49. Knowledge@Wharton, "Lehman's Demise and Repo 105: No Accounting for Deception," March 31, 2010, http://knowledge.wharton.upenn.edu/article.cfm? articleid=2464.htm.

50. Lehman was not rescued because the Fed and U.S. Treasury hoped its collapse could be contained and because they expected other Wall Street firms to buy it. Driving these conclusions was a political backlash from free market "conservatives" in Congress and the Bush administration who opposed government bailouts of private firms. The expectations, theories, and hopes were wrong on all counts.

51. Gretchen Morgenson, "Behind Insurer's Crisis, Blind Eye to a Web of Risk," *New York Times*, September 27, 2008, www.nytimes.com/2008/09/28/business/28melt.html; Michael J. de la Merced and Andrew Sorokin, "Report Details How Lehman Hid Its Woes as It Collapsed," *New York Times*, March 12, 2010, www.nytimes.com/2010/03/12/business/12lehman.html?hp.htm.

52. Between September 2008 and the bottom in March 2009, U.S. stock markets fell about 44 percent in value. Shares in other global markets fell by similar amounts, except for China, where shares fell by "only" 30 percent and bottomed in November 2008. During one week in October 2008, U.S. stocks fell by 22 percent.

53. James B. Stewart, "Eight Days," *The New Yorker* 85, no. 29 (September 21, 2009).

54. For details on the events of this period, see Stewart, "Eight Days." For an analysis of past congressional votes on financial rescue packages, see J. Lawrence Broz, "Congressional Politics of Past Financial Rescues," *American Journal of Political Science* 49, no. 3 (July 2005): 479–496. For an analysis of congressional voting in 2008, see Atif Mian et al., "The Political Economy of the U.S. Mortgage Default Crisis," http://papers.ssrn.com/s013/papers.cfm?abstract_id=1291524.htm.

55. For details, see www.federalreserve.gov/monetarypolicy/bst_crisisresponse.htm; www.federalreserve.gov/monetarypolicy/bst_liquidityswaps.htm; www.newyorkfed.org/markets/pdcf_faq.html; www.newyorkfed.org/markets/tslf_faq.html.

56. For details of the sequence of actions, see Dick Nanto, "The U.S. Financial Crisis: The Global Dimension with Implications for U.S. Policy," Congressional Research Service, January 30, 2009, 66–76. For discussion of different levels of financial crisis impact, see Jorge Ivan Canales-Kriljenko et al., "A Tale of Two Regions," *Finance and Development*, March 2010, 35–36.

57. Landon Thomas Jr. and Nicholas Kulish, "Europe Looks to Aid Package as Spain's Debt Rating Is Cut," *New York Times*, April 28, 2010, www.nytimes.com/2010/04/29/business/global/29euro.html?src=un&feedurl=http%3A%2F%2Fjson8.nytimes.com%2Fpages%2Fbusiness%2Findex.jsonp. Spain's (54 percent) and Portugal's (77 percent) overall debt levels are considerably lower than Greece's, but current budget deficits are roughly comparable.

58. Nicholas Kulish, "Merkel Tested as Escalating Greek Crisis Hurts Euro," *New York Times*, April 28, 2010, www.nytimes.com/2010/04/29/world/europe/29germany.html?hp.

59. Richard Baldwin, ed., *The Great Trade Collapse: Causes, Consequences, and Prospects* (Geneva: Center for Trade and Economic Integration, 2009); Organisation for Economic Co-operation and Development (OECD), *Policy Responses to the Economic Crisis: Investing in Innovation for Long-Term Growth*, June 2009, 9, https://community.oecd.org/docs/DOC-1445; Dick Nanto, "The Global Financial Crisis: Foreign and Trade Policy Effects" (Washington, DC: Congressional Research Service, April 7, 2009), 6.

60. Bureau of Labor Statistics, www.bls.gov/cps/tables.htm. The total job loss through early 2010 was more than 8 million.

61. The turnaround in the U.S. and global economy corresponds closely with the passage of the stimulus bill. Jackie Calmes and Michael Cooper, "New Consensus Sees

Stimulus Package as Worthy Step," *New York Times,* November 20, 2009, www.nytimes .com/2009/11/21/business/economy/21stimulus.html?_r=1. See also David Leonhart, "Judging Stimulus by Jobs Data Reveals Success," *New York Times,* February 16, 2010, www.nytimes.com/2010/02/17/business/economy/17leonhardt.html. For details on the actual spending in the stimulus program, see www.recovery.gov/Pages/home.aspx.

62. Catherine Rampell and Javier Hernandez, "Signaling Jobs Recovery, Payrolls Surged in March," *New York Times,* April 2, 2010, www.nytimes.com/2010/04/03/business/ economy/03jobs.html?hpw. Michael Grunwald, *The New, New Deal,* New York: Simon & Schuster, 2012.

63. Pelin Berkman et al., "Differential Impact," *Finance and Development* (March 2010): 29–31.

64. A breakdown of the U.S. stimulus spending is available at www.theatlantic.com/ slideshows/feds/; additional data are available at www.theatlantic.com/past/docs/ images/issues/200905/fed-map.gif.

65. OECD, Policy Responses to the Economic Crisis, 17–24.

66. For details on the Chinese stimulus, see "A Time for Muscle-Flexing," *The Economist,* March 19, 2009, www.economist.com/displayStory.cfm?Story_ID=E1_TPPNG-DRN; "Reflating the Dragon," *The Economist,* November 13, 2008, www.economist .com/displayStory.cfm?Story_ID=E1_TNGDGJJR; "Lending Binge," *The Economist,* August 6, 2009, www.economist.com/displayStory.cfm?story_id=14161839.

67. Carmen Reinhart and Kenneth Rogoff, "The Aftermath of Financial Crises," *American Economic Review* 99 (May 2009): 466–472. Carmen Reinhart and Kenneth Rogoff, *This Time is Different,* Princeton: Princeton University Press, 2009, 223–239.

68. "Counting Their Blessings," *The Economist,* December 30, 2009, www.economist .com/business-finance/displaystory.cfm?story_id=15172941.

69. Keith Bradsher, "Signs of Possible Recovery Buoy Chinese Exporters," *New York Times,* October 15, 2012.

70. "Perhaps a Reason to Be Cheerful?," *The Economist,* February 19, 2009, www .economist.com/business-finance/displaystory.cfm?story_id=E1_TPTQVRQJ; "Follow the Money," *The Economist,* August 27, 2009, www.economist.com/displayStory .cfm?story_id=14327673.

71. Shaohua Chen and Martin Ravillion, "The Impact of the Global Financial Crisis on the World's Poorest," VoxEU.org, April 30, 2009, www.voxeu.org/index.php? q=node/3520.

72. For an overview of the relationship of financial crises to global politics, see Benn Steil and Robert Litan, *Financial Statecraft: The Role of Financial Markets in American Foreign Policy* (New Haven: Yale University Press, 2008), 81–158.

73. An excellent overview of the dollar as key currency is Eric Helleiner and Jonathan Kirshner, "The Future of the Dollar: Whither the Key Currency?," in Helleiner and Kirshner, eds., *The Future of the Dollar* (Ithaca: Cornell University Press, 2009), 1–23. See also David Andrews, ed., *International Monetary Power* (Ithaca: Cornell University Press, 2006).

74. Paul Krugman, "Will There Be a Dollar Crisis?," *Economic Policy* 51 (2007): 437–467.

75. Barry Eichengreen, *Exorbitant Privilege,* Oxford: Oxford University Press, 2011.

76. This analysis relies on the insights of Helleiner and Kirshner, *The Future of the Dollar.*

77. Benjamin Cohen, "Dollar Dominance, Euro Aspirations: Recipe for Discord?," *Journal of Common Market Studies* 47, no. 4 (2009): 741–766.

78. This is not a new situation; for decades several nations have held U.S. dollars to pay for U.S. trade deficits.

79. Benjamin Cohen, "The Future of Reserve Currencies," *Finance and Development,* September 2009, 26–29, considers the potential for a fragmented reserve currency world.

80. David A. Singer, *Regulating Capital* (Ithaca: Cornell University Press, 2007), 67–95.

81. Nicholas Bayne, "Financial Diplomacy and the Credit Crunch: The Rise of Central Banks," *Journal of International Affairs* 62, no. 1 (Fall 2008): 1–16.

82. Martin Donnelly, "Making Government Policy: A Case Study of the G8," in Nicholas Bayne and Stephen Woolcock, eds., *The New Economic Diplomacy* (Aldershot, U.K.: Ashgate, 2007), 93–103. The G-7 included Canada, France, Germany, Italy, Japan, the United Kingdom, and the United States. The G-8 is the G-7 plus Russia. The G-20 adds Argentina, Australia, Brazil, China, India, Indonesia, Mexico, Saudi Arabia, South Africa, South Korea, and Turkey, making it now composed of nineteen nations plus the European Union. The G-20 provides a forum for discussions among three groups: national political leaders, finance ministers, and central bank governors.

83. G20 Information Center, University of Toronto, http://www.g20.utoronto.ca/summits/index.html.

84. Richard Samans et al., "Running the World after the Crash," *Foreign Policy,* 184, (January/February 2011) 80–83; Maria Monica-Wihardja, "Is the G20 Failing?" East Asia Forum, October 3, 2012, http://www.eastasiaforum.org/2012/10/03/is-the-g20-failing/; *The Economist,* "Grading the G20," November 3, 2011, http://www.economist.com/blogs/dailychart/2011/11/grading-g20.

85. See Gideon Rachman, "A Modern Guide to G-ology," *The Economist,* November 13, 2009, www.economist.com/theworldin/displaystory.cfm?story_id=14742524; David McCormick, "Picking Up the Pieces: The Global Crisis and Implications for U.S. Economic Policymaking," in Nicholas Burns and Jonathan Price, eds., *The Global Economic Crisis* (Washington, DC: Aspen Institute, 2009), 105–120.

86. For a sense of this, see *The Economist,* "Law and Disorder," October 13, 2012, http://www.economist.com/node/21564565.

87. The Economist, "Too Big Not to Fail," February 18, 2012, http://www.economist.com/node/21547784.

88. *The Economist,* "Counterparty Controversy," May 12, 2012, http://www.economist.com/node/21554522.

89. *The Economist,* "Defining the State," October 6, 2012. http://www.economist.com/node/21563953.

90. "Foul-weather Friends," *The Economist,* December 17, 2009, www.economist.com/business-finance/displaystory.cfm?story_id=15124793. Japan has resisted the creation of more strict regulatory rules because this could hurt the competitive position of its banks. Hiroko Tabuchi, "Japan's Banks Object to Adopting Restrictions Like Those in Europe and the U.S.," *New York Times,* April 23, 2010, B5.

91. Daniel Drezner, *All Politics Is Global: Explaining International Regulatory Regimes* (Princeton: Princeton University Press, 2007).

92. Enrique Carrasco, "The Global Financial Crisis and the Financial Stability Board: The Awakening and Transformation of an International Body," University of

Iowa Legal Studies Research Paper No. 10–06, January 2010, http://ssrn.com/abstract=1543508. See also Bayne, "Financial Diplomacy and the Credit Crunch," 10–11. The Brookings Institution, "Assessing the Financial Stability Board," September 23, 2011, http://www.brookings.edu/events/2011/09/23-financial-stability. The Web site for the Financial Stability Board is www.financialstabilityboard.org. A list of institutions represented on the FSB can be found at www.financialstability board.org/members/links.htm. Charles Goodhart, *The Basel Committee on Banking Supervision,* Cambridge: Cambridge University Press, 2011.

93. Moritz Schularick, "How China Helped Create the Macroeconomic Backdrop for Financial Crisis," *Financial Times Blog,* February 24, 2009, http://blogs.ft.com/econo mists forum/2009/02/how-china-helped-create-the-macroeconomic-backdrop-for-financial-crisis/; Niall Ferguson and Moritz Schularick, "Chimerica and the Global Asset Boom," *International Finance* 10, no. 3 (2007): 215–239.

94. A podcast regarding these issues is provided by Brad Setser, "China's Difficult Choices," Council on Foreign Relations, June 2, 2009, www.cfr.org/publication/19546/chinas_difficult_choices.html.

95. Brad Setser, "China: The New Financial Superpower," Council on Foreign Relations, August 3, 2009, http://blogs.cfr.org/setser/2009/08/03/china-new-financial-super power-%E2%80%A6; Brad Setser, "China: Creditor to the Rich," *China Security* 4, no. 4 (Autumn 2008): 17–23. The United States and China have developed a kind of G-2 forum for discussion of economic issues, now named the "Strategic and Economic Dialogue." Between 2009–2012, the dollar-RMB exchange rate has remained within a 9% spread.

96. Brad Setser, "A Neo-Westphalian International Financial System?," *Journal of International Affairs* 62, no. 1 (Fall/Winter 2008): 21. More precisely, the Chinese maintain the peg to a basket of currencies.

97. Setser and Pandey, "China's $1.5 Trillion Bet," 15–16. Additional data are available at http://blogs.cfr.org/setser/2009/01/03/secrets-of-safe-part-1-look-to-the-uk-to -find-some-of-chinas-treasuries-and-agencies. See also Knowledge@Wharton, "Attached at the Wallet: The Delicate Financial Relationship between the U.S. and China," April 29, 2009, http://knowledge.wharton.upenn.edu/article.cfm?articleid=2230. A significant part of Chinese holdings in September 2008 were in the debt of Freddie Mac and Fannie Mae. The role this played, if any, in the decision by the Fed to purchase assets of these government-related entities is unclear.

98. "Report on Foreign Portfolio Holdings of U.S. Securities," June 30, 2011, 8, http://www.treasury.gov/resource-center/data-chart-center/tic/Pages/fpis.aspx.

99. Some of the pathways for change are discussed in Oliver Blanchard and Gian Maria Milesi-Ferretti, "Global Imbalances in Midstream?" IMF Staff Position Note SPN 09/20, December 22, 2009.

100. For details on U.S. savings, see David Leonhart, "To Spend or Save? Trick Question," *New York Times,* February 10, 2009. For analysis of the needed changes in the U.S. economy, see Greg Ip, "Time to Rebalance," *The Economist,* April 2009, www .economist.com/surveys/displaystory.cfm?story_id=15793036. For changes in China, see The World Bank, *China 2030,* Washington, 2012.

101. Susan Lund et al., "The Looming Deleveraging Challenge," *McKinsey Quarterly,* January 2010, 1–7.

102. Nicholas Lardy, *Sustaining China's Economic Growth after the Global Financial Crisis,* (Washington: Peterson Institute, 2012); Eduardo Porter, "China's Vanishing Trade

Imbalance," *New York Times,* May 1, 2012, www.nytimes.com/2012/05/02/business/economy/chinas-vanishing-trade-imbalance.html?pagewanted=2&ref=eduardoporter.

103. After 2010, the Chinese did allow a limited rise in the value of the RMB. But China will be wary of this policy, remembering the damage to the Japanese economy as a result of a significant revaluation of the yen-dollar relationship in the 1980s. Eswar Prasad and Lei Ye, *The Renminbi's Role in the Global Monetary System,* Global Economy and Development at Brookings, 2012.

104. Moritz Schularick, "The End of Financial Globalization 3.0," *The Economists' Voice,* January 2010, 1–5, www.bepress.com/ev; Brad Setser, "Debating the Global Roots of the Current Crisis," VoxEU.org, January 28, 2009, www.voxeu.org/index.php?q=node/2915.

105. Bill Powell, "Chinese Give Tim Geithner a Warm Welcome—to a Point," CNNMoney.com, June 2, 2009, http://money.cnn.com/2009/06/02/news/economy/gethner_goes_to_china.fortune/index.htm.

106. Setser, "A Neo-Westphalian International Financial System?," 18. Of course, the Fed has the special advantage of creating money with a computer keystroke.

107. Stephen Cohen and J. Bradford Delong, *The End of Influence: What Happens When Other Countries Have the Money* (New York: Basic Books, 2010). For an examination of the use of financial power in international politics, see Jonathan Kirshner, *Currency and Coercion* (Princeton: Princeton University Press, 1997); David M. Andrews, ed., *International Monetary Power* (Ithaca: Cornell University Press, 2006).

108. For an examination of U.S.-China relations in light of the financial crisis, see Daniel Drezner, "Bad Debt: Assessing China's Financial Influence in Great Power Politics," *International Security* 34, no. 2 (Fall 2009): 7–45. See also Matthew Burrows and Jennifer Harris, "Revisiting the Future: Geopolitical Effects of the Financial Crisis," *Washington Quarterly* 32, no. 2 (April 2009): 27–38. A view more favorable to U.S. prospects is Michael Beckley, "China's Century? Why America's Edge Will Endure," *International Security,* 36.3 (Winter 2011/12) 41–78.

109. Gregory Chin and Eric Helleiner, "China as a Creditor: A Rising Financial Power?," *Journal of International Affairs* 62, no. 1 (Fall 2008): 87–102. China's rising structural power also derives from its expanding political and economic relationships around the world.

110. Eric Pfanner, "Criticizing Capitalism from the Pulpit," *New York Times,* September 25, 2008, www.nytimes.com/2008/09/26/business/worldbusiness/26euro.html; Willem Buiter, "Lessons from the North Atlantic Financial Crisis," unpublished paper available at www.willembuiter.com/NAcrisis.pdf

111. One estimate for the current crisis places the injection of state resources into the "private" economy in the United States, Britain, and the EU at $14 trillion. Andrew Haldane, "Banking on the State," *BIS Review* 139 (2009): 1.

112. Perhaps the clearest evidence for the partnership of states and firms comes from the financial crisis itself, which exposed the long-standing but previously underreported interactions between government officials and private firms. See Jo Becker and Gretchen Morgenson, "How Geithner Forged Ties to Financial Club," *New York Times,* April 27, 2009, http://dealbook.blogs.nytimes.com/2009/04/27/geithner-as-member-and-overseer-forged-ties-to-finance-club/?scp=2&sq=jp%20becker%20overseer&st=Search; Green, "Inside Man," 36–51; Simon Johnson and James Kwak, *13 Bankers* (New York: Pantheon, 2010).

113. The enormous buildup of Chinese state-owned dollar assets, including the global investment of those assets, involves substantial forms of negotiation and partnership among China, the United States, and global financial firms. Setser, "A Neo-Westphalian International Financial System?"

114. For example, states in Asia have come to act as investors in the global economy seeking to increase investor yields. Datz, "Governments as Market Players," 35–49.

115. Ian Bremmer, "State Capitalism and the Crisis," *McKinsey Quarterly,* July 2009, 1–6; Ian Bremmer, "State Capitalism Comes of Age," *Foreign Affairs* 88, no. 3 (May–June 2003): 40–56; Ian Bremmer, *The End of the Free Market,* New York: Portfolio, 2010.

116. Charles Roxburgh et al., "The New Power Brokers," McKinsey Global Institute, July 2009.

117. Eric Helleiner, *States and the Reemergence of Global Finance* (Ithaca: Cornell University Press, 1994).

118. Miles Kahler, ed., *Capital Flows and Financial Crises* (Ithaca: Cornell University Press, 1998); T. J. Pempel, *The Politics of the Asian Financial Crisis* (Ithaca: Cornell University Press, 1999).

11 Sino-American Trade Relations: Privatizing Foreign Policy

Steven W. Hook and Franklin Barr Lebo

Before You Begin

1. In what ways did the U.S. policy of engagement with China reflect general changes in U.S. foreign policy after the Cold War?

2. How did the composition of Congress and the worldview of the president affect the prospects for trade "normalization" between the United States and the People's Republic of China (PRC)?

3. Which interest groups and nongovernmental organizations became active as advocates or opponents of closer economic relations between the two countries?

4. To what extent did the outcome of the debate on normalization of trade and U.S. support for China's entry into the World Trade Organization (WTO) reflect economic disparities between business interests and nonprofit nongovernmental organizations?

5. What have been the key trends in China's trade relations, particularly those with the United States, since the PRC joined the WTO in December 2001? What have been the responses of key government actors and interest groups to those trends?

6. What does this case tell us generally about the formulation and content of U.S. foreign policy after the Cold War? Can the lessons from this case be applied to other foreign policy arenas, such as national security, particularly since the start of the global war on terrorism in September 2001?

Introduction: The Chinese Challenge

More than a decade after the People's Republic of China (PRC) joined the World Trade Organization (WTO), the PRC and the United States maintain the world's most robust, and complicated, bilateral economic relationship. While China has recorded annual growth rates of 10 percent for more than two decades, the U.S. economy—still the largest in the world—has grown at a much slower pace. The resulting shift in the economic balance of power, hampered by record U.S. budget deficits and foreign debts, has been further aggravated by political paralysis in Washington.

These domestic problems have only made mutually beneficial Sino-American trade ties more crucial. While seeking to soothe relations with its largest creditor and third-largest destination of U.S. exports, President Obama has sought relief on a dozen WTO pending cases that allege unfair trade practices in such areas as intellectual property, monetary policy, the extraction of rare earth metals, and the protection of China's automotive industry.[1] Some observers cited Obama's need for tough rhetoric on the 2012 campaign trail to combat the fiery charges of Mitt Romney, his Republican challenger, that the PRC was a "currency manipulator." Others observed that the White House was simply maintaining its long-term push for faster progress in trade liberalization.[2] Whichever the case, the PRC responded by filing eight WTO suits against Washington for its allegedly punitive trade policies. [3]

Despite allegations of "long-standing mutual mistrust," the outlook for bilateral relations was far from bleak.[4] Ongoing initiatives by the US-China Strategic and Economic Dialogue (S&ED) and the US-China Joint Commission on Commerce and Trade (JCCT) made considerable progress on bilateral trade.[5] High-level talks and negotiations followed on a plethora of issues.[6] By 2011, the Office of the U.S. Trade Representative acknowledged that China had implemented antidumping regulations, stuck to the agreement for eliminating nontariff measures, and issued rules to bring its import license regime into compliance with WTO standards.[7] In February of 2012, Beijing began to investigate thousands of cases of online intellectual property (IP) rights violations.[8] Meanwhile, major Chinese electronics firms such as Foxconn raised wage levels and improved working conditions in ways that "could create a ripple effect that benefits tens of millions of workers."[9] Although backsliding in Beijing remained a concern, Pascal Lamy, director general of the WTO, proclaimed a "new chapter in China's reform."[10] By the end of 2012, sufficient progress had been made for Chinese leaders to insist that their efforts not go unnoticed.[11]

At the same time, however, the PRC had grown wary of its role as a source of financial salvation for the ailing Eurozone.[12] Its bailouts, combined with other concessions, effectively ruptured China's balance of trade.[13] The global financial crisis that began in 2007 continued to dampen world trade and fueled volatility in Sino-American trade. After falling sharply to $227 billion in 2009 due to the "great recession," the U.S. trade deficit with China reached an all-time high of $295 billion in 2011 before falling to an estimated $261 billion in 2012.[14] Far from being on firm ground, Chinese leaders feared higher infla-tion as they allowed the value of the renminbi (RMB), China's currency, to appreciate on global capital markets.[15]

It would be a mistake to assume that only economic matters are relevant in this complex trading relationship. Other issues, such as China's military moderniza-tion program and continuing tensions over Taiwan and the South China Sea, have caused American leaders to reassess the United States' regional security strategy in East Asia.[16] Obama, having declared a geostrategic "pivot" toward East Asia, has been forced to consider precisely what it means for China to be a "responsible stakeholder" in the international system.[17] Such scrutiny, for instance, has led to U.S. pressure on China to support weapons nonproliferation efforts in its bilateral trade with Iran. Close U.S. ties with Taiwan, including a $5.8 billion weapons sale in 2011, along with Washington's continuing demand for improved human rights in China, continue to aggravate trade negotiations.[18] These concerns, however, have been tempered by U.S. economic dependence on China.[19]

To understand how Sino-American trade relations have evolved, in this chapter we explore the political process that led to establishment of permanent, normal trade relations (PNTR) between China and the United States—a vital stepping stone for China's entry into the WTO. Both the Chinese leadership and the Clinton administration considered the two steps critical, and both con-sidered bilateral trade relations a high foreign policy priority. The administra-tion of President Bill Clinton needed support from Congress to deliver the U.S. end of the bargain, however, and gaining it was far from a sure thing. Private interest groups on both sides of the trade issue mobilized on behalf of their policy preferences as the legislative process unfolded. The mobilization of those interests and the uneven resources they brought to bear in shaping the U.S. decision played key roles in determining the outcome.

From its founding in 1949 through the end of the Cold War, the PRC's relations with the United States were overshadowed by ideological competition and the East-West balance of power. China-US tensions moderated in the 1970s, when the Nixon-Kissinger "opening" to China was followed by the rise of the reformist Deng Xiaoping as China's leader. Bilateral relations continued to be plagued, however, by U.S. complaints about China's repression of human rights, neglect of environmental problems, weapons transfers, and maintenance of protectionist trade policies. Conversely, Chinese leaders frequently opposed the United States at the United Nations and openly criticized Washington as "hegemonic."

Upon taking office in January 1993, President Clinton wanted to revive Sino-American relations. He sought specifically to "engage" the PRC, primarily through closer economic ties, in hopes that a more interdependent relationship would benefit U.S. firms and consumers while also eliciting greater cooperation from Beijing on issues of concern to Washington. Clinton's engagement strategy played an important part in his overall foreign policy, which shifted the nation's strategic focus from the military concerns of the Cold War to the geoeconomics of a new era. In the president's view, the United States needed to exploit its status as the world's largest economy by making U.S. firms more competitive in the rapidly integrating global marketplace. Toward that end, the Clinton administration identified several "big emerging markets," including China, that warranted special attention in guiding U.S. foreign economic policy.[20] Engagement required severing the link between China's human rights policies and its status as a trading partner. As Clinton stated in May 1994,

> That linkage has been constructive during the past year. But I believe, based on our aggressive contacts with the Chinese in the past several months, that we have reached the end of the usefulness of that policy, and it is time to take a new path toward the achievement of our constant objectives. We need to place our relationship into a larger and more productive framework.[21]

The president's policy was based on the neoliberal presumption that China's inclusion in global economic and political regimes would encourage Beijing to moderate its internal behavior and conform with international standards. The alternative policy of estrangement—isolating China diplomatically and economically—was viewed as less likely to produce compliance and restraint in Beijing. Beyond increasing bilateral trade and promoting restraint in China's behavior domestically, engagement raised the possibility of also eliciting China's cooperation in solving transnational problems.

A general shift in U.S. foreign policy in the 1990s produced concrete changes in policy formulation. During the Cold War, the State and Defense Departments largely controlled the machinations of foreign policy. The end of the Cold War not only altered the mission of those institutions, it also raised the profile of other agencies in the shaping of foreign policy. These included the Treasury and Commerce Departments; the Office of the United States Trade Representative; and a variety of federal agencies in law enforcement, environmental protection, and health and labor policy. As the foreign policy profile of these institutions grew, so did that of groups outside government in the United States and abroad. With a greater capacity to shape the U.S. foreign policy agenda, interest groups on both sides of the engagement debate mobilized in the late 1990s. Their efforts—often highly visible but frequently behind the scenes—typified the increased activism and policy advocacy of hundreds of organizations in myriad issue areas after the Cold War.

Business interests, in particular, benefited directly from the new opportunities inherent in the engagement policy. Dozens of US-based multinational corporations praised and actively supported the strategy. From their perspective, China's population of more than 1.2 billion was a vast potential market for goods and services that could only be tapped if the governments of China and the United States maintained cordial relations. Echoing the Clinton administration's logic, they predicted that expanded economic contacts would force China's leaders to maintain stable relations overseas and to cooperate on political issues.

Many nonprofit nongovernmental organizations (NGOs), meanwhile, strongly opposed engagement. Human rights groups argued that Beijing should not be "rewarded" as long as it defied human rights standards. NGOs focused on the environment demanded that engagement only proceed after the Chinese government implemented stronger measures to protect air and water quality at home and embraced multilateral environmental initiatives overseas. Religious groups also became vocal on the issue, calling attention to the PRC's suppression of spiritual movements and religious institutions. US-based labor groups weighed in, arguing that engagement would lead to the exodus of U.S. jobs and manufacturing capacity to the PRC.

This mobilization of interest groups occurred at a time when Congress was evenly split over China and highly polarized in general.[22] As Figure 11.1 illustrates, an ad hoc coalition of moderate Republicans and Democrats supported normalized trade with China, with overlapping but divergent priorities in mind: For moderate Republicans, the economic opportunities associated with gaining greater access to the world's largest market were compelling. Moderate Democrats thought engaging China through bilateral agreements and multilateral institutions would improve the chances for democratic reform and for gaining the PRC's cooperation in great power diplomacy.

Figure 11.1 Congress and Support for US-China Trade

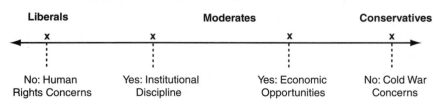

Liberals	Moderates		Conservatives
x	x	x	x
No: Human Rights Concerns	Yes: Institutional Discipline	Yes: Economic Opportunities	No: Cold War Concerns

Timeline
US-China Trade Relations

October 1949	Mao Zedong's communist forces defeat the Chinese nationalist government. The United States refuses to recognize the People's Republic of China (PRC), recognizing instead Nationalist Party exiles in Taiwan as the leaders of China.
February 1972	President Richard Nixon visits Beijing, initiating bilateral relations between the United States and the PRC.
September 1976	Mao Zedong dies.
1978	Deng Xiaoping launches a series of market- oriented economic reforms while maintaining strict control over the PRC's political system.
January 1979	President Jimmy Carter formally recognizes the PRC and abrogates the U.S. treaty with Taiwan.
June 1989	Government forces crush pro-democracy protesters in Tiananmen Square. The United States and other governments respond by imposing economic sanctions against China.
May 1994	President Bill Clinton adopts a policy of engagement toward China, arguing that closer economic relations are more likely than isolation to produce cooperation from Beijing.
February 1997	Jiang Zemin assumes leadership of the PRC and continues Deng's policies of economic reform and political repression.
1998	China applies for membership in the World Trade Organization (WTO).
November 1999	Clinton endorses China's entry into the WTO in return for a series of bilateral trade concessions from Beijing.
May 2000	By a vote of 237–197, the House of Representatives approves H.R. 4444, granting permanent normal trade relations (PNTR) to China.
September 2000	The Senate approves the China trade bill by a vote of 83–15.
October 2000	Clinton signs the legislation formally establishing normal trade relations between the United States and China.
November 2001	The WTO approves China's application.

(continued)

Timeline *(continued)*

US-China Trade Relations

December 2001	China officially joins the WTO.
March 2002	President George W. Bush raises U.S. tariffs on foreign steel, prompting complaints by China and other steel producers and leading to possible sanctions by the WTO.
March 2004	U.S. Trade Representative Robert B. Zoellick files a case with the WTO alleging preferential treatment by China of domestic firms in the electronics industry. The case is subsequently settled outside of the WTO through bilateral negotiation.
2005	China overtakes Britain as the world's fourth-largest economy.
March 2006	U.S. Trade Representative Rob Portman files a case with the WTO alleging that unfair levying of import taxes on U.S. auto parts favors China's domestic manufacturers. The United States and co-complainants subsequently prevail, and China repeals its noncompliant laws in September 2009.
2006	China becomes world's largest carbon dioxide emitter.
February 2007	U.S. Trade Representative Susan C. Schwab files a case with the WTO alleging preferential treatment by China of domestic firms in the steel, wood, and paper industries.
January 2009	China becomes the world's third-largest economy after experiencing 8.7 percent growth from July–September in 2009. It is predicted to overtake Japan to become the second-largest economy possibly by 2010.
2009	The United States receives favorable rulings and/or favorable settlement agreements in five WTO cases against China. For example, U.S. Trade Representative Ron Kirk wins a WTO suit in December, holding China violated trade rules by restricting the domestic distribution of U.S. films, music, and print media.
September 2009	China eases restrictions on film, publishing, entertainment, online games, multimedia, and other foreign investments in the culture industry.
2010	US and China rely increasingly on the WTO for dispute resolution.
2011	U.S. trade deficit with China reaches all-time high of $295 billion.
2012	China's newly appointed General Secretary of the Chinese Communist Party, Xi Jinping, scheduled to assume the presidency of the PRC in March, 2013.

This consensus was threatened, however, by congressional critics at each end of the political spectrum. While conservative Republicans retained Cold War–type hostilities toward Beijing's communist government and objected to its defiant stance on security issues, liberal Democrats opposed rewarding Chinese leaders who monopolized power, violated human rights, harmed the environment, and exploited labor.

Background: The Course of Sino-American Relations

This reshaping of US-China trade relations occurred more than a half century after the birth of the PRC in the mid–twentieth century. China, as the world's most populous state and its newest communist country, was then a primary source of concern to Washington. The Sino-Soviet friendship treaty of 1950 and the Korean War exacerbated U.S. apprehension, so that American leaders soon incorporated the PRC into the anticommunist containment policy designed in 1946 to prevent the spread of Soviet influence and power. Asia evolved as an arena of ideological competition in the 1950s and 1960s, with the wars in Korea and Vietnam taking center stage in the global Cold War. The United States refused to recognize the communist regime in Beijing and instead considered Nationalist Party exiles in Taiwan the true rulers of China. This policy of nonrecognition lasted until the 1970s, when the Nixon administration initiated bilateral relations with the PRC.

By the time Washington formally recognized the PRC in 1979, when Jimmy Carter was president, key changes in the economic structures of China had occurred. Following the death of Mao Zedong in 1976, Deng Xiaoping, a leader of the growing technocratic movement, assumed power and initiated a series of market-oriented economic reforms geared toward bringing China into the modern era.[23] In 1978, Deng began privatizing a small percentage of state-owned enterprises and overhauled the agricultural sector by permitting the sale of surplus commodities at market prices. The PRC under Deng continued to punish dissidents, however, and to deny political rights in general to the Chinese people. When the United States recognized the PRC, it adopted a trade policy that required annual review of China's behavior in several areas, including foreign economic relations and the protection of human rights. The reviews rendered China's "most favored nation" (MFN) trade status—which allowed Beijing the same terms of trade accorded other major trading partners of the United States—dependent upon its overall behavior. The MFN reviews became an annual ritual in Congress and were routinely criticized by China's leaders. The Chinese felt that the PRC was being unfairly singled out among U.S. trading partners and that the United States was unduly interfering in their domestic and foreign affairs. Despite the PRC's widely publicized violations of human rights, Congress renewed its MFN trade status every year in the 1980s, largely because of the fast-growing trade between the two states and the rapid growth of the Chinese economy as Deng's economic reforms took effect.[24] Security concerns also figured in U.S. calculations; closer relations with China were seen as vital to containment of Soviet expansionism.

The Chinese government's assault on pro-democracy protesters in Tiananmen Square in June 1989 sparked renewed debate in Congress and the general public regarding human rights in China. Approximately 1,300 protesters were killed in the assault, and thousands more were arrested and imprisoned.[25] Questions regarding the government's treatment of political dissidents, its suppression of political and religious freedoms in Tibet, and its ongoing hostility toward Taiwan were also raised in Congress. Of additional concern to U.S. leaders was the Chinese government's conduct of bilateral trade with the United States. The Chinese domestic market had opened to some foreign goods, particularly high-technology products that facilitated the PRC's modernization drive. China, however, remained largely closed to foreign goods with equivalents that could be produced by Chinese workers. To gain access to Chinese consumers foreign companies had to establish joint ventures with Chinese firms. U.S. complaints related to a wide range of barriers that prevented US-based firms from competing in the PRC. The most common barriers were high tariffs, which averaged nearly 20 percent on all imports but were much higher on some goods, including automobiles and agricultural products. In addition, the Chinese government imposed a variety of nontariff barriers—such as quotas, import licenses, technical standards, and domestic content provisions—that further discouraged foreign competition. Corporate leaders also complained that the limited number of import-export companies in the PRC further impaired their ability to gain commercial licenses and establish transportation networks in the country.

In October 1991 the White House authorized the Office of the United States Trade Representative to launch the most sweeping market access investigation in that agency's history. In August 1992 the investigation confirmed a wide range of direct and indirect trade barriers hindering U.S. competition. The United States threatened to impose an unprecedented $4 billion in trade sanctions against Beijing if the protectionist measures remained in place. The threat of sanctions was dropped two months later, however, after Chinese officials promised to reform their trade policies and to make their regulations more transparent and understandable to foreign multinational corporations (MNCs) and governments. The symbiotic relationship of mutual need and opportunism between Washington and Beijing led to MFN renewals every year during the Bush administration.

Campaigning against President George H. W. Bush in 1992, Clinton vowed to make MFN status for China genuinely conditional. He viewed the human rights issue as central to U.S. foreign policy and demanded that China's MFN renewal be accompanied by strict legislation requiring reforms in Chinese law and in its behavior at home and overseas. Candidate Clinton promised to impose trade sanctions against China if its leaders did not adhere to internationally recognized standards of human rights. Clinton argued on the campaign trail that Bush had coddled the "butchers of Beijing" and tolerated their repressive rule and persecution of pro-democracy advocates.

Soon after the November 1992 elections, however, Clinton's approach toward China changed. As president he adopted a more cooperative stance based on closer economic ties between the PRC and the United States. Clinton then became a strong supporter of China's entry into the World Trade Organization, the global trade body whose open markets policy he strongly supported. In addition, Clinton endorsed the establishment of normalized trade relations to eliminate the annual reviews of China's MFN status.

Clinton's shift must be placed squarely within the context of the PRC's emergence as a global economic superpower. Between 1979 and 1999 real gross domestic product (GDP) in China grew at an annual rate of 9.7 percent, one of the fastest rates in the world.[26] Between 1978 and 1999 the country's annual trade volume increased in absolute terms from $21 billion to $361 billion. China had become the tenth-largest trading economy by 2000 and was projected by the World Bank to be second only to the United States in total trade by 2020. As China's trade steadily grew, it maintained a large trade surplus—estimated at $21 billion in 1999—and a level of foreign reserves that exceeded $150 billion by 2000. China also became the world's second-largest destination for foreign direct investment (FDI) in the 1990s, attracting more than $45 billion in 1998 alone, primarily from the United States and Japan. This trend reflected strong investor confidence in the sustainability of the Chinese economy, even as real growth in GDP slowed modestly and China's neighbors continued to recover from the regional economic crisis of 1997 and 1998. The scope of private investing in China widened throughout the decade, as the government loosened restrictions on capital transfers and became increasingly receptive to FDI, as well as portfolio investments (that is, trade in stocks, bonds, and international currencies).

The U.S. market was a major stimulant for the Chinese economy. In terms of bilateral trade, China exported more than $81 billion in goods to the United States in 1999. Of this total, $17 billion was in the form of manufactured goods. Footwear, office machines, telecommunications equipment, and apparel were the other major Chinese exports. Bilateral trade grew more lopsided during the 1990s, as China's trade surplus grew each year—from $10 billion in 1990 to nearly $70 billion by 1999. The United States exported just $13 billion in goods to the PRC in 1999, primarily in the form of aircraft, electrical machinery, fertilizers, computers, and industrial equipment.[27] Noticeably absent from this list are automobiles and agricultural products, both of which were subject to rigid trade barriers. It was argued that this would likely change if China were to be granted permanent normal trade relations with the United States. The Agriculture Department estimated that U.S. exports of wheat, rice, corn, cotton, and soybeans to China would have increased by $1.5 billion annually between 2000 and 2009 if barriers had been removed.[28]

The large and growing bilateral trade gap between Beijing and Washington stimulated protests by the U.S. government, which faced strong pressure from labor unions, farmers, and corporate leaders to reverse the imbalance. Many members of Congress and nonprofit NGOs, meanwhile, questioned why the United States continued to tolerate the Chinese government's ongoing violations of human rights, its neglect of environmental standards, and its transfers of military equipment to so-called rogue states. Their criticism was punctuated by the trade disparity, which only widened after the engagement policy was put into practice.

Clinton's Engagement Policy

While calling for improvements in the PRC's human rights record, Clinton argued that US-China trade relations should not depend on political concerns. In May 1994 he renewed China's favorable trade status and by executive order proclaimed that future U.S. trade with China would not be linked directly to human rights. He predicted that U.S. engagement of the PRC, largely through closer economic ties, would elicit greater respect for human rights in China. Toward this end, the basis of US-China trade would be redefined in legislation formalizing the change in policy. When Clinton announced this shift, the link between human rights and trade with China was effectively severed. Concerns over China's human rights policies persisted, however, along with economic tensions. The next year, in 1995, China exported $48.5 billion worth of goods to the United States, while receiving only $10 billion in U.S. imports.[29] The Clinton administration and Congress, which after the November 1994 midterm elections was dominated by the Republican Party, concluded that a trade war had to be avoided.

Debate over U.S.-China trade intensified in 1995. Human rights groups became more outspoken in February, when Human Rights Watch (HRW) released its annual report, concluding that Chinese officials had failed to improve their human rights record since Clinton's proclamation of the engagement policy. In addition to the human rights and labor groups pressuring Washington, U.S.-based multinationals, which had opposed isolating China for its human rights practices, now pushed for sanctioning China over its trade practices. The bilateral trade deficit had become a serious problem. US-based music and software companies believed they had lost an estimated $500 million in potential profits since the early 1980s as a result of piracy of intellectual property. Even so, many of Clinton's economic advisers believed that a return to estrangement would be more harmful than the potential damage from the problems associated with engagement.

The controversy over intellectual property rights proved especially divisive. Washington threatened a 100 percent tariff on certain items if piracy continued. The result was a $3 billion package of sanctions. In retaliation, Beijing imposed higher tariffs against the U.S. automobile industry, which was already largely denied access to the Chinese market. The Chinese Civil Aviation Administration contracted with European aircraft manufacturers in a deal that exceeded $1.5 billion, spurning Boeing, which had taken its export monopoly in China for granted.[30] U.S. officials also expressed concerns about China's sales of nuclear technologies to developing countries, but the engagement strategy remained intact.[31]

After the death of Deng Xiaoping in February 1997, the new premier, Jiang Zemin, pledged to maintain Deng's formula of economic integration abroad and tight political control at home. Public opinion began to swing against engagement as Chinese officials continued to defy international human rights standards.[32] The PRC's burgeoning trade surplus with the United States provoked outrage among U.S. workers and trade unions. As a result, liberals motivated by human rights and conservatives opposed to the large U.S. trade deficit created ad hoc, anti-engagement coalitions (see Table 11.1). Clinton again argued that economic withdrawal from China would have disastrous consequences for the U.S. economy and would only make matters worse for Chinese dissidents and workers.

Table 11.1 Interest Groups in the US-China Trade Relations Debate

Supporters	Opponents
Business groups	Human rights advocates
Transportation industries	Environmental groups
Telecommunications sector	Religious groups
Financial markets	Trade unions

Proponents of Engagement: Business Groups and MNCs

Outside the U.S. government, most advocates of the Clinton administration's engagement strategy were in the business sector. This was no surprise given the immense size of the Chinese consumer market, which remained largely untapped because of the incremental nature of the country's economic reforms and restrictions on foreign competition. Among the pro-engagement advocates were individual multinational corporations, trade groups, and multisector organizations such as the U.S. Chamber of Commerce. Much of their advocacy took the form of traditional lobbying, but they also committed large sums of money to support the reelection campaigns of like-minded members of Congress and to promote candidates challenging incumbents opposed to normalized trade relations between China and the United States. The groups were also able to advance their interests through soft money donations to the major political parties.

One of the first groups to promote expanded trade with China was the US-China Business Council, which played an active role in commercial relations between Nixon's visit to China in 1972 and formal U.S. recognition in 1979. Created in 1973 as the National Council for US-China Trade, this group consisted of about 270 corporate executives who maintained economic interests in China. In the late 1990s the council supported PNTR status for China and its accession to the WTO. A similar group, the Business Roundtable, composed of the chief executive officers of major US-based multinationals, spent nearly $6 million on an advertising campaign to promote normalized trade relations. Another $4 million was budgeted for campaign contributions in 1996 and 1998 to congressional candidates supporting free trade with China.[33] The U.S. Chamber of Commerce also launched a major effort to support China's entry into the WTO and PNTR status.

Among the most active corporate supporters of normalized trade relations were the transportation industries, primarily aircraft and automotive firms, which eagerly sought greater access to the Chinese domestic market. Boeing was one of the earliest U.S. corporations to do business in China. Following Nixon's 1972 visit, the Chinese Civil Aviation Administration ordered ten passenger jets from the Seattle-based manufacturer. Since then, the Chinese government has purchased about three hundred Boeing aircraft. Despite being snubbed in favor of European contractors in 1996, in 1998 Boeing held a 72 percent market share in China. Commercial flights to and from China increased by more than 20 percent annually from 1988 to 1998, so free trade with China would undoubtedly benefit Boeing.

Meanwhile, the "big three" U.S. automakers contributed large amounts of capital and time to the attempt to open the Chinese automobile market to foreign competition. The Chinese domestic auto market was still in the early stages of development in the 1990s, and importation of foreign-made cars was highly restricted. Nonetheless, the vast potential of the Chinese market attracted great attention from US-based manufacturers. Private automobile purchasing in China grew more than 300 percent in the 1990s, but there remained a vast amount of room for growth in this sector.

General Motors (GM) was the most instrumental among US-based automotive firms in developing the auto market in China. In 1997 GM entered into a joint venture with the Shanghai Automotive Industry Corporation that created nearly two thousand manufacturing and administrative jobs. Together the companies invested $1.5 billion in the project.[34] Predictably, GM strongly supported normalized trade relations and China's entry into the WTO. The Chrysler Corporation, meanwhile, entered the Chinese market in 1987 by forming a partnership with Beijing Auto Works. The 1998 merger of Chrysler and Daimler Benz, the German automaker, was expected to increase the conglomerate's market share in China. By 2000, the Ford Motor Company had yet to maximize its potential in China. Although Ford had entered the Chinese automotive market before the 1949 revolution, its reentry was slow. Ford opened its first dealership on the mainland in 1993, but by 1998 it controlled less than 1 percent of the market in China.[35]

China, like much of the developing world, was also fertile ground for growth in the technology and communications sectors in the 1990s. In this respect US-based corporations played a key role in facilitating China's development and application of information technologies, a cornerstone of its development strategy. The San Diego–based Qualcomm Corporation, for example, partnered with two of the three largest state-owned communications companies, China Telecom and China Unicom, in an effort to develop the

Chinese wireless communications market. By 2000 only a small part of the market had been penetrated, but as sharing information becomes a necessity in the rapidly integrating business environment, the use of wireless phones and satellite communications networks will prove vital. Qualcomm's assistance helped standardize the industry by licensing intellectual property and creating a prototype system, Code Division Multiple Access, that all domestic telecommunications firms could use. Not only did Qualcomm reap royalties for its services, but its assistance also made wireless communications more accessible to the business sector. Other major communications and high-technology firms followed Qualcomm into China. Nortel, Motorola, and Lucent Technologies invested in joint ventures with Chinese counterparts. It was commonly estimated at the time that the total wireless market would exceed $16 billion in annual sales once fully exploited.[36]

Other proponents of normalized trade relations came from the financial markets, which may be viewed as something of a collective multinational corporation. Investors can be individual stockholders, corporations, brokerage firms, or mutual fund managers. Recipients of these private investments use the capital to develop new products, expand production, and open new retail outlets. As noted earlier, FDI and portfolio investments played a key role in spurring the PRC's economic growth. As more multinationals set up shop in China, even through the mandated joint ventures with Chinese firms, the country attracted additional private investment. As a result, leaders of US-based financial institutions were among the most ardent supporters of normalized trade relations and Chinese entry into the WTO.

Opponents of Engagement: NGOs and Conservatives

Many conservative members of Congress argued that Clinton's engagement policy would merely reward a "revisionist" Chinese state bent on military expansionism at the expense of U.S. interests. In their view, a policy of isolating the PRC was preferable to one of actively engaging its government. Nonprofit NGOs were also active in the debate, their views in most cases differing strongly from the pro-engagement stance of business-related groups. Among other things, the groups demanded that political, environmental, and labor disputes between China and the United States be resolved before trade relations were normalized. The nonprofit NGOs were highly fragmented because of their wide range of interests and policy preferences. With more limited resources than the corporations and business groups, the NGOs faced an uphill battle in the policy debate. Nonetheless, they posed a strong challenge to the Clinton administration's engagement policy and were able to shape the terms of the legislation that Congress ultimately passed and President Clinton signed.[37]

Lacking the economic clout of business and trade groups, human rights organizations promoted their positions primarily through the release of detailed studies of the Chinese government's human rights conduct. Their reports were especially vital because of the severe press restrictions in the PRC, which prevented Chinese journalists from investigating and exposing human rights violations. In addition to its annual reports on human rights, Human Rights Watch published frequent studies that criticized the PRC's strict control of religion, the news media, and the private affairs of its citizens.[38]

Another human rights NGO that played a major role was Freedom House, based in New York City. Freedom House's annual reports, along with those published by Human Rights Watch, were closely monitored within the U.S. government, by corporate leaders, and by nonprofit interest groups. The reports were especially critical of the Chinese government's human rights policies; the PRC consistently received the group's lowest ranking in its annual surveys of political and civil rights. In its 1997–1998 report, Freedom House declared that the Chinese Communist Party "holds absolute power, has imprisoned nearly all active dissidents, uses the judiciary as a tool of state control, and severely restricts freedoms of speech, press, association, and religion."[39]

Amnesty International (AI) also published reports and sponsored demonstrations to draw attention to human rights abuses in the PRC. Most notably, AI launched a media campaign in 1999 commemorating the ten-year anniversary of the Tiananmen Square massacre and circulated a list of 241 political prisoners still detained by the Chinese government. Members of AI continued to write to political prisoners in China, as well as to government officials, urging the prisoners' release. While remaining nonpolitical, AI cited continuing human rights abuses as evidence that the engagement policy had failed.[40]

NGOs also expressed concern that the engagement policy ignored the environment in China, where air and water pollution had steadily worsened during the country's modernization drive. This trend was especially regrettable given that environmental quality was a noneconomic issue on which the Chinese and U.S. governments could potentially agree. China, however, made a Faustian bargain on the environment to achieve economic growth.[41] In particular, it relied on coal-burning power plants as the primary source of electricity, a practice that led to high levels of fossil fuel emissions that affected air quality far beyond China's borders. Greenpeace, arguably the most influential environmental group in the world, urged the U.S. government to include environmental provisions in any legislation to normalize trade relations and in any U.S. endorsement of Chinese entry into the WTO. Also of concern was the worsening water quality in the Dongjiang River, the Pearl River Delta, and the South China Sea. Greenpeace joined other environmental NGOs in opposing the massive Three Gorges Dam in Hubei Province, which forced the relocation of approximately 1.5 million people by January 2010.

Most of these environmental concerns remained outside the PNTR and WTO debates, primarily because of the Chinese government's rejection of foreign interference in what it considered its sovereign authority over internal economic development. The environmental groups succeeded, however, in raising the profile of these issues and putting pressure on US- and foreign-based corporations to consider the ecological effects of their projects in China. As in other parts of the world, the environmental groups were most effective in appealing directly to public opinion through Internet campaigns and the sponsorship of mass protests and demonstrations.[42]

Religious groups in the United States were also active in the debate over trade relations with China. Of particular concern to them was the persecution of individuals and groups that expressed support for religious principles and institutions. By their nature, such expressions are contrary to the ideology of the Chinese Communist Party. "Freedom of religion is under threat in China," proclaimed the United Methodist Church's General Board of Church and Society. "Catholic churches, mosques, Buddhist temples and indigenous religions are being harassed. . . . We call on Congress to vote against the extension of permanent normal trade relations to China until substantial improvements in religious freedom are achieved."[43]

The groups were particularly outraged at the Chinese government's outlawing in July 1999 of Falun Gong, a spiritual movement that promotes "truthfulness, benevolence, and forbearance," primarily through the ancient meditative practice of *qigong*. Government officials in China labeled Falun Gong a "cult" whose leaders were organizing politically, and illegally, in opposition to the Communist Party. An estimated ten thousand Falun Gong followers surprised Chinese authorities in April 1999 by surrounding the government compound in Beijing to protest their lack of official recognition. The group was officially banned in July, and Chinese authorities arrested large numbers of its followers, closed its facilities, and confiscated its literature.[44]

American labor groups were vocal in their opposition to engagement. These groups sought to sway public opinion against normalized trade relations with China through public information campaigns and public demonstrations. In an unusual show of unity, more than ten thousand labor union advocates from different industrial sectors held a rally in April 2000 at the U.S. Capitol. Their demonstration was designed to convince undecided members of Congress that public opposition to normalized trade relations was extensive and that normalized relations would have real human cost in the form of displaced workers. Their presence also reminded office seekers that the trade unions represented a large and potentially crucial voting bloc.

The AFL-CIO and the United Auto Workers (UAW) led in promoting the trade union position, often invoking reasons beyond the economic self-interest of their members. AFL-CIO president John Sweeney frequently spoke out against Chinese entry into the WTO and normalized trade relations. Testifying to Congress in March 2000, Sweeney argued that an affirmative vote on PNTR "would reward the Chinese government at a time when there has been significant deterioration in its abysmal human rights record."[45] The AFL-CIO devoted much of its lobbying effort—and its budget—to the China trade issue. Advertisements it ran in eleven congressional districts were crucial in garnering public support for its position. For its part, the UAW initiated a lobbying campaign to oppose PNTR for similar reasons and cited the use of child labor and forced labor by political prisoners as justification for a reversal in U.S. trade policy. Of particular concern to the UAW was the opposition of the Chinese government to the formation of independent trade unions in the country.

With the U.S. trade deficit widening in China's favor, labor leaders also argued that normalized trade relations would jeopardize the country's long-term economic growth and harm thousands of firms as well as workers. Labor cited piracy of intellectual property, global environmental destruction, and the treatment of workers in China as additional reasons to oppose PNTR and China's entry in the WTO. Their primary emphasis as they pressed the issue before Congress, however, was on the effects of normalized trade relations on their members. This appeal carried considerable weight among members of Congress who represented urbanized districts with large blue-collar populations.

Final Debates and Congressional Action

As the antagonists for and against engagement tussled, the U.S. government played a paradoxical role in informing the debate. While the White House promoted the cause of engagement, the State Department released annual reports that were consistently critical of the Chinese government. According to the department's 1999 report,

> [t]he Government's poor human rights record deteriorated markedly throughout the year. The government intensified efforts to suppress dissent, particularly organized dissent. . . . Abuses included instances of extrajudicial killings, torture and mistreatment of prisoners, forced confessions, arbitrary arrest and detention, lengthy incommunicado detention, and denial of due process.[46]

The State Department's findings were affirmed by human rights NGOs. Freedom House's review of human rights in China during 1999 noted that Chinese "authorities escalated a crackdown on political dissidents, labor and peasant activists, and religious leaders."[47] To President Clinton, the arguments of the nonprofit NGOs and the State Department only strengthened his argument that the Chinese government should be engaged. Thus in 1999 and 2000 the president intensified his efforts to apply the engagement policy by supporting Chinese accession to the WTO and normalized trade relations between China and the United States.

China's Drive for WTO Membership

The WTO had barely come into existence when Chinese officials declared their interest in joining. They took the first step in that direction in 1995 by forming a working party to prepare a formal application. That part of the process was completed in 1998, after which China began formal negotiations for membership. All WTO applicants must undergo a two-part screening. First, they negotiate directly with the WTO on compliance with the trade body's regulations for open markets, protection of foreign firms and capital, and transparency of commercial regulations. These terms were originally set forth in the 1947 General Agreement on Tariffs and Trade (GATT), which was revised several times before becoming the World Trade Organization after the completion in 1994 of the Uruguay Round of global trade talks. In the second phase, WTO applicants negotiate directly with their primary trading partners. These bilateral negotiations are often the primary hurdle facing prospective WTO members. Chinese officials acknowledged that gaining the blessing of the United States would be its highest hurdle in the WTO accession process. Once applicants complete bilateral talks, they draft a protocol of accession to be considered by WTO member states (which numbered 135 at the time

China's application was under review). Two-thirds of the states must approve the protocol for the applicant to gain entry into the organization.

Talks between Chinese and U.S. trade negotiators progressed early in 1999 despite a series of unrelated political controversies and diplomatic crises that strained relations. The full extent of the 1996 presidential campaign scandals over illegal contributions, many of which involved Chinese citizens, was widely known by 1998. The scandals provoked charges in Congress of undue Chinese influence in the Clinton administration. Making matters worse, U.S. bombers mistakenly destroyed the Chinese embassy in Belgrade in May 1999 as part of the North Atlantic Treaty Organization's effort to stem Serbia's crackdown against Kosovo. Chinese officials condemned the attack, and some even alleged that the bombing was deliberate. Trade talks were suspended for four months after the incident, and during that time the two governments again clashed over Taiwan's status, weapons proliferation in North Korea, and other regional issues.

These incidents compelled Clinton to step up his efforts to conclude a trade pact with China. Talks resumed in September 1999, leading to a comprehensive bilateral agreement that was signed by both governments in November. Under the terms of the deal, the United States endorsed China's WTO membership in return for a wide range of Chinese concessions on bilateral trade. Among other concessions, Chinese leaders agreed to the following:

- allow full trading and distribution rights to U.S. firms doing business in China;
- reduce average tariffs on "priority" agricultural goods from 32 percent to 15 percent by 2004;
- phase out quotas on foreign versus domestically produced goods and suspend other nontariff barriers;
- permit greater access to the Chinese market by US-based automobile companies by 2006; and
- improve the treatment of foreign firms operating in China.[48]

The Chinese government had long acknowledged that reaching a trade accord with the United States was essential if its goal of obtaining WTO membership was to be accomplished. If China had joined the trade body without a positive U.S. vote, its ability to play a meaningful role would have been greatly limited, and chronic differences between China and the United States would have remained. Thus the WTO served a useful function for U.S. officials, whose efforts to gain Chinese cooperation on bilateral trade had previously been frustrated.

While negotiating with the United States, Chinese officials were simultaneously engaged in trade talks with other industrialized countries in their drive for WTO accession. Of particular interest was the European Union (EU), whose progress toward regional economic integration had taken a great leap forward in 1999 with the introduction of the euro as a common currency. Under the terms of the 1992 Maastricht Treaty, the major European states (except for the United Kingdom) agreed to coordinate all facets of their fiscal and monetary policies. Such coordination included the conduct of trade relations, which the union would pursue with one voice. A "bilateral" trade deal between the EU and the PRC was within reach, although EU members demanded many of the same market-opening concessions that China had granted the United States. The China-EU accord was reached on May 19, 2000, when the EU formally endorsed China's bid to join the WTO in return for promised reforms in the PRC's trade practices. Through this single agreement, Beijing garnered the blessings of France, Germany, Italy, and twelve other Western European countries. The pact with the Europeans added momentum to China's drive for permanent normalized trade relations with the United States, an issue soon to be before Congress.

The PNTR Debate in Congress

Under U.S. law, Congress was not required to play a direct role in the bilateral negotiations on U.S. support for China's WTO membership. Congress was also not required to ratify the pact signed by President Clinton. That did not mean, however, that Congress was irrelevant to the process. To the contrary, given its other constitutional powers to regulate trade—specifically its authority to grant or deny "normal" status to U.S. trading partners—Congress effectively held the key to China's entry into the WTO. Furthermore, legislation passed during the Cold War imposed explicit conditions on U.S. trade with communist states. Those conditions would violate the basic principle of the WTO that terms of trade among all its members be maintained consistently and unconditionally. For that reason, a bilateral trade agreement between the United States and China approved by both houses of Congress was the last major hurdle in Chinese membership in the multilateral WTO. The Clinton administration, therefore, directed its efforts early in 2000 toward gaining Congress's approval for PNTR with Beijing.

Clinton assigned lobbying duties to Secretary of Commerce William Daley and the deputy chief of staff, Stephen Ricchetti. The president also recruited former presidents Gerald Ford, Jimmy Carter, and George H. W. Bush to endorse the bill, along with Federal Reserve Chairman Alan Greenspan and leading foreign policy advisers in the State and Defense Departments. Clinton's sense of urgency owed much to the setbacks and frustrations that plagued his second term in office. His impeachment by the House of Representatives for the Monica Lewinsky sex scandal had crippled Clinton domestically. In foreign policy, his goal of achieving a comprehensive Middle East peace treaty was proving beyond reach, and his conduct of the military intervention in Kosovo received more criticism than praise. Clinton, therefore, looked to the China trade pact to define his legacy in foreign affairs.

Fortunately for Clinton, the political winds in Congress were in his favor. Under the trade bill introduced on May 15 in the House of Representatives (H.R. 4444), the United States would extend PNTR status to China upon its accession to the WTO. In approving the bill on May 17, the House Ways and Means Committee included an "anti-import surge" amendment that protected U.S. firms in the event of sudden increases in Chinese imports of specific commodities. The House Rules Committee further amended the bill on May 23. Among other provisions of the amended bill, a commission would be established to monitor and report on the PRC's human rights and labor practices. In addition, the U.S. trade representative would annually evaluate China's compliance with WTO regulations, and a special task force would confirm that Chinese exporters were not shipping goods manufactured by prison laborers to the United States. Finally, the House bill called for increased technical assistance to the PRC's efforts to enact legal reforms, and it urged the WTO to consider Taiwan's application to join the trade body immediately after China's accession.

Lobbying efforts peaked as the bill awaited a final vote in the full House. On the day before the vote was taken, about 200 business lobbyists met on Capitol Hill to coordinate their strategy for swaying undecided members.[49] On May 24, the House approved H.R. 4444 by a vote of 237–197. Although a majority of the 224 Republicans in the House voted for the bill, most of the 211 Democrats voted against it. Opponents came largely from urban areas with large populations of industrial workers and a strong labor union presence. On both sides of the aisle, support was primarily from members representing suburban or rural districts. Approval in the Senate was virtually assured, although its timing was uncertain given the Senate's approaching summer recess, other legislation on its schedule, and the distraction of a presidential election campaign.

Many prominent senators opposed the measure, although Senate approval was considered a given. Sen. Paul Wellstone, D-Minn., for example, spoke out against normal trade with China because of the PRC's continuing repression of human rights and religious freedoms. Republican critics included Fred Thompson, R-Tenn., who sought without success to include an amendment that would link PNTR to Chinese restraint on nuclear weapons proliferation. Jesse Helms, R-N.C., chairman of the Committee on Foreign Relations, argued that PNTR status would reward Chinese leaders for maintaining the communist system he had long condemned. As in the House, supporters and opponents of PNTR crossed party lines to an extent otherwise unseen in the 106th Congress.

As the Senate vote approached in September 2000, the lobbying by interests on both sides of the China trade issue resumed, although with less intensity than before the House vote. Among pro-PNTR interest groups was the American Electronics Association, one of the largest and most influential high-tech trade associations in the United States, which stepped up its lobbying campaign in early September. Representing small and medium-sized industrial firms, the National Association of Manufacturers met with Senate Majority Leader Trent Lott, R-Miss., and Sen. John Breaux, D-La., and received their assurances that the bill would be approved. Once their position was made known, other business groups relaxed their lobbying efforts.[50]

The Senate was under strong pressure from the Clinton administration and business groups to pass the legislation without amendments. Clinton warned senators that amendments to the bill would force a new round of negotiations—first with the Chinese government and then with the House of Representatives. The outcome of those talks would be highly uncertain, and the legislation would be in the hands of a new Congress and a new presidential administration in 2001. The Senate soundly rejected a series of proposed amendments linking China's trade status to improvements in human rights, religious freedom, labor standards, and weapons proliferation. The final bill, identical to that passed by the House, moved quickly toward a vote on the Senate floor.

As expected, the Senate approved the measure on September 19 in an 83–15 vote and sent it to the White House for Clinton's signature. Again, support and opposition to the bill had crossed party lines to an unusual extent, with seven Democrats joining eight Republicans in opposing the legislation. Whereas the Democrats were primarily concerned with labor issues, Republican opponents most often cited the security threat posed by the PRC. Critics of China in both parties raised concerns about human rights. Clinton signed the legislation on October 10, and normalized US-China trade relations became a reality.

Having gained the blessing of the world's foremost economic power, China joined the WTO on December 11, 2001. Its government then embarked on a series of economic reforms, to be phased in over the following decade, that would align the nation's trade policies with WTO standards and those of other member states. Among other commitments, Chinese officials agreed to reduce average tariff levels on industrial as well as agricultural products to 8.9 percent and 15.2 percent, respectively, by 2010.[51] The PRC also pledged to limit subsidies for agricultural production, grant full trade and distribution rights to foreign enterprises, respect intellectual property rights, and open its banking system to foreign-based financial institutions. Taken together, once enacted these reforms would remove the barriers to the entry of goods, services, and foreign investments into China.

Conclusion: The Privatization of Foreign Policy

China's entry into the WTO was followed by rapid increases in its overseas trade. Between 2001 and 2011, China's overall trade increased seven-fold, from $510 billion to approximately $3.5 trillion.[52] The volume of Chinese imports and exports grew at roughly the same levels until 2005, when exports rose over the previous year by more than 28 percent ($762 billion), whereas imports increased by only 18 percent ($660 billion). After both imports and exports fell in 2009 due to the global financial crisis, by 2010 they were both back on the rise at 38.7 percent ($1.39 trillion) and 31.3 percent ($1.58 trillion) respectively. Imports and exports continued this trend in 2011, rising approximately 13 percent ($1.6 trillion) and 17.0 percent ($1.90 trillion) respectively. Likewise, the Chinese economy's real growth, as measured by GDP, continued at an annual average rate of approximately 10 percent through 2011.[53] Such robust growth, which China had enjoyed in previous years while its neighbors endured a protracted economic crisis, also stood in stark contrast to the recessions experienced by Western economies, including that of the United States. Significantly, China had become the world's leading recipient of foreign direct investment (FDI) by 2002, and it retained its status as one of the top destinations for FDI through 2011.

Among the key factors in this surge in China's global trade was the United States, whose imports from China grew from $100 billion in 2000 to nearly $400 billion in 2011.[54] Exports from the United States to China also increased during the same period, from $16 billion to about $104 billion, leaving a trade deficit of just over $295 billion in 2011. The growth in U.S. exports was welcomed in Washington, but the resulting annual trade deficits, the largest ever recorded between two trading partners, fueled renewed charges that China needed to deepen its commitment to open markets.[55] According to the Office of the United States Trade Representative in 2011, in many economic sectors "the prevalence of interventionist policies and practices, coupled with the large role of state-owned enterprises in China's economy, continued to generate significant concerns among U.S. stakeholders."[56] As noted above, the United States has repeatedly filed WTO complaints against China, resulting in positive, if incremental, improvements in reducing domestic restrictions in areas such as intellectual property–laden U.S. products in the film, publishing, and entertainment industries.[57]

Yet, this large and protracted trade imbalance has provided ammunition to U.S. critics of normalized trade relations and China's WTO membership. These critics also have stressed human rights reports, which indicate a lack of improvement in China's record since it joined the WTO. For example, in 2011 Freedom House reported deteriorating human rights in the PRC "due to increased Communist Party efforts to restrict public discussion of political, legal, and human rights issues, including through the systematic disappearance of dozens of leading social-media activists and lawyers and growing online censorship among domestic social-networking services."[58] According to Amnesty International's 2012 Report, "China's economic strength during the global financial crisis increased the country's leverage in the domain of global human rights—mostly for the worse."[59]

American importers, in particular, have had a difficult time ensuring that workers' rights are not abused. Factories in China have notoriously developed sophisticated methods for hiding violations.[60] In the past, labor unions in the United States claimed that such findings prove that Clinton's logic of inducing reform in China through engagement was unfounded. Although the AFL-CIO unsuccessfully called on the Bush administration to put greater pressure on China, the Obama administration has been more receptive to calls for a linkage between the PRC's economic policies and its overall relationship with Washington.[61] Such pressure has yielded promising results. As the AFL-CIO noted in 2012,

> Collective action by Chinese workers, including strikes, has been successful in many cases and . . . China's industrial workers are fashioning their own system of industrial relations, largely without the assistance of the existing law and labor relations institutions.[62]

This is welcome news to pro-engagement groups in the United States that continue to favor closer bilateral trade ties with China. The US-China Chamber of Commerce, for example, facilitated in 2012 the "U.S.-China CEO and Former Senior Officials' Dialogue (Track II)" in Beijing.[63] Yet thorny issues remain. The US-China Business Council and other trade groups remain concerned about Chinese policies that insulate domestic firms from competition. For their part, Chinese officials have expressed dismay at the "political background check" of Chinese corporations seeking to do business with the United States.[64] Despite these sticking points, the continued centrality of the bilateral trade relationship between the United States and China is beyond dispute.

The PRC's global ambitions are much broader than this picture might suggest. Beijing has adopted international engagement as a key component of its own foreign policy agenda and on many occasions has demonstrated a willingness not only to cooperate with the democratic allies of the United States, but to exert pressure on more controversial governments in Iran, Syria, and Libya. Even as Chinese leaders have asserted their territorial rights over disputed waterways near China's borders, they have chosen not to spark political hostilities that could lead to military confrontation in the Asia-Pacific region.[65]

China, meanwhile, remains a competitor of the United States in Asia, as first evidenced by its signing of a free trade agreement with the Association of Southeast Asian Nations (ASEAN) in November 2004. China has since deepened its economic ties with its regional partners, despite the many differences that continue to divide them. Other examples of China's expanding global reach, which is often aimed at satisfying its voracious energy appetite, include a liquid natural gas agreement with Australia, massive infusions of development assistance to resource-rich states across Africa, and energy agreements with Venezuela and Brazil. Indeed, from 2009 to 2011, the PRC simultaneously invested more than any other state in advanced energy and remained the largest global producer and consumer of coal.[66]

The continuing debate over US-China trade relations serves as a microcosm of a larger phenomenon in the formulation of post–Cold War U.S. foreign policy. A variety of new issues, actors, and policy calculations emerged in the 1990s to replace the challenge that the Soviet Union formerly posed. Of particular concern to this study is the heightened effect of foreign economic relations on the policy agenda of the first post–Cold War administration. With the easing of security concerns, U.S. leaders identified competitiveness in the rapidly integrating global economy as a pressing national interest. A related trend was the growing role of international and domestic nonstate actors seeking to promote their interests in this more fluid, pluralistic environment. The global war on terrorism, while altering the strategic environment since September 2001, has not altered this more general shift in world politics.

All these elements greatly complicate the U.S. policy-making environment, which had already been altered by the diffusion of foreign policy responsibilities beyond the State and Defense Departments. As the foreign affairs bureaucracy has grown to empower economic-oriented agencies, such as the Treasury and Commerce Departments, the opportunities for private interest groups to penetrate the policy-making process have greatly increased. This trend is reflected in Congress, whose committees concerned with foreign economic relations are a focus of heightened interest group lobbying and political pressure. The outcome of this legislative process reflects the more complex setting in which "intermestic" issues—those crossing foreign and domestic boundaries—dominate the agenda. In this respect, the debate over US-China trade relations typifies the new and more complex era in U.S. foreign policy.

Key Actors

Amnesty International   Nongovernmental organization; opposed to the Clinton administration policy of engagement with China because of Beijing's political repression of dissidents.

Bill Clinton   President; an advocate of engagement and normalized trade relations with China.

General Motors Corporation   The largest US-based automaker and a proponent of normalized trade relations with China; involved since 1997 in a joint venture with Shanghai Automotive Industry Corporation.

Human Rights Watch   Nongovernmental organization whose annual reports highlighted ongoing political repression in China despite closer economic relations with the United States.

Qualcomm Corporation   A San Diego–based business; proponent of normalized trade relations with China; partnered with two Chinese companies to modernize the country's telecommunications network.

John Sweeney   AFL-CIO president; an outspoken opponent of normalized trade relations on the basis of Chinese trade restrictions, the country's human rights record, and the potential loss of jobs in the United States.

United Methodist Church Issued a report condemning the Chinese government's crackdown on religious freedom and opposing closer trade relations.

US- China Business Council An industry-based group strongly in favor of engagement.

Notes

1. World Trade Organization, "Disputes by Country/Territory," 2012, www.wto.org/english/tratop_e/dispu_e/dispu_by_country_e.htm.

2. Mark Landler, "In Car Country, Obama Trumpets China Trade Case," *New York Times,* September 18, 2012.

3. World Trade Organization, "Disputes by Country/Territory."

4. Susan V. Lawrence and Thomas Lum, Congressional Research Service, "U.S.-China Relations: Policy Issues," March 11, 2011, 1–2.

5. For the Strategic and Economic Dialogue, see www.treasury.gov/initiatives/Pages/china.aspx; for the U.S.-China Joint Commission on Commerce and Trade, see www.ustr.gov/about-us/press-office/fact-sheets/2009/october/us-china-joint-commission-commerce-and-trade.

6. Office of the United States Trade Representative, "2011 Report to Congress on China's WTO Compliance," December 2011, www.ustr.gov/webfm_send/3189.

7. Ibid., 11.

8. BBC Worldwide Monitoring, "China Probing 185 Websites for Piracy, Illegal Activities," April 27, 2012.

9. Keith Bradsher and Charles Duhigg, "Signs of Changes Taking Hold in Electronics Factories in China," *New York Times,* December 26, 2012, A1.

10. Pascal Lamy, "A New Chapter in China's Reform and Opening," World Trade Organization, December 11, 2011, www.wto.org/english/news_e/sppl_e/spp1211_e.htm.

11. Ben Blanchard, "China Slams 'Distorted' View of Copyright Piracy Problem," Reuters.com, November 11, 2012.

12. Stephen King, "This Time China Has No Lifeline to Throw Us: The Eurozone Crisis Is Threatening the Entire World Economy," *The London Times*, October 10, 2012.

13. Scott Murdoch, "Fall in Exports Revives China Economic Fears," *The Australian*, December 11, 2012.

14. U.S. Census Bureau, Foreign Trade Division, Data Dissemination Branch, www.census.gov/foreign-trade/balance/c5700.html#2011.

15. Annie Lowrey, "A Tightrope on China's Currency," *New York Times,* October 22, 2012.

16. Aaron L. Friedberg, *A Contest for Supremacy: China, America and the Struggle for Mastery in Asia* (New York: Norton, 2012).

17. Kerry Dumbaugh, Congressional Research Service, "China-U.S. Relations: Current Issues and Implications for U.S. Policy," September 22, 2006, 3–5. See also Lawrence and Lum, "U.S. China Relations: Policy Issues."

18. Ewen MacAskill and Jonathan Watts, "Obama Urges China to Improve Human Rights Record Amidst Dissident Row," *The Guardian*, April 30, 2012.

19. Steven Lee Myers and Andrew Jacobs, "On a Tightrope, President Prods China on Rights," *New York Times*, April 30, 2012.

20. Jeffrey E. Garten, *The Big Ten: The Big Emerging Markets and How They Will Change Our Lives* (New York: Basic Books, 1997).

21. White House, Office of the Press Secretary, press conference transcript, May 26, 1994.

22. For an elaboration on this domestic balance of power, see the various essays in Scott Kennedy, ed., *China Cross Talk: The American Debate over China Policy Since Nationalization* (Lanham, MD: Rowman and Littlefield, 2003).

23. See Andrew Nathan, *China's Transition* (New York: Columbia University Press, 1997).

24. China's economic output grew by an average of 10 percent annually in the 1980s, with much of this growth based on foreign commerce. See Claude E. Barfield, "U.S.-China Trade and Investment in the 1990s," in *Beyond MFN: Trade with China and American Interests*, ed. James R. Lilley and Wendell L. Willkie II (Washington, DC: AEI Press, 1994), 63.

25. William R. Keylor, *The Twentieth Century World: An International History*, 3rd ed. (New York: Oxford University Press, 1996), 479–80.

26. The figures in this section are derived from Wayne M. Morrison, Congressional Research Service, "China-U.S. Trade Issues," July 20, 2000, 2–5.

27. U.S. Census Bureau, Foreign Trade Division, "U.S. Trade in Goods with China," May 7, 2000, www.census.gov/foreign-trade/balance/c5700.html.

28. Department of Agriculture, Economic Research Service, "China's WTO Accession to Significantly Boost U.S. Agricultural Exports," press release, February 2000.

29. John T. Rourke and Richard Clark, "Making U.S. Foreign Policy toward China in the Clinton Administration," in *After the End: Making U.S. Foreign Policy in the Post–Cold War World*, ed. James M. Scott (Durham, NC: Duke University Press, 1998), 203.

30. Ibid., 208.

31. During a November 1997 visit to the White House, Jiang Zemin agreed to halt the sharing of nuclear technology with Iran, among other concessions. A similar concern among congressional critics involved the Clinton administration's support for sharing satellite launch technology with China. White House officials certified in May 1999 that such technology exports to China would not harm U.S. firms in this sector or threaten U.S. strategic interests.

32. For a review of the shift in public opinion and its relationship to Sino-American relations, see "Support for NTR/MFN Status," in *Americans on Globalization: A Study of US Public Attitudes*, Center on Policy Attitudes, University of Maryland, College Park, March 28, 2000, www.pipa.org/OnlineReports/Globalization/AmericansGlobalization_Mar00/AmericansGlobalization_Mar00_apdxa.pdf.

33. Susan Schmidt, "Businesses Ante Up $30 Million," *Washington Post*, October 26, 2000, A26.

34. China Business World Online News Service, "Joint Venture Project with GM," February 25, 1997, www.cbw.com/business/quarter1/automoti.htm.

35. Richard Pastore, "Motorskills: Emerging Markets," *CIO Magazine Online*, September 15, 1998, www.cio.com/archive/enterprise/091598_ford.html.

36. Lester J. Gesteland, "Foreign Firms to Benefit from China Unicom U.S. $16 Billion CDMA Market," *China Online*, December 13, 1999.

37. For more information regarding the impact of NGO pressure on government policies, see Margaret E. Keck and Kathryn Sikkink, *Activists beyond Borders* (Ithaca: Cornell University Press, 1998).

38. For recent critiques, see Human Rights Watch, "China: Release Whistleblowing Doctor: Year-Long Pattern of Harassment Comes to Light," June 10, 2004, www.hrw .org/english/docs/2004/06/10/china8794.htm; and idem, "China: Stifling the Memory of Tiananmen," June 4, 2004, www.hrw.org/english/docs/2004/06/03/china8732.htm.

39. Freedom House, *Freedom in the World, 1997–1998* (Piscataway, NJ: Transaction, 1998), 190–191.

40. *Amnesty International Annual Report, 1999: China,* www.amnesty.org/ailib/ aireport/ar99/asa17.htm.

41. Elizabeth Economy, "Painting China Green," *Foreign Affairs* 78 (March/April 1999): 16.

42. For examples of environmental NGOs' Internet lobbying activities, see the Greenpeace Website, www.greenpeace.org, and that of the Sierra Club, www.sierraclub.org.

43. United Methodist Church, General Board of Church and Society, "An Appeal of Conscience by Religious Leaders to Members of the U.S. Congress," September 19, 2000, www.umc-gbcs.org/issues/letter.php?letterid=42.

44. Although most religious groups opposed the engagement policy, some sided with the Clinton administration in arguing that toleration of faith would be more likely once the PRC became more integrated into the global economy. One example was a Quaker group, the Friends Committee on National Legislation, which became active during the 1990s on many aspects of Sino-American relations.

45. Federal News Service, "Prepared Testimony of John J. Sweeney before the Senate Finance Committee," March 23, 2000.

46. State Department, Bureau of Democracy, Human Rights and Labor, *Country Reports on Human Rights Practices, 1999,* February 25, 2000, www.state.gov/www/ global/human_rights/1999_hrp_report/china.html.

47. See the Freedom House Website, www.freedomhouse.org.

48. Wayne M. Morrison, National Council for Science and the Environment, "U.S.-China Trade Issues," CRS Issue Brief for Congress, January 3, 2001, www.cnie.org/nle/ econ-35.html.

49. Anne E. Kornblut, "House OK's Normalizing China Trade, Bipartisan Vote Praised and Assailed," *Boston Globe,* May 25, 2000, A1.

50. Edward Daniels, "Manufacturing Advocate Confident China Trade Bill Will Pass," States News Service, August 23, 2000.

51. Although China's record on reducing tariff barriers remained mixed as of 2010, these twin goals had been achieved. See Wayne M. Morrison, "U.S.-China Trade Issues," CRS Issue Brief for Congress, June 21, 2010, www.fas.org/sgp/crs/row/RL33536.pdf.

52. U.S.-China Business Council, *U.S.-China Trade Statistics and China's World Trade Statistics,* www.uschina.org/statistics/tradetable.html. For 2011 and 2012 statistics see www.tradingeconomics.com.

53. *CIA World Factbook,* www.cia.gov/library/publications/the-world-factbook/ index.html.

54. U.S.-China Business Council, *U.S.-China Trade Statistics.*

55. Office of the United States Trade Representative, "2011 Report to Congress on China's WTO Compliance," December 2011, www.ustr.gov/webfm_send/3189. Amid

these complaints from Washington, the USTR indicated a silver lining because "Chinese leaders had taken many impressive steps to implement a set of sweeping commitments."

56. Ibid., 2.

57. The first complaint against China filed in 2004 with the WTO involved the semiconductor industry; it was settled through bilateral negotiation. For a full listing of World Trade Organization disputes by country/territory through 2012, see www.wto .org/english/tratop_e/dispu_e/dispu_by_country_e.htm.

58. Freedom House, "Freedom in the World: China, 2012," www.freedomhouse.org/report/freedom-world/2012/china-0.

59. Amnesty International, "China Report 2012," www.amnesty.org/en/region/china/report-2012.

60. Dexter Roberts and Pete Engardio, "Secrets, Lies, and Sweatshops," *Business Week*, November 27, 2006.

61. AFL-CIO, *The AFL-CIO Workers' Rights Case against China, Global Economy*, accessed April 5, 2007, www.aflcio.org/issues/jobseconomy/globaleconomy/chinapetition.cfm.

62. AFL-CIO: America's Unions, "Labor Rights in China," December 2012, www .aflcio.org/Issues/Trade/China/Labor-Rights-in-China.

63. U.S. Chamber of Commerce, "2012–2013 Asia Program of Work," 2012, www .uschamber.com/sites/default/files/reports/020147_Asia_ProgramofWork_final_.pdf.

64. Brian Wingfield, "China Urges U.S. to End Political Vetting of Its Firms." Bloomberg.com, December 12, 2012.

65. Daniel Ten Kate and Shamim Adam, "China, ASEAN Downplay Sea Disputes as Economic Concerns Grow." *Bloomberg Businessweek*, November 18, 2012.

66. Enrst & Young, "Renewable Energy Country Attractiveness Indices." *Ernst & Young*, www.ey.com/GL/en/Industries/Cleantech/RECAI-May-2012—All-Renewables-Index; Also see Kelly Sims Gallagher and Joanna I. Lewis, "China's Quest for a Green Economy," in *Environmental Policy: New Directions for the 21st Century*, 8th ed., ed. Norman J. Vig and Michael E. Kraft (Washington, DC: CQ Press, 2013), 321–343.

12 The Politics of Climate Change: Will the US Act to Prevent Calamity?

Rodger A. Payne and Sean Payne

Before You Begin

1. What is the American national interest regarding climate change? How do leaders balance economic concerns against environmental issues?

2. Which organizations, coalitions, and leaders most influence climate change policy in the United States? What interests do they pursue?

3. What role do cities and states play in shaping American policy on climate change?

4. Will the United States likely play a pivotal role in ongoing international negotiations about climate change?

5. Is the United States likely to reduce its greenhouse gas emissions without a formal new climate treaty? What policy processes might lead to a reduction in emissions?

Introduction: The U.S. Perspective

The scientific evidence linking carbon dioxide and other so-called greenhouse gases to global warming is now viewed as overwhelming. That was made abundantly clear in the very troubling "Summary for Policymakers" included in the most recent report of the Intergovernmental Panel on Climate Change (IPCC), which was produced by 2,500 scientists from over 130 countries. The panel's fourth assessment found that the data about global temperature increases are "unequivocal." Moreover, the IPCC declared that "most of the observed increase in globally averaged temperatures since the mid-20th century is *very likely*"—defined as greater than 90 percent likely—"due to the observed increase in anthropogenic greenhouse gas concentrations." The IPCC specifically finds that human fossil fuel consumption and "land-use change"—caused by deforestation, for example—are primarily responsible for an "atmospheric concentration of carbon dioxide in 2005 [that] exceeds by far the natural range over the last 650,000 years."[1]

Unsurprisingly, global climate change is now recognized as a very high political priority item on the international agenda. Former U.S. President Bill Clinton, for instance, has declared that "The most profound security threat we face today is global warming."[2] United Nations Secretary General Ban Ki-moon similarly refers to climate change as the "the greatest collective challenge we face as a human family."[3] Numerous countries are now debating the most effective and affordable means of heading off disastrous consequences. It is generally agreed that climate change must be addressed collectively because neither the causes nor consequences can be isolated even to a small set of nation-states.

The first major step was taken in February 2005, when the Kyoto Protocol to the Framework Convention on Climate Change (FCCC) went into effect after ratification by 168 countries and the European Union (EU). The treaty requires meaningful reductions in greenhouse gas emissions, as parties committed to reducing emissions by 5.2 percent by 2012. Though the Kyoto deal was struck in 1997, no U.S. presidential administration has ever forwarded it to the Senate for ratification. President Clinton's negotiators aggressively and openly sought significant additions to the agreement, but could not obtain a deal before his term expired. President George W. Bush's administration considered Kyoto "fatally flawed" and refused to partake in ongoing international talks designed to achieve additional reductions.[4] Well in advance of the December 2009 Copenhagen climate summit, the twenty-seven nations of the EU and Japan agreed to cut their greenhouse gas emissions by 20 percent or more from their 1990 levels by 2020.[5] President Barack Obama claims that the United States wants to help the world head off climate change, but the results to date have been modest. Because the United States emits nearly one-fourth of the pollutants that contribute to global warming, it is nearly impossible to imagine an international treaty that can successfully address this worldwide problem without Washington's endorsement and cooperation.[6] Domestic and international politics in large part explain U.S. behavior in climate change negotiations over the past two decades.

Background: The Emergence of the Global Warming Issue

In 1827, French scientist Jean-Baptiste Fourier recognized that Earth's atmosphere traps significant amounts of the sun's heat in much the same way that glass panels trap heat in a greenhouse. It is now well-established science

Timeline
The Kyoto Protocol

1896	Swedish scientist Svante Arrhenius publishes "On the Influence of Carbonic Acid in the Air upon the Temperature of the Ground."
1957	American oceanographer Roger Revelle warns that humans are conducting a "large-scale geophysical experiment" on the planet by emitting substantial quantities of greenhouse gases.
October 1985	The findings of the first major international conference on global warming, held at Villach, Austria, warn, "As a result of the increasing concentrations of greenhouse gases, it is now believed that in the first half of the next century a rise of global mean temperature could occur which is greater than any in man's history."
June 1988	NASA's James E. Hansen testifies before Congress that "the greenhouse effect is here and affecting our climate now."
November 1988	The first meeting is held of the Intergovernmental Panel on Climate Change, an interdisciplinary group of scientists, scholars, policy makers, and diplomats that regularly issues reports about climate change science, the effects of those changes, and possible means of mitigating the consequences of global warming.
May 12, 1989	President George H. W. Bush announces US support for climate change negotiations.
June 1992	The United Nations Framework Convention on Climate Change (FCCC) is presented to the "Earth Summit" at Rio de Janeiro, Brazil. The treaty does not require states to make binding commitments to reduce greenhouse gas emissions.
October 1992	The United States becomes the first industrialized nation to ratify the FCCC.
March 21, 1994	The FCCC becomes international law three months after the fiftieth ratification.
July 5, 1997	The U.S. Senate passes the Byrd-Hagel Resolution (95–0) opposing U.S. acceptance of any climate change commitment that excludes the developing world or would seriously hurt the U.S. economy.

(continued)

Timeline *(continued)*
The Kyoto Protocol

December 11, 1997	More than 150 nations, including the United States, agree to the Kyoto Protocol to the FCCC. The agreement commits industrialized nations to an average 5 percent reduction in greenhouse gas emissions, using 1990 levels as the base.
November 12, 1998	President Bill Clinton signs the Kyoto Protocol.
March 2001	Bush administration officials declare the Kyoto Protocol "dead" and announce U.S. withdrawal from international negotiations.
2002	Canada, the European Union, and Japan ratify the Kyoto Protocol. California becomes the first U.S. state to restrict greenhouse gas emissions from motor vehicles.
November 2004	Russia ratifies the Kyoto Protocol, which enters into effect three months later.
December 2005	New York and six other states organize a Regional Greenhouse Gas Initiative to reduce greenhouse gas emissions in the northeastern United States.
August 2006	California requires industry to lower greenhouse gas emissions, committing to 25 percent cuts in current levels by 2020.
January 2007	An industry-backed coalition, the United States Climate Action Partnership, releases a report calling for mandatory reductions in greenhouse gas emissions.
February 2007	California and four neighboring states form the Western Climate Initiative to reduce greenhouse gas emissions.
April 2007	The U.S. Supreme Court rules that carbon dioxide and other greenhouse gases are pollutants, the Environmental Protection Agency (EPA) has the authority to regulate them, and states have the right to sue the EPA to force such decisions.
June 26, 2009	By a 219–212 vote, the House of Representatives passes the American Clear Energy and Security Act, cosponsored by Reps. Henry A. Waxman (D-CA) and Edward J. Markey (D-MA).
September 2009	The EPA proposes to focus its first greenhouse gas–permitting requirements on large industrial facilities.

| December 2009 | Copenhagen summit concludes with a nonbinding U.S. agreement with China, India, and other nations establishing a 2° Celsius limit on future warming and a commitment of $100 billion over ten years to help poor countries adapt to climate change. |
| December 2012 | Doha climate talks end with Kyoto Protocol amended to extend to 2020. About 15% of global emissions are covered, primarily because of European and Australian agreement. Canada withdraws from the treaty. |

that carbon dioxide (CO_2), methane, nitrous oxide, and especially water vapor create a greenhouse effect, which modulates the planet's climate. Without this atmosphere, Earth would be cooler by at least 60 degrees Fahrenheit, and life as it is known today would not exist. In the 1890s, however, Swedish scientist Svante Arrhenius and American P. C. Chamberlain identified a potential problem: the buildup of carbon dioxide in the atmosphere because of the burning of fossil fuels. Since the beginning of the Industrial Revolution, the combustion of coal, oil, and natural gas and other human activities have increased carbon dioxide concentrations in Earth's atmosphere by about 35 percent. In 1957 oceanographer Roger Revelle noted, "Human beings are now carrying out a large-scale geophysical experiment of a kind that could not have happened in the past nor be reproduced in the future."[7]

More than half a century has passed since Revelle made his observation, and the scientific community now believes that it has a solid understanding of the results of this grand experiment in atmospheric science. For many years, and after decades of genuinely impressive research, a scientific consensus now agrees about the phenomenon commonly known as global warming. The latest IPCC assessment notes the cumulative result of the research, "a *very high confidence* that the globally averaged net effect of human activities since 1750 has been one of warming."[8] Scientists expect climate change to become even more apparent and pronounced through the twenty-first century. As economies and populations grow worldwide, fossil fuel consumption increases. By the year 2100, carbon dioxide concentrations in the atmosphere are expected to be at least double the levels present at the beginning of the Industrial Revolution.

Although no one can be certain of the effects of these developments, many scientists have long warned of the polar ice caps melting at rapid rates, ocean currents changing dramatically, and precipitation and storm patterns shifting significantly. The global consequences of these changes could include severe flooding of coastal areas, disruption of agricultural patterns, emergence of new and threatening disease patterns, creation of millions of "environmental refugees," and great damage to the planet's biological diversity. In other words, the effects of climate change are likely to be numerous, adverse, costly, and potentially severe.[9]

International Negotiations

The ten warmest years of the twentieth century occurred during its last fifteen years. The ten warmest years recorded since 1850 occurred in the period from 2000 to 2012.[10] Thus, with ever-increasing urgency, many national governments behave as if global warming is an extremely serious ecological threat to the planet.

In 1988, global warming emerged as a major issue in many countries, including the United States. Temperatures were much warmer than normal, North America experienced major drought, and forest fires raged through Yellowstone National Park. In June 1988, James E. Hansen, director of the National Aeronautics and Space Administration's (NASA) Goddard Institute of Space Studies, made headlines when he declared to the Senate Committee on Energy and Natural Resources, "The greenhouse effect is here and affecting our climate now."[11] Many scientists were publicly critical of that comment, arguing that the assertion was not clearly supported by the available evidence. Nonetheless, after Hansen's testimony, "media coverage of global warming ignited."[12] Many political figures around the world soon began recommending that nations pay more attention to the problem. Prime Minister Margaret Thatcher of the United Kingdom, for example, worried that human activity was "creating a global heat trap which could lead to climatic instability."[13]

In 1988, the United Nations Environment Program (UNEP) and the World Meteorological Organization—with the strong support of the United States and other governments—created the Intergovernmental Panel on Climate Change. Holding its first meeting in November 1988, the IPCC engaged nearly 200 top-notch scientists in assessing global warming by creating working groups on science (chaired by the United Kingdom), impacts (chaired by the Soviet Union), and response strategies (chaired by the United States). In addition to the impressive pool of atmospheric scientists, hundreds of economists, diplomats, and public servants also ultimately participated in IPCC working groups.

Almost immediately, states sought international action. In March 1989, France, Norway, and the Netherlands cosponsored a meeting on global environmental issues that was attended by representatives from two dozen countries, including seventeen heads of state. That month, twenty-two nations, including Canada, France, Italy, and Japan, called for the negotiation of a climate change convention; in May 1989, just months into George H. W. Bush's presidency, the United States announced support for such negotiations. In July, the leaders of the Group of Seven (G-7) industrialized countries (Canada, France, Germany, Italy, Japan, the United Kingdom, and the United States) met in Paris and held what some observers called the "environmental summit." The resulting G-7 declaration "strongly advocate[d] common efforts to limit emission of carbon dioxide and other greenhouse gases."[14]

The IPCC working groups reported their initial findings to the UN General Assembly and the Second World Climate Conference in fall 1990 at Geneva. These first assessments reflected a scientific consensus that the greenhouse effect was real and was being exacerbated by human activity. They also paid immediate policy dividends: On December 21, 1990, the General Assembly adopted Resolution 45/212 establishing the Intergovernmental Negotiating Committee (INC) to serve under its auspices and coordinate bargaining among nations.

Many observers believed that international negotiators could model a climate change treaty on the Montreal Protocol. During the 1980s, a series of negotiations led to an agreement to address the class of man-made chemicals known as chlorofluorocarbons (CFCs), which were thinning the atmospheric ozone layer. Under the 1987 Montreal Protocol, a baseline emissions year was established, and then production and use of CFCs were reduced in relation to this target and ultimately banned. Following this precedent, a 1988 Toronto Conference statement recommended that global carbon dioxide emissions be reduced by 20 percent from 1988 levels by the year 2005.[15] In 1990 Prime Minister Thatcher promised that the United Kingdom had "set itself the demanding target of bringing carbon dioxide emissions back to this year's level by the year 2005."[16] Similarly, "a large majority of the industrialized states represented at the conference" meeting in Bergen, Norway, in May 1990 "agreed that they would stabilize the emission of CO_2 and other important greenhouse gases at 1990 levels by the year 2000."[17]

Knowledgeable onlookers realized that despite such commitments, it would be very difficult to duplicate the success of the Montreal Protocol.[18] The stage for the older agreement was set in 1985, when a British Antarctic Survey report made worldwide news by establishing the existence of a dramatic "hole" in the ozone layer.[19] The news media helped build public awareness and concern by describing the many potential dangers of the exposure to ultraviolet radiation resulting from ozone depletion. The agreed cause of the ozone hole was CFC emissions. By the mid-1980s, those chemicals were used primarily in the manufacture of foam insulation (about 25 percent of all CFC uses), as aerosol propellants (33 percent), as refrigerants (25 percent), and as cleansers in the electronics industry (16 percent).[20] These uses were not centrally important to the global economy; a small number of countries produced and consumed the overwhelming majority of the chemicals, and only about twenty companies manufactured billions of dollars worth of CFCs. Developing countries produced just 4 percent of CFCs—and China and India together consumed only about 2 percent of the world total. The U.S. Environmental Protection Agency (EPA) had already banned nonessential CFC use in 1978, and in 1986 U.S. industry leader DuPont announced that it could likely develop and market substitutes for CFCs within a decade. The United States even assumed an international leadership role in the negotiations. In all, this was a welcoming context in which to negotiate an agreement.

The economic and political situation facing the INC participants in the 1990s was dramatically different, and negotiators were aware of the substantial barriers to cooperation on global warming. Despite evidence backed by a fairly strong scientific consensus, many Americans continued to contest the need to act upon what they considered uncertain information. A small number of scientists willing to challenge the assembled evidence pointing toward global warming assumed prominent positions in the public debate. Many of them were funded by oil companies, such as Exxon Mobil. Additional resistance stemmed from the consumption of fossil fuels by virtually every nation and the expense and difficulty of adopting substitutes. Coal and petroleum use was and remains integral to the economic livelihood of dozens of countries. Fossil fuels provide power for electricity generation, heating, automobiles, and a substantial proportion of worldwide industrial activity. Politically potent business interests have strong stakes in the status quo, as do national producers of fossil fuels, such as the members of the Organization of Petroleum Exporting Countries (OPEC).[21]

Despite these challenges, during the 1990s negotiators worked toward a meaningful climate change treaty after the General Assembly created the INC. From February 1991, the INC met five times to draft a Framework Convention on Climate Change in advance of the UN Conference on Environment and Development, which was held in June 1992 at Rio de Janeiro, Brazil. Because INC negotiators knew that the Earth Summit, as the gathering is popularly known, was symbolically important, they effectively operated under a deadline and made rapid progress in the sessions leading up to the June conference. During the negotiations, however, the United States refused to agree to targeted greenhouse gas emission reductions and legally binding timetables; therefore, the FCCC did not include such provisions. As the world leader in emissions, the United States could effectively block any requirements by threatening not to go along with the treaty.

In the final FCCC agreement presented at the Rio conference, the industrialized nations (listed in a document designated "Annex I") agreed merely to "aim" to return their greenhouse gas emissions to 1990 levels by the year 2000. The Annex I countries were also charged with developing national policies to mitigate greenhouse gas emissions, although they were allowed the option of "joint implementation." In practice, this meant they could obtain credit for reductions by helping other nations—potentially including those in the developing world—reduce their emissions. The convention also created transparency measures requiring countries to provide to the FCCC secretariat inventories of greenhouse gas emissions and reports on their development of national emission reduction plans. Poor countries had attempted to secure pledges of increased development assistance to help them acquire the means to reduce their emissions, but the agreement did not include a provision for such aid. Yet the world's richest nations were required "to provide new and additional financial resources to meet the agreed full cost" for developing countries to meet their transparency requirements. At the Earth Summit, the Global Environment Facility (GEF) was named as the interim agency to pool and distribute these financial resources. In 1999, after significant restructuring, the GEF became the treaty's permanent financial mechanism.

More than 150 states signed the agreement in Rio, and 191 countries and the EU are members as of December 2012. The United States was the first industrialized nation to ratify the convention, which entered into force in March 1994, three months after the fiftieth ratification. The FCCC established a Conference of the Parties (COP), composed of all member states, which meets regularly to discuss key unresolved issues. At the spring 1995 COP-1 meeting in Berlin, the Alliance of Small Island States (AOSIS) pressed mightily for a protocol that would require emissions reductions. AOSIS diplomats have strong interests in climate change because their nations are vulnerable to future increases in sea level caused by melting polar ice caps. COP-1 did not yield emissions reductions, however, as very few states were prepared to make a formal commitment. In December 1995, the IPCC released its Second Assessment Report, which bolstered the arguments of countries seeking firm reduction requirements.[22] Nonetheless, the 1996 COP-2 meeting in Geneva also failed to reach agreement on this issue. The Clinton administration made an important concession, however, by committing the United States to legally binding reductions on greenhouse gas emissions; the precise figures were to be negotiated.

The December 1997 COP-3 meeting in Kyoto, Japan, yielded the first legally binding commitments by countries to reduce greenhouse gas emissions. Under the Kyoto Protocol, countries were assigned varying reduction goals, and the timetable for reaching the goals was expressed as an average over the five years from 2008 to 2012. The United States agreed to a target of a 7 percent reduction in greenhouse gas emissions from the 1990 base year. The actual U.S. obligation to reduce emissions was mitigated significantly by the acceptance of its plan to credit countries for the successful management of so-called carbon "sinks" (mainly forested areas that absorb carbon dioxide) by employing environmentally friendly land-use techniques and innovative forestry practices. The major negotiating parties remained deeply divided about many proposed provisions, and as a result the Kyoto Protocol actually reflected only limited agreement. To their credit, the states overcame most divisions about the specific emissions reductions that would be required and the various gases that the treaty would cover.

The Kyoto deal did not, however, successfully resolve two key U.S. concerns, which were influenced as much by domestic as by international political factors. First, the agreement ignored the U.S. demand that developing countries be required to reduce greenhouse gas emissions. The United States worried that developed states might make significant and costly reductions but see their efforts diluted by states like China and India substantially increasing their fossil fuel consumption and greenhouse gas emissions even as they gained a comparative economic advantage.[23] Poorer countries argued that they should be exempted from making reductions: they had not contributed much to the atmospheric changes that dated back to the start of the Industrial Revolution, and they expelled only a small fraction of the emissions of wealthier countries on a per capita basis.[24] Many nongovernmental organizations agreed that it was unjust for wealthy countries to demand reductions in the use of fossil fuels by the world's most impoverished inhabitants.

Second, the United States strongly favored market-friendly emissions trading and joint implementation plans. Economists often argue that such approaches reduce the costs of pollution abatement because they encourage greater efficiency as compared with regulatory approaches. Most American businesses vulnerable to environmental regulation prefer market-based mechanisms, such as "cap-and-trade" approaches, which typically allow businesses to buy and sell pollution permits in order to meet local, regional, or national caps on pollution. However, influential environmental groups, such as Friends of the Earth, argue against global adoption of such mechanisms. These groups fear that industrialized states will refuse to make any technological or resource-use changes if they have the option of "joint implementation." Polluters from advanced countries might merely build new factories in nonindustrial nations to offset treaty obligations.[25] In the end, resolution of this particular dispute was deferred until future COP meetings.

Domestic politics influenced U.S. positions on these points as Congress seemed determined not to allow the Clinton administration to commit to any real emissions reductions. On July 25, 1997, the Senate voted 95–0 in support of S.Res. 98, cosponsored by Democrat Robert Byrd, from coal-rich West Virginia, and newcomer Chuck Hagel (R-NE). The nonbinding resolution indicated the sense of the Senate that it would not ratify any protocol that would "result in serious harm to the economy" or that would "mandate new commitments to limit or reduce greenhouse gas emissions for the Annex I Parties, unless the protocol or other agreement also mandates new specific scheduled commitments to limit or reduce greenhouse gas emissions for Developing Country Parties within the same compliance period."[26] The resolution also required that any future agreement forwarded to the Senate for approval be accompanied by a detailed explanation of regulatory or other legal action that would be needed for implementation, as well as a detailed financial analysis of the costs to the economy.

The Clinton administration signed the Kyoto accord in November 1998, but pointed to the Byrd-Hagel resolution and indicated that it would not submit the agreement to the Senate for "advice and consent" until gaining commitments from developing countries not yet covered by the treaty obligations to reduce their greenhouse gas emissions. This delay was globally significant; for the Kyoto Protocol to become binding, it had to be ratified by at least fifty-five countries "which accounted in total for at least 55 per cent of the total carbon dioxide emissions for 1990 of the Parties included in Annex I."[27]

While countries debated whether to ratify Kyoto, they continued to meet to address unresolved issues. In several successive COP meetings through the late 1990s, negotiators engaged in ongoing talks about enforcement of the Kyoto-mandated emissions reductions, emissions trading proposals, and possible credits for greenhouse gas "sinks." In the various meetings, Clinton's negotiators sought both joint implementation and developing-country participation. The parties were apparently close to a deal concerning implementation questions at the November 2000 COP-6 meeting at The Hague, but the bargaining collapsed over the issue of carbon "sinks" and "reservoirs." The United States, Canada, and Japan wanted generous credits for various land uses and forestry practices, whereas the EU nations wanted to limit such credits.[28] The meeting was widely viewed as a failure, and environmental groups largely blamed the United States, which some argued was trying to gain climate credits for ordinary agricultural practices.

Thus, as the Clinton presidency ended, many environmentalists hoped that a new administration would be able both to convince the next Senate to ratify the Kyoto Protocol and to negotiate a follow-on compliance and implementation agreement with the rest of the world.

The Bush–Exxon Mobil Years

Republican George W. Bush entered the White House in 2001 after narrowly defeating Vice President Al Gore in a drawn-out and contentious political process. Gore was an environmentalist and strong supporter of Kyoto. Bush, by contrast, had worked in the oil industry before serving as governor of Texas, and was opposed to the Kyoto accord, claiming that it provided unfair trade advantages to unregulated economic competitors like China.

On the day of Bush's inauguration, the IPCC released a new report on the scientific basis of global warming that predicted temperature increases substantially greater than prior reports had expected.[29] The next round of negotiations on Kyoto was delayed from May until July at the new president's request, so that his administration would have time to evaluate and develop U.S. climate policy. Internally, there was some support in the administration for regulating carbon dioxide, but support for the Kyoto Protocol was weak at best. Secretary of the Treasury Paul O'Neill circulated a memo promoting a comprehensive domestic approach to global warming, but he too thought the treaty reflected bad policy.[30] The new EPA administrator, Christine Todd Whitman, publicly advocated a regulatory approach, which would include carbon dioxide, and by March media reports suggested that the administration might announce a plan to regulate greenhouse gas emissions from power plants.

However, the prospect of a new regulatory scheme met strong opposition from conservatives who were skeptical about climate science and from industry groups that opposed new environmental standards. Faced with the risk of alienating Republican support in an evenly divided Senate, the White House simply dumped the regulatory proposal from the agenda.[31] The president told key Republican senators, "I do not believe . . . that the government should impose on power plants mandatory emissions reductions for carbon dioxide, which is not a 'pollutant' under the Clean Air Act."[32] Two weeks after abandoning the domestic plan to regulate emissions, Administrator Whitman further announced that the administration considered the Kyoto Protocol "dead" and that the United States had "no interest in implementing that treaty."[33] Environmentalists and many European governments were furious. Although the Bush administration avoided any mandatory international or domestic climate measures, it did pursue two distinct climate-related strategies. Publicly, the administration promoted "business friendly" voluntary programs, such as the Climate Leaders and Climate Vision programs, which did nothing to slow the annual increase in U.S. emissions.[34] Behind the scenes, the administration worked to manipulate public debate about the scientific evidence on climate change. For example, the administration stripped the entire global warming section from the final 2002 EPA report on air pollution.[35] The manipulation was widespread. At a January 2007 House Oversight and Government Reform Committee hearing, the Union of Concerned Scientists (UCS) and Government Accountability Project presented survey results finding that many federal scientists and officials had been subjected to political pressures to downplay the risks of global warming. Rep. Henry Waxman (D-CA), a newly empowered committee chair, condemned the apparent "orchestrated campaign to mislead the public about climate change."[36]

The Bush administration was certainly not working alone in trying to shape the domestic debate to its liking. Exxon Mobil Corporation—then the largest company in the United States—distributed millions of dollars to dozens of think tanks that the leading British scientific academy, the Royal Society, said "misrepresented the science of climate change by outright denial of the evidence."[37] Exxon Mobil's role can perhaps be readily explained by the fact that its products emit more carbon dioxide than all but five countries. Greenpeace released State Department briefing papers from the period 2001–2004, obtained through a Freedom of Information Act request, revealing that the Bush administration sought the company's "active involvement" on climate policy. One briefing note written for Under Secretary of State Paula Dobriansky claimed that the president "rejected Kyoto in part based on input" from an industry group substantially funded by Exxon Mobil.[38]

The International Community Moves Forward

With U.S. withdrawal from the climate negotiations, the EU grabbed the leadership mantle in hopes of ensuring the Kyoto Protocol's implementation. In June 2001, European environment ministers unanimously passed a resolution affirming their countries' intentions to ratify the treaty, and they began to court Russia and Japan in an effort to put the treaty into force without the United States. At July 2001 COP-6 meetings in Bonn, the strategy seemed to work, as the EU was able to bring the parties together on a compromise over implementation rules. To reach a deal, the Europeans acceded to the Japanese position on carbon-trapping "sinks" and compromised on a Russian desire for emissions trading. These developments likely would have pleased Clinton negotiators, but the Bush administration was unmoved. U.S. officials reiterated complaints that the treaty did not go far enough to require action by developing countries, such as China and India.[39] Under Secretary Dobriansky was booed at the conference when she claimed that the United States remained committed to preventing climate change.[40]

The EU nations collectively ratified the Kyoto Protocol in May 2002, and Japan and Canada followed later that year. After a lengthy bargaining period, Russian president Vladimir Putin was able to extract Europe's backing for his country's accession to the World Trade Organization in exchange for a promise to ratify Kyoto.[41] This meant that the agreement had sufficient Annex I membership, and the treaty became binding on parties in February 2005. The international community proved capable of negotiating and ratifying climate deals without U.S. cooperation. Given the volume of U.S. emissions, however, its future position on this issue remained centrally important.

Subnational Action

After the Bush administration pronounced Kyoto "dead," many members of Congress fruitlessly pursued legislative means to limit U.S. greenhouse gas emissions. In fact, 511 bills, resolutions, and amendments "specifically addressing climate" change were introduced in Congress from 2001 through 2008.[42] Fully 235 pieces of legislation were introduced in the 110th Congress alone after Democrats took majority control of both chambers after the November 2006 elections. Despite this energetic activity, not a single piece of binding legislation addressing climate change was passed during the Bush years.

Absent federal action on emissions reductions and climate change, numerous local and state governments moved to combat climate change, typically through collective initiatives and often modeled on the goals and mechanisms of the Kyoto Protocol. For instance, more than 1,000 executives from cities in every state signed the US Mayors Climate Protection Agreement, committing local governments to work independently to meet Kyoto standards and to promote state and national governments to adopt climate legislation.[43] Moreover, the Pew Center on Global Climate Change found that states took the lead on climate policy in the first decade of the twenty-first century. By 2011, thirty-six states had adopted comprehensive climate action plans or had them in development.[44] California especially has been at the forefront of these efforts as the first state to enact a comprehensive climate plan that includes regulating power plant emissions and a statewide cap-and-trade program and in pushing for progressive car efficiency standards.[45] Because California has such a large market share of automobiles and gasoline consumption in the US, regulations in that state can affect the economy as a whole. And California legislators were explicit that this was their goal.[46] Auto regulations provide a strong example. In July 2002, Sacramento passed the first legislation in the United States to restrict greenhouse gas emissions from noncommercial vehicles.[47] The statute required that new "maximum" but "economically feasible" auto emission standards be set by 2005, so as to be incorporated into new car models sold by 2009.[48] Twelve states announced plans to follow California's rules, prompting a lawsuit in 2005 by automakers to block implementation of the new standards.

In December 2007, a federal judge upheld California's law regulating auto emissions, affirming the state's right to establish strict air standards if granted a waiver from the EPA.[49] Later the same month, however, the EPA denied California's waiver—the first time ever in thirty years under the Clean Air Act. Though the denial prompted outcries from states and Congress, then–EPA head Stephen L. Johnson defended the decision: "The Bush administration is moving forward with a clear national solution, not a confusing patchwork of state rules."[50]

Building on the advances made by California's clean car law, many other states began to look for regional solutions to combat global warming. The first regional plan to gain national attention involved northeastern states, and was initiated by Gov. George Pataki (R-NY). In April 2003, Pataki invited the governors of nearby states to participate in developing a "cap-and-trade" program for reducing greenhouse gas emissions. Connecticut, Delaware, Maine, Massachusetts, New Hampshire, New Jersey, Rhode Island, and Vermont joined New York in forming the Regional Greenhouse Gas Initiative (RGGI) and began negotiating a plan loosely based on the Kyoto Protocol to lower emission levels. The nine northeastern and mid-Atlantic state members (Maryland joined in 2007, but New Jersey withdrew in 2011) embraced a plan that caps power plant emissions through 2014 and will reduce them 2.5 percent annually, or by 10 percent in total, by 2018.[51] The initiative held its first permit auction in September 2008, capping emissions from 233 power plants.[52] The RGGI could serve as a model for a national cap-and-trade plan. In February 2007, the governors of Arizona, California, New Mexico, Oregon, and Washington followed the pathway blazed by RGGI and collectively formed the Western Climate Initiative (WCI), with the goal to reduce greenhouse gas emissions 15 percent below 2005 levels by 2020.[53] By 2008, the WCI had grown to include seven western state partners and four Canadian provinces. Gov. Arnold Schwarzenegger (R-CA) lauded the agreement as showing "the power of the states to lead our nation."[54] The initial plan of the initiative instituted limits on the importation of coal-fired power from other states, required greenhouse gas emission reporting, and planned to open a cap-and-trade program among the member states. Support for the WCI waned with the financial crisis, however, and in 2011 all of the U.S. states involved, with the exception of California, officially withdrew from the agreement. The remaining members plan to go forward and implement a cap-and-trade system in January 2013.[55]

States won a significant legal victory in 2007 when the Supreme Court issued its decision in the case of *Massachusetts v. Environmental Protection Agency*. The matter began in 1999 when a group of environmental scientists petitioned the EPA to regulate carbon dioxide and other greenhouse gases under the 1970 Clean Air Act, which Congress renewed in 1990. The Bush administration refused to regulate carbon dioxide, however, claiming it was not a pollutant and that the EPA therefore had no authority to impose standards. The EPA rejected the petition in 2003 and questioned the relationship between automobile emissions and global climate change. The agency's decision was upheld in 2005 by a 2–1 ruling in the U.S. Court of Appeals, but California, New York, ten other states, and three cities joined the environmentalists to challenge the ruling. In April 2007, the Supreme Court ruled 5–4 that carbon dioxide and other greenhouse gases are pollutants, that the EPA has the legal authority to regulate emissions, and that states have the right to sue the EPA over its refusal to do so.[56] Despite the ruling, the EPA delayed issuing rules on greenhouse gases and sought public comments, effectively pushing any administrative action on climate change onto the succeeding president.

Business Reconsiders

President Bush called global climate change a "serious challenge" in his January 2007 State of the Union speech, which marked the first time he had referenced the problem in his annual agenda-setting address.[57] However, the administration did not suddenly reverse course and embrace mandatory domestic and international greenhouse gas reductions. Likewise, longtime industry opponents of greenhouse regulations, like Exxon Mobil, continued to fund groups working against regulation while attempting to change their public image.[58] Many other businesses, however, began taking dramatically different positions.

In 2006, ten major corporations, including Alcoa, BP America, Caterpillar, DuPont, General Electric, and Wal-Mart, joined with environmental groups to form the United States Climate Action Partnership (USCAP). Notably, USCAP's January 2007 report advocated mandatory greenhouse gas reductions. The chair of Duke Energy, Jim Rogers, said at its press conference, "It must be mandatory, so there is no doubt about our actions. . . . The science of global warming is clear. We know enough to act now. We must act now."[59] This message appears to be spreading in the business community, as Apple and a number of utility companies withdrew from the Chamber of Commerce in 2009 because of the group's opposition to domestic climate change policy. Nike and Johnson & Johnson likewise publicly expressed their disapproval of the Chamber's anti-environmental activism.[60]

In the mid-1980s, the Montreal Protocol negotiations gained tremendous momentum once DuPont and other chemical companies abandoned all-out opposition to an ozone accord and signaled their willingness to live with regulation—and to research and develop potentially profitable substitutes for CFCs.[61] Similar bottom-line concerns help explain why some companies are now reversing course on climate change. Many simply want their brand to be "greened," while power companies promoting nuclear energy or other alternatives have more direct financial interests. As company president John Hofmeister explains, "From Shell's point of view, the debate is over. When 98 percent of scientists agree, who is Shell to say, 'Let's debate the science'?"[62] Industry's reversal can also be explained by the unpredictable political situation that the state initiatives have created. Many companies prefer a single national policy, likely based on market mechanisms such as cap-and-trade. Even Exxon Mobil vice president for public affairs Kenneth P. Cohen acknowledges, "One thing heavy industry cannot live with is a patchwork quilt of regulations."[63]

The Obama Era

After eight years of federal inaction on climate change, the 2008 U.S. presidential election clearly held the promise of change, regardless of which candidate won the presidency. Both major-party candidates, Republican senator John McCain and Democratic senator Barack Obama, had previously cosponsored legislation to reduce carbon emissions. Both candidates also publicly stated the need for increased U.S. cooperation with the international community.[64] Obama had the more ambitious proposal, as his plan called for an 80 percent reduction in greenhouse gases, $150 billion in clean energy investments, and a national cap-and-trade system. Campaigning in New Hampshire in October 2007, Obama stated, "No business will be allowed to emit any greenhouse gases for free. Businesses don't own the sky, the public does, and if we want them to stop polluting it, we have to put a price on all pollution."[65] Two weeks after his victory, Obama told the Bi-Partisan Governors Global Climate Summit,

> Few challenges facing America and the world are more urgent than combating climate change. . . . Now is the time to confront this challenge once and for all. Delay is no longer an option. Denial is no longer an acceptable response.[66]

The Obama administration entered the White House with a strong climate agenda, but this policy energy was soon overshadowed by a prolonged economic and political crisis and a contentious battle over healthcare legislation. However, the administration was able to push forward climate-oriented reforms through executive orders, direct command-and-control regulation, and through coupling reforms to other legislation. The first step the new president took was to create a cabinet with a record of supporting climate change policy. Additionally, the White House created a new Office of Energy and Climate Change Policy and appointed as its head Clinton's EPA administrator Carol Browner. Other initial appointments included alternative energy expert and Nobel laureate Steven Chu as secretary of energy, environmental policy analyst John P. Holdren as assistant for science and technology, and experienced environmental regulator Lisa Jackson as EPA administrator. These appointments stood in stark contrasted to the oil industry ties of many Bush-era officials.[67]

The new administration acted on climate issues almost immediately with a set of presidential memorandums issued in January 2009. One directed the Department of Transportation (DOT) to establish tougher fuel efficiency standards for vehicles. Another ordered the EPA to reconsider the Bush administration's denial of California's waiver application, which would allow states to set higher restrictions on vehicle greenhouse gas emissions.[68] In February, the Energy Department was directed to implement aggressive efficiency standards for household appliances. The DOT order led to a new national policy announced in May that increased fuel efficiency and limited greenhouse gas emissions from cars and trucks. The new fuel standards resulted from bargaining among the states requesting the EPA waiver, automakers, and the administration. In the deal, California agreed to amend its 2002 car emissions law to conform to the new national standard beginning in 2012.[69] In June, the EPA granted California its waiver to set its own emission standards, and in October the president signed an executive order requiring all federal agencies to set a greenhouse gas emissions reduction target for 2020.

Perhaps the most significant initiative the administration launched involves EPA preparation to regulate greenhouse gas emissions directly under the Clean Air Act, as prompted by *Massachusetts v. Environmental Protection Agency*.[70] Throughout 2009, the Obama administration set into motion the various steps required for the EPA to regulate greenhouse gases. Due to the sometimes arcane proposal, commentary, and oversight procedures involved in creating or changing regulatory rules, the federal bureaucratic process to establish EPA standards advanced slowly in incremental steps. In April 2009, the EPA announced that it expected to find carbon dioxide and five other greenhouse gases to be pollutants and a threat to human health and welfare. An "endangerment finding" is a necessary precondition to regulate emissions under the Clean Air Act. When congressional Republicans asked for a delayed finding and questioned the underlying science, Administrator Jackson refused:

> We know that skeptics have and will continue to try to sow doubts about the science. . . . But raising doubts—even in the face of overwhelming evidence—is a tactic that has been used by defenders of the status quo for years.[71]

In September, the EPA finalized a new rule that began requiring mandatory reporting of greenhouse gasses from large emitters. The agency also announced a proposal to regulate large emitters, primarily power plants. While the proposed "tailoring rule" exempts small businesses and family farms, the EPA assumed "authority for the greenhouse gas emissions of 14,000 coal burning power plants, refiners and big industrial complexes that produce most of the nation's greenhouse gas pollution."[72] The final endangerment finding was released in December 2009 to coincide with the opening of the Copenhagen climate conference.

The issuing of the final endangerment finding by the EPA sparked both legislative and legal opposition by groups opposed to climate regulation. In 2010, Texas and Virginia led a coalition of fourteen states and industry groups in opposing the endangerment finding, seeking, in effect, to undo the Supreme Court's decision in *Massachusetts v. E.P.A.* Texas Republican Governor Rick Perry said that "the EPA's misguided plan paints a big target on the backs of Texas agriculture and energy producers and the hundreds of thousands of Texans they employ."[73] The U.S. Court of Appeals in Washington DC, however, upheld the EPA's endangerment finding and agreed that the agency is required to regulate greenhouse gases under the Clean Air Act. The appellate court also upheld the EPA's authority to regulate auto and power plant emissions.[74] The ruling, all the same, does not guarantee regulation, as Congress could pass legislation modifying or curtailing the EPA's authority. Despite the EPA movement on this issue, Carol Browner explains that the Obama administration would prefer that Congress act to address climate change:

> The best path forward is through legislation, rather than through sort of the weaving together the various authorities of the Clean Air Act, which may or may not end in a cap-and-trade program. You can get the clearest instruction by passing legislation.[75]

Yet, a statutory solution seems beyond the reach of a politically dead-locked Congress. While the 111th Congress moved closer to enacting binding climate legislation than any prior session, the body still fell far short of implementing greenhouse gas controls into law. In June 2009, in fact, the House of Representatives passed the first U.S. legislation ever seeking to control greenhouse gases. The American Clean Energy and Security Act (ACES), introduced by Reps. Henry Waxman (D-CA) and Edward Markey (D-MA), included support for alternative energy and efficiency targets, but it most significantly established an economy-wide cap-and-trade system for greenhouse gases and established both concrete and bold emission targets—a 17 percent reduction from 2005 levels by 2020 and an 83 percent cut by 2050.[76] The bill faced significant opposition from both House Republicans and private groups, and the final product reflected intense last-minute deal-making and political compromise.[77] Because the compromises included limits on the EPA's authority, some environmental groups called on Congress to reject the bill. On June 26, however, the House narrowly passed ACES 219–212, with forty-four Democrats voting against the bill and only eight Republicans voting in favor.

The Senate took up climate legislation next, but proponents faced major political obstacles. Indeed, Senate Democrats split the provisions of the House bill into two separate proposals, with the less controversial energy provisions in the American Clean Energy Leadership Act and the cap-and-trade provisions in the Clean Energy Jobs and American Power Act. Democrats were able to move both bills out of committee, but once on the Senate floor, they stalled. John Kerry (D-MA), Joseph Lieberman (I-CT), and, for a short time, Lindsey Graham (R-SC) worked to build a consensus before bringing the legislation to a vote, but they faced strong opposition from Senate Republicans and some Democrats.[78] On climate change, Senate Democrats are split between the members from the coasts and the so-called "Brown Dogs" from the Midwest and Great Plains, which rely on coal and manufacturing. In August 2009, ten Brown Dog senators sent Obama a letter stating that they would not support any climate legislation lacking trade protections for industries in their states.[79] After the death of Senator Edward Kennedy (D-MA) and the subsequent unexpected special election victory by Scott Brown (R-MA), who became the forty-first Republican senator, Democrats could no longer gather the 60 votes needed to guarantee cloture and bring any bill to a vote. Republicans successfully employed this version of the filibuster at an unprecedented rate in the

111th Congress, and in July of 2010, Senate Majority Leader Harry Reid (D-NV) announced that upcoming energy legislation would not include the climate provisions from the bills, effectively killing climate change legislation until the next Congress.[80]

Though no climate legislation was passed, the Obama administration was able to pass some related measures it supported by coupling them to other legislation, most significantly the auto industry bailout and the Recovery Act. The American and global auto industries were severely affected both by the global financial downturn in 2008 and by rising fuel costs. American car companies were hit particularly hard because many had made luxury and large size the focus of their vehicle lines, long neglecting fuel economy. When the financial crisis hit, the "big three" U.S. auto companies faced bankruptcy and pleaded with Washington for emergency loans to remain solvent. As part of the bailout, Chrysler and General Motors were restructured under the guiding hand of the Obama administration. GM emerged as majority-owned by the U.S. government, while Chrysler emerged majority-owned by the United Autoworkers union with Fiat in management.[81] Both companies were required to reduce costs and develop more fuel- and energy-efficient vehicles. The administration also implemented a "cash-for-clunkers" program to stimulate demand for fuel-efficient cars and remove some inefficient ones from the roadways.[82] The Recovery Act, passed in February 2009 to stimulate the national economy, contained modest support for other projects that could reduce greenhouse emissions, including investments for energy efficiency and smart grid development.

The 2010 midterm elections proved to be a resounding defeat for House Democrats, with Republicans gaining a net of sixty-three seats and reclaiming the House majority for the 112th Congress. Republicans also gained six seats in the Senate, bringing their total caucus to forty-seven members, ensuring a virtual deadlock in that chamber, given the continued common use of the cloture procedure to block Senate votes on legislation. Nonetheless, the 112th Congress, in session 2011 and 2012, saw the introduction of more than 100 bills dealing with climate change—fifty-two to strengthen climate provisions, but also fifty-five to block or hinder ongoing or future climate regulation, with most of the latter aimed at stripping the EPA of its power. Others were proposed to limit or preclude ongoing U.S. participation in international negotiations.[83] None of the bills passed, however, reflecting the general gridlock in Washington during this period.

Looking forward to Barack Obama's second term, it is unclear whether the administration will be able to expand on the modest energy- and climate-related reforms it pursued successfully in the first term. The 2012 presidential election resulted in a narrow but clear victory for Obama, but climate change was rarely an issue in the long political cycle. The 113th Congress remains split between Republicans and Democrats. In the House, Democratic candidates won more votes nationally than their Republican opponents, but gerrymandering and other factors meant that they were only able to recover eight seats. Republicans continue to hold a strong majority. Democrats also gained two seats in the Senate, but the forty-five-member Republican caucus can continue to block legislative action unless the rules about the filibuster are dramatically changed.

A number of unusual weather events in 2012 began to bring climate change back into mainstream political conversation, where it had been vastly overshadowed by the economic crisis and other issues for most of Obama's first term. In the US, 2012 was the hottest year on record, according to data provided by the National Climatic Data Center.[84] Arctic sea ice is at the lowest point ever measured and springtime snow melted at an even faster rate.[85] Much of the US was also devastated by the most severe drought in 25 years, lasting from 2010 to 2012, due in large part due to record low levels of snowfall in North America.[86] Most politically significant, however, was the devastation inflicted by Hurricane Sandy in late October, the largest Atlantic hurricane on record. The storm flooded lower portions of New York City, New Jersey, and surrounding areas, and according to the best estimates, caused at least $50 billion in damages and killed as many as 121 people.[87] Sandy has emerged as a powerful symbolic call for action on climate change, both in the US and around the world, but it remains to be seen whether it will spur legislation. In his victory speech on election night, President Obama placed global warming among the most significant challenges facing the US: "We want our children to live in an America that isn't burdened by debt, that isn't weakened by inequality, that isn't threatened by the destructive power of a warming planet."[88]

Conclusion: Climate Change Policy into the Future

The COP-18 climate conference, held at Doha, Qatar from November 26 to December 8, 2012, did not yield a comprehensive new binding agreement requiring nations to reduce greenhouse gas emissions throughout the twenty-first century. Instead, the delegates from nearly 200 nations agreed on a package deal called the "Doha Climate Gateway." Under this accord, the expiring Kyoto Protocol was extended to 2020. However, many parties to that original climate treaty did not make a new commitment, including Canada, Japan, New Zealand, and Russia. Canada, in fact, has formally withdrawn from the Kyoto Protocol. Australia and the European Union countries, plus about ten other states, agreed to extend their commitment to Kyoto but did not increase their emission reduction obligations. Altogether, the remaining Kyoto parties emit only about 15 percent of the greenhouse gases released into the atmosphere each year.

The Kyoto treaty is supposed to be replaced by a universal climate agreement that is scheduled to be concluded by 2015 and implemented in 2020. Under the new agreement, which will be negotiated over the next few years, all states will be bound to make emissions reductions, not merely the advanced industrial nations. Given that China's per capita emissions have nearly equaled the per capita emissions of Europe, this is a significant change.[89] In the U.S, it is not difficult to imagine President Obama signing a treaty in 2015, just as Bill Clinton signed Kyoto years ago. However, the consent of the Senate will not be won without a difficult political battle involving major economic stakeholders.

Additionally, at Doha, the wealthiest countries agreed to contribute $100 billion annually by 2020 to compensate poorer countries for the "loss and damage" related to climate change. Although wealthy states had previously promised to provide climate-related economic and technical assistance, this was the first time that they acknowledged culpability for their past emissions. At the COP-15 meetings in Copenhagen in 2009, for instance, affluent states had promised to provide $100 billion per year by 2020 to help poor states adapt to climate change. Until 2020, the latest deal "encourages" rich nations to provide at least $10 billion annually leading up to implementation of a new agreement.[90] Again, these international promises will not be fulfilled until nations like the US affirm them domestically.

Within the US, forward movement to address climate change will likely continue to face many political obstacles. Even the scientific findings remain subject to intense partisan battles. For instance, just after the Doha Climate Gateway was negotiated, many details of the IPCC's Fifth Assessment were posted on a website called Stop Green Suicide by a climate skeptic who is also one of the 800 expert reviewers of the report. The scientist who leaked the draft document was attempting to undermine the report, not due until September 2013, by emphasizing a small detail about the potential warming caused by the sun's variable cosmic rays. His "whistleblowing" seemed at first glance to cast real doubt about the significance of the human contribution to global warming, and the story was quickly picked up by partisan political blogs and other media outlets.

However, in this case, the point the skeptic was attempting to make was quickly debunked and media attention soon refocused on the IPCC's apparent increasing level of confidence in linking human contributions to climate change. The draft document outlining the latest scientific consensus claims that it is "virtually certain" that global warming "is caused by human activities, primarily by the increase in CO_2 concentrations."[91] By "virtually certain" the scientists mean that they are 99% sure that humans' emissions are to blame for ongoing changes. The Fourth Assessment had expressed "very high confidence," which indicated 90% certainty.

The latest opinion poll findings suggest that the public largely understands the significance of these scientific claims—and acknowledges the need for meaningful policy responses. A December 2012 survey released by the Associated Press-GfK found that about four in five Americans believe climate change will be a serious problem for the US if "nothing is done to reduce global warming in the future."[92] In that poll, 57 percent of respondents replied that the U.S. government should do "a great deal" about global warming, and another 20 percent replied that the US should take "some" action.

Climate change is destined to remain on the foreign policy agenda for the foreseeable future. The ongoing and often passionate domestic and international political battles will determine whether or not the US takes action. If the scientists are correct, then the fate of the world will hinge on the result of these efforts.

Key Actors

George H. W. Bush   President; favored participation in the negotiation of the Framework Convention on Climate Change but refused to agree to specific emissions reductions.

George W. Bush   President; rejected the Kyoto Protocol because of concerns about the cost of compliance and because it required emissions reductions from advanced countries but not from less-developed nations.

Robert Byrd   Senator (D-WV); cosponsored S.Res. 98, which warned that the United States should not abide by a climate agreement that exempted developing countries.

Bill Clinton   President; favored the Kyoto Protocol but did not forward the agreement to the Senate because he knew it would likely meet defeat.

James E. Hansen   Director, NASA's Goddard Institute for Space Studies; outspoken scientist about the threat of global warming for more than twenty years.

Edward Markey   Representative (D-MA); cosponsored first climate legislation to pass either body of Congress.

Barack Obama   President; favors international and domestic limits on greenhouse gas emissions, but has not yet concluded policy actions that secure long-range reductions.

George Pataki   Governor (R-NY); worked with governors of other northeastern states to join New York in developing a regional initiative to reduce greenhouse gas emissions.

Arnold Schwarzenegger   Governor (R-CA); negotiated deals with his state legislature and neighboring states to cut greenhouse gas emissions and develop a regional cap-and-trade plan.

Henry Waxman   Representative (D-CA); cosponsored first climate legislation to pass either body of Congress.

Notes

1. Emphasis in the original. "Contribution of Working Group I to the Fourth Assessment Report of the Intergovernmental Panel on Climate Change," *Climate Change 2007: The Physical Science Basis, Summary for Policymakers* (Geneva: Intergovernmental Panel on Climate Change, February 2007), 2, 4, and 8, www.ipcc.ch/pdf/assessment-report/ar4/wg1/ar4-wg1-spm.pdf.

2. Quoted in Hannah K. Strange, "Clinton: Climate Change 'Greatest Threat,'" UPI.com, May 11, 2006, www.upi.com/Business_News/Security-Industry/2006/05/11/Clinton-Climate-change-greatest-threat/UPI-35051147366205/#ixzz2FR3hM5Cn.

3. Ban Ki-moon, "Remarks at 39th Plenary Assembly of the World Federation of United Nations Associations," August 10, 2009, www.un.org/apps/news/infocus/sgspeeches/search_full.asp?statID=555.

4. White House, Office of the Press Secretary, "President Bush Discusses Global Climate Change," June 11, 2001, georgewbush-whitehouse.archives.gov/news/releases/2001/06/20010611-2.html.

5. BBC News, "Where Countries Stand on Copenhagen," 2009, news.bbc.co.uk/2/hi/science/nature/8345343.stm.

6. Energy Information Administration, U.S. Department of Energy, *Emissions of Greenhouse Gases in the United States* (Washington, DC: U.S. Department of Energy, November 2006), 2, ftp://ftp.eia.doe.gov/pub/oiaf/1605/cdrom/pdf/ggrpt/057305.pdf.

7. Spencer Weart, "Roger Revelle's Discovery," *Discovery of Global Warming,* American Institute of Physics, August 2003, www.aip.org/history/climate/Revelle .htm.

8. Emphasis in the original. "Contribution of Working Group I," 5. The study defines this as at least a 9 out of 10 chance.

9. See IPCC, "Summary for Policymakers," *Climate Change 2007: Impacts, Adaptation, and Vulnerability. Contribution of Working Group II to the Fourth Assessment Report of the Intergovernmental Panel on Climate Change,* ed. M. L. Parry et al. (Cambridge: Cambridge University Press, 2007), 7–22.

10. Goddard Institute for Space Studies, "NASA Finds 2011 Ninth Warmest Year on Record," December 16, 2008, www.giss.nasa.gov/research/news/20120119/.

11. Robert H. Boyle, "You're Getting Warmer," *Audubon,* November–December 1999, www.audubonmagazine.org/global.html.

12. Craig Trumbo, "Longitudinal Modeling of Public Issues: An Application of the Agenda-Setting Process to the Issue of Global Warming," *Journalism and Mass Communication Monographs* 152 (August 1995): 1–57.

13. Margaret Thatcher, "Speech to the Royal Society," Fishmongers' Hall, London, September 27, 1988, www.margaretthatcher.org/document/107346.

14. David Bodansky, "Prologue to the Climate Change Convention," in *Negotiating Climate Change: The Inside Story of the Rio Convention,* ed. Irving M. Mintzer and J. A. Leonard (New York: Cambridge University Press, 1994), 52.

15. "News: Changing Atmosphere Conference," *Global Climate Change Digest* 1, no. 2 (August 1988), www.gcrio.org/gccd/gcc-digest/1988/d88aug1.htm.

16. Margaret Thatcher, "Speech at the 2nd World Climate Conference," Geneva, November 6, 1990, www.margaretthatcher.org/document/108237.

17. Information Unit on Climate Change, UN Environment Program, "The Bergen Conference and Its Proposals for Addressing Climate Change," May 1, 1993, www .unfccc.int/resource/ccsites/senegal/fact/fs220.htm.

18. See Marvis S. Soroos, *The Endangered Atmosphere: Preserving a Global Commons* (Columbia: University of South Carolina Press, 1997), chap. 6.

19. Richard Elliot Benedick, *Ozone Diplomacy: New Directions in Safeguarding the Planet* (Cambridge: Harvard University Press, 1991), 18–20.

20. Ibid., 119.

21. OPEC's eleven members collectively produce about 40 percent of the world's oil and hold about 75 percent of proven petroleum reserves.

22. IPCC reports are available at www.ipcc.ch.

23. China has emerged as the top source of emissions. See BBC, "Climate Change: Copenhagen in Graphics," November 24, 2009, news.bbc.co.uk/2/hi/science/nature/ 8359629.stm.

24. Per capita, Americans emit four times the greenhouse gases of Chinese people and sixteen times as much as Indians. See International Energy Agency, "CO_2 Emissions from Fuel Consumption, Highlights" 2009, 89–91, www.iea.org/c02highlights/C02high lights.pdf.

25. Peter Zollinger and Roger Dower, "Private Financing for Global Environmental Initiatives: Can the Climate Convention's 'Joint Implementation' Pave the Way?" *World Resources Institute Archive,* 1996, pubs.wri.org/pubs_content_text.cfm ?ContentID=372.

26. "S. Res. 98—Expressing the Sense of the Senate Regarding the United Nations Framework Convention on Climate Change," *Congressional Record,* June 12, 1997, S5622, www.gpo.gov/fdsys/pkg/CREC-1997-06-12/html/CREC-1997-06-12-pt1-PgS5622.htm.

27. See Article 25 of the Kyoto Protocol, www.unfccc.int/resource/docs/convkp/kpeng.html.

28. See Hermann E. Ott, "Climate Change: An Important Foreign Policy Issue," *International Affairs* 77 (2001): 277–296.

29. IPCC, Working Group I, Third Assessment Report, "Summary for Policymakers," *Climate Change 2001: The Scientific Basis* (Geneva: IPCC, 2001), www.ipcc.ch/ipccreports/tar/wg1/index.php?idp=5.

30. See Ron Suskind, *The Price of Loyalty; George W. Bush, the White House and the Education of Paul O'Neill* (New York: Simon and Schuster, 2004), 103–6.

31. Douglas Jehl and Andrew C. Revkin, "Bush, in Reversal, Won't Seek Cut in Emissions of Carbon Dioxide," *New York Times,* March 14, 2001, www.nytimes.com/2001/03/14/us/bush-in-reversal-won-t-seek-cut-in-emissions-of-carbon-dioxide.html.

32. George W. Bush, "Text of a Letter from the President to Senators Hagel, Helms, Craig, and Roberts," White House, Office of the Press Secretary, March 13, 2001, georgewbush-whitehouse.archives.gov/news/releases/2001/03/20010314.html.

33. Eric Pianin, "U.S. Aims to Pull Out of Warming Treaty," *Washington Post,* March 28, 2001, A1.

34. Environmental Protection Agency, "Executive Summary," *U.S. Greenhouse Gas Inventory Reports,* April 2009, ES-4, www.epa.gov/climatechange/emissions/usinventoryreport.html.

35. Jeremy Symons, "How Bush and Co. Obscure the Science," *Washington Post,* July 13, 2003, B4.

36. Ibid.

37. David Adam, "Royal Society Tells Exxon: Stop Funding Climate Change Denial," *The Guardian,* September 20, 2006, www.guardian.co.uk/environment/2006/sep/20/oilandpetrol.business.

38. John Vidal, "Revealed: How Oil Giant Influenced Bush," *The Guardian,* June 8, 2005, www.guardian.co.uk/climatechange/story/0,12374,1501646,00.html.

39. William Drozdiak, "U.S. Left Out of Warming Treaty; EU-Japan Bargain Saves Kyoto Pact," *Washington Post,* July 24, 2001, A1.

40. "U.S. Isolated after Global Warming Deal Reached," *USA Today,* July 23, 2001, www.usatoday.com/news/world/2001/07/23/warming.htm.

41. Peter Baker, "Russia Backs Kyoto to Get on Path to Join WTO," *Washington Post,* May 22, 2004, A15.

42. Pew Center on Global Climate Change, "What's Being Done in Congress," 2009, www.pewclimate.org/what_s_being_done/in_the_congress.

43. United States Conference of Mayors, "List of Participating Mayors," 2012, www.usmayors.org/climateprotection/list.asp.

44. Pew Center on Global Climate Change, "Climate Change 101: State Action," January 2011, www.c2es.org/docUploads/climate101-state.pdf.

45. "California Gets Landmark Green Law," BBC News, July 22, 2002, news.bbc.co.uk/2/hi/americas/2143615.stm.

46. William Booth, "Calif. Takes Lead on Auto Emissions," *Washington Post,* July 22, 2002, A1.

47. "California Gets Landmark Green Law."

48. Booth, "Calif. Takes Lead on Auto Emissions."

49. John M. Broder, "Federal Judge Upholds Law on Emissions in California," *New York Times,* December 13, 2007, www.nytimes.com/2007/12/13/washington/13emissions.html.

50. John M. Broder and Felicity Barringer, "E.P.A. Says 17 States Can't Set Emission Rules," *New York Times,* December 20, 2007, www.nytimes.com/2007/12/20/washington/20epa.html.

51. RGGI Inc., "States Initiate Bidding Process for March 2010 CO_2 Allowance Auction," January 12, 2010, www.rggi.org/docs/Auction_7_notice_news_release.pdf.

52. "Ten States with a Plan," *New York Times,* September 24, 2008, www.nytimes.com/2008/09/25/opinion/25thu2.html.

53. Pew Center on Global Climate Change, "Climate Change 101: State Action."

54. Timothy Gardner, "Western States United to Bypass Bush on Climate," *Reuters,* February 26, 2007, www.reuters.com/article/idUSN2630275420070226.

55. "Frequently Asked Questions" *Western Climate Initiative,* www.westernclimateinitiative.org/the-wci-cap-and-trade-program/faq.

56. Robert Barnes and Juliet Eilperin, "High Court Faults EPA on Inaction on Emissions; Critics of Bush Stance on Warming Claim Victory," *Washington Post,* April 3, 2007, A1.

57. White House, Office of the Press Secretary, "President Bush Delivers State of the Union Address," January 23, 2007, georgewbush-whitehouse.archives.gov/news/releases/2007/01/20070123–2.html.

58. David Adam, "ExxonMobil Continuing to Fund Climate Sceptic Groups, Records Show," *The Guardian,* July 1, 2009, www.guardian.co.uk/environment/2009/jul/01/exxon-mobil-climate-change-sceptics-funding.

59. "Companies Spell Out Warming Strategy," *MSNBC,* January 23, 2007, www.msnbc.msn.com/id/16753192/.

60. Michael Burnham and Anne C. Mulkern, "Enviros Waging 'Orchestrated Pressure Campaign' on Climate Bill—U.S. Chamber CEO," *New York Times,* October 9, 2009, www.nytimes.com/gwire/2009/10/09/09greenwire-enviros-waging-orchestrated-pressure-campaign-28715.html.

61. Soroos, *The Endangered Atmosphere,* 159–161.

62. Steven Mufson and Juliet Eilperin, "Energy Firms Come to Terms with Climate Change," *Washington Post,* November 25, 2006, A1.

63. Quoted in Steven Mufson, "Exxon Mobil Warming Up to Global Climate Issue," *Washington Post,* February 10, 2007, D1.

64. Pew Center on Global Climate Change, "Voter Guide: International Climate Agreements," 2009, www.pewclimate.org/voter-guide/international.

65. Jeff Zeleny, "Obama Proposes Capping Greenhouse Gas Emissions and Making Polluters Pay," *New York Times,* October 10, 2009, www.nytimes.com/2007/10/09/us/politics/09obama.html.

66. Office of the President-Elect, "President-elect Barack Obama to Deliver Taped Greeting to Bi-Partisan Governors Climate Summit," November 18, 2008, http://change.gov/newsroom/entry/president_elect_barack_obama_to_deliver_taped_greeting_to_bi_partisan_gover/.

67. Katty Kay, "Analysis: Oil and the Bush Cabinet," BBC News, January 29, 2001, news.bbc.co.uk/2/hi/americas/1138009.stm.

68. Bryan Walsh, "Obama's Move on Fuel Efficiency: A Clean Win for Greens," *Time,* January 26, 2009, www.time.com/time/health/article/0,8599,1874106,00.html. See the EPA's "Climate Change" homepage for a complete rundown of recent initiatives, www.epa.gov/climatechange/index.html.

69. Pew Center on Global Climate Change, "Federal Vehicle Standards," www.c2es.org/federal/executive/vehicle-standards.

70. Linda Greenhouse, "Justices Say E.P.A. Has Power to Act on Harmful Gases," *New York Times,* April 3, 2007, www.nytimes.com/2007/04/03/washington/03scotus.html.

71. John M. Broder, "Greenhouse Gases Imperil Health, E.P.A. Announces," *New York Times,* December 17, 2009, www.nytimes.com/2009/12/08/science/earth/08epa.html.

72. Ibid.

73. Robin Bravender, "Texas, Skeptics Seek Court Review of EPA's 'Endangerment' Finding," *New York Times,* Feb. 16, 2010, www.nytimes.com/gwire/2010/02/16/16greenwire-texas-skeptics-seek-court-review-of-epas-endan-12442.html.

74. Matthew L. Wald, "Court Backs E.P.A. Over Emissions Limits Intended to Reduce Global Warming," *New York Times,* June 26, 2012, www.nytimes.com/2012/06/27/science/earth/epa-emissions-rules-backed-by-court.html.

75. Darren Samuelsohn, "Obama Prefers Congress to EPA in Tackling Climate—Browner," *New York Times,* February 23, 2009, www.nytimes.com/cwire/2009/02/23/23climatewire-obama-prefers-congress-to-epa-when-it-comes-t-9800.html.

76. Suzanne Goldenberg, "Barack Obama's U.S. Climate Change Bill Passes Key Congress Vote," *The Guardian,* June 27, 2009, www.guardian.co.uk/environment/2009/jun/27/barack-obama-climate-change-bill.

77. The compromises included instituting protectionist trade policies, removing EPA authority to regulate G-H-Gs, and allowing the Department of Agriculture to regulate carbon offsets. Greg Hitt and Naftali Bendavid, "Obama Wary of Tariff Provision," *Wall Street Journal,* June 29, 2009, online.wsj.com/article/SB124621613011065523.html.

78. Center for Climate and Energy Solutions. "111th Congress Climate Change Legislation," www.c2es.org/federal/congress/111.

79. John M. Broder, "Climate Bill Is Threatened by Senators," *New York Times,* August 6, 2009, www.nytimes.com/2009/08/07/us/politics/07climate.html.

80. Center for Climate and Energy Solutions. "111th Congress Climate Change Legislation."

81. "Automotive Industry Crisis," *New York Times,* May 25, 2011. topics.nytimes.com/top/reference/timestopics/subjects/c/credit_crisis/auto_industry/index.html.

82. "Five Ways The Obama Administration Revived the Auto Industry by Reducing Oil Use," Think Progress, Aug 28, 2012, www.thinkprogress.org/climate/2012/08/28/754561/five-ways-the-obama-administration-revived-the-oil-industry-by-reducing-oil-use/.

83. Center for Climate and Energy Solutions, "Bills of the 112th Congress Concerning Climate Change," www.c2es.org/federal/congress/112/climate-change-legislative-proposals.

84. "Book It: 2012, The Hottest U.S. Year on Record," *Climate Central,* December 13, 2012, www.climatecentral.org/news/book-it-2012-the-hottest-year-on-record-15350.

85. Richard Harris, "As Arctic Ice Melts, So Does the Snow, and Quickly," *All Things Considered,* September 24, 2012, www.npr.org/2012/09/24/161701420/as-arctic-ice-melts-so-does-the-snow-and-quickly.

86. National Climatic Data Center, "State of the Climate, Drought, October 2012," November 15, 2012, www.ncdc.noaa.gov/sotc/drought/.

87. Jeanine Prezioso and Jonathan Allen, "Hurricane Sandy's NYC Death Toll Rises To 43; Northeast Still Cleaning Up after Devastation," *The Huffington Post,* November 11, 2012, www.huffingtonpost.com/2012/11/11/northeast-cleans-up-from-hurricane-sandy-death-toll-nyc-_n_2115375.html.

88. Roberta Rampton and Timothy Gardner, "Obama to Weigh Energy Boom, Climate Change in Second Term," *Chicago Tribune,* Nov. 7, 2012, articles.chicagotribune.com/2012–11–07/classified/sns-rt-us-usa-campaign-energybre8a625s-20121107_1_climate-change-oil-and-gas-climate-bill.

89. Connie Hedegaard, "Why the Doha Climate Conference Was a Success," *The Guardian,* December 14, 2012, www.guardian.co.uk/environment/2012/dec/14/doha-climate-conference-success.

90. Roger Harrabin, "UN Climate Talks Extend Kyoto Protocol, Promise Compensation," BBC News, December 8, 2012, www.bbc.co.uk/news/science-environment-20653018. See Copenhagen Accord, December 2009, www.unfccc.int/files/meetings/cop_15/application/pdf/cop15_cph_auv.pdf.

91. Leo Hickman, "Landmark Climate Change Report Leaked Online," *The Guardian,* December 14, 2012, www.guardian.co.uk/environment/2012/dec/14/ipcc-climate-change-report-leaked-online.

92. Seth Borenstein, "AP-GfK Poll: Belief in Global Warming Rises with Thermometers, Even among US Science Doubters," *AP-GfK,* December 14, 2012, www.ap-gfkpoll.com/uncategorized/our-latest-poll-findings-18.

13 National Security Surveillance: Unchecked or Limited Presidential Power?

Louis Fisher

Before You Begin

1. How does the Constitution balance the needs of national security against the rights and liberties of the individual?

2. In the field of national security, does the president possess "inherent" powers that are immune from legislative and judicial controls?

3. What principles should guide government in balancing the need for national security wiretaps against the constitutional right of privacy?

4. If Congress legislates in the area of foreign intelligence surveillance and selects a procedure that is "exclusive," can the president ignore the statutory command?

5. Is it sufficient for the president to notify eight lawmakers and have them briefed about national security wiretaps conducted without a judicial warrant?

6. What role should federal courts play in supervising and approving national security wiretaps?

Introduction

On December 16, 2005, the *New York Times* reported that in the months following the September 11 terrorist attacks, President George W. Bush secretly authorized the National Security Agency (NSA) to listen to international calls involving Americans and others inside the United States without a court-approved warrant. The agency had been monitoring international telephone calls and international e-mail messages over the past three years in an effort to obtain evidence about terrorist activity.[1]

NSA's statutory purpose, however, was to spy on communications abroad, not on American citizens or domestic activities. During the Nixon administration, it had crossed the line by engaging in domestic surveillance. After September 11, NSA violated the Foreign Intelligence Surveillance Act (FISA) of 1978, which requires the executive branch to seek warrants from the FISA Court to engage in surveillance in the United States. NSA's activity

Timeline

National Security Surveillance

October 25, 1978	Congress enacts the Foreign Intelligence Surveillance Act (FISA) to authorize and control national security surveillance.
September 11, 2001	Terrorists attack the United States, after which President George W. Bush authorizes warrantless national security surveillance (called the Terrorist Surveillance Program, or TSP).
December 16, 2005	The *New York Times* breaks the story on the existence of the TSP.
July 20, 2006	A federal district judge in California denies the government's motion to have a case dismissed that challenges the TSP.
July 25, 2006	A federal district judge in Illinois dismisses a lawsuit against a Bush administration program that involves the collection and monitoring of phone numbers.
August 17, 2006	A federal district judge in Michigan rules that the TSP violates the Constitution and federal statutes. She is reversed by the Sixth Circuit, and on February 19, 2008, the Supreme Court declines to take the case.
May 1, 2007	In congressional testimony, the director of national intelligence, Michael McConnell, appears to revive the administration's reliance on inherent powers after it had announced, earlier in the year, that it would abide by FISA.
July 2, 2008	A federal district court holds that FISA preempts the state secrets privilege offered by the administration to block court action.
July 10, 2008	Congress enacts legislation to provide immunity to the telecoms that assisted in NSA surveillance.
2009–2012	Litigation continues against NSA, especially in *Al-Haramain Islamic Foundation, Inc. v. Bush* and *Hepting v. AT&T.* The Supreme Court in 2012 accepts an electronic surveillance case, *Clapper v. Amnesty International.*
June 15, 2012	FISA Amendments Act Reauthorization Act of 2012 is introduced in the House of Representatives.
September 12, 2012	The House approves the FISA Reauthorization Act by a 301–118 vote.
December 28, 2012	The Senate approves the FISA Reauthorization Act by a 73–23 vote. President Obama signs it two days later.

raised the fundamental issue of whether the administration could violate statutory restrictions (FISA) by invoking "inherent" powers supposedly available to the president under Article II of the Constitution or even claim extraconstitutional powers.

Background: Previous Illegal NSA Activities

In 1967, when the U.S. Army wanted NSA to eavesdrop on American citizens and domestic groups, the agency agreed to carry out the assignment. NSA began to put together a list of names of opponents of the Vietnam War. Adding names to a domestic "watch list" led to the creation of Minaret—a tracking system that allowed the agency to follow individuals and organizations involved in the antiwar movement.[2] NSA was now involved in a mission outside its statutory duties, using its surveillance powers to violate the First and Fourth Amendments.

On June 5, 1970, President Richard Nixon met with the heads of several intelligence agencies, including NSA, to initiate a program designed to monitor what the administration considered radical individuals and groups in the United States. Joining others at the meeting was Tom Charles Huston, a young attorney working at the White House. He drafted a forty-three-page, top-secret memorandum that became known as the Huston Plan. Huston put the matter bluntly to President Nixon: "Use of this technique is clearly illegal; it amounts to burglary."[3] His plan directed NSA to use its technological capacity to intercept—without judicial warrants—the communication of U.S. citizens using international phone calls or telegrams.[4] Although Nixon, under pressure from FBI director J. Edgar Hoover, withdrew the Huston Plan, NSA had been targeting domestic groups for several years and continued to do so. Huston's blueprint, kept in a White House safe, became public in 1973, after Congress investigated the Watergate affair and provided documentary evidence that Nixon had ordered NSA to illegally monitor American citizens. To conduct its surveillance operations, NSA entered into agreements with U.S. companies, including Western Union and RCA Global. U.S. citizens, expecting that their telegrams would be handled with utmost privacy, learned that American companies had been turning over the telegrams to NSA.[5]

After the Church Committee disclosed the illegal NSA activities, the agency supposedly underwent a sea change in attitude toward the statutory and constitutional issues and vowed to remain within the bounds of U.S. law.[6]

Whatever lessons the agency learned in the 1970s were forgotten or subordinated decades later, especially in the period after September 11.

Establishing Limits on Wiretaps

Presidential authority to engage in eavesdropping for national security purposes without obtaining a warrant from a judge had never been properly clarified by statute or judicial rulings. In this legal vacuum, presidents often expanded their powers in time of emergency. On May 21, 1940, on the eve of World War II, President Franklin D. Roosevelt sent a confidential memo to his attorney general, Robert H. Jackson, authorizing and directing him to obtain information "by listening devices" to monitor the conversations or other communications "of persons suspected of subversive activities against the Government of the United States, including suspected spies." Roosevelt told Jackson to limit these investigations "to a minimum and to limit them in so far as possible to aliens."[7]

In the landmark case of *Olmstead v. United States* (1928), the Supreme Court decided that the use of wiretaps by federal agents enforcing prohibition to monitor and intercept phone calls did not violate the Constitution. The Court reasoned that the taps—small wires inserted in telephone wires leading from residences—did not enter the premises of the home or office. Without physical entry there was neither "search" nor "seizure" under the Fourth Amendment.[8] This strained analysis drew a scathing dissent from Justice Louis Brandeis, who accurately predicted that technology would soon overwhelm the Fourth Amendment unless the Court met the challenge with open eyes.

Over the next few decades, federal courts wrestled with new forms of technological intrusion, ranging from "detectaphones" (placing an instrument against the wall of a room to pick up sound waves on the other side of the wall) to placing concealed microphones inside homes. Other variations of electronic eavesdropping blossomed. Police used "spike mikes," small electronic listening devices pushed through the wall of an adjoining house until they touched the heating duct of a suspect's dwelling. Law enforcement officers with earphones could listen to conversations taking place on both floors of the house.[9]

In 1967 the Supreme Court put a halt to these practices by returning to basic principles. By a 7–1 majority, it declared unconstitutional the placing of electronic listening and recording devices on the outside of public telephone booths to obtain incriminating evidence. Although there was no physical entrance into the area occupied by the suspect, the Court ruled that the individual had a legitimate expectation of privacy within the phone booth. In a decision broad enough to accommodate technological advances, the Court held that the Fourth Amendment "protects people, not places."[10] In response to this decision, Congress passed legislation in 1968 requiring law enforcement officers to obtain a judicial warrant before placing taps on phones or installing bugs (concealed microphones). If an "emergency" existed, communications could be intercepted for up to forty-eight hours without a warrant, in cases involving organized crime or national security. This legislation on wiretaps and electronic surveillance is often referred to as "Title III authority."

The 1968 statute established national policy on domestic wiretaps. The executive branch claimed that warrantless surveillances for national security purposes were lawful as a reasonable exercise of presidential power. A section of Title III stated that nothing in it limited the president's constitutional power to "take such measures as he deems necessary to protect the Nation against actual or potential attack or other hostile acts of a foreign power, to obtain foreign intelligence information deemed essential to the security of the United States, or to protect national security information against foreign intelligence activities." Nor should anything in Title III "be deemed to limit the constitutional power of the President to take such measures as he deems necessary to protect the United States against the overthrow of the Government by force or other unlawful means, or against any other clear and present danger to the structure or existence of the Government."[11] Congress, feeling an obligation to say something, chose general language to largely duck the issue. It would soon find it necessary to reenter the field and pass comprehensive legislation on national security surveillance to limit the president.

What pushed Congress to act was a Supreme Court decision in 1972, which held that the Fourth Amendment required prior judicial approval for surveillances of domestic organizations.[12] The Court carefully avoided the question of surveillances over foreign powers, whether within or outside the United States. As to the language in Title III about national security wiretaps, the Court regarded that section as merely disclaiming congressional intent to define presidential powers in matters affecting national security and not to be taken as authorization for national security surveillances.

The FISA Statute

It was now necessary for Congress to pass legislation governing national security wiretaps. In 1973, in announcing a joint investigation by three Senate subcommittees, the lawmakers taking the lead explained,

Wiretapping and electronic surveillance pose a greater threat to the constitutional rights of American citizens than ever before. A recent survey of public attitudes shows that 75 percent of the American people feel that "wiretapping and spying under the excuse of national security is a serious threat to people's privacy."[13]

Extensive hearings were conducted to determine the procedures that would simultaneously protect security interests and individual rights. Legislation reported from the Senate Judiciary Committee in 1977 required the attorney general to obtain a judicial warrant authorizing the use of electronic surveillance in the United States for foreign intelligence purposes. Congress was filling a gaping hole. The federal government had never enacted legislation to regulate the use of electronic surveillance within the United States for foreign intelligence purposes, nor had the Supreme Court ever expressly decided the issue of whether the president had constitutional authority to authorize electronic surveillance without a warrant in cases concerning foreign intelligence.[14]

The bill enacted in 1978 was the Foreign Intelligence Surveillance Act (FISA). To provide a judicial check on executive actions, it created what is known as the FISA Court. The chief justice of the United States would designate seven district court judges to hear applications for, and grant orders approving, electronic surveillance anywhere within the United States. After September 11, Congress increased the number of judges to eleven. No judge designated under this law "shall hear the same application for electronic surveillance under this Act which has been denied previously by another judge designated under this subsection."[15] The chief justice would also designate three judges from the district courts or appellate courts to make up a court of review with jurisdiction to review the denial of any application made under this statute.[16] Significantly, procedures under FISA "shall be *the exclusive means* by which electronic surveillance, as defined in section 101 of such Act, and the interception of domestic wire and oral communications may be conducted."[17]

The 1978 legislation required the government to certify that "the purpose" of the surveillance was to obtain foreign intelligence information. The USA PATRIOT Act of 2001 changed the requirements placed on federal officers when applying for a search order. The new language allowed application if a "significant purpose" was to obtain foreign intelligence information. The objective was to make it easier to obtain permission from the FISA Court, not to bypass it altogether. Legislation after September 11 made other changes to FISA. Under the 1978 law, the attorney general could order emergency electronic

surveillance without a warrant provided that he informed a judge having jurisdiction over national security wiretaps and obtained a warrant within twenty-
four hours. Congress lengthened the emergency period to seventy-two hours
in legislation reported by the Intelligence Committees.[18]

The Administration Responds to the Leak

The Bush administration could have chosen to say nothing about the leak in
the *New York Times;* it could refuse either to acknowledge or deny the existence
of the surveillance program. That approach is frequently used with public
disclosures about other classified operations. In this case, the administration
decided to have President Bush publicly defend the program as essential for the
protection of U.S. security. One administration official explained that making
the president the only voice "is directly taking on the critics. The Democrats
are now in the position of supporting our efforts to protect Americans, or
defend positions that could weaken our nation's security."[19] Sen. Patrick Leahy,
ranking Democrat on the Judiciary Committee, responded to that tactic: "Our
government must follow the laws and respect the Constitution while it protects
Americans' security and liberty."[20]

During the operation of NSA surveillance, the Bush administration offered
to brief eight members of Congress and the chief judge of the FISA Court. The
lawmakers (called the "Gang of Eight") included the chairs and ranking members of the two Intelligence Committees, the Speaker and minority leader of
the House, and the Senate majority and minority leaders. Rep. Nancy Pelosi,
California, at that time the Democratic leader in the House, acknowledged that
she had been advised of the program shortly after it began and had "been provided with updates on several occasions."[21]

On December 17, 2005, in a weekly radio address, President Bush defended
what he called the Terrorist Surveillance Program (TSP). He acknowledged
that he had authorized NSA, "consistent with U.S. law and the Constitution, to
intercept the international communications of people with known links to al
Qaeda and related terrorist organizations."[22] His program was, in fact, inconsistent with, and in violation of, statutory law. Gradually it became clear that
when President Bush referred to "U.S. law" or "authority," he meant law created
within the executive branch, whether or not consistent with law passed by
Congress. In his radio address, Bush underscored what he considered to be his
independent constitutional powers: "The authorization I gave the National

Security agency after September 11 helped address that problem [of combating terrorism] in a way that is fully consistent with my constitutional responsibilities and authorities."[23] He said he had "reauthorized this program more than 30 times since the September 11 attacks."[24] Bush expressed his determination to continue the program as "a vital tool in our war against the terrorists."[25]

In a news conference on December 19, Bush stated, "As President and Commander in Chief, I have the constitutional responsibility and the constitutional authority to protect our country. Article II of the Constitution gives me that responsibility and the authority necessary to fulfill it." He noted that Congress after September 11 had passed the Authorization for Use of Military Force (AUMF) to grant him "additional authority to use military force against Al Qaida."[26] Also on December 19, Attorney General Alberto Gonzales held a press briefing on the NSA program, claiming that "the President has the inherent authority under the Constitution, as Commander-in-Chief, to engage in this kind of activity."[27] When asked why the administration did not seek a warrant from the FISA court, which Congress created as the exclusive means of authorizing national security eavesdropping, Gonzales replied that the administration continued to seek warrants from the FISA court but was not "legally required" to do so in every case if another statute granted the president additional authority.[28] It was the administration's position that the AUMF provided that additional authority.

Gonzales emphasized the need for "the speed and the agility" that the FISA process lacked: "You have to remember that FISA was passed by the Congress in 1978. There have been tremendous advances in technology" since that time.[29] Why did the administration not ask Congress to amend FISA to grant the president greater flexibility, as was done several times after 1978 and even after September 11? Gonzales replied he was advised "that would be difficult, if not impossible."[30] Why not try and put the burden on Congress to pass legislation necessary for national security?

The Sole-Organ Doctrine

On January 19, 2006, the Justice Department produced a forty-two-page white paper defending the legality of the NSA program. It concluded that the NSA activities "are supported by the President's well-recognized inherent constitutional authority as Commander in Chief and sole organ for the Nation in foreign affairs to conduct warrantless surveillance of enemy forces for intelligence purposes to detect and disrupt armed attacks on the United States."[31] Later in the paper, the Justice Department linked "sole organ" to the 1936 Supreme Court decision of *United States v. Curtiss-Wright*.[32]

Nothing in *Curtiss-Wright* supports exclusive, plenary, unchecked, inherent, or extraconstitutional powers for the president. The only question before the Court was the constitutionality of Congress delegating part of its authority to the president to place an arms embargo in a region in South America. The case therefore involved *legislative,* not presidential, power. In imposing the embargo, President Franklin D. Roosevelt issued a proclamation that relied solely on statutory—not constitutional—authority. He acted pursuant to the authority "conferred in me by the said joint resolution of Congress."[33] The issue in *Curtiss-Wright* was whether Congress could delegate legislative power more broadly in international affairs than it could in domestic affairs. In 1935, the Court had struck down the delegation by Congress of *domestic* power to the president.[34] None of the briefs submitted to the Court in the *Curtiss-Wright* case discussed the availability of independent, inherent, or extraconstitutional powers to the president.[35]

Nevertheless, in extensive dicta wholly extraneous to the legal issue before the Court, Justice George Sutherland discussed the availability of inherent and extraconstitutional powers for the president in foreign affairs. His arguments drew from an article he published as a U.S. senator from Utah and from a book he published in 1919. Sutherland's historical analysis has been dismissed as unreliable and erroneous by many scholars.[36] His use of John Marshall's speech in 1800, referring to the president as "sole organ," is a glaring example of a statement made for one limited purpose taken wholly out of context to make the case for a proposition that Marshall never believed at any time in four decades of public life.

On March 7, 1800, in the House of Representatives, Marshall called the president "the sole organ of the nation in its external relations, and its sole representative with foreign nations."[37] The intent was not to advocate inherent or exclusive powers for the president. His objective was merely to defend the authority of President John Adams to carry out an extradition treaty. The president was not the sole organ in formulating the treaty, which required joint action by the president and the Senate. He was the sole organ in implementing it. Article II of the Constitution specifies that it is the president's duty to "take Care that the Laws be faithfully executed." Under Article VI, all treaties made "shall be the supreme Law of the Land."[38]

Once on the Supreme Court as chief justice, Marshall held consistently to his position that the making of foreign policy is a joint exercise by the executive and legislative branches, whether by treaty or by statute, not a unilateral or exclusive authority of the president. With the war power, for example, Marshall looked solely to Congress—not the president—for the authority to take the country to war. He had no difficulty identifying which branch possessed the war power: "The whole powers of war being, by the constitution of the United States, vested in congress, the acts of that body can alone be resorted to as our guides in this enquiry."[39] In an 1804 case, Marshall ruled that when a presidential proclamation issued in time of war conflicts with a statute enacted by Congress, the statute prevails.[40]

In addition to citing constitutional arguments, the Justice Department in 2006 looked to statutes as legal justification for NSA eavesdropping. It argued that "Congress by statute has confirmed and supplemented the President's recognized authority under Article II of the Constitution to conduct such warrantless surveillance to prevent catastrophic attacks on the homeland." In responding to the September 11 attacks, Congress enacted the AUMF to authorize the president to "use all necessary and appropriate force against those nations, organizations, or persons he determines planned, authorized, committed, or aided the terrorist attacks" of September 11, in order to prevent "any future acts of international terrorism against the United States."[41] Moreover, the Justice Department argued that although FISA "generally requires judicial approval of electronic surveillance, FISA also contemplates that Congress may authorize such surveillance by a statute other than FISA." To the Justice Department, AUMF met that requirement.[42] Any congressional statute interpreted to impede the president's ability to use electronic surveillance to detect and prevent future attacks by an enemy "would be called into very serious doubt" as to its constitutionality. If this constitutional question "had to be addressed, FISA would be unconstitutional as applied to this narrow context."[43] According to this reading, statutory law could not restrict what the president decided to do under his Article II powers.

There is no evidence that any member of Congress, in voting on the AUMF, thought that it would in any way modify the requirements of FISA or give the president new and independent authority to conduct warrantless national security wiretaps. When Congress decides to amend a statute or grant new powers, it does so explicitly, not by implication. It is a canon of statutory construction that "repeal by implication" is disfavored. Changing law requires specific, conscious, and deliberate action by Congress.

A Hospital Visit

After initiating the Terrorist Surveillance Program, it was the policy of the administration to reauthorize it periodically after internal review of its legality. In March 2004, the Office of Legal Counsel (OLC) in the Justice Department concluded that the program had a number of legal deficiencies and recommended that it not be reauthorized until changed. The presidential order to reauthorize the program had a line for the attorney general to sign. Attorney General John Ashcroft and Deputy Attorney General James Comey agreed with the OLC analysis and recommendation. When Ashcroft was hospitalized with a serious illness and placed in intensive care, he transferred the powers of attorney general to Comey until he could recover and resume the powers of his office.

On the evening of March 10, 2004, in his capacity as acting attorney general, Comey was heading home with his security detail at about 8 o'clock. He received a call from Ashcroft's chief of staff that White House Counsel Gonzales and White House chief of staff Andrew Card were on their way to the hospital. Comey thought that Gonzales and Card, knowing of the legal objections OLC had raised about the TSP, might try to convince Ashcroft to reverse Justice's position and agree to sign the reauthorization form. Comey called his chief of staff and told him to get as many of Comey's people as possible to the hospital immediately. He called FBI director Robert Mueller and asked that he come to the hospital.

When Comey's car reached the hospital, he raced up the stairs to Ashcroft's room and found Mrs. Ashcroft standing by the bed. As Comey explained to the Senate Judiciary Committee on May 15, 2007, he was concerned that, given Ashcroft's illness, there might be an effort to ask him to sign the form and overrule what Justice had decided, when he was in no condition to do that.[44] Comey tried to get Ashcroft focused on the issue, in preparation for the arrival of Gonzales and Card. Mueller had directed FBI agents not to have Comey removed from Ashcroft's room under any circumstance. OLC head Jack Goldsmith and a senior Justice official, Patrick Philbin, arrived and entered Ashcroft's room.

Within a few minutes Gonzales and Card arrived. Gonzales, holding an envelope, told Ashcroft why they were there and why they wanted him to approve the reauthorization of the TSP. Ashcroft lifted his head off the pillow and defended the position that Justice had taken. He said his opinion did not matter because he was not the attorney general. Pointing to Comey, he said he was the attorney general. Gonzales and Card, without acknowledging Comey, left the room. At that point Mueller arrived and Comey explained what had happened.[45]

Card then called Comey and told him to come to the White House immediately. Comey said that after the conduct he had just witnessed, he would not come without a witness. Card responded, "What conduct? We were just there to wish him well."[46] Comey called Solicitor General Ted Olson, explained the circumstances, and asked him to accompany him to the White House and witness what was said. Comey and Olson arrived at the White House that evening at 11 o'clock. Comey told the Judiciary Committee that he was very upset and angry because he thought Gonzales and Card had tried to take advantage of a very sick man who lacked the official authority to do what they asked of him.[47]

Card, Gonzales, Comey, and Olson discussed the situation. Card said he had heard reports that there might be a number of resignations at the Justice Department over the incident. Comey said he could not stay if the administration decided to engage in conduct that the Justice Department concluded had no legal basis.[48] Other possible resignations included FBI director Mueller, Comey's chief of staff, Ashcroft's chief of staff, and quite likely Ashcroft.[49] The mass resignations were averted when President Bush met with Comey and Mueller in the Oval Office two days later, in the morning, to receive a briefing on Justice's counterterrorism work. As Comey was leaving, Bush asked to see him privately in a separate room for about fifteen minutes. Bush did the same with Mueller. The result of those two meetings, in Comey's understanding, was that he was to do "the right thing" as he saw it.[50] To Comey, that meant that Justice would not sign the reauthorization form until it was satisfied that the program had been sufficiently altered to pass legal muster. Pending the review by Justice, the White House went ahead with the TSP without the approval of Comey or the Justice Department.[51] After two or three weeks, and the acceptance of changes urged by Justice, the reauthorization form received the signature of the attorney general.[52]

Hayden's Testimony

Michael V. Hayden appeared before the Senate Intelligence Committee on May 18, 2006, to testify on his nomination to be Central Intelligence Agency (CIA) director. Previously he had served as NSA director at the time that the Terrorist Surveillance Program was initiated. At the hearing, Hayden defended the legality of the NSA wiretap program on constitutional, not statutory, grounds. He did not attempt to use the AUMF as legal justification. In recalling his service at NSA after September 11, Hayden told the committee that when he talked to NSA lawyers "they were very comfortable with the Article II arguments and the president's inherent authorities." When they came to him and discussed the lawfulness of the NSA program, "our discussion anchored itself on Article II."[53] The attorneys "came back with a real comfort level that this was within the president's authority [i.e., Article II]."[54] This legal advice was not put in writing, and Hayden "did not ask for it." Instead, "they talked to me about Article II."[55] There is no evidence that the NSA general counsel was asked to prepare a legal memo defending the TSP—no paper trail, no accountability, just informal talks.

Hayden repeatedly claimed that the NSA program was legal and that the CIA "will obey the laws of the United States and will respond to our treaty obligations."[56] What did Hayden mean by "law"? National policy decided by statute or a treaty? A policy made solely by the president? During the hearing, he treated "law" as the latter—something that can be derived from Article II or inherent powers: "I had two lawful programs in front of me, one authorized by the president, the other one would have been conducted under FISA as currently crafted and implemented."[57] In other words, he had two avenues before him: one authorized by statutory law, the other in violation of it. He told one senator, "I did not believe—still don't believe—that I was acting unlawfully. I was acting under a lawful authorization."[58] He meant a presidential directive issued under Article II, even against the exclusive legislative policy set forth in FISA.

Hearing Hayden insist that he acted legally in implementing the NSA program, a senator said, "I assume that the basis for that was the Article II powers, the inherent powers of the president to protect the country in time of danger and war." Hayden replied, "Yes, sir, commander in chief powers."[59] Hayden implied that he was willing to violate statutory law in order to carry out what he called presidential law. After September 11, CIA director George Tenet asked whether, as NSA director, he could "do more" to combat terrorism with surveillance. Hayden answered, "Not within current law."[60] In short, the administration knowingly and consciously decided to act against statutory policy. It knew that the NSA eavesdropping program it wanted to conduct was illegal under FISA but decided to go ahead.

At one point in the hearing, Hayden referred to the legal and political embarrassments of NSA during the Nixon administration, when it conducted warrantless eavesdropping against domestic groups. In discussing what should be done after September 11, he told one group, "Look, I've got a workforce out there that remembers the mid-1970s." He asked the Senate committee to forgive him for using "a poor sports metaphor," but he advised the group in this manner: "Since about 1975, this agency's had a permanent one-ball, two-strike count against it, and we don't take many close pitches."[61] The TSP was a close pitch. Perhaps with further public disclosures one can answer the question: Did NSA take a close pitch and strike out?

Challenges in Court

A number of private parties challenged the legality and constitutionality of NSA's eavesdropping. To show the injury necessary to have a case litigated, plaintiffs argued that the contacts they used to have with clients over the telephone were now impossible because of NSA monitoring. To maintain contact, they would have to travel to see clients personally, even in countries outside the United States. The government sought to have all such lawsuits dismissed on the ground that litigation would inevitably disclose "state secrets" injurious to the nation. That argument had been weakened when the Bush administration decided to publicly acknowledge the existence of the TSP and publicly defend its legality.

In a major case in California, decided on July 20, 2006, a federal district judge held that the state secrets privilege did not block action on the lawsuit and that plaintiffs had shown sufficient injury to establish standing. The judge denied the government's motion to have the case dismissed or go to summary judgment on the issue of the state secrets privilege. Under summary judgment, a court does not begin the time-consuming process of depositions and trial but rather goes immediately to the legal issue before it. As a result of the judge's rulings, the lawsuit was allowed to proceed—a significant defeat for the Bush administration.[62]

In this case, the plaintiffs alleged that AT&T and its holding company had collaborated with NSA in conducting a massive, warrantless surveillance program that illegally tracked the domestic and foreign communications of millions of Americans. The plaintiffs charged violations of the First and Fourth Amendments of the Constitution, of FISA, various sections of other federal laws, and California's Unfair Competition Law. In attempting to have the case dismissed, the government advanced three arguments based on the state secrets privilege:

(1) the very subject matter of this case is a state secret; (2) plaintiffs cannot make a prima facie case for their claims without classified evidence and (3) the privilege effectively deprives AT&T of information necessary to raise valid defenses.[63]

To the court, the first step in determining whether a piece of information is a "state secret" requires this judgment: Is the information actually a "secret"?[64] The court pointed to public reports about the TSP in the *New York Times* on December 16, 2005. It noted that President Bush, the following day, confirmed the existence of the program and publicly described the mechanism by which the program was authorized and reviewed. Attorney General Gonzales had talked about the program in public briefings and public hearings, and the Justice Department publicly defended the TSP's legality and constitutionality. Based on this public record, the court said, "it might appear that none of the subject matter in this litigation could be considered a secret given that the alleged surveillance programs have been so widely reported in the media."[65]

The court recognized that just because a factual statement has been made public does not guarantee that the statement is true or that the activity was not a genuine secret. Even if a previously secret program has been leaked, verification of the program by the government could be harmful.[66] Also, media reports may be unreliable.[67] However, in this case the administration had "publicly admitted the existence of a 'terrorist surveillance program,' which the government insists is completely legal." Moreover, given the scope of the TSP, the court found it "inconceivable" that it could exist without the acquiescence and cooperation of a telecommunications provider. The size of AT&T and its public acknowledgment that it performs classified contracts and employs thousands who have government security clearances provided enough verifiable public information to avoid adopting the state secrets privilege as an absolute bar to litigation.[68] Under this reasoning, the court concluded that the plaintiffs were entitled "to at least some discovery."[69] As to whether plaintiffs had shown injury and established standing to sue AT&T, the court concluded that they "have sufficiently alleged that they suffered an actual, concrete injury traceable to AT&T and redressable by this court."[70] On those grounds, the court allowed the case to proceed, with each side at liberty to request additional documents to support its position.

A week later, the government prevailed in an NSA case decided in Illinois. A U.S. district court dismissed a class-action lawsuit against a Bush administration program that involved the collection and monitoring of phone numbers rather than actual conversations (the program that the *New York Times* revealed in December 2005). The administration neither confirmed nor denied the existence of this program on phone numbers, and several telephone companies denied that they had given customer calling records to NSA.

The district judge noted that "no executive branch official has officially confirmed or denied the existence of any program to obtain large quantities of customer telephone records, the subject of the plaintiffs' lawsuit."[71] By invoking the state secrets privilege, the government this time prevented the plaintiffs from seeking additional facts or documents to establish that they had been harmed or would suffer harm in the future. The judge ruled that the plaintiffs could seek relief only from the elected branches.

In the California case, the federal court merely let the case continue, without deciding on the merits. However, on August 17, 2006, District Judge Anna Diggs Taylor, in Michigan, ruled that the TSP violated the Constitution and federal statutes. Like the judge in California, Taylor took note that the existence of the program, the lack of warrants, and the focus on communications in which one party was in the United States had been admitted by the administration.[72] Contrary to the arguments of NSA, Taylor was persuaded that the plaintiffs were able "to establish a prima facie case based solely on Defendants' public admissions regarding the TSP."[73] As to injury, the plaintiffs had provided documentation that "they are stifled in their ability to vigorously conduct research, interact with sources, talk with clients and, in the case of the attorney Plaintiffs, uphold their oath of providing effective and ethical representation of their clients."[74] Plaintiffs cited additional injury by having to travel to meet with clients and others relevant to their cases.

NSA argued in court that it could not defend itself "without the exposure of state secrets." Judge Taylor disagreed, pointing out that the Bush administration "has repeatedly told the general public that there is a valid basis in law for the TSP." Moreover, NSA contended that the president had statutory authority under the AUMF and the Constitution to authorize continued use of the TSP, and presented that case "without revealing or relying on any classified information."[75] Taylor found that the agency's argument that it could not defend itself in this case "without the use of classified information to be disingenuous and without merit."[76]

She said that the Fourth Amendment was adopted "to assure that Executive abuses of the power to search would not continue in our new nation."[77] She cited cases that described a private residence as a place where society particularly recognizes an expectation of privacy. Other cases emphasized that executive officers of the government could not be trusted to be neutral and disinterested magistrates or the sole judges of the extent of their prosecutorial powers. In enacting FISA, Congress insisted on a body outside the executive branch—the FISA Court—to provide independent review. Yet she concluded that the TSP "has undisputedly been implemented without regard to FISA . . . and obviously in violation of the Fourth Amendment."[78]

The next constitutional issue explored was the principle of separation of powers. Judge Taylor recalled the Framers' resentment of the General Warrants authorized by King George III, which helped to precipitate the break with England. She cited the language of Justice Jackson in the 1952 steel seizure case that emergency power was consistent with free government "only when their control is lodged elsewhere than in the Executive who exercises them."[79] Taylor concluded that President Bush, by acting in a manner forbidden by FISA, functioned outside the law decided by legislative deliberations and attempted to combine the powers of government into one branch.

The Bush administration defended the TSP by relying on the AUMF. Judge Taylor observed that the statute "says nothing whatsoever of intelligence or surveillance." She asked whether the authority for the TSP could be implied in the AUMF. In the cases of FISA and Title III on wiretaps, Congress had adopted those statutes "as the exclusive means by which electronic surveillance may be adopted." Prior warrants must be obtained from judges. FISA allowed for a fifteen-day exception in time of a declared war, but here the government argued that the TSP could function for more than five years without congressional authorization. The implication by the government that the AUMF somehow modified FISA, without direct and explicit amendment, "cannot be made by this court,"[80] said the judge. She also dismissed arguments by the administration that relied on inherent powers and broad readings of Article II and the president's powers of commander in chief. There are no "powers not created by the Constitution. So all 'inherent powers' must derive from that Constitution." The argument that "inherent powers justify the program here in litigation must fail."[81]

The government appealed her decision to the Sixth Circuit. On July 6, 2007, the appellate court reversed Judge Taylor on the ground that the plaintiffs lacked standing to bring the suit. Writing for a 2–1 panel, Judge Alice M. Batchelder concluded that if litigation in a state secrets case "would necessitate admission or disclosure of even the existence of the secret, then the case is nonjusticiable and must be dismissed on the pleadings," that is, without proceeding to trial, gaining documents through the discovery process, and reaching the merits.[82] On February 19, 2008, the Supreme Court declined to take this case.

In the *Hepting* case, after the district court held against the administration, the Ninth Circuit reversed and on October 9, 2012, the Supreme Court refused to take the case.[83] Greater success by private plaintiffs against NSA warrantless surveillance was gained in the *Al-Haramain* case. On December 22, 2010, a federal judge ordered the government to pay nearly $2.6 million in lawyers' fees and damages to officials of an Islamic charity in Oregon. Some details of this case are covered in the section "The Immunity Issue," below.

Legislative Remedies

After the *New York Times* disclosed NSA's eavesdropping program, Congress drafted legislation to put the policy on firm legal footing. One element was to impose some type of legislative oversight to replace the skimpy "Gang of Eight" procedure that the Bush administration had followed.[84] However, the administration also was ready to use the *Times* disclosure to press for greater authority, claiming that FISA was out of date and had not kept pace with changing technology. Executive officials testified that it was impractical after September 11 to expect the administration to obtain individual warrants every time it needed to listen to a conversation of someone suspected of being connected with al Qaeda. It urged legislation to recognize by statute what it considered to be the president's inherent authority to conduct warrantless eavesdropping to collect foreign intelligence. Critics of this approach advised Congress that it would be better to have no legislation than to grant the president such sweeping, unchecked power.[85]

By early March 2006, Republicans on the Senate Intelligence Committee said that they had reached agreement with the White House on proposed legislation to impose new forms of congressional oversight. The bill would allow wiretapping without warrants and increase the current three-day limit for emergency surveillance to forty-five days. If the administration found it necessary to exceed forty-five days, the attorney general would have to certify that continued surveillance was necessary to protect the country and explain why the administration would not seek a warrant. His statement would go to a newly created, seven-member "terrorist surveillance subcommittee" of the Senate Intelligence Committee, which would receive full access to details of the program's operations. Democrats attacked the bill as an abdication of legislative power and an effort to bless the NSA program before Congress, and the public, had understood its reach or manner of operation. Sen. John D. Rockefeller IV,

D-W.Va., vice chairman of the Intelligence Committee, described the panel as "basically under the control of the White House."[86]

The seven members of the new subcommittee went to the White House to receive a two-hour briefing on the TSP and were scheduled to visit NSA to learn more. Under the rules set by the White House, the seven senators were not permitted to share what they learned with the other eight senators on the Intelligence Committee. Senator Rockefeller had traveled to NSA the previous week and spent almost seven hours getting information from more than a dozen NSA lawyers, policy makers, and technicians. He told reporters he learned more from that visit than from the White House presentation, which consisted of "flip-chart jobs and not very impressive."[87]

As debate on the legislation continued, the hope of reaching an early consensus vanished. Republican leaders thought there would be an advantage in passing legislation just before the November 2006 elections, to allow voters to compare the national security credentials of the two parties, but there were too many bills and too many contradictions. The Senate bill crafted by Sen. Arlen Specter, R-Pa., seemed to many to be too close to what the White House wanted. On the House side, debate was spread among six rival surveillance bills.[88] Strong objections were raised to allowing the FISA Court to decide the constitutionality of the NSA program.[89] How would that be done? Secret briefs submitted to the FISA Court by the administration, followed by secret oral argument and eventually the release of a declassified, sanitized ruling? Why should constitutional issues be decided in that manner?

With Congress about to recess for the elections, the differences between the various bills were too large to bridge. Members of both parties were reluctant to recognize Article II/inherent powers of the president to conduct warrantless wiretaps. It proved impossible to submit legislation to Bush for his signature.[90] The House managed to pass a bill, 232–191, but it was too unlike the Senate bill to permit quick resolution in conference committee.[91] Democratic victories in the November elections put an end not only to Republican control of Congress but to the Republican-drafted bills on national security surveillance.

Mid-Course Correction?

In the midst of some setbacks in federal courts, the administration announced in January 2007 that it would not continue to skirt the FISA Court but would instead seek warrants from it, as required by statute. In a January 17 letter, Attorney General Gonzales informed the Senate Judiciary Committee that on January 10 a judge of the FISA Court issued orders authorizing the government "to target for collection international communications into or out of the United States where there is probable cause to believe that one of the communicants is a member or agent of al Qaeda or an associated terrorist organization." As a result of those orders, "any electronic surveillance that was occurring as part of the Terrorist Surveillance Program will now be conducted subject to the approval of the Foreign Intelligence Surveillance Court."[92] This statement seemed to comply with FISA, but did it contemplate a one-time, blanket judicial approval for all future national security wiretaps within this category? Gonzales called these orders "innovative, they are complex, and it took considerable time and work for the Government to develop the approach that was proposed to the Court and for the Judge on the FISA Court to consider and approve these orders."[93] He concluded: "Under these circumstances, the President has determined not to reauthorize the Terrorist Surveillance Program when the current reauthorization expires."[94]

Gonzales's appearance before the Senate Judiciary Committee on January 18, 2007, provoked further confrontation. He would not agree to provide more documents to explain the decision.[95] He appeared to concede that the administration not only broke the law but knew it had done so: "The truth of the matter is we looked at FISA and we all concluded there's no way we can do what we have to do to protect this country under the strict reading of FISA."[96] There were reports that FISA Court orders would be shown to House and Senate leaders and selected committees, including Intelligence and Judiciary, although access by the latter seemed restricted to chairs and ranking members.[97]

The tentative and possibly temporary accommodation by the administration undermined its position in court that the NSA cases should be considered moot and dismissed. Had the administration entered into a final and binding agreement, or one that could be revisited later and reversed? At a hearing on January 31, 2007, before the Sixth Circuit, one of the judges asked: "You could opt out at any time, couldn't you?" The deputy solicitor general acknowledged the possibility.[98]

Swerving Again: McConnell's Testimony

On May 1, 2007, Director of National Intelligence Michael McConnell testified before the Senate Intelligence Committee and signaled that the administration might not be able to keep its pledge to seek warrants through the FISA Court. McConnell had served as NSA director from 1992 to 1996. On the one hand, his written statement appeared to endorse FISA as the foundation for conducting national security wiretaps. The pending bill, he said, "seeks to restore FISA to its original focus on protecting the privacy interests of persons in the United States."[99] Yet he also stated that FISA's requirement to obtain a court order, "based on a showing of probable cause, slows, and in some cases prevents altogether, the Government's efforts to conduct surveillance of communications it believes are significant to the national security."[100] The Justice Department, in its testimony, objected to what it considered to be the impractical requirement of obtaining a warrant from the FISA Court for each national security surveillance. Such an approach was "infeasible" and would impose "intolerable burdens on our intelligence efforts.[101]

Senior officials in the Bush administration told the committee that the president had independent authority under the Constitution to order this type of surveillance without warrants and without complying with statutory procedures. McConnell referred several times to Article II as a source of inherent presidential authority. When asked by Sen. Russ Feingold, D-Wis., whether the administration would no longer sidestep the FISA Court, McConnell replied. "Sir, the president's authority under Article II is in the Constitution. So if the president chose to exercise Article II authority, that would be the president's choice." He wanted to highlight that "Article II is Article II, so in a different circumstance, I can't speak for the president what he might decide."[102] Why would an administration witness tell a congressional committee that Article II is in the Constitution, and that Article II is Article II? Those are obvious—too obvious—points. Moreover, Article II directs the president to "take Care that the Laws be faithfully Executed."

McConnell's testimony is similar to that of Michael Hayden, when he was nominated to be CIA director. Both men seemed to be coached to repeat the words "Article II, Article II, inherent, inherent," as though such assertions and claims stated with sufficient frequency would take on substance without further explanation. An assertion is an assertion until the witness offers a persuasive and informed argument, which neither McConnell nor Hayden attempted to do.

The Immunity Issue

On August 5, 2007, just before a scheduled one-month recess, Congress passed an amendment to FISA that gave the administration the discretion it had sought, although only for a period of 180 days. The legislation was called the Protect America Act.[103] A key issue in drafting permanent legislation was whether to grant retroactive immunity to the telecom firms that had provided technical assistance for NSA surveillance.[104] In October 2007, the Senate Intelligence Committee voted to give the telecoms legal immunity from lawsuit because they had "acted in good faith" and believed the TSP was legal and presidentially authorized.[105] The companies had their own offices of general counsel responsible for independently determining what was legal or not. They could have complied with the law instead of deferring to presidential assertions that were in direct violation of the law. Administration officials stated that the letters to the companies requesting their assistance "said very forcefully" the surveillance program was "being directed by the president, and this has been deemed lawful at the very highest levels of the government."[106] Why would telecoms agree to violate statutory law because executive officials decided that the NSA initiative had been "deemed lawful"?

On February 21, 2008, President Bush argued that "[if] we do not give liability protection to those who are helping us, they won't help us. And if they don't help us, there will be no program. And if there's no program, America is more vulnerable."[107] A week later he said, "You cannot expect phone companies to participate if they feel like they're going to be sued."[108] If the phone companies wanted protection from legal action they could have complied with the procedures set forth in the FISA statute. They were legally at risk because they decided to violate the law.

On July 10, 2008, Congress passed legislation to give the telecoms retroactive immunity. The statutory language is quite unusual. First, the statute reaffirms that the procedures set forth in FISA are the "exclusive means" by which electronic surveillance and interception of certain communications may be conducted.[109] If FISA established the exclusive means, the telecoms (and the administration) should have complied with it. Yet Title VIII of the 2008 statute provides "Protection of Persons Assisting the Government." The title covers civil actions filed in federal or state court that allege that (1) an electronic communications service provider furnished assistance to an element of the intelligence community," and (2) "seeks monetary or other relief from the electronic communications service provider related to the provisions of such assistance."[110]

This type of civil action may not be maintained in court "if the Attorney General certifies to the district court of the United States in which such action is pending" that the company being sued was provided a certification in writing over the period from September 11, 2001, through January 17, 2007, regarding the need to detect or prevent a terrorist attack, and that the company's activity was "(i) authorized by the President; and (ii) determined to be lawful."[111] A blank check to the president? No. The statute provides that the written certification shall be given effect "unless the court finds that such certification is not supported by substantial evidence provided to the court pursuant to this section." A court must conduct an inquiry into the quality and substance of the evidence supporting the certification.

Under these conditions and despite the immunity provision, litigation continued. One of the major cases involved the Al-Haramain Islamic Foundation, based in Oregon. On a routine discovery request, the company obtained a top-secret calling log that showed it was a target of warrantless surveillance. After the Treasury Department inadvertently gave the document to Al-Haramain, it insisted that the company return it, which it did. On November 16, 2007, the Ninth Circuit ruled that the company could not refer to the document because it was covered by the state secrets privilege, yet allowed the case to move forward on other grounds, including the extensive public disclosures by the Bush administration about the TSP.[112]

The next question in this case was whether a statute passed by Congress (FISA) trumped a program created by the administration (TSP). On July 2, 2008, a federal district court held that FISA preempted the state secrets privilege. In other words, a statutory policy necessarily overrode a claim or assertion by an administration, including the claim and assertion of state secrets. FISA "limits the power of the executive branch to conduct such activities [foreign intelligence surveillance] and it limits the executive branch's authority to assert the state secrets privilege in response to challenges to the legality of its foreign intelligence surveillance activities."[113] Pursuant to this reasoning, the federal court denied the administration's motion to dismiss the case.

The litigation continued into 2009, giving the district judge an opportunity to review a sealed document within his chambers.[114] He then wanted to give attorneys representing Al-Haramain access to the sealed document and ordered the Justice Department to provide security clearances to two of the plaintiff's attorneys. The dispute escalated in May 2009 when the administration announced that although the two attorneys were suitable for top-secret clearances, they did not "need to know" information the court decided they *did* need to know.[115] Access to examine classified documents always includes two steps: clearance and a need to know. An individual may have clearance without a need to know. In this case, the judge concluded the two attorneys had a need to know to promote the adversarial process. Of course, the collision raised the question of who runs the courtroom: the judge or the defendants?[116] The dispute was finally resolved when the executive branch decided it could pursue the case without relying on classified documents.

On December 21, 2010, the judge ordered the government to pay nearly $2.6 million for the lawyers who represented Al-Haramain and to the officials at the now-shuttered charity. Jon Eisenberg, a lawyer who represented the charity, said: "We brought this case to try and get a declaration from the judiciary that the executive branch is bound by the law."[117] The judge criticized the Bush administration for secretly approving a wiretapping program that operated outside judicial scrutiny and in violation of the surveillance policy enacted by Congress.[118]

Legislative and Judicial Actions in 2012

The FISA Amendments Act of 2008 reauthorized FISA but provided that it would expire on December 31, 2012, unless Congress enacted new legislation. In 2012, House and Senate committees reported legislation to extend the sunset to June 1, 2017. Opponents of the bill objected that a provision (Section 702) permits the administration to engage in warrantless surveillance of non-U.S. persons located abroad. Section 702 allows the collection of foreign intelligence even if a U.S. person inside the United States is a party to the communication. Other sections of the bill require a court order for targeting U.S. persons reasonably believed to be outside the United States.[119]

Members of Congress wanted to know whether the communications of U.S. citizens could be, incidentally, collected. The administration answered that it was not possible to determine the number of U.S. citizens affected. Because of this uncertainty, some lawmakers wanted the reauthorization to cover a shorter period of time.[120] A bipartisan group of U.S. senators expressed concern that "Americans engaged in harmless communications with foreigners could be monitored without a warrant or other privacy protections."[121] On September 20, the Senate Judiciary Committee reported an amended bill authorizing FISA for only two and a half years. On September 12, 2012, the House passed the reauthorization bill by a vote of 301 to 118. Complicating the prospects of reauthorization was a hold that Senator Ron Wyden (D-OR) placed on the bill in June. He identified two concerns: (1) the director of national intelligence would not answer his question about the number of Americans whose communications had been reviewed pursuant to the FISA Amendments Act of 2008, and (2) concern that the government could engage in "back-door searches" of Americans' communications collected under Section 702. He indicated he might accept a short-term extension to pass the bill. However he was unsuccessful, as a five-year extension of the Act was approved by a Senate vote of 73–23 on December 28. On December 30, President Obama signed the FISA Amendments Act Reauthorization Act of 2012.[122]

On May 21, 2012, the Supreme Court announced it would hear a case concerning the government's use of electronic surveillance to monitor the international communication of people suspected of having ties to terrorist groups. Amnesty International, the American Civil Liberties Union, and other groups and individuals said that the FISA Amendments Act of 2008 violated their rights under the Fourth Amendment. Plaintiffs included journalists and lawyers who represent prisoners held at Guantánamo Bay. Because of electronic surveillance, some of the plaintiffs said they now meet clients and sources only in person, creating additional costs in terms of time and expenses.[123] The case is called *Clapper v. Amnesty International.*

On October 29, 2012, the Court heard oral argument. The principal issue is whether the plaintiffs have standing to challenge the 2008 statute. The administration argued that persons who would have standing would be those who are notified that the government intends to introduce information when it prosecutes them, and that such a person would be someone who is abroad and is not a U.S. citizen.[124] Several Justices expressed concern about the steps an attorney would have to take when contacting a client by phone or e-mail. Justice Anthony Kennedy told the government's attorney: "I think the lawyer would engage in malpractice if he talked on the telephone with some of these clients, given this statute."[125] The precautions taken by attorneys are also taken by journalists and human rights researchers whose work is overseas.[126] As a safeguard, they may decide to speak with contacts in generalities rather than in specifics.[127] The conversations need not be with individuals suspected of terrorist activities. They can be with journalists abroad.[128]

Conclusion

In times of emergency, government officials will push boundaries to do what they think is necessary, whether legal or not. Sometimes their judgments are sound, persuading other branches of government, and the public, to register their support. On other occasions the zeal for quick action and prompt results runs roughshod over fundamental constitutional principles, placing in jeopardy the rights and liberties that government officials are sworn to respect and protect. The TSP was devised to circumvent what some executive officials saw as an outmoded FISA, but if that was their concern they should have come to Congress and ask for remedial legislation. Congress passed many emergency statutes in the months after September 11, including the AUMF and the USA PATRIOT Act. It would not have been difficult for the executive branch to persuade Congress to amend FISA to take account of technological changes after 1978. Many changes had indeed been made to FISA, including some after the September 11 terrorist attacks.

Instead of pursuing a legislative strategy, executive officials preferred to act unilaterally on the basis of inherent presidential power, a field of constitutional law filled with doubts, ambiguities, and open invitations to executive abuse. Claims of inherent presidential power always come at the cost of checks and balances, separation of powers, and the types of structural safeguards the Framers adopted to ensure that a concentration of power does not endanger the liberties of citizens. The very purpose of a Constitution is to confer power and limit it. Inherent power, by definition, recognizes no limits. The principles of government announced in 1787 were sound then, when the Framers drafted the Constitution. They are even more crucial today, when governmental power has grown to dimensions the Founders never imagined.

Key Actors

George W. Bush   As president, he authorized warrantless national security surveillance after September 11 and decided not to comply with the exclusive procedures of the Foreign Intelligence Surveillance Act.

James Comey   Deputy attorney general, acting attorney general during the illness of John Ashcroft.

Alberto Gonzales   White House counsel at the time the warrantless surveillance was authorized; later became attorney general.

Michael V. Hayden   NSA director at the time the Terrorist Surveillance Program was initiated.

Michael McConnell   Previously NSA director and later director of national intelligence; in that capacity oversees all intelligence agencies.

Barack Obama   As president, his administration supported the extension of FISA in 2012 and also the electronic surveillance challenged in *Clapper v. Amnesty International.*

Notes

1. James Risen and Eric Lichtblau, "Bush Lets U.S. Spy on Callers without Courts," *New York Times,* December 16, 2005, A1.

2. James Bamford, *Body of Secrets: Anatomy of the Ultra-Secret National Security Agency* (New York: Random House, 2002), 428–429.

3. Keith W. Olson, *Watergate: The Presidential Scandal That Shook America* (Lawrence: University Press of Kansas, 2003), 16.

4. Bamford, *Body of Secrets,* 430.

5. Ibid., 431–439.

6. Ibid., 440.

7. Louis Fisher and Katy J. Harriger, *American Constitutional Law,* 10th ed. (Durham, NC: Carolina Academic Press, 2013), 748.

8. 277 U.S. 438 (1928).

9. Fisher and Harriger, *American Constitutional Law,* 747, 748–749.

10. *Katz v. United States,* 389 U.S. 347, 351 (1967).

11. 82 Stat. 214 (1968).

12. *United States v. United States District Court,* 407 U.S. 297 (1972).

13. "Warrantless Wiretapping and Electronic Surveillance," Report by the Subcommittee on Surveillance of the Senate Committee on Foreign Relations and the Subcommittee on Administrative Practice and Procedure of the Senate Committee on the Judiciary, 94th Cong., 1st Sess. 2 (February 1975) (Senators Edmund Muskie, Ted Kennedy, and Sam Ervin).

14. Ibid., 7, 9.

15. 92 Stat. 1788, sec. 103(a) (1978).

16. Ibid., sec. 103(b).

17. Ibid., sec. 201(f) (emphasis added).

18. 115 Stat. 1402, sec. 314(a) (2001).

19. David E. Sanger, "In Address, Bush Says He Ordered Domestic Spying," *New York Times,* December 18, 2005, 30.

20. Ibid.

21. Ibid.

22. "Bush on the Patriot Act and Eavesdropping," *New York Times,* December 18, 2005, at 30.

23. Ibid.

24. Sanger, "In Address," 30.

25. Ibid.

26. *Weekly Compilation of Presidential Documents,* December 19, 2005, 1885.

27. Press briefing by Attorney General Alberto Gonzales and General Michael Hayden, principal deputy director for national intelligence, 2, www.whitehouse.gov/news/releases/2005/12/print/20051219–1.html.

28. Ibid.

29. Ibid.

30. Ibid., 4.

31. U.S. Justice Department, "Legal Authorities Supporting the Activities of the National Security Agency Described by the President," January 19, 2006, 1.

32. Ibid., 6–7.

33. 48 Stat. 1745 (1934).

34. *Panama Refining Co. v. Ryan,* 293 U.S. 388 (1935); *Schechter Corp. v. United States,* 295 U.S. 495 (1935).

35. Louis Fisher, "Presidential Inherent Power: The 'Sole Organ' Doctrine," *Presidential Studies Quarterly* 37 (March 2007): 139, 144.

36. Ibid., 144–150.

37. 10 *Annals of Congress* 613 (1800), cited in *United States v. Curtiss-Wright Corp.,* 299 U.S. 304, 319 (1936).

38. Fisher, "Presidential Inherent Power," 140–142.

39. *Talbot v. Seeman,* 5 U.S. 1, 28 (1801).

40. *Little v. Barreme,* 2 Cr. (6 U.S.) 170, 179 (1804).

41. U.S. Justice Department, "Legal Authorities Supporting the Activities of the National Security Agency," 2.

42. Ibid., 2–3.

43. Ibid., 3.

44. Transcript of May 15, 2007, hearings on U.S. attorneys firings by the Senate Committee on the Judiciary, CQ Transcriptions. The transcript is not numbered, but the remark by Comey appears on page 13.

45. Ibid., 14–15.

46. Ibid., 16.

47. Ibid., 17.

48. Ibid., 19.

49. Ibid., 20–21.

50. Ibid., 21

51. Ibid., 32.

52. Ibid., 43.

53. Hearing of the Senate Select Committee on Intelligence on the Nomination of General Michael V. Hayden to be Director of the Central Intelligence Agency, May 18, 2006, transcript, 35.

54. Ibid., 69.

55. Ibid.

56. Ibid., 74.

57. Ibid., 88.

58. Ibid., 138.

59. Ibid., 144.

60. Ibid., 68.

61. Ibid., 61.

62. *Hepting v. AT&T Corp.,* 439 F.Supp.2d 974 (N.D. Cal. 2006).

63. Ibid., 985.

64. Ibid., 986.

65. Ibid., 989.

66. Ibid., 990.

67. Ibid., 991.

68. Ibid., 992.

69. Ibid., 994.

70. Ibid., 1001. For newspaper stories on this decision, see Arshad Mohammed, "Judge Declines to Dismiss Lawsuit against AT&T," *Washington Post,* July 21, 2006, A9; John Markoff, "Judge Declines to Dismiss Privacy Suit against AT&T," *New York Times,* July 21, 2006, A13.

71. *Terkel v. AT&T,* 441 F.Supp.2d 899, 912 (N.D. Ill. 2006); Adam Liptak, "Judge Rejects Customer Suit over Records from AT&T," *New York Times,* July 26, 2006, A13; Mike Robinson, "Judge Dismisses Lawsuit on AT&T Data Handover," *Washington Post,* July 26, 2006, A6.

72. *American Civil Liberties v. National Sec. Agency,* 438 F.Supp.2d 754, 765 (E.D. Mich. 2006).

73. Ibid.

74. Ibid.

75. Ibid.

76. Ibid., 766.

77. Ibid., 774.

78. Ibid., 775.

79. Ibid., 778 (citing *Youngstown Sheet & Tube v. Sawyer,* 343 U.S. 579, 652 [1952]).

80. Ibid., 779.

81. Ibid., 781.

82. *ACLU v. National Sec. Agency,* 493 F.3d 644, 650 n.2 (6th Cir. 2007).

83. Brendan Sasso, "Court Turns Aside Wiretapping Suit," *The Hill,* October 10, 2012, 12.

84. David D. Kirkpatrick, "Republicans Seek to Bridge Differences on Surveillance," *New York Times,* March 1, 2006, A13.

85. Eric Lichtblau, "Administration and Critics, in Senate Testimony, Clash over Eavesdropping Compromise," *New York Times,* July 27, 2006, A19.

86. David D. Kirkpatrick and Scott Shane, "G.O.P. Senators Say Accord Is Set on Wiretapping," *New York Times,* March 3, 2006, A1.

87. Walter Pincus, "Panel on Eavesdropping Is Briefed by White House," *Washington Post,* March 10, 2006, A4.

88. Jonathan Weisman, "Republican Rift over Wiretapping Widens: Party at Odds on Surveillance Legislation," *Washington Post,* September 6, 2006, A3.

89. Jonathan Weisman, "House GOP Leaders Fight Wiretapping Limits," *Washington Post,* September 13, 2006, A7.

90. Keith Perine and Tim Starks, "House Panels Approve Surveillance Bill," *CQ Weekly,* September 25, 2006, 2556.

91. Eric Lichtblau, "House Approves Powers for Wiretaps without Warrants," *New York Times,* September 29, 2006, A18.

92. Attorney General Alberto Gonzales to Senators Patrick Leahy and Arlen Specter, Chairman and Ranking Member of the Senate Committee on the Judiciary, January 17, 2007, 1.

93. Ibid.

94. Ibid., 2.

95. David Johnston and Scott Shane, "Senators Demand Details on New Eavesdropping Rules," *New York Times,* January 18, 2007, A18.

96. Ibid. See also Dan Eggen, "Spy Court's Orders Stir Debate on Hill," *Washington Post*, January 19, 2007, A6.

97. Tim Starks, "Oversight Committees to Review Documents on NSA Wiretapping," *CQ Weekly*, February 5, 2007, 402; Mark Mazzetti, "Key Lawmakers Getting Files about Surveillance Program," *New York Times*, February 1, 2007, A11; Dan Eggen, "Records on Spy Program Turned over to Lawmakers," *Washington Post*, February 1, 2007, A2.

98. Adam Liptak, "Judges Weigh Arguments in U.S. Eavesdropping Case," *New York Times*, February 1, 2007, A11.

99. "Modernizing the Foreign Intelligence Surveillance Act," statement by J. Michael McConnell, Director of National Intelligence, before the Senate Select Committee on Intelligence, May 1, 2007, 1.

100. Ibid., 5.

101. "The Need to Bring the Foreign Intelligence Surveillance Act into the Modern Era," statement by Kenneth L. Wainstein, Assistant Attorney General, National Security Division, Department of Justice, before the Senate Select Committee on Intelligence, May 1, 2007, 8.

102. James Risen, "Administration Pulls Back on Surveillance Agreement," *New York Times*, May 3, 2007, A16.

103. P.L. 110–55, 121 Stat. 552 (2007).

104. Helen Fessenden, "Senate Democrats Seek to Regroup Quickly on Surveillance Law Rewrite," *The Hill*, September 11, 2007, 8.

105. Eric Lichtblau, "Senate Deal on Immunity for Telephone Companies," *New York Times*, October 18, 2007, A22; Ellen Nakashima and Shailagh Murray, "Senate Panel Approves New Surveillance Bill," *Washington Post*, October 19, 2007, A2.

106. Eric Lichtblau, "Key Senators Raise Doubts on Eavesdropping Immunity," *New York Times*, November 1, 2007, A16.

107. *Weekly Compilation of Presidential Documents*, vol. 44, 259.

108. Ibid., 291.

109. P.L. 110–261, 122 Stat. 2459, sec. 102 (2008).

110. Ibid., 122 Stat. 2467, sec. 801(5).

111. Ibid., 122 Stat. 2469, sec. 802.

112. *Al-Haramain Islamic Foundation, Inc. v. Bush*, 507 F.3d 1190, 1193 (9th Cir. 2007).

113. *In re National Sec. Agency Telecommunications Rec.*, 564 F.Supp.2d 1109, 1121 (N.D. Cal. 2008).

114. *In re National Sec. Agency Telecommunications*, 595 F.Supp.2d 1077 (N.D. Cal. 2009).

115. Order, *In re National Sec. Agency Telecommunications Rec.*, MDL Docket No. 06–1791 VRW, May 22, 2009, 3.

116. Jim Abrams, "Access to Top-Secret Papers at Issue in Wiretapping Case," *Washington Post*, May 31, 2009, A3; "U.S. Resists Order in Wiretapping Case," *New York Times*, May 31, 2009, 20; Carrie Johnson, "Showdown Looming on 'State Secrets,'" *Washington Post*, May 26, 2009, A4.

117. Eric Lichtblau, "U.S. Ordered to Pay Group of Muslims," *New York Times*, December 22, 2010, A23.

118. Ibid.

119. Edward C. Liu, "Reauthorization of the FISA Amendments Act," Congressional Research Service, Report R42725, September 12, 2012.

120. "FAA Sunsets Extension Act of 2012," S. Rept. No. 112–174, 112th Cong., 2d Sess. (2012), 8, 10–12; "FISA Amendments Act Reauthorization Act of 2012, H. Rept. No. 112–645, 112th Cong., 2d Sess. (2012), 18–22; "The FAA Sunsets Extension Act of 2012, 112th Cong., 2d Sess. (2012), 15–16.

121. Ellen Nakashima, "Debate looms on electronic-intercept law," *Washington Post,* December 9, 2012, A3.

122. "Bill Summary & Status, 112th Congress (2011—2012), H.R.5949, Major Congressional Actions—THOMAS Library of Congress," www.lawfareblog.com/wp -content/uploads/2013/01/Bill-Summary-Status-112th-Congress-2011–2012-H.R.5949 -Major-Congressional-Actions-THOMAS-Library-of-Congress.pdf.

123. Adam Liptak, "Supreme Court Agrees to Hear Case on Surveillance," *New York Times,* May 22, 2012, A19.

124. *Clapper v. Amnesty International USA, et al.,* No. 11–1025, oral argument, U.S. Supreme Court, October 29, 2012, 4–5.

125. Ibid., 26.

126. Ibid., 37 (statement by Jameel Jaffer, on behalf of plaintiffs).

127. Ibid., 38.

128. Ibid., 40.

14 The Rights of Detainees: Determining the Limits of Law

Linda Cornett and Mark Gibney

Before You Begin

1. Why is there so much political contention over the rights of detainees held in connection with the war on terrorism?

2. Why, and on what basis, did the administration of George W. Bush act so aggressively to assert executive privilege in defining the rights of detainees in its war on terrorism?

3. Why, and on what basis, have critics challenged the executive branch's authority to define the rights of detainees without "interference" from Congress or the judiciary?

4. Is the war on terrorism equivalent to other wars—such as World War II or the Vietnam War—that the United States has fought? Does it justify the president's claims to exceptional war powers and military jurisdiction over detainees? Or is the war on terrorism better understood rhetorically, like the "war on drugs" or the "war on poverty," and better fought in the criminal court system, as with the Oklahoma City bombings?

5. How does the separation of powers play out in this case?

6. What deference, if any, should the courts show the president in executing the war on terrorism? What would constitute the "end of hostilities" in this war and mark the expiration of the president's "war powers"?

7. What role did such nongovernmental organizations as the Center for National Security Studies play in defining the rights of detainees?

8. What role have the news media played in shaping the political controversies surrounding the detainees? Should media outlets have published the classified materials leaked to them, in the interest of transparent government and informed debate?

Introduction: Responding to Terrorism

On September 11, 2001, members of the al Qaeda network hijacked four commercial airliners. Two were flown into the World Trade Center towers in New York, one dived into the Pentagon outside Washington, DC, and one crashed in a field in Pennsylvania after passengers attempted to wrest control of the plane from the hijackers. The attacks killed approximately 3,000 people, unsettled the U.S. economy, and shook Americans' sense of security. Shortly thereafter, President George W. Bush promised that the United States would

> direct every resource at [its] command, every means of diplomacy, every tool of intelligence, every instrument of law enforcement, every financial influence, and every weapon of war to the disruption and to the defeat of the global terror network . . . before they strike [again].[1]

Under the assumption that extraordinary times call for extraordinary measures, the administration set out to expand its capabilities to execute what it called the "war on terrorism."

On September 14, the president declared a national emergency and requested that Congress give the administration the authority and tools to act decisively on all fronts of this new war.[2] Four days later, Congress responded to Bush's call with S.J. Res. 23, granting the executive branch broad authority to act against those responsible for the attacks of September 11 and to act to prevent future attacks, which the administration interpreted as the authority to combat terrorism whenever and wherever the threat arose. A short four weeks later, on October 24, Congress passed the USA PATRIOT Act—formally the Uniting and Strengthening America by Providing Appropriate Tools Required to Intercept and Obstruct Terrorism Act—to enhance the executive branch's law enforcement and intelligence-gathering capabilities, as well as its authority. Although it is multifaceted, the primary thrust of the act is to broaden the power of executive agencies to define, investigate, detain, and punish terror suspects with lower thresholds of evidence and less judicial oversight.

The administration moved equally aggressively in the international arena. On September 21, 2001, in a nationally televised address before Congress, Bush demanded that the Taliban government in Afghanistan immediately and unconditionally surrender any and all al Qaeda members on its soil, dismantle al Qaeda training camps, and give the United States unfettered access to suspected al Qaeda facilities. When this request was rebuffed, on October 7 the United States initiated a military campaign against Afghanistan, aided by

Timeline

The Rights of Detainees

September 11, 2001

Al Qaeda members hijack commercial airliners and crash them into the World Trade Center towers and the Pentagon. One plane believed destined for Washington, DC, crashes in rural Pennsylvania.

September 12, 2001

The Justice Department begins using federal immigration laws to detain aliens suspected of having ties to the September 11 attacks or connections to terrorism, or who are encountered during the course of an investigation conducted by the Federal Bureau of Investigation.

September 14, 2001

President George W. Bush declares a state of emergency and vows to devote the full resources of the United States to the "war on terrorism."

September 18, 2001

Congress passes S.J. Res. 23, "Authorizing Use of United States Armed Forces against Those Responsible for Recent Attacks against the United States."

October 7, 2001

The United States attacks Afghanistan to overthrow the Taliban government and root out al Qaeda.

October 24, 2001

Congress passes the USA PATRIOT Act, expanding the executive branch's intelligence-gathering and law enforcement powers.

December 6, 2001

A broad coalition, led by the Center for National Security Studies, files a lawsuit under the Freedom of Information Act to compel the U.S. government to release information about September 11 detainees.

January 11, 2002

The Defense Department begins transporting prisoners captured in the course of the war in Afghanistan to U.S. bases in Cuba. Among the prisoners is Yaser Esam Hamdi, a U.S. citizen.

January–February 2002

Memoranda from the White House counsel and Justice Department lawyers argue that the prisoners taken in Afghanistan do not qualify for protections under the Geneva Conventions. State Department lawyers strongly dissent. The White House announces that although the prisoners do not merit these legal protections, the Geneva Conventions would govern the actions of U.S. military personnel toward them and in Afghanistan.

(continued)

Timeline *(continued)*

The Rights of Detainees

February 19, 2002	In *Rasul et al. v. Bush,* the Center for Constitutional Rights files a writ of habeas corpus in the U.S. District Court for the District of Columbia on behalf of Shafiq Rasul and other foreign nationals held at Guantánamo Bay.
March 3, 2002	The U.S. District Court for the District of Columbia dismisses *Rasul* and other Guantánamo Bay suits for lack of jurisdiction. The case is appealed.
May 8, 2002	José Padilla, a U.S. citizen, is arrested as he enters the country at Chicago's O'Hare International Airport. He is detained as a material witness in the September 11 investigations.
June 9–11, 2002	Padilla is designated an "enemy combatant" by order of President Bush and is transferred from the U.S. criminal justice system to a navy brig in South Carolina. Lawyers for Padilla and Hamdi file petitions for a writ of habeas corpus in the U.S. District Court for the Eastern District of Virginia.
August 2, 2002	Judge Gladys Kessler of the U.S. District Court for the District of Columbia orders the Justice Department to release the names of the September 11 detainees and their attorneys but allows the department to keep other details of their cases secret.
October 2, 2002	Congress passes a joint resolution authorizing the use of U.S. armed forces against Iraq.
January 8, 2003	The U.S. Court of Appeals for the Fourth Circuit overturns the lower court finding in *Hamdi v. Rumsfeld* and rules that the president can designate U.S. citizens enemy combatants and hold them without access to counsel, if the president believes a person's behavior constitutes a threat to national security. The case is appealed to the U.S. Supreme Court.
March 19, 2003	The United States attacks Iraq based on Bush administration claims that Iraq possesses weapons of mass destruction and maintains ties with terrorists who might use such weapons against the United States.
June 17, 2003	The U.S. Court of Appeals for the District of Columbia accepts the Bush administration's contention that

	"disclosure of even one name could endanger national security" and reverses the lower court ruling requiring the government to release limited information about the September 11 detainees. The U.S. Supreme Court declines, without explanation, to take up the case on appeal.
April 5, 2004	The Center for Constitutional Rights directly files two habeas corpus briefs with the Supreme Court and one in district court on behalf of Rasul and his coplaintiffs.
April 28, 2004	The Supreme Court begins hearing oral arguments in *Hamdi v. Rumsfeld, Rumsfeld v. Padilla,* and *Rasul et al. v. Bush.*
June 28, 2004	The Supreme Court hands down rulings in *Hamdi v. Rumsfeld* and *Rasul et al. v. Bush* that essentially affirm the rights of detainees to due process before a neutral judge to challenge their detention as enemy combatants. The Court rejects Padilla's petition for due process on a technicality.
October 11, 2004	Hamdi is released from U.S. custody and flown to Saudi Arabia.
December 30, 2005	Congress passes the Detainee Treatment Act, which drastically curtails the courts' habeas corpus jurisdiction over detentions at Guantánamo.
June 29, 2006	In its decision in *Hamdan v. Rumsfeld,* the Supreme Court strikes down the military commissions President Bush established to try suspected members of al Qaeda.
September 28, 2006	Congress passes the Military Commissions Act, which provides statutory authorization for military commission trials for Guantánamo Bay detainees and eliminates judicial jurisdiction, effectively stripping detainees of the right to file habeas corpus petitions in federal court.
June 18, 2008	In its decision in *Boumediene v. Bush,* the U.S. Supreme Court strikes down the Military Commissions Act, holding that detainees have a constitutional right to habeas protection.
June 20, 2009	Barak Obama is sworn in as president and immediately signs three executive orders to prepare for the closure of Guantánamo Bay detention center, but meets broad opposition from various quarters.
March 7, 2011	Obama announces that military commissions will resume prosecution of alleged terrorists in the Guantánamo detention facility.

Afghan forces of the Northern Alliance, to depose the Taliban government and root out al Qaeda. On March 19, 2003, the Bush administration carried its war on terrorism to Iraq, largely based on the claim that Iraq possessed weapons of mass destruction. The consequences of the administration's actions have been many and complex; however, one of the most immediate effects of the executive's expanded law enforcement, intelligence, and military efforts and capabilities has been a dramatic expansion in the number and variety of people detained by the government. The nature of these detentions raises the question: What legal rights do detainees in the war on terrorism have? What follows is a depiction of the continuing struggle to answer that question.

Background: Detainees in the War on Terrorism

Detainee, by definition, refers to "any person deprived of personal liberty except as a result of conviction for an offense."[3] The rights of detainees are intrinsically important in a democracy that has traditionally privileged liberty above virtually all other values. The rules governing the state's authority to deprive individuals of their liberty are a central theme in the U.S. Constitution. In addressing issues related to detainees, the Court of Appeals for the Fourth Circuit noted in January 2003 that, indeed,

> [The] Constitution is suffused with concern about how the state will wield its awesome power of forcible restraint. And this preoccupation was not accidental. Our forebears recognized that the power to detain could easily become destructive "if exerted without check or control."[4]

The Bush administration's war on terrorism has significantly expanded the number and variety of detainees under the authority of the U.S. government to include the September 11 detainees; foreign "enemy combatants" at Guantánamo Bay, Cuba; prisoners held in American-run prisons in Iraq and Afghanistan; and finally, foreign nationals who have been detained and interrogated as part of a policy known as "extraordinary rendition." An examination of some of the controversies surrounding the rights of detainees brings into stark relief a number of broader, enduring debates about the appropriate balance between national security and civil liberty; the relationship between national interest and international law; and the responsibilities of each of the branches of government to balance competing interests and values when setting national security policy.

September 11 Detainees

In the months following the September 11 attacks, U.S. authorities detained approximately 1,200 foreign nationals, most on visa violations.[5] Many were arrested by the Immigration and Naturalization Service at the direction of Attorney General John Ashcroft and detained as "special interest cases." Some were held for days, weeks, and even months without being charged with a crime. All were denied the opportunity to post bond and given very limited opportunities to communicate with family members or seek legal counsel. The government refused even to release their names, arguing that disclosing such information "would give terrorists a virtual roadmap to [the government's] investigation that could allow terrorists to chart a potentially deadly detour around [its] efforts."[6] Ashcroft further directed chief immigration judge Michael Creppy to close proceedings in deportation hearings of the special interest cases, a policy later ruled unconstitutional by the Court of Appeals for the Sixth Circuit. A broad coalition of civil liberties advocates, led by the Center for National Security Studies, sought to compel the Justice Department to release information about the detainees under the Freedom of Information Act (FOIA). In August 2002, Judge Gladys Kessler of the U.S. District Court for the District of Columbia agreed that although the government's national security concerns were legitimate, "the public's interest in learning the identity of those arrested and detained is essential to verifying whether the government is operating within the bounds of the law."[7] The judge ordered the Justice Department to release the names of the detainees and their attorneys but allowed the department to keep the details of their cases secret.

In June 2003, the U.S. Court of Appeals for the District of Columbia overturned that decision on appeal, accepting the administration's contention that "disclosure of even one name could endanger national security"[8] and in general deferring to the executive on questions of national security. The court asserted that

> when government officials tell the court that disclosing the names of the detainees will produce harm, it is abundantly clear that the government's top counterterrorism officials are well suited to make this predictive judgment. Conversely, the judiciary is in an extremely poor position to second guess the government's views in the field of national security.[9]

The U.S. Supreme Court declined, without explanation, to take up the case on appeal.

The government never charged any of the September 11 detainees with terror-related crimes, and most of them have been released or deported. Regardless, the USA PATRIOT Act substantially increased the Justice Department's authority to detain noncitizens without charge or counsel and, in fact, prescribes mandatory detention for "certified" aliens—that is, people whom the attorney general "has reasonable grounds to believe" represent a security threat or are found by the attorney general and the secretary of state to associate with "foreign terrorist organizations" to commit, incite, prepare, plan, gather information on, or provide material support for terrorist activities.[10] The legislation also explicitly limits judicial oversight of the executive branch's decisions, but it allows detainees to petition the attorney general for a reconsideration of their status every six months.

Critics warned that the administration's increasingly broad authority to secretly arrest and detain terror suspects is a dangerous precedent and provides opportunities for abuse. An internal Justice Department investigation by Inspector General Glenn Fine seemed to lend credence to those fears. In April 2003, Fine reported "significant problems" with the treatment of the September 11 detainees. For example, while recognizing that the Justice Department was operating under extremely difficult circumstances, he charged that the Federal Bureau of Investigation (FBI) in New York had made too little effort to distinguish between aliens who might have knowledge of terrorist threats and aliens encountered coincidentally, resulting in the detention of minor visa violators under very restrictive conditions. The report decried the FBI's "hold-until-cleared" and blanket "no bond" policies, which kept many of these detainees in confinement for extended periods. Fine also found evidence of a disturbing pattern of physical and verbal abuse by some correctional officers.[11]

Guantánamo Bay Detainees: Foreign Nationals, Enemy Combatants

The war in Afghanistan produced another category of detainee: enemy combatant. Beginning January 11, 2002, the military started transferring several hundred prisoners to an interrogation facility, dubbed "Camp X-Ray," at Guantánamo Bay, Cuba. Arguing that these detainees represented the "worst of the worst," General Richard B. Myers, chairman of the Joint Chiefs of Staff, described the Guantánamo Bay detainees as "people who would gnaw through hydraulic lines at the back of a C-17 to bring it down."[12] Many of these inmates, some of whom have now been detained for years, were subjected to constant interrogation, surveillance, and severe restrictions on their physical movements. Although the great majority were captured in Afghanistan during or immediately following hostilities there, a sizable number arrived after being turned over to the United States by other governments, based on suspected ties to al Qaeda.[13] As of October 5, 2012, a total of 779 enemy combatants have been held at Guantanamo Bay. Of these, 604 were eventually transferred, 9 died, and 166 remain at the base. Interestingly enough, the Bush administration transferred many more detainees (532) than has the Obama administration (72).[14] The Bush administration maintained that the detainees at Guantánamo Bay should not have access to U.S. courts or constitutional protections. It based its argument on the grounds that the facility where the detainees were being held is outside the territorial boundaries of the United States and that constitutional protections do not apply extraterritorially. Memos written by Deputy Assistant Attorneys General Patrick Philbin and John Yoo laid out the administration's view. As one former administration lawyer later described it, the base at Guantánamo Bay "existed in a legal twilight zone"—or "the legal equivalent of outer space."[15] Moreover, the government argued, the unprecedented threat that global terrorist networks posed required a suspension of the usual rules governing detainees. Holding prisoners without rights, Solicitor General Theodore Olson argued before the Supreme Court, "serves the vital objectives of preventing combatants from continuing to aid our enemies and gathering intelligence to further the overall war effort."[16]

The Bush administration also claimed exemption from judicial oversight based on the president's powers as commander in chief. The U.S. government classified all of the detainees as "enemy combatants" and steadfastly maintained that only the president can determine who is an enemy combatant and the conditions under which such detainees will be held. In a reply brief in *Rasul et al. v. Bush*, the case challenging the Guantánamo Bay detentions, the government spelled out its position:

> The detained petitioners are aliens held abroad. Accordingly, none of their claims—including their premature challenges to the Military Order—are within the subject matter jurisdiction of this Court, or *any* United States court. . . . The extraordinary circumstances in which this action arises and the particular relief that petitioners seek implicate core political questions about the conduct of the war on terrorism that the Constitution leaves to the Commander-in-Chief.[17]

In effect, the administration argued that the chief executive has total discretion over the designation of enemy combatants and that it can hold enemy combatants without benefit of counsel and with no right to challenge their detention until the "end of hostilities." Moreover, the administration argued that its judgments could not be second guessed by the judiciary. Allowing detainees access to the federal courts, Olson argued before the Supreme Court, would "place the federal courts in the unprecedented position of micromanaging the executive's handling of captured enemy combatants from a distant zone."[18]

In addition to the position that the Guantánamo detainees were without protection under domestic law, the Bush administration also maintained that as enemy combatants, they were not protected under the Geneva Conventions. In early 2002, Secretary of State Colin Powell and State Department attorneys argued within the administration that the case of each detainee would need to be individually reviewed to determine whether the conventions applied to that person. A January 9, 2002, memo from the Justice Department's Office of Legal Counsel argued, however, that the Geneva Conventions did not apply to the detainees. It also stated that the detainees were not covered by the 1996 War Crimes Act, a measure specifying the conditions under which U.S. citizens, including U.S. officials, can be prosecuted for war crimes. In a January 25, 2002, memo, White House Counsel Alberto Gonzales agreed with the Justice Department's interpretation that the Geneva Conventions (as well as the War Crimes Act) did not apply to al Qaeda or Taliban detainees. Following protests by Secretary Powell and his primary legal aide, William Howard Taft IV, the White House responded with a compromise position in February 2002: Although the protection of the Geneva Conventions did not apply to captured al Qaeda and Taliban fighters, the United States would adhere to the conventions in its conduct of the war in Afghanistan "to the extent appropriate and consistent with military necessity."[19] Regardless, the government did hold out the promise that at least some of the Guantánamo Bay detainees would receive trials before a military tribunal, although at the same time it maintained that it would not be bound to release any detainees even if the tribunal acquitted them.

The conditions under which the Guantánamo detainees were held and interrogated attracted renewed attention when gross abuses of detainees in Iraq's Abu Ghraib prison—where the Geneva Conventions ostensibly *did* apply—came to light in early 2004. Investigations into the Iraqi prisoner abuse scandal suggested the more aggressive interrogation techniques that Defense Secretary Donald Rumsfeld had approved for use at Guantánamo Bay were "exported" to Iraq when officials became frustrated by the paltry quantity and quality of intelligence being generated during a sustained Iraqi insurgency.[20]

Of particular interest were a set of interrogation rules developed under Major General Geoffrey Miller that were first employed in Guantánamo Bay but later brought to Iraq.[21]

> [The] "72-point matrix for stress and duress" . . . laid out the types of coercion and the escalating levels at which they could be applied. These included the use of harsh heat or cold; withholding food; hooding for days at a time; naked isolation in cold, dark cells for more than 30 days; and threatening (but not biting) by dogs. It also permitted limited use of "stress positions" designed to subject detainees to rising levels of pain.[22]

The Red Cross issued several reports to U.S. military authorities warning of the conditions at the Guantánamo Bay prison. In addition to potential abuses, the Red Cross specifically stated that the indeterminate nature of the detentions at Guantánamo was taking a heavy psychological toll on detainees and had resulted in thirty suicide attempts since the prison opened.[23]

Subsequent studies revealed that the purported danger and intelligence value of the Guantánamo detainees may have been systematically overstated by the Bush administration. According to the *New York Times*,

> In interviews, dozens of high-level military, intelligence, and law-enforcement officials in the United States, Europe, and the Middle East said that contrary to the repeated assertions of senior administration officials, none of the detainees at the United States Naval Base at Guantanamo Bay ranked as leaders or senior operatives of Al Qaeda. They said only a relative handful—some put the number at about a dozen, others more than two dozen—were sworn Al Qaeda members or other militants able to elucidate the organization's inner workings. While some Guantanamo intelligence has aided terrorism investigations, none of it has enabled intelligence or law-enforcement services to foil imminent attacks, the officials said.[24]

The article further charged that based on a top-secret study conducted at Guantánamo by the Central Intelligence Agency (CIA), the administration knew as early as September 2002 that "many of the accused terrorists appeared to be low-level recruits who went to Afghanistan to support the Taliban or even innocent men swept up in the chaos of the war."[25]

Abu Ghraib and the Issue of Torture

Another category of detainees consists of those held at various US-run military facilities in Iraq and Afghanistan, where it is estimated that tens of thousands have been incarcerated for various periods of time during the course of both wars. However, there is one name that stands out from all of these: Abu Ghraib. In an April 28, 2004 broadcast of *60 Minutes II,* the entire world was shown the despicable and illegal treatment carried out against detainees at the Abu Ghraib prison in Iraq. The Bush administration immediately protested that the acts depicted were nothing more than the work of a few "bad apples" and vigorously denied that the abuses had deeper roots in policy. Faced with growing public criticism, Bush issued an apology for these atrocities a few days later. After meeting privately with King Abdullah II of Jordan, President Bush told a group of reporters and journalists what he had told the king: "I told him I was sorry for the humiliation suffered by Iraqi prisoners and the humiliation by their families."[26] There followed immediately a veritable flood of apologies from members of his cabinet, including Secretary Powell, national security adviser Condoleezza Rice, and Secretary Rumsfeld.

As the scandal unfolded and investigations into its causes strengthened, particularly in Congress, a paper trail began to emerge tracing the evolution of Bush administration policies regarding the status and treatment of detainees. A number of legal memoranda from Justice Department lawyers and the White House counsel surfaced that interpreted the limitations on the detention and interrogation of prisoners in the war on terrorism extremely narrowly. Indeed, in a leaked memo dated January 25, 2003, White House Counsel Alberto Gonzales advised the president on how to preserve the government's flexibility in the detention and interrogation of suspects:

> As you have said, the war on terrorism is a new kind of war. . . . The nature of the war places a high premium on other factors, such as the ability to obtain information from captured terrorists and their sponsors in order to avoid further atrocities against American civilians, and the need to try terrorists for war crimes such as wantonly killing civilians. In my judgment, this new paradigm renders obsolete Geneva's strict limitation on questioning enemy prisoners and renders quaint some of its provisions.[27]

Other legal memos appear to explore ways to circumvent domestic and international laws prohibiting torture. One emphasizes the evidentiary hurdles to the prosecution of torture:

> To convict a defendant of torture [under federal criminal law], the prosecution must establish that: (1) the torture occurred outside the United States; (2) the defendant acted under the color of law; (3) the victim was within the

defendant's custody or physical control; (4) the defendant specifically intended to cause severe physical or mental pain and suffering; and (5) that the act inflicted severe mental pain and suffering.[28]

Each of these requirements presented new opportunities to further narrow the definition of torture. For example, the intent clause was interpreted to require that inflicting severe pain or suffering contrary to the law be the primary *intent* of the defendant. "Thus, even if the defendant knows that severe pain will result from his actions, if causing such harm is not his objective, he lacks the requisite specific intent . . .; a defendant is guilty of torture only if he acts with the express purpose of inflicting severe pain or suffering." Likewise, the memo argues, federal law "makes plain that the infliction of pain or suffering per se . . . is insufficient to amount to torture. Instead, the text provides that the pain or suffering must be 'severe,'" which government lawyers interpreted to mean "death, organ failure, or the permanent impairment of a significant bodily function."[29] The memorandum further maintains that under the president's authority as commander in chief, torture is lawful as long as it is carried out to protect U.S. national security and that interference by Congress or the courts would be unconstitutional. Another memo, prepared by the Justice Department, explains,

> Even if an interrogation method [might arguably constitute torture under these narrow definitions], and application of the statute was not held to be an unconstitutional infringement of the President's Commander-in-Chief authority, we believe that under current circumstances certain justifications [including military necessity or self-defense] might be available that would potentially eliminate criminal liability.[30]

That memo also attempts to draw a legal distinction between torture, which it acknowledges is illegal, and lesser forms of cruel, inhuman, or degrading treatment or punishment, which the memo claims are to be deplored and prevented but are not so universally and categorically condemned as to be illegal. A lengthy portion of the memo goes on to explore a range of cruel, inhuman, and degrading actions just short of torture, which Justice Department lawyers argue would not violate domestic and international prohibitions on torture if applied. For example, forcing someone onto their hands and knees and kicking them in the stomach might not be construed as torture, but rape or sexual assault would.[31] Some groups within the administration were offended by these arguments. There was, reportedly, "almost a revolt" by the military's judge advocates general, or JAGs, including lawyers who report to the chairman of the Joint Chiefs of Staff. In frustration, they made their concerns public, charging that there was "a calculated effort to create an atmosphere of legal ambiguity about how the [Geneva] Conventions should be applied."[32] State Department lawyers also objected. Taft, the State Department's legal adviser, hastily added his own memo to the debate, arguing that the Justice Department's legal advice to President Bush was " 'seriously flawed,' its reasoning 'incorrect as well as incomplete,' and all of it 'contrary to the official position of the United States, the United Nations and all other states that have considered the issue.' "[33]

Although the administration argued that these memos were "theoretical" rather than operational, it has become increasingly clear that the Secretary of Defense did expand the scope and nature of permissible interrogation techniques and admitted that he hid some detainees from the Red Cross at the request of Director of Central Intelligence George Tenet.[34] It is also undeniable that gross abuses, reported by the Red Cross and confirmed in detail in a report by Major General Antonio Taguba,[35] were rife in Iraq prisons. Although the administration vigorously denied that it in any way condoned torture, some observers have concluded that the atmosphere of legal ambiguity at the very least opened the door for abuses. One report, prepared by three senior army generals and commonly known as the Fay Report, after its chair, General George R. Fay, asserts that "a list of interrogation techniques approved by Defense Sec[retary] Rumsfeld for use at the U.S. detention facility at Guantanamo Bay, Cuba, migrated improperly to Abu Ghraib and contributed to some of the abuses there."[36] A four-member independent panel headed by James A. Schlesinger reiterated that "leadership failures at the highest levels of the Pentagon, Joint Chiefs of Staff and military command in Iraq contributed to an environment in which detainees were abused at Abu Ghraib prison and other facilities."[37] Public trust in the administration's appeal for wide latitude in dealing with detainees in the war on terrorism reached new lows in the wake of these revelations.

Extraordinary Rendition and Secret Prisons

Although information has been difficult to obtain, there is now strong evidence that the executive branch has also held prisoners in a number of secret detention facilities offshore. Some of those detainees were taken into custody through a process known as "extraordinary rendition," in which the U.S. government has abducted persons suspected of supporting international terrorism—often in collusion with friendly governments—and taken them to other foreign countries for "interrogation" purposes.

The two best known cases involve Maher Arar and Khaled El-Masri. Arar is a dual citizen of Syria and Canada. He was living in Canada when he took a family vacation to Tunis in September 2002. Responding to his employer's request to return, Arar took a plane that had a stopover in New York. There, he was taken aside by immigration authorities and interrogated for more than a week. Following this, Arar was flown to Syria, where he was detained for ten months and subjected to torture throughout the period, before finally being released and allowed to return to his family in Canada. After a full inquiry, the Canadian government exonerated Arar of having any connection to terrorism and awarded him nearly $10 million in restitution. On the other hand, the U.S. government has refused to acknowledge any wrongdoing, and to this day Arar remains on the government's terrorist watch list. Furthermore, Arar's attempt to obtain a remedy under U.S. law has not been successful either. In November 2009, the U.S. Court of Appeals for the Second Circuit ruled that "special factors counseling hesitation" barred Arar's claim that his constitutional rights were violated when American officials sent him to Syria.[38] The U.S. Supreme Court later declined to hear Arar's appeal.

Khaled El-Masri is a German citizen of Lebanese descent who was arrested by Macedonian authorities during a family vacation and turned over to CIA operatives. He was flown to Kabul, Afghanistan, and detained there for five months. While in detention, he was tortured. Ultimately, he was flown to a remote area of Albania and released. El-Masri subsequently filed suit in U.S. district court against former director of central intelligence Tenet, three corporate defendants, ten unnamed employees of the CIA, and ten unnamed employees of the defendant corporations. The government sought dismissal of the suit on the basis of the "state secrets" doctrine—namely, that to defend itself in the case, the government would be forced to disclose sensitive military secrets and operations. This district court ruled in favor of the United States and dismissed his case. On appeal, El-Masri claimed that both the Council of Europe and President Bush himself had publicly acknowledged the existence of the extraordinary rendition program. Thus there was no longer any "secret" to which the "state secrets" doctrine could be applied. The Fourth Circuit Court of Appeals disagreed and upheld the dismissal on the grounds that pursuit of El-Masri's claim might still involve the disclosure of some sensitive military information.

The Legal Wrangling over Guantánamo

At the outset, it was not clear what role (if any) the American judiciary would play in the "war on terrorism." For one thing, there is a longstanding principle in U.S. law that courts will not involve themselves in issues involving the conduct of American foreign policy, and this is particularly true during times of war. One of the most notorious examples in U.S. history was the Supreme Court's ruling during World War II in *Korematsu v. United States*,[39] which upheld the internment of Japanese nationals. However, in the present case, and with some notable exceptions (see the discussion of Arar and El-Masri above), U.S. courts have come to play a vigorous and vital role. We now turn to the (ongoing) tug of war between the political branches, on the one hand, and the U.S. Supreme Court, on the other. Among the questions we will address are the following: How broad is the latitude that the president can expect in the execution of the war on terrorism? Does the doctrine of separation of powers limit judicial oversight of the president's treatment of various categories of detainees, or does it demand it instead? Do the courts have jurisdiction over enemy combatants on territory outside the United States but effectively and fully under U.S. military control? What (if any) are the rights of detainees in Afghanistan and Iraq? What (if any) protections are available for targets of extraordinary rendition?

Rasul et al. v. Bush

Rasul et al. v. Bush was a consolidated action brought by a group of British, Australian, and Kuwaiti nationals being detained by the U.S. government at Guantánamo Bay.[40] Relying primarily on the Supreme Court's decision in *Johnson v. Eisentrager* (1950),[41] the U.S. District Court for the District of Columbia dismissed their suit for want of jurisdiction, holding that aliens detained outside the sovereign territory of the United States may not invoke a petition for a writ of habeas corpus.[42] The Court of Appeals for the District of Columbia affirmed the dismissal, holding that "the 'privilege of litigation' does not extend to aliens in military custody who have no presence in any territory over which the United States is sovereign."[43]

The Supreme Court reversed the court of appeals decision.[44] The majority opinion emphasized the historic purpose of the writ to justify and reaffirm "the federal courts' power to review applications for habeas relief in a wide variety of cases involving Executive detention, in wartime as well as in times of peace."[45] Traditionally, the writ has been seen as the primary protection against executive restraint. The Court affirmed that "[a]t its historical core, the writ of habeas corpus has served as a means of reviewing the legality of Executive detention, and it is in that context that its protections have been strongest."[46] Congress has generally supported this broad interpretation, the Court noted, "extending the protections of the writ to all cases where any person may be restrained of his or her liberty in violation of the Constitution, or of any treaty or law of the United States."[47] The fact that the petitioners are aliens and are located outside the United States did not matter to the Supreme Court.

For the Court, the crux of the matter was the proper scope of *Eisentrager* in defining the rights of detainees. That case arose during the close of the Second World War. The plaintiffs were a group of twenty-one German nationals who had been captured in China for engaging in espionage against the United States. Following a trial and conviction by a U.S. military commission sitting in China, the prisoners were shipped to the Landsberg prison in Germany. Their legal challenges ultimately reached the Supreme Court, which ruled that the detainees were not entitled to any legal remedy under U.S. law.

The Supreme Court in 2004 found important distinctions between the detainees in *Eisentrager* and *Rasul et al.*:

> Petitioners in [*Rasul et al.*] differ from the *Eisentrager* detainees in important respects. They are not nationals of countries at war with the United States, and they deny that they have engaged in or plotted acts of aggression against the United States; they have never been afforded access to any tribunal, much less charged with and convicted of wrongdoing; and for more than two years they have been imprisoned in territory over which the United States exercises exclusive jurisdiction and control.[48]

Justice Anthony M. Kennedy, in a concurring opinion, added that also unlike the *Eisentrager* case, Guantánamo Bay is in every practical respect a U.S. territory, and it is one far removed from any hostilities.[49] Moreover, the detainees at Guantánamo Bay face the possibility of indefinite detention, and without any benefit of a legal proceeding to determine their status, whereas the Germans were tried and convicted by a military tribunal.

Justice Antonin Scalia filed a dissenting opinion, joined by Chief Justice William Rehnquist and Justice Clarence Thomas. For Scalia, the crux of the case was that the Guantánamo Bay detainees are not located within the territorial jurisdiction of *any* federal district court, and thus the protections afforded under the habeas statute do not extend to them. Scalia went on to describe the "breathtaking" and, in his view, frightening consequences of the majority's decision:

> It permits an alien captured in a foreign theater of active combat to bring a [habeas corpus] petition against the Secretary of Defense. Over the course of the last century, the United States has held millions of alien prisoners abroad. . . . A great many of these prisoners would no doubt have complained about the circumstances of their capture and the terms of their confinement.[50]

For good or for ill, the major thrust of this and the other Supreme Court decisions regarding the detainees was to reassert the judiciary's authority in defining and defending due process in the administration's war on terrorism. However, the decisions also highlighted the role of Congress in defining the reaches of both the administration and the judiciary through the legislative process. Because many of the legal controversies that made their way to the courts depended on differing interpretations of previous laws, breaking the stalemate between the executive and judiciary would require new legislation. The legislature was quick to respond to the call. Before the Guantánamo detainees could take advantage of the Court's ruling, Congress passed new legislation that (seemingly) took away the very rights that the courts had granted detainees. Furthermore, the Justice Department had asked the federal appeals court to restrict Guantánamo detainees' access to their lawyers who, the administration charged, were causing threats to security at Guantánamo by "caus[ing] unrest among the detainees and improperly serv[ing] as a conduit to the news media."[51]

Congress Responds

Following the Supreme Court's decision in *Rasul,* in December 2005 Congress passed the Detainee Treatment Act (P.L. 109–148, 119 Stat. 2680), which added a new subsection (e) to the habeas statute, which reads: "Except as provided in section 1005 of the [Detainee Treatment Act], no court, justice, or judge" may exercise jurisdiction over

1. an application for a writ of habeas corpus filed by or on behalf of an alien detained by the Department of Defense at Guantanamo Bay, Cuba; or
2. any other action against the United States or its agents relating to any aspect of the detention by the Department of Defense of an alien at Guantanamo Bay, Cuba who

(A) is currently in military custody; or

(B) has been determined by the United States Court of Appeals for the District of Columbia Circuit . . . to have been properly detained as an enemy combatant.

The Detainee Treatment Act (DTA) attempted to limit the judiciary's role to the D.C. Circuit Court, and then only for the purpose of determining whether the designation of "enemy combatant" was supported by the evidence that the administration provided. The only reason the federal courts were able to take up these issues again stemmed from ambiguity in the act about whether or not it would apply to cases pending when the legislation was passed.

The Supreme Court Counters

In June 2006, the Supreme Court took up the matter of the DTA in the case of *Hamdan v. Rumsfeld*.[52] Salim Ahmed Hamdan, allegedly Osama bin Laden's former chauffeur, was an enemy combatant held at Guantánamo Bay who challenged the legality of the military tribunals the Bush administration created to try the detainees. The Court agreed with the substantive claim that the proposed military commissions were inconsistent with the procedures established under both the Uniform Code of Military Justice and the Geneva Conventions. It also affirmed the Court's authority to hear the case despite provisions in the DTA that eliminated most avenues for judicial oversight in matters related to the detainees. Although the government claimed that the DTA had removed the Supreme Court's jurisdiction, the Court disagreed. Rather, it pointed to a provision of the DTA that stated that subsections (e)(2) and (e)(3) of section 1005 "shall apply with respect to any claim . . . that is pending on or after the date of the enactment of this Act [DTA Sec. 1005(h)]." However, no provision of the DTA stated whether subsection (e)(1) applied to pending cases. The Court found evidence in the legislative record that the omission of pending cases from the exemption from judicial review was purposeful. Therefore, it refused to dismiss Hamdan's suit, while adroitly sidestepping separation of powers issues being raised by both sides of the continuing controversy.

Congress Responds to the Hamdan Decision

Congress responded to *Hamdan* almost immediately by passing the Military Commissions Act of 2006 (P.L. 109–366, 120 Stat. 2600) (2006) (MCA), which the president signed into law on October 17, 2006. Subsection 7(a) of the MCA, entitled "Habeas Corpus Matters," added a new amendment, which reads as follows:

> (1) No court, justice or judge shall have jurisdiction to hear or consider an application for a writ of habeas corpus filed by or on behalf of an alien detained by the United States who has been determined by the United States to have been properly detained as an enemy combatant or is awaiting such determination.
>
> (2) Except as provided in [section 1005(e)(2) and (e)(3) of the DTA], no court, justice, or judge shall have jurisdiction to hear or consider any other action against the United States or its agents relating to any aspect of the detention, transfer, treatment, trial, or conditions of confinement of an alien who is or was detained by the United States and has been determined by the United States to have been properly detained as an enemy combatant or is awaiting such determination.

Furthermore, in a pointed response to the Court's ruling on *Hamdan,* a new subsection (b) provides:

> The amendment made by subsection (a) shall take effect on the date of the enactment of this Act, and shall apply to all cases, without exception, pending on or after the date of the enactment of this Act which relate to any aspect of the detention, transfer, trial, or conditions of detention of an alien detained by the United States since September 11, 2001.

Congress again clearly and consistently favored executive privilege in the conduct of the war on terrorism.

The Supreme Court Counters—Once Again

Not to be deterred, the final word (we believe) on this matter was delivered by the Supreme Court in its decision in *Boumediene v. Bush.*[53] The Bush administration argued that under the provisions of the Military Commissions Act, courts no longer had jurisdiction to hear any claims filed by enemy combatants, and it petitioned the Court to dismiss the case. The Supreme Court declined to do so. Instead, what it did was to reaffirm the importance of having a judicial check over executive actions, and it arrived at this position by ruling for the very first time that detainees at Guantánamo Bay had a constitutional right to habeas corpus protection.

The Court proceeded in three steps. The first consisted of an extended history of the role that habeas corpus has played in both British and American political history as a means of protection against executive abuses. The second step consisted of addressing the claim whether habeas protection extends to nonnationals being detained outside the United States. As noted earlier, the strongest argument against this proposition was that the Supreme Court had already answered this question in *Eisentrager,* when the Court denied habeas corpus protection in a case filed by a group of German soldiers held in a military camp (Landsberg) in occupied Germany. For the majority in *Boumediene,* there were several factors that differentiated between these two situations. For one thing, Guantánamo Bay is under complete American jurisdiction and control, which was not the case with Landsberg. Another rationale is that while the German prisoners had been given a hearing that established their role as combatants, no such proceedings had ever taken place for the Guantánamo detainees. Finally, the Court was also disturbed that many of the claimants had already spent years in prison—with no apparent end in sight.

Finally, the Supreme Court directly addressed the constitutional requirements for suspending habeas corpus, once it concluded that it was indeed the intention of Congress "to circumscribe habeas review."[54] The U.S. Constitution provides in Article 1, Section 9, that "[t]he privilege of the Writ of Habeas Corpus shall not be suspended, unless when in Case of Rebellion or Invasion the public Safety may require it." Even then, the majority ruled, any suspension of the writ would have to be accompanied by some other means by which executive authority could be challenged. In the Court's view, the protections afforded under the Detainee Treatment Act simply did not meet this standard and thus operates as an unconstitutional suspension of the writ. In its analysis, it pointed to a number of shortcomings in the military tribunals established by the political branches, including the lack of effective legal counsel; the fact that the detainee might not even be aware of critical legal allegations that have been filed against him; and finally, the admissibility of hearsay evidence. Furthermore, although the DTA did establish a level of judicial review through the Court of Appeals for the District of Columbia, the Supreme Court ruled this process inadequate, most notably the fact that the procedure established by Congress did not afford the detainee the opportunity to present relevant exculpatory evidence that was not a part of the record in earlier proceedings.

Boumediene v. Bush is a landmark decision in at least two ways. First, it represents a monument to judicial perseverance. Notwithstanding repeated efforts by

Congress and the president, the American judiciary has refused to be sidelined in the government's conduct of the "war on terrorism." In that way, this decision and its progeny have reaffirmed the principle first established by Chief Justice John Marshall in *Marbury v. Madison:* "It is emphatically the province and duty of the judicial department to say what the law is."

Second, *Boumediene* establishes for the very first time that nonresident foreign nationals have rights under the U.S. Constitution. It is not clear how far (literally) the holding in *Boumediene* will be taken, but it is noteworthy that in a subsequent case, *Maqaleh et al. v. Gates,*[55] involving habeas petitions filed by a group of detainees captured outside Afghanistan and then transferred to the Bagram Airfield in Afghanistan, the U.S. District Court for the District of Columbia was willing to extend *Boumediene* and grant habeas hearings—at least with respect to non-Afghan nationals.

What also remains unclear is whether the *Boumediene* ruling will serve as a true check on the political branches or whether the habeas hearings will be pro forma. One vital question that has yet to be agreed upon is the level of judicial review. Initially, a substantial majority (59%) of the habeas claims were successful at the district court level. However, following the D.C. Circuit Court of Appeals ruling in *Al-Adahi v. Obama,*[56] which overturned a district court decision granting habeas relief, the tide has turned in the opposite direction and, as of this writing, no enemy combatant has been successful since this ruling.[57]

The Obama Administration Joins the Debate

The election of Barack Obama to the presidency substantially changed the direction—if not the charged tone—of the debate. Dramatically, on the day he was sworn into office, President Obama promised to close Guantánamo within a year's time and within days signed several executive orders to prepare for the closure of the detention center. A year later, however, the administration was still weighing its options. In January 2010, a Justice Department–led task force recommended that roughly half of the detainees be repatriated or relocated to a third country; that thirty-five or so be prosecuted in federal courts or reconstituted military tribunals in the United States; and that fifty be detained indefinitely in a new facility in Illinois.[58] Each of these options faced obstacles: Few countries were stepping forward to take in the detainees eligible for repatriation or relocation; Republicans and other critics vociferously opposed bringing detainees "to America's heartland" for prosecution or permanent relocation; and human rights groups were equally opposed to the prospect of indefinite detention.

Apparently conceding defeat, the Obama administration resumed the use of military commissions to prosecute alleged terrorists in the Guantánamo facility in 2011. The political contest over the future of the detainees continues. In the absence of any agreement, even detainees who have been cleared for transfer by the Department of Defense administrative review board remain in limbo.

Conclusion

The debate over the rights of detainees has raged so furiously and on so many fronts because the stakes are so high. The fundamental interests and values of the United States hang in the balance. Does terrorism represent a clear and present threat to U.S. national security? Does the threat terrorism poses require limitations on legal rights and freedoms? What is the appropriate trade-off between security and freedom? Does the nature of the threat render international institutions and laws obsolete? What are the proper roles of the president, Congress, and the courts in striking the right balance between competing interests and values? And finally, what does it mean to say that the United States is a nation that follows the rule of law?

Key Actors

John Ashcroft   Attorney general; fundamentally reoriented the Justice Department after September 11, 2001, to give priority to security and to emphasize prevention over prosecution; had primary responsibility over the September 11 detainees.

George W. Bush   President; sought expanded powers for executive agencies based on "war footing" of the country after September 11 and the president's constitutional role as commander in chief.

Colin Powell   Secretary of state; offered views on U.S. obligations under international law that were often contrary to the views of the Justice Department and the Defense Department.

Donald Rumsfeld   Secretary of defense; had primary responsibility for the detention and interrogation of all persons designated "enemy combatants."

U.S. Supreme Court   Court of last resort; ruled on the legal limits of the executive branch's detention policies in the Bush administration's war on terrorism.

Notes

1. "Address to a Joint Session of Congress and to the American Public," September 20, 2001, www.whitehouse.gov/news/releases/2001/09/20010920–8.html.

2. Ibid.

3. "Imprisoned persons," by contrast, refers to people who have been "deprived of personal liberty as a result of conviction for an offense." UN General Assembly, "Body of Principles for the Protection of All Persons under Any Form of Detention or Imprisonment," General Assembly Resolution 43/173, passed December 9, 1988.

4. Opinion written by Chief Judge T. Harvie Wilkinson III, *Hamdi v. Rumsfeld,* 316 F. 3rd 450, 464 (4th Cir. 2003).

5. The number is approximate because the government has never released complete information about the detainees.

6. Steve Fainaru, "Court Says Detainees' IDs Can Be Kept Secret; Panel: 9/11 Realities Outweigh Disclosure," *Washington Post,* June 18, 2003.

7. *Center for National Security Studies et al. v. Department of Justice,* No. 01–2500, www.cnss.org/discoveryopinion.pdf.

8. Fainaru, "Court Says Detainees' IDs Can Be Kept Secret."

9. Neil A. Lewis, "Threats and Responses: The Detainees: Secrecy Is Backed on 9/11 Detainees," *New York Times,* June 18, 2003.

10. USA PATRIOT Act of 2001, Pub. L. No. 107-56, 115 Stat. 272, §§ 41–412 (2001).

11. Office of the Inspector General, *The September 11 Detainees: A Review of the Treatment of Aliens Held on Immigration Charges in Connection with the Investigation of the September 11 Attacks* (Washington, DC: U.S. Department of Justice, April 2003).

12. Tim Golden and Don Van Natta, Jr., "U.S. Said to Overstate Value of Guantanamo Detainees," *New York Times,* June 21, 2004.

13. Neil A. Lewis, "Bush's Power to Plan Trial of Detainees Is Challenged," *New York Times,* January 16, 2004.

14. Data provided by David Remes (remesdh@gmail.com).

15. John Barry, Michael Hirsh, and Michael Isikoff, "The Roots of Torture," *Newsweek International,* May 24, 2004.

16. *Rasul et al. v. Bush,* No. 03–334, Brief for the Respondents in Opposition, www.usdoj.gov/osg/briefs/2003/0responses/2003–0334.resp.html.

17. Emphasis in original. *Rasul et al. v. Bush,* No. 02–0299 (CKK), Respondent's Motion to Dismiss Petitioner's First Amended Writ of Habeas Corpus, U.S. District Court for the District of Columbia, March 18, 2002, accessed April 23, 2004, www.ccr-ny.org/v2/legal/september_11th/docs/GovernmentResponseToRasulPetition.pdf.

18. Patti Waldmeir, "Court Tries to Balance Guantanamo Detainee Rights with Security Goals," *Financial Times,* April 21, 2004.

19. Michael Isikoff, "Memos Reveal War Crimes Warnings," *Newsweek,* May 17, 2004, www.msnbc.msn.com/id/4999734/site/newsweek/site/newsweek.

20. Under mounting pressure from human rights groups as well as Congress, the Defense Department has released a number of previously classified documents outlining the government's interrogation policies. See "Working Group Report on Detainee Interrogations in the Global War on Terrorism: Assessment of Legal, Historical, Policy, and Operational Considerations," March 6, 2003, http://i.a.cnn.net/cnn/2004/images/06/09/pentagonreportpart1.pdf, and an untitled and incomplete report at http://i.a.cnn.net/cnn/2004/images/06/09/pentagonreportpart2.pdf.

21. General Miller assumed command of the Guantánamo base after interrogators complained that his predecessor was too soft on the detainees.

22. Barry, Hirsh, and Isikoff, "The Roots of Torture."

23. Associated Press, "Guantanamo Suicide Bids May Be Tied to General," MSNBC, June 22, 2004, www.msnbc.msn.com/id/5261632.

24. Golden and Van Natta, "U.S. Said to Overstate Value."

25. Ibid.

26. Elizabeth Bumiller and Eric Schmitt, "President Sorry for Iraq Abuse: Backs Rumsfeld," New York Times, May 7, 2004.

27. Alberto Gonzales, memorandum for the president, "Decision Re: Application of the Geneva Conventions on Prisoners of War to the Conflict with Al Qaeda and the Taliban," www.library.law.pace.edu/research/020125_gonzalesmemo.pdf.

28. "Working Group Report on Detainee Interrogations in the Global War on Terrorism: Assessment of Legal, Historical, Policy, and Operational Considerations," March 6, 2003, www.ccr-ny.org/v2/reports/docs/PentagonReportMarch.pdf. See also the Memorandum for the General Counsel for the Department of Defense, www.dod.gov/news/Jun2004/d20040622doc8.pdf.

29. "Working Group Report on Detainee Interrogations in the Global War on Terrorism: Assessment of Legal, Historical, Policy and Operational Considerations," April 4, 2003, www.defenselink.mil/news/Jun2004/d20040622doc8.pdf.

30. Jay S. Bybee, "Memorandum for Alberto R. Gonzales Re: Standards of Conduct and Interrogation under 18 U.S.C.§§ 2340–2340A," August 1, 2002, news.findlaw.com/wp/docs/doj/bybee80102mem.pdf.

31. Ibid.

32. Barry, Hirsch, and Isikoff, "The Roots of Torture."

33. R. Jeffrey Smith, "Military Legal Advisers Also Questioned Tactics," Washington Post, June 24, 2004, A7, quoting from Taft, memo to White House counsel regarding comments on the applicability of the Geneva Convention to al Qaeda and Taliban prisoners, February 2, 2002. The Taft memo is available at www.fas.org/sgp/othergov/taft.pdf.

34. Memos are available at www.dod.gov/releases/2004/nr20040622–0930.html.

35. Antonio Taguba, "Article 15–6 Investigation of the 800th Military Police Brigade," made available to the public in May 2004, http://news.findlaw.com/hdocs/docs/iraq/tagubarpt.html.

36. Greg Jaffe, "Army Blames Confusion in Iraq for Iraqi Abuse," Wall Street Journal, August 27, 2004, A3.

37. Eric Schmitt, "Defense Faulted by Panel in Prison Abuse," New York Times, August 24, 2004, 1.

38. David Cole, "Getting Away with Torture," New York Review of Books, January 14, 2010, 39.

39. Korematsu v. United States, 323 U.S. 214 (1944).

40. Rasul et al. v. Bush, 542 U.S. 466 (2004). Mention must also be made of two companion cases handed down the same day as Rasul. The first is Hamdi v. United States, 542 U.S. 507 (2004). Yaser Esam Hamdi, who was born in Louisiana but raised in the Middle East, was captured in a war zone in Afghanistan in 2001. After his American citizenship became known, Hamdi was transferred to Guantánamo Bay but then later taken to a naval brig in South Carolina. The Bush administration claimed the authority to detain Hamdi as an "enemy combatant." In its ruling, the Court held that such detention would

have to be accompanied by due process rights, which had not been afforded to Hamdi. In the words of Justice Sandra Day O'Connor, who wrote the majority opinion, the war on terrorism does not provide the president with a "blank check." Following the Court's ruling, in October 2004 Hamdi was released from U.S. custody and flown to Saudi Arabia. He remains there under house arrest. The other companion case, *Padilla v. United States,* 542 U.S. 426 (2004), also involved a U.S. citizen. José Padilla was arrested at O'Hare Airport in Chicago on June 10, 2002, and charged with conspiring with al Qaeda to carry out a terrorist attack in the United States by means of detonating a radioactive bomb. Padilla was then brought to New York but eventually transferred to a naval brig in Charleston, South Carolina. Padilla's attorney challenged his detention by filing a petition for habeas corpus in New York. In its ruling, the Supreme Court held that because of Padilla's detention in South Carolina, the habeas petition was wrongly filed. Padilla ultimately spent three and a half years in solitary confinement as a designated "enemy combatant." Then, in November 2005, a new set of criminal charges was filed against him. The new indictment made no mention of a "dirty bomb." Rather, Padilla was charged with being a member of a "North American cell group" that worked to support jihadist campaigns in Afghanistan and elsewhere. In August 2007, Padilla and two codefendants were convicted of conspiracy to provide material support for terrorists and sentenced to seventeen years and four months in prison.

41. *Johnson v. Eisentrager,* 339 U.S. 763 (1950).

42. *Rasul v. Bush, Habib v. Bush,* and *Al Odah v. Bush,* 215 F. Supp. 2d 55 (D.D.C. 2002).

43. *Rasul v. Bush, Habib v. Bush,* and *Al Odah v. Bush,* 321 F. 3d 1134 (D.C. Cir. 2003).

44. *Rasul et al. v. Bush,* 542 U.S. 466 (2004).

45. Ibid. at 474.

46. Ibid. (citations omitted).

47. Ibid. at 473 (referencing Habeas Act of February 5, 1867).

48. Ibid. at 476.

49. Ibid. at 565, Justice Anthony Kennedy concurring.

50. Ibid. at 567, Justice Antonin Scalia dissenting.

51. William Glaberson, "U.S. Asks Court to Limit Lawyers at Guantanamo," *New York Times,* April 26, 2007, A1.

52. *Hamdan v. United States,* 548 U.S. 557 (2006).

53. *Boumediene v. Bush,* 553 U.S. 723 (2008).

54. Ibid. at 776.

55. *Maqaleh et al. v. Gates,* Civil Action No. 06–1669, U.S. District Court for the District of Columbia (June 3, 2009).

56. *Al-Adahi v. Obama,* 613 F. 3d 1102 (D.C. Cir. 2010).

57. Mark Denbeaux et al., "No Hearing Habeas: D.C. Circuit Restricts Meaningful Review," Seton Hall Public Law Research Paper No. 2145554, http://papers.ssrn.com/s013/papers.cfm?abstract_id=2145554.

58. Peter Finn, "Justice Task Force Recommends about 50 Guantanamo Detainees Be Held Indefinitely," *Washington Post,* January 22, 2010.

15 The International Criminal Court: National Interests versus International Norms

Donald W. Jackson and Ralph G. Carter

Before You Begin

1. What is the International Criminal Court (ICC), and why do many countries, including principal allies of the US, believe that it is needed?

2. Why was the U.S. position so contrary to positions its allies took?

3. Is there merit to the U.S. position in this case? Have there been any major reasons for us to change the U.S. position? Why or why not?

4. Should advocates of the ICC be concerned that the cases brought to the ICC so far have involved failed or failing states in Africa?

5. Should international law, or the global rule of law, sometimes supersede national interests? If so, when? Why or why not?

6. What does this study of the ICC suggest about the future of international law or tribunals in the twenty-first century?

7. Has the simple passage of time demonstrated either the effectiveness of the ICC or its inadequacy?

Introduction: The Rise of International Law

From 1989 to 1991, a process of disintegration began that led to the dissolution of the Soviet empire and ultimately to the demise of the Soviet Union itself. Some of the early beneficiaries of this change seemed to have been international institutions and international law, as was illustrated by Soviet-US cooperation during the 1990–1991 Persian Gulf crisis and war. With the apparent end of the Cold War, the US-led international coalition that drove Iraqi forces from Kuwait justified and coordinated its actions through the United Nations (UN) and the application of international law. Events in the late 1980s and early 1990s led President George H. W. Bush to declare that an increasingly democratic "new world order" had arrived, a time when "the international system would be based on international law and would rely on international organizations such as the United Nations to settle international conflicts."[1]

An illustration of this trend toward international institutions—though perhaps not of the new world order envisioned by Bush—occurred on July 17, 1998, when 120 states voted at a UN diplomatic conference in Rome to create the International Criminal Court (ICC), with powers to try perpetrators of genocide, crimes against humanity, and war crimes. Only seven states voted against creating the ICC: China, Iraq, Israel, Libya, Qatar, Yemen, and the United States. Within four years, more than the sixty nations needed for implementation of the court had ratified the agreement. On July 1, 2002, the Rome Statute for the International Criminal Court entered into force, despite the persistent opposition of the United States. How did the United States come to find itself on "the other side" of international law and abandoned by most of its traditional allies?

What has been the actual trial experience of the International Criminal Court since its entry into force on July 1, 2001? As of December 2012, the ICC has been engaged in sixteen actual or potential cases involving seven situations. But so far only two trials have come to conclusion—resulting in one conviction and one acquittal.

Background: The Rise of International Tribunals

International courts are not unique to the twenty-first century. The Hague Peace Conference of 1899, convened for the primary purpose of promoting peace and stability by limiting or reducing armaments, also created the Hague Convention for the Pacific Settlement of International Disputes and the Permanent Court of Arbitration.[2] With the League of Nations in 1920 came the Permanent Court of International Justice, which rendered thirty judgments and issued twenty-seven advisory opinions from 1922 to 1946.[3] But, despite the tragedy of World War I and the global economic depression that came little more than a decade later, these were idealistic times for the prospects of the rule of law.

After World War II, idealism for the rule of law continued as the United Nations created the International Court of Justice (or World Court), but two exceptions to this international court's jurisdiction remained: The court's decisions generally applied only to states, not individuals, and, moreover, it was possible for states, through reservations, to avoid the court's obligatory jurisdiction.[4]

Timeline
International Criminal Court

1946	The UN General Assembly passes Resolution 95 (I), recognizing the principles contained in the 1945 London Charter as binding precedents in international law. It also passes Resolution 96 (I), making genocide a crime under international law. Trials are held in Nuremberg and Tokyo of Germans and Japanese accused of crimes against peace, war crimes, and crimes against humanity. In the U.S. Senate, the Vandenberg and Connally amendments ensure congressional support for U.S. acceptance of the jurisdiction of the new International Court of Justice (or World Court).
1989	Sixteen Caribbean and Latin American nations propose a permanent international criminal court for the prosecution of narco-traffickers.
1991	The International Law Commission prepares a draft code of international crimes.
1993	The UN Security Council passes Resolution 808, providing for the establishment of the International Criminal Tribunal for the Former Yugoslavia.
1994	The UN Security Council passes Resolution 955, creating the International Criminal Tribunal for Rwanda. The International Law Commission prepares a draft statute for an international criminal court.
1995	The UN General Assembly creates the Preparatory Committee for the Establishment of an International Criminal Court.
March 26, 1998	Sen. Jesse Helms, R-NC, sends a letter to Secretary of State Madeleine Albright vowing that any agreement that might bring a U.S. citizen under the jurisdiction of a UN criminal court would be "dead on arrival" in the Senate.
March 31–April 1, 1998	Defense Department leaders meet in Washington, DC, with military attachés of more than one hundred countries to warn them of the possible jurisdiction of an international criminal court over their soldiers.
June–July 1998	At a conference in Rome, delegates discuss and then vote 120–7 to establish the International Criminal Court.

(continued)

Timeline *(continued)*

International Criminal Court

June 14, 2000	Helms introduces the American Servicemembers' Protection Act (S. 2726), which would prohibit U.S. officials from cooperating with the proposed ICC. Majority Whip Tom DeLay, R-Texas, introduces the same measure in the House of Representatives (H.R. 4654).
December 31, 2000	The Clinton administration signs the Rome Statute establishing the ICC, so the United States can be considered an original signatory and participate in decisions about implementation of the new tribunal.
May 6, 2002	The administration of George W. Bush formally declares that it does not intend to submit the Rome Statute to the Senate for ratification and renounces any legal obligation arising from the Clinton administration's signing of the treaty.
July 1, 2002	The Rome Statute for the International Criminal Court enters into force without the participation of the United States, but with more than sixty accessions.
August 2, 2002	The American Servicemembers' Protection Act becomes law with the signature of Bush.
March 11, 2003	The first judges of the ICC are inaugurated, and Philippe Kirsch of Canada, who chaired the diplomatic conference in Rome, becomes the court's first president.
March 24, 2003	Luis Moreno Ocampo of Argentina is elected the first chief prosecutor of the ICC.
July 1, 2003	The Bush administration announces its intention to eliminate military aid to the thirty-five countries that have not signed bilateral agreements exempting U.S. citizens from being rendered to the jurisdiction of the ICC.
October 13, 2005	Uganda: Arrest warrant against Joseph Kony, alleged commander-in-chief of the Lord's Resistance Army issued unsealed, but arrest not yet effected.
January 29, 2007	Democratic Republic of the Congo (D.R.C): The ICC announces its first case for prosecution. Thomas Lubanga Dyilo of the Union of Congolese Patriots is charged with three counts of enlisting, conscripting, and using children under the age of fifteen as combat soldiers in the D.R.C.

February 6, 2008	D.R.C.: Mathieu Ngudjolo Chui, a commander of the Nationalist and Integrationist Front (FNI) in the D.R.C., is arrested in Kinshasa and turned over the next day to the ICC. He is later charged with war crimes and crimes against humanity (among them murder, sexual slavery, rape, use of child soldiers, and intentional attacks on civilian populations) in the village of Bogoro.
March 4, 2009	Sudan: The ICC announces the issuance of arrest warrants for Sudanese President Omar al-Bashir for crimes against humanity and war crimes in the conflict involving the Darfur region of Sudan. Second warrant of arrest is issued on July 12, 2010, but no arrest has yet been effected.
February 3, 2010	Sudan: The ICC's 2009 decision not to include genocide charges against Omar al-Bashir, due to a legal technicality, is overturned; this opens the possibility that genocide could be added to the charges against him.
March 31, 2010	Kenya: Pre-Trial Chamber II grants the prosecutor's *proprio motu* request to open an investigation into a situation in Kenya.
November 22, 2010	Central African Republic: Trial commences against Jean-Pierre Bemba Gombo, alleged president and commander-in-chief of the Movement for the Liberation of Congo, after his arrest was effected on May 24, 2008. Bemba is being tried on two counts of crimes against humanity (murder and rape) and three counts of war crimes (murder, rape, and pillaging).
November 30, 2010	Côte d'Ivoire: Laurent Gbabgo, former president of the Côte d'Ivoire, is transferred into ICC custody following the issuance of warrant of arrest.
June 27, 2011	Libya: Warrant of Arrest issued for Saif Al-Islam Gaddafi, son of Muammar Gaddafi.
March 14, 2012	D.R.C.: The ICC's Trial Chamber I finds Thomas Lubanga Dyilo guilty of recruiting, conscripting and using child soldiers in the armed wing of Union of Congolese Patriots. The judges find that children had been used in armed conflict in 2002 and 2003 in the Ituri region of the D.R.C.
June 15, 2012	Ms. Fatou Bensouda (of The Gambia), formerly ICC deputy prosecutor, is sworn in as the second chief prosecutor of the ICC

(continued)

Timeline *(continued)*
International Criminal Court

July 10, 2012	D.R.C.: Lubanga is sentenced to a term of fourteen years; however, he is given credit for the six years already served in detention at the time of his sentencing. Lubanga is not required to pay reparations to the victims of his crimes for he is found to be indigent.
October 3, 2012	D.R.C.: Lawyers for Lubanga file two notices of intention to appeal. One appeal asks for the reversal of the conviction and the acquittal of Lubanga. The other asks for his sentence to be set aside or reduced.
December 18, 2012	D.R.C.: Mathieu Ngudjolo Chui is acquitted of charges of war crimes and crimes against humanity, The ICC's Trial Chamber II finds that the prosecution could not prove beyond a reasonable doubt that Ngudjolo Chui was in command of the militia at the time of the attacks, and the credibility of some witnesses is questioned.

The idea for the International Criminal Court did not arise in a political vacuum and was not a dream of idealistic abstractions; rather, it followed a series of precedent-setting tribunals. Between 1919 and 1994, five ad hoc international commissions, four ad hoc international criminal tribunals, and three international or national prosecutions of "crimes" arising during World Wars I and II were convened. The first commission sought to prosecute German and Turkish officials and military officers for war crimes and crimes against humanity during World War I. Crimes against humanity generally consisted of the abusive or murderous treatment of civilians by military personnel. This commission's efforts resulted in a few token convictions in the German supreme court.[5]

After the ineffective United Nations War Crimes Commission was created in 1942, the Allies signed the London Charter for the Prosecution and Punishment of the Major War Criminals of the European Axis, in August 1945. The principles contained in the 1945 agreement were later recognized as binding precedents in international law by UN General Assembly Resolution 95 of December 11, 1946. The London Charter created the International Military Tribunal (IMT), consisting of four judges (one from each of the four powers—France, the Soviet Union, the United Kingdom, and the United States). The jurisdiction of the IMT included the following crimes:

- crimes against peace—Article 6[a] of the London Charter: planning, preparation, initiation or waging a war of aggression or a war in violation of international treaties or agreements;
- war crimes—Article 6[b] of the London Charter, though the most definitive statement appears in the Charter of the International Military Tribunal (annexed to the London Charter): violations of the laws or customs of war, to include murder, ill-treatment, or deportation to slave labor of civilian populations in occupied territory, murder or ill-treatment of prisoners of war or persons on the seas, killing of hostages, plunder of public or private property, wanton destruction of cities, or devastation not justified by military necessity; and
- crimes against humanity—Article 6[c] of the London Charter: murder, extermination, enslavement, deportation, and other inhumane acts committed against any civilian population, or persecutions on political, racial or religious grounds in execution of or in connection with any crime within the jurisdiction of the tribunal.[6]

The IMT's role concluded with the Nuremberg trials in 1946. The tribunal found eighteen of twenty-one prominent Nazi defendants guilty; twelve of the eighteen were given the death penalty, and the other six were imprisoned for terms ranging from ten years to life.[7]

With the occupation of Japan, the International Military Tribunal for the Far East (IMTFE) was created in Tokyo in 1946. Its list of punishable crimes was essentially the same as that for the IMT in Germany.[8] The results were generally similar as well: all twenty-five defendants were found guilty; seven were executed, sixteen were given life imprisonment, and two were given shorter prison terms.[9]

The London Charter and the Nuremberg precedent were affirmed in 1946 by the UN General Assembly in Resolution 95 (I). In December 1946 the assembly unanimously adopted Resolution 96 (I), which expressly made genocide—derived from the London Charter's definition of crimes against humanity—a crime under international law. Two years later the General Assembly adopted the Convention on the Prevention and Punishment of the Crime of Genocide.[10] In the United States, the genocide convention was submitted to the Senate for ratification in 1949, but U.S. ratification (with reservations) came almost forty years later, in 1988.

Much of the substantive international criminal law as applied by the IMT at Nuremberg was expanded and codified in the Geneva Conventions of 1949. In 1948, the UN General Assembly invited the International Law Commission to study the possibility of creating an international criminal court with jurisdiction over the crime of genocide and other crimes that might be defined by international conventions. Because of the Cold War, however, it was not until 1989 that the idea of an international criminal court was again brought before the General Assembly.[11]

U.S. Concerns

The protection of U.S. sovereignty vis-à-vis international law has been a long-standing issue. In 1945, President Harry Truman had to reassure the Senate that Article 43 of the UN Charter, which obligated members to make available to the Security Council "armed forces, assistance, and facilities," would not rob Congress of its right to declare war. In 1946 it took two amendments to ensure Senate support for U.S. acceptance of the jurisdiction of the World Court. The Vandenberg amendment specified that the court's jurisdiction would not apply to "disputes arising under a multilateral treaty, unless (1) all parties to the treaty affected by the decision are also parties to the case before the court, or (2) the United States specially agrees to jurisdiction."[12] The more famous reservation was the Connally amendment, which drew the line of the World Court's obligatory jurisdiction at "disputes with regard to matters which are essentially within the domestic jurisdiction of the United States of America as determined by the United States of America."[13] In the eyes of its critics, this amendment essentially said that the United States would obey the World Court when the U.S. government happened to agree with it. In 1959 the Connally amendment was revisited, when the American Bar Association's Committee on World Peace through Law tried to repeal it. That effort died when the Senate Foreign Relations Committee voted to postpone the matter indefinitely.[14]

These were not the only instances of U.S. unwillingness to be bound by international law. For example, in 1977 the United States and Panama reached agreement on two treaties that returned sovereignty of the Panama Canal and the Canal Zone to Panama and guaranteed neutral operation of the waterway. In approving the treaties, however, the Senate added the DeConcini amendment, which reserved the right of the United States to intervene militarily in Panama to keep the canal open if the United States (not Panama) decided that such a step was necessary.[15] Not surprisingly, the Panamanians were outraged by this infringement on their national sovereignty, and it nearly scuttled the treaties. In 1984, when the World Court ruled that the United States was illegally trying to overthrow the government of Nicaragua, the United States announced its withdrawal from the court's jurisdiction, for a period of two years, regarding any of its actions in Central America. To be fair, other countries have also rejected the obligatory jurisdiction of the World Court, and many states that have accepted obligatory jurisdiction have attached reservations to their acceptance.[16]

Creation of the ICC

Unlike the Nuremberg and Tokyo trials, the idea for the permanent International Criminal Court was not something that victors in a war imposed on the vanquished. Instead, the genesis of the ICC came from smaller powers in the international system. In 1989, sixteen Caribbean and Latin American nations suggested international criminal prosecutions for narco-traffickers.[17] In 1990 a committee of nongovernmental organizations, including the World Federalist Movement, prepared a draft statute for an international court and submitted it to the Eighth United Nations Congress on the Prevention of Crime and the Treatment of Offenders. In 1991 the UN International Law Commission prepared a draft code of international crimes. These events culminated in November 1994, when the commission produced its draft statute for an international criminal court.[18]

At that time, the international legal community was reacting to allegations of horrendous human rights violations in civil wars in Yugoslavia and Rwanda. In 1993 UN Security Council Resolution 808 provided for the establishment of the International Criminal Tribunal for the Former Yugoslavia, to "prosecute persons responsible for serious violations of international humanitarian law committed in the territory of the former Yugoslavia since 1991."[19] The International Criminal Tribunal for Rwanda was established by UN Security Council Resolution 955, with jurisdiction starting January 1, 1994. The mandate of the Rwanda tribunal was to prosecute charges of genocide and crimes against humanity.[20] These tribunals were temporary and dealt only with the specific conflicts in those countries; however, in 2012, both tribunals were still dealing with those conflicts.

In December 1995, the UN General Assembly created a Preparatory Committee for the Establishment of an International Criminal Court. The committee, known as PrepCom, first met in March 1996. Its membership was open to all the member states of the United Nations, UN specialized agencies, and the

International Atomic Energy Agency.[21] The Clinton administration had been a strong supporter of the temporary tribunals for Yugoslavia and Rwanda and had pushed the general issue of criminal prosecution for persons accused of war crimes. In 1997 it created the position of ambassador-at-large for war crimes in the State Department and named David Scheffer to the post, thereby making him the top U.S. representative to PrepCom. It is most notable that in his September 1997 address to the UN General Assembly, President Bill Clinton endorsed the establishment of a permanent international criminal court "to prosecute the most serious violations of international humanitarian law."[22]

The working draft at the last PrepCom meeting was the Zutphen Text, which had been produced during a January 1998 meeting in the Netherlands. The goal was to prepare for an international conference in the summer of 1998 that might lead to the creation of such a court. That document called for a court that would *complement* national criminal courts. The crimes within the proposed jurisdiction of the international court were not yet determined, but the proposals included genocide, aggression, war crimes, and crimes against humanity. The definition of these crimes varied in different proposals. The draft statute included bracketed language wherever PrepCom had been unable to reach consensus. Near the completion of the last PrepCom meeting, the 175-page draft statute contained 99 articles and about 1,700 bracketed words or provisions.[23] The proposals also included a list of sexual offenses under war crimes, including rape, sexual slavery, enforced prostitution, enforced pregnancy, and enforced sterilization.

Yet the most difficult issues touched on in Rome involved delimiting domestic criminal jurisdiction relative to the criminal jurisdiction of the international court and the means by which cases would reach the ICC. The domestic-international jurisdictional issue involved "complementarity," which is the idea that international prosecution ought to occur only when a state fails to take responsibility for its own good faith investigation and prosecution of crimes defined by the statute. The statute provided that a case would be admissible before the ICC only when a domestic judicial system was "unwilling or unable" to conduct the proper investigation or prosecution. In addition, a U.S. proposal on complementarity required the prosecutor for the international court to notify state parties and to make a public announcement when a case had been referred. A state could then step forward and inform the prosecutor that it was taking responsibility for prosecution. In the U.S. proposal, the assertion of domestic responsibility for prosecution would delay international criminal jurisdiction for a period of six months to one year, thus giving home governments more time to try accused individuals. One of the concerns expressed before the PrepCom was the length of this delay.[24]

Other issues concerning the means by which cases might come to the court were more vexing. The draft statute provided that the ICC prosecutor would initiate an investigation only when the UN Security Council referred a case or when a state party that had accepted the jurisdiction of the ICC filed a complaint with the prosecutor. Those favoring a strong ICC wanted the prosecutor to have independent authority to investigate and file charges. At the other end of the controversy were those who, like the United States, preferred that the Security Council determine the agenda of the prosecutor and the ICC. That, of course, would give the United States and the four other permanent members of the Security Council—Russia, the United Kingdom, France, and China—a veto over the ICC's jurisdiction.

U.S. Reaction

In February 1998, Ambassador Scheffer, who was acting as chief negotiator for the United States on the creation of an international court, identified three issues involving the relationship between a court and the UN Security Council that needed to be addressed. The first issue was the need for the two institutions to operate compatibly, with neither undermining the legitimate pursuits of the other; the second involved the council's power to refer situations to the ICC; and the third was the council's role in assisting the court with the enforcement of its orders. Scheffer also made note of the unique position of the United States in the world. Either alone or in concert with its NATO allies and the United Nations, the U.S. military often "shoulders the burden of international security." As he put it, "It is in our collective interest that the personnel of our militaries and civilian commands be able to fulfill their many legitimate responsibilities without unjustified exposure to criminal legal proceedings."[25] State Department spokesman James Rubin followed up on Scheffer's view, adding, "We need to ensure that, in pursuit of justice, a permanent court does not handcuff governments that take risks to promote international peace and security and to save lives."[26]

Nonetheless, Sen. Jesse Helms (R-NC), chairman of the Senate Committee on Foreign Relations, proved to be a key opponent of the ICC. In a March 26, 1998 letter to Secretary of State Madeleine Albright, he vowed that any compromise that might bring an American citizen under the jurisdiction of a UN criminal court would be "dead on arrival" in the Senate. He declared that there should be no flexibility with respect to a U.S. veto over the court's power to prosecute U.S. citizens.[27] A week later, Helms again publicly encouraged the State Department to take aggressive actions to block the establishment of the ICC.

Helms's letter and public statements were the most dangerous warning shots. On March 31 and April 1, 1998, in Washington, DC, Defense Department leaders held meetings with military attachés of more than 100 countries. Their message was that an international criminal court could "target their own soldiers—particularly when acting as peacekeepers—and subject them to frivolous or politically motivated investigations by a rogue prosecutor or an overzealous tribunal." It was by all accounts quite an unusual briefing for Pentagon officials.[28]

A contrasting take on the court's ability to prosecute appeared in the *Times of India*. Having read the State Department's comment that "the permanent court must not handcuff governments that take risks to promote peace and security," an Indian columnist considered the conduct of U.S. forces in the My Lai massacre in Vietnam and an alleged massacre of one thousand civilians by U.S. Army Rangers in Mogadishu, Somalia: "Shouldn't the ICC be allowed to prosecute those involved in such crimes? . . . Or, like the Security Council, will it become a victim of double standards?"[29] Going into the 1998 Rome meeting to draft the ICC statute, about forty-two so-called like-minded countries—including Canada, most European nations, and many countries in Africa, Asia, and Latin America—favored a stronger and more independent international court and prosecutor.[30] According to the *Economist*,

> After nearly four years of intense negotiations among some 120 countries, the effort to set up the world criminal court has run smack into the ambivalence that has always been felt by the world's biggest powers about international law: they are keen to have it applied to others in the name of world order, but loath to submit to restrictions on their own sovereignty.[31]

The Rome Conference

In June 1998, representatives from 162 nations gathered in Rome to see whether they could agree on the creation of a permanent international criminal court.[32] The five-week conference opened with four days of speeches, during which U.S. Ambassador to the United Nations Bill Richardson reiterated the U.S. position that the Security Council should control the work of the ICC by referring critical situations for investigation and by instructing countries to cooperate. The ultimate goal, he said, would be to create a court that "focuses on recognized atrocities of significant magnitude and thus enjoys near universal support."[33] At that time, the United States' position put it in the company of China, France, and Russia, three of the other permanent members of the Security Council; only the United Kingdom had come out in favor of a stronger and more independent court. On the other side with respect to the most critical issues, the group of like-minded countries had by then grown to about sixty members. They were especially intent on creating an independent prosecutor and a court with sufficient jurisdiction and authority to actually bring those who committed human rights crimes to account. More than 200 accredited nongovernmental organizations monitored the conference. A coalition of these organizations had been working for years in the interest of creating a permanent court. The most prominent were Amnesty International, Human Rights Watch, and the European Law Students Association.

During the conference, an enormous amount of time was spent pursuing the elusive goal of consensus among the 162 nations. In part, consensus was sought because each nation had a single vote in the conference, which meant a simple majority vote would not take into account the relative size, power, or influence of individual countries. Hours were sometimes spent on one clause of one section of one article, with delegates from country after country making statements that usually were repetitive and often only seemed to serve the purpose of giving that delegate the chance to claim a few minutes at the microphone. The U.S. delegation worked hard to persuade its traditional allies to accept U.S. conditions for the treaty, especially during the final week of the conference. Indeed, the behind-the-scenes "buzz" was that the United States was actually threatening poor states with the loss of foreign aid and its NATO allies with a reduction of U.S. military support, including the withdrawal of troops.[34]

Motivated by Senator Helms's "dead on arrival" letter, throughout the conference the "U.S. delegation seemed increasingly gripped by a single overriding concern"—that no American could be tried before the court without the consent of the U.S. government.[35] Philippe Kirsch of Canada, chairman of the Committee of the Whole of the conference, noted about the U.S. delegation,

> It was amazing. Nothing could assuage them. . . . They seemed completely fixated on that Helms/Pentagon imperative—that there be explicit language in the Treaty guaranteeing that no Americans could ever fall under the Court's sway, even if the only way to accomplish that was going to be by the U.S. not joining the treaty. . . . Clearly, they had their instructions from back home—and very little room to maneuver.[36]

Many of the world's countries, however, were more willing than the United States to be subject to the international rule of law. Even the country's most powerful European allies, who had also participated in military "humanitarian" interventions, were far friendlier to the idea of the court than was the United States. The reasons for such differences were no doubt complex, but among them was the fact that since World War II, European countries had been moving from the tradition of individual sovereignty toward "European" institutions transcending nationhood. Examples of this trend were the adoption of the European Convention on Human Rights (1950)—and the subsequent empowerment of a European Court of Human Rights—and the emergence of the Court of Justice of the European Union (EU) as a powerful force.

In the last days of the Rome Conference, Ambassador Scheffer issued a public plea:

> We stand on the eve of the conference's conclusion without having found a solution. We fear that governments whose citizens make up at least two-thirds of the world's population [chiefly China and the United States] will find the emerging text of the treaty unacceptable. The world desperately needs this mechanism for international justice, but it must be a community, not a club.[37]

The final draft document for an international criminal court was distributed early on July 17 by Chairman Kirsch. It appeared to offer more to the sixty or so like-minded countries that favored a strong court than it did to the United States. The draft provided for obligatory jurisdiction of the court upon ratification of the treaty by a country for the crime of genocide, crimes against humanity, war crimes, and the crime of aggression. The United States was willing to accept obligatory jurisdiction only for the crime of genocide. Jurisdiction over war crimes was limited by a new draft article allowing states that signed the Rome Statute to opt out of the court's jurisdiction over war crimes for a period of seven years following the creation of the court. Consistent with its objective of blocking the creation of an institution that it could not control, or whose jurisdiction it could not veto, the United States sought a comprehensive opt-out provision that would allow it to be permanently exempt from the court's jurisdiction over war crimes. France agreed to support the draft proposal when the seven-year opt-out provision was added. The United Kingdom also supported the draft.

On July 17, the United States again voiced its opposition in the Committee of the Whole to a criminal tribunal beyond its control when it offered an amendment to the proposal. India also offered amendments that would have made the use of nuclear weapons a war crime and that limited the power of the Security Council over the court. Norway, however, moved to table the proposed amendments, and its motions were adopted. The vote against taking up the U.S. amendment was 113–17. The United States could not even muster the support of its closest allies. In the final conference plenary session, the United States demanded a vote on the draft treaty. The Russian Federation joined France and the United Kingdom in voting for the statute, leaving China and the United States the only permanent Security Council members in opposition. Israel also voted against the draft, in part because it made the relocation of a civilian population in an occupied territory a war crime, a provision too close for its comfort. Iraq, Libya, Qatar, and Yemen also voted against the statute.

As the conference ended, the United States was clearly the big loser. The final vote was 120 countries for the treaty, 7 against, and 21 abstentions. As approved, the court would exercise its jurisdiction over individuals suspected of treaty crimes if the country where the alleged violation occurred or the country of which the accused was a national was a party to the treaty (Article 12). States would accept the jurisdiction of the court on a case-by-case basis. The United States strongly opposed these provisions because they might—as the United States had feared all along—subject American troops to prosecution for alleged crimes committed in countries that had accepted the jurisdiction of the court, without first requiring the consent of the U.S. government.

Most countries felt that there were sufficient safeguards in the treaty to address U.S. concerns. The new court would only take cases involving major human rights violations carried out as part of a plan, policy, or widespread practice, not actions by individuals acting on their own. The court would act only when the appropriate domestic jurisdictions were unable or unwilling to deal with alleged crimes themselves (the complementarity principle).

Early on, the United States had favored a proposal that would have charged the Security Council with referring cases to the court, in part so the U.S. veto in the council could be used to protect U.S. citizens from prosecution. Most countries, however, eventually supported the compromise put forth by Singapore that would allow the Security Council to defer a case for a period of twelve months, with the possibility of extension. The United States eventually accepted this proposal, a version of which was included in the final draft.

The final draft called for a prosecutor with independent power to investigate and initiate prosecutions, as well as for the initiation of cases by a state party or by referral of the Security Council. The United States had fought hard against this provision, but a strong and independent prosecutor was one of the fundamental requirements of the sixty or so like-minded countries. The draft statute did call for a court review panel that would have the power to reject cases arising from an abuse of prosecutorial power, but that safeguard was not enough to satisfy the United States.

The draft also provided for jurisdiction over internal armed conflicts, such as that in Bosnia, which most delegations, including the United States, believed to be absolutely essential for a credible international court. Furthermore, the draft included among war crimes and crimes against humanity the crimes of rape, sexual slavery, enforced prostitution, enforced pregnancy, and enforced sterilization. Aggression was made a treaty crime, but it was left to be defined at later preparatory meetings. This decision was a concession to the members of the Non-Aligned Movement, but the draft did not include the prohibition of nuclear weapons, which the movement also strongly supported. The draft also left out chemical and biological weapons, as a concession to several Arab countries.

The Rome Statute provided that when ratified by at least sixty nations, the new International Criminal Court would enter into force, to be located at The Hague, in the Netherlands, where the ad hoc tribunal for the former Yugoslavia also is located. By April 11, 2002, sixty-six countries had ratified the treaty, and July 1, 2002, was set as the date that the agreement would enter into force.

The rift between the United States and its major European allies over the creation of the court widened and deepened following the Rome Conference and the July 2002 entry into force of the ICC. Although Europeans, like the Americans, put their troops in harm's way as peacekeepers in global hotspots, the general consensus among Europeans seems to be that the principle of complementarity protects them from unwanted or unwarranted international prosecution. U.S. government officials have been unwilling to put their trust in this principle. Many of the institutional details of the ICC were not finalized at the Rome Conference. Follow-up PrepCom sessions in 2000 sought to complete the rules of evidence and procedure and the specifications for the elements of crimes recognized in principle by the Rome Statute. The United States had to sign the statute by December 31, 2000—the last day for nations to become signatories of the original treaty—in order to participate in future PrepCom meetings. On the last day of 2000, President Clinton instructed Ambassador Scheffer to sign the treaty on behalf of the United States. In a press release, Clinton noted that he still had concerns about "significant flaws" in the treaty, but he hoped that they could be overcome in subsequent negotiations before the court became a reality. He said it was important for the United States to sign the treaty to "reaffirm our strong support for international accountability. . . . With signature, we will be in a position to influence the evolution of the court. Without signature, we will not."[38]

Reaction to the U.S. signature was swift. Human rights groups praised it. Richard Dicker, associate counsel of Human Rights Watch, said Clinton's action had "offered the hope of justice to millions and millions of people around the world by signaling United States' support for the most important international court since the Nuremberg tribunal." On the other hand, Senator Helms warned that the president's "decision will not stand."[39] The incoming administration of George W. Bush also opposed the signature. In a May 6, 2002, letter from U.S. Under Secretary of State John Bolton to UN Secretary-General Kofi Annan, the Bush administration formally declared that it would not submit the Rome Statute for Senate ratification and renounced any legal obligations arising from the previous administration's signing of the treaty.[40]

The ICC at the Turn of the Twenty-First Century

UN Secretary-General Kofi Annan hailed the adoption of the Rome Statute as a "giant step forward."[41] One of the proponents of U.S. participation in the court argued that

> America does not commit genocide, war crimes, or crimes against humanity. Nor do our NATO allies. . . . We thus have nothing to fear from the prosecution of these offenses, nothing to make us hesitate when the pleas of the victims of mass slaughter fill our television screens and their plight hounds our conscience.[42]

Furthermore, proponents have pointed out that should American troops cross the line, the principle of complementarity would protect them from international prosecution as long as the United States took action against them.[43] Nonetheless, others have disagreed. One opponent called the treaty "a pernicious and debilitating agreement, harmful to the national interests of the United States."[44] On July 23, 1998, Ambassador Scheffer spoke at a hearing before the Senate Committee on Foreign Relations and outlined the U.S. objections to the Rome Statute. The four main concerns of the United States were as follows:

- the fact that U.S. military personnel could be brought before the ICC prosecutor;
- the degree of Security Council control over prosecutions initiated by the ICC prosecutor;
- the ambiguity of the crimes over which the ICC would exercise jurisdiction, particularly the crime of aggression, which could conceivably extend to some U.S. troop deployments, and the alleged crime of settlement in an occupied territory, which would arguably implicate Israeli leaders for activities in the West Bank and the Gaza Strip; and
- the relationship between the ICC and domestic judicial processes.[45]

At the Senate hearing, Senator Helms made his position clear: The United States should block any organization of which it is a member from providing funding to the ICC; renegotiate its status of forces agreements and extradition treaties to prohibit treaty partners from surrendering U.S. nationals to the ICC; refuse to provide U.S. soldiers to regional and international peacekeeping operations when there is any possibility that they will come under the jurisdiction of the ICC; and never vote in the Security Council to refer a matter to the ICC.[46]

These concerns about protecting individual members of the U.S. armed forces may have been a stalking horse for another, broader concern. At the end of the hearing,

> Helms picked off the examples defiantly[;] he was going to be damned if any so-called International Court was ever going to be reviewing the legality of the U.S. invasions of Panama or Grenada or of the bombing of Tripoli and to be holding any American presidents, defense secretaries, or generals to account.[47]

Still, by early August 1998, more than twenty editorials and op-eds had run in major U.S. newspapers broadly supporting the creation of the ICC.

But controversy continued over who was to receive blame for genocide and other war crimes and what to do after such crimes had occurred. On June 14, 2000, Senator Helms introduced the American Servicemembers' Protection Act (S. 2726), which would prohibit U.S. officials from cooperating with the ICC. That same day, then–Majority Whip Tom DeLay (R-TX) introduced the measure in the House of Representatives (H.R. 4654). It mandated that the president ensure that any Security Council resolution authorizing a peacekeeping operation exempt U.S. personnel from prosecution before the ICC. Additionally, it required the president to certify to Congress that U.S. personnel are immunized by each country participating in the operation. The bill proposed that no U.S. military assistance be provided to governments that are parties to the ICC (with the exception of the NATO allies and Israel), although the president could waive this provision. With these "big sticks," Senator Helms denounced "the ICC's bogus claim of jurisdiction over American citizens."[48]

Despite the protection that complementarity offered the United States and other nations, Senator Helms wanted to leave nothing to chance. On November 29, 2000, his spokesman held a press conference at UN headquarters in New York. There he said Helms would make passage of the American Servicemembers' Protection Act a top priority in the Congress convening in January 2001. On that same day, a letter signed by a dozen former U.S. foreign policy officials was released, supporting Helms's bill; the letter claimed that U.S. world leadership "could be the first casualty" of the new ICC.[49] Among the signatories were former U.S. Secretaries of State James Baker, Henry Kissinger, and George Shultz and former U.S. Ambassador to the UN Jeane Kirkpatrick. As the writer James Carroll concluded in the *Boston Globe*, "That James Baker is a party to the Helms campaign signals that an incoming [George W.] Bush administration would prefer to be shackled by a xenophobic Congress than to be constrained by multilateral and equitable agreements with other nations."[50]

On July 12, 2002, shortly after the ICC entered into force and at the behest of the United States, the UN Security Council passed Resolution 1422, which restricted the ICC from commencing or proceeding with investigations or prosecutions of "peacekeepers" and other officials of states not then part of the ICC for a period of twelve months. The U.S. ambassador to the UN, John Negroponte, announced that the United States would continue to seek bilateral agreements exempting U.S. citizens from the jurisdiction of the ICC.[51]

On August 2, 2002, President Bush signed into law the American Servicemembers' Protection Act (ASPA), which had been included as part of the 2002 supplemental appropriations bill. It provided that the United States cut off military assistance to countries that had not signed bilateral agreements with the United States by July 1, 2003, ensuring that they would not surrender a U.S. citizen to the jurisdiction of the ICC or cooperate with the ICC in the apprehension or rendition of them. The law also, however, authorized the president to waive this provision on grounds of "national interest."

The ASPA specifically exempted NATO members and a few other allies but potentially applied to more than fifty other countries. As of June 2003, forty-five countries had signed bilateral agreements, but few of these were adherents to the Rome Statute.[52]

In February 2003, the first eighteen ICC judges were elected, after as many as eighty-five state adherents to the Rome Statute cast thirty-three ballots. The judges took their seats on March 11, 2003, and on that same day, career diplomat and attorney Philippe Kirsch of Canada, who had led the Rome Conference in 1998, was elected the first president of the ICC. On March 24, 2003, Luis Moreno Ocampo of Argentina was elected the first chief prosecutor of the ICC. Ocampo, a lawyer experienced in criminal and human rights law and anticorruption programs, participated in the 1980s in the prosecution of the Argentine military leaders allegedly responsible for the Falklands War. He also served as president of the Latin American section of Transparency International.[53]

On July 1, 2003, the Bush administration announced its intention to cut off military aid to thirty-five countries that had failed to sign bilateral agreements. At the same time, it granted waivers for varying periods of time to twenty-two countries. In May 2005, the State Department reported that 100 bilateral agreements had been signed. However, by late October 2012, 121 countries had ratified the Rome Statute. Despite this impressive number of state ratifications, six of the ten largest states by population—China, India, the United States, Indonesia, Pakistan, and Russia—have not ratified the statute as of this writing. Bangladesh is the most recent state of quite large population (over 160 million people) to have ratified, and Tunisia in North Africa and Jordan in the Middle East are the only states in the their conflict-prone part of the world to have ratified the statute. Other recent adherents to the Rome Statute of the ICC include Chile (2009), the Philippines (a country with approximately 100 million people that ratified in 2011), and Guatemala (2012). Still, states representing about half of the world's population have refused to participate in the ICC.[54]

It is most notable that the first sixteen cases involving seven situations before the International Criminal Court all come from Africa. The alleged crimes so far have involved the following:

1. Democratic Republic of Congo: War crimes in the D.R.C. (the conscription and employment of child soldiers), which has resulted in the first conviction and sentence by the ICC in the case against Thomas Lubanga Dyilo; war crimes and

crimes against humanity (murder, sexual slavery, rape, cruel or inhuman treatment, use of child soldiers, intentional attacks on civilian populations, etc.), which resulted in the acquittal of Mathieu Ngudjolo Chui due to lack of evidence beyond a reasonable doubt and witnesses with questionable credibility.[55]

2. Uganda: War crimes and crimes against humanity in Uganda (the use of child soldiers and the rape, assault, and murder of civilians), but so far the ICC has failed to arrest Joseph Kony, the leader of the Lord's Resistance Army.

3. Central African Republic: War crimes and crimes against humanity (rape, torture, murder, and pillaging) for which the trial of Jean-Pierre Bemba Gombo began in November 2010.

4. Kenya: The situation in Kenya for which a Pre-Trial Chamber granted the prosecutor's request to open an investigation *proprio motu* (or on his own initiative) in March 2010.

5. Libya: The situation in Libya that the UN Security Council unanimously referred to the ICC in February 2011, for which a decision has yet to be made regarding whether Saif Al-Islam Gaddafi should be prosecuted for crimes against humanity before the ICC or whether he should be prosecuted in Libya under the principle of complementarity.

6. Côte d'Ivoire: A case involving the prospective prosecution of Laurent Gbabgo, former president of that country.

7. Sudan: War crimes, crimes against humanity, and genocide (most notably the death and destruction in Darfur). Twelve arrest warrants have been issued, but so far only four of those indicted are in custody, and no case has yet come to a conclusion.[56] The most interesting case so far has been the 2009 indictment of Sudanese President Omar al-Bashir for war crimes and crimes against humanity.[57] A perceived legal technicality kept the crime of genocide from being added to the charges. In February 2010, the court reversed its prior interpretation that a genocide indictment was not possible, thereby opening the possibility that genocide charges could be added to the other two indictments.[58] Following these indictments, President al-Bashir traveled without incident to Egypt, Mauritania, Saudi Arabia, and Qatar, but he did not go to New York for the 2009 UN General Assembly meeting. Furthermore, he was asked not to attend international meetings in South Africa, Uganda, Nigeria, and Turkey so as not to put those host countries on the spot.[59] Still, numerous state governments—not just other North African states but France as well—press the argument that pursuing his arrest is counterproductive to

seeking his cooperation with peace negotiations and peacekeeping operations in Darfur. His case thus frames a fundamental and ongoing quandary: What is more important, justice for specific victims or peace in the region?

So where does the United States stand regarding the ICC? In October 2008, John Bellinger, the legal adviser to the secretary of state, said at an international law society meeting that the fundamental concerns regarding the ICC had been remarkably consistent across three presidential administrations, and that—absent major political changes—it continued to be unlikely that the United States would ratify the Rome Statute. However, he added that the U.S. government shared the concerns of ICC supporters regarding impunity for serious war crimes and crimes against humanity. Thus the U.S. government adopted a more nuanced approach and was not trying to kill the ICC. Finally, he noted that the U.S. government was prepared to cooperate with ICC prosecutions in appropriate circumstances (Darfur being his cited example), and that it opposed an Article 16 UN Security Council resolution to defer the prosecution of Omar al-Bashir.

The election of Barack Obama to the presidency in 2008 signaled a shift in U.S. government policy in many areas, but that shift is not apparent regarding the ICC. Although a strong proponent of the rule of law, then-Senator Obama said on October 6, 2007,

> The United States has more troops deployed overseas than any other nation and those forces are bearing a disproportionate share of the burden in the protecting of Americans and preserving international security. Maximum protection for our servicemen and women should come with that increased exposure. Therefore, I will consult thoroughly with our military commanders and also examine the track record of the Court before reaching a decision on whether the U.S. should become a State Party to the ICC.[60]

Speaking in August 2009, Secretary of State Hillary Clinton said that it was a "great regret" that the United States had not yet become a member of the ICC.[61] Although the Obama administration appears not to be as hostile to the ICC as the administration of George W. Bush had been, so far it appears not to be a high priority for President Obama to reopen the issue of the US becoming a member.

Despite the oft-stated fears of malicious prosecution of U.S. military personnel, part of the unspoken U.S. opposition to the independent operation of the ICC may be the fear of indictments of senior U.S. governmental officials for a variety of war crimes.[62] Such fears may be real, but they may be slightly misplaced. The more likely source of such indictments would be other states' national courts acting on the basis of universal jurisdiction. In 1998, former Chilean general Augusto Pinochet was arrested in Britain on a Spanish indictment for crimes that occurred during his presidency. After being held for over a year, he was released because of health problems and never turned over to Spain. Pinochet died in Chile in December 2006, before any prosecution could be effected under Chilean law, however unlikely that prospect may have been.

Actions taken by the U.S. government against suspects in the global war on terrorism raised the possibility of similar prosecutions of former senior U.S. officials. In 2004, human rights groups sought prosecution in German courts of U.S. Defense Secretary Donald Rumsfeld for war crimes, but the prosecution was dismissed the next year. In 2006, prosecutions in Germany were sought not only against Rumsfeld but also against Director of Central Intelligence George Tenet and Attorney General Alberto Gonzales for war crimes against detainees. Again, the prosecution was dismissed the following year.[63] In October 2007, several human rights groups filed a complaint in Paris charging Rumsfeld with authorizing torture, an action that was brought under the 1984 Convention against Torture (which has been ratified by both France and the United States).[64] However, the French case against Rumsfeld was dismissed in February 2008.[65] So while no prosecutions of high-level U.S. officials have taken place, the possibility exists that those who gave certain orders—for example, to aggressively interrogate (i.e., possibly torture) detainees—may be held liable at some future point in a court of law, but as time passes such prosecutions become increasingly unlikely.

In March 2010, Harold Koh, the former dean of Yale Law School who became the legal adviser to the Department of State under President Obama, spoke at an academic conference on international law and addressed the U.S. position on the ICC. He was chiefly concerned with the prospective Assembly of States Parties that was to take place in Kampala, Uganda in June 2010. The key issue there was the definition of the crime of aggression under the Rome Statute of the ICC. The two principal U.S. concerns were (1) that the definition of aggression would politicize and weaken the ICC, and (2) how charges of aggression should be brought. On the second concern, the U.S. position continued to support the role of the Security Council, as it had at the Rome conference in 1998, suggesting that neither an investigation nor prosecution of the crime of aggression should occur unless there was a Security Council resolution that aggression had occurred. The obvious point that the US is a permanent member of the Security Council with veto power is inescapable, but it is only fair to note that the role of the United States in peacekeeping, given its military power, makes it particularly sensitive to the possibility of politically driven prosecutions.

Conclusion: The United States and International Law

Israeli diplomat Abba Eban once said international law was "the law which the wicked do not obey and the righteous do not enforce." Whether the United States has lined up on the side of the wicked or of the righteous regarding the prospects for the ICC probably lies in the eye of the beholder. There is no question that U.S. political culture values the rule of law: Presidents George H. W. Bush and Bill Clinton both saw reliance on international law as a mainstay of the post–Cold War era. Clinton wanted to use international law to punish war criminals and those guilty of genocide and crimes against humanity, and he said so when he endorsed the creation of the ICC in his UN General Assembly address in September 1997. Yet by the time of the Rome Conference the following summer, U.S. diplomats were swimming against the international tide by trying to ensure some degree of U.S. control over the ICC or its prosecutor, hence the U.S. support for the role of the UN Security Council. The inability to prevail on this issue produced the final vote that placed the United States in the somewhat unusual company of China, Iraq, Israel, Libya, Qatar, and Yemen. What accounts for this seeming about-face? The answer is national interests in the form of sovereignty concerns in the U.S. Congress. And we have seen that the Obama administration continues to support the role of the Security Council, as have both Republican and Democratic administrations before it.

In 1946, prominent senators ensured that the World Court would not act contrary to U.S. interests, as defined by the United States. Fifty-two years later, congressional emphasis on U.S. national sovereignty at the expense of international law, the United Nations, and a host of nongovernmental organizations reappeared in the ICC case. Once powerful legislators staked out the priority of preserving U.S. sovereignty, the nature of policy making on the issue changed for the Clinton administration. The question was no longer whether the United States could agree with its friends and allies on an important issue in international law, but whether any set of procedures could be found that could ensure Senate ratification of such a treaty. Moreover, the George W. Bush administration was willing to work outside the norms of international law when perceived

U.S. national interests seemed to dictate such a course of action. So far, the only investigations and prosecutions by the ICC have been in African countries, and about half of the world's population remains outside its jurisdiction, facts that do not speak well for or enhance the image of the ICC.

Key Actors

George W. Bush President; rescinded the Clinton administration's signature of the Rome Statute, signed the American Servicemembers' Protection Act, and ordered the cutoff of military aid to thirty-five countries that refused to sign bilateral agreements protecting U.S. service personnel from possible prosecution by the ICC.

Bill Clinton President; unexpectedly ordered Ambassador David Scheffer to sign the ICC treaty so the United States could be considered an original signatory.

Hillary Clinton Secretary of state; has expressed her aspiration for U.S. participation in, or cooperation with, the ICC.

Jesse Helms Senator (R-NC), the chairman of the Committee on Foreign Relations; was an early and active opponent of U.S. participation in the ICC.

Harold Koh Legal adviser, U.S. Department of State; has favored a key role for the UN Security Council in prosecuting crimes of aggression.

Barack Obama President; endorsed the premise that the U.S. military deserves some form of protection from an aggressive or irresponsible ICC prosecutor, thus favoring an integral role for the UN Security Council.

David Scheffer Ambassador-at-large for war crimes; led the U.S. effort to modify the ICC treaty so the United States would have some control over the court's future actions.

Notes

1. John T. Rourke, Ralph G. Carter, and Mark A. Boyer, *Making American Foreign Policy*, 2nd ed. (Guilford, CT: Brown and Benchmark, 1996), 87.
2. Sir Arnold Duncan McNair, *The Development of International Justice* (New York: New York University Press, 1954), 4.
3. George Schwarzenberger, *International Law, as Applied by International Courts and Tribunals* (London: Stevens and Sons, 1986), 4:138.
4. Ian Brownlie, *Basic Documents in International Law*, 4th ed. (Oxford: Clarendon Press, 1995), 446. Reservations are legal statements of the conditions under which parties will agree to a treaty. Often during a debate over the ratification of a treaty, states will declare in advance certain circumstances under which they say a treaty will not

apply to them or their actions. Accepting these conditions is the political cost of getting that state to agree to the treaty. "Obligatory jurisdiction" means that states are obliged to obey a court's jurisdiction. With obligatory jurisdiction, the states cannot deny that a court has jurisdiction in a case or matter. Through reservations, states can set the terms and conditions under which they will accept a court's jurisdiction.

5. M. Cherif Bassiouni, "From Versailles to Rwanda in Seventy-Five Years: The Need to Establish a Permanent International Criminal Court," *Harvard Human Rights Journal* 10 (1997): 11–62; Gerhard von Glahn, *Law among Nations: An Introduction to Public International Law* (New York: Macmillan, 1992), 878.

6. Von Glahn, *Law among Nations,* 880.

7. John E. Findling, ed., *Dictionary of American Diplomatic History,* 2nd ed. (New York: Greenwood Press, 1989), 260.

8. Bassiouni, "From Versailles to Rwanda," 34.

9. Findling, *Dictionary of American Diplomatic History,* 259.

10. Von Glahn, *Law among Nations,* 354–357.

11. Michael P. Scharf, *Balkan Justice: The Story behind the First International War Crimes Trial since Nuremberg* (Durham, NC: Carolina Academic Press, 1997), 13–15.

12. *Congressional Record,* August 1, 1946, 10618.

13. Von Glahn, *Law among Nations,* 615–616.

14. *Congress and the Nation, vol. 1, 1945–1964* (Washington, DC: Congressional Quarterly, 1965).

15. John T. Rourke, Ralph G. Carter, and Mark A. Boyer, *Making American Foreign Policy* (Guilford, CT: Dushkin Publishing Group, 1994), 209–210.

16. Von Glahn, *Law among Nations,* 192.

17. Scharf, *Balkan Justice,* 15.

18. Bassiouni, "From Versailles to Rwanda," 55–56.

19. Ibid., 43.

20. Ibid., 46–47.

21. See the Rome Conference/PrepCom document at www.un.org/law/icc/prepcomm/prepfra.htm.

22. Anne-Marie Slaughter, "Memorandum to the President," in *Toward an International Criminal Court?,* ed. Alton Frye (New York: Council on Foreign Relations, 1999), 7.

23. James Bone, "U.S. Seeks to Limit War Crimes Court," *Times* [London], March 30, 1998.

24. Human Rights Watch, "Justice in the Balance: Recommendations for an Independent and Effective International Criminal Court," 1998, www.hrw.org/reports98/icc.

25. David Scheffer, "An International Criminal Court: The Challenge of Enforcing International Humanitarian Law," address to the Southern California Working Group on the International Criminal Court, February 26, 1998, www.unausa.org/issues/scheffer.asp.

26. Agence France-Presse, "Paris, Washington in Agreement on UN Genocide Court," April 4, 1998.

27. Senate Committee on Foreign Relations, "Helms Declares UN Criminal Court 'Dead on Arrival' without U.S. Veto," press release, March 26, 1998.

28. Eric Schmitt, "Pentagon Battles Plans for International War Crimes," *New York Times,* April 14, 1998.

29. Siddharth Varadarajan, "Imperial Impunity: U.S. Hampers World Criminal Court Plan," *Times of India,* April 23, 1998.

30. Alessandra Stanley, "Conference Opens on Creating Court to Try War Crimes," *New York Times,* June 15, 1998, A1.

31. "A New World Court," *The Economist,* June 13–19, 1998, 16.

32. Bertram S. Brown, "The Statute of the ICC: Past, Present, and Future," in *The United States and the International Criminal Court: National Security and International Law,* ed. Sarah B. Sewall and Carl Kaysen (Lanham, MD: Rowman and Littlefield, 2000), 62. Donald Jackson was an accredited correspondent at the Rome Conference. Statements not otherwise attributed in this section are based either on direct observation or on contemporaneous conversations with conference participants, nongovernmental organization representatives, or journalists.

33. UN press release, L/ROM/11, June 17, 1998.

34. Alessandra Stanley, "U.S. Presses Allies to Rein in Proposed War Crimes Court," *New York Times,* July 15, 1998.

35. Lawrence Weschler, "Exceptional Cases in Rome: The United States and the Struggle for an ICC," in Sewall and Kaysen, *The United States and the International Criminal Court,* 91.

36. Ibid., 105.

37. David Scheffer, press release distributed at the conference, July 15, 1998.

38. Steven Lee Myers, "U.S. Signs Treaty for World Court to Try Atrocities," *New York Times,* January 1, 2001.

39. "War Crime Pact OK'd by Clinton," *Dallas Morning News,* January 1, 2001, 10A.

40. Coalition for the International Criminal Court, *ICC Monitor,* September 2002, www.iccnow.org/publications/monitor.html.

41. "Permanent War Crimes Court Approved," *New York Times,* July 18, 1998.

42. Kenneth Roth, "Speech One: Endorse the International Criminal Court," in Frye, *Toward an International Criminal Court?,* 31–32.

43. Ibid., 31.

44. John Bolton, "Speech Two: Reject and Oppose the International Criminal Court," in Frye, *Toward an International Criminal Court?,* 37.

45. Slaughter, "Memorandum to the President," 8.

46. Michael Scharf, "Rome Diplomatic Conference for an International Criminal Court," *ASIL Insight,* June 1998, www.asil.org/insights/insigh20.htm.

47. Weschler, "Exceptional Cases in Rome," 111.

48. Coalition for the International Criminal Court, August 29, 2000, www.iccnow .org; United Nations Association–USA, June 20, 2000, www.unausa.org/dc/info/ dc062000; "The International Criminal Court: Protecting American Servicemen and Officials from the Threat of International Prosecution," Hearing before the Committee on Foreign Relations, United States Senate, 106 Congress, 2nd Session, June 14, 2000, www.gpo.gov/fdsys/pkg/CHRG-106shrg67980/html/CHRG-106shrg67980.htm.

49. Myers, "U.S. Signs Treaty for World Court to Try Atrocities."

50. James Carroll, "How Helms Is Sparking a Real Crisis," *Boston Globe,* December 5, 2000, A23.

51. Coalition for the International Criminal Court, *ICC Monitor,* September 2002.

52. Ibid.

53. Coalition for the International Criminal Court, *ICC Monitor,* April 2003, www .iccnow.org/publications/monitor.html.

54. Coalition for the International Criminal Court, "States Parties to the Rome Statute of the ICC," July 2009, accessed January 18, 2010, www.iccnow.org/documents/ RATIFICATIONSbyRegion_21_July_20091.pdf.

55. International Criminal Court Press Release, "Alleged Congolese Militia Leader Found Not Guilty in Second ICC Trial," December 18, 2012, accessed December 27, 2012, www.iccnow.org/documents/CICC_PR_Ngudjolo_Dec2012.pdf.

56. Coalition for the International Criminal Court, "Cases & Situations," accessed January 18, 2010, www.iccnow.org/?mod=casessituations.

57. International Criminal Court, accessed September 30, 2008, www.icc-cpi.int/en_menus/icc/press%20and%20media/press%20releases/Pages/index.aspx; "On 14 July 2008, the Prosecutor Luis Moreno-Ocampo, requested Pre-Trial Chamber I to issue an arrest warrant for Omar Hassan Ahmad al-Bashir in the Darfur situation in Sudan. In his Application, the Prosecutor stated that there are reasonable grounds to believe that al-Bashir bears criminal responsibility for genocide, crimes and war crimes committed in Darfur in the past five years. The Application lists ten counts, and alleges among other things that al-Bashir masterminded and implemented a plan to destroy in substantial part the Fur, Masalit and Zaghawa groups, on account of their ethnicity." Coalition for the International Criminal Court Factsheet, accessed September 30, 2008, www.coalitionfortheicc.org/documents/CICCFS_Situations_Overview_eng_14july2008.pdf.

58. "ICC Overturns Decision to Exclude Genocide Charges in Al-Bashir Arrest Warrant," accessed February 3, 2010, www.iccnow.org.

59. Marlise Simons, "Sudan's Leader May Be Accused of Genocide," *New York Times,* February 4, 2010, A10.

60. Citizens for Global Solutions, "'08 or Bust," October 6, 2007, accessed July 24, 2008, http://globalsolutions.org/08orbust/quotes/2007/10/31/quote484.

61. Lisa Gambone, "Hillary Clinton: 'Great Regret" US not in ICC," August 6, 2009, accessed October 19, 2012, foreignpolicyblogs.com/2009/08/06/hillary-clinton-great-regret-that-us-is-not-in-icc/.

62. Although there are many new books on the policies regarding interrogation techniques embraced by the Bush administration, two notable ones are Philippe Sands's *Torture Team: Rumsfeld's Memo and the Betrayal of American Values* (New York: Palgrave Macmillan, 2008) and Jane Mayer's *The Dark Side: The Inside Story of How the War on Terror Turned into a War on American Ideals* (New York: Doubleday, 2008).

63. Adam Zagorin, "Exclusive: Charges Sought against Rumsfeld over Prison Abuse," *Time,* November 10, 2006, accessed July 25, 2008, www.time.com/printout/0,8816,1557842,00.html.

64. Center for Constitutional Rights, "Donald Rumsfeld Charged with Torture during Trip to France," October 26, 2007, accessed July 28, 2008, www.ccrjustice.org/newsroom/press-releases/Donald-rumsfeld-charged-torture-during-trip-france.

65. According to the Center for Constitutional Rights, the case was dismissed at the suggestion of the French Ministry of Justice, even though Rumsfeld was at the time a private citizen on a personal visit in France. See "Open Letter Submitted to French Minister of Justice in Rumsfeld Torture Case," May 21, 2008, accessed July 28, 2008, www.ccrjustice.org/files/OpenLetterKouchnerDatiFinal.pdf.

Conclusion

Ralph G. Carter

Change we can believe in? Despite the rhetoric of Barack Obama's presidential campaign in 2008, the foreign policy actions of President Obama's first term seemed more a difference of style than a sharp change in substance. Although Obama reached out in new ways to diverse international audiences and was generally perceived abroad as more willing to listen to others than was President George W. Bush, his policies proved to be largely centrist and pragmatic in nature. With some exceptions, most Republicans in Congress found they could usually support the president's requests—at times more easily than could members of the more liberal wing of his own party. Thus the sharp partisan differences found in domestic policy making (see, e.g., health care reform or the fiscal cliff debates) were not generally found in foreign policy making. Time will tell whether that pattern remains in place for his second term, as he said very little about looming foreign policy issues—outside of perhaps energy policy noted in the context of global climate change—in his second inaugural address.

As in the previous editions of this volume, these case studies illustrate the array of external challenges and opportunities, substantive issues, internal political situations, and policy-making dynamics likely to confront U.S. foreign policy makers well into the twenty-first century. Although each of these fifteen cases offers a unique perspective on policy making, patterns can be discerned in the internal and external policy-making environments.

On the Outside: Shifts in External Challenges

Foreign policy is made by those who act in the name of the state, and they do so in relation to the external and internal environments. Although the concept of viewing "the state as an actor in a situation" is not new, it continues to be helpful.[1] The external environment presents either opportunities to embrace or problems to solve. How foreign policy makers react to such external situations often depends on the internal environment. Why they get involved in a situation makes a difference, and how their preferences correspond to those of the people, opinion makers, and the media plays a major role in decision making.

The Cold War era was dominated by the politics of national security. To U.S. foreign policy makers, the Soviet threat overrode all other foreign policy issues. Persistent images of a relentless enemy and the potentially catastrophic costs of a policy mistake typically led administration officials to neither seek nor encourage input from others who might know less about the external situation.[2] Although some observers perceived that presidential policy-making preeminence ended with the Vietnam War,[3] most would agree that such presidential preeminence ended along with the Cold War. Without the threat of nuclear annihilation looming over policy discussions, reasonable people could disagree about what the United States should do in foreign affairs.[4] So in the post–Cold War, post–September 11, and post–Great Recession era, the external situation neither stifles foreign policy debate nor deters the participation of potential policy-making actors. Although during the Cold War many "realists" seemed to think that only the external environment mattered, there now seems little question that both the external and internal political situations significantly influence U.S. foreign policy makers.

In the present era, fewer traditional external challenges and opportunities confront U.S. foreign policy makers, but new ones have arisen. Financial crises can threaten the viability of even mature states—like Greece and others—and require new responses from international actors like the European Union and the G-20. The global terrorist threat has concentrated itself in a front line called "AfPak" while at the same time fragmenting globally into diverse al Qaeda franchises that operate on their own. Regime change and nation building, rogue regimes, nuclear proliferation, genocidal civil wars, drug smuggling, and global environmental degradation are but a few examples of the challenges policy makers face. Other examples are more positive, such as structuring beneficial trade relations; helping people and states through multilateral assistance; and creating new, cooperative international institutions to handle complex problems. For U.S. policy makers, the difficult questions are whether the United States should respond to a given situation and, if so, how?

On the Inside: The New Foreign Policy Challenges

The answers to whether and how the United States should respond are usually found in the internal political situations facing foreign policy makers.

As James Scott sums it up, "A changing agenda and increasing interdependence and transnational ties make foreign policy making more like domestic policy making: subject to conflict, bargaining, and persuasion among competing groups within and outside the government."[5] This statement echoes a remark made by President Bill Clinton: "The more time I spend on foreign policy . . . the more I become convinced that there is no longer a clear distinction between what is foreign and domestic."[6] During the Cold War, the president and his advisers directed foreign policy, but in the present era members of Congress and other powerful groups have become highly visible participants in the process. There are now numerous actors clamoring to act in the name and best interest of the United States.

Interbranch Leadership: Presidential-Congressional Interactions

In the present period, some actions remain clearly presidential, such as decisions to go to war, to deploy or remove troops from a combat zone, or to assassinate terrorist leaders. In other instances, Congress seems to be calling the tune, such as in limiting what the president can promise in global climate change talks, setting the parameters of acceptable terms in financial bailouts and stimulus packages, or telling the president the United States will not participate in the International Criminal Court.

Today presidents and members of Congress openly vie for influence over many policy issues, with each branch doing its best to shape the outcome. The possible results of this pattern of interbranch leadership include cooperation, constructive compromise, institutional competition, or confrontation and stalemate.[7] The cases in this volume illustrate all four of these variants. For example, the Indian nuclear accord case reflects institutional cooperation, the China trade case reveals constructive compromise, institutional competition is at the heart of the climate change case, and confrontation and stalemate mark the ICC case. The judicial branch also occasionally becomes a major player in these policy disputes, as the National Security Agency (NSA) eavesdropping and the detainees cases demonstrate.

Each branch of government uses direct and indirect tactics to accomplish its goals. Direct tactics reflected here include members of Congress introducing legislation to change U.S. policy (as in the NSA eavesdropping, China trade, global financial crisis, ICC, and detainees cases), presidents using the military (as in the terrorism, targeted assassinations, and Iraq cases), and promoting diplomatic negotiations (as in the Iranian, North Korean, Chinese defector, Indian nuclear, and ICC cases). Sometimes, when both branches want to "frame" issues in a favorable way, indirect tactics are chosen. Thus, from Sen. Jesse Helms's perspective, the ICC was not about the United States being a law-abiding member of the international community (as the administration suggested), but about threats to U.S. sovereignty. Once issues are successfully framed in the negative, no one wants to be depicted as supporting them. On the other hand, sometimes negative frames fail to take hold, as the appeal of embracing the world's largest democracy (India) overrode concerns about reversing long-standing nonproliferation policy. The executive and legislative branches also try to anticipate the reaction of the other, whether it is an administration trying to gauge congressional reactions in cases like ICC participation or a Democratically controlled Congress testing how much it can press the Obama administration, as in the global financial crisis case.

The actions of other administration officials, and occasionally the courts, also complicate interbranch leadership. Senior administrative officials played pivotal roles in the decisions to pursue war with Iraq, eavesdrop without warrants, and detain enemy combatants. The courts were pivotal in deciding the ability of the administration to pursue warrantless wiretaps or to detain enemy combatants and U.S. citizens and immigrants in the war on terrorism.

New Influences: The Societal Actors

Government officials do not act in a political vacuum. They are often the targets of interest group representatives, who usually believe that their concerns are identical to those of the collective nation (as in the Indian nuclear, Chinese trade, and detainees cases). The news media report on politics, and how the news is reported can sway public opinion (e.g., in the cases of NSA eavesdropping and the detainees). The public's opinion is then used to impress a policy preference on policy makers (as in the Egyptian Revolution and financial crisis cases). In most of these cases, experts who serve as opinion leaders line up on one or both sides of an issue, trying to get their preferred policies enacted. The question becomes, "Who has the ear of policy makers?"

Stimuli: Underlying Factors

Governmental and nongovernmental actors often disagree on foreign policy issues because they respond to different stimuli and thus frame issues differently.[8] To one person, the China trade issue is a human rights problem, while to another it is a jobs issue. At other times agreement can be reached on the definition of an issue but not on the policy solution. For instance, nuclear proliferation concerns virtually everyone, but should Iran and North Korea be the targets of "hard'" or "soft" power responses? Why should India (or Israel, for that matter) be treated differently? As the product of a political process, foreign policy is influenced by what government officials think they should do—enact good policy or garner institutional prestige and stature—and what they think they must do—address the potential preferences of citizens and voters.[9]

Sometimes these differences are simply the products of partisanship and ideology. In the late 1940s and early 1950s, politics seemed to stop "at the water's edge."[10] The last two decades, however, have brought increasingly ideological partisanship to foreign affairs.[11] Cases such as warrantless eavesdropping and how to get out of Iraq pitted more liberal Democrats against the more conservative Republican administration. Now, at times, they pit congressional Democrats against their copartisans in the White House. Although Obama's preference for centrist foreign policy has dampened this ideological divide in a Democratically controlled Congress, it has not ended it.

Looking to the Future

Each case in this collection touches on the unifying theme that U.S. foreign policy making is becoming more open, pluralistic, and partisan. Responding to increasingly diverse motivations, more and more governmental and nongovernmental actors are getting involved. As foreign policy becomes increasingly intermestic and more like domestic policy, reasonable people can be expected to disagree and try to shape policy based on their own values and attitudes. Such behavior has long been commonplace for "low politics," that is, such intermestic issues as immigration, weapons procurement, and foreign trade. Without the overriding fear of global annihilation, there seem to be few reasons for congressional and societal actors to defer to the president or other officials of the executive branch for many "high politics" issues involving core national interests. These other actors bring their ideas, attitudes, passions, ideological beliefs, and partisanship with them as they try to affect policy making. In terms of any search for consensus, the short-term trends do not look promising as the foreign policy process continues to become more political.

With more open and pluralistic foreign policy making, those who oppose the president's policy preferences will seek to exploit any internal divisions within an administration. Members of Congress, interest groups, nongovernmental organizations, and media pundits will seek policy allies in the administration. It is interesting to observe to what degree officials' loyalties to the president outweigh their occasional differences with his policy preferences. Future presidents will have to find policy positions that feel right to them, keep their administration's officials "on message," and convince the country that their policy prescriptions are the best for the nation.

The 2008 elections paired a Democratically controlled Congress with a Democratic president. Quickly, all concerned realized that this situation did not represent a free pass to create whatever policies they desired. Despite the common partisan tie, the structural differences remained. Even when from the same party, presidents and members of Congress respond to different cues and motivations. Thus, even under the best of circumstances, presidents can be expected to have difficulties with Congress regarding foreign policy. As a noted congressional scholar argues,

> The Constitution establishes a fluid decision process that cannot ensure a creative governmental response to issues that confront the country. The system of separation of powers, with its checks and balances, works to constrain the enactment of public programs. Partisanship (embodied in divided or unified government), the responsiveness of government to electoral considerations, the character of congressional organization, and the quality and commitment of presidential leadership conspire in distinctive ways to create a policy process prone to delay and deadlock.[12]

In such an environment, anything controversial will further complicate policy making. After September 11, 2001, George W. Bush bet his presidency on his war on terrorism. While it began with great domestic and international support, that support began to wane after the invasion of Iraq. For his part, it appears Obama has bet his presidency on recovery from the global financial crisis and some measure of success regarding the defense challenges present in Afghanistan and Pakistan. Winning the Nobel Peace Prize in his first year in office showed how much the international arena welcomed his presence in the White House, but many policies remain largely unchanged since the George W. Bush presidency. Again, navigating the difficult issues intertwined in the global climate change debate was the sole major foreign policy issue highlighted in Obama's second inaugural speech.

Thus some things have not changed in this post–Cold War, post–September 11, and now post–Great Recession era. U.S. foreign policy making continues to grow more pluralistic, partisan, and political in the twenty-first century. The good news is that U.S. foreign policy is becoming representative of more organized interests and points of view, more democratic in nature, and somewhat more transparent in process. The bad news for policy makers is that the road to foreign policy enactment and successful implementation shows all the signs of being an increasingly bumpy ride. To paraphrase Winston Churchill's seafaring analogy, democracies are like rafts—they are virtually unsinkable, but they proceed slowly and one's feet always get wet. In this more open process, foreign policy making will almost always be slower, but one hopes that it will be surer in its outcomes.

Notes

1. See Richard C. Snyder, H. W. Bruck, Burton M. Sapin, Valerie M. Hudson, Derek H. Chollet, and James M. Goldgeier, *Foreign Policy Decision Making (Revisited)* (New York: Palgrave Macmillan, 2002).

2. See Richard Melanson, *American Foreign Policy since the Vietnam War,* 2nd ed. (Armonk, NY: M. E. Sharpe, 1996).

3. See Thomas Franck and Edward Weisband, *Foreign Policy by Congress* (New York: Oxford University Press, 1979); James M. Scott and Ralph G. Carter, "Acting on the Hill: Congressional Assertiveness in U.S. Foreign Policy," *Congress and the Presidency,* no. 2 (Autumn 2002): 151–169; and Ralph G. Carter, "Congressional Foreign Policy Behavior: Persistent Patterns of the Postwar Period," *Presidential Studies Quarterly* 16, no. 2 (Spring 1986): 329–359.

4. For a good discussion of these themes, see James M. Scott and A. Lane Crothers, "Out of the Cold: The Post–Cold War Context of U.S. Foreign Policy," in *After the End: Making U.S. Foreign Policy in the Post–Cold War World,* ed. James M. Scott (Durham, NC: Duke University Press, 1998), 1–25.

5. James M. Scott, "Interbranch Policy Making after the End," in Scott, *After the End,* 401.

6. Quoted in Ralph G. Carter, "Congress and Post–Cold War U.S. Foreign Policy," in Scott, *After the End,* 129–130.

7. Scott and Crothers, "Out of the Cold," 11.

8. James M. Lindsay, *Congress and the Politics of U.S. Foreign Policy* (Baltimore, MD: Johns Hopkins University Press, 1994).

9. For more on congressional policy motivations, see R. Douglas Arnold, *The Logic of Congressional Action* (New Haven, CT: Yale University Press, 1990); Aage Clausen, *How Congressmen Decide* (New York: St. Martin's Press, 1973); Richard F. Fenno, *Congressmen in Committees* (Boston: Little, Brown, 1973); or John W. Kingdon, *Congressmen's Voting Decisions,* 3rd ed. (Ann Arbor: University of Michigan Press, 1989).

10. See Carter, "Congressional Foreign Policy Behavior."

11. Carter, "Congress and Post–Cold War U.S. Foreign Policy," 128.

12. Leroy N. Rieselbach, "It's the Constitution, Stupid! Congress, the President, Divided Government, and Policymaking," in *Divided Government: Change, Uncertainty, and the Constitutional Order,* ed. Peter F. Galderisi (Lanham, MD: Rowman and Littlefield, 1996), 129.

Index

Khamenei, Ayatollah, 107
Khan, Samir, 54, 55
Khatami, Mohammad,
112, 114–115, 126
Khomeini, Ayatollah Ruhollah, 108–109,
110, 112–113, 118, 120, 121, 126
Ki-moon, Ban, 348
Kirkpatrick, Jeane, 453
Kirsch, Philippe, 447, 448, 454
Kissinger, Henry, 109, 453
Kleptocracy, 232
Koh, Harold, 259, 269, 457, 459
Korean Peninsula Energy Development
Organization (KEDO),
146–147, 159
Korean War, 133, 138, 156, 323
Korean Worker's Party of
North Korea, 137
Korematsu v. United States, 424
Kosachev, Konstantin, 197
Kosovo, military intervention in, 337
Krakow, 198
Kremlin, 120
Kristol, William, 72
Kucinich, Dennis, 31
Kurds, 90, 95
Kyoto Protocol, 348, 356, 358–360, 370
Kyrgyzstan, 198

L
Labor Department, 3
Lamy, Pascal, 317
Landsberg prison, 425
Lantos, Tom, 175
Lavrov, Sergei, 120, 199, 200, 203, 209,
211, 212, 214
League of Nations, 436
Leahy, Patrick, 384
Lee, Barbara, 21
Lehman Brothers, 287, 289, 305
Lehrer, Jim, 235
Leiter, Mike, 49
Levin, Carl, 21, 30
Libby, I. Lewis "Scooter," 72
Liberation Act of 1998, 72
Libya, 183, 455
Lieberman, Joseph, 95, 367
Lindsay, James, 70

Linyi City, 256
Locke, Gary, 260, 261, 269
London Charter for the Prosecution and
Punishment of the Major War
Criminals of the European
Axis, 440
Lott, Trent, 5, 18, 20, 338
Lucent Technologies, 330
Lugar, Richard, 29, 79, 81–82, 173, 174
Lynch, Marc, 237, 239

M
Maastricht Treaty, 336
Macclesfield Bank, 252
Magnitsky, Sergei, 213–214
Makarov, Nikolai, 208
Maliki government, 90–91
Maqaleh et al. v. Gates, 430
Marbury v. Madison, 430
Market-emphasis capitalism in Asia, 304
Markey, Edward, 175, 177, 367, 372
Marshall, John, 386–387, 430
Martha's Vineyard, 17
Martial law, 226
*Massachusetts v. Environmental
Protection Agency,* 362–363,
365–366
McCain, John, 30, 80, 95, 197,
212, 239, 364
McChrystal, Stanley A., 28–29,
30, 31, 34
McConnell, Michael, 397–398, 403
McCurry, Michael, 18, 145
McFaul, Michael, 207, 209, 212, 241
McKiernan, David, 28
McRaven, Admiral William,
50–52, 54, 63
McVeigh, Timothy, 55
Medvedev, Dmitry, 120, 197,
200–201, 204, 206, 211, 215
Medvedev-Putin strategy, 201
Merrill Lynch, 287, 289
Methane, 351
Middle East Partnership Initiative, 233
Military Commissions Act of 2006
(MCA), 427–428
Miller, Geoffrey, 419
Minaret, 380

⑤SAGE research**methods**

The essential online tool for researchers from the world's leading methods publisher

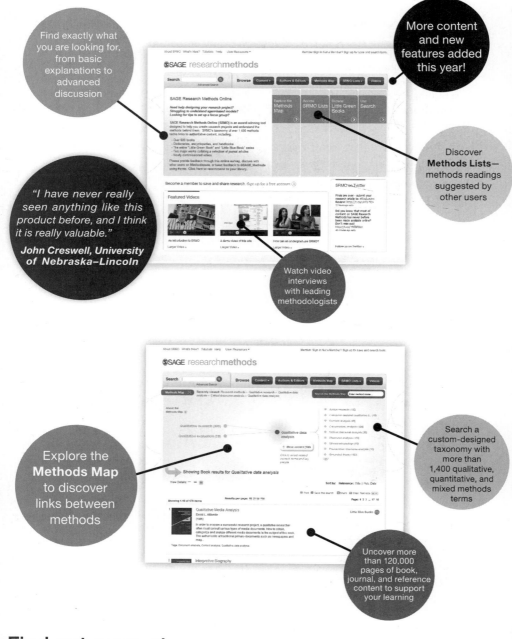

Find exactly what you are looking for, from basic explanations to advanced discussion

More content and new features added this year!

"I have never really seen anything like this product before, and I think it is really valuable."

John Creswell, University of Nebraska–Lincoln

Discover Methods Lists—methods readings suggested by other users

Watch video interviews with leading methodologists

Explore the Methods Map to discover links between methods

Search a custom-designed taxonomy with more than 1,400 qualitative, quantitative, and mixed methods terms

Uncover more than 120,000 pages of book, journal, and reference content to support your learning

Find out more at
www.sageresearchmethods.com